Electronic Evidence and Electronic Signatures

OBserving Law – IALS Open Book Service for Law

First published by LexisNexis Butterworths, 2007

Second edition published by LexisNexis Butterworths, 2010

Third edition published by LexisNexis Butterworths, 2012

Fourth edition published by the Institute of Advanced Legal Studies for the SAS Humanities Digital Library, School of Advanced Study, University of London, 2017

Fifth edition published by the Institute of Advanced Legal Studies for the SAS Humanities Digital Library, School of Advanced Study, University of London, 2021

ISBN (hardback): 978-1-911507-26-0
ISBN (print): 978-1-911507-22-2
ISBN (epub): 978-1-911507-23-9
ISBN (mobi): 978-1-911507-25-3
ISBN (web PDF): 978-1-911507-24-6

Institute of Advanced Legal Studies
University of London
Charles Clore House
17 Russell Square
London WC1B 5DR

http://ials.sas.ac.uk

Electronic Evidence and Electronic Signatures

Fifth edition

Stephen Mason
of the Middle Temple, Barrister

and

Daniel Seng
Associate Professor and Director of the Centre for Technology, Robotics, AI and the Law, Faculty of Law, National University of Singapore

Editors

Contributors

Burkhard Schafer, Professor of Computational Legal Theory, School of Law, University of Edinburgh and Director of the SCRIPT Centre for IT and IP Law

Steven J. Murdoch, Professor of Security Engineering and Royal Society University Research Fellow in the Information Security Research Group, Department of Computer Science, University College London

Luciana Duranti, Professor of Archival Studies, School of Information, the University of British Columbia and Director of the InterPARES Project

Dr Allison Stanfield, Managing Director and Solicitor, Lantern Legal

Alisdair Gillespie, Professor of Criminal Law and Justice, Law School, Lancaster University

Jessica Shurson, BA, JD, LLM

Dr Nigel Wilson, Barrister, Australis Chambers

Andrew Sheldon MSc, Director of Innovations, CCL Solutions Group Limited

Hein Dries, Vigilo Consult

Lynne Townley, LLB (Hons), LLM, Barrister, Lecturer, Bar Professional Training Course, City Law School, University of London

A note on our Creative Commons licence

The authors, the editors and the publisher have collectively continued to make available the fifth edition of *Electronic Evidence and Electronic Signatures* under a Creative Commons licence. We made this carefully considered decision because we want to promote a better understanding of electronic evidence, and wish to facilitate the greater accessibility and availability of our combined scholarship. We commend the Institute of Advanced Legal Studies, University of London, for its strong and continued support for academic education, learning and scholarship and the advancement of knowledge.

Free legal resources on the Internet

Most readers familiar with the common law will be aware of some of the free legal sources on the Internet. For the uninitiated, the World Legal Information Institute (http://www.worldlii.org) is a good start. Many of the more recent cases cited in this book, but by no means all, are available on the various independent jurisdiction-specific websites that are linked to the World Legal Information Institute, which in turn is coordinated by the Australasian Legal Information Institute (http://www.austlii.edu.au), the first of its kind. Note also The Free Access to Law Movement (http://www.falm.info). Additional links can be found on any university library website, including the website of the Institute of Advanced Legal Studies, London. It must be emphasized that the free sources of case law that are available are not comprehensive.

Citations of websites

Readers will be familiar with the changing nature of URLs. Every effort has been made to ensure, where a URL is given, that it was live at the time of publication.

References have been made to Wikipedia on the basis that this source is relatively accurate for information of a technical nature. Readers will be aware that these pages are open to being updated and changed regularly. Although it is sometimes customary to provide the date a page was last viewed on the Internet, it is taken as a given that the reader does not need this information, given the dynamic nature of the Internet.

Practitioner texts

Practitioner texts are cited without reference to the date in the body of the text. This is because the practitioner texts that are cited are updated each year. It is suggested that the reader checks the updated version of the text if they are going to rely on any comments, given that citation of such texts in this publication fixes the year of publication, but this may change between editions.

Errors and omissions

While we, our authors and the publisher have tried hard to ensure all typographical and other errors have been corrected, we are aware that we might have missed some. For this reason, we will be delighted if you let us know if you notice an error. In addition, if you detect any relevant case law, legislation, guidelines or reports that we have missed, we will appreciate it if you inform us of any helpful and pertinent materials.

This edition is dedicated to

Colin Tapper

Emeritus Professor, Magdalen College, University of Oxford

one of the first to write about the topic; mentor

Contents

Software is reliable and robust

'If it please your Lordship,' Dr Huld continued, representing the defendant, Positively Open Limited, 'my client is certain that their system, called EarthSkyMeet, is robust.'

Dr Huld sat down. He tilted his head slightly back, nose in the air, projecting an air of complacent self-satisfied certainty. Sergeant of the Lawe, Sergeant Chaucer stood up.

'Your Lordship, my learned friend has made many claims about the software and the system used by his client in the absence of any evidence. It is my contention that a fair trial cannot take place unless Positively Open Limited is required to disclose the evidence my expert witnesses have requested.'

The judge, Marcus Fabius Quintilian, put on his spectacles and looked at the papers before him. 'Well, Sergeant Chaucer,' he said, 'this is a long list.'

'It is, my Lord.'

'It is a very long list, Sergeant Chaucer.'

'It appears so, my Lord. It comprises three lists, as my learned friend is aware, my Lord. The three lists have been brought into a single list, my Lord.'

'This is your third application, Sergeant Chaucer.'

'It is, my Lord.'

'Well, Sergeant Chaucer, I don't know, you know. What say you, Dr Huld?'

Sergeant Chaucer sat down with an audible sigh of exasperation. Dr Huld stood up, smiling.

'As we all know, your Lordship, if there was a computer error, it is obvious the claimant would have been aware of it. My learned friend has not explained why his client did not notice the errors – if, in reality, they are errors, as he alleges. It is my submission that my learned friend is merely seeking to obtain more irrelevant information. This is just another fishing expedition, my Lord. My client's system is robust. It is reliable. Indeed, as we all know, the evidential presumption is with my client – it is *presumed* to be reliable. It is for the claimant to provide evidence to substantiate their challenge that the system is not reliable.'

At this point Sergeant Chaucer stood up. Dr Huld did not like being interrupted.

'Sergeant Chaucer, Dr Huld must be right.'

Dr Huld reluctantly sat down.

'If my learned friend is correct, your Lordship, then the professors that wrote the article that I submitted before this hearing ...'

'Ah,' the judge interrupted Sergeant Chaucer, 'but we have the Law Commission's recommendation from 1997. It remains in place.'

'Well, your Lordship, if you dismiss the sage knowledge of four learned professors with their combined experience and knowledge, there is little I can do to persuade you, other than to reinforce the need for a fair trial.'

'That's all very well, Sergeant Chaucer, but any issues that fail to be dealt with at trial can be remedied at appellate level.'

'Yes, your Lordship, but the finder of fact acts as a moral agent, and central to this is that the findings by a court must be justifiable and meet the demands of rationality and ethics.'

'That may be, Sergeant Chaucer, but all your client has done is contend the system must be wrong. As I have written, *inspectio etiam ipsa saepe falsum deprendit*.'

'Alas, your Lordship, the statement you wrote in Book 5 of *Institutio Oratoria*, that "simple inspection also often reveals a forgery" is no longer relevant – especially in relation to digital data. My client cannot point to any evidence to say the claimant's computer system might be at fault. My client knows nothing about the claimant's computer system, so my client is put in an impossible position. My client's difficulty is compounded, because my learned friend asserts that his client's system is robust, yet he resists the disclosure of the documents we have requested. It is the absence of such records that suggest poor quality software and poor system management. In addition, my learned friend compounds the difficulty by contending the system is robust – yet when pressed, refuses to produce a technical witness to testify on oath that the system is perfect – or even to offer a definition of what he means by the word reliable.'

'Well, Sergeant Chaucer' the judge replied, 'we are told that the disclosure exercise you are requesting is very expensive.'

'So my learned friends contends, your Lordship, and, if I may say, without any evidence to support the claim that the exercise is expensive. In fact, the requests for disclosure are nothing more than should be expected to be produced from an efficient and well-run system such as EarthSkyMeet. The claimant spent vast amounts of money on a complex computer system that purports to be more efficient and, no doubt, with the intention of increasing profits. Given this, your Lordship, it is my submission that they must face the foreseeable consequences of being required to deliver up relevant evidence in the event of litigation. The claimant is an organization of some size. They have a department that works on litigation continuously. Litigation is a normal part of their business. It is a poor excuse for a powerful organization to allege that the expense of providing routine information relating to the IT system they use is disproportionate to the fairness of legal proceedings.'

Preface

Stephen

This is my last comment on the presumption that computers are 'reliable'. This presumption was reintroduced into English law by the Law Commission in 1997 without any evidence to demonstrate the truthfulness of the assertion. Judges treat the presumption as a legal presumption.

The presumption is not restricted to the jurisdiction of England and Wales. Many common law jurisdictions throughout the world include such a presumption – without defining it – in legislation. Lest the reader think this presumption is restricted to common law jurisdictions, many of the lawyers I know in what are called civil or administrative law systems assure me that although such a presumption does not exist in law, nevertheless the vast majority of judges assume that computers are reliable.

The continued relevance of the presumption has been scrutinized by the first four articles published in the 2020 issue of the *Digital Evidence and Electronic Signature Law Review*. A further article, published in the same journal in 2021, puts forward practical recommendations for judges when dealing with the disclosure or discovery of electronic evidence. It is sincerely to be hoped that judges will begin to treat this topic with the seriousness it deserves.

The ignorance relating to this topic is exacerbated when judges make comments about the simplicity of electronic evidence, as illustrated in Chapter 5. In this respect, the education of judges and lawyers in electronic evidence is essential, as argued in my editorial of the *Digital Evidence and Electronic Signature Law Review* in 2010 and in the commissioning and publication of two articles in 2013: Denise H. Wong, 'Educating for the future: teaching evidence in the technological age' (2013) 10 *Digital Evidence and Electronic Signature Law Review* 16 and Deveral Capps, 'Fitting a quart into a pint pot: the legal curriculum and meeting the requirements of practice' (2013) 10 *Digital Evidence and Electronic Signature Law Review* 23.

The failure to deal with these two issues by the legal profession has finally led me to adopt the view taken by Bertolt Brecht in the following lines from his poem 'An die Nachgeborenen' (To those born after), where he writes, from the translation by Tom Kuhn and David Constantine, with the assistance of Charlotte Ryland, *The Collected Poems of Bertolt Brecht* (Liveright Publishing Corporation, 2015):

> Auch der Zorn über das Unrecht
> Macht die Stimme heiser.
>
> Anger, even at injustice
> Makes your voice hoarse.

Stephen and Daniel

Our aim with this revised text is to provide an accurate guide to the state of the law and the technology. Although the focus is on the law of England and Wales, we recognize that a great deal of important case law and legislation in other jurisdictions is relevant to the issues discussed, and for that reason the text includes references to other jurisdictions when appropriate.

We also acknowledge that the topic remains in flux, which requires all of the authors to be constantly alert to the need to refine the content of chapters to better reflect the purpose of the text. As we have indicated previously, we are in no doubt that the text will continue to evolve.

We have encouraged our authors to take a new look at the chapters they have agreed to update, and we thank Luciana and Allison for substantially revising the chapter on authentication, Nigel, Andrew and Hein for beginning the review of the chapter on proof, and Alisdair and Jessica for updating the chapter on encryption, including the citation of the case from France and a brief discussion of the position in Belgium by way of comparison.

We concluded that the text of the chapter dealing with the characteristics of electronic evidence was better divided between the introductory chapter and the chapter on proof and, bearing in mind the increasing use of 'artificial intelligence' in software, we decided that the time was now right to provide an introduction to the topic.

We have introduced a new chapter dealing more fully with electronic signatures. Sadly, the vast majority of lawyers still do not understand the topic. (Stephen can teach electronic signatures to a hall of lawyers in 30 seconds.) Stephen's book *Electronic Signatures in Law* was first published by LexisNexis Butterworths in 2003, followed by a second edition published by Tottel in 2007, a third edition published by Cambridge University Press in 2012, and the fourth edition published by the Institute of Advanced Legal Studies for the SAS Humanities Digital Library, School of Advanced Study, University of London in 2016. Sadly, Stephen has not been able to find a lawyer or legal academic willing to join him for a fifth edition with a view to taking over the entire text, so this book will no longer be published. With this in mind, we agreed it was appropriate to incorporate the relevant text on electronic signatures into this book. The text has been reduced and updated accordingly.

Stephen Mason
Langford, Bedfordshire
2021

Daniel Seng
Singapore
2021

Acknowledgments

Stephen

As always, I thank the Institute of Advanced Legal Studies for continuing to renew my Associate Research Fellowship (since 2003), which has permitted me unlimited use of the IALS Library and Information Services, and to those members of staff who have unfailingly helped me when I have not been able to find what I was looking for. In addition, I thank the members of staff of the library at the Honourable Society of the Middle Temple, who kindly helped me during the pandemic when travelling to London to visit the library in person was not an easy option.

Chapter 5, 'The presumption that computers are "reliable"', has been modestly updated. I thank the following for reviewing the text:

Dr Chris Elliott, FREng, System Engineer and Barrister

Dr Michael Ellims

Dr David Jackson, CEng, MIET, FBCS, Global Technical Director, Altran Technologies

Peter Bernard Ladkin, Professor i.R. of Computer Networks and Distributed Systems, Bielefeld University and CEO of tech-transfer companies Causalis Limited and Causalis Ingenieurgesellschaft mbH

Martin Newby, Emeritus Professor of Statistical Science, City, University of London

Derek Partridge, Professor Emeritus, University of Exeter

Lorenzo Strigini, Professor of Systems Engineering, City, University of London

Harold Thimbleby, Professor and See Change Digital Health Fellow, Swansea University, Wales, and Visiting Professor, UCL, London, Emeritus Professor, Gresham College, London

Martyn Thomas CBE, FREng, Emeritus Professor, Gresham College, London; Visiting Professor of Software Engineering at Aberystwyth University, Wales

I also thank Daniel for reviewing the chapter, putting me right where I missed points or failed to more fully understand. I appreciate the time that each of those mentioned above has given to consider and enhance the text. The discussion is vastly improved because of their comments, observations and corrections, and I have continued to adopt the vast majority of their recommendations. Nevertheless, any faults are mine.

I continue to remain indebted to Dr John Mitchell of LHS Business Control Limited and Professor Fred Piper, now an Honorary Member of the Information Security Group, previously of the Department of Mathematics, Royal Holloway College, University of London, both of whom reviewed the technical chapters of digital signatures for the first edition of *Electronic Signatures in Law* in 2003, now incorporated into this text. I also thank Alan Liddle, Director, DCS Consulting and Dr Arnis Parsovs, a researcher at the University of Tartu, Estonia, who have kindly provided me with further helpful technical comments relating to digital signatures. I remain responsible for the text.

My thanks also to Daniel and Bev Littlewood, Emeritus Professor of Software Engineering, Centre for Software Reliability, City, University of London for their comments on the various versions of the vignette I worked on for this edition.

As I step down from this text and hand over the responsibility to Daniel, I take this opportunity to thank the Laura Ashley Foundation (now the Ashley Family Foundation) for awarding me a grant of £500 in November 1986 towards the cost of travel and books when I was accepted by City University to take the Diploma in Law. I also thank the London Borough of Redbridge for providing me with a discretionary grant of £2,330 to enable me to take the Vocational Court for the Bar at the Inns of Court School of Law. This covered the cost of the course and a payment towards living expenses.

I would also like to mention that John Gregory and Thomas J. Smedinghoff each monitor and run mailing lists (John: e-communications law and policy, listed at the University of Ottawa: ulc_ecomm-l (@listserv.uottawa.ca), and Tom: American Bar Association, Business Law Section, Identity Management Legal Task Force) for those interested in matters pertaining to electronic communications and policy in general terms. I thank both John and Tom for their friendship over the years and for running these lists, and I thank all of those who have contributed to and have raised questions about policies, legislation and case law during the years that I have been part of these lists. I have benefitted from the discussions that have taken place, and I have gained insights that are often specific to a particular jurisdiction.

I also thank the School of Law, University of Tartu in Estonia for appointing me Visiting Lecturer, where I have had the privilege of teaching with Tõnu Mets on the LLM between 2017 and 2021, and to the Faculty of Law, National University of Singapore, for appointing me Visiting Professor to teach in January 2021.

My thanks to Burkhard, who has kindly added to his commitments by contributing to this text since the second edition, especially in helping to develop the intellectual framework for analysing electronic evidence; to Alisdair, whose knowledge of the landscape of criminal activity is of great help; to Andrew and Hein who have, over the years, discussed technology with me and kindly alleviated my ignorance when I ask what appear to be simple or silly questions (of course, no question is silly – it is the answer that might be stupid). Also to Allison, who, like me, cannot understand why the legal profession ignores this topic. Allison agreed to be a joint editor with me of the *Digital Evidence and Electronic Signature Law Review*, and I thank her for her support over the years.

It has been a pleasure to work with Daniel and our fellow authors in successive editions of this text. I thank all of the authors, past and present, for agreeing to take part in exploring the nuances of electronic evidence – so relevant for today's world. If we are fortunate, we meet people whom we trust to offer guidance and advice, and to improve our understanding of the topics we write and speak about. For me, Nicholas Bohm and Timothy S. Reiniger, Esq are two such people. I have always been able to approach Nicholas and Tim in the certain knowledge that I can rely on their sound judgment. I thank them both for their friendship and willingness to listen and advise.

In a similar way, I have had the great good fortune to know Daniel for many years now. Daniel is a friend, and I appreciate his willingness to critically explore my more recherché ideas over the years, and to gently correct me when I get something wrong. I thank him sincerely for his willingness to join me as a joint editor for the fourth and fifth editions, and for his commitment to take on responsibility for the text in the future.

I remain thankful to my wife, Penelope, for her forbearance over the editions.

Daniel

I first wish to thank Professor Colin Tapper of Oxford University for setting me on the path to scholarship in evidence law. As a Rupert Cross scholar and an eternally indebted student of Professor Tapper, who was one of the first scholars in the Commonwealth to conduct a systematic examination of the issues of electronic evidence, I have always looked to his concise scholarship and his legal precision as guidance and inspiration for my own writings.

I also wish to thank my wife, Xu Le, for her patience, understanding and support as I worked on this text.

And finally, I wish to thank Stephen for his friendship, generosity and kindness in granting me the extraordinary privilege to be his co-editor, and to expand my authorial contributions in the various chapters of this treatise on electronic evidence. It is both a joy and an honour to be in the aura of Stephen's indefatigable enthusiasm, intellectual acuity, receptiveness to new ideas and statesmanship that made this entire treatise possible. In continuing my involvement with this treatise since the first edition, I have personally benefited much from Stephen's mentorship and his willingness to share his thoughts, his research and his scholarship with me. Although Stephen claims that this will be the last edition he will be involved in, I have never ruled out the possibility of persuading him to join me for the next. To use the words of the great Helen Keller, in our journey to elucidate the complexities of electronic evidence, I would rather walk with a friend in the dark, than alone in the light.

Joint

We thank Chris Gallavin, Professor of Law and Deputy pro-Chancellor at Massey University for his work for this text, having taken responsibility for the chapter on New Zealand from the second edition, and the lead in the chapter on hearsay for the fourth edition. Chris was not able to take part in this edition because of the extent of his commitments.

We also thank Dr George R. S. Weir, Computer and Information Sciences, University of Strathclyde for taking part in the third and fourth editions. Unfortunately, because of the lack of time during the 2020 pandemic, George was not able to continue with the project.

We appreciate those authors who have joined us in this edition: uniquely Professor Luciana Duranti has been President of the Society of American Archivists (in the late 1990s) and the Association of Canadian Archivists (2016–2018); Dr Nigel Wilson, who, as we updated the text, was appointed Director, Market Regulation, Government and Conveyance at Water Find Pty Ltd, and Professor Steven J. Murdoch, who is also a bye-fellow of Christ's College, Innovation Security Architect at the OneSpan Innovation Center, a member of the Tor Project, and a Fellow of the IET and BCS (Steven was the expert for Mr Job, working pro bono, whom Stephen represented, also pro bono, in

Job v Halifax PLC (not reported) Case number 7BQ00307 (judgment published in the *Digital Evidence and Electronic Signature Law Review* 6 (2009) 235–245)).

We mention that Lynne Townley is a PhD candidate at City, University of London on the topic of *The RECOGNITION and development of 'Honour Crime' Policy and Practice in England and Wales*. Her supervisors are Professor Andrew Choo, City University of London, and Assistant Professor Mara Maligodi, Faculty of Law, Chinese University of Hong Kong. Jessica Shurston is a PhD candidate at Queen Mary, University of London, on the topic of *Legal Jurisdiction and the Globalization of Evidence: A Theory of Data Sovereignty for Law Enforcement Access to Data across Borders*. Her supervisors are Professor Ian Walden and Professor Julia Hörnle.

We thank all of our other authors for staying with the text and working on it, although their workload increased during the pandemic: Allison, Alisdair, Andrew, Burkhard and Hein; your continuing to take part in the book is greatly appreciated. You have collectively helped to make this book what we aspire it to be.

Finally, our thanks to Sandy Dutczak, the IALS Digital Projects and Publications Manager at the Institute of Advanced Legal Studies, who has seen this text through the publishing process, together with Lorraine Slipper (copyeditor), Jamie Bowman (production controller) and Robert Davies (project editor) – for which we give our additional thanks. We also thank Steven Whittle, predecessor to Sandy Dutczak, who was instrumental in the formation of the SAS Humanities Digital Library.

Table of statutes

R

Northern Ireland

Table of European Legislation

Directives

Table of International Legislation

Table of Other Enactments

Table of cases

Antigua and Barbuda

Australia

Federal

Capital Territory

Industrial Relations Court of Australia

New South Wales

Northern Territory

South Australia

Queensland

Tasmania

Quebec

Saskatchewan

China

Denmark

England and Wales

A

H

Court of Justice of the European Union

European Court of Human Rights

European Patent Office Technical Board of Appeal

Fiji

France

Germany

Greece

Hong Kong

India

International Court of Justice

Ireland

Israel

Italy

Japan

Lithuania

New Zealand

Nigeria

Northern Ireland

Norway

Papua New Guinea

Permanent Court of Arbitration

Portugal

Russian Federation

Scotland

Tonga

Turkey

United States of America

Federal

Court of Appeals for the Armed Forces

Alabama

Arizona

California

1

The sources and characteristics of electronic evidence and artificial intelligence

Steven J. Murdoch, Daniel Seng, Burkhard Schafer and Stephen Mason

1.1 Given the ubiquity of electronic devices and the evidence that they produce, lawyers are required to offer appropriate advice to clients in relation to data in electronic form. Trying to persuade lawyers that they need to keep up to date with technology is far from new.[1] In 1904, judges and lawyers were urged to make themselves aware of photography because 'they might otherwise accept what appears to be pure untouched work as reliable which was all the time outrageously worked on'.[2] And in 1959, an academic noted that 'hundreds of important cases involving disputed typewriting have been tried but there are still lawyers here and there who apparently have never heard of them and courthouses where a disputed typewriting has never been considered'.[3] Although written more than 60 years ago, the statement is undoubtedly still true today in many jurisdictions.

1 For instance, the observations by Hallett LJ in the case of *R. v Hallam (Sam)* [2012] EWCA Crim 1158, [2012] 5 WLUK 518 illustrate the failure to understand that a proper forensic investigation requires the use of the correct equipment, otherwise evidence will be tainted and therefore subject to being rejected by a trial judge – for which, see a more detailed discussion below.
2 'Photographs as Evidence' (1904) 66 ALJ 17.
3 Winsor C. Moore, 'The questioned typewritten document' (1959) 43(4) Minn L Rev 727, 727–728 n 3.

1.2 Electronic evidence and computer forensics are relatively recent additions to the means of proof in legal proceedings. Unlike many older forensic disciplines that were often introduced into the trial process with little or no legal debate and scrutiny, electronic evidence has caused considerable, and often controversial, discussion among legal professionals. Different legal systems have reacted in various ways to this new challenge.[1] Some systems have introduced new legislation to specifically address electronic evidence. Other systems try to establish a 'closest match' to existing evidentiary concepts and have applied wherever possible existing rules analogously: for instance, whether electronic evidence was admissible depended on whether it was similar to proof by (paper) document or proof by visual inspection. Most systems adopt a combination of both strategies. Where new legislation is introduced, the emphasis is on the differences between electronic and traditional forms of evidence. This can prevent lawyers from utilizing their collective institutional experience in evaluating and interpreting such evidence, often creating a sense of confusion and uncertainty. Where analogous approaches are used, the emphasis is on the similarities between traditional and digital evidence. Although this permits lawyers to draw on their experience in assessing the strength of the competing narratives that are argued by the parties, this can result in the inappropriate application of evidentiary rules. In

Steven J. Murdoch, Daniel Seng, Burkhard Schafer and Stephen Mason, 'The sources and characteristics of electronic evidence and artificial intelligence', in Stephen Mason and Daniel Seng (eds.), *Electronic Evidence and Electronic Signatures* (5th edn, University of London 2021) 1–50.

either case, it is important for lawyers to be aware of the distinctive characteristics of electronic evidence to enable them to confidently and reliably evaluate its use.

1 See Stephen Mason (ed), *International Electronic Evidence* (British Institute of International and Comparative Law 2008) for the outline of the following jurisdictions: Argentina, Austria, Belgium, Bulgaria, Croatia, Cyprus, Czech Republic, Denmark, Egypt, Estonia, Finland, France, Germany, Greece, Hungary, Iceland, Italy, Japan, Latvia, Lithuania, Luxembourg, Malta, Mexico, Netherlands, Norway, Poland, Romania, Russia, Slovakia, Slovenia, Spain, Sweden, Switzerland, Thailand and Turkey.

1.3 Various devices are capable of creating and storing data in digital form, and such data may serve as evidence. The aim of this chapter is to introduce the reader to the technologies, their underlying principles and the general characteristics that set evidence in digital form apart from evidence in analogue or physical form. The content of this chapter does not deal with any of these matters in depth. Neither does it aim to be a comprehensive review of the devices and technologies that create electronic evidence. Rather, the aim is to provide a broad brush introduction to the relevant technical issues, and to highlight features that a digital evidence professional and a legal professional should be concerned about when investigating electronic evidence and dealing with electronic evidence issues.

Digital devices

1.4 Historically, the term 'computer' was often used to describe almost any form of processing unit. Now, digital computation and storage facilities are characteristic of many devices that seem far removed in form and function from traditional computers. Such devices include games consoles, wearable technologies (such as fitness trackers and smart watches) and 'smart' domestic components (such as smart energy meters and automated central heating systems). Most of these digital devices share important features with more recognizably conventional computing devices such as desktop computers, laptops and computer tablets. These features are based on what is sometimes called an input–processing–output model:

> The device receives an *input* of some sort, by way of a local file, sensor, mouse, keyboard or through a communication channel (such as a network connection).
>
> It *processes* the information.
>
> It produces an *output* to a display, local file or printer, for instance.
>
> It must be able to *store* (and/or relay) information.
>
> It must be able to *control* what it does.

1.5 In the following, we detail the role played by the main components of digital devices.

Processors

1.6 The digital device contains one or more processors, each of which varies in the extent to which it is dedicated to a specific task. An example of a highly specific processer is one responsible for efficiently moving data between the network and the digital device, such as the network interface controller (NIC) chip. Another specific processor is the trusted platform module (TPM), responsible for certain tasks related to securing the digital device. In contrast, the main processor of a digital device, also called the central processing unit (CPU), is not designed with any specific purpose and is the functional core constituent of every such device. Sitting somewhere between highly specialized (such as a TPM) and highly generic (for example, a CPU) is a graphical processing unit (GPU). As the name suggests, a GPU is designed to display complex and fast-moving 2D and 3D graphics. In recent years GPUs have become more capable and are now able to perform certain tasks more efficiently than CPUs, notably machine-learning tasks. Each processor is itself made up of a number of constituent parts. Together, these parts receive data, perform logical or arithmetic operations and output the results. The results are passed to another processor, a local storage facility or a display unit, or 'uploaded' via a network connection to another device.

Mobile devices

1.7 Hand-held devices are now ubiquitous. These include tablets and smartphones that combine personal computer functionality with telephone and camera capabilities. Such devices are computers, since they have one or more processors, memory, a keypad or mouthpiece (input), and a screen or earpiece (output). Like computers, hand-held devices have volatile and non-volatile memory. The non-volatile memory stores the system software and application software, and the user's data. The volatile memory is used by software to store data that is currently being worked on. (A more detailed discussion of memory and storage follows.) While data that is stored in volatile memory will be lost when the device loses power, turning 'off' a hand-held device usually places the device in a mode that uses a small amount of power to retain data in volatile memory and enables it to continue with essential tasks. Non-volatile memory in modern devices will usually be flash memory, a form of solid-state memory chip that is capable of retaining content without power. Other types of specialist mobile device include digital music players and ebook readers that can use wireless technology to download large volumes of data from a main computer.

1.8 All these devices, together with laptop computers, are increasingly used by organizations as components in an extended information technology infrastructure. Where relevant, such devices may be investigated for electronic evidence, although the amount of information that can be obtained will vary. For instance, while one may find only a list of the most recent telephone numbers called from an ordinary mobile telephone, a smartphone will probably yield substantial amounts of data, including emails and other data from a network that might aid an investigation.

1.9 The examples given above emphasize the types of electronic evidence that can be revealed by means of a forensic examination, including hidden or deleted data. Only a highly skilled person could remove all traces of evidence on a digital device, and such skills are very rare. Some forensic techniques exist that can recover data even when it has been strictly overwritten on disk. Whether these techniques will be used or implemented will depend on the type and value of the data sought to be recovered.

Embedded devices

1.10 The ubiquity of the microprocessor has led to the increasing use of embedded devices. An embedded device or embedded system is a computer system in its own right that combines a processor, memory, and input and/or output peripheral devices to execute a dedicated function within a larger mechanical or electrical system. The three functions – processor, memory and peripheral interfaces – may in turn be combined into a specialized or dedicated microprocessor known as a microcontroller. Unlike multitasking computers, embedded devices typically handle one highly specialized task, but can be combined with other similar devices to form highly complex structures, such as the different embedded devices that together enable an autonomous car to drive. Embedded devices control many systems in common use today,[1] and have consumer, industrial, automotive, home appliance, medical, telecommunications, commercial and military applications.[2] These include, among other things, white electronic goods, burglar alarms, industrial robots, spectrometers and neutron transmission monitors,[3] breath alcohol intoximeters,[4] radar devices,[5] traffic control systems[6] and hotel telephone call-billing systems. Consequently, any evidence produced using or generated by any of these devices is electronic evidence.[7] The versatility and range of these Internet of Things devices means that data from embedded systems is a rapidly increasing source of data.

1 Around 98 per cent of all microprocessors produced each year are used in embedded devices. See Michael Barr, 'Real men program in C', Embedded, 1 August 2009, https://www.embedded.com/real-men-program-in-c/.
2 Embedded system (Wikipedia), https://en.wikipedia.org/wiki/Embedded_system#Applications.
3 *R v Wood (Stanley William)* [1982] 6 WLUK 191, (1983) 76 Cr App R 23, [1982] Crim LR 667, [1983] CLY 636; *PP v Ang Soon Huat* [1990] 2 SLR(R) 246.
4 *Castle v Cross* [1984] 1 WLR 1372, [1985] 1 All ER 87, [1984] 7 WLUK 180, [1985] RTR 62, [1984] Crim LR 682, (1984) 81 LSG 2596, (1984) 128 SJ 855, [1985] CLY 3048.
5 *The Statue of Liberty Owners of Motorship Sapporo Maru v Owners of Steam Tanker Statue of Liberty* [1968] 1 WLR 739, [1968] 2 All ER 195, [1968] 1 Lloyd's Rep 429, [1968] 3 WLUK 65, (1968) 112 SJ 380, [1968] CLY 1546.
6 By way of example, see Thomas Novak and Christoph Stoegerer, 'Embedded system platform for safety-critical road traffic signal applications' in Friedemann Bitsch, Jérémie Guiochet and Mohamed Kaâniche (eds) *Computer Safety, Reliability, and Security*, 32nd International Conference, SAFECOMP 2013, Toulouse, France, 14–27 September, Proceedings (Springer 2013), 138–145.
7 Daniel Seng, 'Computer output as evidence' [1997] SJLS 130, 135–137, 173–175.

1.11 From a forensic perspective, particularly problematic types of embedded device are medical or similar devices that are embedded in biological bodies, sometimes in humans – in the form of intelligent pacemakers – but also sometimes in other animals.[1] Both are sometimes collectively referred to as examples of the 'Internet of Bodies', in juxtaposition to the Internet of Things.[2] For obvious reasons, collecting evidence from these devices while the host is still alive poses significant legal, ethical and technological challenges.

1 https://expmag.com/2020/06/health-tracking-implants-can-create-bionic-cows-are-humans-next/.
2 Andrea M. Matwyshyn, 'The Internet of Bodies' (2019) 61 Wm & Mary L Rev 77.

1.12 Data from embedded devices can have a high level of forensic relevance. These systems regularly operate in autonomous ways and collect data (sometimes including video or audio data) without the need for human intervention. Furthermore, the user or owner will often have only very limited ways to obtain access to, delete or manipulate the data on these devices. If the system in which these devices are embedded is mobile, they will regularly generate geolocation data that can help locate the user and reveal their activity at a specific moment in time. Embedded devices also pose investigative challenges;[1] sometimes, knowledge of the characteristics of the hardware and the surrounding environment are needed to correctly access and interpret the data on these devices. The diversity of the types of device available and their proprietary nature, which will be protected by trade secrets, can make it difficult to establish general protocols and methods.

1 Ronald Van der Knijff, 'Embedded systems analysis' in Eoghan Casey (ed) *Handbook of Digital Forensics and Investigation* (Academic Press 2010), 383–435.

1.13 Data preservation in embedded systems poses particular challenges. It will not always be obvious if embedded systems are switched on or off, which other components of a particular system they are connected to, or if those components can change the data on the target device. For example, carrying an object with an embedded device from a crime scene to a police station can cause a change in geolocation data through the mere act of movement. Sometimes, extraction of the device or its chips will be impossible or overly expensive, and sometimes it is not possible to switch off the device without risking harm to others (as with a traffic control system).

Software

1.14 Software consists of programs that give instructions to the digital device. There are three main categories of software: firmware, system software and application software.

Firmware

1.15 Firmware is software that is highly specialized to the component that it controls, and will usually be written by the same organization that produces the hardware component. Firmware may be stored on the component itself or may be stored as part of the system software and loaded onto the component when the digital device is switched on. Firmware is responsible for controlling the component and its interaction with other components that are part of the digital device.

System software

1.16 As the name suggests, system software is required for the basic operation of a device. The set of software programs that manage the basic operation of a digital device is called the operating system. The operating system controls the flow of data, allocates memory and manages any hardware components of the device, such as the display, input device(s), network interaction, etc. The operating system also permits the user to manage any user-specific files, enabling multiple users to share the use of the digital device, and acts as an interface between the hardware and the application software.

Application software

1.17 Broadly speaking, for more traditional computing devices such as desktop computers, smartphones, laptops and tablets, the application software (or 'apps' as they are also known) provides the user-facing side of the system. This is 'special purpose' software that enables the user to undertake specific kinds of tasks on the computer. These include word processing, desktop publishing, web browsing, emailing, social networking, preparing and delivering presentations, performing complex sets of numerical calculations, among others. Examples of application software include Microsoft Word, Outlook, PowerPoint, Excel, Chrome and LibreOffice. These and other application programs represent the main reasons for which most people use computers and smart mobile devices (that is, to perform specific tasks, which are made simpler by means of the computer and its application software). For other digital devices, the user may only engage the application software through a limited range of functions, such as status checks on a fitness tracker or energy consumption on a smart meter.

The clock

1.18 One further component must be discussed in relation to the operation of digital devices: the clock. The clock serves two functions:

> (1) It is a device that produces pulses of electrical signals that oscillate between a high state and a low state to ensure that events are synchronized and occur in a predictable order. The clock coordinates all the components of the device, including the processor and other digital circuits. Each step in any operation must follow in sequence, although some operations run at different speeds. All parts of the circuit are synchronized to the pulses of the electronic clock. The frequency of pulses is controlled by a phase locked loop (PLL), which, in turn is regulated by a quartz crystal. The speed at which the crystal oscillates, the step-up ratio of the PLL and the number of steps that each instruction requires will determine the speed at which the computer operates.
>
> (2) Also known as a real-time clock, RTC or system clock, the clock also often serves to keep the time of day and date in a human sense. Larger computer systems synchronize their clocks with a reliable time source available over the Internet, using a system interface such as the Network Time Protocol. This allows devices attached to the Internet to synchronize their time settings (taking into account geographical locations and time zones) with Internet time servers. There are two important reasons to provide for the synchronization of time. The first is to ensure that events occur on time, and in the correct sequence. This permits events to be scheduled and enables the fact that they have occurred to be registered accurately. The second is to enable the retrieval of information concerning past events, including establishing when the events occurred and the sequence in which they occurred. This is only possible if accurate time stamps are available. Examples include the time-stamping mechanism relating to authentication, digital signatures and the diagnosis of faults recorded on system event logs. Likewise, email systems and other messaging systems generally time-stamp messages using Coordinated Universal Time, so that the client email system can display the date and time of the message using the client's local time zone.

1.19 In most implementations the built-in real-time clock is powered by a battery and runs continuously even when the device is switched off. Devices that have lain for a long time without being powered on may not 'boot up' when they are switched on, because the battery has run down and may require recharging or replacing. We should also note that the clock in digital devices is often imprecise. Usually, the clock can be adjusted (and even incorrectly set) manually. This can result in the system clock being slightly incorrect (through 'drift' in timekeeping) relative to the actual time in the local region. Such inaccuracy may affect uses of the clock for event scheduling and logging, since both aspects may depend on the time as derived from the system clock. Where the accuracy of time is important, the clock usually requires occasional adjustment to bring the time back into line with better reference sources (such as Internet time servers). This is a matter of some significance, since unquestioned and out-of-context assumptions about the accuracy or otherwise of a clock may result in a misleading conclusion.

Time stamps

1.20 From the perspective of electronic evidence, the system clock often plays a vital role in time-stamping events. For instance, the operating system uses the date and time settings to annotate its record of events such as the creation or modification of a file. In computers, such information is often referred to as file 'metadata' (the data that describes or interprets the base data), since the date and time information is associated with the file, but is not part of the data in the file or data that the user has any direct control over. Time stamps are also recorded against system events such as user logins, password changes and – depending on the purpose of the device – sensor-recorded events such as the number of steps walked by the device wearer and the wearer's pulse rate. The time and date information associated with such events is recorded in system log files (event logs). Such logs are often an important source of event sequence information and afford insights on purported specific user activity.

1.21 As noted earlier, the system clock in a computer can be set by the user and may not be configured to maintain the correct current time (such as by using the Network Time Protocol). Incorrect time settings will be reflected in the date and time stamps subsequently recorded by the system. Obviously, this potential anomaly must be considered when dealing with data that is time-stamped. Since the time zone is also set in the system, an incorrect choice of zones may result in an incorrect current date or time. In addition, because of the critical role the clock plays, it features a great deal in electronic evidence, particularly where it is manipulated by the defendant to hide changes made to critical evidence.[1]

1 Chet Hosmer, 'Proving the integrity of digital evidence with time' (2002) 1(1) Intl J of Digital Evidence; Chris Boyd and Pete Forster, 'Time and date issues in forensic computing – a case study' (2004) 1(1) Digital Investigation 18; Malcolm W. Stevens, 'Unification of relative time frames for digital forensics' (2004) 1(3) Digital Investigation 225.

Memory and storage

1.22 In order to retain programs, output results and other data on which programs operate, digital devices rely on storage. There are generally speaking two forms of storage: primary storage and secondary storage. Primary storage is storage that is directly accessible by the processor. In general, this takes the form of semiconductor memory, such as:

(1) An internal storage chip known as *random access memory* (RAM).[1] This chip is capable of repeatedly storing (writing) and retrieving stored data (reading) at very high speeds.

(2) An internal storage chip that is capable of storing data once, but does not allow the data to be rewritten. Once data has been entered, this type of chip only allows the data to be read. This is called *read-only memory* (ROM).[2]

(3) An internal storage chip that stores data and behaves as a ROM during its normal operation, but permits data to be erased and replaced. This form of device is known as *erasable programmable read-only memory* (EPROM).[3] A flash ROM is a type of EPROM.

1 Random-access memory (Wikipedia), https://en.wikipedia.org/wiki/Random-access_memory.
2 Read-only memory (Wikipedia), https://en.wikipedia.org/wiki/Read-only_memory.
3 EPROM (Wikipedia), https://en.wikipedia.org/wiki/EPROM.

1.23 Secondary storage is storage that is not directly accessible by the processor. Where data on which it is stored is required, the processor will use its input/output channels to obtain access to the secondary storage and transfer the required data into the primary storage. Unlike RAM, secondary storage is non-volatile: it retains its data when the device is powered down. Hard disk drives (HDDs), solid-state drives (SSDs) and Universal Serial Bus (USB) 'thumb drives' used as storage media are typical forms of secondary storage. They may be permanently attached to the computer (internal storage) or attached when required (external storage). Other forms of external storage may be less proximal to the computer, such as network-attached storage (NAS),[1] tape drives or 'cloud' storage. Because secondary storage is non-volatile, the hard disk and associated offline storage media are a significant source of electronic evidence for a device. But the fact that primary memory such as RAM is volatile does not mean that its data cannot be retrieved. An experiment on 'freezing' RAM chips before physical removal and transfer to a different computer revealed an unusual context in which it was possible to recover RAM data from the treated chips.[2]

1 Network-attached storage (Wikipedia), https://en.wikipedia.org/wiki/Network-attached_storage.
2 J. Alex Halderman, Seth D. Schoen, Nadia Heninger, William Clarkson, William Paul, Joseph A. Calandrino, Ariel J. Feldman, Jacob Appelbaum and Edward W. Felten, 'Lest we remember: cold boot attacks on encryption keys' in *Proceedings of the 17th Conference on Security Symposium* (USENIX Association 2008); and (2009) 52(5) Communications of the ACM 91, https://www.usenix.org/legacy/event/sec08/tech/full_papers/halderman/halderman.pdf.

Data storage facilities

1.24 The increasingly varied methods of storing digital data and the variety of storage contexts mean that locating relevant data as prospective evidence may not be a simple matter. Data may be stored locally on a computing device, such as on hard disks, DVDs or CDs, flash drives, memory sticks or micro memory devices (commonly found in smartphones). But data may also be stored remotely on NAS, remote networks or 'cloud' facilities. Of concern to many digital investigators is the difficulty inherent in locating and obtaining legal access to data that is stored remotely from an individual's computer.

1.25 A further level of complexity has developed since 2009 with a significant increase in distributed data storage. A well-known example is blockchain. In these approaches to data storage, distributed ledgers are maintained across a considerable number of machines (the 'nodes'). Replicating data on such a scale provides for the quality of the data and makes the storage medium particularly resilient to attacks directed against availability and integrity. Authenticity of the copies at each node are provable through computation, creating a system of 'computational trust' in which no node has priority over another. The inherent transparency of the blockchain and similar decentralized data storage technologies offers advantages in forensic investigations.[1] However, the use of encryption can also pose challenges. From a legal perspective, the decentralized nature of the storage causes similar problems to cloud computing when it comes to questions of applicable jurisdiction, while concepts such as computational trust and data replication pose further challenges to traditional evidential concepts such as the original/copy dichotomy.[2]

1 Blockchain technology was accepted as a means of authentication in China in the case of *Hangzhou Huatai Yimei Culture Media Co., Ltd. v Shenzhen Daotong Technology Development Co., Ltd.* (2018) Zhe 0192 Civil Case, First Court No. 81, Hangzhou Internet Court of the People's Republic of China, translated by Dr Jiong He, Digital Evidence and Electronic Signature Law Review (2019) 16, 61–70.
2 Joseph Ricci, Ibrahim Baggili and Frank Breitinger, 'Blockchain-based distributed cloud storage digital forensics: where's the beef?' (2019) 17(1) IEEE Security & Privacy, 34–42; S. Naqvi, 'A126: Challenges of cryptocurrencies forensics: a case study of investigating, evidencing and prosecuting organised cybercriminals' in *ARES 2018: Proceedings of the 13th International Conference on Availability, Reliability and Security* (27 August–30 August 2018), 1–5, http://www.open-access.bcu.ac.uk/6093/1/Challenges%20of%20cryptocurrencies%20forensics.pdf.

1.26 The common data storage contexts are summarized in the table below.

Memory type	Volatile	Local
RAM	Yes	Yes
HDD (internal) SSD (internal)	No	Yes
HDD (portable) SSD (portable)	No	Perhaps
Flash/USB	No	Perhaps
CD/DVD	No	Perhaps
Network	No	Perhaps
Cloud	No	Typically No

Data formats

1.27 Digital data may be broadly classified into binary data, where the information is represented in binary form, and text data, including alpha, numeric and punctuation data. Text can be entered into the computer by a range of methods:

(i) The typing of letters, numbers and punctuation, mainly when using a keyboard.

(ii) Scanning a page with an image scanner and converting the image into data by using optical character recognition (OCR)[1] software.

(iii) Using a bar code. The bar code represents alphanumeric data and is read with an optical device called a wand or scanner. The scanned code is converted into binary signals, enabling a bar code translation component to read the data.

(iv) Reading the magnetic stripe on the back of a credit card.

(v) Using voice data, where a person speaks into a microphone capable of recording the sounds. This form of data, as well as video data, is encoded in binary form.

(vi) Converting from speech to text. Here, the user speaks into a microphone that is connected to the computer and a dedicated software application analyses the input signal and converts this to a textual representation of the spoken words.

1 Optical character recognition (Wikipedia), https://en.wikipedia.org/wiki/Optical_character_recognition.

1.28 To enable a user to view text and numbers, and to see images or hear sound, the binary form of the data must be converted using a code. Computers manipulate binary (base 2) information, but for human convenience it is more common to represent computer numbers in the octal (base 8) or hexadecimal (base 16) system. A range of codes exists to represent text data in numerical form (to enable machine processing).[1] Some of the codes in common use are the American Standard Code for Information Exchange (ASCII),[2] Extended Binary Code Decimal Interchange Code (EBCDIC),[3] Unicode Transformation Format–8 (UTF-8)[4] and Unicode Transformation Format-16 (UTF-16).[5] UTF-8 and UTF-16 are capable of encoding the characters standardized by the Unicode Consortium, including all commonly used characters in currently spoken languages, but the two standards differ in how text data is represented in binary form. Computers running Microsoft Windows commonly use ASCII and UTF-16, and most others use ASCII and UTF-8. EBCDIC is commonly found on IBM mainframe computers and some applications designed for such systems, particularly banking software. Tools are available to display binary data used in computers to enable a digital investigator to view features that are normally not visible to the computer user. For instance, documents stored in the Microsoft Word format contain application metadata that are normally not visible. By using certain types of software program, a digital evidence professional is able to view all aspects of the data and such data may reveal crucial information that may help an investigation.

1 Character encoding (Wikipedia), https://en.wikipedia.org/wiki/Character_encoding.
2 ASCII (Wikipedia), https://en.wikipedia.org/wiki/ASCII; Vinton Cerf, 'RFC 20 – ASCII format for Network Interchange' (Internet Engineering Task Force, 16 October 1969), https://tools.ietf.org/html/rfc20.
3 EBCDIC (Wikipedia), https://en.wikipedia.org/wiki/EBCDIC; J. M. Winett, 'RFC 183 – The EBCDIC Codes and Their Mapping to ASCII' (Internet Engineering Task Force, 21 July 1971), https://tools.ietf.org/html/rfc183; R. T. Braden, 'RFC 338 – EBCDIC/ASCII Mapping for Network RJE' (Internet Engineering Task Force, 17 May 1972), https://tools.ietf.org/html/rfc338.
4 UTF-8 (Wikipedia), https://en.wikipedia.org/wiki/UTF-8; F. Yergeau, 'RFC 3629 – UTF-8, a transformation format of ISO 10646' (Internet Engineering Task Force, November 2003), https://tools.ietf.org/html/rfc3629.
5 UTF-16 (Wikipedia), https://en.wikipedia.org/wiki/UTF-16; P. Hoffman and F. Yergeau, 'RFC 2781 – UTF16, an encoding of ISO 10646' (Internet Engineering Task Force, February 2000), https://tools.ietf.org/html/rfc2781.

Starting a computer

1.29 Every time a digital device is switched on, various components must interact with each other for it to begin working. This is called the start-up process or 'booting' the system. Most devices have a program stored in the non-volatile memory called variously a boot loader, boot process, boot strap or initial program load. It is this program that enables the system to start. In general terms, this is how it works:

> (1) When the system is powered on, control is first transferred to the bootstrap loader, bootstrap or boot loader.[1] On a PC, this is sometimes known as the basic input and output system (BIOS),[2] a small program located permanently in the non-volatile memory of the device.
>
> (2) The boot loader tests the various components of the system, verifying that they are active and working. The results of the various tests it carries out may appear on the system output. The boot process can also clear local primary memory of all historical data and metadata. It then loads up a second-stage boot loader which it has found on booting the device (a non-volatile storage device) to continue the start-up process. On a PC, the BIOS locates the first (or default) secondary storage device, looks for an operating system on the storage device and passes control to the operating system's boot record (a set of instructions starting at a specific location on the storage device).
>
> (3) The second-stage boot loader takes control of the system. It loads and tests the configuration of the device before loading the operating system.
>
> (4) Finally, the operating system will display any startup dialogue (for instance, the identity of the mobile telephone service provider) and, if the user is authorized (for instance, by providing a code), grant access to application-level programs. The user can then take control of the device through an application.

1 Booting (Wikipedia), https://en.wikipedia.org/wiki/Booting.
2 BIOS (Wikipedia), https://en.wikipedia.org/wiki/BIOS.

Networks

1.30 Gone are the days when most computers stood alone on a desk. The majority of computers are now connected, or are intermittently connected, to other computers or a network. Given the trails left by the assortment of logs and files in computers, going online can produce electronic evidence in abundance, including the use of email, connection to the Internet and the websites viewed, and the transfer of files between computers. Other sources of electronic evidence can be obtained from server logs, the contents of devices connected to the network and the records of traffic activity. In many instances, even if a digital device has been destroyed or disposed of, relevant evidence may still be retrieved through the network to which the device has been connected.

Types of network

The Internet

1.31 The Internet was developed from its precursor, the ARPANET, which was created in 1969 to facilitate collaboration between research institutions, initially within the US and then later internationally. A wide range of applications have been developed to make use of the Internet, but the introduction of the World Wide Web in 1989, which provides a relatively easy-to-use way to share information, contributed to the dramatic growth of the Internet. When a digital device connects to the Internet, it uses a set of protocols called Transmission Control Protocol/Internet Protocol (TCP/IP).[1] This set of communication standards can be regarded as a common language that enables various types of network to communicate, each with the other. A digital device connected to a network is referred to as a 'host'. The device uses a modem or an NIC[2] to send and receive information, although medium-sized and large organizations will have a Local Area Network (LAN)[3] gateway to the Internet. Application software running on hosts provides services to users, building on the functionality that TCP/IP provides. The network itself does not have any knowledge of what the application is doing – only the application software running on the hosts at the ends of the connection interprets the data being carried over the network. This, called the end-to-end principle, is desirable because new Internet applications can be created without having to request the permission of the organizations running the network. Similarly, application software need not be concerned with the details of how the network transfers data from one end of the communication to another, and so networks may change the way they work provided they still preserve the functionality that applications expect.

1 Internet protocol suite (Wikipedia), https://en.wikipedia.org/wiki/Internet_protocol_suite; Vinton Cerf, 'RFC 675 – Specification of Internet Transmission Control (Internet Engineering Task Force, December 1974), https://tools.ietf.org/html/rfc675; F. Baker, 'RFC 1812 – Requirements for IP Version 4 Routers' (Internet Engineering Task Force, June 1995), https://tools.ietf.org/html/rfc1812.
2 Network interface controller (Wikipedia), https://en.wikipedia.org/wiki/Network_interface_controller.
3 Local area network (Wikipedia), https://en.wikipedia.org/wiki/Local_area_network.

1.32 A further component of the modern communication infrastructure is the server. These are hosts that run application software, but rather than providing a service to the individual sitting in front of the computer, they provide a range of customers with a service over the network, for instance hosting an organization's web service or email facility. Some servers permit anyone to obtain access to their resources without limitation. Other servers restrict access to some resources to authorized users only, usually by means of a username and password. Sources of electronic evidence from servers include the data necessary to provide the web service hosted by the servers, as well as the logs recording when a user connects to a server, whether to get access to the Internet or to download email.

IP addresses

1.33 The purpose of an Internet Protocol (IP) address is to identify a particular device connected to the Internet. Each unit of data (packet) sent over the Internet includes the IP address of the device for which the packet is intended (the destination). The devices responsible for directing packets to the correct destination (routers) use this destination IP address to make decisions on how best to dispatch packets. Routers may also be responsible for filtering traffic that is not permitted and keeping logs of activity. Packets also contain the IP address allocated to the device that sent the packet (the source), to allow that packet to be replied to. IP addresses currently in use take one of two forms: version 4 (IPv4), for example 198.51.100.42, and version 6 (IPv6), for example 2001:0db8:85a3:0000:0000:8a2e:0370:7334. For a device to be able to communicate over the public Internet directly, that device needs to be allocated a public IP address. Each public IP address should be allocated to at most one device worldwide. If two or more devices are allocated the same public IP address, then problems are likely to occur, so network providers put in place technical and procedural controls to prevent this occurring.

1.34 IP addresses may also be private. Such IP addresses are allocated to devices which do not directly connect to the Internet. Devices allocated a private IP address may only communicate with the public Internet via an intermediary which has been allocated a public IP address. There are many devices worldwide, each allocated a private IP address, but packets with a source or destination IP address that is private should not be sent over the public Internet. Network providers also have in place technical and procedural controls to prevent this occurring.

1.35 There are just over 4 billion possible IPv4 addresses, and far more IPv6 addresses.[1] To ensure that no two devices are allocated the same public IP address, IP addresses are distributed by a central organization: the Internet Assigned Numbers Authority (IANA). IANA delegates large groups of IP addresses to regional authorities, which in turn delegate smaller groups of IP addresses to network operators. For example, the regional authority for Europe is Réseaux IP Européens (RIPE), the regional authority for North America is the American Registry for Internet Numbers (ARIN) and the regional authority for the Asia Pacific region is the Asia Pacific Network Information Centre (APNIC). Information about which network operator is responsible for a particular group of IP address is listed in a WHOIS database maintained by the relevant regional authority. Public IP addresses are frequently used to attribute behaviour to individuals, but IP addresses identify Internet-connected devices, not people. There are three main ways in which one IP address can correspond to multiple people, all of which may occur simultaneously.

1 Specifically, 340,282,366,920,938,463,463,374,607,431,768,211,456 or approximately 3 followed by 38 zeros.

1.36 First, the operator of a network may allocate a given public IP address to different devices at different points in time. This scheme of IP address allocation is known as dynamic allocation. The period of time for which an IP address is dynamically allocated to a given device could be anything from a few hours to a few months. An alternative scheme of IP address allocation is static allocation, where the network operator allocates the same IP address to a particular device, if that is feasible. Even if static allocation is used, there may still be changes in which a device is allocated a particular IP address for operational reasons.

1.37 Second, the operator of a network may allocate private IP addresses to a group of devices, then connect these devices to the public Internet via an intermediary device with a single public IP address. From the perspective of the public Internet, all devices within this group will share the same IP address. This configuration is common for a home network: all devices within the home have private IP addresses, and the home router performs Network Address Translation (NAT) to allow all these devices to share the single public IP address allocated to the home router. In addition, operators of mobile networks (carriers) commonly use NAT to share a single public IP address between hundreds or even thousands of different customers. This scheme is known as Carrier-Grade NAT (CGN). CGN (sharing a public IP address between different customers) can be used in combination with home NAT (sharing a public IP address, which may itself be shared, with multiple devices using a home router). NAT is common for IPv4 connections because there are not enough IPv4 addresses for every device connected to the Internet to have its own address. IPv6 has more than enough addresses, but network providers may nevertheless decide to apply NAT.

1.38 Third, a single device may have multiple users – sequentially or concurrently. These multiple users may be authorized by the owner of the device or may be unauthorized (that is, they have hacked into the computer and are using it without authorization). From the perspective of the public Internet, all users of a device will share the same public IP address that the device uses to connect to the Internet (directly or indirectly). Redirecting communication via another computer is known as proxying the connection.

1.39 In summary, a single public IP address may be used by different customers at different times. At any one time, a single public IP address may be used by multiple customers (CGN). Each customer may be sharing their IP address over many devices (NAT). Each device may have many users (authorized or unauthorized), at the same time or at different times. Consequently, attributing Internet activity requires consulting a wide range of stored logs, each of which have limitations in terms of the extent that they may be relied upon.[1]

1 Richard Clayton, 'Anonymity and traceability in cyberspace', PhD thesis, University of Cambridge, November 2005, https://www.cl.cam.ac.uk/techreports/UCAM-CL-TR-653.html.

Corporate intranets

1.40 An intranet, usually run by a large organization, is a private network that in principle is only available to members and employees of the organization or others with authorization to obtain access to and use the information contained on the network. The intranet may look like a smaller version of the Internet, providing websites, mail servers and time servers among other facilities. Usually situated within the corporate firewall, an intranet is built to support the internal needs of the organization, as well as to improve workforce connectivity and business operations. As such, it generally aims to keep those outside the organization from gaining access, and is usually well protected.

Wireless networking

1.41 A further development in this form of networking is wireless technology. One implementation of wireless networking is Wi-Fi[1] (a mark used by the Wi-Fi Alliance), mainly through the 2.4 GHz and 5 GHz radio bands based on the 802.11 communications standard.[2] Another wireless technology standard, known as Bluetooth,[3] is a standard for exchanging data between devices over short distances using ultra high frequency (UHF) radio waves in the 2.402 GHz to 2.480 GHz band. From an evidential perspective, logs exist to record the use of wireless networks, affording evidence of the use that a device has made of a network.

1 Wi-Fi (Wikipedia), https://en.wikipedia.org/wiki/Wi-Fi.
2 The number 802 is the name given to the interoperability standard developed by the Institute of Electrical and Electronic Engineers for Local Area Networks and Metropolitan Area Networks, and Wi-Fi is based on 802.11, which is a subset of the 802 standard relating to wireless local area networks.
3 Bluetooth (Wikipedia), https://en.wikipedia.org/wiki/Bluetooth.

Cellular networks

1.42 A cellular network or mobile network is a communications network that enables portable devices such as cellular telephones to communicate with each other. The network is made up of a number of cell sites (base stations) within a defined geographical area. An individual connected to a cell site can make and receive calls over the network. Each cell site is connected to a central computing infrastructure, comprising telephone exchanges or switches, which are in turn connected to the public telephone network. This infrastructure processes the calls by routing them to their destination, and retains logs for the purpose of sending out bills, maintenance and, if necessary, carrying out investigations. The most recent developments in cellular technology include General Packet Radio Services (GPRS),[1] the third generation (3G),[2] the Universal Mobile Telecommunications System (UMTS),[3] the fourth generation (4G,)[4] the Long-Term Evolution (LTE)[5] standard and the fifth generation (5G) standard,[6] developments that provide for faster transmission rates and enable applications such as mobile web access, IP telephony, gaming services, high-definition mobile TV and video conferencing. Many mobile service providers plan to introduce these new systems to replace the Global System for Mobile Communications (GSM)[7] standard, which is now considered to have exploitable security flaws.

1 General Packet Radio Service (Wikipedia), https://en.wikipedia.org/wiki/General_Packet_Radio_Service.
2 3G (Wikipedia), https://en.wikipedia.org/wiki/3G.
3 UMTS (telecommunication) (Wikipedia), https://en.wikipedia.org/wiki/UMTS (telecommunication).
4 4G (Wikipedia), https://en.wikipedia.org/wiki/4G.
5 LTE (telecommunication) (Wikipedia), https://en.wikipedia.org/wiki/LTE (telecommunication).
6 5G (Wikipedia), https://en.wikipedia.org/wiki/5G.
7 GSM (Wikipedia), https://en.wikipedia.org/wiki/GSM; H. Haverinen and J. Salowey (eds.), 'RFC 4186 – Extensible Authentication Protocol Method for Global System for Mobile Communications (GSM) Subscriber Identity Modules (EAP-SIM)' (Internet Engineering Task Force, January 2006), https://www.ietf.org/rfc/rfc4186.txt.

1.43 A mobile telephone has several numbers that identify the device. The manufacturer includes an electronic serial number (ESN)[1] or the International Mobile Equipment Identity (IMEI)[2] number as a code to uniquely identify mobile devices. The International Mobile Subscriber Identity (IMSI)[3] number is a unique identification number, usually located in the SIM card of the telephone, to identify the subscriber of a cellular network. To prevent the subscriber from being identified, this number is rarely sent. What is sent in its place is the Temporary Mobile Subscriber Identity (TMSI),[4] which is randomly generated and assigned to the telephone the moment it is switched on to enable communications between the mobile device and the base station. Finally, the mobile identification number (MIN) or mobile subscription identification number (MSIN)[5] is the unique telephone directory number for the mobile subscription that is used to identify a telephone. It is derived from the last part of the IMSI.

1 Electronic serial number (Wikipedia), https://en.wikipedia.org/wiki/Electronic_serial_number.
2 International Mobile Station Equipment Identity (Wikipedia), https://en.wikipedia.org/wiki/International_Mobile_Station_Equipment_Identity.
3 International mobile subscriber identity (Wikipedia), https://en.wikipedia.org/wiki/International_mobile_subscriber_identity.
4 Mobility management (Wikipedia), https://en.wikipedia.org/wiki/Mobility_management#TMSI.
5 Mobile identification number (Wikipedia), https://en.wikipedia.org/wiki/Mobile_identification_number.

1.44 To ensure the telephone company knows the correct base station to which to direct the call, the position of the telephone is constantly tracked when it is switched on. Thus, there is a broad range of electronic evidence associated with the use of a mobile telephone, including where the telephone was located geographically, details of calls made and received, and the contents of text messages.[1] Where a telephone is capable of being used in other ways, such as making micro-payments, data relating to such services are also capable of being retrieved.[2]

1 In *R v Brooker* [2014] EWCA Crim 1998 also cited as *AG's Ref: 071 of 2014, R v B (R C A) (2014)* (available on the LexisNexis database), Brooker falsely accused her former partner, Paul Fensome, of various crimes including rape and assault. Cell site analysis determined that Brooker was not at various locations as she claimed. In addition, because Mr Fensome retained all of the text messages exchanged with Brooker, it was possible to establish that the relationship between the two was not as alleged by Brooker.

2 Svein Yngvar Willassen, 'Forensics and the GSM mobile telephone system' (2003) 2(1) Intl J of Digital Evidence.

Cloud computing

1.45 Cloud computing is not new. Back in the 1960s, computer bureaus would allow companies to rent time on a mainframe as a 'time-sharing' service. With the rise of the personal computer, which made affordable computer ownership possible, it fell into relative obscurity, but became popular again in the early 2000s.[1] Today, cloud computing refers to the use of high-speed and high-capacity network access to make computer system resources available to users at any time and anywhere, without direct active management by the users – who may be individuals or corporations.[2] These resources tend to be data storage (cloud storage), computing power and applications, and are provided as service models in which the cloud computing providers offer various 'services' according to different service models, such as 'Software as a service' (SaaS), 'Platform as a service' (PaaS) and 'Infrastructure as a service' (IaaS).[3] By sharing resources among users, cloud providers bring the economies of scale to users and enable them to avoid or minimize the cost of putting IT infrastructure into place. The 'pay-as-you-go' model also offers users the ability to increase or reduce their use of the resources depending on their needs.

1 Steve Ranger, 'What is cloud computing? Everything you need to know about the cloud explained', ZDNet, 13 December 2018, https://www.zdnet.com/article/what-is-cloud-computing-everything-you-need-to-know-about-the-cloud/.

2 Cloud computing (Wikipedia), https://en.wikipedia.org/wiki/Cloud_computing.

3 See NIST (National Institute for Standards and Technology) at https://csrc.nist.gov/publications/detail/sp/800-145/final#:~:text=Cloud%20computing%20is%20a%20model,effort%20or%20service%20provider%20interaction.

1.46 When reference is made to data that is being stored 'in the cloud', it does not mean that there is no tangible form for the data. The data still has to reside on the servers that companies set up in their data centres or, as is predominantly the case, multiple data centres that are geographically distributed. This architecture is intended to improve the performance, resilience and reliability of cloud computing services, especially since the data is constantly transferred and replicated across data centres, thereby providing for data redundancy. It also raises issues of security, data ownership, confidentiality, privacy and jurisdiction,[1] because resources are always available online (and sometimes in different geographical areas) and the service provider can accidentally or intentionally obtain access to the data on its servers at any time, or use the data for unauthorized purposes.[2] This also subjects cloud service providers to court orders and warrants that mandate that they share information with third parties, which in turn behoves the use of encryption by users to protect their data stored on the cloud. Organizations as users have also changed the way they use the cloud,[3] for instance combining cloud resources with on-premises resources (hybrid cloud) to better manage their resources. This has also affected the way electronic evidence on the cloud is located and collected for forensic purposes. A further discussion follows.

1 Miranda Mowbray, 'The fog over the Grimpen Mire: cloud computing and the law' (2009) 6(1) Scripted Journal of Law, Technology and Society 133, https://script-ed.org/archive/volume-6/issue-61-1-193/.
2 For example, see Mark D. Ryan, 'Cloud computing privacy concerns on our doorstep', Communications of the ACM (January 2011) 54(1), 36, DOI: 10.1145/1866739.1866751.
3 See NIST at https://csrc.nist.gov/publications/detail/sp/800-145/final#:~:text=Cloud%20computing%20is%20a%20model,effort%20or%20service%20provider%20interaction.

The Internet of Things

1.47 While the Internet was originally conceived as a network to enable people to communicate with one another, today it is also being used as a network to allow interrelated computing devices to transfer data between each other without requiring human interaction or intervention. This development is referred to as the Internet of Things (IoT).[1] In the consumer market, IoT is associated with products such as always-on speakers, home security systems and smart thermostats. In organizations, IoT has been used in the health care sector, manufacturing and logistics to enable the integration of sensors, trackers and other processing devices. The ubiquity of IoT has led to evidential discovery claims in the US being made against the companies that collect and store the data recorded by IoT devices.[2] At the same time, the advent of IoT has raised serious concerns about the adequacy of security in its implementation, which in turn raises questions about individual privacy and the quality of the electronic evidence collected by such devices.

1 Internet of Things (Wikipedia), https://en.wikipedia.org/wiki/Internet_of_things.
2 For example, see Nadeem Bohsali, 'Alexa: hear no evil', Blog Post, Richmond Journal of Law and Technology, 13 February 2020, https://jolt.richmond.edu/2020/02/13/alexa-hear-no-evil/.

The deep web and the dark web

1.48 The role of the Internet is simply to carry data from one computer to another, but for this to be a useful service to a user, application software must be created. For example, an email client allows its user to send and receive messages, and a web browser allows its user to view pages on the World Wide Web. Certain Internet applications, such as the web browser, are now considered to be a standard part of Internet provision. However, not all web pages can be viewed using only a web browser. Additional software can be used to increase the level of convenience or security for individuals providing or obtaining access to information. Such web pages make up the 'dark web'.[1]

1 Dark web (Wikipedia), https://en.wikipedia.org/wiki/Dark_web.

1.49 One example of dark-web software is corporate virtual private networks (VPNs), where web pages are available only to employees. The VPN software ensures that only authorized individuals can obtain access to the web pages and that, through the use of encryption, eavesdroppers are unable to view the content of pages being viewed. While a corporate VPN meets the criteria for the dark web, the term is more often associated with software designed to protect the identity of those providing the content of web pages. One of the most popular technologies of this type is Tor onion services, where website addresses end in .onion. Like a VPN, Tor onion services protect the content of web pages through encryption, but, unlike a VPN, Tor also hides the IP addresses of both the individual providing the web page and the individual obtaining access to the web page.

1.50 The additional level of security that Tor offers, as compared to a VPN, is desirable for people who want to share material censored in their country, and indeed Tor is used for this purpose. However, Tor onion services gained notoriety for enabling online marketplaces selling illicit products. When used for illegal purposes, the privacy Tor offers disrupts investigations of law enforcement authorities into the operator of the marketplace, as well as the sellers and purchasers of products. Cryptocurrencies are also used on such marketplaces, to reduce the risk that payments will be traced through the banking system.[1] Tor's security is far from perfect, however, and law enforcement authorities have shut down Tor onion sites participating in illegal activities and have discovered the identities of both the operators of the sites and their users. Examples include one of the first popular marketplaces for illegal drugs, The Silk Road, set up in 2011 and shut down by the FBI in 2013.[2] Law enforcement authorities are rarely explicit about the methods they use to trace individuals involved in dark websites, but approaches undoubtedly include some combination of the following:

(1) Exploiting design flaws and security vulnerabilities in software installed on the computer serving the dark web pages and/or the computers used to access them.

(2) Monitoring networks used by people suspected of being involved in running or using the website, and looking for patterns of use. Such timing patterns are not hidden by Tor's encryption and so can provide information about who is using which service.

(3) Gathering information from the dark website and linking this activity to another website to which an identity can more easily be attributed.

(4) Recruiting informants involved in the running of services and inducing them to collect information on behalf of law enforcement authorities.

(5) Tracing flows of cryptocurrencies until they can be linked to an identity.

1 For example, see Dr Clare Jones, Associate Professor Banking and Finance Law, Bristol Law School, Faculty of Business and Law, University of the West of England, Bristol, 'Digital currencies and organised crime update', https://core.ac.uk/download/pdf/323892795.pdf.

2 *United States of America v Ross William Ulbricht, a/k/a Dread Pirate Roberts, a/k/a Silk Road, a/k/ a Sealed Defendant 1, a/k/a DPR*, 858 F.3d 71 (2nd Cir 2017).

1.51 The use of encryption for providing access to a website and for making payments increases the complexity of collecting and interpreting evidence. Some of this evidence will be statistical in nature and so particular care is needed when applying probabilistic reasoning to reach conclusions. However, the underlying principles behind attributing Internet activity remain the same regardless of whether a standard website or a dark website are used. The nature of the dark web makes it difficult to assess how it is being used, but while it is used for illegal activities, the normal World Wide Web is still the preferred option for online crime.[1] The notoriety of illicit marketplaces attracts media attention, but it is probable that these make up only a small proportion of the around

175,000 Tor onion services (as of August 2020).[2] The technologies used for the dark web are not restricted to just providing websites. There are also dark-web equivalents of instant messaging networks, and file sharing.

1 In 2019, 0.2 per cent of child sexual abuse images assessed by the Internet Watch Foundation were hosted on onion services. See IWF 2019 Annual Report at https://www.iwf.org.uk/report/iwf-2019-annual-report-zero-tolerance; Chandrika Nath and Thomas Kriechbaumer, 'The darknet and online anonymity', POSTNOTE 488 (Parliamentary Office of Science & Technology, March 2015), https://post.parliament.uk/research-briefings/post-pn-488/.
2 https://metrics.torproject.org/hidserv-dir-onions-seen.html.

1.52 The dark web is frequently confused with the deep web. While it is necessary to use special software to obtain access to the dark web, the deep web refers to content that can be viewed using a normal web browser but which is password-protected or otherwise restricted in terms of who can view it. These pages include web mail, online banking, private social media pages and profiles, web forums that require registration for viewing and services that must be paid for to enable access ('paywalls'), such as video on demand and online content.[1] The deep web cannot be included in the index of search engines because their indexing software does not possess the passwords and other credentials that would allow them to obtain access to the deep web. Consequently, such content is less visible than that on the rest of the World Wide Web. Most search engines also do not include the dark web in their index, but this is because these search engines have made the business decision that dark web content is not sufficiently popular, rather than because they are not able to do so. There are, however, specialized search engines which can find pages on the dark web. Addresses of pages on the dark web can also be shared through links on standard web pages and through email, chat rooms or word of mouth. Content on the dark web can also be restricted through password protection, which would result in this content being inaccessible even to dark-web search engines.

1 Deep web (Wikipedia), https://en.wikipedia.org/wiki/Deep_web.

Common network applications

Email

1.53 A significant amount of correspondence undertaken within organizations and between organizations and individuals takes the form of the exchange of email. Email is, essentially, an unstructured form of communication, whose content determines its purpose. Email is an important source of electronic evidence. However, emails should be treated with some discretion, because a person can conceal his identity and hide behind a false email address with relative ease. It is very straightforward to send an email that appears to come from someone other than the real source. Forging emails might be effortless, but email is freely admitted into legal proceedings, both criminal and civil.

1.54 To obtain access to email, it is necessary to interact with two different services, one for outgoing mail and one for incoming mail. These services may or may not be provided by the same server. To read email, the individual must direct the email program to connect to a mail server using one of a number of protocols, the most common of which are: Post Office Protocol (POP),[1] Internet Message Access Protocol (IMAP)[2] and a Proprietary Microsoft Protocol called Messaging Application Programming Interface (MAPI).[3]

1 Post Office Protocol (Wikipedia), https://en.wikipedia.org/wiki/Post_Office_Protocol; J. Myers and M. Rose, 'RFC 1939 – Post Office Protocol – Version 3' (Internet Engineering Task Force, May 1996), https://tools.ietf.org/html/rfc1939.
2 Internet Message Access Protocol (Wikipedia), https://en.wikipedia.org/wiki/Internet_Message_Access_Protocol; M. Crispin, 'RFC 3501 – Internet Message Access Protocol – Version 4rev1' (Internet Engineering Task Force, March 2003), https://tools.ietf.org/html/rfc3501.
3 MAPI (Wikipedia), https://en.wikipedia.org/wiki/MAPI.

1.55 The POP protocol (POP3 is the most widely used version) permits the user to read her email by downloading it from a remote server onto the storage facility of her local computer or device. Once the email has been downloaded from the server, it is optionally deleted from the live server, but probably not from the backup server that will invariably be used by the mail service provider for the purpose of recovering from a failure for any reason. By contrast, the IMAP protocol (IMAP4 being the most widely used) enables the user to leave all her email on the mail server by default. Both POP and IMAP protocols require a user to have a username and a password before the user can obtain access to the mail download service. In addition, the protocol servers may keep logs of who checked emails and when they were checked. The existence of logs will enable an investigator to look for evidence of email traffic even where a user has deleted all of her emails.

1.56 Outgoing email uses a different protocol called Simple Mail Transfer Protocol (SMTP),[1] although MAPI also supports outgoing email. The servers supporting SMTP do not normally require a user to use a password. This makes it very easy for an individual to forge a message. However, the SMTP server may keep a log of the messages that pass through the system.

1 Simple Mail Transfer Protocol (Wikipedia), https://en.wikipedia.org/wiki/Simple_Mail_Transfer_Protocol; J. Klensin (ed.), 'RFC 5321 – Simple Mail Transfer Protocol' (Internet Engineering Task Force, October 2008), https://tools.ietf.org/html/rfc5321.

1.57 When an email is sent from a computer, it will pass on to one of a number of Message Transfer Agents (MTA). The MTAs act in the same way as post offices handling physical mail. A local MTA will receive the email. Upon receipt, it will add to the top of the email message received the current time and date, the name of the MTA and additional information. This information is in what is called the header of the email. As the message passes through various MTAs, each MTA will add further date and time stamps to the header. The most recent information will be at the top of the header. Another item of information that tends to be collected in the header is the IP address of the computer or system connecting to the server. Technically astute users of email who may wish to hide their identity can send messages through anonymous or pseudonymous re-mailing services. When email is sent through such a re-mailing agent, the header information may be stripped before the message is sent on to its destination. However, other forms of electronic evidence are transferred during such a process, and it is possible for forensic investigators to attempt to find evidence that may be useful.[1]

1 See Craig Earnshaw and Sandeep Jadav, 'E-mail tracing' (2004) 15(3) Computers & Law, 7 for an introduction.

Instant messaging

1.58 Instant messaging (IM) is a form of online communications service that enables the user to transmit a variety of text, voice and image messages to other individuals in real time over the Internet. This form of communication is similar to a conversation over the telephone, but the users communicate by typing messages into the software. The technology also permits the user to share files. Instant messaging has become popular because the software implementing the service can be downloaded at no cost, and is easy to install and use. Popular instant messaging software includes WhatsApp, Facebook Messenger, WeChat, Viber, LINE and Telegram. Data from such systems is also increasingly used as evidence in legal proceedings.[1]

1 For example, see *U.S. Commodity Future Trading Commission v Amaranth Advisors, L.L.C.*, 554 F Supp 2d 523 (SDNY 2008); *CX Digital Media, Inc. v Smoking Everywhere, Inc.*, 2011 WL 1102782 (SD Fla Mar 23, 2011).

1.59 Depending on the type of software used, the program will, when a message is initiated, connect the two devices, either via a direct point-to-point configuration or via a client–server configuration, through the ports of the devices. There are two significant problems with this in respect of producing reliable electronic evidence. First, in a client–server configuration the instant message server may not necessarily log such messages, which means that such conversations can be considered conceptually similar to conversations over the telephone. Second, the program may have a feature that allows for messages to pass through legitimate open ports if others are not available. Whether such conversations are recorded will depend on the software used. In an earlier variation of Instant Messaging known as Internet Relay Chat (IRC),[1] conversations take place in a similar way to a conference call. IRC is mainly designed for group communications, though it also allows for one-on-one communications via private messages. It frequently suffers from the same issues as instant messaging, in that the servers relaying messages are not necessarily configured to log conversations.

1 Internet Relay Chat (Wikipedia), https://en.wikipedia.org/wiki/Internet_Relay_Chat; C. Kalt, 'RFC 2812 – Internet Relay Chat: client protocol' (Internet Engineering Task Force, April 2000), https://tools.ietf.org/html/rfc2812; and 'RFC 2813 – Internet Relay Chat: server protocol' (Internet Engineering Task Force, April 2000), https://tools.ietf.org/html/rfc2813.

1.60 Since instant messaging requires various intermediaries to relay the messages from sender to recipient, to resist the interception of the message and loss of privacy, many instant messaging software packages have implemented encryption. These implementations may vary in the level of security they provide: some implementations secure the messages as between users (end-to-end encryption), but others only encrypt the messages in transit (link encryption), which enables the service provider to gain access to them. This allows the service provider to implement filtering, blocking and other editorial features, and also enables a party to require the service provider to preserve or disclose evidence.[1]

1 For instance, see the US cases of *Duhn Oil Tool, Inc. v Cooper Cameron Corporation*, 609 F.Supp.2d 1090 (E.D. Cal. 2009), reconsidered in *Duhn Oil Tool, Inc. v Cooper Cameron Corporation*, 2009 WL 3381052; *People for the Ethical Treatment of Animals, Inc. v Dade City's Wild Things, Inc.*, 2017 WL 5187770 (M.D. Fla. Nov. 9, 2017).

Peer-to-peer networking

1.61 As personal computers have developed, so has their capacity and power increased. As a result, there is less of a dividing line between a client and a server. This is because any host can be made a server by installing appropriate software onto the computer. This software then permits other clients to obtain access to the resources of the computer over the network. This is called peer-to-peer networking (P2P),[1] and is often the subject of litigation regarding intellectual property, especially regarding the downloading of music and films without payment. For instance, in Hong Kong a *Norwich Pharmacal*[2] order was granted in the case of *Cinepoly Records Co Ltd v Hong Kong Broadband Network Ltd*[3] in respect of a number of IP addresses, and in the case of *Polydor Ltd v Brown*[4] summary judgment was granted against the second defendant, Mr Bowles, for copyright infringement after a *Norwich Pharmacal* order was made against various Internet service providers whose subscribers' IP addresses had been identified as being used for allegedly infringing activity. In both cases the infringers were identified by the Internet service providers from their electronic records of the IP addresses assigned to their subscribers at the date and time when the allegedly infringing activity was taking place.[5]

1 Geoff Fellows, 'Peer-to-peer networking issues – an overview' (2004) 1(1) Digital Investigation 3; Peer-to-peer (Wikipedia), https://en.wikipedia.org/wiki/Peer-to-peer; G. Camarillo (ed.), 'RFC 5694 – Peer-to-peer (P2P) architecture: definition, taxonomies, examples, and applicability' (Internet Engineering Task Force, November 2009), https://tools.ietf.org/html/rfc5694.

2 *Norwich Pharmacal Co v Customs and Excise Commissioners* [1973] 3 WLR 164, [1973] 2 All ER 943, [1973] 6 WLUK 112, [1973] FSR 365, [1974] RPC 101, (1973) 117 SJ 567, [1973] CLY 2643. See generally Paul Torremans, *Holyoak and Torremans Intellectual Property Law* (9th edn, Oxford University Press 2019).

3 [2006] HKCFI 84, [2006] 1 HKLRD 255, HCMP 2487/2005 (26 January 2006).

4 [2005] EWHC 3191 (Ch), [2005] 11 WLUK 760, (2006) 29(3) IPD 29021.

5 For a similar case in Denmark, see Per Overbeck, 'The burden of proof in the matter of alleged illegal downloading of music in Denmark' (2010) 7 Digital Evidence and Electronic Signature Law Review 87; Per Overbeck, 'Alleged illegal downloading of music: the Danish Supreme Court provides a high bar for evidence and a new line of direction regarding claims for damages and remuneration' (2011) 8 Digital Evidence and Electronic Signature Law Review 165; similar comments were made by Baker DJ in *VPR Internationale v Does 1-1017*, 2011 WL 8179128; Thomas M. Dunlap and Nicholas A. Kurtz, 'Electronic evidence in torrent copyright cases' (2011) 8 Digital Evidence and Electronic Signature Law Review 171.

Social networking

1.62 The advent of Web 2.0 has seen an enormous increase in websites that permit users to provide their own content. This varies in type from uploaded video clips (on sites such as YouTube), photographs (on sites such as Flickr), personal musings in the form of blogs (personal Web logs), and interactive exchanges with a wider audience in the form of social networking sites (such as Facebook and Twitter) and their more business-oriented alternatives (such as LinkedIn). As social networking has increased in popularity, with a significant increase in participating users, several contexts arise in which the content of an individual's social network contribution may constitute evidence. For instance, an individual may be located at a specific place by means of his geotagged submissions to such a site,[1] and photographs uploaded to a social networking site often retain their geotag data and reflect the time and place at which they were taken. Many sites with contributions that contain such information have been used for the purposes of grooming[2] and blackmail.[3]

1 Jiebo Luo, Dhiraj Joshi, Jie Yu and Andrew Gallagher, 'Geotagging in multimedia and computer vision – a survey' (2011) 51(1) Multimed Tools Appl 187, https://doi.org/10.1007/s11042-010-0623-y.
2 *R. v Scott (Michael Lawrence)* [2008] EWCA Crim 3201, [2008] 12 WLUK 671; *R. v B (C)* [2010] EWCA Crim 3009, [2010] 12 WLUK 262.
3 *R. v Breakwell (Jake)* [2009] EWCA Crim 2298, [2009] 10 WLUK 647.

1.63 In a different vein, data from social media can also play an evidential role in both criminal and civil proceedings. This is obviously the case when the social media contribution itself constitutes a crime or a tort, for instance defamation, copyright violations or incitement to terrorist offences. More indirect use of such evidence can establish an alibi by locating an individual at a specific time and place in the same way as indicated above. In child custody cases, social media data has been used to demonstrate that a child was regularly left unsupervised late at night during schooldays, and social media information has provided evidence of spousal infidelity in divorce proceedings.[1] An individual's social network contributions may also help to determine political or social prejudices that in turn shed light on the character of a trial witness. The evidence may be recovered from the witness's contributions to social networking sites, depending on their availability and accessibility. If an individual has made such contributions under an alias, a digital evidence professional may be able to establish his true identity by matching his online contributions to the same content that is found on the individual's storage media.

1 By way of example, see *Lachaux v Lachaux* [2017] EWHC 385 (Fam), [2017] 4 WLR 57, [2017] 3 WLUK 67, [2018] 1 FLR 380, [2017] 2 FCR 678, [2017] CLY 984.

1.64 Finally, in addition to the content of individual contributions, the social network of a person can itself be of evidential value, for instance in investigations of terrorist organizations, criminal networks or any other situation where the law requires evidence of membership of a group or participation in a form of coordinated action. In such cases, it is increasingly common to use network analysis or similar artificial intelligence tools to identify structures within social media networks.[1]

1 Michael Chau and Jennifer Jie Xu, 'Mining communities and their relationships in blogs: a study of online hate groups' (2007) 65(1) International Journal of Human-Computer Studies 57; Stephen Kelley, Mark Goldberg, Malik Magdon-Ismail, Konstantin Mertsalov and Al Wallace, 'Defining and discovering communities in social networks', https://core.ac.uk/download/pdf/209214163.pdf.

Types of evidence available on a digital device

1.65 A digital evidence professional can make a range of evidence available from a digital device. This section provides an outline of some of the types of evidence that can be gleaned.

Files

1.66 A wide range of application software is used on computers, laptops, tablets and mobile telephones, including programs that enable a user to send messages, prepare spreadsheets, databases and text documents, take digital photographs, and create multimedia and presentations. This data, referred to as files on the digital device or on networks, will store messages, spreadsheets, databases, texts, photographs, multimedia and presentations, and may themselves be electronic evidence. A great deal of data can be retrieved, depending on the method of storage, the media on which it is stored and the manner in which the device manages data storage.

Metadata

1.67 Metadata is, essentially, data about data. For instance, the metadata in relation to a piece of paper as a physical document may be:

> Explicit from perusing the paper itself, such as the title of the document, the date, the purported name of the person(s) who wrote it, who received it and the location of the document.
>
> Implicit, which includes such characteristics as the types of type (font) used, such as bold, underline or italic, the location of the document such as a coloured file to denote a particular type of document, and document labels that also act as pointers to allow the person using the document to deal with it in a particular manner, such as a confidential file, for instance.

1.68 All files, including email communications, spreadsheets, websites and word processing documents, will contain metadata in one form or another. In fact, a file has to have metadata to help the interpretation of the purpose of the digital document. Such data can be taken automatically from the originating application software, or can be supplied by the person who originally created the record. The list of information that is available includes, but is not limited to: when and how a document was created (purported time and date), the file type, the name of the purported author (although this will not necessarily be reliable information, because the person whom the document metadata names as 'author' might be someone entirely different from the person who actually wrote the document[1]), the location from which the file was opened or where it was stored, when the file was last opened (purported time and date), when it was last modified, last saved and last printed, the identity of the purported previous authors, the location of the file on each occasion it was stored, the details of who else may be able to obtain access to it, and, in the case of email, blind carbon copy (bcc) addresses.

1 For instance, where a document is revised on a number of occasions, on different computers and by different people, the name of the author will probably bear no resemblance to the authorship of the document. In *IG Markets v Crinion* [2013] EWCA Civ 587, [2013] 5 WLUK 621, [2013] CP Rep 41, Times, 31 July 2013, [2013] CLY 387, also known as *Crinion v IG Markets Ltd*, the judgment of the trial judge, HH Judge Simon Brown QC, was taken word-for-word from the closing submissions of Mr Chirnside, counsel for the claimant, written in a Word file. The trial judge adjusted the text, and the 'properties' file in the Word version of the judgment indicated that the 'author' was 'SChirnside'. Also, the person originating a document may not use a new file, but may create the document by opening an old file, deleting the majority of the text, then creating the genesis of the new text; further, the name of the author may not be accurate if the person creating the document had logged onto the computer using somebody else's account, and there may be occasions when a person uses software on their own computer that has been installed and registered in another name – although if the metadata is correct, it can directly lead to a killer that has murdered a number of people over a long period of time: https://en.wikipedia.org/wiki/Dennis_Rader.

1.69 Because metadata is generally created automatically by the software and without the knowledge of the user, it is therefore also more difficult to alter, manipulate or delete. Imagine that Alice writes a document on a computer. The software will add metadata that is associated with this document, for instance the time when the document was created. The file where this information is stored is the metadata that records the time of the event of writing. Since it is not an intentional creation by the author, but an automatic, software-generated artefact that is often invisible to the user, she may not know about this data, and even if she did, she may not know how to alter or delete it.

1.70 However, it must be said that metadata is not infallible. Its interpretation requires making assumptions about the environment in which it was created. If the real-time clock on the device was not accurate (for instance, the clock in a laptop that has crossed time zones without being adjusted for this, or if the clock is slow, or has been deliberately changed), the metadata as recorded will be false. Since the environment can in this sense 'lie', informed criminals can intentionally manipulate the data. For instance, experienced phishing attackers who use email may not only forge the sender's address in the emails they send, but may also manipulate the entire header to conceal the place from which the email originates. Finally, since metadata is the unintentional creation of information by the environment, examiners or other third parties who are operating in the same environment will also create metadata, and so potentially contaminate the evidence. A careless digital evidence professional, or an IT administrator of a company who is alerted to potentially illegal activity by an employee, can by the very act of opening and looking at the file create new metadata and overwrite the old (a new time when the document was created, according to the computer), thereby erasing potentially useful metadata about the illegal activity such as the actual date and time it was committed.

Types of metadata

1.71 In broad terms, there are three main types of metadata:[1]

> (1) Descriptive metadata describe a resource for a particular purpose, such as a disclosure or discovery exercise. The metadata may include such information as title, key words, abstract and the name of the person purporting to be the author. To understand the history of the document more fully, it would be necessary to obtain information about how and when the system recorded the name of the purported author.
>
> (2) Structural metadata describe how a number of objects are brought together. Some examples of structural metadata include 'file identification' (e.g. to identify an individual chapter that forms part of a book or report); 'file encoding' (to identify the codes that were used in relation to the file, including the data encoding standard used (ASCII, for instance)); the method used to compress the file and the method of encryption, if used; 'file rendering' (to identify how the file was created, including such information as the software application, operating system and hardware dependencies); 'content structure' (to define the structure of the content of the record, such as a definition of the data set, the data dictionary, files setting out authority codes and such like); and 'source' (to identify the relevant circumstances that led to the capture of the data).
>
> (3) Administrative metadata, which provides information to help with the management of a resource. Administrative data is further divided into rights management metadata and preservation or record-keeping metadata.

1 For more information on metadata, see Dublin Core Metadata Initiative, http://dublincore.org/; National Information Standards Organization, 'Understanding Metadata' (NISO Press 2004), http://www.niso.org/standards/resources/UnderstandingMetadata.pdf; Michael Day, 'DCC Digital Curation Manual Instalment on Metadata' (UKOLN v1.1 2005), https://www.dcc.ac.uk/sites/default/files/documents/resource/curation-manual/chapters/metadata/metadata.pdf.

1.72 The metadata can be fundamentally linked to and be a part of the electronic document, be included in the systems used to produce the document, or be linked to it from a separate system. Metadata can be viewed in a variety of ways, one of which is to look at the 'properties' link in the application that created the document, or by using software specifically written for this purpose. Some metadata can also be removed with specialist software. This can be useful when sending files to third parties, but can attract additional expense if a court orders the data to be delivered up in its original format, as in the case of *Williams v Sprint/United Management Company*.[1] Before passing electronic spreadsheet documents in Excel form to the plaintiffs, Sprint modified the electronic files by, among other things, deleting metadata from the electronic files that included the spreadsheets, and preventing the recipients from viewing certain data contained in the spreadsheets by locking the value of certain cells. Sprint was ordered to produce the unlocked versions of the spreadsheets in the manner in which they were maintained, including their metadata. In his judgment, the judge discussed metadata and whether it formed a sufficient part of a document in electronic form for it to be given up to the other party.[2]

1 230 F.R.D. 640 (D.Kan. 2005).
2 230 F.R.D. 640 at 646–48 (D.Kan. 2005).

1.73 A further illustration of the importance of metadata is the case of *Campaign Against Arms Trade v BAE Systems PLC*.[1] On 29 December 2006, a senior officer of the Campaign Against Arms Trade (CAAT), Ms Feltham, sent an email containing privileged legal advice to the members of the CAAT steering committee using a private and internal email distribution list to 12 members of the steering committee and 7 members of CAAT's staff. A copy of the email was somehow sent to BAE Systems PLC (BAE). By a letter dated 9 January 2007 and received the next day, solicitors for BAE returned a printed paper copy of the email to CAAT's solicitors. This was the first time that CAAT came to know of the leak. CAAT sought and obtained a *Norwich Pharmacal* order against BAE. In giving judgment, Mr Justice King noted that the printed email returned to CAAT was incomplete (because the email metadata were missing). As described by Mr Justice King:[2]

> It was a redacted version of that which had come into the possession of the Respondent and/or its own solicitors. All the routing information, the header address and so forth, which would give details of the email accounts through which the email had been received and sent before arriving at the Respondent and its solicitors, had been removed. Such removal must have been done either by the Respondent or by its solicitors acting on its instructions.

1 [2007] EWHC 330 (QB), [2007] 2 WLUK 617.
2 [2007] EWHC 330 (QB) at [31].

1.74 The source of the leak could be the result of only two possibilities – one of the authorized recipients of the email or an unauthorized interception of the email. BAE had objected to the order, arguing that CAAT should have investigated the authorized recipients and their personal electronic data to trace the source before seeking the order. Mr Justice King rejected this argument:

> 46. … Ms Feltham … explains that there was a major practical and logistical problem as regards access to the computers used by members of the steering committee. Unlike the staff they are not employees of the Applicant but volunteers who do not work in the office or use computer systems belonging to

> the Applicant. Some are members of other organizations who access emails from accounts and equipment owned by their employers. Some are based outside London. This all means that to have investigated further on the lines suggested by the Respondent, the Applicant would have needed access to computers to which the Applicant has no right of access and in any event the Applicant would have needed the 'costly services of a computer expert to go on a fishing expedition for emails which might or might not have been sent which moreover would have been very time consuming.'

1.75 The unrealistic claim by BAE that CAAT ought physically to examine every computer to trace the route of the email fails to grasp the fundamental issue that electronic data knows no geographical or physical bounds. Returning the email without the metadata is similar to returning a letter received through the post in an envelope, yet refusing to deliver up the envelope. That the routing and other technical data available in relation to an email is 'similar' to the data included on an envelope is an understatement, because the email metadata is far more extensive than the metadata contained on an envelope. In this instance, Mr Justice King concluded that the order sought ought to be granted, although not in the terms requested.

1.76 This application illustrates the importance of the metadata associated with an electronic object. Documents in electronic form include metadata as a matter of course, and it seems unrealistic for the recipient to refuse to deliver up the full document, including the associated metadata, in such circumstances.

1.77 A case from the US serves to highlight how concerns relating to the preservation of data are viewed, as well as the relevance of metadata. In the case of *Armstrong v Executive Office of the President, Office of Administration,*[1] the Executive Office of the President and related White House departments intended to require all federal employees to print out their electronic communications on paper to discharge their obligations under the provisions of the Federal Records Act. This was challenged by researchers and non-profit organizations on the grounds that this amounted to a destruction of federal records. The United States Court of Appeals, District of Columbia Circuit upheld the challenge, noting that the hard copy printed version 'may omit fundamental pieces of information which are an integral part of the original electronic records, such as the identity of the sender and/or recipient and the time of receipt'.[2]

1 1 F.3d 1274 (D.C. Cir. 1993).
2 1 F.3d 1274 (D.C. Cir. 1993) at 1277.

Social context and metadata

1.78 A significant amount of electronic data is created through communication between people separated by geographical, political, social and cultural boundaries. While the Internet has brought people previously separated by distance into interaction, it also creates a new form of 'distance' between the communicators. Some communication practices do not translate well to this new medium, such as facial expressions and tone of voice. Evidence is not created in a vacuum, however. It has meaning, and can be interpreted only with knowledge of the context in which it was created. The exchange 'I hate you all and wish you were dead' in a dispute between a teenager and his parents about cleaning a room will be interpreted by most people acquainted with a similar cultural background as insignificant and not serious. The same words found on a carefully written letter will carry a different meaning. Therefore, consideration has to be given to whether an email, a Twitter post or an exchange on a discussion forum is more similar to a letter or to a direct verbal exchange.

1.79 Consider the case of *Chambers v Director of Public Prosecutions*.[1] Paul Chambers was a registered Twitter user with the handle '@PaulJChambers'. He was due to fly to Belfast from Doncaster Robin Hood Airport to meet another Twitter user, identified as '@Crazycolours', on 15 January 2010.[2] On 6 January 2010, Chambers became aware of problems at Doncaster Robin Hood Airport because of adverse weather conditions, and he and Crazycolours subsequently entered into the following exchange on Twitter:

> @Crazycolours: I [Chambers] was thinking that if it does then I had decided to resort to terrorism
>
> @Crazycolours: That's the plan! I am sure the pilots will be expecting me to demand a more exotic location than NI

1 [2012] EWHC 2157 (Admin), [2013] 1 WLR 1833, [2013] 1 All ER 149, [2012] 7 WLUK 933, [2013] 1 Cr App. R 1, (2012) 176 JP 737, [2012] Info TLR 193, [2012] ACD 114, [2013] CLY 625.
2 The facts are taken from the judgment of Lord Judge LCJ in *Chambers v Director of Public Prosecutions* [2012] EWHC 2157 (Admin); Lilian Edwards, 'Section 127 of the Communications Act 2003: threat or menace?' (2012) 23(4) Computers & Law 21.

1.80 The court noted that in the context of the bad weather, these comments from Chambers seemed to be a reference to the possibility of the airport closing. No reply from Crazycolours was produced in court. Two hours later, when Chambers found out that the airport had closed, he posted the following message, available to the 600 or so followers of his Twitter postings:

> Crap! Robin Hood Airport is closed. You've got a week and a bit to get your shit together otherwise I am blowing the airport sky high!!

1.81 On 11 January 2010, five days after the comments were posted, the managers at Robin Hood Airport found the comments and passed what was regarded as a 'non-credible' threat (because the tweet featured Chambers' name and because he was due to fly from the airport in the near future) to the airport police, who in turn referred the matter on to the South Yorkshire police.

1.82 The South Yorkshire police arrested Chambers on 13 January on suspicion of involvement in a bomb hoax while he was at work, seven days after the offending message was tweeted. Interviewed under caution, Chambers repeatedly asserted that this Tweet was a joke, or meant to be a joke and not intended to be menacing. He said that he did not see any risk at all that it would be regarded as menacing, and that if he had, he would not have posted it. In interview he was asked whether some people might get a bit jumpy and responded 'yah. Hmm mmm'. Chambers was charged with the offence of sending by a public electronic communication network a message of a 'menacing character' contrary to s 127(1)(a) and (3) of the Communications Act 2003 and was found guilty. His appeal to the Crown Court in Doncaster was dismissed, and on further appeal the question was whether the words he used were a 'menacing message sent through a public communication medium' and thus in violation of s 127(1)(a) and (3) of the Communications Act 2003.

1.83 The ensuing prosecution showed just how difficult this determination can be. Some security officers at the airport were willing to dismiss it outright as 'venting', while others were concerned enough to inform the police. The court of first instance, applying an abstract, decontextualized dictionary definition of 'menace', convicted Chambers. On appeal, the members of the Court of Appeal noted, however, that '[b]efore concluding that a message is criminal on the basis that it represents a menace, its precise terms, and any inferences to be drawn from its precise terms, need to be examined in the context in and the means by which the message was sent'.[1] The Court of Appeal reversed the decision of the lower court and allowed the appeal against conviction because it was posted as a conversation piece for Chambers' followers, drawing attention to himself and his predicament. It was not addressed to anyone at the airport or anyone responsible for public security. The communication was airing the grievance that the airport was closed when the writer wanted it to be open, and identified the person making the 'threat' in ample time for it to be reported and extinguished.

1 *Chambers v Director of Public Prosecutions* [2012] EWHC 2157 (Admin) at [31].

1.84 For the Court of Appeal to consider the social context in which the electronic evidence was to be understood must be correct. The visual form in which this evidence appears may not be a true account of the social meaning that informed the users when the evidence was created. For instance, a Tweet may look like a warning, but it is certainly not understood as such by the participants. Since judges and jurors will often have very different technological experiences, it is tempting to lead sociological or psychological evidence on these issues, but procedural rules on admissibility may well prevent this.

Imaging

1.85 Any digital forensic investigation will begin by 'imaging' the device on which electronic evidence may reside. The imaging process is a non-destructive process that creates an exact external digital copy of any data on the device. Subsequently, all data investigation should be performed on the imaged copy and not on data stored on the original device.

System and program logs

1.86 As previously noted, many services and devices keep records or logs of activity for business and operational purposes. In most modern operating systems such as Windows and Linux, virtually anything and everything happening on and to the system is recorded in the form of logs in some manner. This includes information about system events, including the startup of applications and various classes of error messages. Information in the logs may help to determine, for instance, how an unauthorized computer user obtained access to a system with the intent of stealing information from the computer. It may also be possible to configure the systems log (syslog) such that the log messages can be sent to another networked system while retaining a local copy. As a result, if a hacker acquires system adminstrator privileges on a networked UNIX operating system,[1] for instance, and wants to erase something from the local logs, he would not be able to erase the data from the remote logs to remove all traces of his intrusion unless he also has the appropriate privileges on the remote machine.

1 In UNIX-type systems, the 'superuser', that is the account for the system administrator, is known as 'root'. This account has all rights or permissions to all files and programs in all modes.

1.87 Unlike UNIX-type operating systems such as Linux and macOS, the Windows operating system also includes a 'registry'. This is a store of data that contains a great deal of information, including a comprehensive database containing information on every program that is compatible with Windows that has been installed on the computer. It also includes information about the purported user of the computer, the preferences exercised by the user, information about the hardware components and information about the network (if it is connected to a network). The values stored in the registry are designed primarily to be processed by the computer, but can be converted to a human-readable form. An example of the type of information that the registry can provide to an investigator is the AutoComplete data for a user of Internet Explorer visiting a particular website, such as her name, address, telephone number, email address and passwords. In addition, it is possible to establish when the user last downloaded a file from the Internet, together with the first page she visited from the registry.[1]

1 Although it does not follow that a user clicked on a website address that has been recorded in a temporary cache file, for which see the case of *State of Connecticut v Julie Amero* (Docket number CR-04-93292; Superior Court, New London Judicial District at Norwich, GA 21; 3, 4 and 5 January 2007). For an exhaustive analysis of this case, see Stephen Mason (ed.), *International Electronic Evidence*, xxxvi–lxxv.

Temporary files and cache files

1.88 When a digital device connects to the Internet, a range of information about its activities may be recorded and retained locally, including the websites and any newsgroups that have been visited, and the content that was viewed. For the purpose of enabling the browser to improve user experience and speed up browsing, temporary copies of websites that have been visited are stored in cache folders. These folders contain fragments of the web page, including images and text. Some browsers will retain more than one local file containing location information about the websites visited.

1.89 It is important to understand the legal consequences of temporary files and cache files. This is exemplified in the case of *Atkins v Director of Public Prosecutions.*[1] In this case, Dr Atkins, a university lecturer at the University of Bristol, Department of English, had browsed the Internet for indecent photographs of children and had saved a number of such photographs as files in the J directory of his computer. He was convicted of one offence of having in his possession indecent photographs of children on the J directory of his computer and nine other offences for the temporary files that his browser had placed in the cache folder. In allowing an appeal, Simon Brown LJ and Blofeld J held that Dr Atkins should not have been convicted of possession in respect of the photographs stored in the cache, because he was not aware of its existence or what it did, and therefore could not be said to have knowingly had possession of these particular photographs. The court ordered that the case be remitted with a direction to convict Dr Atkins of the offences where he deliberately saved photographs in the J directory.[2]

1 *Atkins v DPP* [2000] 1 WLR 1427 (QB), [2000] 2 All ER 425, [2000] 3 WLUK 213, [2000] 2 Cr App R 248, (2000) 97(13) LSG 42, (2000) 144 SJLB 148, Times, 16 March 2000, Independent, 17 April 2000, [2000] CLY 993, also known as *DPP v Atkins*; for a US case based on similar facts with an identical outcome, see *United States v Kuchinski* 469 F.3d 853 (9th Cir. 2006).
2 In *Clifford v Chief Constable of the Hertfordshire Constabulary* [2011] EWHC 815 (QB), [2011] 4 WLUK 7, Mr Justice Mackay observed that the prosecution were fully aware of this issue, but prosecuted Mr Clifford in any event: a prosecution that was eventually determined to be malicious; see also *Clifford v Chief Constable of the Hertfordshire Constabulary* [2008] EWHC 3154 (QB), [2008] 12 WLUK 568 and *Clifford v Chief Constable of the Hertfordshire Constabulary* [2009] EWCA Civ 1259, [2009] 12 WLUK 16.

1.90 In addition to browser caches, Windows and UNIX systems also have paging file or swap space. This is an area of non-volatile storage space that is used as virtual memory. In the event that the applications being run on the system require more RAM than the system has available, low-priority applications are copied to the virtual memory and the RAM they are using is thereby freed for use by applications with a higher priority. Swap space is rarely cleaned during the normal operation of the system. This means that when a system needs to be forensically analysed, it is often the case that useful data associated with applications, which may not even be running at the time, can be found by analysing the content of the swap space. This can also apply to data that is normally stored on the standard file system in an encrypted form. Depending on the application and the precise circumstances, some applications may allow unencrypted copies of the data to be stored in the swap file.

Deleted or 'lost' files

1.91 File systems keep a record of where data are located on a storage medium. The way data are stored will differ, depending on the software and the architecture of the method used to allocate blocks of storage for files (the file system architecture). In simple terms, the location of data on a storage medium is controlled by a file system. For instance, the storage medium can be divided into partitions and media blocks, and where this is the case, the file will be stored in a particular location in a partition. When a file is deleted, only the system's pointers in the filing system are deleted: the instruction to delete removes the pointer to the location of the file, but does not actually delete the file. Even where part of a file has been overwritten, it is often possible to recover part of the deleted file if the set of media blocks containing that file has not been completely overwritten. For this reason, in the majority of cases it is possible to recover data that has been deleted, depending on the amount of medium-writing activity that has been performed between the deletion of the file and the recovery process.[1]

1 Andy Jones and Christopher Meyler, 'What evidence is left after disk cleaners?' (2004) 1(3) Digital Investigation 183; 'Deleted File Recovery' (NIST), https://www.nist.gov/itl/ssd/software-quality-group/computer-forensics-tool-testing-program-cftt/cftt-technical/deleted.

1.92 File systems also keep a record of those parts of the medium that are unusable or 'bad', so that no data will be written there. But a user may intentionally mark portions of the medium as 'bad' to hide substantial amounts of data in those portions. Such data could not be seen without the use of an appropriate media diagnostic or examination tool (since the operating system will automatically avoid making any use of these 'bad sectors'). Alternatively, when a device that is claimed to be non-functional is forensically restored or unlocked, it may be possible to discover or infer evidence of wrongdoing on the device. This is illustrated by the case of *Sectrack NV v Satamatics Ltd*[1] concerning the misuse of confidential information. One of the defendants was in possession of a Blackberry device, which he claimed was frozen or locked. When the device was 'unlocked', it automatically downloaded various emails that the defendant had received, which implicated him in the misuse of confidential information.[2] Since this case, manufacturers of hand-held devices have developed extensive backup systems that permit the backing up of device data to other devices and storage facilities. In the future, without the use of encryption, it will be relatively difficult to delete data sufficiently for it to be beyond recovery.

1 [2007] EWHC 3003 (Comm), [2007] 12 WLUK 558.
2 [2007] EWHC 3003 (Comm) at [7].

1.93 However, it does not follow that the recovered data is genuine or trustworthy evidence just because it is found. There are numerous contexts in which data may be lost or damaged, and this will affect the credibility of any resulting data that is recovered. Examples include the corruption or loss of original or deleted data because of errors in the program, and interference with the data from extrinsic sources.[1] Further, it should be observed that the reliability of the recovered data as evidence would also be affected by the way in which a digital evidence professional carries out the examination and recovery process. If the process of investigation affects the evidence, it will be less reliable.

1 Peter Sommer, 'Downloads, logs and captures: Evidence from cyberspace' [2002] CTLR 33; Eoghan Casey, 'Error, uncertainty, and loss in digital evidence' (2002) 1(2) Intl J of Digital Evidence; Caroline Allinson, 'Audit trails in evidence – a Queensland case study' (2001) 1 JILT; and 'Audit trails in evidence: analysis of a Queensland case study' (2003) 2 JILT.

Simulations, data visualizations, augmented and virtual reality

1.94 There is an increasing use of computer-generated sequences as a method of presenting evidence in legal proceedings. Often these are designed to predict the behaviour or outcome of an incident, based on mathematical models that are built on the well-known behaviour of natural systems in chemistry, biology, physics and engineering.[1]

1 Computer simulation (Wikipedia), https://en.wikipedia.org/wiki/Computer_simulation; see 'Computer generated animations and simulations' in Chapter 2 for a more detailed discussion of the legal issues and citation of relevant authorities, legal and non-legal.

Encryption and obfuscated data

1.95 Encryption has been known and used since ancient times, especially to protect military communications.[1] But the advent of computers and the Internet has intensified the use of cryptography to secure information and communications. The underlying concept remains the same, however: since sensitive information in its unencrypted form may be read by people with unscrupulous motives or be exposed to interceptors, encryption converts the information in its unencrypted form (referred to as plaintext) into a form which is non-readable by unauthorized parties (referred to as ciphertext). Only authorized parties can decrypt the ciphertext back into its readable form. Encryption is classically combined with authentication, allowing the recipient to verify who created the information and that it has not been tampered with in transit. The data that allows a recipient to verify the authenticity of a message is known as a digital signature, but this is quite separate from the legal concept of a signature.

1 John F. Dooley, *History of Cryptography and Cryptanalysis: Codes, Ciphers, and Their Algorithms* (Springer 2018), 13–18.

1.96 Encryption and authenticity verification are achieved through the use of a third piece of information known as a key. There are two main types of keys in cryptographic systems: symmetric key and asymmetric (or public) key schemes. In symmetric key schemes, the key that is used to encrypt and/or authenticate the plaintext is the same key used to decrypt and/or verify the ciphertext. In other words, both the sender and recipient must share the same key in order to achieve secure communication. In asymmetric key schemes, the private part of the key is used to decrypt information or create a digital signature, and the public part of the key is used to encrypt the information or verify the authenticity of a message with a corresponding digital signature. Asymmetric and symmetric cryptographic systems are often combined to take advantage of the efficiency of symmetric cryptography and the flexibility of asymmetric cryptography.

1.97 For instance, the Hypertext Transfer Protocol Secure (HTTPS), an extension of the Hypertext Transfer Protocol (HTTP), is used to secure communications over the Internet by authenticating a website, protecting the privacy of the sender and the recipient, and preserving the privacy and authenticity of the data exchanged while the data is in transit.[1] The authentication aspect of HTTPS is achieved by a trusted third party digitally signing a server-side document (known as a digital certificate) that certifies that the public key is owned by the sender responsible for the website, while the privacy aspect of HTTPS is achieved by the encryption of the data transmitted between the sender and recipient using symmetric cryptography keys that are unique to each connection.[2]

1 HTTPS (Wikipedia), https://en.wikipedia.org/wiki/HTTPS.
2 Transport Layer Security (Wikipedia), https://en.wikipedia.org/wiki/Transport_Layer_Security.

Artificial intelligence and machine learning

1.98 Using a definition dating back to the 1970s, artificial intelligence (AI) can, in a suitably technology-neutral way, be defined as '[The automation of] activities that we associate with human thinking, activities such as decision-making, problem solving, and learning'.[1] While the term first appeared in the 1950s, interaction between law and AI entered the academic mainstream in the 1980s and 1990s through organizations such as JURIX[2] and the International Association for Artificial Intelligence and Law.[3] These were the halcyon days of the 'symbolic manipulation' approach to AI, exemplified through the quest for 'expert systems' that contained symbolic representations of expert knowledge in their knowledge base, usually in the form of 'If/Then' rules, and that were able to perform logical operations on it. Systems of that type (which are still around today and continue to be developed and refined) include programs that help crime investigators to structure the evidence they collect as part of an investigation, evaluate its probative weight and turn it into logically compelling arguments.[4] More complex systems combine rule-based knowledge representation with statistical or probabilistic reasoners, for instance Bayesian networks, to analyse and evaluate a broader range of evidence types.[5] While these systems help investigators to analyse and structure evidence, they do not generate new types of digital evidence. As a result, they are outside the scope of this chapter.

1 Richard Bellman, *An Introduction to Artificial Intelligence: Can Computers Think?* (Boyd & Fraser Publishing Company 1978), 3–4.
2 http://jurix.nl/.
3 http://www.iaail.org/.
4 Ephraim Nissan, *Computer Applications for Handling Legal Evidence, Police Investigation and Case Argumentation* Volume 5 (Springer Science & Business Media 2012); Jeroen Keppens and Burkhard Schafer, 'Knowledge based crime scenario modelling' (2006) 30(2) Expert Systems with Applications 203.
5 Floris Bex, Peter J. van Koppen, Henry Prakken and Bart Verheij, 'A hybrid formal theory of arguments, stories and criminal evidence' (2010) 18(2) Artificial Intelligence and Law 123, DOI: 10.1007/s10506-010-9092-x.

1.99 The results of approaches that started to emerge in the mid-1990s to enable a way of knowledge representation and knowledge sharing that preserved more of the meaning, or semantics, of our knowledge are closer to being digital evidence generated by AI. This became of particular importance with the emergence of the semantic Web and its aim to establish 'a common framework that allows data to be shared and reused across application, enterprise, and community boundaries',[1] one of the significant technologies underpinning the World Wide Web. Ontology-based legal AI would then try to represent the knowledge of an investigator, or the knowledge we have about a particular crime, by building taxonomies and classification networks. Such a formal ontology would, for instance, allow the software to reason about the information it finds on a website to determine if the text falls under the category of 'committing incitement', which in turn falls under the category of 'committing a criminal offence'. Ontology-based AI systems have been used, for instance, to enable search engine indexing services to autonomously identify websites that host content that violates banking regulations or are in other ways fraudulent, or to identify whether a set of digital VAT receipts are likely to support a claim for VAT fraud.[2] This part-automation of the investigative process can raise issues for the law of evidence, for instance how rules on searches can be analogized: whether it makes sense to attribute 'reasonable suspicion' to the software agent, or whether this resides with its human (police) operators, for instance. However, more recent developments in AI have moved beyond these 'symbolic' approaches to knowledge representation and reasoning to probabilistic or statistic approaches, using machine learning as a way to implement them.

1 https://www.w3.org/2001/sw/SW-FAQ.
2 John Kingston, Burkhard Schafer and Wim Vandenberghe, 'No model behaviour: ontologies for fraud detection' in V. Richard Benjamins, Pompeu Casanovas, Joost Breuker and Aldo Gangemi (eds.) *Law and the Semantic Web* (Springer 2005), 233–247; Dimitris Kanellopoulos, Sotiris Kotsiantis and Vasilis Tampakas, 'Towards an ontology-based system for intelligent prediction of firms with fraudulent financial statements', *2007 IEEE Conference on Emerging Technologies and Factory Automation (EFTA 2007)* (IEEE 2007).

1.100 Before examining machine learning in more detail, it should be noted that many forensic subdisciplines have relied for a long time on complex statistics software programs for data analysis that can no longer be verified by human experts, thus already creating the problem of 'black box' algorithms that are a main concern for current AI systems. Forensic DNA analysis, and in particular advanced methods such as low copy number DNA testing, requires complex statistical analysis that is carried out by computer programs.[1] Similarly, forensic use of neuroimaging such as FMRI scans rely on complex statistical software tools that mediate between the 'raw data' collected by sensors and the visual representation of a brain for the human analyst. Even though, especially in the latter case, significant parts of the evidence are computer-generated, new evidential requirements for electronic evidence have not normally been applied to the use of computer technology within established forensic disciplines. To the extent that the accuracy and reliability of these programs has been discussed at all, they have been dealt with through certification and standardization, rather than a forensic computing analysis of individual machines and their use in an individual case.

1 Wing K. Fung, Yue-Qing Hu and Yuk-Ka Chung, 'On statistical analysis of forensic DNA: theory, methods and computer programs' (2006) 162(1–3) Forensic Science International 17, DOI: 10.1016/j.forsciint.2006.06.025.

1.101 Machine learning (ML) refers to the broad category of computational approaches to solving problems through applying statistical techniques to identify patterns in data, rather than having a developer explicitly specify detailed steps to follow. In this way, machine learning systems can be said to demonstrate artificial intelligence; that is, their approach contains some characteristics of the approach a human would take to carry out such a task. Machine learning works by 'allow[ing] systems to learn directly from examples, data, and experience'.[1]

1 Royal Society, 'Machine learning: the power and promise of computers that learn by example' (April 2017) 19, https://royalsociety.org/~/media/policy/projects/machine-learning/publications/machine-learning-report.pdf.

1.102 There are three main permutations of ML. First, in supervised machine learning the machine system is trained with data items that each have an associated label. The ML system learns the relationship between data items and labels and is then able to estimate the most likely label that should be associated with data items it has not encountered. For example, a ML system could be provided with many photographs of street signs that each have been transcribed by a human, then be tasked with identifying photographs of street signs encountered by a self-driving car. Second, in unsupervised machine learning data is not labelled. The ML system identifies patterns within the data items in order to group items that are similar or to summarise the important characteristics of the data. For example, supermarket customers could be grouped into categories based on their shopping habits, so as to direct advertising more effectively. Third, with reinforcement learning the ML system interacts with the physical world or a system of rules and develops a strategy that achieves a specified objective. For example, a robot could be given the task of reaching a point as quickly as possible, given access to a collection of motors and sensors.[1]

1 Royal Society, 'Machine Learning', 20.

1.103 Because ML is a general technique for automating useful tasks that require human intelligence for successful completion, the range of applications possible with ML are wide and varied. Law enforcement authorities such as police officers may be equipped with body-worn video cameras that record crucial evidence in real time[1] and can execute automated facial recognition.[2] Patrol cars are equipped with in-car cameras that automatically read number plates to find matches for vehicles and their owners.[3] The gathering of criminal intelligence and predictive policing are also being helped by advancements in ML.[4] In banking, logistics, medicine, electronic commerce and other industries, ML systems are used in applications that range from fraud and accident detection to productivity improvement, from diagnostics and safety assurances to customization of goods and services, to enable rapid and accurate decision making.[5] For this reason, the range of evidence that is generated by ML devices is practically limitless. This in turn engenders a careful review of the nature of such evidence, including an examination of the authentication of such evidence and whether the admission of it in legal proceedings breaches the rule against hearsay.[6]

1 Ben Bowling and Shruti Iyer, 'Automated policing: the case of body-worn video' (2019) 15(2) Int JLC 140; *DPP v Young* [2018] EWHC 3616 (Admin), [2018] 12 WLUK 67 (accepting body-worn video as evidence).

2 See *R. (on the application of Bridges) v Chief Constable of South Wales* [2019] EWHC 2341 (Admin), [2020] 1 WLR 672, [2020] 1 All ER 864, [2019] 9 WLUK 9, [2020] 1 Cr App R 3, [2019] HRLR 16, [2019] ACD 122, Times, 9 December 2019, Times, 11 December 2019, [2019] 11 CLY 1389, regarding a challenge to privacy and data protection from police use of automated facial recognition technologies on body-worn videos.

3 For instance, see *R. v Doyle (Hugh), R v Wood (Carl), R. v Lincoln (William)* [2017] EWCA Crim 340, [2017] 2 WLUK 194, admitting automatic number plate recognition evidence as part of the evidence of the movement of accused's cars; *R. v Brown (Nico)* [2019] EWCA Crim 1143, [2019] 1 WLR 6721, [2019] 7 WLUK 41, [2019] 2 Cr App R 25, [2020] Crim LR 71, [2019] CLY 647, admitting automatic number plate recognition evidence.

4 Walter L. Perry, Brian McInnis, Carter C. Price, Susan C. Smith and John S. Hollywood, 'Predictive policing: the role of crime forecasting in law enforcement operations' (Rand Corporation 2013), https://www.rand.org/content/dam/rand/pubs/research_reports/RR200/RR233/RAND_RR233.pdf; Patrick Perrot, Gendarmerie Nationale, Ministry of Interior, Paris, France, 'What about AI in criminal intelligence? From predictive policing to AI perspectives', European Police Science and Research Bulletin, Issue 16, Summer 2017, 65–76, https://bulletin.cepol.europa.eu/index.php/bulletin/article/download/244/208/; Albert Meijer and Martijn Wessels, 'Predictive policing: review of benefits and drawbacks' (2019) 42(12) International Journal of Public Administration 1031, https://www.tandfonline.com/doi/full/10.1080/01900692.2019.1575664.

5 Artificial intelligence in industry (Wikipedia), https://en.wikipedia.org/wiki/Artificial_intelligence_in_industry.

6 See Daniel Seng and Stephen Mason, 'Artificial intelligence and evidence' (2021) 33 SAcLJ 241.

Simulations, data visualizations, augmented and virtual reality

1.104 In addition to collecting and evaluating evidence, an important role of AI and related technologies is to help communicate complex data to the trier of facts. This can range from data visualization tools that, for instance, make channels of email communication within an alleged criminal network visible, to visual recreation of crime scenes or dynamic reconstructions of putative events.[1] This technology is described using a variety of terms, including 'computer simulations', 'computer animation' and 'data visualization'. Where the simulation allows for the creation of a three-dimensional sequence in which the viewer can participate, move around the computer-simulated environment and look at the incidents from different viewpoints, the technology is described as 'virtual reality' or 'augmented reality', the distinction being that in augmented reality the virtual representations of objects is also overlaid with real-world objects and items to alter one's perception of the real-world environment.[2] This can be achieved through the use of virtual reality headsets, which offer a particularly radical way to enable judges or jurors to 'relive' putative events in 3D space.[3]

1 The reader should read the text in this part in combination with the detailed discussion of the legal issues in 'Computer-generated animations and simulations', Chapter 2. Minhua Ma, Huiru Zheng and Harjinder Lallie, 'Virtual reality and 3D animation in forensic visualization' (2010) 55(5) Journal of Forensic Sciences 1227; Isabella Aquila MD, Ph.D., Matteo A. Sacco MD, Giuseppe Aquila MS, Roberto Raffaele MS Alfredo Manca, Giuseppe Capoccia, Fabrizio Cordasco MD and Pietrantonio Ricci MD, Ph.D., 'The reconstruction of the dynamic of a murder using 3D motion capture and 3D model buildings: the investigation of a dubious forensic case' (2019) 64(5) Journal of Forensic Sciences 1540; see 'Computer-generated animations and simulations' in Chapter 2 for a more detailed discussion of the legal issues and citation of relevant authorities, legal and non-legal.

2 Augmented reality (Wikipedia), https://en.wikipedia.org/wiki/Augmented_reality.

3 Till Sieberth, Akos Dobay, Raffael Affolter and Lars C. Ebert, 'Applying virtual reality in forensics – a virtual scene walkthrough' (2019) 15(1) Forensic Science, Medicine and Pathology 41.

1.105 Factual data from an investigation is input into a forensic computer simulation software, which then associates the data with the 'generic world knowledge' in the knowledge base of the AI. This can then reproduce crime scenes and demonstrate how an alleged activity at various points in time could have taken place, while observing physical constraints such as gravity and other considerations.[1] The jurors may then 'see' how a car collided with a wall after swerving around an animal,[2] or how a person killed the victim, so that the reconstruction matches the pathologist report about, for example, the trajectories of bullets and our general knowledge of human anatomy, behaviour of firearms or the law of optics when taking aim.[3] These reproductions usually combine computer graphics, natural language processing, computer vision, motion tracking and forensic computing to turn defence and prosecution hypotheses into 'observable' stories that can then be tested.

1 G. D. Sloan and J. Talbott, 'Forensic application of computer simulation of falls' (1996) 41(5) Journal of Forensic Sciences 782.

2 Kristin L. Fulcher, 'The jury as witness: forensic computer animation transports jurors to the scene of a crime or automobile accident' (1996) 22 U Dayton L Rev 55.

3 Lars C. Ebert, Tuan T. Nguyen, Robert Breitbeck, Marcel Braun, Michael J. Thali and Steffen Ross, 'The forensic holodeck: an immersive display for forensic crime scene reconstructions' (2014) 10(4) Forensic Sci Med Pathol 623.

1.106 While these technologies can help to communicate complex facts to laypeople during a trial, there are concerns about their 'authenticity' for evidential purposes, and also their potential prejudicial effect, even in cases where the reconstructions are as faithful as possible.[1] Computer simulations do not fall easily within any of the existing categories of evidence because they are synthetic evidence: they are not contemporaneous records of the facts but are produced after the relevant events have occurred.[2] One problem that can arise is that the reconstruction will add details that are neither supported by eyewitness evidence, nor by universal scientific facts from the AI's knowledge base, but are default design choices made by the programmers. For instance, this can include choosing a colour scheme when visualizing brain activity from a scan, or having an intact headlight on a car directly before a crash, even though there is no direct witness statement to substantiate such an assertion. Sometimes these design choices are salient for evaluation of the event; at others they subtly influence juror perception.[3] Therefore, computer simulations should be seen for what they are – representations of opinions about facts. They should be treated as expert evidence and should be admitted only when reasonably required and with the judge's permission to resolve the proceedings.[4] While computer simulations have been admitted in both criminal and civil cases,[5] their limited use has been permitted only as mechanisms to enable the disputed issues to be refined, and only when the raw data that serve as the source of simulations are of sufficiently high quality.[6]

1 The legal issues are discussed in more detail in 'Computer-generated animations and simulation', Chapter 2.

2 Moya Clifford and Katie Kinloch, 'The use of computer simulation evidence in court' (2007) 24 Computer Law and Security Report 169.

3 See 'Computer-generated animations and simulation', Chapter 2 for relevant citations.

4 The foundational legal issues are discussed in more detail in 'Computer-generated animations and simulation', Chapter 2.

5 For example, see *R. v Maloney (Gerald)* [2003] EWCA Crim 1373, [2003] 5 WLUK 565; *The Owners of the Ship Pelopidas v The Owners of the Ship TRSL Concord* [1999] 2 All ER 737 (Comm), [1999] 2 Lloyd's Rep 675, [1999] 10 WLUK 259, [2000] CLY 4677; *Owners of the Global Mariner v Owners of the Atlantic Crusader, sub nom. Global Mariner, The, Atlantic Crusader, The* [2005] EWHC 380 (Admlty), [2005] 2 All ER (Comm) 389, [2005] 1 Lloyd's Rep 699, [2005] 3 WLUK 782, [2005] 1 CLC 413, (2005) 155 NLJ 594, [2005] CLY 3794.

6 Clifford and Kinloch, 'The use of computer simulation evidence in court', 173.

Transparency and explainability

1.107 Machine learning systems apply probabilistic reasoning and statistical techniques to solve problems. They therefore introduce the same types of error as in more traditional applications of statistics.[1] For example, the data on which they are trained might not be representative of reality, and so any conclusions drawn may not be accurate, or the uncertainty present in the output of the system might not be properly interpreted. Furthermore, the complexity of machine learning systems introduces sources of error. With the advent of machine learning and its implementation in 'artificial intelligence' systems, concerns have been rightly raised as to whether autonomous or intelligent detection systems are 'traceable, explicable and interpretable'[2] – often referred to in short as 'explainability'. The requirement for explainable autonomous or intelligent systems, reflected as the Principle of Transparency in the IEEE (Institute of Electrical and Electronic Engineers) rulebook on Ethically Aligned Design, ensures that the operation of such systems is transparent to a wide range of users.[3] In addition, depending on the type of machine learning algorithms used and implemented, the degree and extent of the explainability of the results from such algorithms may vary greatly. Statistical multivariate regression or random forest models built on existing data may be more traceable, explicable and interpretable by virtue of their algorithmic design,[4] but they may lack the requisite accuracy and prediction power.[5] On the other hand, deep learning neural network models, with their higher dimensionality architectures, may produce models that have the necessary prediction power,[6] but may suffer from issues of explicability from their relative opacity and an inability to generalize or deal with corner cases.[7] The requisite level of transparency and explainability that is required to provide the foundational substantiation for admitting evidence produced by such systems in legal proceedings will depend on the purposes for which the evidence is adduced.

1 Colin Aitken, Paul Roberts and Graham Jackson, 'Communicating and interpreting statistical evidence in the administration of criminal justice: 1. Fundamentals of probability and statistical evidence in criminal proceedings' (Royal Statistical Society), https://www.maths.ed.ac.uk/~cgga/Guide-1-WEB.pdf.

2 IEEE, Ethically Aligned Design, Principle 4 – Transparency (March 2018), 29, https://standards.ieee.org/content/dam/ieee-standards/standards/web/documents/other/ead_v2.pdf.

3 IEEE, Ethically Aligned Design, Principle 4 – Transparency.

4 For instance, see Rich Caruana and Alexandru Niculescu-Mizil, 'An empirical comparison of supervised learning algorithms' in *ICML 2006, Proceedings of 23rd International Conference on Machine Learning* (Association for Computing Machinery 2006), 161–168, https://www.cs.cornell.edu/~caruana/ctp/ct.papers/caruana.icml06.pdf; Vijay Khadse, Parikshit N. Mahalle and Swapnil V. Biraris, 'An empirical comparison of supervised machine learning algorithms for Internet of Things data' in *2018 Fourth International Conference on Computing Communication Control and Automation (ICCUBEA)* (IEEE 2018), https://ieeexplore.ieee.org/document/8697476.

5 For example, see Michal Hrabia, 'Deep learning vs. machine learning', 8 February 2020, https://towardsdatascience.com/deep-learning-vs-machine-learning-e0a9cb2f288.

6 Decision tree learning (Wikipedia), https://en.wikipedia.org/wiki/Decision_tree_learning.

7 But see Geoffrey Hinton, Oriol Vinyals and Jeff Dean, 'Distilling the knowledge in a neural network', in NIPS Deep Learning Workshop (2015), https://arxiv.org/pdf/1503.02531.pdf; Minsuk Kahng, Pierre Y. Andrews, Aditya Kalro and Duen Horng Chau, 'ActiVis: visual exploration of industry-scale deep neural network models' (2018) 24(1) IEEE Transactions on Visualization and Computer Graphics http://arxiv.org/abs/1704.01942.

AI adversarial attacks

1.108 As AI systems are increasingly used, there is a need to verify that they work reliably and appropriately, especially when they are used in open environments which may expose the systems to real-world data on which they have not been previously trained. When this happens, a system may produce unexpected results or behave in an unexpected way. Where AI systems are being set to continue to 'learn' from their new environment and update their models, this may also cause a system to 'unlearn' its models and crystallize the unexpected results or behaviour as correct or expected responses.[1]

1 Royal Society, 'Machine learning', 112.

1.109 Considerable research is being undertaken to investigate AI systems for such weaknesses. Known as 'adversarial attacks', these generally attempt to expose AI systems to novel environments and track their unexpected behaviour. While 'good' adversarial attacks attempt to detect such weaknesses to increase the robustness of AI systems, 'bad' adversarial attacks may exploit such weaknesses for gain or to cause disruption. When evidence is generated from AI systems that have or could have been compromised, questions regarding the robustness, transparency and explainability of AI systems will be valid when authenticating or evaluating such evidence.

Defining electronic evidence

1.110 Defining what we mean by 'electronic' evidence is not an easy task. The type of evidence that we are dealing with has also been variously described as 'digital evidence' or 'computer evidence'. All three terms express some aspects of our pre-theoretical intuition that this type of evidence has some distinctive features that set it apart from other means of proof. However, defining what these distinguishing features are is far from straightforward. The rapid technological change in the field of information technology means that any definition narrowly tailored to the current state of technology faces the risk of becoming obsolete rapidly. Definitions that are suitably future-proof by contrast tend to be too abstract and will cut across traditional divisions and categories in the law of evidence. For our purpose, we will take as our approach the need of the lawyer to turn certain artefacts – digital objects – into evidence that can be used as proof in legal proceedings. Based on this, we can develop a workable definition that will suit most applications and purposes.

1.111 Various definitions of electronic evidence exist. These include 'information of probative value that is stored or transmitted in binary form'[1] and 'information stored or transmitted in binary form that may be relied on in court'.[2] In his treatise, Casey defines digital evidence as:

> any data stored or transmitted using a computer that support or refute a theory of how an offense occurred or that address critical elements of the offense such as intent or alibi.[3]

1 Scientific Working Groups on Digital Evidence and Imaging Technology, 'Model Quality Assurance Manual for Digital Evidence Laboratories' (v3, 13 September 2012), https://www.swgde.org/documents/published.
2 International Organisation on Computer Evidence, 'G8 proposed principles for the procedures relating to digital evidence' (2000), http://web.archive.org/web/20030207173420/http://ioce.org/G8_proposed_principles_for_forensic_evidence.html. This definition was adopted by the US Department of Justice Office of Justice Programs, National Institute of Justice, in *Electronic Crime Scene Investigation: A Guide for First Responders* (US Department of Justice 2001) and *Forensic examination of digital evidence: A guide for law enforcement* (US Department of Justice 2004).
3 Eoghan Casey, *Digital Evidence and Computer Crime* (3rd edn, Elsevier 2011), 7.

1.112 Although the emphasis of this definition is on criminal investigations, it is a wider definition than the previous definitions, and it usefully explicates certain important aspects of electronic evidence. For instance, the reference to 'data' is to information that is held in electronic form, such as text, images, audio and video files. Also, the word 'computer' must be understood in its widest possible sense, and incorporates any device that stores, manipulates or transmits data. In addition, the definition implies that the evidence must be relevant and admissible, a question that can only be answered after we know what the electronic evidence, whether admissible or inadmissible, actually is. A project funded by the EU entitled 'European Informatics Data Exchange Framework for Court and Evidence' (March 2014 – October 2016)[1] set out a number of definitions of electronic evidence in 'D2.1 – EVIDENCE Semantic Structure', 1.2, and offered a definition at 1.6.1 that is strikingly similar to the one set out below:

> Electronic evidence is any data resulting from the output of an analogue device and/or a digital device of potential probative value that are generated by, processed by, stored on or transmitted by any electronic device. Digital evidence is that Electronic evidence which is generated or converted to a numerical format.

1 http://www.evidenceproject.eu/.

1.113 With the aim of offering a wider-ranging definition that includes civil and criminal cases, we propose the following definition:

> Electronic evidence: data (comprising the output of analogue devices or data in digital form) that is generated, processed, stored or communicated by any digital device, computer or computer system or conveyed over a digital transmission system that has the potential to make the factual account of either party more probable or less probable than it would be without the evidence.

1.114 This definition has three elements. First, the reference to 'data' includes all forms of evidence created, processed or stored in a device that can, in its widest meaning, be considered a computer.[1] It is used here in a non-technical sense, meaning roughly 'a gathered body of facts'. While computer scientists often distinguish between 'data' and 'programs', this distinction is not helpful for our purposes. For instance, in a copyright case, if a defendant has allegedly installed an unauthorized operating system, the presence of the system on his computer is electronic data for our purposes.[2] Second, the definition includes the various devices by which data can be stored or transmitted, including analogue devices that produce an output. Ideally, this definition will include any form of a digital device, whether it is a computer (as we presently understand the meaning of a computer), telephone systems, wireless telecommunications systems and networks such as the Internet, and mobile devices and embedded systems such as smart cards and navigation systems. Third, the definition restricts the data to information that is relevant to the process by which a dispute, whatever the nature of the disagreement, is to be decided by an adjudicator, whatever the form and level the adjudication takes. This part of the definition includes one aspect of admissibility – relevance only – but does not use 'admissibility' in itself as a defining criterion, because some evidence will be admissible but excluded by the adjudicator within the remit of their authority, or inadmissible for reasons that have nothing to do with the nature of the evidence. This could be, for instance, because of the way it was collected, such as in violation of privacy or in breach of legal professional privilege. However, the definition is limited to those items of evidence offered by the parties as part of the fact-finding process. This contextual, teleological aspect of the definition excludes, for instance, electronic documents that are created during a trial in a purely administrative capacity, such as email reminders of the date of the hearing sent to the parties by the court administrators. Of course, the very same data can become 'electronic evidence' if offered in an appeal to show that the information was not sent out in a timely fashion, if this is part of the complaint.

1 Excluding the human brain, which has also been compared to a computer, though this line is becoming increasingly difficult to maintain, especially with the increasing feasibility of human–computer interfaces.

2 Obviously, we also do not use 'data' in the way it is sometimes understood in telecommunications, where only digital, but not analogue, information is sometimes referred to as data.

1.115 A particularly important form of evidence in all developed legal systems is proof by document. Consequently, electronic documents are a particularly important form of electronic evidence.[1] They are also a particularly good example to illustrate some of the pertinent characteristics of electronic evidence. Because of the importance of documents for our daily life, and the way we handle them as folders, documents and photocopies, many of the most important software applications intentionally mimic the 'look and feel' of traditional, paper-based stationery when dealing with electronic documents. We therefore create digital objects that are called documents and have the same visual appearance as documents typed on paper. We 'turn' their 'pages' (as with some electronic readers for ebooks and ejournals), 'put' them in files and folders, and discard them in digital 'waste paper' baskets or trash bins. Email also intentionally mimics the traditional letter, from the letter icon on the inbox to the pencil icon for 'writing' a new message. This inauthentic familiarity can create the misleading impression that the electronic document exists somewhere on the computer as a single, complete whole, and maintains its structural integrity even when the file is closed or the computer is switched off, in the same way a paper document continues to exist when it is put out of sight into a folder. This overly naive view underestimates the differences between electronic and paper-based documents, and potentially also overestimates their reliability. The converse, however, can equally happen, where a more sophisticated user sees through the processes that intentionally create the appearance of a paper document and dismisses all electronic evidence as essentially deceptive, spurious and unreliable, rather than as a new kind of document. This becomes a particular problem for those jurisdictions whose evidence law has formal definitions of 'document' and proof by document, for instance the German *Urkundenbeweis*. In these jurisdictions, legal rather than factual issues can increase the chasm between electronic and traditional documents and bridging legislation is required to make electronic documents also 'documents-in-law'.

1 William Kent, *Data and Reality* (2nd edn, 1stBooks 2000) for an interesting discussion of how humans perceive and process information, and how humans impose this outlook on data processing machines.

1.116 A better and more realistic approach is to acknowledge that documents in electronic form have particular characteristics that affect both the test for authenticity (or provenance), should authenticity be in issue, and the way the electronic evidence is secured and handled at the pre-trial stage. It is the thesis of this text that evidence in electronic form ought to be subject to a more rigorous mechanism than would normally be associated with a document extant on physical media. John D. Gregory has observed that the integrity of physical documents is 'often protected fairly casually',[1] yet the same could not be said of documents that are created, modified, communicated, stored and deleted in electronic form. For instance, a forensic document examiner can analyse the chemical properties of the ink on a paper document to determine if more than one writing utensil was used, or if the composition of the ink is consistent with the time at which the document was allegedly created, or the material properties of the paper. Once the document is written, changes or alterations will also leave physical traces. With paper documents, we therefore have a clear understanding, routinely recognized in evidence law, that the original document[2] and copies of it are objects with different physical properties. This crucial distinction becomes problematic in the electronic medium, where not only are copy and original indistinguishable, but the very act of working on 'a' document will also automatically and routinely create numerous copies on the computer without the knowledge of the author, copies that can persist and override earlier drafts even when the document is completed. As outlined above in the discussion about metadata, documents in electronic form have a number of features that present particular challenges that a paper carrier in the physical world does not.

1 John D. Gregory, 'Authentication rules and electronic records' (2002) 81 Can Bar Rev 529, 533.
2 For the meaning of 'original', see Steven W. Teppler, 'Digital data as hearsay' (2009) 6 Digital Evidence and Electronic Signature Law Review 7, 9 n 18; Stephen Mason, 'Electronic evidence and the meaning of "original" ' (2009) 79 Amicus Curiae 26, http://sas-space.sas.ac.uk/2565/; Luciana Duranti

and Corinne Rogers, 'Trust in digital records: an increasingly cloudy legal area' (2012) 28(5) Computer Law and Security Review 522, 527 with further references.

The dependency on machinery and software

1.117 The reader can easily read the content of a traditional document long after it was created with little or no additional costs; the only things necessary are good eyesight and a knowledge of the language in which the document is written. Data in electronic form by contrast is dependent on hardware and software. The data requires an interpreter to enable it to be rendered into human-readable form. A user cannot create or manipulate electronic data without appropriate hardware. Therefore, an electronic document should not be treated as an object 'somewhere there' on the digital device, in the same way as a paper book is in a library. Instead, the electronic document is better understood as a process by which otherwise unintelligible pieces of data that are distributed over the storage medium are assembled, processed and rendered legible for a human user. In this sense, the electronic document is nowhere: it does not exist independently from the process (software) that recreates it on the device (hardware) every time a user opens it on screen. If those electronic documents were produced in the 1990s, many thousands of the programs used to create them are now no longer available commercially, and even if such software were available, it might be impossible to load it on a modern operating system. An additional problem for older data is that it might be necessary to have a specific machine with specific software loaded in order to read the data.[1] This can cause additional expense to a party, as in the case of *PHE, Incorporated dba Adam & Eve v Department of Justice*,[2] where PHE was ordered to review information contained in a database, even though no program existed to enable it to obtain the information requested by the Department of Justice.

1 For instance, the jazz club Ronnie Scott's, based in Soho, London, was refurbished in 2005–2006. As each part of the club was renovated, so large numbers of recordings of jazz musicians and singers, such as Dizzy Gillespie, Ella Fitzgerald, Chet Baker, Sarah Vaughan and Buddy Rich, that had been recorded during live performances were discovered. Some of the recordings were made on tapes that could only be played on machines that were no longer in the possession of the club. Report by Bob Sherwood, 'Ronnie Scott's jazz club to release archive of the greats' *Financial Times* (London, 28 June 2006) 1.
2 139 F.R.D. 249 (D.D.C. 1991); a similar problem was considered by Vinelott J in *Derby & Co Ltd v Weldon (No. 9)* [1991] 1 WLR 652, [1991] 2 All ER 901, [1990] 7 WLUK 300, [1992] CLY 3472.

The mediation of technology

1.118 Data in electronic form must be rendered into human-readable form through the mediation of a set of technologies. This means differences occur in how the same source object is displayed in different situations. A good example common to all users of the Internet is that a website can look very different depending on what type of screen and what browser is used, among other things. As a result, there can be no concept of a single, definitive representation of a particular source digital object. This can have obvious legal repercussions. An electronic contract document carelessly drafted may informally refer to the 'paragraphs' of the document without enumerating them since the formatting on the author's computer makes them plainly visible through line breaks in the text. Sent by email to the buyer and opened on her machine with a different software program, this formatting data may be unreadable and the paragraphs no longer apparent. Another example can be found in the changed representations of emojis (ideograms used in an electronic message similar to older ASCII emoticons). For instance, in 2016 Apple controversially changed a 'hand gun' emoji into a 'water pistol' emoji. However, when a message containing this emoji is sent to a non-Apple device, it could appear on the recipient's machine as a cartoon image of a real gun.[1] If a message such as 'bring <gun emoji> to our meeting' or 'retract that or I come with my <gun emoji>' is sent, what was intended by the sender as a light-hearted joke may look like a threat for some recipients, depending on what device they are using.

1 Bonnie Malkin, 'Water pistol emoji replaces revolver as Apple enters gun violence debate' *The Guardian* (London, 2 August 2016), https://www.theguardian.com/technology/2016/aug/02/apple-replaces-gun-emoji-water-pistol-revolver-violence-debate.

1.119 With traditional evidence, the act of observing or analysing a crime scene should not be allowed to alter it – a problem commonly known as 'contamination'. In contrast, with electronic evidence the mere act of starting a computer and opening a document changes it, for instance by altering its metadata. Different observers using only marginally different machinery may recreate different versions of the object in question, and it is not an easy issue to decide which one of them should be regarded as 'more authentic'.

1.120 To manage this issue, we can adopt the approach taken with eyewitness evidence. We know that different observers of the same event will always provide subtly different accounts as to what happened. Furthermore, an observer will unintentionally and inevitably alter his memory of the events every time he tries to remember them. In the same way in which we try to minimise these effects through appropriate protocols and procedures – for instance, processes for an identification line-up or the interviewing of witnesses – protocols and procedures used by the digital evidence professional can minimize, but not eliminate, the distortion that the investigation creates. This means that it is crucial to identify appropriate standards, protocols, benchmarks and procedures, and the relevant hardware and software to be used, in relation to the management and use of any item of electronic evidence.

Speed of change

1.121 Technology in operating systems, application software and hardware changes rapidly. As a result, data in digital form may reach a point when they cannot be read, understood or used with new software or hardware. For instance, a software company may no longer produce software that is backward compatible or 'downward compatible' (where new versions of software are able to operate with older products). Technical obsolescence is a major problem that affects every aspect of the legal process, especially because the rate of change has now become so rapid.

1.122 The incessant speed of change has another consequence, again best explained by contrasting electronic evidence with traditional evidence. Eyewitness identification evidence is one of the oldest, if not the oldest, form of evidence used in trial. Despite this, the way we elicit and interpret eyewitness evidence in legal proceedings has changed little over the centuries, and legal systems regularly keep culturally obsolete concepts such as the oath or dock identification for their ritual value. Fingerprint evidence is younger, with little over a hundred years of forensic use. But since its inception, while the basics of the discipline have remained the same, important changes in the way in which we interpret fingerprint evidence have been made, as have the features that we look for when establishing a match. A fingerprint expert trained 90 years ago would probably need at least a refresher course. DNA evidence is younger still, but in its 30-year history there have been considerable changes in the way in which DNA is collected, analysed and interpreted. An expert trained in the 1980s would require considerable retraining to be able to deal with current technology and equipment. For electronic evidence, the pace of change is faster still. This makes it all the more difficult to keep lawyers and other non-experts briefed of the relevant developments, and increases reliance on experts. It also means that it is essential that an expert has up-to-date knowledge and receives constant training, which may be more important than 'experience' in this field. A problem related to the rapid changes witnessed is the horizontal diversification of software and hardware. If a DNA expert analyses a blood sample, she need not know in advance the age, nationality or gender of the donor. By contrast, the digital evidence professional needs to know, and be trained for, the specific type of device and software that she is asked to analyse.

1.123 The ability of those investigating crimes is also hampered, for instance, by the speed at which the technology changes. In particular, obtaining relevant electronic tools to analyse a device forensically can be difficult for two reasons: first, the tools needed have yet to be devised, and second because, even if they are available, such tools can be expensive. In the case of *R. v Hallam (Sam)*,[1] Sam Hallam's conviction for three offences of murder, conspiracy to commit grievous bodily harm and violent disorder was quashed. One of the grounds of appeal was that Hallam was in possession of two mobile telephones, both of which were seized by the police. One of the telephones, a 3G telephone, contained evidence that suggested that Hallam's alibi was probably correct, and that the memories of both Hallam and his alibi witness as to the date they were together were defective. Neither telephone was the subject of forensic analysis. The observations by Hallett LJ, delivering the judgment of the court, illustrate the lawyers' naivety in the forensic investigation of the data.[2] She said:

> 65. ... For reasons which escape us [the mobile phones] do not seem to have been interrogated by either the investigating officers or the defence team. We can understand why cell site evidence in relation to the use of the phones may have been of limited value given the close proximity of the masts, the various scenes, and the homes of those involved. However, given the attachment of young and old to their mobile phones, we cannot understand why someone from either the investigating team or the defence team did not think to examine the phones attributable to the appellant. An analysis of mobile phone evidence played a part in the investigation ...
>
> 67. One reason proffered for the failure to examine the phone was that in 2004 the Metropolitan Police did not have the technology in-house to examine 3G telephones. However, given our limited knowledge, we would have thought that even a cursory check might have produced some interesting results. Further, it might be thought that the appellant would have alerted his defence team to the fact that he had taken photographs on his new phone in the days before and after the murder which might have jogged his memory and helped establish his whereabouts.

1 [2012] EWCA Crim 1158, [2012] 5 WLUK 518.
2 This highlights the need for lawyers to ensure they are competent to practice, for which see in particular Denise H. Wong, 'Educating for the future: teaching evidence in the technological age' (2013) 10 Digital Evidence and Electronic Signature Law Review 16; and Deveral Capps, 'Fitting a quart into a pint pot: the legal curriculum and meeting the requirements of practice' (2013) 10 Digital Evidence and Electronic Signature Law Review 23.

1.124 Because the electronic evidence in the telephone supported the defendant's alibi and contradicted the eyewitness testimony, which Hallett LJ had described as 'rock solid', the court concluded that this was a case of mistaken identity and acquitted the defendant.[1]

1 [2012] EWCA Crim 1158 at [77].

Volume and replication

1.125 Electronic documents are easy to manipulate: they can be copied,[1] altered, updated, or deleted (and deleted in the electronic environment does not mean expunged). The integration of telecommunications and computers to form computer networks (such as wide area networks and the Internet) further allows for data to be created and exchanged in far greater volumes than had previously been possible, and across physical and geographical boundaries. In essence, email, instant messaging and Internet communications are a 'duplicate and distribute' technology.[2] Once computers are networked together in this fashion, an electronic document may be transmitted and numerous copies distributed around the world very rapidly. By way of example, in *AMP v Persons Unknown*[3] the claimant's mobile telephone was stolen or lost. It was not protected with a password. A number of photographs were stored on the telephone, some of which were of an explicit sexual nature. Shortly after the telephone went missing or was stolen, digital images were uploaded on various social media websites, enabling others to download and share the images. Some of the social media sites removed the images when requested, but the images were seeded onto a Swedish BitTorrent node and continued to circulate. Ramsey J decided that the claimant was entitled to an interim injunction to prevent the distribution of the digital images, either by conventional downloading from a site or by downloading using the BitTorrent protocol. To reflect the ease with which the images could be obtained and distributed, the injunction was granted in the following terms:

> 50. I therefore grant an interim injunction in the following terms against persons unknown being those people in possession or control of any part or parts of the files listed in Schedule C to the order who are served with this order:
>
> (1) shall immediately cease seeding any BitTorrent containing any part or parts of the files listed in Schedule C of this Order.
>
> (2) must not upload or transmit to any other person any part or parts of the files listed in Schedule C of this Order.
>
> (3) must not create any derivatives of any of the files listed in Schedule C of this Order.
>
> (4) must not disclose the name of Claimant (or any other information which might lead to her identification) or the names of any of the files listed in Schedule C of this Order.

1 The copying of large numbers of electronic documents (around 56,000) formed part of the allegations in *Vestergaard Frandsen A/S v Bestnet Europe Limited* [2007] EWHC 2455 (Ch), [2007] 10 WLUK 659, (2008) 31(1) IPD 31005, which is a judgment in relation to an application by the defendants to strike out the action on the grounds that it was vexatious and an abuse of the process; George L. Paul and Jason R. Baron, 'Information inflation: can the legal system adapt?' (2007) 13(3) Rich J L & Tech 1.
2 Social media websites and text messages sent on mobile telephones and other devices were used to foment rioting in the UK in 2011: *R. v Blackshaw (Jordan Philip)* [2011] EWCA Crim 2312, [2012] 1 WLR 1126, [2011] 10 WLUK 465, [2012] 1 Cr App R (S) 114, [2012] Crim LR 57, (2011) 108(42) LSG 19, Times, 25 October 25, 2011, [2011] CLY 3030.
3 [2011] EWHC 3454 (TCC), [2011] 12 WLUK 641, [2011] Info TLR 25, (2012) 156(2) SJLB 31.

1.126 The ease of communication and replication of electronic documents has increased the potential volume of data that need to be identified to obtain relevant documents pertaining to litigation or the prosecution of a criminal offence. For instance, as part of the Enron investigation, the Federal Energy Regulatory Commission made public a dataset corpus containing 500MB of electronic messages.[1] Yet 'traditional' messages like these are a minuscule minority of all the electronic data (and potential evidence) that is routinely created by machines, such as monitoring and routing Internet traffic. In addition to the sheer volume of this data, it poses the additional problem that in its raw form it is not intelligible to humans – most of the data are instructions sent between and for use by machines. To turn them into evidence for legal proceedings requires a significant amount of translation or 'sense making' by a suitably qualified expert.

1 Available at the Library of Congress website: https://www.loc.gov/item/2018487913/.

1.127 To deal effectively with this amount of data, other computer tools such as data-mining software will routinely be required. These methods of analysis carry their own problems of accuracy, reliability, prejudicial effects and so on. Link analysis software, for instance, can create from this data a picture of a network that shows how people in the company formed communication circles that can be interpreted as the core of a conspiracy, simply as a result of the way in which the software arranges and visualises the information or other design choices not supported by the actual evidence.[1] On the other hand, other forensic disciplines routinely use scientifically validated sampling techniques.[2] At present, there is still a tendency not to use the same sampling protocols for at least some types of electronic evidence, in particular the type of data that can in principle be assessed directly by humans. This can force witnesses, such as police officers, to visually inspect potentially large amounts of disturbing illegal material. However, some jurisdictions have begun to use statistical methods of (electronic) evidence collection more systematically. 'Predictive coding' or 'technology assisted review' uses Bayesian probability theory and ML to scan electronic documents for data relevant to the case, and automatically identifies 'good candidates' for further examination by humans. Used mainly in civil electronic disclosure or discovery, it acquired approval from the courts in 2016.[3] And prosecutors, lawyers and judges have likewise started to use ML-driven case-tracking and management systems to manage case filing, information and caseloads.[4]

1 Cathleen McGrath, Jim Blythe and David Krackhardt, 'Seeing groups in graph layouts' (1996) 19(2) Connections 22.
2 If 300,000 suspicious pills are seized, only a small sample of them will be tested to determine if they are illegal drugs, and a statistical confidence value reported. Colin G. G. Aitken and David Lucy,

'Estimation of the quantity of a drug in a consignment from measurements on a sample' (2002) 47(5) J Forensic Sci 968.

3 *Pyrrho Investments Ltd v MWB Property Ltd* [2016] EWHC 256 (Ch), [2016] 2 WLUK 413; *Brown v BCA Trading Ltd* [2016] EWHC 1464 (Ch), [2016] 5 WLUK 371; Clive Freedman, 'Technology assisted review approved for use in English High Court litigation' (2016) 13 Digital Evidence and Electronic Signature Law Review 139.

4 For instance, see Joint Technology Committee – National Center for State Courts, Introduction to AI for Courts, 7–8, 27 March 2020, https://www.ncsc.org/__data/assets/pdf_file/0013/20830/2020-04-02-intro-to-ai-for-courts_final.pdf.

1.128 The ability to transfer evidence rapidly can also create issues relating to jurisdiction. Many computer users now routinely upload all their files for backup purposes to Internet-based providers. Business data may be processed using cloud computing technology. On the other hand, the automatic uploading of data also means that the user of a device loses control over the information she has created. It can become increasingly difficult to delete or rid oneself of information once it has been created on a device and the information is uploaded onto the cloud.

Storage and disclosure

1.129 Generally, the media upon which electronic data are stored is fragile. Electronic storage media is inherently unstable, and unless the media is stored correctly, it can deteriorate quickly without showing external signs of deterioration. It is also at risk from accidental or deliberate damage and accidental or deliberate deletion.

1.130 Computers, systems and digital devices now operate largely in a networked environment. Devices such as smartphones, computers, laptop computers, mobile telephones, personal digital assistants (PDAs) and tablets are linked by applications (facsimile transmissions, voice over Internet protocol (VoIP), email, peer-to-peer software and instant messaging) that run over networks (the Internet, intranets, wireless networking, cellular networks and dial-up). It follows that almost everything anybody does on a device that is connected to a network is capable of being distributed and duplicated with consummate ease. As a result, the same item of digital data can reside almost anywhere. The ramifications for lawyers and law enforcement authorities are obvious. The relevant document may be available, but it might not be clear where it resides. This affects how a criminal investigation is conducted, and how much effort a party to a civil case will have to devote to finding relevant documents for discovery or disclosure.

1.131 An early example from the US, *Zubulake v UBS Warburg LLC*, serves to illustrate some of the problems faced by a large organization in locating relevant documents in electronic form, especially historical email correspondence. Zubulake, a director and senior salesperson with UBS Warburg LLC, commenced legal proceedings for gender discrimination when she was dismissed from her job. Among other things, she alleged that her manager Chapin treated her differently. She sought disclosure of UBS email communications to support her action.[1] The parties disagreed about the extent of the disclosure of emails, although it was not in dispute that email was an important means of communicating since each salesperson received approximately 200 emails each day. Securities and Exchange Commission Regulations required UBS to store emails. UBS used two storage methods: backup tapes for disaster recovery and optical disks.

This meant that there were three possible places that relevant email communications could be found: in files that were in use by employees, emails archived on optical disks, and emails sent to and from a registered trader (internal emails were not recorded) that were stored on optical storage devices. Ninety-four backup tapes were identified as being relevant for the purposes of disclosure. UBS used a backup program that took a snapshot of all emails that existed on a given server at the time the backup was taken: namely, at the end of each day, every Friday night and on the last business day of the month. Because emails were backed up intermittently, some emails were not stored, in particular where a user received or sent an email and deleted it on the same day.

1 *Zubulake v UBS Warburg LLC* 217 F.R.D. 309 (S.D.N.Y. 2003); *Zubulake v UBS Warburg LLC* 216 F.R.D. 280 (S.D.N.Y. 2003).

1.132 Scheindlin J determined that Zubulake was entitled to disclosure of the emails because they were relevant to her claim, and ordered UBS to produce all relevant emails that existed on the optical disks or its servers at its own expense, and from five backup tapes selected by Zubulake. A consulting firm restored and searched the tapes for US$11,524.63. Additional expenses included the time it took lawyers to review the emails, which brought the total cost to US$19,003.43. Some 1,541 relevant emails were discovered. Fewer than 20 relevant emails were found on the optical disks. In July 2003, Zubulake made a further application for the remaining backup tapes to be restored and searched. UBS estimated that the cost would be US$273,649.39 and applied for the costs to be shifted to Zubulake. In considering the seven-factor test (which is not relevant for the purposes of this particular discussion), the judge noted that a significant number of relevant emails existed on backup tapes, and there was evidence that Chapin had deleted relevant emails. Scheindlin J decided that Zubulake should pay 25 per cent of the cost of restoring the backup tapes, but UBS were required to pay all other costs.

1.133 The purpose of describing this example is to illustrate the problems that multinational organizations have in locating relevant evidence in electronic form. The nature of the distributed environment means that a range of practical problems have begun to emerge in determining what material needs to be disclosed or discovered to the other side. First, it is necessary to prevent the destruction of evidence, and then it is necessary to establish where the evidence is likely to be, before undertaking the exercise of sifting through the various sources to identify relevant documents. This will invariably require a party to locate where all backup tapes are situated, whether held on the premises, with third parties in off-site remote storage or on individual computers, servers, in an archive or a disaster recovery system. The types of storage media that will need to be identified and located include tapes, disks, drives, USB sticks, tablets, laptops, PCs, PDAs, smartphones, mobile telephones, pagers and audio systems (including voicemail), to name but a few.[1] The fragility and the ubiquity of electronic storage has made the modern-day discovery exercise a formidable process.

1 Detective Inspector Simon Snell, Head of the High Tech Crime Unit in Devon and Cornwall, is reported to have indicated that criminals are using satellite navigation systems, games consoles and hand-held computers to try and hide their activities; see 'Abuse images "hidden on sat-navs"', BBC News, 22 January 2008, http://news.bbc.co.uk/1/hi/england/devon/7201785.stm.

Concluding remarks

1.134 This chapter provides an overview of the nature of digital evidence, and introduces the most important concepts and terms that are needed to understand the discussion in the chapters to follow. It also introduces the main components and aspects of digital devices that a forensic investigator has to consider. The chapter also reveals a tension that is inherent in technologically mediated evidence. If we describe digital evidence on a sufficiently high level of abstraction, the continuity with other, older forms of evidence becomes apparent, thereby permitting analogies with the existing common law rules on evidence. For instance, memory, in this sense, is memory, whether gathered from an eyewitness and stored in a biological medium or from a digital device and stored in silicon. From a legal and regulatory perspective, these high-level abstractions fulfil an important role – they create legal stability and predictability for businesses and citizens alike. However, as soon as we move to a higher level of detail, these similarities all but disappear. Electronic evidence is always technologically mediated and technology dependent. We can get data from a book written centuries ago needing nothing more than knowledge of the language. By contrast, acquiring data from an electronic storage device requires appropriate tools and procedures, and can therefore fail, even for systems that are but a few years old. This can mean that laws quickly fail to understand the nature of the technology they try to regulate, and therefore quickly become obsolete. This can create the impression that the law is constantly behind technological developments, and where parliaments or courts try to respond, they more often than not exacerbate the situation with poorly drafted laws or ill-considered rules. The challenge for lawyers and policy makers is to find a middle ground between stable and technology-neutral, but overly abstract and imprecise laws, and highly specific rules that try, but often fail, to be responsive to the latest technological development and therefore risk obsolescence. This first chapter tries to help find such a middle ground by combining high-level and abstract definitions and discussions of historical continuities with more technology-specific discussions, and demonstrating both the similarities as well as the differences between traditional evidence and electronic evidence.

2

The foundations of evidence in electronic form

Stephen Mason and Daniel Seng

2.1 By taking into account the defining characteristics of the digital world, the use and admissibility of evidence in digital form have largely been accomplished through the definition and redefinition of legal concepts in the malleable rules of evidence. This chapter sets out to review the rules of evidence in the categorization of, means of proof of, treatment of and weight given to electronic evidence. An overview of the issues of hearsay, the treatment of software code as the witness, the presumption that computers are 'reliable' and authentication of electronic evidence are covered in detail in other chapters.

Direct and indirect evidence

2.2 The purpose of adducing evidence in legal proceedings is to prove the facts in issue. Facts in issue can also be properly inferred from any facts that are presented. Where evidence is used to prove the facts in issue, it is direct evidence. Where evidence is used to prove facts from which the facts in issue may be inferred, it is indirect evidence. If the facts in issue involve proving the existence of an electronic record, the electronic record itself constitutes direct evidence. Direct evidence refers to evidence which proves the facts in issue, and indirect evidence, or circumstantial evidence, is defined as evidence which proves facts which are relevant to the facts in issue.

2.3 Unless the existence, character or circumstance of the generation or storage of an electronic record is itself a fact in issue, it is more frequently the case that electronic evidence is used as indirect evidence to prove certain facts from which the facts in issue may be inferred. For instance, if an electronic record is adduced in evidence to show that A owes B a debt, the electronic record as indirect evidence only proves that there is a record that A owes B a debt, and it is necessary to make the additional inference that A actually owes B a debt.

Evidence in both digital and analogue form

2.4 Although there are differences in form and format between the analogue or non-electronic version of an item of evidence and its electronic equivalent, if the differences are not material, courts will not reject electronic evidence in favour of other forms of evidence.

2.5 The differences may be material depending on the facts in issue: the alternative representations of data in digital form and in human-readable form, on a screen or printed piece of paper, may become significant. In the Tasmanian case of *Maynard*,[1]

Stephen Mason and Daniel Seng, 'The foundations of evidence in electronic form', in Stephen Mason and Daniel Seng (eds.), *Electronic Evidence and Electronic Signatures* (5th edn, University of London 2021) 51–84.

the trial magistrate declined to admit a printout purporting to indicate the dates and times when the accused obtained access to data stored in the computer on the basis that not all of the data that were evident on the computer screen were fully replicated on the printout. In a motion to review, Wright J upheld the magistrate's decision. The judge observed that if all the data were relevant, the prosecution could have recorded the data on the screen by video. In this case, it was demonstrated that the information recorded on the printout was incomplete and not an accurate rendition of the data, and it did not involve only minor format changes, as the prosecution sought to contend.

1 (1993) 70 A Crim R 133, also cited as *Rook v Maynard* [1993] TASSC 137, (1993) 2 Tas R 97, (1993) 126 ALR 150.

2.6 In contrast, in *People of the State of New York v Rose*[1] Morse J in City Court, City of Rochester, New York had to consider the use and admissibility of 'computer generated simplified traffic information tickets' or 'e-tickets'. The defendants moved for dismissal of the charges for driving while intoxicated because the State Police had issued the charges in the computer-generated simplified information form rather than the multi-copy handwritten simplified traffic information form used across New York State. In a carefully reasoned judgment, Morse J set out how the system worked, and determined that the computer terminal used by the police generated each e-ticket with simplified traffic information for the defendants, printed duplicate originals of the e-ticket and affixed the arresting officer's electronic signature to the e-ticket. Although there were minor format differences, such as the colour and the number of sides on which the e-tickets were printed, these differences were not sufficient to persuade the judge that the e-tickets conformed substantially to a paper ticket. Thus, the motion for dismissal was denied.

1 11 Misc.3d 200 (2005), 805 N.Y.S.2d 506, 2005 N.Y. Slip Op. 25526.

2.7 A similar consideration arose in *Griffiths v DPP*,[1] where photographs taken with a speed camera on photographic film were admitted as evidence of a vehicle being driven at a speed greater than the speed limit. The evidence was also available in digital form, and the defence argued that the digital data should have been disclosed as well as the printed photographs. It was revealed that the camera technician had carried out a secondary check to confirm the speed of the vehicle on the digital files of the photographs. The judge indicated that the photographs were real evidence – they showed the times at which the vehicle crossed a number of pre-measured lines painted on the road – and that by using all this information it was possible to carry out the secondary check from the photographs themselves; it was not necessary to carry out the secondary check on the digital files. For this reason, it was held that whether the digital data were disclosed to the defendant or not was irrelevant.[2]

1 [2007] EWHC 619 (Admin), [2007] 3 WLUK 572, [2007] RTR 44, [2007] CLY 3537.
2 [2007] RTR 44 at [34].

Metadata and electronic evidence

2.8 There is a distinction between a document in digital form (and the content of the digital document as a printout) and the metadata logically associated with the document in digital form. The metadata may be relevant, either as indirect evidence in relation to the document in digital form, or it may itself be relevant as direct evidence.

For instance, when there are multiple versions of a digital document, the metadata as indirect evidence will enable the parties to identify the most relevant version of the document. On the other hand, where there is an allegation that the user manipulated the metadata of the file, such as its date–time stamp, to his own advantage, the correct date and time of the file becomes the fact in issue and the metadata is the direct evidence. In such a case the metadata may need to be rendered into human-readable form.

Means of proof

2.9 All direct and indirect evidence used to prove a fact in issue or a relevant fact takes one (or more) of the following forms: testimony, hearsay, documents and real evidence.

Testimony and hearsay

2.10 Testimony is the declaration (which must be admissible) in court of a person who actually perceived the fact in issue or facts from which facts in issue may properly be inferred. Thus the human perception of a computer display as narrated via oral testimony is admissible as evidence that a counterfeit computer game was being played in breach of copyright.[1]

1 The image on a screen can constitute sufficient evidence of data copied onto the RAM of a computer used to play counterfeit games to establish an offence of breach of copyright, for which see *Gilham v The Queen* [2009] EWCA Crim 2293, [2010] ECDR 5.

2.11 If, however, the best that a witness can do is to depose as to what someone else said on the fact in issue, it will be hearsay, because it is 'an assertion other than one made by a person while giving oral evidence in the proceedings ... as evidence of any fact asserted'.[1] In the context of digital evidence, what someone else said is typically recorded electronically. Hearsay is generally inadmissible unless it falls within one of the exceptions to the rule against hearsay. (A further treatment of this subject is found in Chapter 3.)

1 *R v Sharp* [1988] 1 All ER 65 at 68, [1988] 1 WLR 7 at 11.

Real evidence

2.12 The term 'real evidence' has been used in three divergent senses: (i) evidence from things as distinct from persons; (ii) material objects produced for the inspection of the court; and (iii) perception by the court (or its results) as any perceptions by the court (or its results) as distinct from the facts perceived,[1] and is best described as 'Material objects other than documents, produced for inspection of the court'.[2] Veronica Cowan considered that there is no authoritative definition of 'real evidence', and suggested that 'where a document is tendered simply to prove the fact that a statement was made (and not to prove a fact stated therein), it is not properly described as "real evidence" '.[3]

1 Hodge M. Malek (ed.), *Phipson on Evidence* (19th edn, Sweet & Maxwell 2018), 1.14. It was used in *R. (on the application of O'Shea) v Coventry Magistrates Court* [2004] EWHC 905 (Admin), [2004] 4 WLUK 120, [2004] ACD 50, (2004) 101(17) LSG 30, Times, 22 April 2004, [2004] CLY 686 regarding computer access logs.
2 Malek, *Phipson on Evidence*, paras 1–14.

3 Veronica Cowan, 'Computer printouts – real evidence or documentary evidence?' [1991] Crim LR 199 at 201, discussing *R v Spiby (John Eric)* [1990] 3 WLUK 150, (1990) 91 Cr App R 186, Times, 16 March 1990, Independent, 2 April 1990, Daily Telegraph, 30 March 1990, [1990] CLY 785.

2.13 To highlight the difference between real evidence and hearsay in electronic evidence, Professor Daniel Seng and Sriram S. Chakravarthi formulated the following categorizations: digital data that is stored on a device, a device that processes data, and a device that processes and stores data.[1] The digital data is hearsay, because the device contains a record of human assertions. As for the second and third cases, where the data is produced without human intervention, it is real evidence. If the data is a record of human assertions, it is hearsay. Although the distinction is a clear one, it can be difficult to apply in practice,[2] as the cases discussed below illustrate.

1 Daniel Seng and Sriram S. Chakravarthi, *Computer Output as Evidence: Consultation Paper* (Singapore Academy of Law 2003), 87–88.
2 Seng and Chakravarthi, *Computer Output as Evidence*, 137–138; a point also made by Adam Wolfson, ' "Electronic fingerprints": doing away with the conception of computer-generated records as hearsay' (2005) 104(1) Michigan L Rev 165.

Evidence in analogue form

2.14 The treatment of evidence in analogue form (which preceded the use and acceptance of digital computers) first received detailed treatment in the case of *R v Ali (Maqsud), R v Hussain (Ashiq)*,[1] where the issue was the admissibility of a tape recording. In admitting the evidence, Marshall J analogized tape recordings with photographs, and noted that just as evidence of things seen through telescopes or binoculars which otherwise could not be picked up by the naked eye had been admitted, the same would apply to devices for picking up, transmitting and recording conversations, noted, at [701] (emphasis added):

> For many years now photographs have been admissible in evidence on proof that they are relevant to the issues involved in the case and that the prints are taken from negatives that are untouched. The prints as seen represent situations that have been reproduced by means of mechanical and chemical devices. Evidence of things seen through telescopes or binoculars which otherwise could not be picked up by the naked eye have been admitted, and now there are devices for picking up, transmitting, and recording, conversations. We can see no difference in principle between a tape recording and a photograph. In saying this we must not be taken as saying that such recordings are admissible whatever the circumstances, but it does appear to this court wrong to deny to the law of evidence advantages to be gained by new techniques and new devices, *provided the accuracy of the recording can be proved and the voices recorded properly identified*; provided also that the evidence is relevant and otherwise admissible, we are satisfied that a tape recording is admissible in evidence. Such evidence should always be regarded with some caution and assessed in the light of all the circumstances of each case. There can be no question of laying down any exhaustive set of rules by which the admissibility of such evidence should be judged.

1 *R v Ali (Maqsud), R v Hussain (Ashiq)* [1966] 1 QB 688, [1965] 3 WLR 229, [1965] 2 All ER 464, [1965] 4 WLUK 27, (1965) 49 Cr App R 230, (1965) 129 JP 396, (1965) 109 SJ 331, [1965] CLY 796.

2.15 Shortly thereafter, Sir Jocelyn Simon P determined in *The Statue of Liberty, Sapporo Maru M/S (Owners) v Steam Tanker Statue of Liberty (Owners)*[1] that the film recording on a radar set of echoes of ships within its range was real evidence, even though it was recorded from a mechanical instrument.[2] The judge considered there was no distinction in the manual operation of a camera by a photographer or the observations of a barometer operator and the equivalent operation by a trip switch, a clock or a dial-recording mechanism. The judge held, at [196], that '[t]he law is bound these days to take cognisance of the fact that mechanical means replace human effort', and accepted that the film comprised real evidence because it recorded the information given out by the radar set, rejecting the submission that the evidence was hearsay.

1 [1968] 1 WLR 739, [1968] 2 All ER 195, [1968] 1 Lloyd's Rep 429, [1968] 3 WLUK 65, (1968) 112 SJ 380, [1968] CLY 1546.
2 Oral evidence of the position of a ship as given by a radar set is acceptable, for which see *Chen Yin Ten v Little* (1976) 11 ALR 353, [1976] WASC 143.

Evidence in digital form

2.16 The characterization of evidence as real evidence or as hearsay becomes more complicated with evidence in digital form, especially when some computational processing is carried out. In *R v Pettigrew (Stewart Douglas), R v Newark (John)*[1] the Court of Appeal held that the printout from a computer operated by an employee of the Bank of England was a hearsay statement. The operator fed bundles of bank notes with consecutive serial numbers into the machine, and the machine automatically rejected any notes that were defective. The machine recorded the first and last serial numbers of each bundle of 100 notes, and the operator also noted the first serial numbers in the bundle on a card as he fed them into the machine. It was the printout from this machine that was sought to be admitted in evidence. The purpose of adducing the evidence was to permit the prosecution to trace the issuance of the notes, and to link bank notes found in the possession of Pettigrew to a particular bundle of notes that had been stolen in a burglary. Counsel for the prosecution argued that the printout was admissible as a business record under the provisions of the Criminal Evidence Act 1965.[2] However, s 1(1)(a) required that for such a record to be admissible as evidence of the truth of any matter dealt with in the record, the information would have to be supplied by a person who had, or may reasonably be supposed to have, personal knowledge of the matters. The members of the Court of Appeal reached the conclusion that the operator did not have personal knowledge of the numbers of the notes that were rejected, because the machine automatically compiled the list.

1 [1980] 1 WLUK 561, (1980) 71 Cr App R 39, [1980] Crim LR 239, [1980] CLY 486; applied in *R v Wiles* [1982] Crim LR 669.
2 The Criminal Evidence Act 1995 was repealed by the Police and Criminal Evidence Act 1984 sch 7 pt III.

2.17 While this was an accurate application of the hearsay rule, the analysis omitted any consideration that the printout might be considered real evidence.[1] Professor J. C. Smith has noted that 'the operator had personal knowledge of the first number of each bundle which he fed into the machine because he recorded that number on a card',[2] and suggested that because the operator had knowledge of the number at a given point in time, it was not material that he forgot it afterwards. Once the first number could be established, it could then be inferred that the new notes bore consecutive serial numbers.[3] Professor Smith considered that this is not hearsay but direct evidence, because there was an absence of human intervention.[4] On the other hand, Professor Colin Tapper took the view that the printout was partly hearsay and partly non-hearsay – the first number is hearsay and the last number and the numbers of the notes that were rejected were not hearsay because they were the output of the device.[5]

1 Colin Tapper, *Computer Law* (4th edn, Longman 1989), 375; printouts were admitted under the provisions of s 1(1) of the Criminal Evidence Act 1965 in *R v Ewing (Terence Patrick)* [1983] QB 1039, [1983] 3 WLR 1, [1983] 2 All ER 645, [1983] 3 WLUK 125, (1983) 77 Cr App R 47, [1984] ECC 234, [1983] Crim LR 472, (1983) 127 SJ 390, Times, 15 March 1983, [1983] CLY 63, although Seng and Chakravarthi, in *Computer Output as Evidence*, 90, point out that 'the electronic records *are* the manifestation of the transaction'.
2 J. C. Smith, 'The admissibility of statements by computer' [1981] Crim LR 387, 388.
3 *R v Pettigrew (Stewart Douglas), R v Newark (John)* (1980) 71 Cr App R 39 at 42. In effect, Professor Smith's point was an argument pursued by counsel for the Crown.
4 Smith, 'The admissibility of statements by computer', 389–390.
5 Colin Tapper, 'Reform of the law of evidence in relation to the output from computers' (1995) 3 Intl J L & Info Tech 87.

2.18 Professor Seng considered that the views of Professors Smith and Tapper were both plausible: 'The difference lies in whether the operator fed the first number into the machine, and whether the machine processed this number.'[1] Seng continued:

> the different views espoused by Professors Tapper and Smith can be resolved as follows: was the machine operating as a data storage device in relation to the first number, or a data processing device? Some form of hybrid function may also be possible, eg, the operator inputs the first number, which the machine records and then verifies against its own reading of the first number. If the machine behaved in this way, perhaps Professor Smith's view is perhaps more accurate. This is all a question of the degree and extent of human intervention.[2]

1 Daniel K. B. Seng, 'Computer output as evidence' [1997] SJLS 139.
2 Seng, 'Computer output as evidence', 140.

2.19 As computers are designed to undertake a wide range of tasks, this means that the evidence available as output of a computer is equally as varied. A review of cases shows that whether electronic evidence is real evidence or hearsay turns on whether the evidence is characterized as being a product of a device's processing functions or of its storage functions.

2.20 In *R v Wood (Stanley William)*,[1] the software in a computer that made calculations of chemical compositions based on spectrometer readings was considered to be a tool, and the printout was an item of real evidence. The basis of admitting a printout of an output as an item of real evidence was explained by Professor Tapper:

> Evidence derived from a computer constitutes real evidence when it is used circumstantially rather than testimonially, that is to say that the fact that it takes one form rather than another is what makes it relevant, rather than the truth of some assertion which it contains.[2]

1 [1982] 6 WLUK 191, (1983) 76 Cr App R 23, [1982] Crim LR 667, [1983] CLY 636. See also the earlier case of *R v McCarthy (Colin Paul), R v Warren (Mark Stephen), R v Lloyd (Leigh Cedric), R v Warren (Robert John)* [1997] 11 WLUK 347, [1998] RTR 374, [1998] CLY 867 and the Singapore case of *PP v Ang Soon Huat* [1990] 2 SLR(R) 246.
2 Tapper, *Computer Law*, 373.

2.21 The same distinction was drawn by Professor Smith as regards the computer printout in *R v Ewing (Terence Patrick)*,[1] between its use as evidence to prove that a thing was done (money had been credited to a bank account) and as evidence that something was recorded as being done (the bank clerk records a payment, as opposed to creating the credit).[2]

1 [1983] QB 1039, [1983] 3 WLR 1, [1983] 2 All ER 645, [1983] 3 WLUK 125, (1983) 77 Cr App R 47, [1984] ECC 234, [1983] Crim LR 472, (1983) 127 SJ 390, Times, 15 March 1983, [1983] CLY 63; see *DPP v Thornley* [2006] EWHC 312 (Admin), [2006] 2 WLUK 68, (2006) 170 JP 385, (2006) 170 JPN 656, (2006) 103(9) LSG 32, [2006] CLY 3578 where a speed violation detection deterrent system, a prescribed device approved by the Secretary of State under the Road Traffic Offenders (Prescribed Devices) Order 1999, was considered.
2 [1983] Crim LR 472 (CA), 473.

2.22 The admissibility of more complex electronic evidence is illustrated in a case about the breath alcohol printout from a portable breath analyser device, the Intoximeter 3000. In *Castle v Cross*,[1] it was determined that the printout was an item of real evidence and not hearsay.[2] The judge compared the device to a speedometer, a calculator or a sophisticated tool. In this instance, the breath alcohol value in the printout comprised information that was produced by the Intoximeter because the data had not passed through a human mind. On the other hand, Kennedy J also remarked that 'where a computer is used in respect of its memory function, it is possible to envisage where it might fall foul of the rule against hearsay'.[3]

1 [1984] 1 WLR 1372, [1985] 1 All ER 87, [1984] 7 WLUK 180, [1985] RTR 62, [1984] Crim LR 682, (1984) 81 LSG 2596, (1984) 128 SJ 855, [1985] CLY 3048.
2 The members of the Court of Appeal in Northern Ireland followed this line, admitting a copy of a printout as being real evidence, in *Public Prosecution Service v Duddy* [2008] NCIA 18, [2009] NI 19.
3 [1984] 1 WLR 1372 (DC) at 1380.

2.23 In *R v Spiby (John Eric)*,[1] Taylor LJ held that there was a distinction between a printout as real evidence and as hearsay. Professor Smith[2] noted the difference between the content of a printout as a mere recording of a fact, such as when data are processed by a computer without any human input of any description,[3] and the content of a printout as being processed in some way by a human being. The printout in this case was a log of telephone calls made, which was generated by a computerized machine called a 'Norex' that monitored the telephone calls of hotel guests in order to work out how much to charge for telephone use. It was held to be real evidence.

1 [1990] 3 WLUK 150, (1990) 91 Cr App R 186, Times, 16 March 1990, Independent, 2 April 1990, Daily Telegraph, 30 March 1990, [1990] CLY 785.
2 Smith, 'The admissibility of statements by computer'.
3 Although no computer works on this basis – the code is written in the main by human beings, and the code comprises the instructions to the computer, upon which basis the computer undertakes activities, and the computer undertakes actions based on the instructions written by human beings.

2.24 In *R v Robson (Kenneth), R v Mitchell (Bernard), R v Richards (Alan)*,[1] a printout of telephone calls made on a mobile telephone was adduced as evidence of the calls made and received in association with the number. The defence's challenge that the evidence was documentary hearsay failed. Orde J held that 'where a machine observes a fact and records it, that record states a fact. It is evidence of what the machine recorded and this was printed out ... The record was not the fact, but evidence of the fact.'[2]

1 [1991] 2 WLUK 381, [1991] Crim LR 362, [1991] CLY 646.
2 [1991] Crim LR 362, 363; Robert Bradgate, 'The evidential status of computer output: confusion compounded' (1992) 9(2) Applied Computer & Communications Law 1; see also *McDonald v R* [2011] EWCA Crim 2933, [2011] 12 WLUK 556 where a printout of telephone calls was admitted in the absence of the electronic records that no longer existed. Records of calls made by a mobile telephone were accepted as real evidence by the Court of Criminal Appeal of the Republic of Ireland in *People v Colm Murphy* [2005] 2 IR 125 (CCA) and in *DPP v Brian Meehan* [2006] IECCA 104, [2006] 3 IR 468 (CCA).

2.25 In the business context, two popular uses of computers are for the formation of records and the recording of the credits and debits of an account. In the latter, the records of computer payment transactions are considered real evidence, as Their Lordships made clear in *R v Governor of Brixton Prison, ex p Levin*.[1] In this appeal against extradition, it was alleged that Levin had used a computer terminal in St Petersburg to gain unauthorized access to a Citibank terminal in Parsipanny, New Jersey to make 40 fraudulent transfers of funds from the accounts of clients of the bank to accounts which he or his associates controlled. Printouts of screen displays of the historical records of computer payment transactions were adduced, and a witness gave evidence as to how the records were created. Lord Hoffmann took the opportunity to make clear the difference between a hearsay statement and evidence of a record of a transaction:

> The print-outs are tendered to prove that such transfers took place. They record the transfers themselves, created by the interaction between whoever purported to request the transfers and the computer program in Parsipanny. The evidential status of the print-outs is no different from that of a photocopy of a forged cheque. [2]

1 [1997] AC 741, [1997] 3 WLR 117, [1997] 3 All ER 289, [1997] 6 WLUK 335, [1998] 1 Cr App R 22, [1997] Crim LR 891, (1997) 94(30) LSG 28, (1997) 147 NLJ 990, (1997) 141 SJLB 148, Times, 21 June 1997, Independent, 2 July 1997, [1997] CLY 2418.
2 [1997] AC 741 at 746; Assafa Endeshaw, 'Admissibility of evidence and jurisdiction relating to online fraud' (1998) 14(1) Computer Law and Security Report 29; Ben Fitzpatrick, 'Computers, hearsay, and the status of extradition proceedings' (1998) Web JCLI 1; Susan Nash, 'The admissibility of evidence in extradition proceedings' (1998) 2(3) E & P 198.

Documents and disclosure or discovery

2.26 In evidentiary discovery (or disclosure as it is called in England and Wales) a 'document' has been construed widely in both criminal and civil proceedings.[1] While the emphasis is on the recording of the content by the application of (usually) text on to (usually) paper, early decisions such as the Court of Appeal in *Lyell v Kennedy (No. 3)*[2] have admitted photographs of tombstones and houses as documents for the purposes of discovery. In *R v Daye (Arthur John)*,[3] Darling J suggested, at [340], that the meaning of 'document' should not be defined in a narrow way:

> But I should myself say that any written thing capable of being evidence is properly described as a document and that it is immaterial on what the writing may be inscribed. It might be inscribed not on paper, but on parchment; and long before that it was on stone, marble, or clay, and it might be, and often was, on metal. So I should desire to guard myself against being supposed to assent to the argument that a thing is not a document unless it be a paper writing. I should say it is a document no matter upon what material it be, provided it is writing or printing and capable of being evidence.

1 For the meaning of a 'document', see Stephen Mason, 'Documents signed or executed with electronic signatures in English law' (2018) 34(4) Computer Law and Security Report 933; also see Malek, *Phipson on Evidence*, para 41–02.
2 (1884) 50 LT 730; for a discussion about the status of legal resources on the Internet, including case reports, see Richard J. Matthews, 'When is case law on the web the "official" published source? Criteria, quandaries, and implications for the US and the UK' (2007) 2 Amicus Curiae 19, 25.
3 [1908] 2 KB 333 (KBD).

2.27 In *Hill v R*,[1] Humphreys J held, at [332–333], 'that a document must be something which teaches you something ... To constitute a document, the form which it takes seems to me to be immaterial; it may be anything on which the information is written or inscribed – paper, parchment, stone or metal.' Likewise, statutes adopt a similarly broad definition of a 'document'. Section 13 of the Civil Evidence Act 1995 defines a 'document' as 'anything in which information of any description is recorded'. The same definition is provided in s 20D(3) of the Taxes Management Act 1970. Schedule 1 of the Interpretation Act 1978 does not define 'document', but defines writing as follows:

> 'Writing' includes typing, printing, lithography, photography and other modes of representing or reproducing words in a visible form, and expressions referring to writing are construed accordingly.

1 [1945] 3 KB 329.

2.28 Audio tapes were accepted by Walton J as a discoverable document in *Grant v Southwestern and Country Properties Ltd*,[1] where a 'document' was defined as having the quality of conveying information. Television film is also considered a document,[2] as are the output of facsimile transmissions[3] and a label on a bottle containing a specimen of blood provided by the accused.[4]

1 [1975] Ch 185, [1974] 3 WLR 221, [1974] 2 All ER 465, [1974] WLUK 81, [1974] 118 SJ 548, [1974] CLY 2941. See also *R v Senat (Martin), R v Sin (Christopher Cho Him)* [1968] 3 WLUK 56, (1968) 52 Cr App R 282, [1968] Crim LR 269, (1968) 112 SJ 252, [1968] CLY 71; *R. v Stevenson (Ronald), R. v Hulse (Barry), R. v Whitney (Raymond)*, [1971] 1 WLR 1, [1971] 1 All ER 678, [1970] 10 WLUK 82, (1971) 55 Cr App R 171, (1971) 115 SJ 11, [1971] CLY 2264; *R v Robson (Bernard Jack), R v Harris (Gordon Frederick)* [1972] 1 WLR 651, [1972] 2 All ER 699, [1972] 3 WLUK 89, (1972) 56 Cr App R 450, [1972] Crim LR 316, (1972) 116 SJ 313, [1972] CLY 642.
2 *Senior v Holdsworth, Ex p Independent Television News* [1976] QB 23, [1975] 2 WLR 987, [1975] 2 All ER 1009, [1975] 3 WLUK 106, (1975) 119 SJ 393, [1975] CLY 1393.
3 *Hastie and Jenkerson v McMahon* [1990] 1 WLR 1575, [1991] 1 All ER 255, [1990] 3 WLUK 425, [1990] RVR 172, (1990) 134 SJ 725, [1991] CLY 2950.
4 *Khatibi v DPP* [2004] EWHC 83 (Admin), [2004] 1 WLUK 531, (2004) 168 JP 361.

2.29 In *Derby & Co Ltd v Weldon (No. 9)*,[1] one of the earliest modern decisions on the point, it was held that data stored on a computer in the form of an online database constitutes a document for the purposes of the obligation to discover under the provisions of Order 24 of the Rules of the Supreme Court. In analysing this point, Vinelott J referred to the Australian case of *Beneficial Finance Corp Co Ltd v Conway*,[2] in which McInerney J held that a tape recording was not a document because the information is not capable of being visually inspected. Vinelott J, however, preferred the opposing view in *Grant v Southwestern and County Properties Ltd*,[3] in which Walton J pointed out that there is no difference between recording a conversation on a tape recorder and in shorthand. Both are methods of recording the same conversation. Vinelott J quoted Walton J with approval as follows:

> the mere interposition of necessity of an instrument for deciphering the information cannot make any difference in principle. A litigant who keeps all his documents in microdot form could not avoid discovery because in order to read the information extremely powerful microscopes or other sophisticated instruments would be required. Nor again, if he kept them by means of microfilm which could [not] be read without the aid of a projector. [4]

1 [1991] 1 WLR 652, [1991] 2 All ER 901, [1990] 7 WLUK 300, [1992] CLY 3472.
2 [1970] VR 321.
3 [1975] 1 Ch 185, [1974] 3 WLR 221, [1974] 2 All ER 465, [1974] 2 WLUK 81, [1974] 118 SJ 548, [1974] CLY 2941; Walton J criticized the reasoning of McInerney J at 196F–197A.
4 *Derby & Co Ltd v Weldon (No. 9)* [1991] 2 All ER 901 (CA) at 906B-C.

2.30 Thus the interposition of a computer to enable the retrieval of data stored in the online database did not disqualify the data from being considered a document. A similar issue for discovery as to the meaning of 'document' in the context of data stored on a computer was discussed in *Alliance & Leicester Building Society v Ghahremani*[1] on a motion to commit Naresh Chopra, a solicitor, to prison for contempt of court. Mr Chopra was alleged to have deliberately deleted part of a file that showed crucial transaction details stored on his computer in contempt of court, when investigations into possible mortgage fraud and negligence were being conducted into his affairs. A court order had directed Chopra to restrain from destroying or altering any document relating to the transaction, and required him to deliver up all such documents in his control. In the contempt proceedings, counsel argued that the word 'document' required there to be some form of visible writing on paper or other material, and because there was no physical document, the order had not been breached. Hoffmann J noted the comments of Vinelott J in *Derby & Co Ltd v Weldon (No. 9)*,[2] and held that 'document' would bear the same meaning in the discovery order. Taking into account the expert evidence, Hoffmann J concluded that it was proved beyond reasonable doubt that Chopra did alter or destroy part of a document[3] and granted the motion, although Chopra was eventually fined instead.[4]

1 [1992] 2 WLUK 256, [1992] RVR 198, (1992) 142 NLJ 313, Times, 19 March 1992, Independent, 9 March 1992, [1993] CLY 3252.
2 [1991] 1 WLR 652, [1991] 2 All ER 901, [1990] 7 WLUK 300, [1992] CLY 3472.
3 *Alliance & Leicester Building Society v Ghahremani* [1992] 32 RVR 198 at 203. The amount of forged evidence has increased. For some examples in the context of England and Wales (this is not an exhaustive list), see *ISTIL Group Inc v Zahoor* [2003] EWHC 165 (Ch), [2003] 2 All ER 252, [2003] 2 WLUK 476, [2003] CP Rep 39, Independent, 7 April 2003, [2003] CLY 451 for a forged document; *Fiona Trust & Holding Corporation v Privalov* [2010] EWHC 3199 (Comm), [2010] 12 WLUK 346, (2011) 108(3) LSG 17 for a forged and backdated agreement and employment contract; *Apex Global Management Ltd v FI Call Ltd* [2015] EWHC 3269 (Ch), [2015] 11 WLUK 248 for forged emails; in the criminal context, see *R v Brooker* [2014] EWCA Crim 1998, also cited as *AG's Ref: 071 of 2014, R v B (R C A)* [2014] EWCA Crim 1998 (this citation is available in the LexisNexis electronic database), where Brooker sent text messages from a second mobile telephone in her possession, claiming that her boyfriend had sent them (Simon de Bruxelles, 'Trainee barrister faces jail for false rape allegations' *The Times*, 6 June 2014, 19; Miranda Prynne, 'Trainee barrister sentenced to three and a half years in prison for false rape allegations', *Daily Telegraph*, 26 June 2014 (Online edition)); *Islamic Investment Company of the Gulf (Bahamas) Ltd v Symphony Gems NV* [2014] EWHC 3777 (Comm), [2014] 11 WLUK 521, for a case of fictitious litigation; *Otkritie International Investment Management Ltd v Urumov (Rev 1 - amended charts)* [2014] EWHC 191 (Comm), [2014] 2 WLUK 286, in which the allegations (and counter-allegations) included, among other things, the forgery of the contents of a laptop and metadata in relation to documents; Steven Morris, 'Barrister becomes first to be jailed for perverting justice', *The Guardian* (London, 20 September 2007).

4 Communications by email between Nicholas Leviseur, counsel for Mr Chopra, and Stephen Mason dated 14 October 2006 and 23 November 2006.

2.31 There is judicial recognition that the acceptance and use of technology will increase the range of objects that fall within the definition of 'document'. In *R v McMullen*,[1] Linden J held that a current account ledger card printed from a computer was a document within the meaning of s 29(2) of the Canada Evidence Act. The judge commented that: 'It is merely a new type of copy made from a new type of record. Though the technology changes, the underlying principles are the same.'[2] On appeal, citing this comment, Morden JA observed that the 'section should be considered as "always speaking" and "be applied to the circumstances as they arise"'.[3] The same view was emphasized by Buxton LJ in *Victor Chandler International v Customs and Excise Commissioners*,[4] where he observed, at [55], that 'the word "document" is not constrained by the physical nature that documents took in 1952, so we are entitled, and indeed bound, to consider the appropriate application of the concept of circulation, etc, of a document in the light of current practice and technology'. In this case, an advertisement contained in a teletext transmission was held to be a document for the purposes of the Betting and Gaming Act 1981. This view was reinforced by Pumfrey J in *Marlton v Tectronix UK Holdings*,[5] when the judge held that a computer database, in as far as it forms part of the business records of a company, is a document for the purposes of the Civil Procedure Rules, and therefore can be disclosed. Calvert Smith J also concluded, in *Kennedy v Information Commissioner*,[6] that the word 'document' in s 32 of the Freedom of Information Act 2000 included information recorded in an electronic medium. The judge said, at [79]:

> It seems clear to me that for the Act to work at all – and in particular for Section 32 to work at all – the word 'document' must now mean what everybody now thinks it means and includes both hard and electronic copies of documents.

1 1978 CanLII 244, 42 CCC (2d) 67, 6 CR (3d) 218.
2 42 CCC (2d) 67 at 69.
3 *R v McMullen* 1979 CanLII 1867 (ON CA), 25 OR (2d) 301, 100 DLR (3d) 671, 47 CCC (2d) 499 (100 DLR (3d) 671 at 676).
4 [2000] 1 WLR 1296, [2000] 2 All ER 315, [2000] 2 WLUK 990, [2001] LLR 401 (2000), 97(11) LSG 36 (2000), 150 NLJ 341, (2000) 144 SJLB 127, Times, 8 March 2000, Independent, 10 March 2000, [2000] CLY 414.
5 [2003] EWHC 383 (Ch), [2003] 2 WLUK 269, [2003] Info Tech LR 258, [2004] CLY 341; Trevor Mascarenhas, 'The extent of disclosure relating to emails', (2003) 3(2) ECL Rep 14.
6 [2010] EWHC 475 (Admin), [2010] 1 WLR 1489, [2010] 1 WLUK 285, [2010] CLY 65.

2.32 As such, a 'document' is a medium upon which information is stored. The medium may sometimes determine the admissibility of the evidence, but the definition of 'document' is considered wide enough to bring any medium into its ambit without causing difficulties.[1] This must be correct, because if information is not stored on a medium, the content is not available without the medium, and therefore the information remains oral evidence. As Lord Milligan in *Rollo (William) v HM Advocate*[2] said, when he indicated that the information stored in a Sharp Memomaster 500 hand-held device was a document:

> Unsurprisingly, the word 'document' in normal usage is most frequently used in relation to written, typed or printed paper documents. Where information is stored by other means on other surfaces we accept that the storing item

> concerned is more readily referred to by reference to the means of storage or surface for storage concerned rather than as a 'document'. Hence reference to, for example, machines or tapes. However, terminological emphasis in description in such cases on the means or surface for recording information does not deprive such alternative stores of information from qualifying as 'documents' any more so than, for example, a tombstone, which is expressly included in the dictionary definition referred to. It seems to us that the essential essence of a document is that it is something concerning recorded information of some sort. It does not matter if, to be meaningful, the information requires to be processed in some way such as translation, decoding or electrical retrieval. [3]

1 Charles Hollander QC, *Documentary Evidence* (13th edn, Sweet & Maxwell 2018), 7–13; in *Taylor v R.* [2011] 2 Cr App Rep 4, [2011] WLR 1809, [2011] 2 Cr App R 4, [2011] 1 WLR 1809, [2011] EWCA Crim 728, [2011] Bus LR 1011, [2011] Lloyd's Rep FC 348, the court determined that digital data came within the scope of the words 'book or paper' in s 206(1)(c) of the Insolvency Act 1986.
2 1997 JC 23, 1997 SLT 958 (HCJ).
3 1997 SLT 958, 960F-G.

Visual reading of a document

2.33 Although the meaning of 'document' has been construed widely, nevertheless it was held by the court in *Darby (Yvonne Beatrice) v DPP*[1] that a visual reading cannot be a document. This must be correct. Unless the reading is stored in some way that enables it to be read at a later date, the reading is merely a transitory phenomenon that can only be captured by a person who provides original testimony by giving evidence about her perception.[2]

1 [1994] 10 WLUK 343, [1995] RTR 294, (1995) 159 JP 533 (DC), Times, 4 November 1994, [1994] CLY 674.
2 *Owen v Chesters* [1984] 11 WLUK 108, (1985) 149 JP 295, [1985] RTR 191, [1985] Crim LR 156, (1985) 82 LSG 443, (1984) 129 SJ 856, [1985] CLY 3054 where a police officer gave evidence of the reading from a breath test machine; see also (this list is not exhaustive) *Denneny v Harding* [1985] 10 WLUK 291, [1986] RTR 350, [1986] Crim LR 254, [1986] CLY 2881; *Mayon v DPP* [1988] 2 WLUK 53, [1988] RTR 281, [1988] CLY 3124; *Greenaway v DPP* [1993] 2 WLUK 40, (1994) 158 JP 27, [1994] RTR 17, (1993) 157 JPN 234, [1994] CLY 3978.

2.34 Oral testimony may be provided in lieu of documentary evidence. In a number of breath specimen cases, the defendants' counsel have submitted that it is necessary to provide the printout as documentary evidence of the output recorded by the machine, and that substitute evidence given by a police officer as to the machine output is not admissible.[1] In *Thom v DPP*,[2] the printout from an Intoximeter was not produced, and the defence objected to testimony by a police officer as to what he had seen on the printout. Clarke J addressed this point as follows, at [14G]:

> I can see no distinction in principle between evidence by a witness that he looked at his watch and read the time at, say, noon, and evidence from a witness that he looked at the Lion Intoximeter and that he read the proportion of alcohol in 100 millilitres of breath as being X.

1 When radar speed meters were introduced in the late 1950s, police officers had to note down the reading in their notebooks, because this was the only method of recording a reading: J. M. W. McBride, 'The radar speed meter' [1958] Crim LR 349.
2 [1993] 1 WLUK 823, (1994) 158 JP 414, [1994] RTR 11, [1994] CLY 3977.

2.35 Likewise, in *Sneyd v DPP*,[1] when the printout from an Intoximeter was not produced, the court accepted the police officer's testimony of what he had seen on the printout provided by the device, rather than what he had seen on the screen. Rejecting the objection on the basis that the testimony was secondary evidence, Richards LJ held, at [32], that 'it is well established that evidence both as to the results of the analysis and as to the reliability of the machine can be given either in the form of a written print-out or orally by the officer who carried out the procedure'. He determined that there was no difference between the oral evidence of the results shown on the printout and oral evidence of the results on the screen of the machine – both were not inadmissible hearsay. In *R (on the application of Leong) v DPP*,[2] Silber J applied the analysis of Richards LJ, holding admissible the oral evidence of the police officer's reading from a printout, at [14]: 'Where, as in the present case, there is evidence that the machine is working properly, there is no reason why the police officer concerned cannot give admissible evidence of what he saw in the print-out.'

1 [2006] EWHC 560 (Admin), [2006] 2 WLUK 635, (2006) 170 JP 545, [2007] RTR 6, (2006) 170 JPN 998, [2006] CLY 799.
2 [2006] EWHC 1575 (Admin), [2006] 6 WLUK 172.

Authentication

2.36 When a document is tendered as evidence of its contents, it is often accompanied by proof that the document 'has some specific connection to a person or organization, whether through authorship or some other relation'.[1] As noted by Austin J: 'Authentication is about showing that the document is what it is claimed to be, not about assessing, at the point of the adducing of the evidence, whether the document proves what the tendering party claims it proves.'[2] Similarly, where any object is tendered in evidence, an adequate foundation for admission will require testimony first that the object offered is the object which was involved in the incident, and further that the condition of the object is substantially unchanged.[3]

1 Kenneth S. Broun (ed.), *McCormick on Evidence*, vol. 2 (7th edn, West Publishing 2013), 83–85 (§221).
2 *Australian Securities and Investment Commission v Rich* (2005) 216 ALR 320, [118], [2005] NSWSC 417.
3 Broun, *McCormick on Evidence*, 13–16 (§213).

2.37 As is the case for any other form of evidence, electronic evidence must be authenticated. The authentication process for electronic evidence is even more critical,[1] and can occasionally be challenging.[2] Undoubtedly the use of technology has afforded us convenience and efficiency. But if parties and investigative authorities choose to use the fruits of technology, they must also accept the need to prove the authenticity and integrity of the evidence produced by technology, even though the cost of such proof might be considered to be high. This is particularly the case where authentication evidence will shed light on the latent assumptions and hidden errors inherent in electronic evidence, which could affect the accuracy of the electronic evidence itself.

1 Seng, 'Computer output as evidence', 159–166; Rosemary Pattenden, 'Authenticating "things" in English law: principles for adducing tangible evidence in common law jury trials' (2008) 12 E & P 290.
2 The challenge of proving that evidence in digital form is authentic was the subject of *R v Cochrane* [1992] 6 WLUK 63, [1993] Crim LR 48 (CA), [1993] CLY 366; Allison Nyssens, 'The law of evidence:

on-line with the computer age?' (1993) 15(10) EIPR 360; see Chapter 6 on authentication for a detailed discussion.

2.38 Authentication evidence may also demonstrate that the errors in question will not have an adverse effect on the evidence itself. For instance, in *DPP v McKeown (Sharon), DPP v Jones (Christopher)*,[1] the clocks on the Intoximeter 3000 used to measure the breath alcohol values of the defendants were not accurate. For this reason, the defendants challenged the admissibility of the printouts from the device. In addressing whether the accuracy of the clocks was relevant to the accuracy of the printout readings, Lord Hoffmann examined the functioning of these devices and concluded that, for the purposes of s 69 of the Police and Criminal Evidence Act 1984,[2] a malfunction is irrelevant unless it affects the way in which the computer processes, stores or retrieves the information used to generate the statement.[3] On the facts, the clock was not part of the processing mechanism of the Intoximeter, and the convictions of the defendants based on the printout readings were upheld.

1 [1997] 1 WLR 295, [1997] 1 All ER 737, [1997] 2 WLUK 386, [1997] 2 Cr App R 155 (HL), (1997) 161 JP 356, [1997] RTR 162, [1997] Crim LR 522, (1997) 161 JPN 482, (1997) 147 NLJ 289, Times, 21 February 1997, Independent, 7 March 1997, [1997] CLY 1093; see also Jonathan S. W. Black, 'Breath testing devices and computer evidence' (1997) 141(10) SJ 236–; C.G., 'Computers: evidence' (1997) 3(3) CTLR T68; 'Computer clock malfunction irrelevant' (1997) 161(14) Justice of the Peace & Local Government Law 325; Renzo Marchini, 'DPP v McKeown (Sharon)' (1997) 8(2) Comps & Law 27; Philip Plowden, 'Garbage in, garbage out – the limits of s.69 of the PACE Act 1984' (1997) 61(3) Journal of Criminal Law 310; Gordon Cropper, 'The evidential breath testing device as a computer' (1997) 2(May) RTI 3; H. L. J. Makin, 'PACE and the intoximeter' (1998) 142(11) S.J. 250.

2 Section 69 of the Police and Criminal Evidence Act 1984 was repealed by s 60 of the Youth Justice and Criminal Evidence Act 1999, although the relevant case law remains a useful authority.

3 [1997] 1 All ER 737 at 744. A study later demonstrated that breath alcohol values measured on the Lion Intoximeter 3000 are not affected if the machine clock is incorrect by more than four minutes: R. C. Denny, 'The Intoximeter 3000 and the four minute fallacy' (1998) 38(2) Medical Science Law 163. Minor typographical errors on a printout do not alter the validity of the results: *Reid v DPP* [1998] 2 WLUK 401, [1999] RTR 357, [1998] Masons CLR 269, Times, 6 March 1998, [1998] CLY 897.

2.39 This does not mean that authentication evidence will always have to be supplied for each item of evidence. In civil proceedings in England and Wales, a party is deemed to admit the authenticity of a document disclosed under the provisions of Civil Procedure Rule (CPR) 31 unless notice is served that the party wishes the document to be proved at trial. Thus where the authenticity of a document is questioned, the party raising the issue is required to do so at an early stage of the proceedings, thereby providing the party submitting the document the opportunity of gathering evidence to prove the veracity of the document.

2.40 See Chapter 6 on authentication for a more detailed discussion.

Best evidence

2.41 The best evidence rule can be considered from two points of view. It can be regarded as an inclusionary rule under which whatever is the best evidence is admissible, thus overcoming exclusionary rules such as the hearsay rule; alternatively, it can be regarded as an exclusionary rule, so that anything which is not the best evidence is inadmissible. Since *Omychund v Barker*,[1] the majority of the cases have used the rule in an exclusionary way to deny the use of copies of documents when the absence of the original was not satisfactorily accounted for.

1 1 Atk 22, 26 ER 15.

2.42 Reaction against this rule began in the nineteenth century,[1] and by the latter part of the twentieth century it was recognized that the best evidence rule was no longer as relevant as it once was. In *Kajala v Noble*,[2] Ackner LJ held that the rule is now confined to written documents in the strictest sense of the term. Echoing the robust comments of Lord Denning MR in *Garton v Hunter (Valuation Officer)*,[3] His Lordship said:

> The old rule, that a party must produce the best evidence that the nature of the case will allow, and that any less good evidence is to be excluded, has gone by the board long ago. The only remaining instance of it is that, if an original document is available in one's hands, one must produce it; that one cannot give secondary evidence by producing a copy. Nowadays we do not confine ourselves to the best evidence. We admit all relevant evidence. The goodness or badness of it goes only to weight, and not to admissibility ... In our judgment, the old rule is limited and confined to written documents in the strict sense of the term, and has no relevance to tapes or films.[4]

1 Malek, *Phipson on Evidence*, 7–42; see the discussion by Sargent J in the New Hampshire case of *Howley v Whipple* 48 N.H. 487 (1869) in respect of best evidence in the case of telegrams.
2 [1982] 3 WLUK 133, (1982) 75 Cr App R 149, [1982] Crim LR 433, [1982] CLY 605.
3 [1969] 2 QB 37, 44, [1969] 2 WLR 86, [1969] 1 All ER 451, [1968] 11 WLUK 46, (1969) 133 JP 162, 67 LGR 229, [1969] RA 11, 15 RRC 145, (1968) SJ 924, Times, 15 November 1962, [1969] CLY 3017.
4 *Kajala v Noble* (1982) 75 Cr App R 149 at 152; whether it is necessary to produce the original when a photocopy is adduced in evidence will depend upon whether the production of the original is relevant and necessary, for which see *Attorney-General v Lundin* [1982] 2 WLUK 231, (1982) 75 Cr App R 90, [1982] Crim LR 296, [1982] CLY 2435.

2.43 By 1990, Lloyd LJ in *R v Governor Ex p Osman (No 1)* observed that the best evidence rule had become a rule of practice or procedure.[1] He also made the following remarks about the rule:

> this court would be more than happy to say goodbye to the best evidence rule. We accept that it served an important purpose in the days of parchment and quill pens.[2] But since the invention of carbon paper and, still more, the photocopier and the telefascimile machine, that purpose has largely gone. Where there is an allegation of forgery the court will obviously attach little, if any, weight to anything other than the original; so also if the copy produced in court is illegible. But to maintain a general exclusionary rule for these limited purposes is, in our view, hardly justifiable. [3]

1 *R v Governor Ex p Osman (No 1) sub nom Osman (No 1)* [1990] 1 WLR 277, [1989] 3 All ER 701, [1988] 3 WLUK 391, (1990) 90 Cr App R 281, [1988] Crim LR 611, (1990) 87(7) LSG 32, (1990) 134 SJ 458, Times, 13 April 1988, Independent, 15 April 1988, Guardian, 19 April 1988 Daily Telegraph, 21 April 1988, [1990] CLY 1175.
2 It will be interesting to know how many ancient documents previously admitted into evidence were actually copies: *A Guide to Seals in the Public Record Office* (2nd edn, HMSO 1968), 30; T. F. Tout, 'Mediæval forgers and forgeries' (1919) Bulletin of the John Rylands Library 208.
3 [1990] 1 WLR 277 (DC) at 308B-C.

2.44 The best evidence rule has been effectively limited to requiring a party having possession of an original document who is relying on it for the statements recorded on the document (primary evidence) not to wilfully refuse to produce the original document as primary evidence, and instead produce copies or substitutes (secondary evidence) in its place.[1]

1 Colin Tapper, *Cross and Tapper on Evidence* (8th edn, Butterworths 1995) 748, ch XVIII, s 1: Proof of the contents of a document. A. The general rule. 1. Statement and illustrations of the general rule. This statement of the rule was removed in subsequent editions. See also *R. v Wayte (William Guy)* [1982] 3 WLUK 247, (1982) 76 Cr App R 110, CA, Times, 24 March 1982, [1983] CLY 659, where photostat copies of two letters were not admissible in circumstances where the party seeking to rely on the documents refused to produce the original letters.

2.45 Where good reasons exist for the failure to produce the original document, secondary evidence, even in the form of oral testimony, is permissible. This may be illustrated by the case of *Taylor v Chief Constable of Cheshire*,[1] a case involving the inadvertent destruction of evidence. In this case, video images of the accused allegedly committing theft from a store were recorded on the store video recorder, and the manager of the store, three police officers and the lawyer for the accused later saw these recordings. When the case was heard, it transpired that new security officers had erased the recording of the video images. The magistrates permitted the witnesses to give evidence of what they saw on the video recording. An appeal was made that the best evidence – the video recording – could not be admitted because it had been destroyed, and that testimonial evidence of the recording was not the best evidence. This was rejected. Although the best evidence in this instance was the video recording, its unavailability did not preclude the admission into evidence of the testimony of those witnesses who viewed the recording. The recollections of the witnesses ought not to be precluded because the best evidence was not available. The evidence offered by the witnesses was, as pointed out by Ralph Gibson LJ, 'direct evidence of what was seen to be happening in a particular place at a particular time', and it was for the trier of the facts to assess its weight, credibility and reliability.[2]

1 [1986] 1 WLR 1479, [1987] 1 All ER 225, [1986] 10 WLUK 244, (1987) 84 Cr App R 191, (1987) 151 JP 103, [1987] Crim LR 119, (1987) 151 JPN 110, (1987) 84 LSG 412, (1986) 130 SJ 953, [1987] CLY 743; P. W. Ferguson, 'Video identification and the best evidence rule' (1987) 51(2) Journal of Criminal Law 125.
2 [1987] 1 All ER 225, 230.

2.46 Since the statutory intercession of the Civil Evidence Act 1995 and the Criminal Justice Act 2003, the best evidence rule has further taken a simplified, statutory form. The judgment of the Court of Appeal in *Masquerade Music Ltd v Springsteen*[1] suggests that the best evidence rule is hardly of any relevance. After considering the best evidence rule in detail and reviewing the case law extensively,[2] Jonathan Parker LJ outlined the position with respect to the best evidence rule in the twenty-first century, at [85]:

> In my judgment, the time has now come when it can be said with confidence that the best evidence rule, long on its deathbed, has finally expired. In every case where a party seeks to adduce secondary evidence of the contents of a document, it is a matter for the court to decide, in the light of all the circumstances of the case, what (if any) weight to attach to that evidence. Where the party seeking to adduce the secondary evidence could readily produce the document, it may be expected that (absent some special circumstances) the court will decline to admit the secondary evidence on the ground that it is worthless. At the other extreme, where the party seeking to adduce the secondary evidence genuinely cannot produce the document,

> it may be expected that (absent some special circumstances) the court will admit the secondary evidence and attach such weight to it as it considers appropriate in all the circumstances. In cases falling between those two extremes, it is for the court to make a judgment as to whether in all the circumstances any weight should be attached to the secondary evidence. Thus, the 'admissibility' of secondary evidence of the contents of documents is, in my judgment, entirely dependent upon whether or not any weight is to be attached to that evidence. And whether or not any weight is to be attached to such secondary evidence is a matter for the court to decide, taking into account all the circumstances of the particular case.

1 [2001] EWCA Civ 563, [2001] 4 WLUK 239, [2001] CP Rep 85, [2001] CPLR 369, [2001] EMLR 25, Independent, 24 April 2001, Daily Telegraph, 17 April 2001, [2001] CLY 392.
2 [2001] EWCA Civ 563, [64]–[85].

2.47 Waller and Laws LJJ concurred. In other words, there is no automatic bar to the failure to admit the original document as primary evidence. Instead, when the original document is no longer available, a copy of the original evidence is admissible, but an adjudicator must consider its weight as secondary evidence.

2.48 The modern application of this rule is illustrated by *Post Office Counters Ltd v Mahida*.[1] In this case, the Post Office sought to claim an alleged deficiency of social security benefits paid out against the defendant, the sub-postmaster general. The deficiency was set out in a schedule prepared by investigators of the Post Office based on checks conducted against the underlying dockets and foils. Subsequently, the dockets and foils were destroyed as part of a routine process. The trial judge accepted the schedule as secondary evidence and found against the defendant. On appeal, the Court of Appeal was concerned that the secondary evidence was of insufficient weight to prove the precise amount of the debt claimed against the defendant. In particular, the Post Office as an institution could not readily be said to have discharged the burden of proving the precise amount of the debt when it was alleged that the defendant had been responsible for this loss, and had denied the defendant the opportunity to check those figures.[2] For this reason, the very basic unfairness should have led the trial judge to consider that the amount of the debt was not proved, and the defendant's appeal was allowed.

1 [2003] EWCA Civ 1583, [2003] 10 WLUK 601, Times, 31 October 2003, [2004] CLY 248.
2 [2003] EWCA Civ 1583 at [27].

Analogue evidence

2.49 Although the best evidence rule is now tightly confined, it applies to both civil and criminal proceedings.[1] But as the statutory formulations of the rule in s 8 of the Civil Evidence Act 1995 and s 133 of the Criminal Justice Act 2003 retain the differentiation between primary and secondary evidence, the ramifications are different, depending on whether the evidence is in analogue or in electronic form.

1 *R. v Wayte (William Guy)* [1982] 3 WLUK 247, (1982) 76 Cr App R 110, CA, Times, 24 March 1982, [1983] CLY 659.

2.50 In the physical world, primary evidence is an original document, and secondary evidence is in the form of copies of the original. The best evidence rule will require the production of the original document to prove the content in question, and the submission of copies is considered inferior evidence. But the fact that copies were made, for instance, by a reprographic process such as photocopying, will not prevent the copies themselves from being originals. In *Miller-Foulds v Secretary of State for Constitutional Affairs*[1] regarding orders issued by Brentford County Court, Pelling J noted the following, at [26]:

> The method of production involved copying an original draft [order] and then sealing the copies thus resulting. The copies, once sealed, were original orders. The original draft was just that: a draft. The fact that the documents that were sealed were produced by photocopying rather than copying out by hand the same document umpteen times is wholly irrelevant, in my judgment, as long as the document itself resulting from the copying process was sealed.

1 [2008] EWHC 3443 (Ch), [2008] 11 WLUK 517. A subsequent application before Lloyd LJ was rejected: [2009] EWCA Civ 1132.

2.51 The concepts of 'primary' and 'secondary' evidence take a different shape when applied to material objects that must be processed to be viewed. Consider, for instance, a photograph taken with a camera containing film, or a plate. The negative or the plate comprises the only copy of the image in reverse.[1] It is the negative or plate that is the material upon which the primary evidence is recorded. However, few people will be satisfied by looking at the primary image, if only because it is not easy to view, and is not intended to be viewed in this form unless by means of a projector, if the primary image is a negative. This means that the printed image is secondary evidence. Any number of copies of the primary object can be made, although no printed copy will be an exact copy of the film or plate. This is because the processes applied and the mix of chemicals used in transforming the negative into a print will determine how accurately the photograph reflects the image, in particular the degree of contrast (that is the range of grey tones) captured on the negative. For example, the degree of contrast will affect how bruising is reproduced on the photograph: a high contrast makes the bruising appear darker and more dramatic, while a low contrast will lessen the effect of the visual image, making the bruise seem somewhat less consequential.

1 A point noted by Smith LJ in *Griffiths v DPP* [2007] RTR 44 at [21].

Digital evidence

2.52 In contrast to the discussion above, the range of evidence in digital form is vast, and it comprises not just printouts of what might be termed conventional files, such as copies of letters, contracts or spreadsheets. Other forms of digital documents include reports from computer databases, the electronic records of transactions and the digital store and reproduction of images, such as the scanned image of an original paper document. The treatment of evidence in digital form calls for different and occasionally difficult considerations.

2.53 First, there may be issues identifying the primary evidence of a digital document. In *Derby & Co Ltd v Weldon (No. 9)*, Vinelott J considered the memory or database of a word processor or computer to be the 'original document',[1] presumably on the basis that these are components 'on which material fed into a simple word processor is stored'.[2] However, Professor Tapper disagrees, and takes the view that the printout from the word-processed electronic document is the original and the document in computer memory is the copy.[3] Both views are possible. Vinelott J's analysis is plausible – where the printout is generated as a physical draft to aid in the editing of the word-processed document. But Professor Tapper's view could also be justified where the object behind the use of the word processor is the generation of the printout as the final, definitive version of the document. In such a case, the authentic printout may be a better form of evidence than the state of the document in internal memory at a later time. This inversion provides a good illustration of the danger of assuming that the printout may not be the best evidence in any given situation.

1 *Derby & Co Ltd v Weldon (No. 9)* [1991] 1 WLR 652 at 658C-D.
2 [1991] 1 WLR 652 at 658C-D.
3 Colin Tapper, 'Evanescent evidence' (1993) 1 Intl J L & Info Tech 35, 42.

2.54 In addition, the use of a digital device need not always produce an 'original document'. Where the 'original document' is created in digital form but is never stored in a more permanent, non-ephemeral manner, the 'original' digital 'document' ceases to exist for all practical purposes. Instant messaging is an example of evidence that might not be stored, which makes it analogous to an oral conversation.

2.55 The issues may be further considered with the following extended illustration. For instance, the original of a physical document, such as a commercial contract between two parties, signed by the authorized representatives of both parties and acknowledged as the original, is primary evidence of the content of the contract. Even if the contract was created on a computer, the physical document will still be the original document as it was signed and adopted by both parties.[1] However, should the contract, which is subsequently acted upon by both parties, exist only in digital form on a computer, the primary evidence of the document will be the digital contract residing on an identified computer storage device such as the hard drive of a computer. Printing out the document on paper will provide copies in a human-readable form, which will in turn comprise secondary evidence of the document.[2]

1 The physical document might have a digital counterpart, as in Austria, for which see Friedrich Schwank 'CyberDOC and e-government: the electronic archive of Austrian notaries' (2004) 1 Digital Evidence and Signature Law Review 30, 32.
2 The schedule produced in *R v Nazeer (Mohammed Azad)* [1998] Crim LR 750, [1998] 2 WLUK 93 cannot be considered to be hearsay or secondary evidence because it was real evidence produced by individuals using different sources of information (including computer records); Claire Barsby, 'Evidence – documentary evidence held on computer', [1998] Crim LR 750.

2.56 Now let us take the matter one stage further. Assume the original digital file is accessed multiple times after the contract is executed, but its file contents are not altered: perhaps particular clauses are copied for other reasons. The metadata for the digital file may have been changed to record the action of opening and closing the file, even if no substantive changes are made. Although the metadata might have been altered, the content of the file in question has not been affected. In these circumstances, it might be considered that the integrity of the original digital data is compromised. But as the content (rather than the metadata) of the digital document is unchanged, the digital document remains the primary evidence, and a printout of that document a faithful copy of the original.[1] The metadata merely records when the file was opened and viewed. Metadata can be compared to a file register in the physical world that records the name of the person to whom the physical file was given, the date and time the person obtained the file, and the date and time it was returned: the register information does not alter the content of the statements made in the file (unless the person obtaining access to the file alters its contents). In such circumstances, the metadata does not affect the integrity of the digital data, which also means the secondary evidence of the file in the form of the printout remains a reliable reproduction of the digital file.

1 Professor Tapper expressed the contrary view, that 'the memory holds the copy and the original is the printed copy' in 'Evanescent evidence', 42. This is correct if the printed version is a document such as a contract, where the contract is subsequently signed by the parties with manuscript signatures and excludes reference to any other version.

2.57 Consider another example: the drafting of a contract by an external lawyer for a multinational company. This task will comprise a number of stages, including: liaising with a number of people internally with different responsibilities to produce an initial draft of the contract; passing it to the other contracting party for comments; and producing a final version to the satisfaction of both parties, after a substantial period of negotiation. In all probability, various versions of the draft contract will exist in storage devices on computers, hand-held devices and backup devices belonging to several companies and their employees, perhaps across different jurisdictions. If the contract is then printed and signed by the authorized representatives of the two parties, the original document will be the printed version. If there is an issue regarding a particular version of the contract at a particular point in the negotiations, the draft digital version of the contract will be original evidence because that electronic copy is the best evidence of that version of the contract, and a printout of that version will be secondary evidence.

2.58 In addition, digital documents may themselves be stored, changed, compiled and collated into new documents, and the new documents may be original documents in themselves. The Canadian case of *R v Bell*[1] is instructional in this regard. In this case, the bank's computer software processed the various transactions of its customers' chequing accounts into a monthly statement for each account. Two identical copies of the monthly statement were printed, one for the customer and one for the bank. The bank retained its copy of the monthly statement, but did not retain a record of the transactions. The trial judge held that a copy of the statement was not admissible because the transaction information stored on a computer was the record, and the original 'record' as a record of the dealings of a financial institution (and its subsequent copy) no longer existed. On appeal, this analysis was rejected. Weatherston JA noted that the form in which information is recorded may change from time to time, and a new form in which information is recorded, such as a compilation or collection of other records, is equally a record of that kind of information. The court found the monthly statement to be such a 'record' that consolidated the transactions of a financial institution and allowed the appeal.[2]

1 (1982) 35 OR (2d) 164 (CA).
2 (1982) 35 OR (2d) 164 (CA) at [13].

Civil proceedings

2.59 The admissibility of secondary evidence in civil proceedings is governed by of s 8 of the Civil Evidence Act 1995, which permits the introduction of copies of documents into evidence for the purpose of proving the statement contained in the document:

> 8.—(1) Where a statement contained in a document is admissible as evidence in civil proceedings, it may be proved—
>
> (a) by the production of that document, or
>
> (b) whether or not that document is still in existence, by the production of a copy of that document or of the material part of it, authenticated in such manner as the court may approve.
>
> (2) It is immaterial for this purpose how many removes there are between a copy and the original.

2.60 A 'document' is in turn defined in s 13 as 'anything in which information of any description is recorded', and a 'copy' of a document as 'anything onto which information recorded in the document has been copied, by whatever means and whether directly or indirectly'. There are two operative parts to s 8. Section 8(1)(a) provides that an admissible statement contained in a document may be proved by the production of the original document. Section 8(1)(b) provides that the same document may be proved by the production of a copy of that document or a material part of it, with the expression 'whether or not that [primary] document is still in existence' completely eviscerating the common law best evidence rule. And although s 8(1) uses the language of 'a statement contained in a document', suggesting that the statutory version of the best evidence rule only applies to documentary evidence used in a testimonial sense, a better reading is that s 8 applies to documentary evidence both as testimonial evidence and as real evidence. This means that s 8 will apply to the analogue record of the measurements of a device (the measurement constitutes the statement of the document)[1] or the printout from an Intoximeter.

1 Such as the film in *The Statue of Liberty, Sapporo Maru M/S (Owners) v Steam Tanker Statue of Liberty (Owners)* [1968] 1 WLR 739, [1968] 2 All ER 195, [1968] 1 Lloyd's Rep 429, [1968] 3 WLUK 65, (1968) 112 SJ 380, [1968] CLY 1546.

2.61 The admissibility of the copied document as secondary evidence is subject to one condition and one qualification. The condition is that, as set out in the proviso to s 8(1), the copied document must be 'authenticated in such manner as the court may approve', just as the primary document must be authenticated. In other words, where the credibility of the digital data is in question, foundation evidence, typically in the form of testimony, will have to be introduced and tested to determine whether the secondary evidence can be accepted as 'a copy' of the original document. The residual judicial control over the admissibility of secondary evidence takes the form of judicial prescription of the requisite authentication evidence to prove that it is an accurate and reliable copy of the whole or a material part of the original document.

2.62 The qualification is that, by s 8(2), the number of removes between the copy and the original document is statutorily deemed to be irrelevant. This detracts from the judicial control role as explained above, and also undermines the judicial assessment of the authentication evidence as to the true accuracy and reliability of the secondary evidence.[1]

1 For a broad discussion of electronic evidence in the civil context, see 'Electronic evidence in civil and administrative proceedings: guidelines and explanatory memorandum' (adopted by the Committee of Ministers of the Council of Europe, 30 January 2019), https://www.coe.int/en/web/cdcj/activities/digital-evidence.

Criminal proceedings

2.63 The starting point for the application of the best evidence rule in criminal proceedings is s 133 of the Criminal Justice Act 2003:

> 133 Proof of statements in documents
>
> Where a statement in a document is admissible as evidence in criminal proceedings, the statement may be proved by producing either-
>
> (a) the document, or
>
> (b) (whether or not the document exists) a copy of the document or of the material part of it, authenticated in whatever way the court may approve.

2.64 The s 133 provisions are identical to those for civil proceedings in the Civil Evidence Act 1995, save for the fact that there is no mention of the number of times a copy is removed from the original in s 133 in the Criminal Justice Act. (It is suggested that the elimination of the number of removes qualification in s 133 is an improvement over the equivalent formulation of the best evidence rule in the Civil Evidence Act, in getting rid of the judicial handicap on assessment of the authentication evidence.) The other difference is that proof in criminal proceedings must rise to the appropriate standard, which is proof beyond reasonable doubt in the case of the prosecution, and proof on the balance of probabilities in the defence case. Otherwise, it should also be noted that, notwithstanding the reference to 'a statement in a document', for the same reasons as outlined above in relation to the Civil Evidence Act 1995, the best evidence provisions should apply equally to a document as real evidence and to a document as testimonial evidence.[1] In other words, as in civil proceedings, secondary evidence of an electronic document is admissible subject to authentication evidence.

1 In *R v Minors (Craig), R v Harper (Giselle Gaile)* [1989] 1 WLR 441, [1989] 1 All ER 208, [1988] 12 WLUK 161, (1989) 89 Cr App R 102, [1989] Crim LR 360, (1989) 133 SJ 420, [1989] CLY 546 it was held that s 24, Criminal Justice Act 1988 applied only to a 'statement in a document' and not to real evidence. Section 24, like s 27, the predecessor provision to s 133, is found in Part II (Documentary Evidence in Criminal Proceedings) of the Criminal Justice Act 1988. That notwithstanding, it could be argued that the holding in *R v Minors (Craig), R v Harper (Giselle Gaile)* should be confined to s 24 (an exception to the hearsay rule) and has no application to the interpretation of s 27 (a restatement of the best evidence rule); J. A. Coutts, 'Admissibility of computer print-outs in evidence' (1989) 53(4) Journal of Criminal Law 454; Lynne Knapman, 'Computer printout – evidence – admissibility – procedure – s.68 PACE 1984', [1989] Crim LR 360; Bernard Robertson, 'Section 69 PACE and the intoximeter' (1989) 153(41) Justice of the Peace & Local Government Law 653.

2.65 The effect is that while the original electronic document, if available, should be adduced into evidence, in practice a copy of the document tends to be adduced as secondary evidence. The copy may be at least one, if not two removes[1] from the original. This should not matter, provided the digital copy has been produced in a way that captures the file in its entirety, including all its attributes, such as the metadata, without altering the original data. (On this point, please see the detailed discussion in Chapter 6 on authentication.)

1 It is usually two removes from the original, if the original is considered to be the operational electronic document that is actively used on the computer system in question, and a copy is previously taken from that operational electronic document (in computer science terms, a 'snapshot' – the state of the system at a particular point in time, considering that some time would have lapsed between the taking of this copy and the current operational version of the electronic document), and a copy is in turn taken from that previous copy for purposes of preparation of proceedings.

2.66 To a certain extent, rather than question whether a document in digital form is an original or a copy, it might be more useful and relevant to refer to the proof of authenticity, or provenance, or reliability of a digital file. This is required under both s 133 of the Criminal Justice Act 2003 and s 8 of the Civil Evidence Act 1995. This in turn encapsulates proof of the integrity of the content of the data. Because of the ease with which a digital document may be migrated from one storage device to another, and thereby undergo formatting and other changes, including content and metadata changes, it is vital to require any such changes to be documented in such a way as to preserve the integrity and authenticity of the copy. Thus it might be more relevant, when referring to digital data, to concentrate on establishing which version of the data is required, particularly whether the making of copies of the digital document is properly documented.

Admissibility

2.67 That evidence takes electronic form has not been an impediment to its admissibility. Judges have admitted digital records of the product of mechanical devices and automatic recordings, photographs,[1] tape recordings,[2] automated film recordings of the movements of a ship as traced by radar,[3] microfilm,[4] printouts of test results undertaken on a breath test machine,[5] video recordings,[6] computer printouts[7] and a recording of an oral statement of testamentary intentions on a DVD.[8] The types and categories of electronic evidence are not closed.

1 *R v The United Kingdom Electronic Telegraph Company (Limited)* (1862) 3 F & F 73, 176 ER 33, where a photograph was admitted to show the nature of the surface of a highway in respect of an allegation of an obstruction, although photographs have to be verified on oath to be considered as more than mere pictures: *Hindson v Ashby* [1896] 2 Ch 1 (CA) 21; *R. v Tolson* (1864) 4 F & F 103, 176 ER 488 where a photograph was admitted in a case of alleged bigamy to illustrate oral testimony (Willes J commented in his summing up to the members of the jury: 'The photograph was admissible because it is only a visible representation of the image or impression made upon the minds of the witnesses by the sight of the person or the object it represents; and, therefore, is, in reality, only another species of the evidence which persons give of identity, when they speak merely from memory' – the jury subsequently entered a verdict of not guilty); D. W. Elliott, 'Mechanical aids to evidence' [1958] Crim LR 5; Chris Nicoll, 'E.D.I. evidence and the Vienna Convention', (1995) Jan Journal of Business Law 21; Elliott Goldstein, 'Photographic and videotape evidence in the criminal courts of England and Canada' [1987] Crim LR 384.

2 *Harry Parker v Mason* [1940] 2 KB 590, [1940] 4 All ER 199, [1940] 8 WLUK 1; *R v Burr and Sullivan* [1956] Crim LR 442; *R. v Ali (Maqsud), R. v Hussain (Ashiq)* [1966] 1 QB 688, [1965] 3 WLR 229 (CA), [1965] 2 All ER 464, [1965] 4 WLUK 27, (1965) 49 Cr App R 230, (1965) 129 JP 396, (1965) 109 SJ 331, (1965) CLY 796; for an example in Scotland, see *Hopes and Lavery v HM Advocate* [1960] Crim LR 566, 1960 JC 104, 1960 SLT 264.

3 *The Statue of Liberty Owners of Motorship Sapporo Maru v Owners of Steam Tanker Statue of Liberty* [1968] 1 WLR 739, [1968] 2 All ER 195, [1968] 1 Lloyd's Rep 429, [1968] 3 WLUK 65, (1968) 112 SJ 380, [1968] CLY 1546.
4 *Barker v Wilson* [1980] 1 WLR 884, [1980] 2 All ER 81, [1980] 2 WLUK 2, (1980) 70 Cr App R 283 (DC), [1980] Crim LR 373, (1980) 124 SJ 326, [1980] CLY 469, in respect of the Bankers' Books Evidence Act 1879.
5 *Castle v Cross* [1984] 1 WLR 1372 (DC), [1985] 1 All ER 87, [1984] 7 WLUK 180, [1985] RTR 62, [1984] Crim LR 682, (1984) 81 LSG 2596, (1984) 128 SJ 855, [1985] CLY 3048.
6 *Kajala v Noble* [1982] 3 WLUK 133, (1982) 75 Cr App R 149, [1982] Crim LR 433 (DC), [1982] CLY 605; *R v Grimer* [1982] 6 WLUK 204, [1982] Crim LR 674, 126 SJ 641 (CA), [1982] CLY 606; *R v Thomas (Steven)* [1986] 7 WLUK 85, [1986] Crim LR 682, [1986] CLY 594 regarding video recording of the route taken made in lieu of maps and still photographs; *XXX v YYY and ZZZ* [2004] EWCA Civ 231, [2004] 2 WLUK 196, [2004] IRLR 471 regarding video recording of a nanny in a home which was also a place of work; *R v Nikolovski* (1996) 111 CCC (3d), [1996] 3 SCR 1197 403.
7 *R v Wood (Stanley William)* [1982] 6 WLUK 191, (1983) 76 Cr App R 23, [1982] Crim LR 667 (CA), [1983] CLY 636 considering the results of an automated analysis; *R v Sinha (Arun Kumar)* [1994] 7 WLUK 34, [1998] Masons CLR 35, [1995] Crim LR 68 (CA), Times, 13 July 1994, Independent, 1 August 1994, [1994] CLY 1137 concerning the alteration of medical data recorded on a computer.
8 *Re Estate of Wai Fun Chan, Deceased* [2015] NSWSC 1107.

2.68 Evidence is admitted into legal proceedings if it is relevant to an issue in dispute, subject to a number of exceptions.[1] It is a matter of law for a judge to determine whether evidence is admissible. Generally, judges are required to determine whether evidence is to be excluded in criminal trials far more frequently than in civil matters, especially where admitting the evidence might not be in the interests of justice.[2] For instance, in *R v Fowden and White*[3] the Court of Appeal held that a video film showing activities that were consistent with the acts of theft had been improperly admitted.[4] The prejudicial value outweighed its probative effect, because the witnesses who identified the accused knew them from a similar case of theft that occurred a week after the events recorded in the video film, and the defence was therefore not able to test the accuracy of the identification without causing prejudice and embarrassment.[5]

1 For a more detailed discussion, see Malek, *Phipson on Evidence*, ch 2 and 7–01 to 7–16.
2 Police and Criminal Evidence Act 1984, s 78; Criminal Justice Act 2003, s 114(1)(d).
3 [1982] 2 WLUK 48, [1982] Crim LR 588, [1982] CLY 607.
4 For the US, see Nicole Chauriye, 'Wearable devices as admissible evidence: technology is killing our opportunity to lie', (2016) 24(2) Cath UJL & Tech 495; Katherine E. Vinez, 'The admissibility of data collected from wearable devices', (2017) 4 Stetson J Advocacy & L 1.
5 In *R v Caldwell, R v Dixon* [1993] 5 WLUK 237, (1994) 99 Cr App R 73, [1993] Crim LR 862, [1995] CLY 933 the members of the court considered it would be useful to have a set of procedures in relation to the use of video recordings for the purposes of identification.

2.69 In civil proceedings, evidence that is admissible can be excluded in accordance with the provisions of CPR 32.1(2), which provides a judge with the explicit general power to exclude evidence when in the role of managing a case:

> 32.1 (1) The court may control the evidence by giving directions as to –
>
> (a) the issues on which it requires evidence;
>
> (b) the nature of the evidence which it requires to decide those issues; and
>
> (c) the way in which the evidence is to be placed before the court.
>
> (2) The court may use its power under this rule to exclude evidence that would otherwise be admissible.

2.70 However, in adopting the argument of the appellants in *Great Future International Ltd v Sealand Housing Corporation*, Arden LJ pointed out, at [24], that the power 'must be used with great circumspection for the purpose of achieving the overriding objective'.[1] The modern tendency is to admit evidence, and then consider its weight, as illustrated by the comment of Cockburn CJ in *The Queen v Churchwardens, Overseers and Guardians of the Poor of the Parish of Birmingham*: 'People were formerly frightened out of their wits about admitting evidence lest juries should go wrong. In modern times we admit the evidence and discuss its weight.'[2]

1 [2002] EWCA Civ 1183, [2002] 7 WLUK 689, [2003] CP Rep 3, [2003] CLY 276.
2 (1861) 1 B & S 763, 767; 121 ER 897.

Weight

2.71 The questions of weight, credibility and sufficiency of the evidence are decisions for the members of a jury, and for the judge where a case is tried without a jury. There are no fixed rules to determine what weight to give to any item of evidence. In *R v Madhub Chunder Giri Mohunt*, Birch J observed: 'For weighing evidence and drawing inferences from it, there can be no canon. Each case represents its own peculiarities and in each common sense and shrewdness must be brought to bear upon the facts elicited',[1] and Lord Blackburn commented in *Lord Advocate v Blantyre* that '[t]he weight of evidence depends on rules of common sense'.[2]

1 (1874) 21 WRCr (India) 13 at19.
2 (1879) 4 App Cas 770 at 792.

2.72 When conducting a trial with members of a jury, the judge may withdraw an issue because the proponent has failed to adduce sufficient evidence in support of the claim. Furthermore, in summing up to the members of the jury at the end of the trial, the judge is required to provide directions on a range of issues, including, but not limited to: who has the burden of proof; what presumptions, if any, apply; when supporting evidence should be considered before putting weight on certain types of evidence; and to offer comments on matters including the weight of the evidence, although it must be made explicit that such comments are meant only to help the members of the jury in reaching their own decision.[1] In addition, there are a number of factors set out in s 114(2) of the Criminal Justice Act 2003 that deal with the assessment of the weight of hearsay in criminal proceedings.

1 Crown Court Compendium, https://www.judiciary.uk/publications/crown-court-compendium-published/.

Video and audio evidence

Testimonial use in legal proceedings

2.73 In exceptional instances, video-recorded and tape-recorded evidence may be used in lieu of testimonial evidence. In civil proceedings, evidence may be given by means of a video link or any other means, subject to leave being obtained from the court.[1] In criminal matters, it is possible to record the initial interview with children[2] and admit the recording in evidence, subject to leave of the court and any editing that the court decides is necessary.[3] Leave is required to adduce a video recording of the testimony of a witness in accordance with the provisions of s 27 of the Youth Justice and Criminal Evidence Act 1999.[4]

1 Civil Procedure Rule 32.3, which is supplemented by Practice Direction 32 – Evidence Annex 3.
2 Section 35A of the Criminal Justice Act 1988 was added by s 54 of the Criminal Justice Act 1991.
3 Criminal Justice Act 1988, s 35A(2).
4 For further details, see the most up-to-date editions of the following practitioner texts: *Archbold: Criminal Pleading, Evidence and Practice* (Sweet & Maxwell); *Blackstone's Criminal Practice* (Oxford University Press); *Archbold: Magistrates' Courts Criminal Practice* (Sweet & Maxwell).

2.74 Video-conferencing and web-conferencing technology have also made it possible to provide testimonial evidence from outside the court.

Identification and recognition evidence

2.75 Surveillance cameras are very much part of life in the twenty-first century, ever since the foundations of their use were laid in the latter decades of the twentieth century. Evidence of images from security cameras can be very helpful in identifying the perpetrators of crimes. Such evidence has been admitted in English courts, mainly in criminal cases.[1] The widespread availability of video-recorded and tape-recorded evidence has opened up the possibility that such evidence may be augmented with more advanced techniques, and the enhancement of the sounds or images, together with the use of techniques such as aural identification and facial mapping, can help to identify the parties in a recording.

1 A list that is not exhaustive includes: *McShane (Yolande Tregenna)* [1977] 7 WLUK 2, (1978) 66 Cr App R 97, [1977] Crim LR 737, (1977) 121 SJ 632, [1978] CLY 636; *R v Fowden and White* [1982] 2 WLUK 48, [1982] Crim LR 588 (CA), [1982] CLY 607; *R v Grimer* [1982] 6 WLUK 204, [1982] Crim LR 674, (1982) 126 SJ 641 (CA), [1982] CLY 606; *R v Dodson (Patrick); R v Williams (Danny Fitzalbert Williams)* [1984] 1 WLR 971, [1984] 4 WLUK 121, (1984) 79 Cr App R 220, [1984] Crim LR 489, (1984) 81 LSG 1677, (1984) 128 SJ 364, [1984] CLY 605; *Stockwell (Christopher James)* [1993] 3 WLUK 119, (1993) 97 Cr App R 260, Times, 11 March 1993, [1994] CLY 914; *R v Clarke (Robert Lee)* [1994] 12 WLUK 118, [1995] 2 Cr App R 425, Times, 26 December 1994, Independent, 30 January 1995, [1996] CLY 1373 also known as *R v Clarke (Bobby Lee)*; *Clare (Richard), Peach (Nicholas William)* [1995] 4 WLUK 107, [1995] 2 Cr App R 333, (1995) 159 JP 412, [1995] Crim LR 947, (1995) 159 JPN 424, (1995) 92(17) LSG 47, (1995) 139 SJLB 117, Times, 7 April 1995, Independent, 7 April 1995, [1996] CLY 1378; *R v Feltis (Jeremy)* [1996] EWCA Crim 776, [1966] 8 WLUK 104; *R v Hookway* [1999] Crim LR 750, also known as *R v H (Stephen James) (A Juvenile)* [1999] Crim LR 750 (CA (Crim Div)); *R v Breddick (Christopher)*, also known as *R v Briddick (Christopher)* [2001] EWCA Crim 984, [2001] 3 WLUK 790, Independent, 21 May 2001; *R v Loveridge (William), R v Lee (Charles Sonny), R v Loveridge (Christine)* [2001] EWCA Crim 973, [2001] 4 WLUK 290, [2001] 2 Cr App R 29, (2001) 98(23) SJLB 120, Times, 3 May 2002, [2001] CLY 983 – in this instance the accused were recorded by video in the court, an act prohibited by s 41 of the Criminal Justice Act 1925, and the recording was also held to have infringed the rights of the accused under article 8 of the Human Rights Act 1998. However, neither infringement was held to have interfered with the right to a fair trial: Elliott Goldstein, 'Photographic and videotape evidence in the criminal courts of England and Canada' [1987] Crim LR 384; Michael C. Bromby, 'At face value?' [2003] 153(7069) NLJ Expert Witness Supplement 302; Rob R. Jerrard, 'Police video of defendants in magistrates' court for comparison with security video recording' (2002) 75(3) Pol J 263.

2.76 Before such evidence is used, there should be a careful examination[1] of the technology in question. A good example of this judicial scrutiny was that done by Steyn LJ in *R v Clarke (Robert Lee)*,[2] where His Lordship analysed the technique of facial mapping[3] by video superimposition. The court carefully considered the reliability of the underlying scientific techniques, noting that the techniques themselves could be fit for debate, and their improper use by an expert in the particular case could in turn affect the probative value of such evidence. It was only after the court was satisfied on these two grounds that the identification evidence from the application of the technique was admitted.

1 The careful examination may be done in a trial within a trial, also called a 'voir dire'.
2 [1994] 12 WLUK 118, [1995] 2 Cr App R 425, Times, 26 December 1994, Independent, 30 January 1995, [1996] CLY 1373, also known as *R v Clarke (Bobby Lee)*.
3 [1995] 2 Cr App R 425 at 430F; Bromby, 'At face value?', 302–304; *R v Jung* [2006] NSWSC 658.

2.77 Issues regarding the reliability and application of these techniques are very much for expert evidence, depending on the nature and sophistication of each technique. But some guidance may be sought that stems from the best practices for handling electronic evidence. For instance, for evidential techniques that involve manipulating and enhancing digital imagery, Gregory Joseph has noted that the following steps must be taken before enhanced digital imagery can usefully be used:[1]

> 1. The original image needs to be properly authenticated.
>
> 2. The original image must remain intact to enable the original to be compared with the enhanced version.
>
> 3. The original image should be preserved in such a way that its integrity cannot be impugned.
>
> 4. The process of enhancement should be fully documented.
>
> 5. The process of enhancement should be carried out in such a way that the process can be repeated by the other party.
>
> 6. The enhanced images should be preserved in such a way that prevents them from being manipulated, thereby preserving their integrity.

1 Gregory P. Joseph, 'Modern visual evidence' (2009) 8(4) L J Seminars Press 4.

2.78 Important lessons were also spelt out regarding the use of voice recognition technologies and techniques for identification purposes in *R v Flynn and St John*.[1] In this case, the prosecution sought to identify the two appellants as conspirators of a robbery through voice recognition techniques. Before the robbery, the police secretly fitted a listening and transmitting device to one of the vehicles it was assumed (correctly) that the conspirators would use for the robbery. Four police officers testified that they recognized the appellants' voices from the 60 minutes of covert recording made by the device. The trial judge ruled admissible the evidence of the police officers and the transcripts of the recording, and placed the evidence before the jury. The appellants challenged the decision of the trial judge to admit the voice recognition evidence of the officers and the judge's failure to give an appropriate direction to this evidence.

1 [2008] EWCA Crim 970, [2008] 5 WLUK 53, [2008] 2 Cr App R 20, [2008] Crim LR 799, [2008] CLY 701; Damian Warburton and Thomas Lewis, 'Opinion evidence; admissibility of ad hoc expert voice recognition evidence: R v Flynn' (2009) 13(1) E & P 50; Ken Shaw, 'The quasi-expert witness: fish or fowl?', (2009) 73(2) Journal of Criminal Law 146; Jeremy Robson, 'A fair hearing? The use of voice identification parades in criminal investigations in England and Wales' [2017] Crim LR 36.

2.79 In giving judgment on appeal, Gage LJ noted that there are two categories of voice recognition evidence: expert evidence using either auditory analysis or acoustic/spectrographic analysis, or lay listener evidence, where the lay listener as a witness is required to possess some special knowledge of the suspect that enables him to recognize the suspect's voice. Such witnesses may be close relatives or friends, but they may also be persons who acquire such familiarity by the frequency of their contact with the suspect. Gage LJ also noted that suspect identification by voice recognition is more difficult than visual identification, that voice identification by experts using sophisticated auditory, acoustic and spectrographic techniques are likely to be more reliable than identification by a lay listener, and that the quality of identification by a lay listener is highly variable. In addition, research has shown that a confident recognition by a lay listener of a familiar voice may nevertheless be wrong, because while an expert is able to draw up an overall profile of the individual's speech patterns, in combination with instrumental analysis and reference research, a lay listener's response is fundamentally opaque because he cannot know and has no way of explaining which aspects of the speaker's speech patterns he is responding to, and has no way of assessing the significance of the individually observed features relative to the overall speech profile. This makes it more difficult to challenge the accuracy of his evidence.

2.80 For all these reasons, the Court of Appeal allowed the appeal, holding that the police officers as lay listeners had a limited opportunity to acquire familiarity with the appellants' voices, and that the quality of the covert recording was poor. In contrast, both experts, one representing the prosecution and the other representing the appellants, were unable to identify the voices as being those of the appellants, further casting doubt on the officers' voice recognition evidence.

2.81 While *R v Flynn and St John* did not close the door on voice recognition evidence, Gary Edmond, Kristy Martire and Mehera San Roquem suggest the following minimal safeguards be required before the prosecution can seek to admit voice recognition evidence from lay listeners:[1]

> 1. The process must be properly recorded, and the amount of time spent in contact with the defendant will be very relevant to the issue of familiarity.
>
> 2. The date and time spent by the police officer compiling a transcript of a covert recording must be recorded. If the police officer annotates the transcript with his views as to which person is speaking, that must be noted.
>
> 3. A police officer attempting the voice recognition exercise must do so without the aid of a transcript that bears another officer's annotations of whom he or she believes is speaking.
>
> 4. It is highly desirable that a voice recognition exercise should be carried out by someone other than an officer investigating the offence.

1 For a critical analysis of this topic and the discussion of further case law, see: David Ormerod, 'Sounding out expert voice identification' [2002] Crim LR 771; Gary Edmond, Kristy Martire and Mehera San Roque, 'Unsound law: issues with ("expert") voice comparison evidence' (2011) 35(1) Melbourne U L Rev 52; Geoffrey Stewart Morrison, 'Distinguishing between forensic science and forensic pseudoscience: testing of validity and reliability, and approaches to forensic voice comparison' (2014) 54(3) Science & Justice 245; Gary Edmond, 'Legal versus non-legal approaches to forensic science evidence' (2016) 20(1) E & P 3; Geoffrey Stewart Morrison, 'Admissibility of forensic voice comparison testimony in England and Wales' [2018] Crim LR 20.

2.82 These safeguards are certainly in line with the issues raised by Gage LJ in *R v Flynn and St John*, and highlight the care with which both the parties and the courts must proceed when seeking to admit computer-generated and computer-augmented evidence, in order to safeguard the evidential process.

Computer-generated animations and simulations

2.83 Digital visual evidence presentation systems (including digital displays, computer-generated graphical presentations, animated graphics and immersive virtual environment technology) have been used in legal proceedings in many jurisdictions. Such tools can be used to present evidence and illustrate hypotheses based on scientific data, or to depict the perception of a witness, or to illustrate what may have occurred (as seen from a specific viewpoint) during a particular incident. Digital reconstruction technology may also be applied in a court to explore and illustrate 'what if' scenarios and questions, to test competing hypotheses and to expose any possible inconsistencies and discrepancies within the evidence.

2.84 Computer animations and interactive virtual simulations are potentially unparalleled in their capabilities for presenting complex evidence.[1] The use of such enabling visualization technologies can affect the manner in which evidence is assimilated and correlated by the viewer. In many instances, visual media can potentially help make the evidence more relevant and easier to understand.[2] In other cases it may be seen to be unfairly prejudicing the members of a jury.

1 Gregory P. Joseph, *Modern Visual Evidence* (L J Seminars Press 2009); Neal Feigenson and Christina Spiesel, *Law on Display: The Digital Transformation of Legal Persuasion and Judgment* (New York University Press 2009); David M. Paciocco seems to fail to have understood this serious issue when commenting that the introduction of computer-enhanced photographs did not require any special evidential foundations or relevant expert evidence: 'Proof and progress: coping with the law of evidence in a technological age', (2013) 11(2) Canadian Journal of Law and Technology 181, 186–187.
2 A. M. Burton, D. Schofield and L. M. Goodwin, 'Gates of global perception: forensic graphics for evidence presentation' in *ACM Multimedia 2005: Proceedings of the 13th Annual ACM International Conference on Multimedia* (Association for Computing Machinery 2005), 103 and Jeffrey Mervis, 'Court views engineers as scientists' (1999) 284(5411) Science 21.

2.85 At first glance, these computer-generated graphical reconstructions may be seen as potentially useful in any court, and they are often treated like any other form of digital evidence regarding their admissibility. In particular, they are admitted as part of expert testimonial evidence or as a special type of real evidence.[1] However, this specific form of digital media warrants special care and attention due to its inherently persuasive nature, and the undue reliance that the viewer may place on evidence presented through a (potentially photorealistic) visualization medium such as this, often to the exclusion of the underlying evidence and the assumptions made in generating these graphical representations. This is often referred to as the 'seeing is believing' tendency.[2]

1 For example, see *R v Clarke (Robert Lee)* [1994] 12 WLUK 118, [1995] 2 Cr App R 425, Times, 26 December 1994, Independent, 30 January 1995, [1996] CLY 1373, also known as *R v Clarke (Bobby Lee)*.
2 Fred Galves, 'Where the not so wild things are: computers in the courtroom, the federal rules of evidence, and the need for institutional reform and more judicial acceptance' (2000) 13(2) Harv J L & Tech 161; Christine O. Spiesel, Richard K. Sherwin and Neal Feigenson, 'Law in the age of images: The challenges of visual literacy' in Anne Wagner, Tracey Summerfield and Farid S. B. Vanegas (eds) *Contemporary Issues of the Semiotics of Law* (Oñati International Series in Law and Society 2005); Richard Sherwin, 'Visual literacy in action: law in the age of images' in James Elkins (ed) *Visual Literacy in Action* (Routledge 2007), 179; Damian Schofield, 'The use of computer generated imagery in legal proceedings' (2016) 9 Digital Evidence and Electronic Signature Law Review 1.

2.86 As courts begin increasingly to use multimedia and cinematic displays, this has profound implications for the legal processes taking place that are intrinsically tied to the application of such technology. It must be questioned whether the decisions made in courts using such technologies are adversely affected by the manner in which the evidence is presented.[1]

1 Jonathan Chambers, 'Shipping law – collision – responsibility for collision – expert evidence – admissibility of expert evidence on seamanship – nautical assessors – plotting – simulations' (1999) 6(1) Int M L 281; Moya Clifford and Katie Kinloch, 'The use of computer simulation evidence in court', (2008) 24(2) Computer Law and Security Report 169; Joanna Gallant and Lauren Shepherd, 'Effective visual communication: scientific principles and research findings', in Samuel H. Solomon, Joanna Gallant and John P. Esser (eds) *The Science of Courtroom Litigation: Jury Research and Analytical Principals* (ALM Publishing 2009); Ken Fowle and Damian Schofield, 'Visualising forensic data: investigation to court' in Dr Andrew Woodward and Professor Craig Valli (eds) *Proceedings of the 9th Australian Digital Forensics Conference* (Security Research Centre 2011); Peer Watterson, 'Appeal court reluctance: complex evidence, obviousness and related matters', (2012) 7(5) JIPLP 358; David-John Gibbs, Stephen Emmitt, Kirti Ruikar and Wayne Lord, 'Recommendations on the creation of computer generated exhibits for construction delay claims' (2014) 30(4) Const LJ 236.

Computer-generated evidence in England and Wales: civil proceedings

2.87 An early occurrence of the use of computer-generated evidence is seen in the civil case of *The Owners of the Ship Pelopidas v The Owners of the Ship TRSL Concord*.[1] In 1996 a collision took place in the Access Channel to Buenos Aires between two vessels: the *Pelopidas* and *TRSL Concord*. The issue for the court to decide was the liability for the collision and the apportionment of that liability. The items of computer-generated evidence submitted were two-dimensional computer-generated simulations of the trajectories of both vessels; these were, in effect, animated maps. A 'black box' on the *Concord* recorded various positioning, speed and heading data at 15-second intervals for the relevant collision time period. Both sides accepted the accuracy of the plot. David Steel J concluded that a fair apportionment of liability was 60:40 in favour of the *Pelopidas*, and stated:

> there is a danger of losing sight of the true value of reconstructions. Of course they enable the Court and the parties to have a broad bird's eye view of the events leading up to collision. But their true probative value is that they may sometimes enable the Court to determine, not what may have happened, but what could not possibly have happened.[2]

1 [1999] 2 All ER 737 (Comm), [1999] 2 Lloyd's Rep 675, [1999] 10 WLUK 259, [2000] CLY 4677.
2 [1999] 2 Lloyd's Rep 675 at 682.

2.88 In stating the above, David Steel J was remarking on his accumulated experience of the usefulness of computer-generated reconstruction evidence.[1] Computer simulations are now more frequently used in civil proceedings.[2]

1 Charles Macdonald QC, 'Case note *Owners of the Ship Devotion v Owners of the Ship Golden Polydinamos*' (1995) 4 Int ML 77, where the members of the Court of Appeal endorsed the comments of the trial judge respecting the use of computer simulations as evidence of a collision.
2 This list is not exhaustive: in criminal proceedings, *R. v Maloney (Gerald)* [2003] EWCA Crim 1373, [2003] 5 WLUK 565; *Mitrasinovic v Stroud* [2020] EWHC 914 (QB), [2020] 4 WLUK 156; others include: *Halliburton Energy Services Inc v Smith International (North Sea) Ltd* [2006] EWCA Civ 1715, [2006] 12 WLUK 379, (2007) 30(2) IPD 30009; *Maersk Oil UK Ltd v Dresser-Rand (UK) Ltd* [2007] EWHC 752 (TCC), [2007] 4 WLUK 50.

Computer-generated evidence in England and Wales: criminal proceedings

2.89 The Court of Appeal has indicated that it favours the use of digital images in criminal proceedings, as indicated in *R v Smith (Peter Kenneth)*[1] by Thomas LJ, at [61]:[2]

> The presentation of the evidence to the jury made no attempt to use modern methods of presentation. The presentation to this court was similar; a large amount of time was wasted because of this. It was incomprehensible to us why digital images were not provided to the jury; the refusal of NAFIS [National Automated Finger Print Identification System] to permit a digital image to be supplied to the court was a further example of the lack of a contemporary approach to the presentation of evidence. The presentation to the jury must be done in such a way that enables the jury to determine the disputed issues.

1 [2011] EWCA Crim 1296, [2011] 5 WLUK 644, [2011] C App R 16, [2011] CLY 602.
2 See also Rosemary Pattenden, 'Fingerprint evidence – United Kingdom', (2011) 15(4) E & P 371; for New Zealand, see *R v Garrett* [2001] DCR 955 and *R v Little* [2007] NZCA 491.

2.90 Because of the critical nature of criminal trials, it is crucial that any computer-generated evidence that is put forward be thoroughly examined.[1] The use of a jury in criminal cases is another important reason for assessing the relevance, accuracy and possible prejudicial effect of computer-generated evidence carefully. For this reason, it is important for defence counsel to be aware of the issues that can arise and be suitably prepared to test the evidence. In *R. v Gardner (Trevor Elton)*,[2] a person was killed during a fire in a block of flats. One of the experts who gave identification evidence for the prosecution used a new technique that deployed computer software to provide an analysis of video surveillance footage, as described by Waller LJ at [34]:[3]

> [The expert] had developed a different technique. He had developed equipment to enable the images on a video surveillance film to be presented so as to extract as much information from it as possible. This included enhancing the film by computer to allow frame by frame examination, the ability to zoom in on part of the frame to alter the contrast and brightness to bring out detail and to run the film backwards and forwards. The second purpose of the equipment is to assist in making comparisons between one frame and another. To help in that [the expert] has developed three techniques. He called the first of them 'image addition'. By means of his computer he takes an image from one sequence of movements and selects from another sequence an image of a person who displays approximately the same stance and is about the same distance from the camera as the first. The second image is superimposed on the first so the viewer can observe whether the two images are like one another and whether there are any differences. The difference, depending on what it is, may show that the images are of different people. The second technique is referred to as 'image subtraction'. [The expert] takes the two images selected because of their comparable poses and distances from the camera and turns the first computerised image into a negative and superimposes the second on it in a positive form. The result is that the features which are common to both images disappear and only what is different remains. [The expert's] third technique is a 'blink comparison' whereby he can switch from one image to another. When there are differences between the two they generate an illusion of movement so that the eye is able to pick up the differences. That technique also enables the viewer to see that when one image is removed an element which had appeared to belong to the picture which has been removed in fact belongs to the picture which remains.

1 For an examination of the issues and case law, see Tony Ward, 'Surveillance cameras, identification and expert evidence' (2012) 9 Digital Evidence and Electronic Signature Law Review 42; Gareth Norris, 'The influence of computer generated animations on juror decision making', (2014) 11 Digital Evidence and Signature Law Review 46.

2 [2004] EWCA Crim 1639, [2004] 6 WLUK 615; Andy Roberts, 'Expert evidence: facial mapping; image analysis' (2004) 68(5) Journal of Criminal Law 372; Ruth Costigan, 'Identification from CCTV: the risk of injustice' [2007] Crim LR 591.

3 The admissibility of such evidence was approved in *R v Breddick (Christopher)*, also known as *R v Briddick (Christopher)* [2001] EWCA Crim 984, [2001] 3 WLUK 790, Independent, 21 May 2001.

2.91 Even though the defence did not have any material in relation to which they could cross-examine the expert witness and enable the jury to judge the accuracy of the expert's analysis and assessment that the person identified in the surveillance footage was the defendant, the court guardedly accepted the admissibility of this evidence. In doing so, Waller LJ also sounded a note of caution regarding new techniques relating to identification. The judge quoted, at [45], the following statement of Lord Hope in *Hopes and Lavery v HM Advocate*:

> If admitting evidence of this kind seems unfamiliar and an extension of established evidential practice, the answer must be that, as technology develops, evidential practice will need to be evolved to accommodate it. Whilst the courts must be vigilant to ensure that no unfairness results, they should not block steps which enable the jury to gain full assistance from the technology.

2.92 But even if juries are to be enabled to benefit from the full spectrum of technological evidence, they are particularly vulnerable, often more so than judges and coroners, to any prejudicial effect and inaccuracy of scientific animations. Perhaps this is because juries do not have the same level of cynicism that years of experience of analysing evidence has given judges and, to a lesser degree, coroners. In the case of *R v Ore*,[1] Tucker J stated the defence's apprehension regarding the admissibility of a computer-generated animation:

> The concern which is expressed by [the defence] … is as to the impact which this evidence will have upon the jury and I understand that concern. [The defence] fears that the weight which the jury may place upon the graphic animation will be disproportionate to its value in the case. [The defence] fears that they may be distracted from concentrating as they ought to do upon the evidence to be given by the expert witnesses on either side and is concerned, naturally, that the graphic animation reproduces simply one particular side of the coin.

1 (1998, Birmingham Crown Court, unreported). Stephen Mason tried to obtain a copy of the transcript of the case for the first edition of this text, but the tapes were destroyed in accordance with the relevant retention and disposal policy (correspondence with Michael Ives of Marten Walsh Cherer Limited). Stephen Mason subsequently corresponded with Sir Richard Tucker, who indicated that he no longer had the notes of this trial, but kindly confirmed the remarks that are attributed to him as quoted in this text.

2.93 The concerns stated above are highly relevant and illustrate real fears about any computer-generated evidence. This is especially true for forensic reconstructions. Hence, any computer-generated reconstructions should be made as precisely and in as unbiased a way as possible, and their use has to be shown to be necessary.[1] Their probative value should outweigh any potential prejudicial effect.

1 In *R. v Maloney (Gerald)* [2003] EWCA Crim 1373, [2003] 5 WLUK 565, a reconstruction was developed using computer simulation software in preparation for an appeal against conviction, a

technology that was not available at the time of trial. The members of the Court of Appeal decided, in the light of the opinion of the expert who undertook the simulation not being conclusive, that the evidence would have no effect upon the safety of the conviction, and the court did not receive it and dismissed the appeal. It is not clear whether Mr Adrian Redgrave, QC, who appeared for the Crown at trial and on the reference to the Court of Appeal (Criminal Division), explored the technical integrity or the assumptions upon which the program was prepared.

2.94 These lessons may be illustrated by the case of *R v Ore*, which introduced one of the first forensic computer-generated animations to an English criminal trial. The Crash Investigation and Training Unit of the West Midlands Police Service produced the animation. The case involved a collision between two vehicles at a junction; one of the drivers was killed as he pulled out in front of an oncoming vehicle. The views of both drivers were partially obscured by large hedges and walls around the junction.[1] Tucker J, who presided over this case, further stated in his ruling on 25 November 1998:[2]

> I am told that this is the first time in which it has been suggested that a jury in a trial such as this should be shown a computer aided animation which pictorially represents a reconstruction of a road traffic accident. It may be that in years to come such displays will be commonplace and that lawyers will marvel that anyone should ever have questioned their admissibility.
>
> … I am satisfied that it would be right to admit this evidence and, indeed, wrong to refuse so to do, provided, as I shall try to do, that I give the jury proper directions as to their approach to this evidence and provided I ensure, so far as I can, that they do not place disproportionate weight upon it. Accordingly, I rule that the evidence is admissible.

1 M. Doyle, 'Working model: helping the police with their enquiries' (1997) CAD User 62 (no longer available online).
2 *R v Ore* (1998, Birmingham Crown Court, unreported).

2.95 A well-known example from Northern Ireland is the computer-generated evidence that was extensively used during the Bloody Sunday Inquiry.[1] In 1972, 13 people were killed during a peaceful demonstration. The original inquiry produced a report within 11 weeks of the incident, and acquitted the soldiers involved. In 1998, a Tribunal of Inquiry was established to reassess the events.[2] Lord Saville, the chair of the tribunal, took full advantage of ensuing improvements in technology, and used a computer software system designed especially for use in the Inquiry to amplify the testimony of witnesses. The Northern Ireland Centre for Learning and Resources produced the computer-generated virtual models, which reconstructed a large area of Londonderry that had been extensively altered since 1972. The user was able to compare the same scene as it appeared at the time of the Inquiry and as it was in 1972. There were 80 locations stored in the system that could be explored, with specific points of view being recalled when switching between the representations. The system could also store oral evidence about location and movement, and export scenes to a mark-up system so that witnesses could draw on top of images. The computer software system that was admitted was deemed to be unbiased and accurate.

1 See The Bloody Sunday Inquiry http://www.bloody-sunday-inquiry.org.uk/.
2 Statement by Tony Blair, Prime Minister: HC Deb 29 January 1998, vol 305, col 501.

2.96 The Bloody Sunday Inquiry computer system was not interactive in three-dimensions. Virtual reality or VR, by definition, is an interactive computer-generated simulated environment with which users can interact using a computer monitor or specialized hardware. The computer system used for the Bloody Sunday Inquiry was interactive in the sense that viewers were able to view images of different scenes at varied times. However, the viewer was not able to move around a full three-dimensional virtual environment of Londonderry itself, since such a three-dimensional virtual model of the area did not exist. But since then, courts in England and Wales have begun to introduce interactive three-dimensional VR crime scene environments for a number of high-profile criminal cases.[1] There is little doubt that, with the increasing complexity of criminal investigations, we will see more use of virtual environments and immersive virtual environments in legal proceedings.

1 Damian Schofield, 'Playing with evidence: using video games in the courtroom' (2011) 2(1) J of Entertainment Computing (Special Issue: Video Games as Research Instruments) 47.

2.97 Virtual environments possess the potential to sway juries and decision makers, even more so than computer animations in general. Creating an environment that allows viewers to take different perspectives and manipulate objects in that environment do indeed allow for 'what if' scenarios to be played out, and could lead to more robust decisions. But the reconstructions of scenes in these environments are based on various assumptions and premises, not all of which can be elucidated or are transparent, or easily accessible for review by opposing experts and by decision makers. Analyses of computer-generated displays show that they can be extremely advantageous in the court, provided they are used appropriately. The consequences of a failure to investigate these issues cannot be underestimated, since errors, inaccuracies, misuse, tampering or biases within visualizations are capable of leading to miscarriages of justice.[1]

1 Marcel Worring and Rita Cucchiara, 'Multimedia in forensics' in *Proceedings of the 17th ACM International Conference on Multimedia* (Association for Computing Machinery 2009), 1153.

3

Hearsay

Daniel Seng and Stephen Mason

3.1 The much-maligned evidential rule of hearsay exclusion has been subject to some interesting challenges in many common law jurisdictions since 2005. An anathema to lawyers of the civil or administrative law system and seemingly largely misunderstood in its complexity by many common law lawyers, the hearsay rule has been supplemented in some respects and undermined in others by various legislative reforms in both civil and criminal proceedings. This chapter does not seek to provide a comprehensive exposé of the hearsay rule. However, in drawing the rule back to its historical foundation we will, in part, consider its relevance in the context of electronic evidence and attempt to demonstrate the application of hearsay to evidence in electronic form.

The rule of hearsay exclusion and its rationale

3.2 We begin with a traditional definition of the hearsay rule. Sir Rupert Cross defined the hearsay rule of evidence in these terms: '[A] statement other than one made by a person while giving oral evidence in the proceedings is inadmissible *as evidence of any fact stated*'.[1] In offering this definition, Sir Rupert Cross intentionally conflates in one definition the rule against self-corroboration with the rule against hearsay in the narrow sense,[2] to both encompass and contrast the situations where the witness who made the statement is either available to testify (the rule against self-corroboration) or unable to testify (the rule against hearsay in the narrow sense). If a witness's earlier statement is sought to be admitted of the facts therein, it is at common law inadmissible except as an informal admission provided against that witness or as part of the *res gestae* rule.[3] And where it is so admitted, it is not as evidence of the truth of the assertions contained in them.[4] If the witness's earlier statement is in the form of electronic evidence, this does not change the application of this rule, and does not engage the rule against hearsay.

1 Sir Rupert Cross, *Evidence* (5th edn, Butterworths 1979) 6, emphasis added. In his first edition, Phipson stated his definition of hearsay as 'Oral or written statements made by persons not called as witnesses are not receivable to prove the truth of the matters stated': Sidney L. Phipson, *The Law of Evidence* (Stevens and Hayes 1892) 117. See also the definition suggested by Charles Cato, who preferred to see hearsay limited to 'unsworn utterances containing narrative assertion, where it is a suggestion for reform'; 'Verbal acts, res gestae and hearsay: a suggestion for reform' (1993) 5(1) Bond LR 72, 73.
2 Roderick Munday, *Cross & Tapper on Evidence* (13th edn, Oxford University Press 2018) 563 (hereinafter *Cross & Tapper*).
3 *Cross & Tapper*, 563.
4 *Cross & Tapper*, 587.

3.3 Turning to the rule against hearsay, the most widely accepted judicial formulation of the rule is as follows:

Daniel Seng and Stephen Mason, 'Hearsay', in Stephen Mason and Daniel Seng (eds.), *Electronic Evidence and Electronic Signatures* (5th edn, University of London 2021) 85–111.

> Evidence of a statement made to a witness by a person who is not himself called as a witness may or may not be hearsay. It is hearsay and inadmissible when the object of the evidence is to establish the truth of what is contained in the statement. It is not hearsay and is admissible when it is proposed to establish by evidence, not the truth of the statement, but the fact that it was made.[1]

1 *Subramaniam v Public Prosecutor* [1956] 1 WLR 965 at 969, [1956] 7 WLUK 26, (1956) 100 SJ 566, [1956] CLY 7051.

3.4 The hearsay rule is prompted when the testimony of a witness as to what a declarant said is admitted in evidence to establish its truth, but not otherwise. Hearsay evidence is thus subject to at least four clear vulnerabilities: belief by the declarant that X exists (the risk of impaired perception), justification for the declarant's statement that 'X exists' (bad memory, ambiguity and insincerity), confirmation that the witness correctly heard the declarant as having said 'X exists' (impaired perception) and justification for the witness in repeating that statement (the duplicated risks of bad memory, ambiguity and insincerity).[1] Hearsay therefore increases these risks because it has to contend not only with the testimony of the witness, but also with the testimony of the declarant. This is because the usual safeguards that apply in relation to ordinary testimony must also apply to second-hand evidence,[2] since there is no link between the testimony of the witness and the declarant's proposition that 'X exists' that is sought to be supported.

1 *Cross & Tapper*, 564. See also John H. Wigmore, *A Treatise on the Anglo-American System of Evidence in Trials at Common Law* (3rd edn, Little Brown 1940) para 478; Edmund M. Morgan, 'Hearsay dangers and the application of the hearsay concept' (1948) 62(2) Harv L Rev 177; Laurence H. Tribe, 'Triangulating hearsay' (1974) 87(5) Harv L Rev 957; and Michael H. Graham, 'Stickperson hearsay: a simplified approach to understanding the rule against hearsay' (1982) 4 U Ill L Rev 887; Edward W. Cleary (ed), *McCormick on Evidence* (West Publishing Co 1984) para 245.
2 That is, evidence that is more than one remove from the first statement, or 'irrespective of the number of intermediate communications between the original source and the testifying witness': Colin Tapper, *Cross & Tapper on Evidence* (12th edn, Oxford University Press 2010) 552 fn 9; the authors of Australian Law Reform Commission, *Uniform Evidence Law* (Report No 102, 2006) refer throughout to 'second-hand' hearsay evidence.

3.5 Thus, some academics have advanced the argument that '[t]he basic rationale of the hearsay rule rests on the right of cross-examination'.[1] 'The central reason for the presumptive exclusion of hearsay statements is the general inability to test their reliability. Without the declarant in court, it may be impossible to inquire into the declarant's perception, memory, narration or sincerity.'[2] However, it should also be noted that cross-examination is only one way to test evidence: if it is the rationale for hearsay, evidence which is inherently reliable or which can be evaluated for reliability without the need for cross-examination could be admitted.[3]

1 *Cross & Tapper*, 565; James Allan, 'The working rationale of the hearsay rule and the implications of modern psychological knowledge' [1991] 44 CLP 217. On the dangers of hearsay evidence, see Morgan, 'Hearsay dangers and the application of the hearsay concept', 178–179. On the perceived virtues of cross-examination, see 2 Bl Comm 373, where Sir William Blackstone stated that examination through '*viva voce*, in the presence of all mankind, is much more conducive to the clearing up of truth', and Matthew Hale, *History and Analysis of the Common Law of England* (J. Nutt 1713) 258, https://constitution.org/1-Constitution/cmt/hale/history_common_law.htm (cited in the US Supreme Court case of *Crawford v Washington*, 541 U.S. 36 (2004)), where it is said that cross-examination 'beats and boults out the Truth much better than when the Witness only delivers a formal Series of his Knowledge without being interrogated'. The Supreme Court of Canada proclaimed cross-examination as 'the optimal way of testing testimonial evidence': *R v Khelawon* 2006 SCC 57 (CanLII), [2006] 2 SCR 787 at [35].

2 *R v Khelawon* [2006] 2 SCR 787, para 2.
3 Elisabeth McDonald, 'Going "Straight to basics": the role of Lord Cooke in reforming the rule against hearsay – from Baker to the Evidence Act 2006', (2008) 39(1) VUWLR 143, 156. Focusing on the right of cross-examination would also mean that the rule against self-corroboration cannot be justified, and that out-of-court statements of witnesses are outside the hearsay rule. See e.g., New Zealand Evidence Act 2006, s 18(1)(b)(i) (defining admissible hearsay as including any reliable statement that is made by a person who is available as a witness).

The right of confrontation

3.6 A further, apparently important but ill-defined foundation of the hearsay rule that is related to the right of cross-examination is the right to confront an accuser as an essential element of the right to a fair trial. It was on this basis that the United States Supreme Court in *Crawford v Washington* held that where cross-examination is not possible for the testimonial statements of witnesses who have since become unavailable, the statements are inadmissible.[1]

1 *Crawford v Washington* 124 S.Ct. 1354 (2004), 541 U.S. 36 (2004).

3.7 The right to confront draws on the notion that the right to humane treatment and procedural integrity both *feel* undermined by the admission of hearsay evidence.[1] Although expressly established in the Constitution of the United States[2] and in the European Convention of Human Rights,[3] a review shows that in other common law jurisdictions there is no 'right' per se of confrontation for hearsay evidence.[4] As the UK Supreme Court explained in *Horncastle*, under the common law system of trial by jury, the conditions relating to the admissibility of hearsay evidence (including exceptions to the hearsay rule), combined with the trial judge's role as gatekeeper in applying them and her general residual discretion to exclude prejudicial or unfair evidence from going before the jury, provide the appropriate assurance in guaranteeing a fair trial.[5] This greatly reduces the influence of this right as justification for the hearsay rule.

1 For discussion of the foundation of this right and its modern legitimacy, see Mike Redmayne, 'Confronting confrontation' in Paul Roberts and Jill B. Hunter (eds) *Criminal Evidence and Human Rights: Reimagining Common Law Procedural Traditions* (Hart Publishing 2012), 283–308 (the text of this chapter is also an LSE Law, Society and Economy Working Paper, No 10/2010, http://eprints.lse.ac.uk/32897/1/WPS2010-10_Redmayne.pdf). See also Toni M. Massaro, 'The dignity value of face-to-face confrontations' (1998) 40(5) U Fla L Rev 863.
2 US Const. amend. VI ('In all criminal prosecutions, the accused shall enjoy the right ... to be confronted with the witnesses against him').
3 European Convention on Human Rights, article 6(3)(d). In *Al-Khawaja v United Kingdom (26766/05) Tahery v United Kingdom (22228/06)* [2011] 12 WLUK 533, [2012] 2 Costs LO 139, (2012) 54 EHRR 23, 32 BHRC 1, [2012] Crim LR 375, Times, 22 December 2011, [2012] CLY 657, it was held that the defendant was entitled to examine the maker of a statement admitted in evidence who was not called as a witness, where the statement was the sole, or at least the decisive, basis for the defendant's conviction.
4 *R. v Horncastle (Michael Christopher)* [2009] UKSC 14, [2010] 2 AC 373, [2010] 2 WLR 47, [2010] 2 All ER 359, [2009] 12 WLUK 249, [2010] 1 Cr App R 17, [2010] HRLR 12, [2010] UKHRR 1, [2010] Crim LR 496, (2009) 153(48) SJLB 32, Times, 10 December 2009, [2010] CLY 658. The UK Supreme Court declined to follow *Al-Khawaja and Tahery*.
5 *R. v Horncastle (Michael Christopher)* [2010] 2 AC 373 at [41].

3.8 United States jurisprudence also suggests waning support for this rationale as justification for the hearsay rule. Even though any 'testimonial' evidence in respect of which there has been or can be no cross-examination is excluded, it has also been held that hearsay exceptions including dying declarations and non-testimonial evidence such as business records and statements in furtherance of a conspiracy are not excluded by the Confrontation Clause.[1] As the Supreme Court itself recognized, the right of confrontation was not absolute and exceptions to the hearsay rule are valid inroads on the right of confrontation.[2]

1 *Crawford v Washington* 124 S.Ct. 1354 (2004) at 1367, 1376.
2 *Crawford v Washington* 124 S.Ct. 1354 (2004) at 1377, citing *U.S. v Burr*, 25 F.Cas. 187 (1807) at 193.

Hearsay and electronic evidence

3.9 For these reasons, we adopt the broader view taken by Stein that the rule against hearsay exists as a rule of evidence that properly allocates the risk of error. Confirmed risks that can be *eliminated or avoided*[1] are part of the fundamental 'principle of maximal inferential individualization', which Stein described as follows:

> (1) No adverse inference should be drawn against the defendant, unless it has been exposed to and survived the maximal individualized testing;
>
> (2) This includes every practical possibility of testing the applicability of the inference in question to the individual defendant's case;
>
> (3) The defendant should accordingly be provided with appropriate immunities from the risk of error.[2]

1 Alex Stein, 'The refoundation of evidence law' (1996) 9(1) CJLJ 279, 326–328.
2 Stein, 'The refoundation of evidence law', 326–327.

3.10 Admitting hearsay thus denies to the party adversely affected by the evidence the opportunity to test all of the inculpatory arguments that transform the evidence.[1] Hearsay evidence is excluded, not because a court could not be assured of its reliability, but that its reliability was effectively unknowable due to, among other things, the absence of an ability to cross-examine. Furthermore, in the interest of fairness to the adversely affected party, as part of the exclusionary strategy of the principle of maximal inferential individualization, such a line of inquiry should not be allowed to begin.[2] This is because admitting hearsay will expose the adversely affected party to the possibility of not being able to test every practical possibility of the hearsay inference to the proponent's case, thereby introducing 'value-preferences' that threaten the overall coherence of the proceedings.[3]

1 Stein, 'The refoundation of evidence law', 326–327.
2 Stein, 'The refoundation of evidence law', 327.
3 Stein, 'The refoundation of evidence law', 326 and following, would describe this as an avoidable risk of error in proceedings.

3.11 Based on the discussion thus far, it could be possible to conclude that electronic evidence will not initiate the hearsay rule because records in digital form are 'non-testimonial' and that the hearsay rule focuses only on the 'human-centric' nature of statements. This would be wrong. In fact, because of the third (and some would argue fourth) industrial revolution and the digital economy, ever-increasing amounts of information are now in digital form.[1] The digital revolution has forced companies and individuals alike to record, use, transform and generate information in complex ways. 'Our reality [is now defined] in written records, oral communications, and immersive experiences' that are in electronic form.[2] Global interconnectedness and reliance on electronic information, especially to cope with the speed of change, has led to the development of increasingly complex information systems that have outpaced much of existing jurisprudence. It follows that it is necessary to fundamentally reconsider their justification and underlying rationale. For the rules of evidence, the question should be the relevance, if any, of the rule against hearsay in relation to this shift in evidence from physical form to digital form. In reality, the difficult application of the hearsay rule of exclusion to electronic evidence has been considered to be complex and confusing.[3]

1 For example, see Peter Lyman and Hal R. Varian, 'How much information?' (2003), https://www2.sims.berkeley.edu/research/projects/how-much-info-2003/printable_report.pdf.
2 George L. Paul, 'Systems of evidence in the age of complexity' (2014) 12(2) Ave Maria L Rev 173.
3 Colin Tapper, 'Reform of the law of evidence in relation to the output from computers' (1995) 3(1) IJLIT 79 for a critique and suggestion that the rule should be abolished.

3.12 In this regard, a useful tool for evaluating electronic evidence under the hearsay rule and for sharpening the evidential analysis is, first, to classify the *type of device* that is used to produce the evidence in question:

> Data processing devices can be classified into the following categories [these are discussed in more detail in Chapter 4]:
>
> [category 1] devices which accept human-supplied input and reproduce human-supplied output,
>
> [category 2] self-contained data processing devices that obtain input or take recordings from the environment without human intervention, and
>
> [category 3] devices which are a hybrid of the two. [1]

1 Daniel Seng, 'Computer output as evidence' (1997) 130 Sing JLS 173.

3.13 After identifying the device, the next step is to analyse the *use* that is made of the output of the device to determine if its use is testimonial: that is, if the output is tendered for the matter stated in the output as a fact, or otherwise.[1]

1 Notwithstanding the statutory abrogation of the hearsay rule, the analysis of whether the use of the evidence is testimonial remains pertinent in relation to the conditions which have to be satisfied for the statement to be admissible. A further discussion follows.

3.14 Category 1 relates to the use of data processing devices primarily to store and record content that is written or spoken by one or more persons. Category 1 devices operate primarily to receive human input and store that same input for subsequent retrieval. When such information is retrieved, most of the time it is principally used *for the testimonial content of the human input.* As an antecedent to the storage and recording functions of these devices, this information may be recorded, digitized, compressed and processed in some way before being stored on the device or some other platform. There may be further processing or ingestion in the form of activation of the device for recording, transcribing or indexing the recording to facilitate its retrieval.

3.15 Evidence produced by Category 1 devices is therefore generally hearsay, even though it is the product of automation, because these devices are used primarily as recording devices for the evidential value of human input. Examples include lists of contacts and their information in mobile devices, text messages and email correspondence between parties – the only difference between paper-based documentation and such records is that their creation, capture and storage are done electronically. The Singapore case of *Aw Kew Lim* illustrates this point well.[1] In this case, the accused were charged with the copyright offence of possession of illegally copied gramophone records for sale. To prove that the accused were owners of the shop that was searched and found to have the records in question, the prosecution tendered in evidence a computer printout from the official government Registry of Companies and Businesses that identified the name of the firm, other company registration information and the names and addresses of the accused as directors. The court ruled that the information about the names of the accused was inadmissible as hearsay. As the court explained, the printout contained information that was derived from some other source such as a database or an original document, which would be inadmissible hearsay, even if that printout had been correctly certified.[2] To put it another way, the printout was admitted because it recorded the fact that '[the six accused] were directors of [company X]'. This is a hearsay use of the electronic evidence enabled by the recordation function of the device.

1 *Aw Kew Lim v PP* [1987] SLR(R) 443, [1987] 2 MLJ 601.
2 *Aw Kew Lim v PP* [1987] SLR(R) 443 at [9].

Electronic evidence and real evidence

3.16 Category 2 devices (records generated by software that have not had any input from a human), simply put, generate evidence that is substantially the product of automation. Digital cameras and video recorders are the ubiquitous example of Category 2 devices. Fundamentally, after some form of manual setup, these devices work autonomously by collecting light information via digital sensors and converting that via digital processing into digital form. After some additional processing, depending on the specifications and features of these cameras and recorders, the digitized images or video streams are stored or recorded. When the images or videos are retrieved, they are used to replicate the input or environment within which these devices are situated.

3.17 English courts appear relatively sanguine in admitting ANPR (automatic number plate recognition) evidence, without raising any noted hearsay challenges.[1] The primary reason for the absence of challenges is that, typically, photographs and video recordings, such as ANPR evidence made from Category 2 devices, are not used 'testimonially': they are considered real evidence. Real evidence is 'an independent species of evidence as [its] production calls upon the court to reach conclusions on the basis of its own perception, and not on that of witnesses directly or indirectly reported to it'.[2] The genesis for its modern application to electronic evidence may be found in *Re The Statue of Liberty*, where the issue was whether the cinematograph film recordings of a navigational traffic radar system were admissible to prove the movements of the vessels that had collided. Sir Jocelyn Simon P held that they were. His Lordship opined, at 195 (emphasis added):

> In my view the evidence in question in the present case has nothing to do with the hearsay rule ... It is in the nature of real evidence, which is conveniently defined in Cockle's Cases and Statutes on Evidence (10th Edn. 1963) ...:

> 'Real evidence is evidence afforded by the production of physical objects *for inspection or other examination by the court.*'
>
> ... The law is bound these days to take cognisance of the fact that mechanical means replace human effort.[3]

1 For example, see *R. v Doyle (Hugh), R. v Wood (Carl), R. v Lincoln (William)* [2017] EWCA Crim 340, [2017] 2 WLUK 194, where hearsay challenges were raised on appeal in relation to the covert listening devices placed on the defendants' cars, but not in relation to the automatic number plate recognition evidence as part of the evidence of the movement of those cars. Likewise, hearsay challenges were raised, but not in relation to the automatic number plate recognition evidence, in *R. v Brown (Nico)* [2019] EWCA Crim 1143, [2019] 1 WLR 6721, [2019] 7 WLUK 41, [2019] 2 Cr App R 25, [2020] Crim LR 71, [2019] CLY 647.
2 *Cross & Tapper*, 58.
3 *The Statue of Liberty Owners of Motorship Sapporo Maru v Owners of Steam Tanker Statue of Liberty* [1968] 1 WLR 739, [1968] 2 All ER 195, [1968] 1 Lloyd's Rep 429, [1968] 3 WLUK 65, (1968) 112 SJ 380, [1968] CLY 1546, admitting as real evidence radar set recordings of nautical traffic.

3.18 It is also for this reason that the digital audio recorder is an example of either a Category 1 *or* a Category 2 device, depending on its use. From a technical standpoint, the analogue sound waves produced by human speech or sounds are captured by the microphones on such recorders, converted into digital form by the use of digital signal processing techniques and then further processed (for instance, compressed, tagged or indexed), before the digitized representation of sound is stored or recorded. Whether the recording made by a digital audio recorder is hearsay will depend on whether it is used as evidence testimonially. For instance, if Amazon Echo recordings of conversations were used as evidence of the incidents that allegedly took place in households being investigated, the recording would be an experiential reproduction of the context of the offences allegedly being committed.[1] In other words, it is used as a surveillance tool – a Category 2 device. On the other hand, if the Echo is used as a dictation tool to record the user as saying 'X exists', such a use as evidence that 'X exists' would be testimonial and would be excluded as hearsay. In those circumstances, it would be a Category 1 device.

1 For example, see Michael Harrigan, 'Privacy versus justice: Amazon's First Amendment battle in the cloud', (2017) 45 W St L Rev 91; Robert D. Lang and Lenore E. Benessere, 'Alexa, Siri, Bixby, Google's Assistant, and Cortana testifying in court', (2018) 74 J Mo B 20; John G. Browninga and Lisa Angeloa, 'Alexa, testify new sources of evidence from the Internet of Things' (2019) 82 Tex BJ 506.

3.19 But while real evidence from Category 2 devices does not amount to 'assertions' that are caught by the hearsay rule, this does not mean that such evidence is automatically admissible. All relevant evidence is generally considered admissible only if a proper foundation has been laid for its admission: this will be by way of satisfying the authentication requirements of the laws of evidence. A more detailed discussion of the authentication evidence in general and specific challenges to the reliability and accuracy of electronic evidence can be found in Chapter 6.

3.20 In many circumstances, the proponent of the electronic evidence, usually the prosecutor, would, in the absence of foundation evidence, seek to circumvent the requirement for foundation evidence by relying on the doctrine of *omnia praesumuntur rite esse acta* or presumption of reliability. However, this presumption is not a suitable substitute for authentication, particularly in relation to complex and sui generis devices and systems. It is often ill-appreciated that foundation evidence must also be sought before there can be reliance on the presumption itself. And the scope and effect of the presumption has often been misunderstood. A more detailed discussion of the presumption of reliability as applied to devices that produce electronic evidence can be found in Chapter 5.

Testimonial and non-testimonial use of information

3.21 A large proportion of electronic evidence, however, will be evidence produced by Category 3 devices (records comprising a mix of human input and calculations generated by software). In this category, the device functions through a mix of human-supplied input and produces data output without further human intervention. The human input could be in the form of the initial calibration of such devices or their internal programming. These are ex facie testimonial input of some form in the absence of further elucidation. Even machine learning systems – the epitome of autonomous systems – have varying levels of reliance and dependence on human-labelled data, choices and configurations to enable their proper autonomous operations.

3.22 The line between Category 2 and Category 3 devices can be hard to draw: the difference is one of degree that represents the relative significance of the level of contribution of human-supplied input and pre-programmed autonomous processes to the eventual output, and the extent to which the testimonial input qualifies the (purportedly) non-testimonial use of the output. In *Wood*, for instance, the admissibility of chromatograph and spectrometer outputs as real evidence was supported by the oral testimony of the chemists who calibrated and operated the machines, as well as the programmers of the program who analysed the chromatograph and spectrometer outputs, leading the courts to characterize the processes of recording, processing and calculating the testing sample as operating without human intervention. The Court of Appeal in *Wood*, in characterizing the test results as real evidence, said:

> This computer was rightly described as a tool. *It did not contribute its own knowledge* [but] merely did a sophisticated calculation which could have been done manually by the chemist and was in fact done by the chemists using the computer programmed by the [programmer] whom the Crown called as a witness. The fact that the efficiency of a device is dependent on more than one person does not make any difference in kind. Virtually every device will involve the persons who made it, the persons who calibrated, programmed or set it up ... and the person who uses or observes the device. In each particular case how many of these people it is appropriate to call must depend on the facts of, and the issues raised and the concessions made in that case. [1]

1 *R v Wood (Stanley William)* [1982] 6 WLUK 191, (1983) 76 Cr App R 23, [1982] Crim LR 667, [1983] CLY 636 at 27 (emphasis added).

3.23 It could be argued that the phrase 'it did not contribute to its own knowledge' (as noted above) is a misleading representation of the testimonial input of the chemists and programmers. When programmers set up instructions (or code) in devices, it is these instructions which are followed by the devices to process the input received. These instructions amount to conditional statements embedded in such devices.[1] But it is clear that the effect of the supporting testimonies of the chemists and programmers is that it is only the non-testimonial parts of the chromatograph and spectrometer outputs – the analysis results – that are being relied on by the courts. In contrast, in *Mehesz v Redman*[2] the electronic evidence of blood alcohol concentration was produced by a chromatograph that had to be calibrated using a pre-prepared standard. The chromatograph was in turn coupled to a data analyser which had to be manually configured by following an instruction manual prior to its use to produce the concentration analysis. Only one of the two analysts who ran the tests testified. He also admitted to not following the instruction manual and making changes to the configuration of the analyser. Bereft of the testimony of the second analyst who ran the second test (two tests were run and the results averaged for the final concentration report), the testimony of the programmer of the data analyser, as well as the instruction manual, the court upheld the objection as to the admissibility of the final printout from the analyser. Zelling J of the South Australian Supreme Court pointed out that because the calibration depended on a standard prepared by somebody, the final result was the average of two analyses and the second person was not called, and because the instructions in the manual were not followed, 'there was no overall evidence called from an expert as to the trustworthiness of the computer itself ... under these circumstances the objection as to hearsay should have been sustained'.[3] Likewise, in *Holt v Auckland City Council*,[4] which concerned a similar setup of a chromatograph with a data analyser (and almost similar lack of evidence), the court held that the final output was 'inadmissible as incorporating hearsay data outside the field of [the analyst's] proven competence'.[5]

1 Steve W. Tepper, 'Testable reliability – a modernized approach to ESI admissibility' (2014) 12(2) Ave Maria L Rev 213, 231–233. For this reason, Tepper argues that *all* output generated by programmed devices is hearsay, 238, 240.
2 (1979) 21 SASR 569.
3 (1979) 21 SASR 569 at 573.
4 [1980] 2 NZLR 124.
5 [1980] 2 NZLR 124 at 128–129.

3.24 There is much to commend in the detailed analyses undertaken in *Mehesz* and *Holt*. They attempt to resolve the different components of the electronic evidence into its testimonial and non-testimonial components, identify the programmers as declarants responsible for each of the components, require each declarant to explain how she was responsible for her respective testimonial component, and justify the results that arise from each non-testimonial component. This analysis approach more accurately reflects the reality that modern-day devices and computers are complex systems[1] subject to inevitable faults and errors,[2] clearly part of the 'heightened reliability and testability' regime proposed by Tepper,[3] and consonant with the principle of maximal inferential individualization advanced by Stein.[4] For instance, if the contents of text messages and email correspondence are to be used testimonially and constitute hearsay, some metadata associated with such messages and correspondence, such as the date and time of transmission and receipt and the routing paths, would be generated by Category 2 devices without human intervention. Such metadata is produced as a consequence of software code, and subject to the tests of authentication, reliability and testability, it could constitute real evidence and be independently admissible.

1 Paul, 'Systems of evidence in the age of complexity'.
2 Peter Bernard Ladkin, 'Robustness of software' (2020) 17 Digital Evidence and Electronic Signature Law Review 15.
3 Tepper, 'Testable reliability', 247–250 (citing in support the decision of *State v Swinton*, 847 A.2d 921 (Conn. 2004) at 924, in which the Supreme Court of Connecticut declared that reliability is an essential precondition of admissibility).
4 'Maximal inferential individualization is the Stein doctrine for describing maximum testing of all individual inferences possible from the evidence. It restates the importance of rules of evidence

and seeks to avoid the use of discretion and ambiguous rules in place of rules of evidence. The point that Stein made is that the rules operate to avoid subjecting the opponent of the evidence to 'the impermissible risk of error', which he called 'a special kind of moral injustice' if it is not avoided (Stein, 'The refoundation of evidence law', 325–326).

3.25 But we caution against treating the test of reliability as the ultimate aim for this hybridized hearsay-authentication analysis of electronic evidence. The concept of 'reliability' is a value-loaded concept that varies depending on, among other things, the specifications of the device, the purposes to which the device has been put and the underlying social concepts that it seeks to protect.[1] For instance, it is well known that devices that operate on neural networks have statistically modelled accuracy, precision and recall measurements of reliability. It is also well known that there are two estimates of such parameters: using the data on hand and using unavailable data. The latter obviously cannot be done ('you do not know what you do not know') and has to be an estimate. This explains why a problem or situation that occurs only outside normal operating parameters (called 'corner cases'), or errors that occur in open environments which subject the device to situations or environments outside normal operating parameters, are so difficult to ascertain. That is not to say that it is impossible to ascertain the 'reliability' of devices and systems: we contend that unexplained and unjustified instances where the device or system is *not* operating as intended is certainly evidence of absence of reliability.

1 For which see Ladkin, 'Robustness of software'.

3.26 Therefore, there is much to be said for treating computing systems and devices as 'the witness'[1] in proceedings. Just as a human witness will be subject to an examination as to his or her experience and qualifications, subjecting the output of a device to the scrutiny of the hearsay rule helps to tease out the embedded human assertions from the results sought to be admitted in evidence – be it the code or its data.[2] If there is no opportunity for the human assertions to be tested – for instance, if the automatically produced analysis is to be relied on but the programmer who wrote the software that generated the analysis is not called to testify – the analysis becomes hearsay.[3] Given that the product of devices will inevitably be based on a multiplicity of, and interplay between, direct and indirect human assertions, not all of which have been validated, let alone completely assessed for their accuracy and correctness,[4] it will be near impossible to call all contributors of these assertions to give evidence in legal proceedings. Therefore, considering that these models entrench various human assertions and even biases, it is more apt to proceed with caution and subject such electronic evidence to closer scrutiny for the 'human input' by placing it into the hybrid Category 3. Of course, this closer scrutiny can be further assisted with a robust approach to authentication of such evidence and to a more effective stance regarding disclosure.

1 For which see, Chapter 4 'Software code as the witness', although note the opinion of Judge Curtis E. A. Karnow in 'The opinion of machines' (2018) 19 Colum Sci & Tech L Rev 136.
2 Arguments have been developed in the US that devices that generate reports as evidence of the accused's commission of an offence, such as breath analysers, would entitle the accused to challenge them on the basis of the Confrontation Clause, as the devices serve as tools of human declarants. See Tepper, 'Testable reliability', citing *Melendez-Diaz v Massachusetts*, 557 U.S. 305, 310–11, 129 S.Ct. 2527, 174 L.Ed.2d 314, 321–22 (2009), at 242–244 in support.
3 See *Mehesz v Redman* (1979) 21 SASR 569; *Holt v Auckland City Council* [1980] 2 NZLR 124.
4 See Chapter 4 and Chapter 5.

Implied assertions

3.27 Since the decision of *Wright v Doe d Tatham*,[1] the law in England and Wales has been that implied assertions from testimonial statements are inadmissible under the rule against hearsay. Although difficult issues may arise in relation to distinguishing implied assertions from the use of such statements as grounding a relevant inference (which falls outside the hearsay rule),[2] this position at common law was later affirmed by a majority of the House of Lords in *R v Kearley*,[3] who held inadmissible, as being irrelevant, calls made to the defendant's number asking to be supplied with drugs as proof that the defendant had intent to supply drugs, or alternatively, inadmissible as hearsay.

1 (1837) 7 A & E 313, 11 ER 1378.
2 See, for instance, *Ratten (Leith McDonald) v Queen, The* [1972] AC 378, [1971] 3 WLR 930, [1971] 3 All ER 801, [1971] 10 WLUK 28, (1972) 56 Cr App R 18, (1971) 115 SJ 889, [1971] CLY 4587.
3 *R. v Blastland (Douglas)* [1986] AC 41, [1985] 3 WLR 345, [1985] 2 All ER 1095, [1985] 7 WLUK 293, (1985) 81 Cr App R 266, [1985] Crim LR 727, [1985] CLY 578; *R v Kearley* [1992] 2 AC 228, [1992] 2 WLR 656, [1992] 2 All ER 345, [1992] 4 WLUK 107, (1992) 95 Cr App R 888, [1992] Crim LR 797, (1992) 89(21) LSG 28, (1992) 142 NLJ 599, Times, 10 April 1992, Independent, 9 April 1992, [1992] CLY 852; see also Diane Birch and Michael Hirst, 'Interpreting the new concept of hearsay' (2010) 69(1) CLJ 72; Greg Taylor, 'Two English hearsay heresies' (2005) 9(2) E & P 110. For the Australian context, see the comments of McHugh J in the Australian case of *Pollitt v R* [1992] HCA 35, (1992) 174 CLR 558 at [21]. Similarly in New Zealand, see *R v Mokaraka* [2002] 1 NZLR 793 (CA).

3.28 In the context of electronic evidence, the circumstances in which the strictness of the rule against implied assertions at common law could apply are legion. In the digital economy, electronic records proliferate with an abundance of unique identification numbers that identify records and documents (e.g. hash numbers, login IDs, registration numbers), labels that identify the nature, origin, provenance or ownership of goods, services or other records (e.g. barcodes and QR codes on product packaging), dates of records and documents and the relationships or identities of persons (e.g. organizational unit attributes and organizational codes used for grouping accounts and corporate entities). In the controversial case of *Myers (James William) v DPP*,[1] the manufacturer's records, made routinely in the course of production, that identified the cars in question as stolen cars because they recorded identification numbers indelibly stamped inside the cylinder blocks, which corresponded to the numbers found in the cylinder blocks of the cars sold by the defendant, were held to be implied assertions and inadmissible as hearsay. A majority of the House of Lords reasoned that the cogency of the records, maintained on microfilm, depended on hearsay, as each witness could not prove that the records were correct or that the numbers which the records contained were in fact the numbers on the car cylinder when it was made by the unknown workmen.[2] While the records in question in *Myers* were microfilm records, even if they were substituted with electronic records, the analysis at common law would remain the same.

1 [1965] AC 1001, [1964] 3 WLR 145, [1964] 2 All ER 881, [1964] 6 WLUK 79, (1964) 48 Cr App R 3488, (1964) 128 JP 481, (1964) 108 SJ 519, [1964] CLY 1461.
2 [1965] AC 1001, see Lord Reid, at 1019; Lord Morris of Borth-y-Gest at 1027; Lord Godson, at 1030. Their Lordships also considered, but dismissed, the application of the business records exception and the public records exception to such records.

3.29 The House of Lords was not unaware of the controversial nature of their decision, but noted that, at common law, the reliability and trustworthiness of records is not an exception to the hearsay rule,[1] and urged legislative reform.[2] However, the statutory treatment of the rule against hearsay is different, depending on whether electronic evidence is adduced in civil proceedings or in criminal proceedings. It is to the statutory rules against hearsay in civil and criminal proceedings and the complex and unique issues that arise in the treatment of electronic evidence that we now turn.[3]

1 For example, see *Kearley*, per Lord Oliver at 276; *Myers*, per Lord Reid at 1023–24.
2 For the virtues or otherwise of this position, see Brenda Marshall, 'Admissibility of implied assertions: towards a reliability-based exception to the hearsay rule' (1997) 23(1) Mon LR 200; Peter Mirfield, 'A final farewell to Kearley', (2012) 128(Jul) LQR 331–337.
3 We observe that the admissibility of the mobile telephone records and chat room records in the following cases does not appear to have been discussed: *R v Davis* [2006] EWCA Crim 1155, [2006] 1 WLR 31300, [2006] 4 All ER 648, [2006] 5 WLUK 528, [2006] 2 Cr App R 322, [2007] Crim LR 70, Times, 1 June 2006, [2006] CLY 989, use of a mobile telephone; *R. v Bailey (Tyrone)* [2008] EWCA Crim 817, [2008] 4 WLUK 498, evidence of a chat room.

Civil proceedings and the requirement to give notice

3.30 In England and Wales, the hearsay rule was abolished for civil proceedings by s 1(1) of the Civil Evidence Act 1995. The Act applies to all civil proceedings,[1] including proceedings in the magistrates' court.[2] A party that intends to adduce hearsay evidence in civil proceedings is required to give the other party or parties notice of his intention and, should it be requested, particulars of the evidence.[3] This requirement to give notice is not unique to England and Wales. A criticism of hearsay evidence said to justify the existence of a rule of exclusion is that admission of hearsay would amount to an unjustified element of surprise causing delay and unwarranted disruption in a proceeding.[4] This criticism has largely been addressed through the power given to any other party to the proceedings, with leave of the court, to call as a witness the person whose hearsay evidence is relied on by the proponent but who is not called as a witness by the proponent, and cross-examine him on the statement.[5] It is noteworthy that pursuant to the notice, hearsay of any degree may be admitted.[6] This is especially relevant in relation to electronic records made in the course of manufacturing or production by various workers, who may or may not be identified, within the organizational hierarchy or chain of responsibility. However, the court may have regard to, among other things, whether the evidence involves multiple hearsay in estimating the weight to be given to such hearsay evidence.[7]

1 Civil Evidence Act 1995, s 11.
2 The Magistrates' Courts (Hearsay Evidence in Civil Proceedings) Rules 1999, SI 1999/681.
3 Civil Evidence Act 1995, s 2.
4 See Chris Gallavin, *Evidence* (LexisNexis 2008) 127. The irony of this justification for the rule of exclusion is that argument over the application of the rule was likely to lead to more delay and greater expense than would otherwise have been the case.
5 Civil Evidence Act 1995, s 3. See also Australia, Evidence Act 1995 (Cth), s 68.
6 Civil Evidence Act 1995, s 1(2)(b).
7 Civil Evidence Act 1995, s 4(2)(c).

3.31 The Act includes a number of exceptions to the hearsay rule that are particularly relevant to documents stored in digital form. Published works dealing with matters of a public nature, public documents and public records are all admissible under the provisions of s 7(2) of the Civil Evidence Act 1995. More distinctively, where a document can be shown to be part of the records of a business or public authority, the document can be received into evidence in civil proceedings without further proof in accordance with s 9, subject to certification procedures[1] that may be dispensed by the court.[2] Subject to the threshold requirement that these records must be part of a 'business', which includes any activity *regularly* carried on over a period of time,[3] the wording of this and similar provisions in other jurisdictions[4] means that the form a technology takes ('records' means 'records in whatever form')[5] will not prevent the admission into evidence of data stored in digital form.

1 Civil Evidence Act 1995, s 9(2).
2 Civil Evidence Act 1995, s 9(5).
3 Civil Evidence Act 1995, s 9(4) (defining 'business'). In contrast in Australia, the business records exception does not apply to records prepared or obtained for the purposes of conducting proceedings, or were made in connection with an investigation leading to criminal proceedings. Australia, Evidence Act 1995 (Cth), s 69(3).
4 See New Zealand Evidence Act 2006, s 20; Australia, Evidence Act 1995 (Cth), s 69.
5 Civil Evidence Act 1995, s 9(4)(a).

3.32 Finally, it is noteworthy that s 9(3) of the Civil Evidence Act enables the absence of an entry in the records of a business or public authority to be proved by affidavit of the relevant officer of that business or authority. This addresses the problem of 'negative hearsay', in which evidential significance is attributed to the absence of the requisite records of a business or public authority. Of course, to enable the requisite conclusions to be drawn, especially in relation to electronic records or electronic databases, the necessary foundation evidence as to, among other things, good record-keeping practices must first be established.

Criminal proceedings

3.33 In England and Wales, the enactment of the Criminal Justice Act 2003 repealed the provisions relating to hearsay in the Criminal Justice Act 1988, and by doing so, abrogated most of the common law of hearsay,[1] substituting in its place a statutory regime for admitting hearsay[2] and multiple hearsay.[3] The operative provision is s 114(1), which reads:

> Admissibility of hearsay evidence
>
> (1) In criminal proceedings a statement not made in oral evidence in the proceedings is admissible as evidence of any matter stated if, but only if—
>
> > (a) any provision of this Chapter or any other statutory provision makes it admissible,
> >
> > (b) any rule of law preserved by section 118 makes it admissible,
> >
> > (c) all parties to the proceedings agree to it being admissible, or
> >
> > (d) the court is satisfied that it is in the interests of justice for it to be admissible.

1 Previously, where a computer recorded the numbers of various components that were fitted to motor cars, the printout was a hearsay statement where it was offered in evidence to prove that a number of components were fitted to a specific motor car: *Myers (James William) v DPP* [1965] AC 1001, [1964] 3 WLR 145, [1964] 2 All ER 881, [1964] 6 WLUK 79, (1964) 48 Cr App R 3488, (1964) 128 JP 481, (1964) 108 SJ 519, [1964] CLY 1461; Michael Hirst, 'Hearsay, confessions and mobile telephones' (2011) 75(6) JCL 482, 483.

2 *Cross & Tapper*, 611.
3 Criminal Justice Act 2003, s 121. Evidence from a Police Incident Log was wrongly admitted under s 117 at trial, but on appeal the members of the court decided that the evidence was correctly admitted under s 121(c): *Maher v DPP* [2006] EWHC 1271 (Admin), [2006] 5 WLUK 333, (2006) 170 JP 441, (2006) 170 JPN 780, [2006] CLY 789.

3.34 The provisions of s 114 serve as an introductory provision to the other provisions in that chapter. The operative scope of s 114 and the other provisions lies in the definition of a 'statement' as a representation of fact or opinion made by a person by whatever means, not made in oral evidence in the proceedings, but sought to be admissible *as evidence of any matter stated.*[1] A matter stated is something which the maker of the statement intended someone (generally the recipient) to believe or to act upon, or to cause a machine to operate.[2] Thus defined, s 114 retains the default exclusion of the hearsay rule in relation to statements intended to be acted on (express assertions), and operates to admit them in criminal proceedings within the parameters set out in s 114(1)(a)–(d) (although a number of common law exceptions are retained in statutory form by virtue of s 118(1) Criminal Justice Act 2003).

1 Criminal Justice Act 2003, s 114(1) read with s 115(2).
2 Criminal Justice Act 1995, s 115(3); *R. v Twist (Andrew Terence)* [2011] EWCA Crim 1143, [2011] 3 All ER 1055, [2011] 5 WLUK 320, [2011] 2 Cr App R 17, (2011) 175 JP 257, [2011] Crim LR 793, [2011] CLY 584.

3.35 In contrast, statements that are not intended to be acted on (implied assertions) fall outside the definition of a 'statement' as defined[1] and are admissible pursuant to the abolition of the common law rules governing the admissibility of hearsay evidence in criminal proceedings.[2] This has the effect of reversing the common law position in *R v Kearley*,[3] but with the proliferation of records of electronic communications and the ubiquity of their use, it has in turn opened up new considerations regarding the scope of the rule as regards implied assertions and their relevance to the issues.

1 See also the definition of 'statement' in New Zealand: Evidence Act 2006, s 4; in Australia, Evidence Act 1995 (Cth), s 59(1). See also Australian Law Reform Commission, *Uniform Evidence Law* (Report No 102, 2006) paras 7.19–7.22, http://www.alrc.gov.au/publications/7.%20The%20Hearsay%20Rule%20and%20Section%2060/unintended-assertions.
2 Criminal Justice Act 2003, s 118(2). See also *R. v Singh (Alexander Sukadave)* [2006] EWCA Crim 660, [2006] 1 WLR 1564, [2006] 2 WLUK 590, [2006] 2 Cr App R 12, (2006) 170 JP 222, [2006] Crim LR 647, (2006) 170 JPN 571, Times, 8 March 2006, [2006] CLY 787, also known as *R. v Singh (Alexander Sukadeve), R. v Singh (Alexander Sukedave)*, at [14].
3 As explained in *R. v Singh (Alexander Sukadave)* [2006] EWCA Crim 660 at [14].

Telephone calls and messages

3.36 We start with the cases that deal with the inclusion of evidence of telephone calls and text messages sent on mobile telephones, especially in relation to cases involving illegal drugs, that have caused some confusion. For instance, in *R v Chrysostomou (Mark)*[1] the trial judge admitted four text messages, apparently sent to the appellant by someone called 'John' who attempted to set up a supply of drugs, as evidence that the appellant was a dealer in drugs. In giving judgment for the court, Aikens LJ agreed that the text messages were not caught by the statutory code on hearsay in the Criminal Justice Act on the basis that the messages were adduced, not to prove, as fact, any matters stated in the messages, but 'as evidence of an underlying state of affairs, which was the basis on which "John" apparently sent the texts to the appellant, namely that the appellant dealt with drugs and so could meet John's demands'.[2] In his commentary, Professor Ormerod agreed with the conclusion reached by Aikens LJ but disagreed with the reasoning, pointing out that the text messages were actually relied upon for the truth of the implied assertion contained in the message that the accused was a dealer in illegal drugs. This, however, did not render the message hearsay because, as Professor Ormerod noted,[3] for a statement to be hearsay, the purpose of making the statement must be to cause another to believe the matter or to act on the matter stated,[4] while 'the purpose of the texter ["John"] was *not* to cause [the appellant] C to believe/act on his being a dealer'.[5]

1 [2010] EWCA Crim 1403, [2010] 6 WLUK 547, [2010] Crim LR 942, [2011] CLY 609.
2 [2010] EWCA Crim 1403 at [28].
3 See the analysis of this precise point by Professor Ormerod: 'R. v Bains: evidence – hearsay – admissibility of mobile phone text messages', in which he cites *R. v Singh (Alexander Sukadave)* [2006] EWCA Crim 660, [2006] 1 WLR 1564, [2006] 2 WLUK 590, [2006] 2 Cr App R 12, (2006) 170 JP 222, [2006] Crim LR 647, (2006) 170 JPN 571, Times, 8 March 2006, [2006] CLY 787, also known as *R. v Singh (Alexander Sukadeve), R. v Singh (Alexander Sukedave)*; *R. v Mayers (Jordan)* [2009] 1 WLR 1915, [2009] 2 All ER 145, [2008] EWCA Crim 2989, [2008] 12 WLUK 373, [2009] 1 Cr App R 30, [2009] Crim LR 272, [2009] CLY 768; *R. v Leonard (Mark Alan)* [2009] 4 WLUK 482, [2009] EWCA Crim 1251, (2009) 173 JP 366, [2009] Crim LR 802, [2009] CLY 756; *R. v Fox (Craig)* [2010] EWCA Crim 1280, [2010] 4 WLUK 461; *R. v Bains (Pardeep Singh)* [2010] EWCA Crim 873, [2010] Crim LR 937; regarding inferences to be drawn from the absence of an entry on a record, see *R. v Shone (Robert Dowson)* [1982] 6 WLUK 185, (1983) 76 Crim LR 72, [1983] CLY 666; M. Khan, 'Hearsay' (1984) 48(1) JCL 25, 25–27; Ben Fitzpatrick, 'Criminal Justice Act 2003: hearsay provisions' (2006) 70(5) Journal of Criminal Law 372; Ben Fitzpatrick, 'Criminal Justice Act 2003: hearsay – implied assertions' (2006) 70(5) Journal of Criminal Law 398.
4 Criminal Justice Act 2003, s 114(1) read with s 115(3)(a), (b).
5 [2010] Crim LR 942 (note), 944 (emphasis added).

3.37 In contrast, in *R. v Leonard (Mark Alan)* the members of the Court of Appeal (Criminal Division) determined that two text messages sent by unknown people to the appellant on two separate mobile telephones were hearsay evidence, and should not have been admitted at trial in support of the case for the Crown that the appellant was a drug dealer (with the prosecution conceding that the evidence would not have been admitted following a consideration of all the factors set out in s 114(2)). The messages were set out as follows:

> The first, timed at 10.24 on 2nd May 2008, reads:
>
> 'Cheers for yday! Well sound gear:-S! feel well wankered today!'
>
> The second text message was from a different phone number and was on the second mobile phone. It was timed at 10.51 on 6th May 2008. It read:
>
> 'Mark, that was a proper dog cunt move mate, that joey was a £5 joey and that was my last £10. Thanks. I dont why I think u would not do that 2 me. I dont.[1]

1 [2009] EWCA Crim 1251 at [3].

3.38 It was assumed that the content described feedback on the quality of the drugs purported to have been supplied (the first one positive and the second one negative). Professor Ormerod considered the decision by the Court of Appeal to be incorrect because the Crown did not rely on the content of the text messages for the truth of whether the quality was good or bad, or the nature of what had been supplied. The issue was whether the appellant was the supplier of a controlled drug, not the quality of the drugs supplied, which was irrelevant.[1] This must be undoubtedly correct, and the argument illustrates the absurdity of the largely arbitrary line between hearsay and non-hearsay statements.

1 See *MK, R v* [2007] EWCA Crim 3150, [2007] 12 WLUK 47, (2008) 172 JP 538, (2008) 172 JPN 757, [2009] CLY 752, where a conversation over a telephone captured by covert recording equipment was not considered to be hearsay, and it was therefore admissible without having to comply with the statutory provisions relating to hearsay.

3.39 The Court of Appeal considered an entire set of electronic messages and their use in inculpating the defendants in *R. v Twist (Andrew Terence)*,[1] where the issue was the admissibility of text messages sent over mobile telephones as evidence against various defendants for a variety of offences. In determining the general approach to take as to whether the hearsay rules in the Criminal Justice Act applied, Hughes LJ set out the following approach:

> i) identify what relevant fact (matter) it is sought to prove;[2]
>
> ii) ask whether there is a statement of **that matter** in the communication. If no, then no question of hearsay arises (whatever other matters may be contained in the communication);
>
> iii) If yes, ask whether it was one of the purposes (not necessarily the only or dominant purpose) of the maker of the communication that the recipient, or any other person, should believe **that matter** or act upon it as true? If yes, it is hearsay. If no, it is not.[3]

1 [2011] EWCA Crim 1143, [2011] 3 All ER 1055, [2011] 5 WLUK 320, [2011] 2 Cr App R 17, (2011) 175 JP 257, [2011] Crim LR 793, [2011] CLY 584; note the criticism of Hirst, 'Hearsay, confessions and mobile telephones', 491–493.
2 Hughes LJ indicated at [11] that it must be a relevant matter.
3 [2011] EWCA Crim 1143 at [17], emphasis in the original.

3.40 Hughes LJ went on, at [18], to indicate that the 'answers to these questions will be case-sensitive. The same communication may sometimes be hearsay and sometimes not, depending on the matter for which it is relied upon and the fact which it is sought to prove.'[1] While correct, this line of argument emphasizes the largely arbitrary nature of the distinction. A text message commenting on the quality of drugs bought will not be a hearsay statement[2] (even if they could amount to an implied assertion that the recipient was a drug supplier, the purpose of the sender(s) did not include causing him or anyone else to believe that he was[3]) and can be adduced in support of a contention that the recipient actually sold drugs. However, a statement to the effect of 'thanks for selling me those drugs' will be inadmissible hearsay because it contains a statement that the recipient had sold drugs. An argument might be made that what was sought to be established was the state of mind of the maker of the message, not whether drugs were actually sold by the recipient of the message. Depending on the issue to be proved, this argument may render the statement admissible.

1 Note the criticism by Hirst, 'Hearsay, confessions and mobile telephones', 491–492.
2 Assuming *Leonard (Mark Alan)* was decided wrongly as it was based on the concession by prosecution, as Hughes LJ noted [2011] EWCA Crim 1143 at [24].
3 [2011] EWCA Crim 1143 at [29].

3.41 The tests set out in *R. v Twist (Andrew Terence)* were considered in the case of *R. v Midmore (Billy Nathan)*,[1] where a WhatsApp message containing an image of a box of sulphuric acid with the caption 'This is the one face melter' was considered by the trial judge to be hearsay. The members of the Court of Appeal determined it was not hearsay. One commentator considered this analysis to be unsound,[2] because in relation to the second question in *Twist* (the question of relevance of the statement), it does not appear that there was a statement of the matter sought to be proved. McKeown suggested that the image, taken with the caption:

> appears to be little more than a straightforward implied representation that One Shot was capable of causing serious harm to a person's face. Yet the court read it as a representation by GM to his girlfriend that he had purchased the One Shot with the intention of using it to cause serious injury to C by throwing it over her face. This surely goes too far, and exposes a risk with the *Twist* formula for identifying hearsay if it is now to be used in relation to implied representations.[3]

1 [2017] EWCA Crim 533, [2017] 4 WLR 107, [2017] 4 WLUK 529, [2017] 2 Cr App R 8, (2017) 181 JP 354, [2017] Crim LR 793, [2017] CLY 512.
2 Paul McKeown, 'Evidence: R. v Midmore' (2017) Crim LR 793.
3 (2017) Crim LR 796.

3.42 McKeown suggested that '[S]ince implied representations may now potentially be hearsay, a question arises as to whether the Twist formula should continue to be followed'[1] and that another approach to identifying hearsay could be as follows:

> (i) What is the matter stated, i.e. what is the express or implied representation in the statement? Where the representation is implied, care should be taken not to read something into it which is not there;
>
> (ii) Is the party seeking to admit the statement for a purpose other than as evidence to establish the matter stated? If so, the statement is not hearsay and is admissible if it is relevant, subject to exclusion;
>
> (iii) If the party is seeking to admit the statement as evidence to establish the matter stated, was one of the purposes of the maker of the statement to cause someone to believe or act, or a machine to operate, etc. on the basis that what is stated is true?
>
> If yes, it is hearsay and inadmissible unless it is relevant and can pass through a statutory exception, subject to exclusion. If no, it is not hearsay and is admissible if it is relevant, subject to exclusion.[2]

1 (2017) Crim LR 798.
2 (2017) Crim LR 798.

3.43 To conclude that anything inferred from a statement is not hearsay, whereas anything directly stated is, is to establish a distinction that dances on the head of a pin. The better approach is to treat all types of assertion – express or intended *and* implied or unintended – as prima facie hearsay and leave their admission to the judge on the basis of an analysis of a list of balancing criteria.

3.44 With the abolition of implied or unintended assertions from the scope of the hearsay rule, not all assertions made with the intention to communicate will be qualifying hearsay statements. The inadmissible hearsay assertion has to be associated with the object for which it is tendered in evidence in support, failing which it could be admissible as an implied or unintended assertion. To amplify McKeown's point, to enable the admission of implied representations as to the supposed mental state of the maker of the statement presupposes the relevance of such mental state in the first place. If sanctioned, this could allow for all statements to be classified as implied statements and bypass the hearsay exclusion against express statements. Indeed this was the concern that was well recognized at common law.[1] In the same vein, Professor Hirst observed that if there is nothing to prove an established relationship, or an incriminating response or reaction from the defendant, the assertion may be inadmissible, regardless of whether it is hearsay or not.[2]

1 *R. v Blastland (Douglas)* [1986] AC 41, [1985] 3 WLR 345, [1985] 2 All ER 1095, [1985] 7 WLUK 293, (1985) 81 Cr App R 266, [1985] Crim LR 727, [1985] CLY 578, holding that statements indicating knowledge of a third party of the commission of a murder were irrelevant to the issue of whether the murder was committed by him or by the accused.

2 Hirst, 'Hearsay, confessions and mobile telephones', 491 fn 25, citing *R. v O'Connell (William)* [2003] EWCA Crim 502, [2003] 2 WLUK 291.

3.45 This illustrates the fundamental weakness of the rule. By excluding unintended assertions, there is a possibility that arbitrary limits may arise in that the difference between a hearsay statement and a non-hearsay statement will rest with the question of whether there exists an intention to communicate. The existence of an intention to communicate is of such little value as to render the distinction meaningless. Furthermore, such a distinction exposes the application of the exclusionary rule to the formulation of a clever submission of a lawyer in that the application of the rule might be avoided by classifying the statement as a reflection of the mindset of the maker as opposed to an intention of the maker, an approach made plausible given the ubiquity and accessibility of electronic devices. In such a case, no real distinguishing factor truly exists.

Representations other than by a person

3.46 Of particular relevance to electronic evidence is s 129 Criminal Justice Act 2003. It reads:

> 129 Representations other than by a person
>
> (1) Where a representation of any fact—
>
> > (a) is made otherwise than by a person, but
> >
> > (b) depends for its accuracy on information supplied (directly or indirectly) by a person, the representation is not admissible in criminal proceedings as evidence of the fact unless it is proved that the information was accurate.
>
> (2) Subsection (1) does not affect the operation of the presumption that a mechanical device has been properly set or calibrated.

3.47 The UK Law Commission considered the admissibility of a computer printout, whether it is hearsay, and whether the printout itself is relevant:

> The question is, on what basis should such evidence be excluded? One view is that it is hearsay, because it is tantamount to a statement made by the person who fed the data into the machine. An alternative view is that the statement by the machine, properly understood, is conditional on the accuracy of the data on which it is based; and that, if those data are not proved to have been accurate, the statement therefore has no probative value at all. The question of hearsay does not arise, because the statement is simply irrelevant.
>
> We believe that the latter view is closer to the truth, and that it is therefore unnecessary to complicate our hearsay rule by extending it to statements made by machines on the basis of human input. On the other hand we do not think it

> would be safe to assume that everyone will share this view. We must anticipate the argument that, if such statements are inadmissible at present, that is because they are hearsay; that, under our recommendations, they would no longer be hearsay, because our formulation of the rule would apply only to representations made by people; and that they would therefore cease to be inadmissible.[1]

1 Law Commission, *Evidence in Criminal Proceedings: Hearsay and Related Topics* (Law Com No 245, 1997) paras 7.48–7.49.

3.48 The effect of s 129 is to treat not as hearsay and as admissible representations of any fact made in a document emanating from a device that is adduced to prove something other than the truth of a statement previously entered into them by a human being.[1] They are admissible subject to proof of the accuracy of any information supplied by a human to such a device,[2] including its proper setup and calibration.[3] But as previously noted, the proper treatment of such representations of facts by devices or machines requires a proper categorization of the function of such devices, and an identification and subsequent characterization of the different parts of the representation, as to whether they emanate from the device or are made by a person or persons.

1 *Cross & Tapper*, 614.
2 Criminal Justice Act 2003, s 129(1) proviso.
3 Criminal Justice Act 2003, s 129(2).

3.49 This may be illustrated by the Australian case of *Hansen Beverage Company v Bickfords (Australia) Pty Ltd.*[1] In this case, working television sets in homes were monitored by a meter system that recorded that a person was physically located in the home when he registered his presence by pressing a button when a television was on. This was for the purposes of establishing the size of the audience that might be watching a particular programme. That the evidence was produced on a printout and was automatically recorded by software was not at issue. It was argued that the evidence was not hearsay as there was no previous representation made by a person, as required by s 59(1) of the Australian Evidence Act 1995. Middleton J, it is suggested correctly, identified the evidence as hearsay because it was a representation of fact that a certain number of people clicked on the buttons. The judge commented:

> Undoubtedly, Hansen seeks to prove the estimated audience sizes for a particular program derived by statistical methods from the data, but such data is not automatically recorded by the meters without the human intervention of deliberately pressing the button to show a person or persons are in the room where the television is on. When the people are in the room they intend to, and do, make the representation to assert the existence of this fact, the existence of which needs to be proved to form the basis of the statistical analysis. It seems to me that the necessary reliance by Hansen on the data derived from the sample homes must involve the representation ... by a person that the person was in the room on the relevant occasion, namely when the television is operating.[2]

1 [2008] FCA 406.
2 [2008] FCA 406 at [125].

Body-worn camera footage

3.50 Body-worn cameras have rapidly become a normal feature of policing.[1] In *McGuinness v The Public Prosecution Service for Northern Ireland*,[2] on appeal by way of case stated from the County Court for the Division of Londonderry, the question arose whether the trial judge was correct to admit the recording from a body-worn video camera, which documented allegations made by the complainant of assault by the appellant, under the hearsay provisions of the Criminal Justice (Evidence) (Northern Ireland) Order 2004, in particular under articles 18(1)(b) and 22(1)(4)(a). Although the complainant withdrew her complaint, the appellant was charged and tried of the offence. The complainant was not called to give evidence, because she was reconciled to the appellant.

1 For a general introduction, see Ben Bowling and Shruit Iyer, 'Automated policing: the case of body-worn video' (2019) 15(2) Int JLC 140.
2 [2017] NICA 30, [2017] 5 WLUK 19.

3.51 In reaching their decision, the members of the Court of Appeal in Northern Ireland considered the tests set out by Lord Ackner in *R. v Andrews (Donald Joseph)*[1] under the doctrine of *res gestae* exception to the hearsay rule where a conversation took place in such circumstances that the possibility of concoction or distortion by the victim could be disregarded:

> 1. The primary question which the judge must ask himself is – can the possibility of concoction or distortion be disregarded?
>
> 2. To answer that question the judge must first consider the circumstances in which the particular statement was made, in order to satisfy himself that the event was so unusual or startling or dramatic as to dominate the thoughts of the victim, so that his utterance was an instinctive reaction to that event, thus giving no real opportunity for reasoned reflection. In such a situation the judge would be entitled to conclude that the involvement or the pressure of the event would exclude the possibility of concoction or distortion, providing that the statement was made in conditions of approximate but not exact contemporaneity.
>
> 3. In order for the statement to be sufficiently 'spontaneous' it must be so closely associated with the event which has excited the statement, that it can be fairly stated that the mind of the declarant was still dominated by the event. Thus the judge must be satisfied that the event, which provided the trigger mechanism for the statement, was still operative. The fact that the statement was made in answer to a question is but one factor to consider under this heading.
>
> 4. Quite apart from the time factor, there may be special features in the case, which relate to the possibility of concoction or distortion. ... The judge must be satisfied that the circumstances were such that having regard to the special feature of malice, there was no possibility of any concoction or distortion to the advantage of the maker or the disadvantage of the accused.
>
> 5. As to the possibility of error in the facts narrated in the statement, if only the ordinary fallibility of human recollection is relied upon, this goes to the weight to be attached to and not to the admissibility of the statement and is therefore a matter for the jury. However, here again there may be special features that may give rise to the possibility of error. ... In such circumstances the trial judge must consider whether he can exclude the possibility of error.[2]

1 [1987] AC 281, [1987] 2 WLR 413, [1987] 1 All ER 513, [1987] 2 WLUK 72, (1987) 84 Cr App R 382, [1987] Crim LR 487, (1987) 151 JPN 254, [1987] CLY 659.
2 [1987] AC 281 at 300G–301F.

3.52 In giving the judgment of the court, Weatherup LJ said, at [36]:

> In the exercise of the discretion whether to exclude the evidence, the Judge considered each of the factors set out in Article 18(2) of the 2004 Order before deciding to admit the body-cam video statement of the complainant under the res gestae exception. The recording was stated to have strong probative value, there was other evidence from the two police officers as to the condition of and the injuries to the complainant, the recording was very important, there was no indication that the complainant was other than reliable, the evidence of the making of the recording was reliable and the complainant was unwilling to give evidence because of reconciliation. As to the appellant's difficulty in challenging the statement and the likely prejudice arising, there was stated to be some such difficulty and some prejudice but not such as to render unfair the admission of the evidence.

3.53 The court noted, at [41], that the prosecution relied on the *res gestae* exception in order to provide support to the complainant in the changed circumstances brought about by the reconciliation of the parties, while seeking to deal with the alleged previous conduct of the appellant. The prosecution had to balance the competing interests when deciding to prosecute the appellant. The trial judge was correct to admit the recording under the statutory provisions.

3.54 The *res gestae* exception at common law has been expressly preserved in the Criminal Justice Act 2003.[1]

1 s 118(4).

3.55 The case of *DPP v Young*[1] has a similar set of circumstances. The complainant was not able to appear to give evidence. The prosecution sought the admission of an audio recording of a 999 call and a recording from a body-worn video camera from one of the police officers attending the scene. Both items of evidence overlapped, because the telephone line on which the 999 call was made remained open up to the time the police officers attended the scene, and the telephone recording contained identical evidence to that in the body-worn video camera recording. Both recordings were admitted as real evidence. No consideration was given to the tests set out in *R. v Andrews (Donald Joseph)*. The defence submitted that there was no case to answer, given, it was argued, that the evidence was tenuous in nature, weak and vague. The lay magistrates accepted the submission and dismissed the case against the defendant. The Divisional Court quashed the decision of the justices. Lord Justice Holroyde, in giving the judgment, indicated, at [19]:

> Having considered the evidence which was before the justices, for my part, I have no doubt that the evidence was sufficient to support a conviction and that the submission of no case to answer should have been rejected. Indeed, I very much doubt whether the submission should ever have been made. There was before the justices clear evidence that Ms Robertshaw made a 999 call to the effect that a man was going berserk at her home. Given the speed with which the police officers arrived on the scene and the overlap of recordings to which I have referred, there could be no realistic doubt but that the man concerned was the respondent. There was then a clear audio recording from which, in my view, a reasonable bench, properly directed, undoubtedly could find that the 999 call recorded an assault actually taking place with the victim of that assault uttering cries of pain against a background of sounds of physical exertion by the respondent. In those circumstances it was, in my judgment, not properly open

> to the justices to allow the submission of no case to answer. Whether at the conclusion of all the evidence they would have convicted is of course a separate matter. The issue they had to determine, and in respect of which in my judgment they fell into error, was whether a reasonable bench, properly directed, could properly convict.

1 [2018] EWHC 3616 (Admin), [2018] 12 WLUK 76.

Business and other documents

3.56 In this regard, it is useful to start with a review of the cases that considered s 24 of the Criminal Justice Act 1988. This provision, concerning the admission in criminal proceedings of business and other documents, was the predecessor provision to s 117 of the Criminal Justice Act 2003. In *Brown v Secretary of State for Social Security*,[1] the Secretary of State adduced evidence of statements from computer records by way of two witnesses where the identity of the persons who supplied the information could not be established. It was submitted on behalf of the appellant that the two statements were inadmissible because they did not comply with the terms of s 24. Section 24 was written to enable business documents to be admissible without the need to call the maker where the documents formed part of records about which the maker could not be expected to know anything in detail, and which were created in the course of trade or business. The members of the Divisional Court, Balcombe LJ and Collins J, agreed that the statements were not admissible under s 24(4) of the Criminal Justice Act 1988 'as there was no evidence that it was impossible that the makers of the statements would have no recollection of the matters referred to in their statements'.[2] In comparison, the members of the Court of Appeal (Criminal Division) in the case of *R. v Derodra (Kishor)*,[3] rightly it is suggested, admitted the contents of a police 'CRIS' report, which was a computerized record of incidents of crime under s 24. In this instance, the person who reported the crime to the police – the lodger of the appellant – could not be found to give evidence of his complaint. It was the statement of the lodger that was to be relied upon testimonially, not that of the police officer who made the relevant entry.[4]

1 [1994] 11 WLUK 283, [1995] COD 260, Times, 7 December 1994, [1994] CLY 904.
2 [1995] COD 260 at 262.
3 [1999] 5 WLUK 342, [2000] 1 Cr App R 41, [1999] Crim LR 978, Independent, 10 June 1999, [1999] CLY 873.
4 *R. v Derodra (Kishor)* [1999] 5 WLUK 342, [2000] 1 Cr App R 41, [1999] Crim LR 978, Independent, 10 June 1999, [1999] CLY 873; note the criticism by Roderick Munday, 'Section 24 of the Criminal Justice Act 1988: the great escape' (1999) 7 Arch News 5.

3.57 In *Vehicle and Operator Services Agency v George Jenkins Transport Limited*,[1] the prosecution had to prove that certain commercial drivers had failed to properly record their journeys with the tachographs in their vehicles, and had worked beyond the number of hours that were permitted without the prescribed rest periods or breaks. To discharge this burden, the prosecution sought to put in evidence a number of drivers' time sheets pursuant to s 24. On a preliminary point, the trial judge ruled them inadmissible and dismissed all charges against the defendants. The prosecutor appealed, and the appeal raised a number of issues regarding the interpretation of these provisions. First, the provisions in s 24, described by Mackay J at [10] as 'criteria or gateway' provisions,[2] must be satisfied before the second issue is addressed, that is whether the documents in question can be admitted in evidence. Mackay J quoted[3] from the judgment of Roch LJ in *R. v Foxley (Gordon)*:

> Section 24 deals with the statements in a document and makes such statements admissible of any fact of which direct oral evidence would be admissible if two conditions are satisfied. The wording of condition (ii) demonstrates that Parliament anticipated that courts would draw inferences as to the personal knowledge of the person supplying the information of the matters dealt with. The purpose of section 24 is to enable the document to speak for itself; the safeguard being the two conditions and the other statutory provisions applicable, for example in the case of a statement made for the purpose of a criminal investigation, one of the requirements of section 23(2) or the requirements of section 23(3) have to be fulfilled.[4]

1 [2003] EWHC 2879 (Admin), [2003] 11 WLUK 528, Times, 5 December 2003, [2004] CLY 3852.
2 *R. v Foxley (Gordon)* [1995] 2 WLUK 75, [1995] 2 Cr App R 523, [1995] 16 Cr App R (S) 879, [1995] Crim LR 636, Times, 9 February 1995, Independent, 3 April 1995 [1995] CLY 918.
3 [2003] EWHC 2879 (Admin) at [24].
4 [1995] 2 WLUK 75, [1995] 2 Cr App R 523 at 536F–G, [1995] 2 Cr App Rep 523, [1995] 16 Cr App R (S) 879, [1995] Crim LR 636, Times, 9 February 1995, Independent, 3 April 1995, [1995] CLY 918.

3.58 In this instance, Mackay J and Kennedy LJ agreed that the documents satisfied the criteria provisions, and were admissible and self-proving in evidence.[1] Kennedy LJ also noted the criticisms that Professor Smith made of the decision in *R. v Foxley (Gordon)*, although it was observed that a further analysis of another case[2] by Professor Smith was capable of applying to the case in hand if it was adjusted slightly.[3]

1 [2003] EWHC 2879 (Admin) at [30], [34].
2 *R. v Ilyas (Mohammed); R. v Knight (Paul)* [1996] 5 WLUK 330, [1996] Crim LR 810.
3 [2003] EWHC 2879 (Admin) at [34].

3.59 Section 24 is succeeded by s 117 of the Criminal Justice Act 2003. Section 117(1) to (5) reads:

> Business and other documents
>
> (1) In criminal proceedings a statement contained in a document is admissible as evidence of any matter stated if—
>
> > (a) oral evidence given in the proceedings would be admissible as evidence of that matter,
> >
> > (b) the requirements of subsection (2) are satisfied, and
> >
> > (c) the requirements of subsection (5) are satisfied, in a case where subsection (4) requires them to be.
>
> (2) The requirements of this subsection are satisfied if—
>
> > (a) the document or the part containing the statement was created or received by a person in the course of a trade, business, profession or other occupation, or as the holder of a paid or unpaid office,
> >
> > (b) the person who supplied the information contained in the statement (the relevant person) had or may reasonably be supposed to have had personal knowledge of the matters dealt with, and
> >
> > (c) each person (if any) through whom the information was supplied from the relevant person to the person mentioned in paragraph (a) received the information in the course of a trade, business, profession or other occupation, or as the holder of a paid or unpaid office.
>
> (3) The persons mentioned in paragraphs (a) and (b) of subsection (2) may be the same person.

(4) The additional requirements of subsection (5) must be satisfied if the statement—

(a) was prepared for the purposes of pending or contemplated criminal proceedings, or for a criminal investigation, but

(b) was not obtained pursuant to a request under section 7 of the Crime (International Co-operation) Act 2003 (c. 32) or an order under paragraph 6 of Schedule 13 to the Criminal Justice Act 1988 (c. 33) (which relate to overseas evidence).

(5) The requirements of this subsection are satisfied if—

(a) any of the five conditions mentioned in section 116(2) is satisfied (absence of relevant person etc), or

(b) the relevant person cannot reasonably be expected to have any recollection of the matters dealt with in the statement (having regard to the length of time since he supplied the information and all other circumstances).

3.60 The provisions of s 117, dealing with the business document exception, are very wide and permit the admission into evidence of multiple hearsay,[1] although the various foundational conditions set out in s 117 must be satisfied. In *R. v Humphris (Andrew James)*,[2] the Crown sought to adduce evidence of the appellant's previous convictions under s 117. For that purpose, they relied on a statement of Police Officer Grimes, who retrieved relevant records from the Essex Police computer facility, the contents of which were in turn derived from staff of the Essex Police Force, who acted under a duty to record information and who either had or may reasonably be supposed to have had personal knowledge of the matters dealt with in the records. These records were attached to Police Officer Grimes' statement. Section 117 provides certain conditions that must be fulfilled before evidence can be admitted. The defence accepted that the provisions of s 117(2)(a) were complied with, but argued that for each record of the appellant's previous conviction, s 117(2)(b) required the statement to have been obtained from each complainant as the relevant person, rather than the police officer who recorded the information. Although Lord Woolfe upheld the conviction of the appellant, he agreed and held that the necessary foundations for the admissibility of the evidence were not properly laid.

1 A point made by Professor Tapper, when he indicated that some electronic information will be collated from other statements, thus constituting multiple hearsay: Colin Tapper, 'Electronic evidence and the Criminal Justice Act 2003' (2004) 10 CTLR 161; an example would be proving the links of the continuity of evidence between the withdrawal of cash from an ATM to demonstrating the entering of the transaction in the customer's account.

2 [2005] EWCA Crim 2030, [2005] 7 WLUK 538, (2005) 169 JP 441, (2005) 169 JPN 718, Times, 19 September 2005, [2006] CLY 813; for a similar point, also see *Maher v DPP* [2006] EWHC 1271 (Admin), [2006] 5 WLUK 333, (2006) 170 JP 441, (2006) 170 JPN 780, [2006] CLY 789.

3.61 Where a document is put in under the provisions of s 114 and s 117, care must be taken over any content that is hearsay.[1] In addition, the trial judge must ensure that the members of the jury understand the purpose of admitting the document. In *R. v Horncastle (Michael Christopher)*,[2] there was an email statement made by an ISP which identified the appellant and his address as being the possible holder of an email account suspected to have been used to send abusive images of children. The ISP acknowledged that this information could have been supplied by the email account holder impersonating the appellant. The prosecution adduced this email to show the address of the place (the appellant's home) where the police raid took place, but not to prove the fact that the account was that of the appellant or used by the appellant. (In fact, no evidence of abusive images of children was found on the appellant's computer, although there was evidence that the appellant's lodger had used the email account.) No directions were given by the trial judge as to the limited purpose for which the ISP's email was adduced. On appeal, Thomas LJ held that the judge's failure to explain the use was a material misdirection, as the jury could have used the ISP's email to link the appellant to the email account. The appellant's appeal was allowed and his conviction was set aside.

1 For an example of where a printout from the Police National Computer was correctly admitted into evidence, all of the conditions under s 117 having been met, see *R. (on the application of Wellington) v DPP* [2007] EWHC 1061 (Admin), [2007] 5 WLUK 5, (2007) 171 JP 497, (2007) 171 JPN 868, [2007] CLY 836.
2 [2009] EWCA Crim 964, [2009] 4 All ER 183, [2009] 5 WLUK 566, [2009] 2 Cr App R 15, (2009) 153(21) SJLB 28, Times, 3 June 2009, [2009] CLY 761; note also *DPP v Leigh* [2010] EWHC 345 (Admin), [2010] 2 WLUK 136, where the prosecution did not rely on a record for the purpose of establishing the veracity of any of the matters recorded.

Judicial discretion to include hearsay

3.62 Notwithstanding the other routes of admissibility in s 114(1), one particularly wide[1] route is to admit hearsay evidence 'in the interests of justice' under s 114(1)(d),[2] subject only to the conditions in s 114(2).

1 For example, see *R. v Humphris (Andrew James)* [2005] EWCA Crim 2030, [2005] 7 WLUK 538, (2005) 169 JP 441, (2005) 169 JPN 718, Times, 19 September 2005, [2006] CLY 813.
2 *R. v Xhabri (Agrol)* [2005] EWCA Crim 3135, [2006] 1 All ER 776, [2005] 12 WLUK 182, [2006] 1 Cr App R 266, 20 BHRC 233, Times, 10 January 2006, [2006] CLY 788; however, note the commentary (and references to other relevant articles): Billal Malik, 'The hearsay rule under the Criminal Justice Act 2003: R v Xhabri (Agrol)' (2006) 10(4) E & P 316; Tom Worthen, 'The hearsay provisions of the Criminal Justice Act 2003: So far, not so good?' [2008] Crim LR 431; Roderick Munday, 'Athwal and all that: previous statements, narrative, and the taxonomy of hearsay' (2010) 74(5) JCL 415; Michael Stockdale and Emma Piasecki, 'The safety-valve: discretion to admit hearsay evidence in criminal proceedings' (2012) 76(4) JCL 314.

3.63 Careful consideration needs to be made of the provisions of s 114(2) regarding evidence in digital form when it is obtained from the Internet and where the evidence relating to the material, such as its authorship and ownership of the website from which it originates, is not known, as in the case of *R. v Bucknor (Ashley Dwayne)*.[1] In this case, the trial judge admitted evidence found by the police on BEBO (https://www.bebo.com), consisting of 46 separate website 'pages'. The material included a number of photographs of Bucknor that he had taken of himself after he had left prison. The photographs had been placed on the page by someone in such a manner as to portray Bucknor as a member of the Organised Criminals (OC) gang. There was a hyperlink to a YouTube page that portrayed the OC gang as violent. The YouTube page was also shown to the jury in the form of a DVD. The prosecution did not have any evidence of the IP address from which the material was uploaded. The trial judge admitted the evidence as part of the background to the case, but on appeal the appellant argued that the judge failed to give a sufficient direction regarding the ownership of the website in question. The members of the Court of Appeal agreed with the submission. The material was clearly hearsay because it seemed likely that the maker as the source of the material was representing as fact or opinion that Bucknor was a member of the OC gang. In considering the issues set out in s 114(2), Hooper LJ, giving the judgment for the court, said that the judge ought to have considered the reliability of the maker of the statement (sub-paragraph (e)), whom the judge failed to identify.[2] Failing to identify the maker meant that it was not obvious how many levels of hearsay were involved. The judge also failed to consider the reliability of the statement that the appellant was a member of the OC. Hooper LJ concluded:

> 44. Furthermore it seems to us on the facts of this case that the judge should have considered how reliable the statement was. He should also have asked whether the prosecution could call the maker of the statement and if not why not.
>
> 45. In our view the judge did not approach section 114 as he should have done. In any event, as we have said, his direction to the jury invited them to reach conclusions which no reasonable jury could have reached. [3]

1 [2010] EWCA Crim 1152, [2010] 5 WLUK 731.
2 [2010] EWCA Crim 1152 at [42]–[43].
3 [2010] EWCA Crim 1152 at [44]–[45].

Judicial discretion to exclude hearsay

3.64 A trial judge also has the ability to refuse to admit a statement in accordance with s 126(1)(b) where 'the court is satisfied that the case for excluding the statement, taking account of the danger that to admit it would result in undue waste of time, substantially outweighs the case for admitting it, taking account of the value of the evidence'.[1]

1 A similar provision exists in s 8, New Zealand Evidence Act 2006.

3.65 The Law Commission described the necessity of this judicial discretion as the power to exclude superfluous hearsay evidence. The concern is not with evidence that is wholly irrelevant, but evidence which has some relevance, yet 'where the probative value of the evidence is so slight that almost nothing is gained by admitting it'.[1] Although this discretion is intended to be exercised only in exceptional cases, the existence of the discretion serves as an important counterweight to address concerns about the expansionary rules for the admission of barely relevant hearsay evidence.[2]

1 Law Commission, *Evidence in Criminal Proceedings: Hearsay and Related Topics* (Law Com No 245, 1997) para 11.18.
2 Law Commission, *Evidence in Criminal Proceedings: Hearsay and Related Topics* (Law Com No 245, 1997) para 11.18.

Concluding observations

3.66 Almost everybody now uses digital data, whether this interaction is by way of the ether – a terminal linked by software to a server located in an unknown location – or from a physical device. Software code has become part of the everyday fabric of the majority of people. This means we are all, wittingly or unwittingly, assessing electronic evidence every day: from whether to trust that incoming email from an unknown source, to dealing with the veracity of content from networking sites.

3.67 The digital world is now awash with evidence: direct statements over the Internet; communications between telephones and other devices; messages made by a known author, anonymously or by somebody who cannot be traced. Every day we are dealing with the multiplicity of direct and indirect assertions (whether factually accurate or not), in the form of statements by one person or relayed, correctly or incorrectly, by others, and the interplay between them and the reality of the physical world. For the first time, we are all assessing evidence every day.

3.68 This chapter seeks to demonstrate the importance for lawyers to be aware of the dangers of admitting hearsay evidence and the need to distinguish between the various hearsay representations and 'representations' made by devices that may be embedded in electronic evidence. The identification of the nature of the device that stored or produced the electronic evidence and the testimonial or non-testimonial use that is made of the evidence remain important steps for determining the admissibility and relevance of the evidence, even in a statutory regime for admitting hearsay. It is only with a careful understanding of the nuances of both the hearsay rules as well as the nature of electronic evidence that the principle of testing the evidence can be observed, to ensure that any rational inference from evidence admitted against the defendant is objective and fair, and that the law, in its quest to establish the truth of what is contained in the statement, has indeed been true to itself.

4

Software code as the witness

Stephen Mason

4.1 The aim of this chapter is to illustrate how software code can affect the examination and introduction of electronic evidence in legal proceedings. The topic is considered in the context of software code as the 'witness'. It is important to understand how software can affect an assessment of the truth in any given set of facts, and software code can be written deliberately to deceive.[1] Failure to appreciate this can lead to unfairness in legal proceedings and incorrect decisions.

1 See the example of Volkswagen AG, Audi AG and Volkswagen Group of America, Inc, described in detail in Chapter 5; for the US, see the excellent article by Andrea Roth, 'Machine testimony' (2017) 126 Yale LJ 1972.

4.2 A digital computer is like a mechanical device, where switches replace gears, and the switches are miniaturized. However, it is impossible to build a mechanical device that reflects the functionality of a modern digital computer, because such a device would require both a machine built on a colossal scale and the use of materials beyond the strengths or machine tolerances of what is possible to manufacture mechanically. To complete the picture, physical digital devices, as indicated in Chapter 1, cannot work without the software written by programmers and the input by users.

4.3 It follows that electronic evidence could be treated as a joint statement that is:

(i) partly made by the person inputting data (such as typing an email or word document, inserting a PIN, filling in forms over the Internet – in essence anything a person does when interacting with a device), and

(ii) partly made by the hundreds of programmers who are responsible for writing the software that produces the data.

4.4 For this reason, there is an argument, as proposed by Steven W. Teppler, that all forms of evidence in digital form remain hearsay,[1] because software code conveys information.[2] Teppler[3] gives us the example of United States Patent Office Number 5,619,571, which includes some uncompiled source code that contains the following lines of code in the application:

```
ptrFIXUP fixupBase = NULL; // Base pointer for fixups

ptrFIXUP fixupMap = NULL; // pointer used to 'walk off of base'

FIXUP IVFixup;    // ISII Verification fixup

memset(&IVFixup,0,sizeof(FIXUP));

// Allocate a buffer to build the IFD (If this fails, we are F'd)[4]
```

1 Assistant Professor Andrea Roth points out, in 'Machine testimony' (2017) 126 Yale LJ 1972 at 1980, that 'the hearsay rule itself could not easily be modified to accommodate machines, given its focus on the oath, physical confrontation, and cross-examination'. This must be right.

Stephen Mason, 'Software code as the witness', in Stephen Mason and Daniel Seng (eds.), *Electronic Evidence and Electronic Signatures* (5th edn, University of London 2021) 112–125.

2 Steven W. Teppler, 'Testable reliability: a modernized approach to ESI admissibility' (2014) 12(2) Ave Maria Law Review213.
3 Steven W. Teppler, 'Digital data as hearsay' (2009) 6 Digital Evidence and Electronic Signature Law Review 7.
4 U.S. Patent No. 5,619,571 (issued Apr. 8, 1997), 17–18, lines 10–14.

4.5 What this comment indicates is an acknowledgment of the possibility of a weakness in the software code that has been written, not that the software code is or will be at fault. In this regard, it is useful to understand more fully the nature of source code. For instance, Svein Willassen explains the complex nature of software as follows:

> Software is written as source code. The source code is written by the programmer, by entering instructions in an editor. The sequence of instructions defines the function of the program, such as taking input from the user, performing calculations, showing output on the screen and so on. This source code is then usually compiled into an executable program (an executable file causes a computer to perform tasks in accordance with the instructions), which is distributed to the users of the program. The source code cannot be derived completely from the executable program.[1]

1 Svein Yngvar Willassen, 'Line based hash analysis of source code infringement' (2009) 6 Digital Evidence and Electronic Signature Law Review 210.

4.6 In the Australian case of *Computer Edge Pty Limited v Apple Computer Inc*,[1] Gibbs CJ offered the following explanation of the various parts of a computer program:

> A computer program is a set of instructions designed to cause a computer to perform a particular function or to produce a particular result. A program is usually developed in a number of stages. First, the sequence of operations which the computer will be required to perform is commonly written out in ordinary language, with the help, if necessary, of mathematical formulae and of a flow chart and diagram representing the procedure. In the present case if any writing in ordinary language (other than the comments and labels mentioned below) was produced in the production of Applesoft and Autostart, no question now arises concerning it. Next there is prepared what is called a source program. The instructions are now expressed in a computer language—either in a source code (which is not far removed from ordinary language, and is hence called a high level language) or in an assembly code (a low level language, which is further removed from ordinary language than a source code), or successively in both. Sometimes the expression 'source code' seems to be used to include both high level and low level language. In the present case, the source programs were written in an assembly code, comprising four elements, *viz.*:
>
> > (a) labels identifying particular parts of the program;
> >
> > (b) mnemonics each consisting of three letters of the alphabet and corresponding to a particular operation expressed in 6502 Assembly Code (the code used);
> >
> > (c) mnemonics identifying the register in the microprocessor and/or the number of instructions in the program to which the operation referred to in (b) related; and
> >
> > (d) comments intended to explain the function of the particular part of the program for the benefit of a human reader of the program.
>
> The writing has been destroyed, although it is possible to reconstruct the mnemonics, but not the labels and comments, which were comprised in it.

> The source code or assembly code cannot be used directly in the computer, and must be converted into an object code, which is 'machine readable,' *i.e.* which can be directly used in the computer. The conversion is effected by a computer, itself properly programmed. The program in object code, the object program, in the first instance consists of a sequence of electrical impulses which are often first stored on a magnetic disk or tape, and which may be stored permanently in a ROM ('read only memory'), a silicon chip which contains thousands of connected electrical circuits. The object code is embodied in the ROM in such a way that when the ROM is installed in the computer and electrical power is applied, there is generated the sequence of electrical impulses which cause the computer to take the action which the program is designed to achieve. The pattern of the circuits in the ROM may possibly be discerned with the aid of an electron microscope but it cannot be seen by the naked eye. Obviously, the electrical impulses themselves cannot be perceived. However the sequence of electrical impulses may be described either in binary notation (using the symbols 0 and 1) or in hexadecimal notation (using the numbers 0–9 and the letters A–F), and it is possible to display the description on the visual display unit of the computer, and to print it out on paper. And, as has been said, it is also possible to reconstruct the mnemonics in the source code. It will have been seen from this account that a program exists successively in source code and in object code, but the object code need not be written out in binary or hexadecimal notation in the process of producing and storing the program.[2]

1 [1986] F.S.R. 537.
2 [1986] F.S.R. 537 at 541–542.

4.7 The term 'source code' is also the subject of a commentary in the case of *Ibcos Computers Ltd v Barclays Mercantile Highland Finance Ltd*[1] by Jacob J:

> The program the human writes is called the 'source code.' After it is written it is processed by a program called a compiler into binary code. That is what the computer uses. All the words and algebraic symbols become binary numbers. Now when a human writes he often needs to make notes to remind himself of what he has done and to indicate where the important bits are. This is true of life generally and for programmers. So it is possible to insert messages in a source code. A reader who has access to it can then understand, or understand more readily, what is going on. Such notes, which form no part of the program so far as the computer is concerned, are called 'comments.' They are a kind of side-note for humans. In the DIBOL and DBL programs with which I am concerned, a line or part of a line of program which is preceded by a semi-colon is taken by the complier as a comment. That line is not translated by the compiler into machine code. The program would work without the comment. It follows that although computers are unforgiving as to spelling in their programs, they do not care about misspelt comments in the source code. If a line of operational code (a 'command line') is modified by putting a semi-colon in front of it, it ceases to be operational. The computer treats the code as a mere comment. Computer programmers sometimes do this with a line which pre-exists when they no longer want that line, but are not sure they may not need it in the future. Or, if the programmer thinks he may want to add a feature to his program in the future he may put in a comment allowing for this. He is unlikely in the latter instance to put in detailed code only to comment it out. A general note will do.
>
> Source code, being what humans can understand, is very important to anyone who wants to copy a program with modifications, for instance to upgrade it. It is the source code which shows the human how it all works, and he or she will also get the benefit of all the comments laid down by the original programmer.

Software houses not surprisingly normally keep their source code to themselves and confidential.[2]

1 [1994] 2 WLUK 353, [1994] FSR 275, [1998] Mason CLR Rep 1, [1995] CLY 854.
2 [1994] FSR 275 at 286.

4.8 There is a distinction between the code written by programmers that provides instructions to the computer and the comments made by the programmer writing the code. If the software code is inaccurate, or if an instruction written by a programmer acts on information or a further instruction that is incorrect, then the code will probably fail to instruct the computer in the way the programmer intended. However, comments by a programmer that do not form part of the instructions cannot necessarily be considered to be part of the code.

The classification of digital data

4.9 The starting point for this analysis is an attempt at classifying software code as digital data. To this end, Professor Ormerod, the commentator in a report on the case of *R. v Skinner (Philip)*,[1] suggested there were three questions to consider for every type of digital data:

(i) Who or what made the representation.

(ii) Whether the representation was hearsay or not.

(iii) Whether the evidence is authentic.[2]

1 [2005] EWCA Crim 1439, [2005] 5 WLUK 506, [2006] Crim LR 56.
2 David C. Ormerod, 'Evidence: information copied from one website to another' [2006] Crim LR 56.

4.10 In *Elf Caledonia Ltd v London Bridge Engineering Ltd*, Lord Caplan noted the following:

> The defenders suggested that there are three categories of use for computers. They can be used to record data without the need of human intervention. The Spectra-Tek programme was described as being of this type. It was said that what this programme prints out may be regarded as real evidence. However Counsel had to concede that even this type of computer exercise depends on the reliability of the material programme. Unless it is properly programmed it will not store and regurgitate facts accurately ...
>
> Another category of computer use was said to be where data is recorded by the computer and the data is put in manually. Thus Piper would regularly send information to the beach and this would be entered in the computer system. It was accepted that to prove this material would involve some hearsay evidence unless the persons who entered the material in the computer were led as witnesses. However the defenders did not explore just what evidence would be required in the situation under consideration. In general it seems to me that there must be many cases where it would not be practicable to lead the person who generated the data and the person who fed it into the computer so that there must be some practical limits as to what proof can be expected in this kind of computer evidence.
>
> It was submitted that the third type of computer situation is where the computer is used by experts to carry out calculations or simulations. It was claimed that in this kind of situation the general rules relating to expert evidence should be applied. Certainly in this kind of situation one can get a distorted result if

> one factor is in-putted wrongly. The kind of computer models used by experts of course generally requires more than normal discrimination and judgment in the selection of in-put material. Thus the expert will have to prove how the input material was arrived at and the justification for selecting what was put in. However I am not sure that the three categories of computer exercise referred to by the defenders' Counsel can be distinguished quite as neatly as he attempts. Even in a simple office system distorted results will arise if the proper material is not fed into the computer. Thus it was argued that the first requirement in considering computer evidence given by an expert is to consider the input. That may be so but it cannot be exclusive to expert computer evidence. Of course it was said that the best evidence of in-put and out-put material is in the print-outs of such material.[1]

1 [1997] ScotCS 1, 898–900, sub nom *Elf Enterprise Caledonia Ltd v London Bridge Engineering Limited* [1997] ScotCS 1, 2.

4.11 Based on this categorization, Professor Ormerod noted that some types of computer-generated representations do not infringe the hearsay rule.[1] If a computer carries out the instructions of the program that has been written by humans to create such data, it may be right to suggest that such data are probably accurate without the need to test whether they are correct. But if the time as noted by a clock on a camera linked to an ATM is to be offered into evidence to link the accused to the murder of the person whose card was used in the ATM, then the time as data will have to be adduced as to its truth, as in the case of *Liser v Smith*,[2] and there will be a need to validate the clock, and verify the time and date set by a human being.[3]

1 Although he accepted that s 129 of the Criminal Justice Act 2003 may need to be considered. For a commentary on s 129, see John R. Spencer, *Hearsay Evidence in Criminal Proceedings* (Hart Publishing 2008) ch 3.
2 254 F.Supp.2d 89 (D.D.C. 2003).
3 Colin Tapper, 'Reform of the law of evidence in relation to the output from computers' (1995) 3 Intl J L & Info Tech 79, 85 fn 44.

4.12 To the same end, Professor Smith distinguished between the types of representation that the code in a device can make,[1] and argued that where the computer is instructed to perform certain functions, many of which are performed in a mechanical way (such as the addition of the time and date on an email), in such circumstances the computer is producing real evidence, not hearsay. In illustrating the point he was making, Professor Smith gave a number of examples where evidence is not hearsay.[2] One example was that of Six's thermometer (commonly known as a maximum minimum thermometer), which he referred to as an instrument and not a machine. This is correct. The thermometer provides three readings: the current temperature, and the highest and the lowest temperatures reached since it was last reset. A human being can give evidence of his observation of the precise location of the mercury against the scale at a given time and date. The witness might be challenged as to the truthfulness of his recollection without calling into question the accuracy of the instrument. Such evidence will not be hearsay. Alternatively, the precision of the scale on the thermometer might be open to scrutiny, in which case it will be necessary to have the instrument tested by an appropriately qualified expert.[3]

1 J. C. Smith, 'The admissibility of statements by computer' [1981] Crim LR 387.
2 Smith, 'The admissibility of statements by computer', 390.
3 This was also discussed by Penelope A. Pengilley, 'Machine information: is it hearsay?' (1982) 13(4) MULR 617, 625.

4.13 Further examples considered by Professor Smith included a camera that records an image, a tape recorder that records sound and a radar speedmeter that records the speed of a vehicle. In 1981, each of these machines was mechanical in construction, with the exception of the radar speedmeter, which also incorporated components that were instruments. None of the examples involved devices controlled by software written by human beings. Although it is possible to alter the image from a camera or the sound from a tape recording, or for a human being to lie about the reading from a radar speedmeter, nevertheless the evidence from such devices would not be hearsay.

4.14 In respect of software, Professor Smith indicated that a programmer may make mistakes (errors are common, for which see Chapter 5 on 'reliability'), but mistakes can also be made when deciding the scale on a thermometer. He went on to suggest that '[t]his consideration goes to weight rather than admissibility. In any event it certainly has nothing to do with the hearsay rule.'[1]

1 Smith, 'The admissibility of statements by computer' 390. One answer to this issue has been proposed by Professor Pattenden – that s 129(1) of the Criminal Justice Act 2003 be replaced 'with a single test of admissibility for all factual representations that are not in substance the statement of a person but "machinespeak", that is, those whose content is the outcome of creating machine-processing': Rosemary Pattenden, 'Machinespeak: section 129 of the Criminal Justice Act 2003' [2010] Crim LR 623, 636–637. Professor Pattenden discusses the conflicting opinions relating to s 129(1) in detail.

4.15 Professor Seng proposed an analysis in 1997:

> Computers which are used as data processing devices can be classified into the following categories: devices which accept human-supplied input and produce output, self-contained data processing devices which obtain input or take recordings from the environment without human intervention, and a hybrid of the two.[1]

1 Daniel Seng, 'Computer output as evidence' [1997] SJLS 130, 173.

4.16 Steven Teppler also accepted that it is possible to categorize data into three types, treating digital data as hearsay:

(i) The memorandum 'created' by a human.

(ii) Digital data generated in part with human assistance.

(iii) Digital data generated without a human being.[1]

1 Teppler, 'Testable reliability', 235–240.

4.17 Teppler has also suggested that a 'fourth potential category, for which there has been no judicial analysis, has recently emerged as a consequence of computer programs that "listen and respond" to questions in natural language and with a "voice" that closely mimics a "real" human'.[1] Arguably, this category fits into category three, for which see below.

1 Teppler, 'Testable reliability', 235.

4.18 The authors of *Archbold* have also divided digital data into three categories:

(i) Where the device is used as a processor of data.

(ii) Where the software records data where there is no human input involved.

(iii) Where there is data recorded and processed by software that has been entered by a person, directly or indirectly. [1]

1 *Archbold: Criminal Pleading, Evidence and Practice* (Sweet & Maxwell), 9–11, 9–14.

4.19 It is proposed that the three categories outlined by Professor Seng, Steven Teppler and the authors of *Archbold* be slightly amended to read as follows:

(i) Content written by one or more people (that is, where the device is used as a processor of data).

(ii) Records generated by the software that have not had any input from a human.

(iii) Records comprising a mix of human input and calculations generated by software.

Each of these categories is discussed below.

Category 1: Content written by one or more people

4.20 Records of electronic content that are written by one or more people include email messages, word processing files and instant messages. Unless the author of the software has included instructions to alter the content of the text that has been typed in by a human, the only function of the device is to store the information that has been input by the human being. However, Teppler suggests that all computer-generated information is hearsay of some sort, and that the data generated by an email program, for instance, remains hearsay because:

> the receiving computer is carrying out the stated intent or declaration of some person who instructed the computer to make the assertion on his or her behalf (e.g., a programmer) to carry out some request (and provided that certain conditions are met) that the receiving computer was told by the sending computer as agent for that person, which in turn was requested by a statement or declaration of the person or sender.[1]

1 Teppler, 'Testable reliability', 240.

4.21 Conceptually this must be right, but the status of the instructions issued by the software code at the material time is rarely relevant. This category, artificial as it might appear to be, enables content that was input by the maker of the statement to be separated from content made by the author of the software program – in the same way that the printed notepaper with the name of the person or organization, together with other information such as address and telephone number, is created by the printer, but is distinct from the content of the letter.

4.22 The content of the software program will not be relevant unless there is a dispute as to what data were entered, when and where they were entered, and by whom. In such circumstances, the relevant witnesses can be called to give oral evidence to determine the truth, failing which a suitably qualified digital evidence practitioner might be called to give evidence about the metadata associated with the document to help ascertain answers to these technical questions.

4.23 By way of example, consider whether a letter typed into a computer is a document produced by a computer. Professor Smith took the view that if the human author printed the document and then read the contents to verify the text, the author authenticates the text. Given this set of facts, the computer is a mere tool. Where the author does not read the printout, the document remains computer output.[1] Professor Seng suggests that 'it is difficult to see how reading what is clearly a computer-produced document converts it into one not produced by a computer. The printout remains clearly a document produced by a computer operated as a data storage device.'[2] Professor Smith indicates that the person can authenticate the text after it has been printed. This does not mean that the act of authentication takes away the fact that the document was created on and remains stored on the device. This distinction can be important, as in the case of electronic wills. The court must establish whether, in the absence of the testator authenticating the will, the testator actually wrote the will and intended it to be their last will and testament. In such cases, it might also be necessary to give consideration to both the content written by the human and the software code that makes up the metadata.

1 *R. v Shephard (Hilda)* [1993] Crim LR 295 (note), 297–298.
2 Seng, 'Computer output as evidence' 178 – Professor Seng begins his discussion (at 177) by asking whether word-processed documents are computer output or recorded computer output.

4.24 Professor Tapper pointed out that computers include such facilities as spell checkers, calculators and automatic paragraph numbering, among other tools. This suggests that a word file (such as a letter) is processed computer output.[1] In his discussion, Professor Smith also discussed the same document being produced by a human typing on a typewriter. If the text – for the sake of illustration, a letter – is written by hand, or typed on a typewriter, or typed into a computer, the resultant content will be the same, other than the type of print, typeface and such like used, although the author might cause the data to remain stored on the device if it was a computer.[2] The person writing the letter by hand or on a typewriter might use a dictionary to check their spelling in the same way that spelling can be checked on a computer using the spell checker. Whether the letter is written by hand, typed on a typewriter or on a computer, the letter will then be complete when printed (in the case of the computer) on paper. The method used to record words on paper must be irrelevant, providing that the only evidence to be relied upon is the text that is recorded on the paper. If other factors are in issue, such as the purported author of the document, then clearly an examination of the digital data might be instructive. Professor Seng takes issue with Professor Smith's characterization that the evidential quality of a letter changes immediately when a recipient reads it, without taking into account any characterization of its source. In such a case, where the computer is behaving as a storage device, the rebuttable presumption is that the code operating to make it behave as such is reliable, and issues as to authentication of this code do not enter the evidential analysis, generally speaking. But there can be other software errors, for which see Chapter 5 on the 'reliability' of computers.

1 Tapper, 'Reform of the law of evidence in relation to the output from computers', 86–88.
2 A point made by Professor Seng, 'Computer output as evidence', 178.

4.25 The Law Commission in their report[1] noted that the 'present law draws a distinction according to whether the statement consists of, or is based upon, only what the machine itself has observed; or whether it incorporates, or is based upon, information supplied by a human being'.[2] It was further noted that the hearsay rule did not apply to tapes, films or photographs, or to documents produced by machines that automatically record an event or circumstance.[3] This was because the court is not being asked to accept the truth of an assertion made by any person, and the evidence is real evidence, not hearsay.

1 Law Commission, *Evidence in Criminal Proceedings: Hearsay and Related Topics* (Law Com No 245, 1997).
2 Law Commission, *Evidence in Criminal Proceedings: Hearsay and Related Topics* (Law Com No 245, 1997) para 7.43.
3 Law Commission, *Evidence in Criminal Proceedings: Hearsay and Related Topics* (Law Com No 245, 1997) para 7.44.

4.26 That humans generally have control over a computer system is demonstrated in the case of *Ferguson v British Gas Trading Limited*,[1] in which the members of the Court of Appeal rejected arguments submitted that letters sent out automatically by a computer were not the fault of British Gas. Computers only work on instructions given to them, and it followed that a person in British Gas, or authorized by British Gas, must have instructed the computer to initiate the letters in question. In this case, British Gas sent letters to the claimant that the court held were capable of amounting to unlawful harassment contrary to the Protection from Harassment Act 1997. In the words of Jacob LJ: 'British Gas says it has done nothing wrong; that it is perfectly all right for it to treat consumers in this way, at least if it is all just done by computer.'[2] Jacob LJ went on to indicate that he did not follow the reasoning of Martin Porter QC, counsel for British Gas, that '[as] the correspondence was computer generated ... [the harassed victim] should not have taken it as seriously as if it had come from an individual'.[3] Jacob LJ noted that computers operate on instructions given to them: 'real people are responsible for programming and entering material into the computer. It is British Gas's system which, at the very least, allowed the impugned conduct to happen.'[4] Likewise, Sedley LJ roundly rejected the pathetic excuse offered by British Gas:

> One excuse which has formed part of British Gas's legal argument for striking out the claim, and which has been advanced as incontestable and decisive, is that a large corporation such as British Gas cannot be legally responsible for mistakes made either by its computerised debt recovery system or by the personnel responsible for programming and operating it. The short answer is that it can be, for reasons explained by Lord Justice Jacob. It would be remarkable if it could not: it would mean that the privilege of incorporation not only shielded its shareholders and directors from personal liability for its debts but protected the company itself from legal liabilities which a natural person cannot evade. That is not what legal personality means.[5]

1 [2009] EWCA Civ 46, [2010] 1 WLR 785, [2009] 3 All ER 304, [2009] 2 WLUK 206, (2009) 106(8) LSG 18, (2009) 153(7) SJLB 34, [2009] CLY 3959.
2 [2009] EWCA Civ 46 at [5].
3 [2009] EWCA Civ 46 at [21].
4 [2009] EWCA Civ 46 at [21].
5 [2009] EWCA Civ 46 at [51].

Category 2: Records generated by the software that have not had any input from a human

4.27 Examples of records generated by software controlling a computer without any input from a human include computer data logs for the purposes of tracking activity and diagnostics, number plate recognition software,[1] automatic connections made by telephone switches and the records of such calls made for billing purposes,[2] records of ATM transactions, machine translation,[3] and objects connected to the Internet, known as Internet of Things.[4] In one case, Antonio Boparan Singh was convicted of dangerous driving. Part of the evidence adduced by the prosecution included evidence from the event data recorder (EDR) – a device fitted to the airbag system of his vehicle. The EDR established that a force equivalent to 42 mph was lost in one-fifth of a second in the crash. This information helped the police to put Singh's speed at around 72 mph.[5]

1 https://www.police.uk/pu/advice-crime-prevention/automatic-number-plate-recognition-anpr/; for judicial consideration of automatic number plate recognition, see *R. v Jackson (Royston)* [2011] EWCA Crim 1870, [2011] 7 WLUK 643; *Attorney General's Reference (Nos 114 and 115 of 2009)* [2010] EWCA Crim 1459, [2010] 6 WLUK 549; *R. v Najib (Amaar)* [2013] EWCA Crim 86, [2013] 2 WLUK 290; *R. v Khan (Imran); R. v Mahmood (Amjed Khan); R. v Kajla (Jaspal)* [2013] EWCA Crim 2230, [2013] 12 WLUK 57, [2014] Crim LR 520; *R. v Welsh (Christopher Mark)* [2014] EWCA Crim 1027, [2014] 5 WLUK 740. Interestingly, the absence of challenges to ANPR evidence in the English courts could be attributed to the fact that, for the large part, the defendants or the parties have admitted to the accuracy of such evidence and so no real dispute arises: see [125], *Makdessi v Cavendish Square Holdings BV ParkingEye Ltd v Beavis* [2015] UKSC 67, [2016] AC 1172, [2015] 3 WLR 1373, [2016] 2 All ER 519, [2016] 2 All ER (Comm) 1, [2016] 1 Lloyd's Rep 55, [2015] 11 WLUK 78, [2015] 2 CLC 686, [2016] BLR 1, 162 Con LR 1, [2016] RTR 8, [2016] CILL 3769, Times, 23 November 2015, [2016] CLY 437, also known as *Cavendish Square Holding BV v Makdessi, El Makdessi v Cavendish Square Holdings BV*; also *D (A Child) (Fact-finding Appeal), Re* [2019] EWCA Civ 2302, [2019] 12 WLUK 409, [2020] 2 FCR 15, [2020] 7 CL 90, also known as *M v X BC*, at [32]. Even so, when a discrepancy arises in relation to ANPR evidence, as in the case of *A (Death of a Baby), Re* [2011] EWHC 2754 (Fam) [66] and [69], where there was testimonial evidence to corroborate the drivers' testimony as to their movements and contradict the ANPR evidence, the independent verifiability of the vehicular movements coupled with the lack of authentication of the ANPR evidence led the court to exercise its discretion and choose to draw no conclusions from the ANPR evidence [158].

2 Rosemary Pattenden, 'Authenticating "things" in English law: principles for adducing tangible evidence in common law jury trials' (2008) 12 E & P 273, suggests that 'self-generated output' can be categorized into two sub-divisions: output that contains no input from human thought, and output that draws directly or indirectly on information fed into the device by a person: 297; Julian Fulbrook, 'Deadly distractions: mobile telephones and transport litigation' (2018) 2 JPI Law 89, in which he cites *Eyres v Atkinsons Kitchens & Bedrooms Ltd* [2007] EWCA Civ 365, [2007] 4 WLUK 369, (2007) 151 SJLB 576, Times, 21 May 2007, [2007] CLY 2955.

3 Nicole E. Crossey, 'Machine translator testimony & the confrontation clause: has the time come for the hearsay rules to escape the stone age?' (2020) 12 Drexal L Rev 561.

4 David Caruso, Michael Legg and Jordan Phoustanis, 'The automation paradox in litigation: the inadequacy of procedure and evidence law to manage electronic evidence generated by the "internet of things" in civil disputes' (2019) 19 Macquarie LJ 157.

5 Mark Cowan, 'Crime files: picking up the pieces on Midland roads' *Birmingham Mail* (Birmingham, 6 October 2010); an insurance company used data recorded from telematics technology installed in a motor vehicle to disprove 31 claims involving seven accidents over five months: Oliver Ralph, 'Black box data expose £500,000 driver fraud' *Financial Times* (London, 11 June 2016) 4; James Wade, 'Emerging technologies in collision investigation' (2016) 4 JPI Law 220; Amelia Murray, 'A £90,000 bogus car insurance claim – and how the fraudsters were caught by their telematics box', *The Telegraph*, 13 January 2018, https://www.telegraph.co.uk/insurance/car/90000-bogus-car-insurance-claim-fraudsters-caught-telematics/.

4.28 It does not follow that the automatic communications that occur between software code are accurate. For instance, the records from a telephone service provider might be admitted to show that calls were made and received,[1] but it does not follow that the same records can be used as a basis for showing that a SIM card used in a mobile telephone, and purportedly its user,[2] were at a particular location or moved from location to location.[3]

1 For an analysis in the context of New Brunswick, Canada, see *Her Majesty the Queen v Dennis James Oland* 2015 NBQB 244 (third ruling); *Her Majesty the Queen v Dennis James Oland* 2015 NBQB 245 (fourth ruling) and the observations by David M. Paciocco, 'Proof and progress: coping with the law of evidence in a technological age' (2013) 11(2) Canadian Journal of Law and Technology 181, which in turn are disputed in Ken Chasse, 'Guilt by mobile phone tracking shouldn't make "evidence to the contrary" impossible', http://www.slaw.ca/2016/10/04/guilt-by-mobile-phone-tracking-shouldnt-make-evidence-to-the-contrary-impossible/.

2 Cell site analysis was the subject of discussion in *R. v Jackson (Royston)* [2011] EWCA Crim 1870, [2011] 7 WLUK 643; Reg Coutts and Hugh Selby, 'Safe and unsafe use of mobile phone evidence' (Public Defenders Criminal Law Conference, Sydney, March 2009), http://www.publicdefenders.nsw.gov.au/Documents/safeunsafemobilephones.pdf, recommend that defence lawyers pay particular attention to the explanation of cell site analysis set out by Blaxell J in *The State of Western Australia v Coates* [2007] WASC 307, [211]–[220]; R. P. Coutts and H. Selby, 'Problems with cell phone evidence tendered to "prove" the location of a person at a point in time' (2016) 13 Digital Evidence and Electronic Signature Law Review 76.

3 Michael Cherry, Edward J. Imwinkelried, Manfred Schenk, Aaron Romano, Naomi Fetterman, Nicole Hardin and Arnie Beckman, 'Cell tower junk science' (2012) 95(4) Judicature 151, 151–52; Aaron Blank, 'The limitations and admissibility of using historical cellular site data to track the location of a cellular phone' (2011) 18(1) Rich J L & Tech 10; Judge Herbert B. Dixon Jr, 'Scientific fact or junk science? Tracking a cell phone without GPS' (2014) 53(1) Judges' J 37; Graeme Horsman and Lynne R. Conniss, 'Investigating evidence of mobile phone usage by drivers in road traffic accidents' (2015) 12 Digital Investigation S30, S37; Alex Biedermann and Joëlle Vuille, 'Digital evidence, "absence" of data and ambiguous patterns of reasoning' (2016) 16 Digital Investigation S86, S94; for the case of Phuong Canh Ngo, see *R v Ngo* [2001] NSWSC 1021 (the sentence); *R v Ngo* [2003] NSWCCA 82 (appeal against conviction); David Patten (Judicial Officer Conducting Inquiry), *Report to the Chief Justice of New South Wales (The Hon J J Spigelman AC) of the Inquiry into the Conviction of Phuong Canh Ngo for the murder of John Newman* (14 April 2009), http://www.lawlink.nsw.gov.au/practice_notes/nswsc_pc.nsf/6a64691105a54031ca256880000c25d7/f1ef2541db38ae82ca25759b00052606/$FILE/Report_Phuong_Ngo_140409.pdf; *Phuong Canh Ngo – Application under Part 7 Crimes (Appeal and Review) Act 2001* [2010] NSWSC 981 (hearing after Report published).

Category 3: Records comprising a mix of human input and calculations generated by software

4.29 An example of records comprising a mix of human input and calculations generated by software is that of a financial spreadsheet program that contains human statements (input to the spreadsheet program) and computer processing (mathematical calculations performed by the spreadsheet program). From an evidential point of view, the issue is whether the person or the software created the content of the record, and how much of the content was created by the software and how much by the human. It is possible that the quality of the software acts to undermine the authenticity of the data, which may in turn affect the truth of the statement tendered in evidence. The algorithms in spreadsheet programs are good examples of where the software code affects the truth of the statement. For a more detailed analysis, see Chapter 6 on authentication.

4.30 Professor Pattenden suggests that 'most representations of fact require human intervention at some point',[1] which must be right. The Law Commission report also indicated:

> By contrast, the law does sometimes exclude evidence of a statement generated by a machine, where the statement is based on information fed into the machine by a human being. In such a case, it seems, the statement by the machine is admissible *only* if the facts on which it is based are themselves proved.[2]

1 Pattenden, 'Machinespeak', 633.
2 Law Commission, *Evidence in Criminal Proceedings: Hearsay and Related Topics* (Law Com No 245, 1997) para 7.46.

4.31 This comment distinguishes between information fed into a machine (the word 'computer' is not used, but the word 'machine' is presumably meant to include a computer or computer-like device) and the instructions contained in software code written by human beings that are essential for a device to work. Where a person inputs information into a computer, and that information is to be relied upon as to the truth of the statement, then the person should give oral evidence of this action. In contrast, the software code that might be used to transform the raw data into information that can be used is not necessarily relevant, depending on the purpose for which it is adduced in evidence. To this end, the Law Commission[1] compared the cases of *R v Wood (Stanley William)*[2] and *R v Coventry Justices, Ex p Bullard.*[3] In *Wood*, the evidence of the analysis by a computer of tests carried out by chemists was not considered to be hearsay because the chemists gave oral evidence of the results of the tests. The calculations performed by the computer were carried out under the instructions of the person who wrote the software code. The chemists were able to give oral evidence of the results of the tests they performed, but the computer software carried out the actual analysis. The calculations relied upon the software code, which was created by a human being (in this case, a Mr Kellie). The software analysed the data in accordance with the instructions given to it by Mr Kellie. The computer was not capable of analysing the data without the software code. The chemists gave oral evidence of the results of the computer program. This means that the truth of the content of the output of the computer was predicated upon the software code created by Mr Kellie.

1 Law Commission, *Evidence in Criminal Proceedings: Hearsay and Related Topics* (Law Com No 245, 1997) para 7.47.
2 [1982] 6 WLUK 191, (1983) 76 Cr App R 23, [1982] Crim LR 667, [1983] CLY 636.
3 [1992] 2 WLUK 233, (1992) 95 Cr App R 175, [1992] RA 79 [1992] COD 285, (1992) 142 NLJ 383, Times, 24 February 1992, Independent, 26 February 1992, Guardian, 11 March 1992, [1992] CLY 2058; 'Print-Out Inadmissible as Hearsay' (1993) 57 JCL 232.

4.32 In comparison, the computer printout in *R v Coventry Justices, Ex p Bullard* included a statement that a person was in arrears with his community charge. This was held to be inadmissible hearsay because the content of the printout contained information that had been put into the computer by a human, and the printout had not been properly proved. The Law Commission, agreeing with the result, would propose a similar analysis as follows:

> An alternative view is that the statement by the machine, properly understood, is conditional on the accuracy of the data on which it is based; and that, if those data are not proved to have been accurate, the statement therefore has no probative value at all. The question of hearsay does not arise, because the statement is simply irrelevant.[1]

1 Law Commission, *Evidence in Criminal Proceedings: Hearsay and Related Topics* (Law Com No 245, 1997) para 7.48.

4.33 In *Mehesz v Redman*,[1] Zelling J concluded that the output of an auto-lab data analyser was hearsay, given that the analysis relied on software where the writer of the software had not been called, and where modifications had been made but the person responsible for the modifications had not been called either. A similar decision was made in *Holt v Auckland City Council*,[2] where evidence of the analysis of the amount of alcohol in a blood sample was excluded by the New Zealand Court of Appeal because the truth of the statement tendered was predicated upon the software code written by a programmer who was not called to give evidence, which meant there was a gap in the continuity of proof. In contrast, in *Wood*, the oral evidence of the results of the tests were read out by the chemists from printouts from the computer (which was real evidence), and if the results were to be challenged for their accuracy, then the integrity of the software program might need to be tested.

1 (1979) 21 SASR 569.
2 [1980] 2 NZLR 124.

4.34 The instructions written by a human in the form of software code can, depending on the circumstances, be just that: instructions to the machine to perform a particular task. This is illustrated in the case of *Maynard*.[1] An item of software, called a trace, had been written to ascertain whether a particular employee was obtaining access to private information in a computer system, and if so, to record the time and date that the employee viewed the data. The employee was subsequently prosecuted. The magistrate refused to admit the evidence of the printout of the trace data, partly because he considered the record of the time and date to be hearsay. On appeal, Wright J rejected this analysis. The person who wrote the code gave evidence at trial, both as to the reason for writing the code and as to how it worked. The judge was of the following opinion:

> it seems to me that once the trace was applied to the respondent's log-on identification, the process then undertaken by the trace was entirely mechanical in that the peregrinations through the database by that computer user was automatically traced through the system and were recorded and stored ready for retrieval in report form as soon as the trace print-out was called for.[2]

1 (1993) 70 A Crim R 133, sub nom *Rook v Maynard* (1993) 126 ALR 150.
2 (1993) 70 A Crim R 133 at 141.

4.35 Wright J then went on to illustrate the separate steps:

> Although much more complex in its operation than the following description suggests, the process, stripped to its essentials, involved (a) The implementation of the trace program and its attachment to the respondent's log-on identification. This was a human function proved by direct evidence from Mr Poulter [the person who wrote the code]. (b) Once attached, the trace followed the log-on identification number and the user and (c) when the user tapped into or called up a particular file from the database, the trace was able to store details of this event in its memory for subsequent retrieval.[1]

1 (1993) 70 A Crim R 133 at 142.

4.36 There was no evidence that suggested that the trace program modified any other programs in the computer, and if there were any such failings, the program designer could have been cross-examined on them. For this reason, the statement was not hearsay.

Challenging the code to test the truth of the statement

4.37 One of the most frequently mounted challenges to evidence in digital form is the admissibility of the output from breath-testing devices. Such challenges are attempted across jurisdictions, but the legislation put in place usually provides that where a device is authorized by an appropriate authority, judges do not have the power to require the prosecution to reveal the software code, or refuse to because, it is claimed, the defence do not provide sufficient evidence to support the challenge that the device might not be reliable.[1] However, in *State of New Jersey v Chun* the Supreme Court in New Jersey in the United States ordered the software of a new breath-testing device – the Alcotest 7100 MK111-C – to be reviewed in detail and tested for scientific validity.[2] After extensive testing, the court concluded that the Alcotest, using New Jersey Firmware version 3.11, 'is generally scientifically reliable', but ordered modifications to enable its results to be admitted into legal proceedings.[3] The analysis of the source code indicated that there was a fault when a third breath sample was taken, which could cause the reading to be incorrect, and the court saw fit to order a change in one of the formulae used in the software. This is a significant decision because the court accepted, albeit implicitly, that the software that controlled the device, written by a human, was defective. This in turn meant that had the code not been remedied, the data relied upon for the truth of the statement would be defective and therefore this would affect the accuracy and truthfulness of the evidence.

1 Peter Hungerford-Welch, 'Disclosure: DPP v Walsall Magistrates' Court'(2020) 4 Crim LR 335; *DPP v Walsall Magistrates' Court DPP v Lincoln Magistrates' Court* [2019] EWHC 3317 (Admin), [2019] 12 WLUK 61, [2020] RTR 14, [2020] Crim LR 335, [2020] ACD 21, [2020] 5 CL 43; *R. (on the application of DPP) v Manchester and Salford Magistrates' Court* [2017] EWHC 3719 (Admin), [2019] 1 WLR 2617, [2017] 7 WLUK 154, also known as *DPP v Manchester and Salford Magistrates' Court.*

2 194 N.J. 54, 943 A.2d 114; an application authorizing the discovery of source code used in the Intoxilyzer 5000 breath test equipment failed for procedural reasons in *State of Florida v Bjorkland*, 924 So.2d 971 (Fla. 2d DCA 2006).

3 943 A.2d 114 at 120.

5

The presumption that computers are 'reliable'

Stephen Mason

5.1 This chapter considers the common law presumption in the law of England and Wales that 'In the absence of evidence to the contrary, the courts will presume that mechanical instruments were in order at the material time'. The Law Commission formulated this presumption in 1997.[1] The concept of 'judicial notice'[2] is also considered in this chapter.

1 The Law Commission, *Evidence in Criminal Proceedings: Hearsay and Related Topics* ((Law Com No 245, 1997), 13.13. The Law Commission has an influence beyond the jurisdiction of England and Wales, for which see two cases from the Supreme Court of India, *Anvar P.V. v P.K. Basheer* [2014] INSC 658 (18 September 2014), where Kurian J said: 'It is relevant to note that Section 69 of the Police and Criminal Evidence Act, 1984 (PACE) dealing with evidence on computer records in the United Kingdom was repealed by Section 60 of the Youth Justice and Criminal Evidence Act, 1999. Computer evidence hence must follow the common law rule, where a presumption exists that the computer producing the evidential output was recording properly at the material time. The presumption can be rebutted if evidence to the contrary is adduced' (correct pagination not available in the pdf version). In *Arjun Panditrao Khotar v Kailash Kushanrao Gorantyal* (2020 SCC OnLine SC 571) Ramasubramanian J outlined the discussions in the Law Commission paper, but failed to consider any of the recent scholarship on this topic.

2 *Halsbury's Laws* (5th edn, 2015) vol 12, paras 712–723.

5.2 The reasons given by the Law Commission for the introduction of this presumption make it clear that the words 'mechanical instruments' include computers and computer-like devices – even though computers and computer-like devices are not mechanical instruments. Judges have, although not exclusively, used the term 'reliable' in relation to computers, and lawyers have also bypassed the use of the word 'reliable' by using the word 'robust'. The purpose of this chapter is to consider the introduction of a presumption of 'in order' or 'reliability' or 'working properly' in relation to mechanical instruments generally, and to explain why the term 'reliable' in relation to computers and computer-like devices is not accurate, although we now have definitive evidence from computer scientists that the words 'reliable' and 'robust' as used by lawyers and judges have been exposed as not having the meaning attributed to them by the legal profession.[1] It must be emphasized that the examples of the failure of computers and similar devices discussed in this chapter are provided to demonstrate the problems that occur, and do not represent the totality of illustrations that could be used, nor the volume of errors that have occurred or will occur in the future. It is suggested that judicial notice be taken of these examples, particularly because they contradict the presumption that computers are 'reliable'.[2]

1 Peter Bernard Ladkin, Bev Littlewood, Harold Thimbleby and Martyn Thomas CBE, 'The Law Commission presumption concerning the dependability of computer evidence' (2020) 17 Digital Evidence and Electronic Signature Law Review 1; Peter Bernard Ladkin, 'Robustness of software' (2020) 17 Digital Evidence and Electronic Signature Law Review 15; Michael Jackson, 'An approach to the judicial evaluation of evidence from computers and computer systems' (2021) 18 Digital Evidence and Electronic Signature Law Review 50.

Stephen Mason, 'The presumption that computers are "reliable" ', in Stephen Mason and Daniel Seng (eds.), *Electronic Evidence and Electronic Signatures* (5th edn, University of London 2021) 126–235.

2 For instance, problems with the century date change problem continue to afflict technology, and in 2038 the problem will occur again, because epoch time on Unix is stored as a 32-bit integer, which will run out of capacity at 3.14 am on 19 January 2038, for which see Chris Stokel-Walker, 'A lazy fix 20 years ago means the Y2K bug is taking down computers now', NewScientist Technology, 7 January 2020, https://www.newscientist.com/article/2229238-a-lazy-fix-20-years-ago-means-the-y2k-bug-is-taking-down-computers-now/; Professor Martyn Thomas, 'What really happened in Y2K?', Gresham College lecture, 4 April 2017, https://www.gresham.ac.uk/lectures-and-events/what-really-happened-in-y2k.

The purpose of a presumption

5.3 The aim of a presumption, which allocates the burden of proof, is to alleviate the need to prove every item of evidence adduced in legal proceedings, to reduce the need for evidence in relation to some issues and to save 'the time and expense of proving the obvious'.[1] In an appeal before the Supreme Court of South Australia, Travers J explained the rationale in the case of *Barker v Fauser*[2] regarding the accuracy[3] of the readings of a weighbridge:

> It is rather a matter of the application of the ordinary principles of circumstantial evidence. In my opinion such instruments can merely provide prima-facie evidence in the sense indicated by *May v. O'Sullivan* [(1955) 92 CLR 654]. They do not transfer any onus of proof to one who disputes them, though they may, and often do, create a case to answer. Circumstantial evidence is something which is largely based upon our ordinary experience of life ... It is merely an application of this principle to our ordinary experience in life which tells us of the general probability of the substantial correctness of watches, weighbridges and other such instruments. If they are instruments or machines of a type which we know to be in common use our experience tells us that this is suggestive of their substantial correctness. Experience also tells us that they are rarely completely accurate, but usually so substantially accurate that people go on using them, and that subject to a certain amount of allowance for some measure of incorrectness, they act upon them.[4]

1 *Holt v Auckland City Council* [1980] 2 NZLR 124, per Richardson J at 128.
2 (1962) SASR 176.
3 The words 'accurate', 'precision' and 'correctness' are often used interchangeably in the everyday sense, but they have different meanings in their technical use. I owe this observation to Professor Martin Newby.
4 (1962) SASR 176 at 178–179.

5.4 This explanation justifies the rationale for the presumption that mechanical instruments were in order at the material time. However, it appears that this presumption exists on the basis of expediency. In admitting evidence from a mechanical instrument or similar device, judges have not justified the presumption on the basis of relevant scientific evidence, but have substituted for it concepts such as 'common use', 'ordinary experience' or 'substantial correctness'.

5.5 Consider the accuracy of a watch. Just because a watch has passed tests of accuracy at one moment in time does not preclude its mechanical parts from failing subsequently. In *Cheatle v Considine*, Travers J put the discussion of the accuracy of mechanical instruments into its overall context:

> My view on the subject of such instruments is that reliance on them is basically an application of circumstantial evidence. The fact that people go on relying upon

> watches, speedometers, or even hearing aids, seems to be some circumstantial proof that all these things do provide some aid or assistance to those who use them, otherwise they would not go on using them. They are not necessarily accurate, and indeed, probably, most of such instruments on being properly tested would reveal some degree of inaccuracy. But I think in the absence of contrary evidence, they are to be regarded as some proof.[1]

1 *Cheatle v Considine* [1965] SASR 281 at 282.

Presumptions and mechanical instruments

5.6 The presumption that scientific instruments work properly has a long history.[1] For instance, scales benefit from the presumption.[2] Timing devices also take advantage of the presumption. In *Plancq v Marks*,[3] in an appeal against conviction for driving a motor car in excess of the speed limit of 20 mph, the evidence of the police officer was challenged. The stopwatch used by the police officer was produced in court. The appeal focused on the ground that the police officer gave opinion evidence as to the speed of the vehicle. This appeal was dismissed on the basis that the police officer was merely giving oral evidence of the actions of the stopwatch, which did not constitute the giving of opinion evidence. The real issue was whether the police officer was telling the truth.

1 R. P. Groom-Johnson and G. F. L. Bridgman (eds), *A Treatise on the Law of Evidence* (12th edn, Sweet and Maxwell 1931), 167, in which the working accuracy of certain scientific instruments, such as watches, clocks, thermometers, aneroids and anemometers, among other 'ingenious contrivances', was recognized in the absence of evidence to the contrary.
2 *Giles v Dodds* [1947] VLR 465, [1947] ArgusLawRp 53; (1947) 53 Argus LR 584.
3 (1906) 94 LT NS 577.

5.7 Arguments that a watch used to prove that the defendant was speeding ought to be tested have been ignored,[1] as in the case of *Gorham v Brice*.[2] The Lord Chief Justice dismissed the appeal against conviction for driving a motor car in excess of the speed limit of 12 mph without considering the point. In comparison, the members of the Divisional Court in *Melhuish v Morris*[3] allowed an appeal against speeding because the speedometer of the police vehicle had not been tested for accuracy.[4] The court in *Nicholas v Penny*[5] subsequently overturned this decision. Lord Goddard CJ commented:

> The question in the present case is whether, if evidence is given that a mechanical device, such as a watch or speedometer – and I cannot see any difference in principle between a watch and a speedometer – recorded a particular time or a particular speed, which is the purpose of that instrument to record, that can by itself be prima facie evidence, on which the court can act, of that time or speed.[6]

1 In communication with the author, Professor Lorenzo Strigini, Professor of Systems Engineering School of Mathematics, Computer Science and Engineering, Department of Computer Science, City University of London, points out that, from an engineering point of view, testing that a watch is accurate enough now (which usually implies that it was accurate until now, unless it has been repaired) is an inexpensive enough exercise that not doing it seems a dereliction of duty.
2 (1902) 18 TLR 424.
3 [1938] 4 All ER 98, [1938] 10 WLUK 7; see also 'Evidence in speed limit cases', The Journal of Criminal Law (1937) 1(2) 181.
4 Evidence that the accused did not exhibit the usual signs of being intoxicated can indicate that a machine is not working properly: *R. v Crown Prosecution Service Ex p. Spurrier* [1999] 7 WLUK 431, (2000) 164 JP 369, [2000] RTR 60, Times, 12 August 1999, [1999] CLY 883, also known as *DPP v*

Spurrier. Police officers can conduct physical tests to ensure a speedometer is working accurately, for which see *Mohammed Aslam Pervez v Procurator* [2000] ScotHC 111.
5 [1950] 2 KB 466, [1950] 2 All ER 89, 66 TLR (Pt. 1) 1122, [1950] 5 WLUK 20, (1950) 114 JP 335, 48 LGR 535, 21 ALR2d 1193, (1950) 94 SJ 437, [1947–51] CLY 9158, also known as *Penny v Nicholas*; 66 Law Quarterly Review (1950) 264, 441; in the South Australian case of *Peterson v Holmes* [1927] SASR 419, Piper J asked, at 421, 'If [appears as "It" is in the report, but this must be a mistake] the speedometer be tested by stop-watches and measured distances, what about the accuracy of the watches and the chain measure?'; 'Proof of excessive speed' (1950) XIV(4) The Journal of Criminal Law 360.
6 [1950] 2 KB 466 at 473.

5.8 The judge went on to suggest that because the defendant was accused of exceeding the speed limit by 10 mph, it 'would be a considerable error in the speedometer if it were as much out as that'.[1] Such a comment was not intended, it is suggested, to create a presumption that such devices are reliable, especially as Lord Goddard CJ commented that 'the justices need never accept any evidence if they do not believe it, or feel that for some reason they cannot accept it'.[2] A similar issue arose in the case of *H. Gould and Company Limited v Cameron*,[3] where the pressure in the tyres of a heavy motor vehicle was tested in July and found to be over the legal limit. The instrument used to test the tyre pressure had itself been tested in March of the previous year, and in August in the year following the reading. The defence argued that the instrument might have developed an error after being tested in March. It was known and accepted that, at certain pressures, the device would be in error of 1 lb over a range of tests between 70 lb and 100 lb. This error had been taken into account in this case. Northcroft J said:

> In a case such as this, where of necessity, a mechanical device must be used to ascertain the pressure within the tyres, it is sufficient, I think, to show that the instrument is used correctly, and that, from its nature and history, it may reasonably be relied upon by the Court. The history of this instrument and the description of its use satisfies me that the learned Magistrate was justified in accepting it, as I do, as a reliable test on this occasion.[4]

1 [1950] 2 KB 466 at 473.
2 [1950] 2 KB 466 at 742. In *R v Amyot* (1968) 2 OR 626, Clare Co.Ct.J accepted the use of a stop-watch to measure the time a vehicle took to travel between marked points on a highway, where the police officer had personally checked the distance between the markings using a cyclometer and made the observations with the stop-watch in an aircraft.
3 [1951] NZLR 314.
4 [1951] NZLR 314 at 316 (40–45).

5.9 The observations by Shadbolt DCJ in the New South Wales case of *Re Appeal of White*[1] put the matter into perspective when hearing an appeal for exceeding the speed limit, where he noted, at 430:

> Courts have been generally loath to be wearied in seeking proof of some absolute measure or requiring it in cases such as this. It is not possible for every child to check his wooden ruler with the standard metre in Canberra nor every grocer his scales with the standard gram. Most of us accept the ruler's accuracy and the weight of the grocer's scales.

1 (1987) 9 NSWLR 427.

5.10 It does not follow, however, that every measuring device is accurate.

Judicial formulations of the presumption that mechanical instruments are in order when used

Judicial notice

5.11 There are a number of reasons for the doctrine of judicial notice:[1] to expedite the hearing of a case where obvious facts do not need proving; to promote uniformity in judicial decision making and to prevent the possibility of a decision which is demonstrably erroneous or false.[2] Brett JA summed up the concept in *R v Aspinall*: 'Judges are entitled and bound to take judicial notice of that which is the common knowledge of the great majority of mankind and of the greater majority of men of business.'[3] In the High Court of Australia,[4] Isaacs J emphasized the guiding principle of the doctrine:

> The only guiding principle – apart from Statute – as to judicial notice which emerges from the various recorded cases, appears to be that wherever a fact is so generally known that every ordinary person may be reasonably presumed to be aware of it, the Court 'notices' it, either *simpliciter* if it is at once satisfied of the fact without more, or after such information or investigation as it considers reliable and necessary in order to eliminate any reasonable doubt.
>
> The basic essential is that the fact is to be of a class that is so generally known as to give rise to the presumption that all persons are aware of it.[5]

1 See Law Commission New Zealand, *Evidence Law: Documentary Evidence and Judicial Notice: A Discussion Paper* (Preliminary Paper No 22, 1994) Chapter IX for a nuanced consideration of the topic; Hodge M. Malek (ed), *Phipson on Evidence* (19th edn, Sweet & Maxwell 2018), chapter 3.
2 Christopher Allen, 'Case comment: judicial notice extended' (1998) E & P 37, 39; David M. Paciocco, 'Proof and progress: coping with the law of evidence in a technological age' (2013) 11(2) Canadian Journal of Law and Technology 181, 188–189; Evidence (Interim) [1985] ALRC 26 [969]; Law Commission New Zealand, *Evidence Law: Documentary Evidence and Judicial Notice: A Discussion Paper* (Preliminary Paper No 22, 1994), [259].
3 (1876) 3 QBD 48 at 61–62.
4 *Holland v Jones* (1917) 23 CLR 149, [1917] VLR 392, 23 ALR 165, 1917 WL 15976, [1917] HCA 26.
5 (1917) 23 CLR 149 at 153.

5.12 The practical approach was considered in *Commonwealth Shipping Representative v Peninsular and Oriental Branch Service*[1] by Lord Summer:

> My Lords, to require that a judge should affect a cloistered aloofness from facts that every other man in Court is fully aware of, and should insist on having proof on oath of what, as a man of the world, he knows already better than any witness can tell him, is a rule that may easily become pedantic and futile.[2]

1 [1923] AC 191, (1922) 13 Ll L Rep 455, [1922] 12 WLUK 85, also known as *Peninsular & Oriental Branch Service v Commonwealth Shipping Representative.*
2 [1923] AC 191 at 211.

5.13 The doctrine of judicial notice is restricted to very clear knowledge,[1] and it can be more severe in its effect than a presumption, as noted by Susan G. Drummond:

> It is a manoeuvre that forecloses further evidence. The judge operates, in this case, as a virtually unlimited authority with limitations imposed only from within the legal hierarchy. Judicial notice can only be contested on appeal and invalidated if it can be demonstrated that the criteria for the application

> of judicial notice were not present (the fact was not notorious, the sources to establish the fact were not indisputable ...). As judicially noticed matters operate in the domain of fact, not law, they have no precedential value.[2]

1 For discussions on the confusing treatment of this doctrine, see G. D. Nokes, 'The limits of judicial notice' (1958) 74 LQR 59 and Susan G. Drummond, 'Judicial notice: the very texture of legal reasoning' 15 No 1 Can JL & Soc'y 1.
2 Drummond, 'Judicial notice: the very texture of legal reasoning', 4.

5.14 Given that it appears as if this doctrine has been extended to electronic evidence in Canada, this observation by Drummond illustrates the importance of ensuring judges more fully understand the nature of the world in which they now live. Thorson JA discussed judicial notice in *R. v Potts* before the Ontario Supreme Court, Court of Appeal:

> Judicial notice, it has been said, is the acceptance by a court or judicial tribunal, without the requirement of proof, of the truth of a particular fact or state of affairs that is of such general or common knowledge in the community that proof of it can be dispensed with.
>
> ...
>
> Thus it has been held that, generally speaking, a court may properly take judicial notice of any fact or matter which is so generally known and accepted that it cannot reasonably be questioned, or any fact or matter which can readily be determined or verified by resort to sources whose accuracy cannot reasonably be questioned.[1]

1 1982 CarswellOnt 56, [1982] OJ No 3207, 134 DLR (3d) 227, 14 MVR 72, 26 CR (3d) 252, 36 OR (2d) 195, 66 CCC (2d) 219, 7 WCB 236, at [15].

5.15 In *R. v Find*,[1] before the Supreme Court of Canada, McLachlin CJC, at [48], held that the threshold for judicial notice is strict:

> Judicial notice dispenses with the need for proof of facts that are clearly uncontroversial or beyond reasonable dispute. Facts judicially noticed are not proved by evidence under oath. Nor are they tested by cross-examination. Therefore, the threshold for judicial notice is strict: a court may properly take judicial notice of facts that are either: (1) so notorious or generally accepted as not to be the subject of debate among reasonable persons; or (2) capable of immediate and accurate demonstration by resort to readily accessible sources of indisputable accuracy.

1 2001 CarswellOnt 1702, 2001 CarswellOnt 1703, 2001 SCC 32, [2001] 1 SCR863, [2001] SCJ No 34, 146 OAC 236, 154 CCC (3d) 97, 199 DLR (4th) 193, 269 NR 149, 42 CR (5th) 1, 49 WCB (2d) 595, 82 CRR (2d) 247, JE 2001-1099, REJB 2001-24178.

5.16 The concept of 'notorious' is considered in *Phipson*:

> the concept covers matters being so notorious or clearly established or susceptible of demonstration by reference to a readily obtainable and authoritative source that evidence of their existence is unnecessary. Some facts are so notorious or so well established to the knowledge of the court that they may be accepted without further enquiry.[1]

1 Malek, *Phipson on Evidence*, para 3:02.

5.17 The judge can conduct her own research, and the United States Court of Appeals, Ninth Circuit reached conclusions regarding automatic programs in this way, as in *U.S. v Lizarraga-Tirado*, where Kozinski CJ said:

> Because there was no evidence at trial as to how the tack and its label were put on the satellite image, we must determine, if we can, whether the tack was computer generated or placed manually. Fortunately, we can take judicial notice of the fact that the tack was automatically generated by the Google Earth program. By looking to 'sources whose accuracy cannot reasonably be questioned' – here, the program – we can 'accurately and readily determine [ ]' that the tack was placed automatically. *See* Fed.R.Evid. 201(b). Specifically, we can access Google Earth and type in the GPS coordinates, and have done so, which results in an identical tack to the one shown on the satellite image admitted at trial.[1]

1 789 F.3d 1107 (9th Cir. 2015), 1109. Although judges should be wary of reaching conclusions without adequate evidence, as in the case of *1475182 Ontario Inc. o/a Edges Contracting v Ghotbi*, 2021 ONSC 3477 (CanLII), where Boswell J incorrectly determined, at [50], that the unique telephone number linked to a cellular telephone, taken together with the International Mobile Equipment Identifier number 'provide, in effect, a digital signature on every message sent by the user of that particular device.'

5.18 In justifying judicial notice, David M. Paciocco comments: 'If a court could not rely on a notorious and incontrovertible material fact because it had not been proved, verdicts would not conform to reality. The repute of the administration of justice would be harmed.'[1] Paciocco went on to illustrate his argument with the following example of how a brake on a motor vehicle operates:

> For example when someone describes putting the brakes on in a car no-one offers expert testimony that the function of brakes is to slow or stop vehicles, that brakes are typically controlled by foot-pedals that are depressed in order to slow or stop the vehicle, or that brakes are depressed gently to come to a gradual stop and aggressively for an emergency stop.[2]

1 Paciocco, 'Proof and progress', 188–189.
2 Paciocco, 'Proof and progress', 189

5.19 There is a distinction between the purpose of a brake on a motor vehicle (which is the fact in issue in the above illustration) and how the braking system operates (if the fact in issue is whether the brakes actually worked). In the example above, Paciocco made assumptions about how braking systems work and failed to understand the nature of the technology. Most braking systems in motor vehicles are controlled by a mix of electronic systems and software code (a fact so notorious that no citation ought to be required[1]). It is more accurate, using a high-level functional description of the brake system, to explain the braking technology in vehicles as involving the use of brakes primarily under the control of electronics or software code. The failsafe fallback strategy for most modern brake systems is that if the electronics or software code fails, the system reverts to a standard hydraulic brake system. It does not necessarily follow that the function is always performed correctly or as normally expected in the situation where the action is mediated by electronic systems. For instance, anti-lock braking systems (ABS), electronic stability control (ESC) and traction control are predicated on interactions between the engine torque output and brake control on individual wheels and so on (such as using data from accelerometers). This means that there is a possible difference between the fact that a braking event took place and whether or not a braking event was requested, and vice versa.[2] This example is far from the strict application of the doctrine as noted in the Supreme Court of Canada by McLachlin CJC. If judicial notice is extended to such an extent, then the question of whether justice is served by this doctrine must be carefully scrutinized.

1 Notwithstanding that it is notorious that anti-lock brake systems are partly controlled by software code and electronic systems, the reader can obtain more information from the Society of Automotive Engineers International, the open access journal *Intelligent Control and Automation* and *IEEE Transactions on Vehicular Technology*.
2 I owe this point to Dr Michael Ellims; see also the following, in which it is demonstrated that braking systems can be controlled by hacking into the motor vehicle computer system: Chris Valasek and Charlie Miller, *Adventures in Automotive Networks and Control Units* (Technical White Paper, 2014), http://www.ioactive.com/pdfs/IOActive_Adventures_in_Automotive_Networks_and_Control_Units.pdf; Dr Charlie Miller and Chris Valasek, *Remote Exploitation of an Unaltered Passenger Vehicle* (2015), http://illmatics.com/Remote%20Car%20Hacking.pdf; Roderick Currie, Developments in Car Hacking (SANS Institute, 2015), https://www.sans.org/reading-room/whitepapers/internet/developments-car-hacking-36607.

A 'notorious' class

5.20 In the Victoria case of *Crawley v Laidlaw*,[1] Lowe J considered, at 374, the basis upon which a presumption might apply – in this case regarding a scientific instrument:

> I do not question that such a presumption is frequently and (in general) tacitly acted on by our Courts; but in my opinion it must appear from evidence before the Court, or from something which stands in place of evidence, *e.g.*, judicial notice, that the instrument in question is a scientific instrument, before the presumption applies.

1 (1930) VLR 370.

5.21 The prosecution sought to adduce evidence from two weighing machines called 'loadometers' to prove a motor truck was carrying a greater weight than that allowed by the regulations. The Police Magistrate who heard the case had dismissed it on the basis that there was no evidence to demonstrate the correctness of the instruments. On appeal, Lowe J concurred, holding that there was no evidence that the devices were scientific instruments, and there was no foundation for a presumption that the instruments worked properly. Emphasizing the need to establish a foundation for the presumption, Lowe J observed:

> I do not doubt that in appropriate cases the Court will use its 'general information and ... knowledge of the common affairs of life which men of ordinary intelligence possess' – *Phipson on Evidence* (6th ed.), p. 19 – and that of the nature of most, if not all, of the instruments mentioned in the paragraph cited from *Taylor*[1] would require no evidence in order to raise the presumption relied on. I think, too, that the Court may, if it thinks it desirable, refer to appropriate standard works of reference in order to inform itself of matters of the kind mentioned of, which it may personally be unaware. But if, after such reference, the Court is still ignorant of the nature of the instrument in question, no help can be got from the presumption relied on. Apparently the learned magistrate did not know, and I myself do not know, what a loadometer is. I may guess from the derivation of the name what the instrument is, but my guess is not evidence.[2]

1 *Taylor on Evidence* (10th edn), s 183, where the author wrote: 'The working accuracy of scientific instruments is also presumed. For example, in the absence of evidence to the contrary, a jury would be advised to rely on the correctness of a watch or clock, which had been consulted to fix the time when a certain event happened; a thermometer would be regarded as a sufficiently safe indication of the heat of

any liquid in which it had been immersed; a pedometer would afford prima facie evidence of the distance between two places which had been traversed by the wearer; and similar prima facie credit would be given to aneroids, anemometers, and other scientific instruments; and blood stains are every day detected by means of known chemical tests:' (1930) VLR 370 at 373–374. This quote uses the term 'correctness'; others seem to refer to 'sufficient accuracy'. A measurement instrument for a continuous quantity has a degree of accuracy (how close the reading is to the real value) and a degree of precision (how tightly spaced the points are on its scale), but its reading will not usually be exactly 'correct'. This may have a bearing on how digital devices are seen. A tiny amount of damage to the mechanical mechanism of a scale might cause it to be slightly off the exact reading of weight, but a tiny mistake in software may change the response to some specific inputs substantially. I owe this insight to Professor Strigini.

2 (1930) VLR 370 at 374.

5.22 Herring CJ made comments similar to Lowe J's in the Victoria case of *Porter v Koladzeij*.[1] This case involved the review of the refusal of a Stipendiary Magistrate to admit evidence of an analogue device to measure the amount of alcohol in a sample of breath. The judge observed that certain instruments of a scientific or technical nature fell into a 'notorious' class that by general experience are known to be trustworthy.[2] He placed a speedometer into this class. However, the evidence from the device to measure breath alcohol was rejected because it was not a standard device, and because the evidence given by the witness regarding the device was not adequate. The judge said that once breath analysis devices were used more often, they would become standard, and then judicial notice would be taken of their existence as scientific or technical instruments,[3] although it was necessary to present relevant evidence to the court:

> Where, however, the instrument in question does not fall within the notorious class, then his Honour made it clear that evidence must be given to establish that it is a scientific or technical instrument of such a kind, as may be expected to be trustworthy, before the presumption can be relied upon.[4]

1 (1962) VR 75.
2 Falling back on 'general experience' is dubious, because few people check the correctness of the instruments they might use. People routinely use imprecise instruments such as house thermometers and speedometers, and seldom have occasions for questioning the readings. Relying on the reading does not make the reading accurate.
3 The Supreme Court in South Australia refused to take judicial notice of the accuracy of the breathalyser in 2012: *Police v Bleeze* [2012] SASCF 54 at [88] and [89].
4 (1962) VR 75 at 78.

5.23 The failure to obtain such evidence can lead to scenarios such as that described by Thomas E. Workman below:

> In Florida, one citizen was tested 13 times on one machine, by one officer, in one hour. These instances occur because in some situations, a machine that registers an error or multiple errors may finally produce a value that has the appearance of being a valid test. The Courts are usually unaware of the history of failures on the machine, and believe that the result is legitimate, when in fact [it] may not be.[1]

1 Thomas E. Workman, Jr, 'Massachusetts breath testing for alcohol: a computer science perspective' (2008) 8 J High Tech L. 209, 217.

5.24 In this context,[1] it is relevant to consider the decision of the Supreme Court in New Jersey in the United States, which ordered the software of a breath-testing device to be reviewed in detail in the case of *State of New Jersey v Chun*.[2] In his judgment, Hoens J began by stating that: 'For decades, this Court has recognized that certain breath testing devices, commonly known as breathalyzers, are scientifically reliable and accurate instruments for determining blood alcohol concentration.' This comment was based on the old technology. With the introduction of a new device, the Alcotest 7100 MK111-C, which was selected by the department of the Attorney General, the court agreed to test the scientific validity of the machine. After extensive testing, the court concluded that the Alcotest, utilizing New Jersey Firmware version 3.11, 'is generally scientifically reliable', but modifications were required to enable its results to be admitted into legal proceedings.[3] The testing of the software revealed the following issues, among others:[4]

> 1. That a mathematical algorithm that corrected for fuel-cell drift did not undermine the reliability of the results, but it was recommended that the machines be recalibrated every six months to ensure fuel cells are replaced regularly.
>
> 2. That a specific buffer overflow error should be corrected.
>
> 3. That a specific number of documents be produced for the purposes of foundation of evidence, as recommended by the court.
>
> 4. That the recommendations by the defendants' experts for reorganizing and simplifying the source code be considered for implementation.

1 These devices are also discussed, in the context of England and Wales, under the heading 'The statutory presumption' below.
2 194 N.J. 54, 943 A.2d 114.
3 943 A.2d 114 at 120.
4 943 A.2d 114 at 134.

5.25 The analysis of the source code indicated that there was a fault when a third breath sample was taken that could cause the reading to be incorrect, and the court saw fit to order a change in one of the formulae used in the software. Save that the extensive analysis of the device and the source code took some time and some expense, little of substance was found to be wrong with the machine. However, there are two significant points that arise as a result of this case: the first is that the software that controlled the device, written by a human, was defective, which in turn meant that the data relied upon for the truth of the statement was defective and therefore affected the accuracy and truthfulness of the evidence; and the decision by the court to intervene by ordering certain changes and modifications to be carried out, one of which was a change in a formula, meant that part of the evidence used against drivers in the future would be a set of instructions provided by the Supreme Court of New Jersey.[1]

1 There is a considerable body of case law relating to challenges of breathalyser devices in the US. Some of the articles that discuss the position are (in addition to those already cited): Charles Short, 'Guilt by machine: the problem of source code discovery in Florida DUYI prosecutions' (2009) 61 Fla L Rev 61, 177; Cheyenne L. Palmer, 'DUIs and apple pie: a survey of American jurisprudence in DUI prosecutions' (2010) 13 UDC L Rev 407; Aurora J. Wilson, 'Discovery of breathalyzer source code in DUI prosecutions' (2011) 7 Wash JL Tech & Arts 121; Kathleen E. Watson, 'COBRA data and the right to confront technology against you' (2015) 42 N Ky L Rev 375.

5.26 However, it is not necessary to rely on a presumption that an instrument is accurate or reliable in lieu of other evidence that the data produced by the instrument is accurate.[1] For instance, a satellite navigation system was the subject of discussion in *Chiou Yaou Fa v Thomas Morris*[2] before the Supreme Court of the Northern Territory of Australia. In this case, the commander of the vessel established his position by using the satellite navigation system, radar and sextant. The court accepted the evidence that a variety of methods were used to establish the position at sea, including the expertise of qualified navigators. Even though the court heard their testimony as to the accuracy of the satellite navigation system, it concluded that it was not necessary to determine, and therefore rely upon, the satellite navigation system as being in the 'notorious' class, and accepted the radar and sextant evidence in its place.[3]

1 In *R. v Ranger* 2010 CarswellOnt 8572, 2010 ONCA 759, [2010] OJ No 4840, 91 WCB (2d) 271, the Ontario Court of Appeal held at [16]: 'it is now notorious that cell phone users engaged in a cell phone call and travelling from point A to point B will find their cell phone signal passes from one cell phone tower to another at different locations along the route from point A to point B', which led the court to consider that the trial judge did not err 'in taking judicial notice that a particular cell phone was in a general location based on the tower that received the signal and that the path along which the cell phone was moving could be determined by reference to the cell phone towers that received the signal transmission in respect of particular calls'.

2 [1987] NTSC 20; 46 NTR 1; 87 FLR 36; 27 A Crim R 342 (8 May 1987).

3 Here are a selection of cases dealing with aerial photography, infra-red rays and images from satellites. International Court of Justice: *Land and Maritime Boundary between Cameroon and Nigeria*, ICJ Reports 1991, 31; *Kasikili/Sedudu Island (Botswana/Namibia)*, ICJ Reports 1999, 1045; *Maritime Delimitation and Territorial Questions between Qatar and Bahrain*, ICJ Reports, 2001, Judgment (Merits), 16 March 2001; *Survey of Recent Court Cases that Consider Remote Sensing Data as Evidence – Case Concerning Frontier Dispute*, ICJ Reports 1986, 554. Permanent Court of Arbitration: *Eritrea/Yemen*, Award 9 October 1998; Award 17 December 1999. Australia: *Witheyman v Simpson* [2009] QCA 388; *McKay v Doonan* [2005] QDC 311; *Maple Holdings Limited v State of Queensland* [2001] QPEC 056. England and Wales: *Associated British Ports v Hydro Soil Services NV* [2006] EWHC 1187 (TCC), [2006] 6 WLUK 575. Singapore: *Virtual Map (Singapore) v Singapore Land Authority* [2008] SGHC 42. USA: *St. Martin v Mobil Exploration & Producing U.S. Inc.*, 224 F.3d 402 (5th Cir. 2000), 31 Envtl. L. Rep. 20, 01155 Fed. R. Evid. Serv. 270 (aerial photography); *Connecticut v Wright*, 58 Conn.App. 136, 752 A.2d 1147 (Conn.App. 2000) (computer-generated engineering map); *Wetsel-Oviatti Lumber Co. Inc., v United States*, 40 Fed.Cl. 557 (1998) (aerial photography); *United States v Kilgus*, 571 F.2d 508 (9th Cir. 1978) (infra-red rays); *Pittson Co. v Allianz Insurance Co.*, 905 F.Supp. 1279 (D.N.J. 1995) rev'd in part on other grounds, 124 F.3d 508 (3d Cir. 1997) (aerial photography); *Ponca Tribe of Indians of Oklahoma v Continental Carbon Co.*, 2008 WL 7211981 (digital orthophoto); *Gasser v United States*, 14 Cl.Ct. 476 (1988) (aerial and satellite photographs); *I & M Rail Link v Northstar Navigation*, 21 F.Supp. 849 (N.D.Ill. 1998) (satellite photography); *Wojciechowicz v United States*, 576 F.Supp.2d 214 (D.Puerto Rico 2008) (satellite photography); *Lisker v Knowles*, 651 F.Supp.2d 1097 (C.D. Cal. 2009) (satellite photography); *United States v Fullwood*, 342 F.3d 409 (5th Cir. 2003) (satellite photography); *Fry v King*, 192 Ohio App.3d 692, 950 N.E.2d 229 (Ohio App. 2 Dist. 2011), 2011 WL 766583 (satellite photography); *State v Reed*, 2009 WL 2991548 (Google Earth evidence rejected); *State of New Jersey in the Interests of J. B. A Minor*, 2010 WL 3836755 (Google Earth evidence admitted); *Swayden v Ricke*, 242 P.3d 1281 (2010), 2010 WL 4977158 (Google Earth images and photographs from 'trail cameras'); *Banks v U.S.*, 94 Fed.Cl. 68 (2010) (satellite photography).

Common knowledge

5.27 Another justification for accepting that a mechanical instrument is in order when it is used is the assertion that it is a type of instrument that is commonly held to be – more often than not – in 'working order'. In discussing mechanical instruments, it does not appear that lawyers or judges have ever concerned themselves with how the instrument has been maintained, or have considered the maintenance history of the instrument. In a case before the full court of the Supreme Court of Western Australia, *Zappia v Webb*,[1] the question was whether an amphometer, used to determine the speed of a vehicle, could be considered an accepted scientific instrument. Jackson CJ discussed this as follows:

> It is, however, common knowledge that amphometers have been widely used in this State for a number of years for the purpose of checking the speed of motor vehicles.[2] As one drives through the country, it is common-place to see large notices by the side of the road warning motorists that amphometers are used

> in the district, and it is not at all uncommon to see a traffic inspector by the side of the road with his amphometer equipment set up. It is also, I believe, generally accepted in the community that an amphometer correctly set up and operated will give a reliable reading of speed, not necessarily precise, but sufficiently accurate for its purpose. There has not been, so far as I am aware, any general complaint about the use or efficiency of these machines, and there must be hundreds of speeding convictions each year resulting from their use.
>
> It seems to me, therefore, that an amphometer is now a well known and accepted speed checking device and that judicial notice should be taken in this State of its use and effectiveness, in general terms.[3]

1 (1974) WAR 15; (1973) 29 LGRA 438.
2 Lie detectors are widely used and are scientifically shown to be useless, for which see Shane O'Mara, *Why Torture Doesn't Work: The Neuroscience of Interrogation* (Harvard University Press 2015), chapter 3 'Can we use technology to detect deception?'; George W. Maschke and Gino J. Scalabrini, *The Lie Behind the Lie Detector* (5th edn, AntiPolygraph.org 2018), https://antipolygraph.org/pubs.shtml.
3 (1973) 29 LGRA 438 at 440–441.

5.28 The Chief Justice referred to the 'common knowledge' of the use of amphometers without referring to any evidence to demonstrate that they were reliable. He also asserted that somehow it was generally accepted that the device would give a reliable reading of speed (without discussing whether the amphometer was calibrated, and if so, to what standard) and concluded that because he was not aware of any complaints about the devices, they were therefore to be considered an accepted speed-checking device.

5.29 In *Castle v Cross*,[1] the prosecution relied on the presumption that mechanical instruments were in order when they were used. In the judgment, Stephen Brown LJ cited a passage from *Cross on Evidence* (1979)[2] regarding this presumption:

> A presumption which serves the same purpose of saving the time and expense of calling evidence as that served by the maxim omnia praesumuntur rite esse acta is the presumption that mechanical instruments were in order when they were used. In the absence of evidence to the contrary, the courts will presume that stopwatches and speedometers and traffic lights were in order at the material time; but the instrument must be one of a kind which it is common knowledge that they are more often than not in working order.[3]

1 [1984] 1 WLR 1372, [1985] 1 All ER 87, [1984] 7 WLUK 180, [1985] RTR 62, [1984] Crim LR 682, (1984) 81 LSG 2596, (1984) 128 SJ 855, [1985] CLY 3048.
2 Page 47 of the fifth edition.
3 [1984] 1 WLR 1372 at 1376H–1377A.

5.30 The Latin tag *omnia praesumuntur rite esse acta* means 'all acts are presumed to have been done rightly and regularly' or 'all things are presumed to have been done regularly and with due formality until the contrary is proved'. Such a presumption cannot operate in a vacuum, as indicated by Stephen Brown LJ's preference for the above formulation in *Cross on Evidence*, which requires the basic fact – proof that the instrument be one of a kind which is common knowledge that they are more often than not in working order – to be established before the presumption could operate, as opposed to the same formulation of the presumption in *Phipson on Evidence*, which did not adopt the basic fact.[1]

1 [1984] 1 WLR 1372 at 1377.

5.31 In this case, counsel for the Crown put forward the case that the device in question, a Lion Intoximeter 3000, was a sophisticated machine that depended in part on software code, but this did not set it in a different class from other sophisticated mechanical devices and instruments. The presumption stood unchallenged because the defence 'argued forcefully that the potential for computer error renders the consideration of evidence stemming from a computer particularly sensitive and places it into a separate class in relation to its admissibility'.[1] It is unclear from the judgment of Stephen Brown LJ whether His Lordship relied on the presumption in admitting the printout from the Lion Intoximeter 3000, because the central issue in this case appears to be the admissibility of the printout as real evidence.

1 [1984] 1 WLR 1372 at 1379D.

5.32 The case of *Anderton v Waring*[1] also concerned the reading from a Lion Intoximeter 3000. In giving the judgment of the court, May LJ stated that the 'Intoximeter ought to have been assumed by the justices to have been in good working order unless the contrary was proved'.[2] Counsel for the prosecution cited from the fourth edition of *Cross on Evidence*:[3] 'In the absence of evidence to the contrary, the courts will presume that [mechanical instruments] were in order at the material time'.[4] However, the barrister omitted to continue, and cite the basic fact that 'the instrument must be one of a kind as to which it is common knowledge that they are more often than not in working order'.[5] This has to be a misapplication of the presumption, because a presumption cannot operate in a vacuum without the basic fact or facts. In addition, the manufacturers of intoximeters (and almost all forms of software) refuse to share their code, so there is no way to establish any such basic fact or facts – in addition to which, the US cases (discussed above) illustrate that such devices are not reliable.

1 [1985] 2 WLUK 274, [1986] RTR 74, (1985) 82 LSG 1417, Times, 11 March 1985, [1986] CLY 2883.
2 [1986] RTR 74 at 80F.
3 Page 47.
4 [1986] RTR 74 at 79E.
5 *Cross on Evidence* (6th edn, 1985), 28; Professor Tapper mentioned this omission in Colin Tapper, 'Reform of the law of evidence in relation to the output from computers' (1995) 3(1) Intl J L & Info Tech 79, 89.

5.33 A more recent reformulation of the presumption has been articulated by Kerr LCJ, as he then was, when he rejected the suggestion that the machine in question ought to be commonly known to be – more often than not – in working order. In *Public Prosecution Service v McGowan*,[1] Kerr LCJ said:

> In so far as the passage from *Cross and Tapper* suggests that for the presumption to operate it will always be necessary that the machine was commonly known to be more often than not in working order, we would not accept it. We consider that the presumption must be that machines such as a cash register are operating properly and in working order in the absence of evidence to the contrary. The presumption of the correct operation of equipment and proper setting is a common law presumption recognised by article 33(2) [Criminal Justice (Evidence) (Northern Ireland) Order 2004]. In the modern world the presumption of equipment being properly constructed and operating correctly must be strong.[2]

1 [2008] NICA 13, [2009] NI 1.
2 [2009] NI 1 at [20].

5.34 Kerr LCJ's deviation from the formulation of the presumption, which requires proof of the basic fact, is unwarranted. Furthermore, Kerr LCJ's formulation of the presumption without the basic fact leads to the extraordinarily broad assumption that all devices and machines are operating properly and in working order, an assumption for which His Lordship did not cite any relevant evidence in support. In particular, there was nothing in the judgment to indicate what he understood by 'equipment', or how the equipment was 'properly constructed', nor did he provide any evidence as to what he meant by 'operating correctly' or 'proper setting'.[1]

1 The assumption of correctness would be verified by recording the performance of the machine, just as when one constructs a quality control chart. I owe this observation to Professor Martin Newby.

Evidential foundations of the presumption

5.35 It is suggested that the correct articulation of the presumption for mechanical instruments is as follows:[1]

> For a mechanical instrument (including stand-alone computers, computer-like devices and digital systems) to benefit from the evidential presumption that it was in working order at the material time, it is necessary for the party seeking to benefit from the presumption to adduce evidence of how the instrument in question works, together with change logs and release notices, changes to the device or system (software, physical and organizational), transaction and event logs, and sworn evidence that (i) the records disclosed are complete records of all the known defects in the device or system, and (ii) that members of staff with access to the device or system have not modified system data in the relevant period.

1 For a more detailed set of recommendations, see Paul Marshall, James Christie, Peter Bernard Ladkin, Bev Littlewood, Stephen Mason, Martin Newby, Dr Jonathan Rogers, Harold Thimbleby and Martyn Thomas CBE, 'Recommendations for the probity of computer evidence' (2021) 18 Digital Evidence and Electronic Signature Law Review 18.

5.36 This formulation is consistent with *Crawley v Laidlaw*[1] and *Porter v Koladzeij*[2] in that if the presumption is to be recognized, it is necessary for the proponent to provide sufficient evidence – the basic fact – to merit the introduction of such a presumption. It this respect, it is pertinent to note the observation by Lord Griffiths in *Cracknell v Willis*[3] that '"trial by machine" is an entirely novel concept and should be introduced with a degree of caution'.[4] He went on to indicate that it would be unthinkable that somebody should be convicted by a machine that is not 'reliable', although he did not make it clear what he meant by 'reliable'.

1 (1930) VLR 370.
2 (1962) VR 75.
3 [1988] AC 450, [1987] 3 WLR 1082, [1987] 3 All ER 801, [1987] 11 WLUK 62, (1988) 86 Cr App R 196, [1988] RTR 1, (1987) 137 NLJ 1062, (1987) 131 SJ 1514, [1988] CLY 3122; work had already been undertaken before 1988: T. R. H. Sizer and A. Kelman (eds), *Computer Generated Output as Admissible Evidence in Civil and Criminal Cases* (Heydeon & Son on behalf of the British Computer Society 1982); Alistair Kelman and Richard Sizer, *The Computer in Court* (Gower 1982).
4 [1988] 1 AC 450 at 459.

5.37 Conversely, in *DPP v McKeown (Sharon), DPP v Jones (Christopher)*[1] Lord Hoffmann voiced the opinion in 1997 that 'It is notorious that one needs no expertise in electronics to be able to know whether a computer is working properly'.[2] This comment, akin to the 'aura of infallibility',[3] is an extreme view that is contradicted by the evidence, and did not bear a great deal of scrutiny at the time the comment was made. The observation by Lloyd LJ in *R v Governor Ex p Osman (No 1), sub nom Osman (No 1), Re*[4] is of a similar nature:

> Where a lengthy computer printout contains no internal evidence of malfunction, and is retained, e.g. by a bank or a stockbroker as part of its records, it may be legitimate to infer that the computer which made the record was functioning correctly.[5]

1 [1997] 1 WLR 295, [1997] 1 All ER 737, [1997] 2 WLUK 386, [1997] 2 Cr App R 155 (HL), (1997) 161 JP 356, [1997] RTR 162, [1997] Crim LR 522, (1997) 161 JPN 482, (1997) 147 NLJ 289, Times, 21 February 1997, Independent, 7 March 1997, [1997] CLY 1093; note the comment by Harvey J in the New Zealand case of *R v Good* [2005] DCR 804 at 65 'that computers are not recently invented devices, are in wide use and are fundamentally reliable'.

2 [1997] 1 All ER 737 at 743b.

3 D. W. Elliott, 'Mechanical aids to evidence' [1958] Crim LR 5, 7.

4 [1990] 1 WLR 277, [1989] 3 All ER 701, [1988] 3 WLUK 391, (1990) 90 Cr App R 281, [1988] Crim LR 611, (1990) 87(7) LSG 32, (1990) 134 SJ 458, Times, 13 April 1988, Independent, 15 April 1988, Guardian, 19 April 1988, Daily Telegraph, 21 April 1988, [1990] CLY 1175.

5 [1990] 1 WLR 277 at 306H.

5.38 The judge did not indicate what evidence was before him to demonstrate that there was no 'internal evidence of malfunction'. Just because a bank or a stockbroker will rely on computer data as part of its records, it does not follow that a judge should accept that such records are what a party asserts they are. Indeed, Professor Seng observed that such comments made by judges are 'extravagant judicial statements … [that] are incomplete and are actually misleading because accurate computer output depends not just on the proper operation of computers, but also proper human use (or abuse) of computers'.[1] There is a significant difference between functioning 'correctly' – meaning, as intended – and *being* correct, namely that the intentions of the programmers were correct and free of any errors.

1 Daniel K. B. Seng, 'Computer output as evidence' [1997] SJLS 130, 167.

5.39 The 'instrument in working order' relies on the presumption that transitions between 'being in working order' and 'not being in working order' are reasonably rare.[1] In other words, the instrument cannot capriciously alternate between giving correct readings and incorrect readings, with arbitrary lengths of the sequences of correct and of incorrect readings. These arbitrary sequences happen rapidly and often with software. Although there is generally a reason for these sequences – something in the exact values and timings of the sequences of inputs determines which outputs will be correct and which ones will be wrong, given the defects in the software – identifying the law that governs them and the software defects causing a problem may be impossibly time-confusing, even for well-equipped experts.

1 This moves into the confusing area of inference, implication and causality. The arguments are based on a conditional probability. The court wants to know that the conditional probability that the device is working correctly is high enough given the evidence about its provenance and circumstances. Very few people understand conditional probability. I owe this observation to Professor Martin Newby.

How judges assess the evidence of devices controlled by software

5.40 When discussing the admission of evidence from devices controlled by software code, judges do not distinguish between a single, highly specialist device that is self-contained and a linked network containing any number of devices each independently operating on its own set of software code. As noted above, when considering cases dealing with specialized devices such as breath-testing machines and blood-testing machines, judges have used nebulous terms in the absence of scientific analysis, such as 'notoriety', 'common knowledge' and 'properly constructed'. There is little evidence to demonstrate that proper evidential foundations have been adduced to permit such presumptions to be admitted. In this regard, it is useful to consider, although not exclusively, the case law in Australia, where these devices have been subjected to stricter judicial analysis.

5.41 The Southern Australian case of *Mehesz v Redman*[1] concerned the method of analysing a blood sample. At trial, the Special Magistrate categorized the blood sample-testing device as a scientific instrument with the presumption that it was in the category of a 'notorious' instrument whose accuracy is presumed. On appeal, Zelling J rejected this on the basis that the device was not a mere calculator, although the interpretation of the data was a result of its software program. There was no evidence to demonstrate that the machine was accurate or reliable. The appellant was tried a second time, convicted again and appealed to the Supreme Court once more. This appeal was referred to the full court.[2] The main argument of counsel for the appellant related to the evidence tendered by the prosecution regarding the analysis of a blood sample, in that the evidence relied on the use of two instruments (a gas chromatograph and the 'Auto-lab system 4B' data analyser) whose accuracy had not been established. King CJ rejected the submission that the Auto-lab was an instrument that could not be relied upon because there was no evidence as to the 'correctness' of its software program. He said:

> The courts do not require such evidence. If the instrument is so well known that its accuracy may be assumed as a matter of common experience, the Court is entitled to presume its accuracy without evidence.[3]

1 (1979) 21 SASR 569.
2 *Mehesz v Redman (no 2)* (1980) 26 SASR 244.
3 (1980) 26 SASR 244 at 247.

5.42 Proof of the accuracy of a particular instrument will 'ordinarily be proved by those who use and test it', and the results obtained are acceptable in evidence 'provided that the expert witness has himself formed an opinion that the methods used are apt to produce the correct result'.[1] Notwithstanding the inability of the operator of a machine controlled by software code to demonstrate the accuracy or otherwise of the code that he does not control and has no ability to alter, this proviso is important. (White J also made a similar point.[2]) This means that the operator of such a machine ought to be able to assess when the machine produces results that are not expected, even if the operator is not able to establish why those results are wrong. If a machine produces results that are not anticipated, the operator is put on notice that the machine (and the software code) might not be reliable. In such circumstances, it will be necessary to have the machine tested before it is relied upon for future analysis.

1 (1980) 26 SASR 244, King CJ at 248.
2 (1980) 26 SASR 244 at 254.

5.43 Dealing with the submission that the prosecution failed to provide proper foundations for the Auto-lab analyser, White J set out the conditions that must be fulfilled before evidence will be admitted regarding the measurements of scientific instruments:

> 1. If the instrument falls within the class of instrument known as notorious scientific instruments, the court will take judicial notice of its capacity for accuracy, so that the operator merely proves that he handled it properly on the particular occasion.
>
> 2. If the instrument is *not* a notorious scientific instrument, its accuracy can be established by evidence: (a) that the instrument is within a class of instrument generally accepted by experts as accurate for its particular purpose; (b) that the instrument, if handled properly, does produce accurate results: ((a) and (b) must be established by expert testimony, that is, by experts with sufficient knowledge of that kind of instrument; and upon proof of (a) and (b), a latent *presumption of accuracy* arises which allows the court to infer accuracy on the particular occasion if it is proved) – (c) that the particular instrument was handled properly and read accurately by the operator on the particular occasion; ((c) can be established by a trained competent person familiar with the operation of the instrument, not necessarily the type of expert who proves (a) and (b)).
>
> 3. Where the actual accuracy of the measurement can be inferred from all of the proved circumstances, it is not necessary to rely upon the presumption arising from (a) and (b), proof of which is superfluous.[1]

1 (1980) 26 SASR 244 at 251–252, original emphasis.

5.44 At the second trial, the prosecution called evidence from Professor Northcote, Chairman of the School of Mathematics and Computers at the Institute of Technology in South Australia, and an expert in mathematics, physics and computers. He gave evidence about the workings of the Auto-lab from his reading of the manufacturer's manual and his understanding of the content of the manual. He was not able to read the software code, because the manufacturer had sealed the program against inspection, tampering and modification. Although Professor Northcote was not an expert in relation to the Auto-lab, the members of the Court of Appeal in the Supreme Court were of the opinion that both Professor Northcote and Mr Vozzo, who gave evidence at both trials, were sufficiently qualified to give evidence, even though neither witness had access to, nor any knowledge of, the software code. The Chief Justice also stated: 'It is sufficient that the expert who uses it is able to say that it is an instrument which is accepted and used by competent persons as a reliable aid to the carrying out of the scientific procedures in question and that he so regards it.'[1] He also prayed in aid the observations of *Wigmore on Evidence*[2] to support this comment:

> (2) Scientific instruments, formulas, etc. The use of *scientific instruments, apparatus, formulas, and calculating-tables,* involves to some extent a dependence on the statements of other persons, even of anonymous observers. Yet it is not feasible for the professional man to test every instrument himself; furthermore he finds that practically the standard methods are sufficiently to be trusted. Thus, the use of a vacuum-ray machine may give correct knowledge, though

> the user may neither have seen the object with his own eyes nor have made the calculations and adjustments on which the machine's trustworthiness depends. The adequacy of knowledge thus gained is recognized for a variety of standard instruments.[3]

1 (1980) 26 SASR 244 at 247.
2 (3rd edn), Volume 2, paragraph 665a.
3 (1980) 26 SASR 244 at 247, original emphasis.

5.45 In this case, the court emphasized that there was evidence other than the trustworthiness of the software code that enabled the evidence from the machine to be admitted as being accurate. White J set out the following analysis of the problem:

> The only defect in the expert evidence of Dr. Northcote and Mr. Vozzo, if defect it be, was their lack of direct knowledge of the internal operations of the sealed instrument. They relied upon what the manufacturer said about its operation. The extreme position would be that only the expert actually supervising the manufacture of the instrument in the United States of America could prove (a) and (b). I do not think that the rules relating to expert evidence encourage that kind of extreme position. Quite apart from questions of expense and delay in the administration of justice, the Court is entitled to rely upon evidence of measurements made by instruments which reputable scientists accept as accurate, whether those scientists have direct knowledge of the reasons for the instrument's accuracy or not, provided they have knowledge that the instrument's measurements are accurate according to a known standard, or are accepted as accurate by reputable scientists.[1]

1 (1980) 26 SASR 244 at 253. Most of these arguments fall short when applied to a large-scale system. In all of the examples where the subject of discussion is notionally a scientific instrument, there is always the possibility of treating it as a black box and testing its calibration with standard inputs, just like the weights and measures inspector turning up with a box of standard weights. These *instruments* essentially have a single input and output, and could be fully characterized experimentally. As soon as this very simple conceptual model does not fit, many other considerations come into play. Primarily that there is no longer the possibility of exhaustively examining all circumstances and factors determining behaviour. I owe this observation to Professor Martin Newby.

5.46 By implication, the court concluded that it would be extreme to establish the reliability of a software controlled device in a court of law by analysing the software code – the very software code that controlled the device and provided the evidence. The court considered that evidence from the operator of the device was sufficient for the trial court to assess the accuracy of the evidence. The appeal was dismissed.

5.47 Given these comments, it is understandable that the court reached the conclusions it did in *Mehesz v Redman (no 2)*. At issue was a self-contained device that was used by trained operators with suitable qualifications. On the basis that the readings from such devices were, at any time, not within the expected range, the suitably trained and qualified operators were expected to use their professional judgement to verify the reliability of the device before submitting the evidence for legal proceedings. In such a case, the court would not require the software code to be challenged.

5.48 The case of *Bevan v The State of Western Australia*[1] illustrates the approach taken when considering the admission of evidence from computers and computer-like devices. One of the grounds of appeal in this case was the admissibility of mobile telephone data in the form of text messages downloaded by a computer software program. An investigating police officer carried out two separate downloading operations using two separate tools, Cellebrite and XRY. At the beginning of the trial, counsel for the accused objected to the text messages being received into evidence. The trial judge held that the text messages were admissible. Questions were raised as to the reliability of the software and of the officer's correct use of it. The Court of Appeal concluded that the trial judge erred in law in admitting the text messages into evidence. This was because the officer did not explain the process of how he downloaded it in any detail at trial: it was the first time he had used the relevant software, and he did not have any formal training in its use. When considering the rebuttable presumption at common law as to the accuracy of 'notorious' scientific or technical instruments, Blaxell J said that 'when evidence from a new type of scientific instrument or process is adduced for the first time, there must be proof of its reliability and accuracy'.[2] He went on to say that:

> When specific evidence of the accuracy of a new instrument is required, this need not come from the manufacturer. It is sufficient that the expert who uses it can say that it is an instrument which is accepted and used by competent persons as a reliable aid in the carrying out of the scientific procedure in question, and that he so regards it.[3]

1 [2010] WASCA 101.
2 [2010] WASCA 101 at [30].
3 [2010] WASCA 101 at [31].

5.49 Blaxell J approved of the observations by White J[1] in *Mehesz v Redman (no 2)* as noted above. He continued:

> To the above principles I add the obvious comment that a court will not be satisfied that an instrument was 'handled properly' on a particular occasion, if it does not understand what was required of the operator for this to be so. Detailed evidence as to the workings of the instrument need not be given ... However, it is necessary that there be sufficient evidence for the court to apprehend what it was that the operator had to do in order to ensure an accurate result.[2]

1 *Mehesz v Redman (no 2)* (1980) 26 SASR 244 at [251]–[252].
2 *Bevan v The State of Western Australia* [2010] WASCA 101 at [33].

5.50 In essence, Blaxell J is saying that if the user of a smartphone can give evidence to demonstrate that he can use the smartphone, it follows that he is sufficiently knowledgeable to give evidence indirectly that the software code that controls the device is 'working properly', 'reliable' or 'accurate'. It is as if the software programs that form the device are irrelevant. Additionally, no attempt was made to define how software code can be determined to be 'working properly', 'reliable' or 'accurate'.

5.51 In *Bevan v The State of Western Australia*, the Court of Appeal heard a second appeal in the same case after a re-trial.[1] The same argument arose regarding the method of downloading the data from the mobile telephone. There was a trial within a trial concerning the evidence of Detective Tomlinson. (Buss J referred to him as a First Class Constable, and set out his qualifications.[2]) Counsel for the appellant conceded that the witness was qualified to operate the equipment used to perform the download, but argued that he was not qualified to give evidence about the accuracy of the download material and the reliability of the material itself. In cross-examination, Detective Tomlinson explained he did not hold a certificate in relation to the Cellebrite and XRY software packages, but that he had been shown how to use them on about ten occasions. The following exchange took place regarding how the software worked:

> Q. Can you tell me how the Cellebrite package actually works.
>
> A. I don't understand the question.
>
> Q. How does it work? Explain to me, a layman, who knows nothing about Cellebrite, how it works.
>
> A. It extracts data from a telephone.
>
> Q. How? How does it do that?
>
> A. It uses software.
>
> Q. And how does that software work?
>
> A. I couldn't tell you.
>
> Q. What about the XRY?
>
> A. The same.
>
> Q. If you don't know how it works, how can you say its [*sic*] reliable?
>
> A. You'd have to ask the manufacturer.
>
> Q. Okay. I'm asking you. How can you say its [*sic*] reliable.
>
> A. I can't.
>
> Q. You can't. And, in fact, on one occasion that you used it in relation to the Nokia, it was unsuccessful.
>
> A. Yes, that's right.[3]

1 [2012] WASCA 153.
2 [2012] WASCA 153 at [18]–[21] and [105].
3 [2012] WASCA 153 at [20]; the last question and answer is at [106(g)].

5.52 In deciding to allow the evidence before the members of the jury, the trial judge said:

> The workings of the instrument need not be given and it seems to me that in this case the notes of the experienced officer, the evidence that this software is regularly used by him establishes the level of accuracy and in his notes at the time that he was – successfully used the program seems to me to meet the tests ... He was a trained, experienced and competent operator and the software was operated properly and, in those circumstances, in this case I think this evidence is admissible and I will allow it to be given by the qualified expert.[1]

1 [2012] WASCA 153 at [21].

5.53 Pullin and Mazza JJA agreed the trial judge did not err in overruling the objection to the tendering of the text messages. In essence, because Detective Tomlinson was qualified as an expert, he could testify about the performance of the machines and the software. It was inferred that as an expert (in the opinion of the court), he considered the process to be accurate, and that because he had performed such actions previously, the actions undertaken on this particular occasion were properly performed – even though the user of the program will not know that it was giving inaccurate results.[1] There was no requirement for the Detective to understand how the software worked, or whether there were any problems with the software he used.[2] Pullin JA said: 'His evidence provided sufficient assurance that the results produced by the machines were reliable and accurate, because he (a trained operator of the machines) observed them to be so.'[3] But it does not follow that any operator of an electronic device will be able to detect if the device was malfunctioning in any way. As noted by Eric Van Buskirk and Vincent T. Liu:

> There is a general tendency among courts to *presume* – without the benefit of meaningful assurance – that forensic software can be trusted to yield accurate digital evidence. As a judicial construct, this presumption is unjustified in that it is not tailored to separate accurate results from inaccurate ones.[4]

1 As in the case of the death of Casey Marie Anthony in 2011, for which see Craig Wilson, 'Digital evidence discrepancies – Casey Anthony trial, 11 July 2011', http://www.digital-detective.net/digital-evidence-discrepancies-casey-anthony-trial/; Tony Pipitone, 'Cops, prosecutors botched Casey Anthony evidence', Clickorlando.com, 28 November 2012, http://www.clickorlando.com/news/cops-prosecutors-botched-casey-anthony-evidence; Jose Baez and Peter Golenbock, *Presumed Guilty: Casey Anthony: The Inside Story* (BenBella Books, updated edition 2013), 46, 180–183, 211, 346–348, 365, 368–371, 400, 426–428; Jess Ashton and Lisa Pulitzer, *Imperfect Justice: Prosecuting Casey Anthony* (William Morrow 2011), 105, 239, 277, 291–292, 298, 315.

2 [2012] WASCA 153; the rationale is set out at [66] and [67].

3 [2012] WASCA 153 at [67].

4 Eric Van Buskirk and Vincent T. Liu, 'Digital evidence: challenging the presumption of reliability' (2006) (1) Journal of Digital Forensic Practice 19, 20, original emphasis.

5.54 They suggest there are two approaches to resolve the problem in the abstract of the paper:

> One is through the proper application of scientific jurisprudence to questions of digital evidence and the other is through some combination of certain broad market and social corrections.

5.55 The important question is:

> *If the device was malfunctioning, how would the operator know?*

5.56 More significantly, the question should be:

> *How would the malfunction manifest itself, if at all, and in a form evident to the operator?*

5.57 In addition to which, it is necessary to allow for human factors: such as whether an operator focusing on getting a job done has the cognitive capacity to notice errors. It is well known that errors cause 'interference', which makes them very hard to recall even if they were noticed – that is, noticing and interpreting the error requires a different sort of thinking than doing the main task, so it interferes and makes it harder to do either properly.

5.58 In the minority, Buss J considered that none of the relevant basic facts and circumstances were proven. The judge considered the applicable legal principles in detail. He cited the relevant case law, and also extracts from *The Science of Judicial Proof* (3rd edn, 1937, para 111) by Professor Wigmore:

> Professor Wigmore enunciated three fundamental propositions applicable to evidence based on the use of a mechanical or scientific instrument constructed on knowledge of scientific laws:

> 1. *The type of apparatus purporting to be constructed on scientific principles must be accepted as dependable for the proposed purpose by the profession concerned in that branch of science or its related art.* This can be evidenced by qualified expert testimony; or, if notorious, it will be judicially noticed by the judge without evidence.
>
> 2. *The particular apparatus used by the witness must be one constructed according to an accepted type and must be in good condition for accurate work.* This may be evidenced by a qualified expert.
>
> 3. *The witness using the apparatus as the source of his testimony must be one qualified for its use by training and experience* (§220).[1]

1 [2012] WASCA 153 at [111]–[129], original emphasis.

5.59 The judge continued:

> *Wigmore on Evidence* (Chadbourn Rev, Vol III, 1970) §795 states the requirements for the admissibility of evidence based on the use of scientific instruments, as follows:
>
> > What is needed, then, in order to justify testimony based on such instruments, is preliminary professional testimony: (1) to the *trustworthiness of the process* or instrument in general (when not otherwise settled by judicial notice); (2) to the correctness of the *particular instrument*; such testimony being usually available from one and the same qualified person.[1]

1 [2012] WASCA 153 at [112], original emphasis.

5.60 And logically, as Professor Thimbleby has indicated,[1] (3) the appropriateness and correctness of the use of the instrument as used in the particular case.

1 In reviewing this chapter for the fifth edition, for which my thanks.

5.61 Buss J rejected the evidence of the constable, partly because he was not qualified to comment on the software and because the 'machines/software' were not so well known that their accuracy may be assumed as a matter of common experience.[1] Evidence was required to demonstrate their accuracy. It followed that the State had to produce evidence from a suitably qualified expert of the trustworthiness of the machines and software in general, and of the correctness of the particular instruments for the purposes of downloading data from mobile telephones.[2] Arguably, had the State produced sufficient evidence to convince a judge of the accuracy of the machines and software, it would not have been necessary to reply on the presumption. Notwithstanding this observation, the approach by Buss J is to be preferred. His brother judges appear to accept the astonishing conclusion that not having any knowledge of how a device works is irrelevant to the results of the analysis. In their approach, the work of software programmers is immaterial. Software code is not germane when determining causation. If this approach were accepted, no longer would decisions in legal proceedings be based on relevant evidence.

1 This is a criterion that ignores how often people trust something that is untrustworthy simply because they are never tempted to challenge its results and scrutinize them with sufficient rigour to be able to tell whether they are correct.

2 [2012] WASCA 153 at [132]–[139].

5.62 Contrast this decision to a similar set of facts discussed by the United States Court of Appeals, First Circuit in the case of *U.S. v Chiaradio*.[1] The Federal Bureau of Investigation (FBI) used a software tool called LimeWire, a commercially available peer-to-peer file sharing program that enables users to transmit files to and from other members of the LimeWire network. The FBI adapted this software for the purposes of investigations into abusive images of children. It was called 'enhanced peer-to-peer software' or EP2P. The software adapted by the FBI differed from LimeWire in three principle respects: (1) the software permitted downloading from only one source at a time, thus ensuring that the entire file was available on the computer of the accused; (2) in the commercially available version, LimeWire responds to a search term by displaying the names of the available files, file types, and the file sharers' IP addresses, whereas EP2P displays the same data and the identity of the Internet Service Provider (ISP), together with the city and state associated with the IP address sharing a particular file, and (3) EP2P was modified so that an agent could easily compare the hash value of an available file with the hash values of confirmed videos and abusive images of children.

1 684 F.3d 265 (1st Cir. 2012).

5.63 The defence requested discovery of the source code at an evidentiary hearing before the District Court. The application was refused. The purpose of the request was to determine whether the reliability of the technology could be credibly challenged; the defence argued that the inability to examine the source code prevented the accused from mounting such a challenge. The District Court denied the motion to compel discovery of the source code and the Appeal Court agreed with the District Court. Agent P. Michael Gordon testified that the software had no error rate; he demonstrated how the results of an investigation could be independently verified, and that the software had never yielded a false positive. The court considered that this alone provided sufficient evidence of the reliability of the tool. The defence also cited the lack of a peer review, but the Appeal Court indicated that the *Daubert*[1] factors were not a definitive checklist, and there was a sound explanation for the absence of peer review:

> The record shows that the source code is purposely kept secret because the government reasonably fears that traders of child pornography (a notoriously computer-literate group) otherwise would be able to use the source code to develop ways either to evade apprehension or to mislead the authorities. This circumstance satisfactorily explains the absence of any peer review.[2]

1 *Daubert v Merrell Dow Pharmaceuticals, Inc.*, 509 U.S. 579 (1993), 113 S.Ct. 2786.
2 684 F.3d 265 (1st Cir. 2012) at 278.

5.64 The evidence in this example enabled the court to resist the discovery of the source code on the basis that the software was proven to be 'reliable' in respect of the specific purposes for which it had been developed, although it is not clear what evidence of its correctness, if any, was offered.[1] That no errors (for example there were no false positives) are found does not mean that there are none.

1 See *People v Collins*, 49 Misc.3d 595, 15 N.Y.S.3d 564 (N.Y. Sup. Ct. 2015), 2015 N.Y. Slip Op. 25227 (evidence based on a forensic statistical tool (FST) excluded on the basis that the device was not generally accepted in the DNA scientific community); a number of judges have declined to follow this decision – one of the most negative is Schwartz J in *People v Carter*, 50 Misc.3d 1210(A), 36 N.Y.S.3d 48 (Table), 2016 WL 239708, 2016 N.Y. Slip Op. 50067(U) (determining that the defendant was not

entitled to a *Frye* hearing because the FST is not new, novel or experimental), although note the order of Caproni J in *United States v Johnson*, Case No. 1:1-er-00565-VEC (S.D.N.Y. 7 June 2016) (order granting request for subpoena for disclosure of FST source code), https://www.courtlistener.com/recap/gov.uscourts.nysd.446412.57.0.pdf.

Mechanical instruments and computer-like devices

5.65 The discussion in this chapter focuses on software code that provides instructions. In the case of firmware, which is software that is incorporated into hardware, the absence of visible programs does not mean that software is absent: the commentary in this chapter applies equally to this form of implementation of software.

The nature of software errors

5.66 It can be said that a computer can be both 'reliable' (but not infallible) and yet perform functions without the authority or knowledge of the owner or software writer. This may be when the code executes in a way, because of a strange or unforeseen conjunction of inputs, which neither the owner nor the writer had imagined. For instance, one Jonathan Moore designed and produced forged railway tickets that were accepted by ticket machines controlled by computers. It took a ticket inspector to notice subtle differences in the colour and material of the ticket, which led to his arrest and prosecution for forgery.[1]

1 Tom Pugh, 'IT expert sentenced for rail ticket forgery', *The Independent* (London, 2 October 2009).

5.67 It is important to understand that programmers are aware of the limitations of their software, as famously articulated by Ken Thompson:

> You can't trust code that you did not totally create yourself. (Especially code from companies that employ people like me.) No amount of source-level verification or scrutiny will protect you from using untrusted code.[1]

1 Ken Thompson, 'Reflections on trusting trust' (1984) 27(8) Turing Award Lecture, Communications of the ACM 761; Donald MacKenzie, *Mechanizing Proof Computing, Risk and Trust* (MIT Press 2004), 299, fn 1.

5.68 These comments are decidedly relevant, given that Thompson demonstrated how to create a C program fragment that would introduce Trojan horse code into another compiled C program by compromising the C compiler. Thomas Wadlow explained this process as follows:

> For example, when compiling the program that accepts passwords for login, you could add code that would cause the [first] program to accept legitimate passwords or a special backdoor password known to the creator of the Trojan. This is a common strategy even today and is often detectable through source-code analysis.
>
> Thompson went one step further. Since the C compiler is written in the Cprogramming language, he used a similar technique to apply a Trojan to the C compiler source itself. When the C compiler is compiled, the resulting binary program could be used to compile other programs just as before; but when the program that accepts passwords for login is compiled with the new compiler

> from clean, uncompromised source code, the backdoor-password Trojan code is inserted into the binary, even though the original source code used was completely clean. Source-code analysis [of the login program] would not reveal the Trojan because it was lower in the tool chain than the login program.[1]

1 Thomas Wadlow, 'Who must you trust?' (2014) 12(5) acmqueue Security 2.

5.69 The description could have continued. The Trojan, as described above, remains easily detected: there is one in the source code of the compiler and one in the object code of the compiler. In Thompson's scheme, he went one step further: modify the compiler to insert the compiler's Trojan. Now the source code Trojan in the compiler (which inserts the Trojan into the login) can be removed. Furthermore, as Thompson points out, you can now remove all trace of the Trojan in all source code. *There is now no readable evidence of any Trojan attack.*[1]

1 My thanks to Professor Thimbleby for this point.

5.70 Just because a person is in physical control of a computer or shop cash till,[1] it does not follow that she will be aware whether it is working 'reliably', 'properly', 'consistently', 'correctly' or 'dependably'.[2] As indicated above, even the writer of the software will not be in such a luxurious position. It therefore follows that the following comment by Kerr LCJ was not correct:

> In the modern world the presumption of equipment being properly constructed and operating correctly must be strong. It is a particularly strong presumption in the case of equipment within the control of the defendant who alone would know if there was evidence of incorrect operation or incorrect setting.[3]

1 Stephen Castell, 'Letter to the editor' (1994) 10 Computer Law and Security Report 158 pointed out that the observation by Lord Griffiths that a till was a 'computer ... of the simplest kind' was, even at the time, an assumption that did not reflect the truth: at 387D, *R. v Shephard (Hilda)* [1993] AC 380, [1993] 2 WLR 102, [1993] 1 All ER 225, [1992] 12 WLUK 273, (1993) 96 Cr App R 345, (1993) 157 JP 145, [1993] Crim LR 295, (1993) 143 NLJ 127, (1993) 137 SJLB 12, Times, 17 December 1992, Independent, 21 January 1993, [1993] CLY 636; Allison Nyssens, 'The law of evidence: on-line with the computer age?' (1993) 15(10) EIPR 360.
2 The use of the word 'dependability' is a global concept that subsumes attributes of reliability, availability, safety, integrity and maintainability, and 'reliability' provides for continuity of correct service: Algirdas Avižienis, Jean-Claude Laprie and others, 'Basic concepts and taxonomy of dependable and secure computing' (2004) 1(1) IEEE Transactions on Dependable & Secure Computing 11, 13.
3 *Public Prosecution Service v McGowan* [2009] NI 1 at [20]; it is acknowledged that many standards in the safety critical community require some element of proof in the tools they use, such as evidence that the supplier tracks and corrects defects, for instance.

5.71 That software code is imperfect and remains so may be illustrated by the comments of an early pioneer in computing, the late Professor Sir Maurice V. Wilkes FRS FREng:

> By June 1949 people had begun to realize that it was not so easy to get a program right as had at one time appeared. I well remember when this realization first came on me with full force. The EDSAC was on the top floor of the building and the tape-punching and editing equipment one floor below on a gallery that ran round the room in which the differential analyzer was installed. I was trying to get working my first non-trivial program, which was one for the numerical integration of Airy's differential equation. It was on one of my journeys between

> the EDSAC room and the punching equipment that 'hesitating at the angles of the stairs' the realization came over me with full force that a good part of the remainder of my life was going to be spent in finding errors in my own programs. Turing had evidently realized this too, for he spoke at the conference on 'checking a large routine'.[1]

1 Maurice V. Wilkes, *Memories of a Computer Pioneer* (MIT Press 1985), 145. For the EDSCA room, see https://en.wikipedia.org/wiki/EDSAC.

5.72 This observation has been repeated many times since.[1] Programmer errors are caused by a mix of novelty (applying software to previously unsolved problems) and the difficulty of the tasks software is required to perform, including their magnitude and complexity.[2] And the errors reach back. Programmers use programming languages, and the languages are themselves subject to errors; there are errors even if the programmers are somehow perfect and ensure there are no errors, because other programmers further back will have left errors. This is why software has always been released in new versions: primarily to correct previously unknown (or ignored) errors.

1 The reader might wish to begin with the following, which is only one of many articles by many eminent people: Les Hatton, 'Characterising the diagnosis of software failure' (2001) 18(4) IEEE Software 34.
2 B. Littlewood and L. Strigini, 'Software reliability and dependability: a roadmap' in A. Finkelstein (ed.), *The Future of Software Engineering*, State of the Art Reports given at the 22nd International Conference on Software Engineering (ACM Press 2000), 177–188.

5.73 To address this problem, the approach of many of the existing software safety standards is to define requirements for and put constraints on the software development and assurance processes.[1] Using the taxonomy of the provision of services, Algirdas Avižienis and colleagues have defined a 'correct service' as one where the service implements the system function. Its failure is an event that occurs when the service does not do what the function provides. This deviation is described as an 'error'. For instance, if the function when using an ATM is to dispense the correct quantity of cash, and the ATM dispenses the correct amounts of cash, then there is a correct service, and the service is carried out in accordance with the function. If the amount of cash withdrawn from an ATM is greater or less than the amount keyed in, or no cash is provided, this is a service failure that can be an error or fault. The authors go on to say:

> Since a service is a sequence of the system's external states, a service failure means that at least one (or more) external state of the system deviates from the correct service state ... In most cases, a fault first causes an error in the service state of a component that is a part of the internal state of the system and the external state is not immediately affected.
>
> For this reason, the definition of an **error** is the part of the total state of the system that may lead to its subsequent service failure.[2] It is important to note that many errors do not reach the system's external state and cause a failure. A fault[3] is **active** when it causes an error, otherwise it is **dormant**.[4]

1 Professor John McDermid and Tim Kelly, 'Software in safety critical systems: achievement and prediction', 2(3) Nuclear Future 34; Peter Bernard Ladkin, 'Duty of care and engineering functional-safety standards' (2019) 16 Digital Evidence and Electronic Signature Law Review 51.
2 Although this permits everything to be an error.
3 The word 'fault' has not been defined or distinguished from error.

4 Algirdas Avižienis and others, 'Basic concepts and taxonomy of dependable and secure computing', 13, original emphasis; for additional discussions on this topic, see John Rushby, 'Critical system properties: survey and taxonomy' (1994) 43(2) Reliability Engineering and System Safety 189, and MacKenzie, *Mechanizing Proof Computing*, 337, fn 16.

5.74 For instance, an ATM might provide a receipt that £100 has been withdrawn, but does not dispense the money. Given this set of facts, clearly a fault has occurred. One reason might be that the sensors or the software code (or both) in the machine failed to detect the lack of movement of cash. The bank might provide a printout of the machine's internal functioning that shows the purported balance of cash held in the machine before the transaction, and again after it. This proves very little. In the New York case of *Porter v Citibank, N.A.*,[1] a similar set of facts occurred. The customer used his card, but no money was dispensed. Employees of the bank testified that on average machines were out of balance once or twice a week. From the point of view of evidence, the information on the printout is restricted to a single transaction. For the bank to prove that the machine actually dispensed £100 (and therefore the customer is lying), it is necessary for the bank to balance the ATM and report the results for the material time. The overall balance might indicate that it had gone down by £100. But the report might be inaccurate. This is because of a number of associated variables, such as (this is not an exhaustive list): there are multiple layers of outsourcing, the fact that people cover up mistakes and the fact that people rely on other people to be diligent in dual-control tasks (whatever they are). Equally, if the machine happens to overpay someone else by £100, the error will cancel out the previous error and the end result might not have been detected by human intervention either. Human cross-checks may suggest that everything appears correct, but the system is failing repeatedly. A further reason for the machine to be in error is that a third party may have successfully inserted code to bypass the software in the machine, leaving the thief to recover the cash after the customer left the scene.[2]

1 123 Misc.2d 28, 472 N.Y.S.2d 582 (N.Y.City Civ.Ct. 1984).

2 Stephen Mason, 'Debit cards, ATMs and negligence of the bank and customer', (2012) 27(3) Butterworths Journal of International Banking and Financial Law 163; Maryke Silalahi Nuth, 'Unauthorized use of bank cards with or without the PIN: a lost case for the customer?' (2012) 9 Digital Evidence and Electronic Signature Law Review 95; Stephen Mason, 'Electronic banking and how courts approach the evidence' (2013) 29(2) Computer Law and Security Review 144.

5.75 For all these reasons and more, it is difficult to show that a computer is working 'properly', even for highly skilled professionals.[1] Part of the problem is that computers fail in discontinuous ways (they cannot fail slightly), which is a characteristic of discrete complexity, unlike most mechanical devices.

1 There is a technique called code verification, where code functionalities are verified as mathematical properties. But this process is time-consuming and limited, although it is faster then fixing a problem later. I owe this observation to Professor Seng.

Why software appears to fail

5.76 People across the world increasingly depend on computers and computer-like devices for mundane uses such as recording (cameras and recorders on mobile telephones), for critical uses such as lifesaving devices that control delicate medical equipment in hospitals and for important infrastructural uses such as systems for the supply of gas, electricity and fuel, underground trains,[1] buses[2] and financial software that assesses risk in financial products.

1 The railway trains on the Jubilee Line of the London Underground were being replaced with new trains from 2011. Many of the new trains failed and left passengers stranded for hours because of software failures: Dick Murray, 'Computer crash caused Jubilee Line "meltdown"', *Evening Standard* (London, 9 November 2011) 11; this problem was also included in one of the series of six programmes by the BBC entitled *The Tube* that was broadcast during the spring of 2012. This is merely one example from across the world.
2 A software problem meant that a new model of the London bus had to be run with its distinctive rear platform shut: 'New Routemaster bus starts running on London roads', BBC News, 27 February 2012, http://www.bbc.co.uk/news/uk-england-london-17173625.

5.77 In the light of the ubiquitous nature of software, it is important to be aware that software code can function as intended by the programmer, but it can also be the cause of failure. Alternatively, software code may fail to function in the way the programmer intended, or it might continue to function but undertake actions that the programmer did not originally intend or instruct the device to undertake. Problems can occur for a number of reasons, such as where software code has a mistake, or because of improper installation, or because the people hired to undertake the work were not sufficiently qualified.[1] A range of consequences might follow, such as the failure of air traffic control systems[2] and lost baggage from baggage handling systems in airports,[3] preventing couples from obtaining mortgages because of incorrect records,[4] dispensing more cash than is recorded via faulty software in ATMs,[5] miscalculating assets in family cases,[6] and causing injuries and deaths.[7] The increasing complexity of software and interconnections act to exacerbate the problems that occur.[8]

1 *Robotic Vision Systems, Inc. v Cybo Systems, Inc.*, 17 F.Supp.2d 151 (E.D.N.Y. 1998).
2 Leonard Lee, *The Day the Phones Stopped: the Computer Crisis – The What and Why of It, and How We Can Beat It* (Donald I. Fine, New York 1991), chapter 7; Independent Enquiry, NATS System Failure 12 December 2014 – Final Report (13 May 2015), paras ES7–ES10, https://www.caa.co.uk/WorkArea/DownloadAsset.aspx?id=4294974241.
3 Michael Schloh, *Analysis of the Denver International Airport Baggage System* (Submitted: 16 February 1996 Advisor: Daniel Stearns) (Computer Science Department, School of Engineering, California Polytechnic State University 1996), http://www5.in.tum.de/~huckle/schloh_DIA.pdf; Paul Stephen Dempsey, Andrew R. Goetz and Joseph S. Szyliowicz, *Denver International Airport: Lessons Learned* (McGraw-Hill 1997); The Department of Homeland Security, Office of the Inspector General, *Lessons Learned from the August 11, 2007, Network Outage at Los Angeles International Airport (Redacted)* (OIG-08-58, May 2008); House of Commons Transport Committee, *The Opening of Heathrow Terminal 5, Twelfth Report of Session 2007–08: Report, Together with Formal Minutes, Oral and Written Evidence* (Ordered by The House of Commons to be printed 22 October 2008; HC 543, published on 3 November 2008).
4 Nicole Blackmore, 'Npower's error cost us our mortgage', *The Daily Telegraph*, Your Money (London, 10 May 2014) 1, 3.
5 Tim Stewart, 'Huge queues as Tesco cash machine gives customers "free money"', *London Evening Standard* (18 August 2009), http://www.standard.co.uk/news/huge-queues-as-tesco-cash-machine-gives-customers-free-money-6702682.html; for other examples, see Stephen Mason, *When Bank Systems Fail: Debit Cards, Credit Cards, ATMs, Mobile and Online Banking: Your Rights and What To Do When Things Go Wrong* (2nd edn, PP Publishing 2014).
6 Owen Bowcott, 'Revealed: divorce software error hits thousands of settlements', *The Guardian* (London, 17 December 2015).
7 Donald MacKenzie, 'Computer-related accidental death: an empirical exploration' (1994) 21(4) Science and Public Policy 233.
8 For instance, consider the widespread effect that the power outage in August 2019, partly because of software failures, had on England: Office of Rail and Road, *Report Following Railway Power Disruption on 9th August 2019* (3 January 2020); Department for Business, Energy & Industrial Strategy, *GB Power System Disruption on 9 August 2019*, Energy Emergencies Executive Committee (E3C): Final Report (January 2020).

Classification of software errors

5.78 The word 'bug' is a term commonly used in the information technology industry to describe a variety of issues.[1] When a technician uses this term, it can have a number of meanings.[2] Professor Thomas offered his view at a lecture he gave in 2015:

> Different researchers and authors may describe faults as 'flaws', 'errors', 'defects', 'anomalies' or 'bugs' but they will almost always mean *functional* faults, which cause the software to crash or to give the wrong results.[3]

1 It must be emphasized that there are a number of definitions of technical terms, but they are not dealt with in any detail in this text. For an insight as to how 'bugs' are dealt with in a contract between commercial entities, see *GB Gas Holdings Limited v Accenture (UK) Limited* [2010] EWCA Civ 912, [2010] 11 WLUK 260, [2011] 1 Costs LO 64, [2011] CLY 269 and *Kingsway Hall Hotel Ltd v Red Sky IT (Hounslow) Ltd* [2010] EWHC 965 (TCC), [2010] 5 WLUK 106, (2010) 26 Const LJ 542, [2011] CLY 2777; in the software world, a 'bug' is also known as an undocumented feature, for which see David Lubar, *'It's Not a Bug, It's a Feature!'* (Addison-Wesley Publishing Company 1995).

2 The members of the team responsible for writing the following report did not use the term 'bug' when they meant 'error': Willis H. Ware (ed), *Security Controls for Computer Systems: Report of Defense Science Board Task Force on Computer Security – RAND Report R-609-1* (Published for the Office of the Secretary of Defense) R-609-1, Reissued October 1979.

3 'Should we trust computers?', lecture given at Gresham College, 20 October 2015, http://www.gresham.ac.uk/lectures-and-events/should-we-trust-computers.

5.79 Lay people, not without some justification, consider the term 'bug' to be a cloak that hides the correct meaning, namely that what is being described is an error, flaw, mistake, failure or fault in a software program or system.[1] Drawing from the work of Professor Ladkin, it is possible to classify most software errors into the following non-exhaustive categories:[2] human errors in coding and software development; software design or specification errors; unintended or unanticipated software interactions, input data flaws and deliberate errors caused by operators or hackers remotely.

1 Causes of failure can also be categorized into human error, environment (including power outages or A/C failure), network failure, software failure and hardware failure: Bianca Schroeder and Garth A. Gibson, 'A large-scale study of failures in high-performance computing systems' (2010) 7(4) IEEE Transactions on Dependable and Secure Computing 338.

2 Peter B. Ladkin, *On Classification of Factors in Failures and Accidents* (Report RVS-Occ-99-02), https://rvs-bi.de/publications/.

Human errors and biases in the software code

5.80 Notwithstanding the best software development tools that catch and identify coding errors, human errors in writing software code account for a large number of software errors. This problem is going to be exacerbated, given the increasing size of written codes. An example of human error in software code is that of *Mariner I*, the spacecraft that was sent to Venus and launched on 22 July 1962. The software code indicated that the booster had failed, and the rocket was destroyed on command from the control centre. In fact, the rocket was behaving correctly and it was the computer system on the ground that was at fault, partly because of a defect in the software and partly because of a hardware failure. The error in the software arose because the person who wrote the software failed to include an overbar in the guidance equations.[1]

1 Peter G. Neumann, *Computer Related Risks* (Addison-Wesley 1995), 26–27 ('Here *R* denotes the radius; the dot indicates the first derivative – that is, the velocity; the bar indicates smoothed rather than raw data; and *n* is the increment. When a hardware fault occurred, the computer processed the

track data incorrectly, leading to the erroneous termination of the launch'); see also the explanation by the National Aeronautics and Space Administration report NSSDC ID: MARIN1, http://nssdc.gsfc.nasa.gov/nmc/spacecraftDisplay.do?id=MARIN1; for more detail on computers and the space age and an analysis of accidents (including this example), see Paul E. Ceruzzi, *Beyond the Limits: Flight Enters the Computer Age* (MIT Press 1989).

5.81 Two further examples are the *Clementine* mission and the *Ariane 5* failure. The *Clementine* mission was a joint project between the Strategic Defense Initiative Organization and NASA. After the spacecraft left lunar orbit, a malfunction in one of the onboard computers on 7 May 1994 caused a thruster to fire until it had used up all of its fuel, leaving the spacecraft spinning at about 80 rpm with no spin control. The spacecraft remained in geocentric orbit and continued testing the spacecraft components until the end of mission.[1] In the case of the *Ariane 5* rocket failure in 1996, the disintegration of the rocket 40 seconds after launch was due to a software failure – because, in the words of Professor Les Hatton, 'the programmers had arranged the code such that a 64-bit floating point number was shoe-horned into a 16-bit integer'.[2] As pointed out by Professor Ladkin, 'Code was reused from the Ariane 4 guidance system. The Ariane 4 has different flight characteristics in the first 30 seconds of flight and exception conditions were generated on both inertial guidance system (IGS) channels of the Ariane 5.'[3]

1 Space Studies Board, National Research Council, *Lessons Learned from the Clementine Mission* (National Academy Press 1997), http://ntrs.nasa.gov/archive/nasa/casi.ntrs.nasa.gov/19980041408.pdf.
2 Les Hatton, 'Ariane 5: A smashing success' (1999) 1(2) Software Testing and Quality Engineering 14; Ariane 501 Inquiry Board report (4 June 1996), http://esamultimedia.esa.int/docs/esa-x-1819eng.pdf and https://www.ima.umn.edu/~arnold/disasters/ariane5rep.html; Charles C. Mann, 'Why software is so bad', (2002) Technology Review 38(b); Derek Partridge, *The Seductive Computer: Why IT Systems Always Fail* (Springer 2011), 99, fn 6.
3 Peter B. Ladkin, *The Ariane 5 Accident: A Programming Problem?* (Article RVS-J-98-02), https://rvs-bi.de/publications/.

5.82 Human bias has also begun to be more fully understood, especially when analysing systems marketed as artificial intelligence, usually developed with a form of machine learning.[1] Hidden biases and flawed datasets are, in all probability, normal.[2]

1 *State v Loomis*, 881 N.W.2d 749 (Wis. 2016), *cert. denied*, 137 S.Ct. 2290 (2017); Danielle Keats Citrona, 'Technological Due Process' (2008) 85 Wash U L Rev 1249 – noting that the automated public benefits systems of Colorado, California and Texas mistranslated codified eligibility requirements and erroneously distributed or withheld public benefits; Kenneth A. Bamberger, 'Technologies of compliance: risk and regulation in a digital age' (2010) 88 Tex L Rev 669 – software designers have created compliance and risk management software with automation biases to favour corporate self-interest; Kathleen E. Watson, 'Note, COBRA data and the right to confront technology against you' (2015) 42 N Ky L Rev 375, 381; Susan Nevelow Mart, 'The algorithm as a human artifact: implications for legal [re]search' (2017) 109 Law Libr J 387; Christian Chessman, 'A "source" of error: computer code, criminal defendants, and the constitution' (2017) 105 Cal L Rev 179 – for corrections in this article, see Duncan A. Taylor, Jo-Anne Bright and John Buckleton, Commentary, 'A "source" of error: computer code, criminal defendants, and the constitution' (2017) 8 Frontiers in Genetics 1; Molly Griffard, 'A bias-free predictive policing tool?: an evaluation of the NYPD's Patternizr' (2019) 47 Fordham Urb LJ 43; Aylin Caliskan, Joanna J. Bryson and Arvind Narayanan, 'Semantics derived automatically from language corpora contain human-like biases' (2017) 356(6334) Science 183; Jieyu Zhao, TianluWang, Mark Yatskar, Vicente Ordonez and Kai-Wei Chang, 'Men also like shopping: reducing gender bias amplification using corpus-level constraints' in *Proceedings of the 2017 Conference on Empirical Methods in Natural Language Processing* (Association for Computational Linguistics 2017), https://

www.aclweb.org/anthology/D17-1323.pdf; Anupam Chander, 'The racist algorithm?' (2017) 115 Mich L Rev 2013; Virginia Eubanks, *Automating Inequality: How High-Tech Tools Profile, Police, and Punish the Poor* (St Martin's Press 2018); Caroline Criado Perez, *Invisible Women: Exposing Data Bias in a World Designed for Men* (Chatto & Windus 2019).

2 In her book *Weapons of Math Destruction: How Big Data Increases Inequality and Threatens Democracy* (Broadway Books 2016, 2017), Cathy O'Neil demonstrates that software applications are written by human beings (mostly men), with choices as to how the software code is written, often on the basis of prejudice, misunderstanding and bias. Software writers define their own reality and then use it to justify the results. In writing software code, programmers routinely lack data for human behaviour, which means they substitute data from dubious statistical correlations that discriminate and whose use might even be illegal. For details of the case law cited, see 'Book Reports' (2017) 14 Digital Evidence and Electronic Signature Law Review 95. For an early example of software that was written and produced biased results because of the bias of the programmer, see Stella Lowry and Gordon Macpherson, 'A blot on the profession' (1988 March) 5 British Medical Journal 657, https://www.ncbi.nlm.nih.gov/pmc/articles/PMC2545288/; Anders Eklund, Thomas E. Nichol and Hans Knutsson, 'Cluster failure: why fMRI inferences for spatial extent have inflated false-positive rates' (2016) 113 Proc Natl Acad Sci 7900. For software bias that promotes male over female vocal artists, see Andres Ferraro, Xavier Serra and Christine Bauer, 'Break the loop: gender imbalance in music recommenders' in *CHIIR '21: Proceedings of the 2021 Conference on Human Information Interaction and Retrieval* (Association for Computing Machinery 2021) 249, https://dl.acm.org/doi/pdf/10.1145/3406522.3446033.

Failure of specification

5.83 The problem might not be in the software code, but with the specification,[1] such as with the loss of the *Mars Climate Orbiter* spacecraft in 1999. On this occasion, the failure resulted from not using metric units in the coding of a ground software file. The thruster performance data used in the software application code entitled SM_FORCES (small forces) was in Imperial units instead of metric units.[2] Roy Longbottom, Head of the Large Scientific Systems Branch of the Central Computer Agency, observed that:

> When the software is first written and assembled, as for hardware, it usually undergoes a series of design quality assurance tests to ensure that the specification is met on facilities, performance and on physical source requirements. It is again fairly easy to check out the broad facilities provided but impossible to forecast and test for all possible modes of operation, combinations and sequences. One difference with hardware is that, the writing of comprehensive tests[3] for the software is often regarded as an overhead, whereas for hardware, comprehensive tests are written as a natural process for identifying constructional defects on all new equipment and for overcoming long term reliability problems. So, when software is first delivered, it is almost certain that the design will not be quite correct or some coding errors will be present.[4]

1 For an example of the failure of a properly structured agreement that included what the customer wanted from the software; see *South West Water Services Ltd v International Computers Ltd* [1999] 6 WLUK 427, [1999] BLR 420, [1999–2000] Info TLR 1, [1998–99] Info TLR 154, [1999] ITCLR 439, [2001] Lloyd's Rep PN 353, [1999] Masons CLR 400, [2000] CLY 870. In *Co-Operative Group (Cws) Ltd. (Formerly Co-Operative Wholesale Society Ltd.) v International Computers Ltd.* [2003] EWHC 1 (TCC), [2003] 12 WLUK 646, [2004] Info TLR 25, (2004) 27(3) IPD 27023, (2004) 148 SJLB 112, Times, 19 January 2004, [2005] CLY 42, the case failed for lack of a contract, but the judge observed, at [260], that 'the initial efforts of ICL to try to meet the requirements of CWS as to when software was required were frustrated by the failure of CWS to specify precisely what its requirements were'.

2 *Mars Climate Orbiter Mishap Investigation Board Phase I Report* (10 November 1999), https://llis.nasa.gov/llis_lib/pdf/1009464main1_0641-mr.pdf.

3 Because of the discontinuous nature of software, the notion of a 'comprehensive test for software' does not exist, even in the high-integrity market. Testing every possible sequence of every possible input is not feasible.

4 Roy Longbottom, *Computer System Reliability* (Wiley 1980), 71. This book may have been published in 1980, but remains true in the twenty-first century. Note chapter 6 regarding faults.

5.84 It is a pervasive characteristic of software code that design will not be quite correct or coding errors will be present, and there will be occasions when a fault cannot be replicated.[1] At the beginning, the attitude taken by NASA towards software code was to consider it of secondary importance. Although this view had changed over time, and a rigorous methodology has since been implemented to provide for the better control and development of software code, NASA has never produced error-free software code.[2]

1 For which see National Transportation Safety Board, *Pipeline Accident Report, Pipeline Rupture and Subsequent Fire in Bellingham, Washington June 10, 1999* (NTSB/PAR-02/02; PB2002-916502; Notation 7264A, Adopted 8 October 2002), 63, https://www.ntsb.gov/investigations/AccidentReports/Reports/PAR0202.pdf.
2 Nancy G. Leveson, 'Software and the challenge of flight control' in Roger D. Launius, John Krige and James I. Craig (eds) *Space Shuttle Legacy: How We Did It and What We Learned* (American Institute of Aeronautics and Astronautics 2013).

Unintended software interactions

5.85 Software code might function correctly, as intended by the programmer, but the interactions between individual components of the software code can be the cause of failure, because the designers of the system fail to account for all potential interactions. This is because the possible number of defects in software relates not only to the components (lines of code), but also to the number of ways in which they interact – the number of interactions increases faster than the number of components, thus making large systems with many components proportionally harder to get right. As the work of Bianca Schroeder and Garth A. Gibson demonstrates, the more complex the system becomes, the more likely it is that different types of failure will occur,[1] and the number of reasons that complexity causes failure also increases.[2] To put the problem into perspective, it is necessary to understand not the number of defects per device but the proportion of design decisions that contain defects.[3] A typical design decision in software looks like this:

```
if some-condition-I-have-decided-when-I-designed-the-software
then
            do something
otherwise
            do something else
```

1 Schroeder and Gibson, 'A large-scale study of failures in high-performance computing systems'.
2 For the same discussion in 1986, see Rudolph J. Peritz, 'Computer data and reliability: a call for authentication of business records under the federal rules of evidence' (1986) 80(4) Northwestern University Law Review 965, 990–999; Stephen Mason and Timothy S. Reiniger, '"Trust" between machines? Establishing identity between humans and software code, or whether you know it is a dog, and if so, which dog?' (2015) 21(5) Computer and Telecommunications Law Review 135; for a specific case study, see Sivanesan Tulasidas, Ruth Mackay, Pascal Craw, Chris Hudson, Voula Gkatzidou and Wamadeva Balachandran, 'Process of designing robust, dependable, safe and secure software for medical devices: point of care testing device as a case study' (2013) 6 Journal of Software Engineering and Applications 1.
3 Nobody is certain how many defects occur per lines of code or number of design decisions, but for a good discussion, see McDermid and Kelly, 'Software in safety critical systems', 34 .

5.86 Illustrating the point with this simple example means that each design decision creates at least two choices for the software to handle, and further design choices will have to be made within the 'do something' bits, as well as in the 'do something else' bit as needed. One decision will have 2 choices, then as it is developed, 4, then 8, 16, 32, 64 and so on, increasing exponentially in complexity. Very quickly the choices go beyond human comprehension. This demonstrates that in software, a very few decisions rapidly create a far more complex thing than humans can reliably analyse and about which they can be confident they have made the right decisions, in even a modest fraction of the possible cases.[1] Since there are typically thousands of design decisions in the software for even relatively small products, there will be millions and millions of design choices, and hence it is easy to overlook hundreds of defects in the final products.[2] An average defect level of one to five defects per thousand lines of code could translate into hundreds if not thousands of defects for devices that have several hundred thousand to a million or more lines of code.[3] This is the typical size of most software that controls aircraft,[4] motor vehicles and many other common systems. The user is affected by how often the software fails. This is because one defect may cause failures frequently, and another defect may very seldom cause failures.[5]

1 I owe this example and analysis to Professor Harold Thimbleby.

2 Hoang Pham, *System Software Reliability* (Springer 2000), 2; Clemente Izurieta and James M. Bieman, 'How software designs decay: a pilot study of pattern evolution', *First International Symposium on Empirical Software Engineering and Measurement (ESEM, 2007)* (Institute of Electrical and Electronics Engineers 2009); Clemente Izurieta and James M. Bieman, 'A multiple case study of design pattern decay, grime, and rot in evolving software systems' (2013) 21 Software Qual J 289; Duc Minh Le, Carlos Carrillo, Rafael Capilla and Nenad Medvidovic, 'Relating architectural decay and sustainability of software systems', in *13th Working IEEE/IFIP Conference on Software Architecture (WICSA 2016)* (Institute of Electrical and Electronics Engineers 2016); National Institute of Statistical Sciences, *Code Decay in Legacy Software Systems: Measurement, Models, and Statistical Strategies*: 'Over time, software code can lose quality and begin having errors and problems working properly. [Note: code does not lose quality on its own, but because programmers continue to alter code.] It is more difficult to keep changing the code and has become much more expensive as well. Eventually the hardware fails and there is no way to update or port the software to newer tools. Lucent Technologies, along with the National Science Foundation, hired NISS to look at a way to quantify, measure, predict and reverse or retard code decay.' For the results, see https://www.niss.org/research/code-decay-legacy-software-systems-measurement-models-and-statistical-strategies.

3 William Guttman, professor of economics and technology at Carnegie Mellon University, is of the view that the figure is nearer 30 errors per 1,000 lines of code on average: Alorie Gilbert, 'Newsmaker: fixing the sorry state of software', *CNET News*, 9 October 2002 (this item no longer seems to be available online); see also *The Economic Impacts of Inadequate Infrastructure for Software Testing: Final Report* (May 2002) prepared for National Institute of Standards and Technology by RTI Health, Social, and Economics Research, https://www.nist.gov/system/files/documents/director/planning/report02-3.pdf; Herb Krasner, *The Cost of Poor Quality Software in the US: A 2018 Report* (Consortium for IT Software Quality 2018), https://www.it-cisq.org/the-cost-of-poor-quality-software-in-the-us-a-2018-report/The-Cost-of-Poor-Quality-Software-in-the-US-2018-Report.pdf.

4 On 2 June 1994, Chinook helicopter ZD 576 crashed on the Mull of Kintyre. The RAF Board of Inquiry held the pilots to be negligent. Some considered that the installation of a Full Authority Digital Engine Control (FADEC) system was to blame, as described in detail in *RAF Justice* (*Computer Weekly*), http://cdn.ttgtmedia.com/rms/computerweekly/DowntimePDF/pdf/rafjust.pdf; Tony Collins, 'Chinook crash: critical internal memo on software flaws', *Computer Weekly*, 4 June 2009, http://www.computerweekly.com/news/2240089594/Chinook-crash-critical-internal-memo-on-software-flaws; the decision of the RAF Board of Inquiry was subsequently reversed: *The Mull of Kintyre Review* (HC Paper 1348, 2011), https://www.gov.uk/government/uploads/system/uploads/attachment_data/file/247259/1348.pdf.

5 P. G. Bishop, 'The variation of software survival time for different operational input profiles (or why you can wait a long time for a big bug to fail)' in *FTCS-23 The Twenty-Third International Symposium on Fault-Tolerant Computing* (IEEE 1993), 98–107.

5.87 Consider, by way of example, the 2003 power outage that affected large portions of the Midwest and Northeast United States and Ontario, Canada. The outage affected an area with an estimated 50 million people and 61,800 megawatts of electric load, and power was not restored for four days in some parts of the United States. Parts of Ontario suffered blackouts for more than a week before full power was restored. The subsequent investigation indicated a number of failures, a significant one being the failure of a computerized energy management system, XA/21 EMS. This system failed to detect the tripping of electrical facilities. After weeks of testing and analysis, a software coding error was discovered. It was a subtle incarnation of a common programming error called a race condition,[1] brought to light by a series of events and alarm conditions in the equipment being monitored. The race condition involved times measured in milliseconds. Mike Unum, manager of commercial solutions at GE Energy, explained the problem: 'There was a couple of processes that were in contention for a common data structure, and through a software coding error in one of the application processes, they were both able to get write access to a data structure at the same time ... And that corruption led to the alarm event application getting into an infinite loop and spinning.'[2]

1 https://en.wikipedia.org/wiki/Race_condition.
2 Kevin Poulsen, 'Tracking the blackout bug', *SecurityFocus*, 7 April 2004; US–Canada Power System Outage Task Force, *Final Report on the August 14, 2003 Blackout in the United States and Canada: Causes and Recommendations* (Merrimack Station AR-1165, April 2004), https://emp.lbl.gov/publications/final-report-august-14-2003-blackout.

5.88 This issue is further magnified by what are called 'legacy' systems. For instance, the computer systems used by airlines are very complex. There are a number of reasons for this: airlines introduced computer systems in the 1950s; as airlines merge, or take over other airlines, they might combine or adopt the computer systems they have inherited; over time, as new functions are added, this process has created systems of great complexity. The banking sector has the same problem. Replacing such systems is not an easy decision, because it would take a considerable amount of money and time, and it is doubtful whether any IT firm has sufficient skills and knowledge to provide all the software needed for a complete replacement.[1]

1 'All systems stop: why big firms like Delta find it so hard to eliminate glitches from their IT systems', *The Economist*, 13 August 2016 (from the print edition), https://www.economist.com/business/2016/08/13/all-systems-stop.

5.89 Consider a practical example. The display on a screen has a meaning, and if that meaning is not veridical, then an accident may result. Where the moon rising over the horizon causes a system to interpret it as a massive ICBM launch, semantic safety is violated: that is, the display (it might be a warning signal or something else) was not veridical. This problem has been linked to the possibility that a nuclear war has been averted by human intervention despite computer warnings of imminent attacks at least twice.[1]

1 I owe this suggestion to Professor Peter Bernard Ladkin. For the incident where software code made it appear the Soviet Union had launched a nuclear missile assault on the USA, see MacKenzie, *Mechanizing Proof Computing*, 23–24 and Eric Schlosser, *Command and Control* (Penguin 2014), 253–254; for an incident where software code made it appear there was a missile attack by the USA against the Soviet Union, see Ron Rosenbaum, *How the End Begins: The Road to a Nuclear World War III* (Simon & Schuster 2011) 7, 225–226, 248; Pavel Aksenov, 'Stanislav Petrov: the man who may have saved the world', *BBC News*, 26 September 2013.

5.90 It should be observed that the increasing use of machine-learning systems complicates this issue, because the software code is instructed to make further decisions when running, which increases the complexity. In addition, the veridicality of machine-learning systems, like neural nets, cannot be easily understood or verified.[1] Machine learning (ML) systems can learn (correctly or incorrectly) after they have been programmed: the errors they can make will typically not have been subject to the sort of scrutiny we expect of standard non-ML software. In particular, ML systems are easy to fool. There is a whole field of 'adversarial ML' which seeks training data to teach ML perverse things. One commonly quoted example is to spray STOP signs with innocuous-looking graffiti, and sign recognition software used in cars will read the STOP sign as 40 mph;[2] a more recent example is to mislead the software in autopilots by inserting split-second images into roadside billboards.[3]

1 I owe this point to Dr Michael Ellims and Professor Martyn Thomas, CBE, FREng.

2 Kevin Eykholt, Ivan Evtimov, Earlence Fernandes, Bo Li, Amir Rahmati, Chaowei Xiao, Atul Prakash, Tadayoshi Kohno and Dawn Song, 'Robust physical-world attacks on deep learning models', CVPR 2018, https://arxiv.org/abs/1707.08945.

3 Ben Nassi, Yisroel Mirsky, Dudi Nassi, Raz Ben Netanel, Oleg Drokin and Yuval Elovici, 'Phantom of the ADAS: securing advanced driver assistance systems from split-second phantom attacks', https://ad447342-c927-414a-bbae-d287bde39ced.filesusr.com/ugd/a53494_04b5dd9e38d540bc863cc8fde2ebf916.pdf.

Input data flaws

5.91 There are also what are known as 'input-data flaws', meaning that the data entered into the machine was not correct, thus ensuring the information coming out is also incorrect – colloquially known as 'garbage-in-garbage-out'. In a well-designed system, the software should check, insofar as that is possible, that the input data is not wrong, corrupted or unexpected, and subject the output to a warning, perhaps via the user interface. This is a common problem in fairly simple systems such as databases, even in critical uses as in the medical field.

Operational errors

5.92 Another manifestation of human error would be operational error. Professor Leveson observed that it is 'often very difficult to separate system design error from operator error: In highly automated systems, the operator is often at the mercy of the system design and operational procedures'.[1] The accuracy of this comment applies to virtually every automated system that includes computers and software code, and has, indirectly, caused significant loss of life. For instance, 'user interface errors' have been blamed for several aviation accidents, where the pilot as the user did not do anything wrong, but did not know the correct way to do what she wanted to do. Even in situations where people are part of a controlled and trained user community, such as ambulance controllers or air traffic controllers, human error rates in many tasks are high enough to stress systems in ways that are unpredictable. Examples of such situations in high stress industries are further explored in the rest of this chapter.

1 Nancy G. Leveson, *Engineering a Safer World: Systems Thinking Applied to Safety* (MIT Press 2012), 39.

The development, maintenance and operation of software

5.93 As general-purpose computing systems have become more powerful and flexible, users have devised new uses for them in ways that the systems developers never envisaged. This, coupled with the increase in complexity and the speed at which computers work, especially in modern automated systems, means that developers can never completely anticipate how users will use their software, or how their software will interact with other systems and software. Even where the developers have tested their systems in the ways that most users use them (and possibly fail to test them against less conventional methods of use), they may subsequently need to issue upgrades that provide more functions, or updates to remedy any defects that have been found. In doing so, the developers will have modified the software and its operating conditions. Such changes will result in new modes of operation that have not been previously tested, causing the users to encounter defects they have not previously experienced. This problem is compounded when complex operations such as banking systems are connected to networks and can be attacked by hackers – internal or external to the organization – or just simply affected by unintentional actions of third parties, such as making errors during recovery from backups.

5.94 While it might appear that exhaustive testing could be the answer to these problems, it is impractical and does not necessarily work, and there is no workable theory that would constitute an adequate test. Professor Thomas notes that 'The main way that software developers assure the quality of their work is by running tests, even though computer scientists have been saying for the past forty years that testing can never show that software is secure or correct'.[1] For even relatively small systems, the number of possible test cases required for comprehensive testing is enormous. It is also not always certain whether or not the software has passed or failed the test, and it is necessary to repeat the tests after all software changes. Furthermore, a single test case can only expose a system to a very specific set of conditions and data values. The number of variations is, in practical terms, unbounded because a robust test must consider, among other things, different data values, the number of simultaneous jobs running, the system memory configuration, the hardware configuration, all of the connected devices or systems, the operators' actions, user errors, data errors, device malfunctions, and so forth. However, just because testing is a complex affair does not mean that testing should not be carried out.[2] This is so especially when people can be killed or injured,[3] as in the case of the sudden unintended acceleration problems experienced by owners of some modern motor vehicles which operate with electronic control systems.[4] Michael Barr, in giving evidence as the expert witness for the plaintiffs in the trial of *Bookout v Toyota Motor Corporation Case*, gave the following in oral testimony:

> [Toyota] didn't [have] a formal safety process like the MIRSA, the big book. They don't follow a recipe for making a safe system.
>
> They also have the defect that they didn't do peer reviews on the operating system code or the monitor CPU codes. And here, ultimately, it comes down to resources. Toyota did not put people and time behind checking up on the suppliers who were supplying this critical software [for their vehicle electronic control systems]. The operating system at the heart of this main CPU and this and second CPU that's doing the monitoring.[5]

1 Martyn Thomas, 'Technology, security and politics' (2016) 25(3) SCSC Newsletter 53.
2 For which see Chris Elliott and Peter Deasley (eds), *Creating Systems that Work: Principles of Engineering Systems for the 21st Century* (The Royal Academy of Engineering 2007).
3 Matt Parker, *Humble Pi: A Comedy of Maths Errors* (Allen Lane 2019) – the title is hardly fitting, given the author refers to a total of 1,517 deaths as a result of software errors, and four deaths relating to the results of a lottery (at 156).
4 For safety critical systems, see B. Littlewood, I. Bainbridge and R. E. Bloomfield, *The Use of Computers in Safety-Critical Applications* (Health and Safety Commission 1998).
5 No. CJ-2008-7969 (Reported by Karen Twyford, RPR): examination and cross examination of Michael Barr 14 October 2013, 80, http://www.safetyresearch.net/Library/Bookout_v_Toyota_Barr_REDACTED.pdf.

Developmental issues and software errors

5.95 In examining the nature of a software fault, even at a time when software was less complex than now, Professor Randell and his colleagues made the following astute observation:

> A detected error is only a symptom of the fault that caused it, and does not necessarily identify the fault. Even where the relationship between the fault and the detected error appears obvious, it will be found that many other possible faults could have caused the same error to be detected.[1]

1 B. Randell, P. Lee and P. C. Treaven, 'Reliability issues in computing system design' (1978) 10(2) ACM Computing Surveys 126, 127; but as Professor Thimbleby has pointed out when reviewing this chapter, simple slips (including programming errors) do not stem from unmastered complexity; they just stem from random events.

5.96 Professor Randell also commented that 'What is significant about software faults is, of course, that they must be algorithmic faults stemming from unmastered complexity in the system design'.[1] This is a telling observation, in that the primary source of software errors lies in its development process. There are numerous issues in the development of software that will generate errors, including but not limited to the speed at which a developer is required to work to write proprietary software within the contractual time frame, the consistent failure within the industry to provide for suitable quality control procedures, the creation of a climate of fear to suppress concerns relating to errors and safety,[2] and the lack of knowledge that programmers may have of the domain in which the software is to work (for instance, the programmer might be knowledgeable about mathematics, but have no knowledge of how acceleration systems work in motor vehicles[3]). In addition, it is extremely difficult to develop good software without well-designed and mature engineering processes, and impossible to do so consistently. Such processes involve the production of essential documents that enable effective communication between members of the development team and those who will accept, install, use and modify the software. The existence of such documents does not guarantee that the software is of high (or adequate) quality, but the absence or lack of rigorous quality control is a strong indication of poor-quality software.[4]

1 Randell and others, 'Reliability issues in computing system design', 127.
2 Nancy G. Leveson, 'Technical and managerial factors in the NASA Challenger and Columbia losses: looking forward to the future', in Daniel Lee Kleinman, Karen A. Cloud-Hansen, Christina Matta and Jo Handelsman (eds) *Controversies in Science and Technology Volume 2: From Climate to Chromosomes* (Mary Ann Liebert Press 2008); for a legal response to this problem, see Richard Warner and Robert H. Sloan, 'Vulnerable software: product-risk norms and the problem of unauthorized access' (2012) Journal of Law, Technology & Policy 45.

3 Michael Ellims, 'On wheels, nuts and software', 9th Australian Workshop on Safety Related Programmable Systems (SCS '04) in Brisbane, 2.1, http://crpit.com/abstracts/CRPITV47Ellims.html.
4 I thank Professor Martyn Thomas CBE for these observations.

5.97 In addition, unrealistic estimates of how long it will take to write and test software also undermine accuracy,[1] which means that those responsible for writing software code will not have the time or resources to be comprehensive in developing the software.[2] It is also necessary to have a comprehensive design that has been subjected to peer review that should precede any coding. Often, the writing of lines of code remains the ready and easily quantifiable measure of progress, which means that writing code starts much too soon, and too little emphasis is placed on good design.

1 This is just one of the problems. Frederick P. Brooks, *The Mythical Man-Month Anniversary Edition* (Addison Wesley Longman, Inc. 1995). For a comprehensive failure, see Slaughter and May, *TSB Review An Independent Review Following TSB's Migration to a New IT Platform* (October 2019), https://www.slaughterandmay.com/news/slaughter-and-may-s-independent-review-of-tsb-s-2018-migration-to-a-new-it-platform/.
2 This is not a recent phenomenon. Even in 1976 it could be said that 'debugging and testing often account for half the cost of a program': Theodore A. Linden, 'Operating system structures to support security and reliable software' (1976) 8(4) ACM Computing Surveys 409, 410–411 (also available as a US Department of Commerce National Bureau of Standards Technical Note 919, https://csrc.nist.gov/csrc/media/publications/conference-paper/1998/10/08/proceedings-of-the-21st-nissc-1998/documents/early-cs-papers/lind76.pdf); and more recently, Robert N. Charette, 'Why software fails' (2005) 42(9) IEEE Spectrum (2005) 42, http://spectrum.ieee.org/computing/software/why-software-fails; Partridge, *The Seductive Computer*; W. Wayt Gibbs, 'Software's chronic crisis', *Scientific American*, September 1994, 86.

5.98 This is not to say that all software programmers are incompetent or that they do not wish to undertake work of a high quality. In their writings about software errors, Algirdas Avižienis and colleagues define 'human-made faults'[1] as including faults of omission, and wrong actions that lead to faults of commission. 'Human-made faults' are, in turn, divided into malicious faults and 'non-malicious' or guileless faults. These faults can be introduced during the development of the system by a developer or during use by an external third party. Guileless faults can be classified as faults resulting from mistakes, and deliberate faults that are brought about because of poor decisions – usually caused when choices are made to accept having less of one thing in order to get more of something else, for instance to preserve acceptable performance, or because of economic considerations. Developers who commit such faults may unintentionally or deliberately violate an operating procedure with or without understanding the consequences of their action.[2]

1 Avižienis and others, 'Basic concepts and taxonomy of dependable and secure computing', 15–18.
2 For instance, management in Boeing was aware that additional software added to the 737 Max, if not correctly dealt with by a pilot within 10 seconds, would lead to catastrophic results, for which see The House Committee on Transportation & Infrastructure, *Final Committee Report: The Design, Development & Certification of the Boeing 737 MAX* (September 2020), 231, https://transportation.house.gov/imo/media/doc/2020.09.15%20FINAL%20737%20MAX%20Report%20for%20Public%20Release.pdf.

5.99 The main part of the problem is that writing software is an exceedingly difficult and challenging field, and the methods used by management to control quality are not necessarily the most competent that can be used. However, writing software is now getting easier. Advanced development environments generate some code automatically, although writing software to perform complex functions that works well in all circumstances continues to be demanding. Many amateurs have had the experience of being able to build software that achieves impressive effects with very little effort. This may well lead them to believe that because they find it easy to program a simple video game or puzzle-solver (whose failures do not matter and will probably go unnoticed), or some simple program that seems reliable enough for their personal, everyday use, then completely finishing or building other complex software systems that are correct must be just as easy.

5.100 A further barrier arises when an organization is collectively incompetent.[1] This in turn means that inherent problems in software used in large organizations may not be identified for a long time. For instance, in 2003 Oates Healthcare began to use a new software product that was written for the company. At that time it was not known that the code written by the programmer was defective, in that it failed to calculate overtime for employees correctly. The problem was identified when a previous employee took legal action against the company five years after the software was implemented. As a result of discovering this problem, the company had to undertake two exercises. First, the simple solution was to write new software code to permit the program to begin calculating overtime correctly from the point in time that the software was amended. Second, because the changes to the software were not capable of affecting the previous calculations, the previous records had to be recalculated manually, which is an admission of poor programming: it would not be necessary do it manually if a computer could do it. Apparently there were over 10 million records that needed to be recalculated.[2]

1 As in the example of the failure of the AAS system: Office of Inspector General, *Audit Report: Advance Automation System: Federal Aviation Administration*, Report Number: AV-1998-113 (15 April 1998), https://www.oig.dot.gov/sites/default/files/av1998113.pdf.
2 Phil Simon, *Why New Systems Fail: Theory and Practice Collide* (AuthorHouse 2009), 7–9.

5.101 A software project can fail partly because of a combination of the failure of management, an unrealistic time frame to develop the software, and a failure to develop and test software properly. There are many examples of such failure, and more importantly, some failures do not come to light until after the project is complete.[1]

1 Robert L. Glass, *Software Runways: Lessons Learned from Massive Software Project Failures* (Prentice Hall PRT 1998), xiii–viv; Lee, *The Day the Phones Stopped*; Nancy G. Leveson, 'Role of software in spacecraft accidents' (2004) 41(4) Journal of Spacecraft and Rockets 564.

Increasing the risk of errors through modification of software

5.102 Software typically goes through modification cycles, called updates or upgrades, to fix existing errors in code or enhance or improve software functionality. One of the major causes of software failure is that, as software code is modified, each modification is capable of increasing the risk of failure. Some of the changes that are meant to fix errors may create another one, resulting in a greater or smaller probability of failure. Where a vendor releases a significant number of new features or a major redesign, there is typically a sudden increase in the probability of failure, after which the risk is reduced once further error updates begin to resolve the errors discovered, thus reducing the risk again over time.

5.103 It is useful to observe that when safety-related software code is modified, there is usually documentation to explain how this risk has been reduced, although this is routine only in the case of dangerous failures, and not necessarily all failures. By way of example, consider the case of *Saphena Computing Limited v Allied Collection Agencies Limited*[1] in which Mr Recorder Havery QC commented:

> In the present case, on the other hand, once the software is fit for its purpose, it stays fit for its purpose. If by any chance a flaw is discovered showing that it is unfit for purpose (which is hardly likely after prolonged use)[2] there is a remedy in damages against the supplier, if solvent, until the expiry of the period of limitation.[3]

1 [1989] 5 WLUK 21, [1995] FSR 616, [1995] CLY 774.

2 Professor Thomas has indicated that even in 1995 there was plenty of evidence that this was not correct.

3 [1995] FSR 616 at 639.

5.104 The problem with this remark is that proprietary software code can be (and indeed often is) affected by updates, which means it does not necessarily stay 'fit for purpose'. It can also be affected by updates in other code, for instance – and quite commonly – in updates to the operating system on which it runs. Flaws can become manifest at any time, and some flaws can remain for years, which means if they are detected by a malicious person or state agency, they can be manipulated for purposes other than that which the users intend. There is a more fundamental flaw in the statement that 'it stays fit for its purpose'. If the software is used unchanged for a different purpose, which may be no more than the original purpose but applied to different data, it may still fail.

5.105 This is illustrated in the Heartbleed exposé.[1] Cryptographic protocols are used to provide for the security and privacy of communications over the Internet, such as the World Wide Web, email, instant messaging and some virtual private networks. A current protocol is called the Transport Layer Security (TLS). To implement this protocol, a developer will use a cryptographic library. One such library, which is open source, is OpenSSL. In 2011, a doctoral student wrote the Heartbeat Extension for OpenSSL, and requested that his implementation be included in the protocol. One of the developers (there were four) reviewed the proposal, but failed to notice that the code was flawed. The code was included in the repository on 31 December 2011 under OpenSSL version 1.0.1. The defect allowed anyone on the Internet to read the memory of any system that used the flawed versions of the OpenSSL software. It was possible for a hacker using this flaw to steal user names and passwords, instant messages, emails and business documents. No trace would be left of the attack. The attack did not rely on access to privileged information or credentials such as username and passwords. Taking into account the length of exposure, the ease by which it could be exploited, the fact that an attack would not leave a trace and that it is estimated to have affected up to two-thirds of the Internet's web servers, this weakness was taken very seriously. On 7 April 2014, the same day the Heartbleed vulnerability was publicly disclosed, a new version that applied a fix to the flaw was released.

1 Zakir Durumeric, James Kasten, David Adrian, J. Alex Halderman, Michael Bailey, Frank Li, Nicholas Weaver, Johanna Amann, Jethro Beekman, Mathias Payer and Vern Paxson, 'The matter of Heartbleed', *IMC '14: Proceedings of the 2014 Conference on Internet Measurement Conference* (Association for Computing Machinery, New York, United States, 2014), 475–488. A more important error was discovered in GNU Bash in September 2014, for which see 'Bourne-again Shell (Bash) remote code execution vulnerability' (original release date 24 September 2014; last revised 30 September 2014), https://www.us-cert.gov/ncas/current-activity/2014/09/24/Bourne-Again-Shell-Bash-Remote-Code-Execution-Vulnerability.

5.106 Software can also be affected by changes in the environment, such as the operating system or other components, rather than any specific application, although it is necessary to distinguish between modification of software in situ and the reuse of software in an environment that is presumed to be similar. An example is the *Ariane 5* incident, where a malfunction arose from a changed environment and assumptions that were poorly understood, rather than a defect in the original development. Where the software is modified in situ, the environment does not change; where software is reused in an environment that is presumed to be similar, the software has not changed, but the environment has. The results in either case are that there may be a mismatch where there was none before.

5.107 Generally speaking, programmers who modify someone else's code often do not fully understand the software, and may also be less well trained than the people who originally wrote it. Software can (if appropriately designed) be relied upon to produce verifiably correct results, but to have such a degree of certainty, it is necessary to be assured that the operating conditions remain identical and that nothing else malfunctions. Peter G. Neumann has indicated that even though the utmost care and attention might be devoted to the design of a system, it may still have significant flaws.[1] This was illustrated in a 1970 report edited by Willis H. Ware. The authors noted, under 'Failure Prediction' within section V System Characteristics, that:

> In the present state of computer technology, it is impossible to completely anticipate, much less specify, all hardware failure modes, all software design errors or omissions, and, most seriously, all failure modes in which hardware malfunctions lead to software malfunctions. Existing commercial machines have only a minimum of redundancy and error-checking circuits, and thus for most military applications there may be unsatisfactory hardware facilities to assist in the control of hardware/software malfunctions. Furthermore, in the present state of knowledge, it is very difficult to predict the probability of failure of complex hardware and software configurations; thus, redundancy [is] an important design concept.[2]

1 Neumann, *Computer Related Risks*, 4; see his text generally for this topic.
2 *Security Controls for Computer Systems: Report of Defense Science Board Task Force on Computer Security – RAND Report R-609-1*, http://www.rand.org/pubs/reports/R609-1/index2.html.

5.108 The authors of the report went on to observe the following in Part C, Technical Recommendations:

> (a) It is virtually impossible to verify that a large software system is completely free of errors and anomalies.
>
> (b) The state of system design of large software systems is such that frequent changes to the system can be expected.
>
> (c) Certification of a system is not a fully developed technique nor are its details thoroughly worked out.
>
> (d) System failure modes are not thoroughly understood, cataloged, or protected against.
>
> (e) Large hardware complexes cannot be absolutely guaranteed error-free.

Security vulnerabilities

5.109 Software vulnerabilities are software errors generally hidden from view. While they generally cause users no harm, they may be exploited by state security services, malicious hackers and professional thieves for various advantages, including theft of personal data (to sell on), control of vulnerable systems, drug smuggling,[1] blackmail and other forms of financial gain. The market in selling packets of software code known as 'exploits' has become significant. Legitimate businesses may sell a vulnerability in a software code to business and government agencies, and hackers may sell a vulnerability to anyone who will buy them. These vulnerabilities, particularly those against which there are no pre-existing defences, known as 'zero day exploits',[2] may be exploited, whether legally or illegally, for criminal investigation as well as for the purposes of cyber espionage, including the violation of confidentiality (stealing information), availability (denial of service for political intimidation or blackmail) and integrity (corrupting information to steal from banks or to cause an embedded computer system to cause accidents).

1 *Hackers Deployed to Facilitate Drugs Smuggling*, Intelligence Notification 004-2013, June 2013, Europol Public Information, https://www.europol.europa.eu/publications-documents/cyber-bits-hackers-deployed-to-facilitate-drugs-smuggling.
2 https://en.wikipedia.org/wiki/Zero-day_(computing).

5.110 To address these vulnerabilities, software vendors often, but not always, issue 'security patches' regularly each month (sometimes referred to as 'software updates' to conceal the nature of the update) in recognition of the failure of their software. Yet these may give rise to more problems. For instance, an important security weakness was discovered in relation to the distribution of software patches (which, ironically, was put in place to address security weaknesses). This meant that attackers who receive the patch first might compromise vulnerable hosts who have yet to receive the patch.[1]

1 Two examples from many: David Brumley, Pongsin Poosankam, Dawn Song and Jiang Zheng, 'Automatic patch-based exploit generation is possible: techniques and implications', *2008 IEEE Symposium on Security and Privacy (sp 2008)* (Oakland, IEEE 2008); Yan Wang, Chao Zhang, Xiaobo, Zixuan Zhao, Wenjie Li, Xiaorui Gong, Bingchang Liu, Kaixiang Chen, Wei Zou, 'Revery: from proof-of-concept to exploitable', *CCS '19: Proceedings of the 2019 ACM SIGSAC Conference on Computer and Communications Security* (New York, Association for Computing Machinery 2019), 1689–1706.

5.111 Software security vulnerabilities are particularly pertinent to businesses and industries that operate or rely on digital security infrastructures. For these industries, there are other issues to consider. The first is whether the design of the security protocol is robust. An example of a failure in this category is with banking systems,[1] and although a design can be modified, at best it is only possible to take a provisional view in respect of this point, because designs constantly change and are therefore liable to failure. The second is whether the security protocol is implemented properly. For instance, a number of ATMs were tested around Cambridge in the UK, and it was found that nonce generation was predictable. A nonce is supposed to be a unique object in a protocol, a one-time 'security code', but it was found that some ATMs were using a small supply of tokens as nonces and reusing them in a predictable order, thereby compromising their security.[2]

1 Steven J. Murdoch, Saar Drimer, Ross Anderson and Mike Bond, 'Chip and PIN is broken' in *31st IEEE Symposium on Security and Privacy* (IEEE Computer Society 2010) 433–446, https://www.cl.cam.ac.uk/research/security/banking/nopin/oakland10chipbroken.pdf; Steven J. Murdoch, 'Reliability of Chip & PIN evidence in banking disputes' (2009) 6 Digital Evidence and Electronic Signature Law Review 98.
2 Megan Geuss, 'How a criminal ring defeated the secure chip-and-PIN credit cards', arstechnica, 20 October 2015, http://arstechnica.com/tech-policy/2015/10/how-a-criminal-ring-defeated-the-secure-chip-and-pin-credit-cards/; Mike Bond, Omar Choudary, Steven J. Murdoch, Sergei Skorobogatov and Ross Anderson, 'Chip and skim: cloning EMV cards with the pre-play attack', paper presented to Cryptographic Hardware and Embedded System (CHES) 2012, Leuven, Belgium, September 2012, https://murdoch.is/papers/oakland14chipandskim.pdf; Houda Ferradi, Rémi Géraud, David Naccache and Assia Tria, *When Organized Crime Applies Academic Results: A Forensic Analysis of an In-Card Listening Device*, https://eprint.iacr.org/2015/963.pdf.

5.112 Furthermore, security may be associated with safety. If there is a safety-related system with security vulnerabilities, it is possible for the safety functions in the system to be deliberately subverted and give rise to a safety issue. For instance, the nuclear industry has developed a draft international standard for safety and security.[1] The vital problem in this area, which nobody has solved, is that while updates of safety functions in code that control nuclear reactors are slow, deliberate and highly analytical, updates for security purposes have to be rapid, to forestall anticipated attempts via zero-day exploits. These two modi are obviously incompatible.

1 Caroline Baylon, with Roger Brunt and David Livingstone, *Cyber Security at Civil Nuclear Facilities: Understanding the Risks*, Chatham House Report (The Royal Institute of International Affairs, September 2015), https://www.chathamhouse.org/publication/cyber-security-civil-nuclear-facilities-understanding-risks.

5.113 It follows that software security vulnerabilities expose the software to manipulations without the authority or knowledge of the software vendor.[1] Many of the vulnerabilities arise specifically from the errors in the original implementation. For instance, it might be possible for a person to control another owner's computer as part of a botnet[2] or enter the control system of an aircraft in flight via the in-flight entertainment system.[3]

1 The Trojan horse problem was recognized very early on, for which see Linden, 'Operating system structures to support security and reliable software', 422–424.
2 Sanjay Goel, Adnan Baykal and Damira Pon, 'Botnets: the anatomy of a case', (2005) 1(3) Journal of Information System Security 45.
3 See *Applicant for a Search Warrant in the case of Chris Roberts at the United States District Court for the Northern District Court of New York* Case number 5:15-MJ-00154 (ATB) dated 17 April 2015, [18]–[19], http://www.wired.com/wp-content/uploads/2015/05/Chris-Roberts-Application-for-Search-Warrant.pdf; https://assets.documentcloud.org/documents/2082796/gov-uscourts-nynd-102002-1-0.pdf; Caleb Kennedy, 'New threats to vehicle safety: how cybersecurity policy will shape the future of autonomous vehicles' (2017) 23 Mich Telecomm & Tech L Rev 343.

5.114 At this point, the reader might consider that such problems can be solved fairly easily – by the introduction of anti-virus software (this is not to imply that all attacks occur through the use of malicious software). But it must be understood that the fundamental nature of most anti-virus software limits its effectiveness – and the anti-virus software itself might not be error-free. A sophisticated attacker will have access to all types of anti-virus software, and he will program round the detection mechanisms and test his code against the anti-virus systems to ensure it is not detected.[1] Most anti-virus software is reactive, in that it searches for known threats. As such, anti-virus software is far from perfect. It can fail to stop some malicious software[2] and should not be relied upon as the sole method of securing a computer.

1 J. A. P. Marpaung, M. Sain and Hoon-Jae Lee, 'Survey on malware evasion techniques: state of the art and challenges', *Advanced Communication Technology (ICACT), 2012 14th International Conference*, PyeongChang, (Global IT Research Institute 2012), 744–749; Chandra Sekar Veerappan, Peter Loh Kok Keong, Zhaohui Tang and Forest Tan, 'Taxonomy on malware evasion countermeasures techniques', *2018 IEEE 4th World Forum on Internet of Things (WF-IoT)* (Institute of Electrical and Electronics Engineers 2018).

2 Daniel Bilar, 'Known knowns, known unknowns and unknown unknowns: anti-virus issues, malicious software and internet attacks for non-technical audiences' (2009) 6 Digital Evidence and Electronic Signature Law Review 123; in 2006, Graham Ingram, the general manager of the Australian Computer Emergency Response Team (AusCERT), told an audience in Sydney, Australia, that popular desktop antivirus applications do not work: Munir Kotadia, 'Eighty percent of new malware defeats antivirus' (19 June 2006), ZDNet Australia; Michael A. Caloyannides, 'Digital evidence and reasonable doubt' (2003) 1(6) IEEE Security and Privacy 89; Dmitry Silnov, 'Features of virus detection mechanism in Microsoft security essentials (Microsoft forefront endpoint protection)' (2013) 4(2) Journal of Information Security 124; also see the annual 'X-Force Trend Statistics' by IBM Internet Security Systems that reinforces the position on the failure of anti-virus software, https://www.ibm.com/security/data-breach/threat-intelligence; the reports produced by the Anti-Phishing Working Group (http://www.antiphishing.org/) illustrate the same problem; reports by AV-Comparatives.org appear to indicate that some of the best products are now very efficient, http://www.av-comparatives.org/; see also 'Common vulnerabilities and exposures', https://cve.mitre.org/.

5.115 It is a truth universally acknowledged that the majority of hackers concentrate on the most widely used software and on vulnerable applications that can be found by using Internet search engines. The development of the Stuxnet virus illustrates that governments are now probably responsible for some of the most effective viruses that are written, although organized criminals can be equally effective.[1] Software need only include a low number of defects to create enough vulnerabilities for hackers to manipulate them to their advantage. Jim Nindel-Edwards and Gerhard Steinke usefully sum up the position:

> It would seem that after decades of software development there would be some assurance that software works as specified in the customer requirements. Is it that software vendors are unwilling to perform sufficient testing? Is it possible to test everything? Finding a certain number of bugs, doesn't mean that the software has no more bugs. On the other hand, not finding any defects doesn't mean there aren't any defects in the software either. Perhaps there are known bugs, but the time and resources to fix these bugs and defects are often not provided and the software is released with known (but not publicly stated) bugs. Is it because there is a low expectation of quality? Is it even possible to get rid of all bugs, especially when we are integrating components from multiple sources and we are dependent on the software that was developed and tested by others?
>
> Software quality assurance is a challenging task. There are many questions raised by software being released with defects. What are the ethical responsibilities of a software vendor releasing software with bugs, especially if it is system-critical software, but also when releasing non system-critical software?[2]

1 Roderic Broadhurst, Peter Grabosky, Mamoun Alazab, Brigitte Bouhours and Steve Chon, 'Organizations and cyber crime: an analysis of the nature of groups engaged in cyber crime' (2014) 8(1) International Journal of Cyber Criminology 1, http://www.cybercrimejournal.com/broadhurstetalijcc2014vol8issue1.pdf; https://www.nationalcrimeagency.gov.uk/what-we-do/crime-threats/cyber-crime; https://www.unodc.org/e4j/en/cybercrime/module-13/key-issues/criminal-groups-engaging-in-cyber-organized-crime.html.

2 Jim Nindel-Edwards and Gerhard Steinke, 'Ethical issues in the software quality assurance function' (2008) 8(1) Communications of the IIMA article 6, 53, 54.

Software testing

5.116 Most software organizations test their products extensively, including in the ways that they anticipate that their customers will use them. Indeed, most software has become so complex that in a process called beta testing, software has been provided to volunteers to test before it is sold as a product. It has also been suggested that the problems of the composition of components in large systems can be mitigated by programmers reusing components in ways that they know from experience tend to work,[1] although this view is not generally accepted.[2] However, there will continue to be malfunctions, because many problems in hardware, software and configuration are only exposed when the system runs under real workloads.[3] A number of issues arise in this respect, including the use of tools to test software fault tolerance or robustness,[4] the degree to which the testing accurately reflects the way users will actually use the software, the unconventional ways in which people may attempt to use the program and testing how the software works when connecting and communicating with different software and hardware. It is well known that testing software is inadequate for uncovering errors, because there is never enough time to cover all the cases, as the illustrations mentioned in this chapter vividly show. Professor Thimbleby has indicated that the only solutions are:

> (1) a very careful approach to reasoning about the requirements that lead to the decisions,
>
> (2) a mathematically rigorous way to analyse the combinations of decisions,
>
> (3) rigorous testing, primarily to uncover whether there were flaws in steps (1) and (2), including in the testing process itself, and
>
> (4) external oversight to avoid mistakes in one's reasoning – this includes processes such as code review by third parties.[5]

1 C. A. R. Hoare, 'How did software get so reliable without proof?' in Marie-Claude Gaudel and Jim Woodcock (eds) *Lecture Notes in Computer Science, vol 1051/1996* (Springer 1996), 1–17.
2 Bev Littlewood and Lorenzo Strigini, 'The risks of software', *Scientific American* 267(5), (November 1992) 62–75, cited by Partridge, *The Seductive Computer*, 205, fn 15; B. Littlewood and L. Strigini, 'Validation of ultra-high dependability – 20 years on' (2011) 20(3) SCSC Newsletter, http://www.staff.city.ac.uk/~sm377/ls.papers/2011_limits_20yearsOn_SCSC/BL-LS-SCSSnewsletter2011_02_v04distrib.pdf.
3 Schroeder and Gibson, 'A large-scale study of failures in high-performance computing systems', 343.
4 Although the availability of such tools does not mean that developers use them to improve their systems, for which see John DeVale and Philip Koopman, 'Robust software – no more excuses' in Danielle C. Martin, editorial production, *Proceedings International Conference on Dependable Systems and Networks* (The Institute of Electrical and Electronics Engineers, Inc. 2002), 145–154; *The Economic Impacts of Inadequate Infrastructure for Software Testing: Final Report* (May 2002), Prepared for National Institute of Standards and Technology by RTI Health, Social, and Economics Research, https://www.nist.gov/system/files/documents/director/planning/report02-3.pdf.
5 Personal communication with the author.

5.117 The problem with a presumption that a computer is deemed to be 'reliable' is that, as systems become more complex, it has become progressively more challenging to test software to reflect the way the users will actually use the product. This is because of the large number of functions that software is required to perform and the unpredictability of its users.[1] Professor Partridge reiterates the point that 'no significant computer program is completely understood',[2] and goes further by indicating that systems are now so complex that humans are no longer able to deal with the problems:

> We might speculate further: if the nature of computer-system complexity really is new and peculiar, a system characteristic that has no parallel in the natural world, then our evolutionary history is unlikely to have equipped us to reason effectively with such systems. Our genetic programs may be totally lacking in mechanisms that can deal effectively with discrete complexity.[3]

1 The rise in fraud that took advantage of the faults in software was rapidly increasing in the 1970s, for which see Linden, 'Operating system structures to support security and reliable software', 410.
2 Derek Partridge, *What Makes You Clever – the Puzzle of Intelligence* (World Scientific 2014), 394 and 407 fn 22.
3 Partridge, *The Seductive Computer*, 192.

5.118 This weakness is now recognized by some of the organizations that produce devices and software. Microsoft and Apple are among a number of companies that have adopted a 'bug' bounty programme to reward professionals who test and find errors in the software.[1] The US Department of Defense has also taken this approach, as has Google in respect of cryptographic software libraries.[2] Yet claims that software code and hardware products have been independently tested does not necessarily lead to the conclusion that they can be relied upon. In his ACM Turing Lecture of 1972, Professor Dijkstra said this of testing:

> Today a usual technique is to make a program and then to test it. But: program testing can be a very effective way to show the presence of bugs, but is hopelessly inadequate for showing their absence.[3]

1 Microsoft Bounty Program, https://www.microsoft.com/en-us/msrc/bounty?rtc=1; https://developer.apple.com/security-bounty/; Project Wycheproof, https://github.com/google/wycheproof; HackerOne, formed by Facebook, Microsoft and Google, https://www.hackerone.com/.
2 DoD Vulnerability Disclosure Policy, available at https://hackerone.com/deptofdefense.
3 https://www.cs.utexas.edu/~EWD/ewd03xx/EWD340.PDF; the lecture was published as an article: Edsger W. Dijkstra, 'The humble programmer', (1972) 15(10) Communications of the ACM 859.

5.119 In other words, good-quality testing might discover the failings of the developer, but is less capable of resolving the issues in the overall design of software: there are significant limits to testing.

Writing software that is free of faults

5.120 As Professor Thomas indicates, it is possible to design and develop software so that it is almost completely free of faults.[1] Many applications are now built without the developer writing any code at all. The coding is done in building the tools that generate the code when given parameters by the developer – and this is premised on the fact that the software tools that generate the code are themselves error free.

1 'Should we trust computers?', lecture given at Gresham College on 20 October 2015, http://www.gresham.ac.uk/lectures-and-events/should-we-trust-computers.

Software standards

5.121 Where an organization produces safety critical software for aeroplanes, motor vehicles, air traffic control or power stations, it will be necessary to conform to the requirements of an international standard on the functional safety of programmable electronic systems.[1] For instance, security in the banking sector relies on certification standards such as FIPS-140 Information Technology Security Evaluation Criteria (ITSEC) and the Common Criteria for Information Technology Security Evaluation. It should be noted that these schemes only focus on aspects of security, and not on overall functionality. It is possible to have an accredited product that implements the security functions well, but its business functions badly.

1 For a discussion, see the NuSAC Study Group on the Safety of Operational Computer Systems, *The Use of Computers in Safety-Critical Applications* (Her Majesty's Stationery Office 1998).

5.122 The ITSEC scheme, which is no longer as active as it once was, assesses a product based on a document prepared by the organization that wants that product to be evaluated. In general terms, a document that is submitted to ITSEC describes what the product is designed to do, the situation in which it is intended to operate, the risks the product is likely to encounter and the mechanism by which the product acts to protect against the risks. It is for ITSEC to determine whether the claims are substantiated. Only the risks identified by the applicant are tested. A product is given one of seven levels from E0 (no formal assurance) to E6 (the highest level of confidence), with each level representing increasing levels of confidence. The assessment and granting of a position on the E scale is a judgement that a certain level of confidence has been met; it is not a measure of the strength of the security in place. It is important to realize that the organization submitting the product for evaluation sets out the criteria by which it will be evaluated, and it may be that this organization will not have included the risks associated with the use of the product by the end user. The evaluation includes an assessment of the confidence to be placed in whether the security features are the correct ones and how effectively they work. This means that a security mechanism might be applied correctly, but it will not be effective unless it is appropriate for the purpose for which it has been designed. In this respect, it is necessary to know why a particular security function is necessary, what security is actually in place and how the security is provided. It does not follow that if a product has a high E level that it will provide a high level of security.

5.123 The 'Common Criteria for Information Technology Security Evaluation' and 'Common Methodology for Information Security Evaluation' comprise the technical basis for an international agreement called the Common Criteria Recognition Agreement. The manufacturer submits its product to an independent licensed laboratory for an assessment. The way a product is evaluated is similar to the way ITSEC undertakes such assessments. There are problems with this, because it creates a conflict of interest: there are no known examples of the revocation of licences of laboratories that conduct evaluations, both parties are able to subvert the process, and determining the name of the organization that conducted the evaluation might be impossible without an order for disclosure. In addition, claims will sometimes be made that a device has been certified when, in fact, it might only have been evaluated. Often, a bank will ask a judge to rely on the certification process without disclosing the relevant report. In the Norwegian case of *Bernt Petter Jørgensen v DnB NOR Bank ASA,*

Journal number 04-016794TVI-TRON, Trondheim District Court, 24 September 2004,[1] Assistant Judge Leif O. Østerbø, who tried the case, said at 121–122 (emphasis added):

> It is *assumed* that the standard security systems that are used are effective. However, according to Jørgensen, no cases have been documented that demonstrate [that] the implementation of the systems are secure.
>
> The court refers in this respect to the fact that banks are subject to supervision and operate a comprehensive internal control work, and the witness Haugstad's explanation that both the standards and the practical implementation are revised thoroughly and regularly. In that regard, Haugestad explained that the systems are subject to annual audits. The Banks Control Center (BSK), in addition to the major international card companies, conducts such audits.
>
> *The court does not find that there is reason to accept that the banks' security systems are in doubt.* Although the implementation of a system necessarily involves opportunities for errors, the court cannot see that this involves significant practical risk for customers with cards.

1 For a translation into English, see (2012) 9 Digital Evidence and Electronic Signature Law Review 117; Nuth, 'Unauthorized use of bank cards with or without the PIN'.

5.124 If the purpose of a trial is to test the evidence, should a judge *assume* that the standard security systems used by the bank were effective in the absence of any evidence? Should a judge accept *untested* assurances that audits actually take place, not knowing whether such audits are conducted internally or by the Banks Control Center, whether the audits revealed problems that might affect the systems for ATMs and PINs, or whether the audits were conducted by people with appropriate qualifications? Given the lack of such evidence, can a judge conclude that there was no reason to doubt the bank's security systems could be at fault?[1] For instance, it has been demonstrated that independent external examination continues to validate and approve devices and cryptographic software code that are open to failure and subversion.[2]

1 Ken Lindup, 'Technology and banking' (2012) 9 Digital Evidence and Electronic Signature Law Review 91.

2 Steven J. Murdoch, Mike Bond and Ross Anderson, 'How certification systems fail: lessons from the Ware Report' (2012) 10(6) IEEE Security & Privacy 40; Kim Zetter, 'In legal first, data-breach suit targets auditor', Wired, 16 February 2009 – the case mentioned in this article was *Merrick Bank Corporation v Savvis, Inc.*, 2010 WL 148201 (for other references, see 2009 WL 2968844 (D.Ariz.) (Trial Motion, Memorandum and Affidavit) (5 June 2009); 2009 WL 4823623 (D.Ariz.) (Trial Motion, Memorandum and Affidavit) (7 July 2009); 2009 WL 4823624 (D.Ariz.) (Trial Motion, Memorandum and Affidavit)) – it is not clear what happened as a result of the legal action. It is probable that the case was settled after the court refused to dismiss the case. Another case, a class action, was initiated in the United States District Court Northern District of Illinois Eastern Division on 24 March 2014: *Trustmark National Bank v Target Corporation*, Case No 14-CV-2069, although it was reported that this action was subsequently withdrawn, for which see Jonathan Stempel, 'Banks pull out of lawsuit vs Target, Trustwave over data breach', Reuters, 1 April 2014.

5.125 Two observations are worthy of note: that standards[1] regarding aviation, space and medical devices are usually much more prescriptive that those used in other domains, and even within the aviation, space and medical industries a great deal of commercial software is developed against no formal process model at all. The relevant standard for medical devices is 'ISO 13485:2003 Medical devices – Quality management systems – Requirements for regulatory purposes' (now revised by 'ISO 13485:2016 Medical devices – Quality management systems – Requirements for regulatory purposes'). This standard has historically placed much less focus on tracing the details of internal product structure than, for instance, DO-178B, Software Considerations in Airborne Systems and Equipment Certification, which is a guideline dealing with the safety of critical software to be used in certain airborne systems. Yet, although having software evaluated against standards is a laudable goal, it does not follow that, by conforming, errors are eliminated.[2]

1 The use of standards is a topic of significant debate, because it is not always certain that they work to improve the quality of software. By way of example, see Patrick J. Graydon and C. Michael Holloway, *Planning the Unplanned Experiment: Assessing the Efficacy of Standards for Safety Critical Software* (NASA/TM - 2015 - 218804, September 2015), https://core.ac.uk/reader/42705578.
2 Timothy J. Shimeall and Nancy G. Leveson, 'An empirical comparison of software fault tolerance and fault elimination' (1991) 17(2) Transactions on Software Engineering 173; P. B. Ladkin, 'Opinion – taking software seriously' (2005) 41(3) Journal of System Safety https://rvs-bi.de/publications/; Harold Thimbleby, Alexis Lewis and John Williams, 'Making healthcare safer by understanding, designing and buying better IT' (2015) 15(3) Clinical Medicine 258.

Summary

5.126 In summary, faults in software and errors relating to the design of software systems are exceedingly common.[1] And while defects in hardware have been relatively rare,[2] they are not unknown.[3] Hardware is increasingly developed using high-level languages similar to those used for software. Furthermore, hardware is being released with firmware which may be reconfigured for other purposes. In addition, hardware faults can also be introduced by the improper use or configuration of software tools designed for developing hardware, which may themselves be error-prone. Like software, hardware errors, too, can be exploited to cause security failures.[4]

1 Richard Cook, 'How complex systems fail', Cognitive Technologies Laboratory, University of Chicago (January 2002), https://www.researchgate.net/publication/228797158_How_complex_systems_fail/link/5caf748a299bf120975f697e/download; L. Strigini, 'Fault tolerance against design faults', in Hassan B. Diab and Albert Y. Zomaya (eds) *Dependable Computing Systems: Paradigms, Performance Issues, and Applications* (John Wiley & Sons 2005), 213–241.
2 Such as the Pentium FDIV or 'floating point' error (strictly speaking, this was a software fault), although Intel could not fix the error other than by issuing a replacement, https://en.wikipedia.org/wiki/Pentium_FDIV_bug. Professor Thomas R. Nicely was the first to publicize this fault: Partridge, *The Seductive Computer*, 98, fn 8.
3 Most complex integrated circuits in wide use will have published lists of 'errata' – for example, Intel publishes regular updates online.
4 For an example, see Apostolos P. Fournaris, Lidia Pocero Fraile and Odysseas Koufopavlou, 'Exploiting hardware vulnerabilities to attack embedded system devices: a survey of potent microarchitectural attacks' (2017) 6 electronics, 52; Lucian Cojocar, Kaveh Razavi, Cristiano Giuffrida and Herbert Bos, 'Exploiting correcting codes: on the effectiveness of ECC memory against Rowhammer', in *2019 IEEE Symposium on Security and Privacy (SP)*, Volume 1 (IEEE 2019), 279–295.

5.127 Every part of a program is different, and must be independently correct. In the case of machines, there are two important differences: things are almost always continuous, and after a time the system is back where it started. When they are not continuous, problems always occur. For example, a wheel turns, and once it has turned, it is (not withstanding wear and tear) likely to be able to turn again. Each time it turns, it gets back to an indistinguishable state. This is called a symmetry. Symmetries are very general ideas. For example, if one moves a cup of coffee a foot to the left, it stays the same and works exactly as before. This is because the world we live in has translational symmetry – everything is the same if it is moved. Wheels have rotational symmetry, and so on. This means that almost all of the design decisions in mechanical devices 'collapse' because of symmetries, and there is not the exponential growth of cases that happens in software. On the other hand, no part of a software program is the same as any other part. Indeed, if it was, one would ask why it was so inefficiently designed. Thus there are no symmetries in software that amplify the 'how it works' thinking that so readily simplifies physical design. The other advantage of physical systems is that where a response is expected to be continuous, it can be verified. Where continuity holds, interpolation tells what the behaviour for any input will be. Digital systems do not have this helpful property.

5.128 In particular, it might be obvious that the behaviour of a stopwatch used by a policeman is the 'same' as the behaviour of the 'same' stopwatch presented in court as evidence, or in the laboratory where it was tested. Thanks to symmetries, moving a watch from the roadside to the laboratory does not change it. There is no symmetry to justify software adduced in court behaving as it did anywhere else. Software is not constrained, as any physical device is, to work in the universe with all its symmetries. Software does not obey any of them, and thanks to human error (known and unknown) in its design, its behaviour cannot be taken for granted.[1]

1 I owe this discussion to Professor Thimbleby.

5.129 Software will continue to be unreliable. By providing a general presumption of reliability to software, the law acts to reinforce the attitude of the software industry that the effects of poor-quality work remain the problem of the end user. In many circumstances, because the user can himself cause errors, the industry may seek to pin the blame on the user, further obfuscating the true origin and source of the errors.[1] For these reasons, it is rare for a customer to take legal action against the software supplier, let alone attempt such an action and be successful.[2]

1 The various pressures are illustrated in Hechler, 'Lost in translation?' . David Hechler is the executive editor of *Corporate Counsel* magazine, and the American Society of Business Publication Editors awarded him the 2014 Stephen Barr Award for this article.

2 For example, see the English cases of *St Albans City and District Council v International Computers Limited* [1996] 4 All ER 481, [1996] 7 WLUK 443, [1997–98] Info TLR 58, [1997] FSR 251, (1996) 15 Tr LR 444, [1998] Masons CLR Rep 98, (1997) 20(2) IPD 20020, Times, 14 August 1996, [1996] CLY 1218 and *Kingsway Hall Hotel Ltd v Red Sky IT (Hounslow) Ltd* [2010] EWHC 965 (TCC), [2010] 5 WLUK 106, (2010) 26 Const LJ 542, [2011] CLY 2777; Alison White, 'Caveat vendor? A review of the Court of Appeal decision in St Albans City and District Council v International Computers Limited', Commentary 1997 (3) The Journal of Information, Law and Technology JILT, https://warwick.ac.uk/fac/soc/law/elj/jilt/1997_3/white/#Salvage. Elizabeth MacDonald considered the position in contract, giving a number of examples in her article 'Bugs and breaches' (2005) 13(1) Intl J L & Info Tech118. National Air Traffic Services initiated action against Electronic Data Systems Ltd, although the outcome is not certain. For an appeal against an application to amend the reply and defence to counterclaim, see *Electronic Data Systems Ltd v National Air Traffic Services* [2002] EWCA Civ 13, [2002] 1 WLUK 128 – Professor Ladkin indicated that the software development could fail, for which see Memorandum by Professor Peter B. Ladkin (ATC 20) submitted to the Select Committee on Environment, Transport and Regional Affairs Fourth Report (ordered by the House of Commons to be printed 27 March 1998), http://www.publications.parliament.uk/pa/cm199798/cmselect/cmenvtra/360-e/36082.htm.

5.130 This discussion apart, the central issue for lawyers is dealing with the presumption that a computer is working properly. The following summary of the problems of software by Professor Partridge help to remind us of the landscape:

> IT systems are everywhere, and will continue to infiltrate the lives of all of us.
>
> We cannot easily check that an IT system is computing correctly.
>
> IT systems all fail: sometimes immediately and spectacularly, sometimes unobtrusively just once in a while, and sometimes in any combination of these two extremes.
>
> IT-system failures vary from production of blatantly incorrect results to failure to produce a desired result.
>
> The interplay of a variety of causes means that all large IT systems are unmanageably complex.
>
> IT-system complexity is discrete complexity rather than complexity based on continua.
>
> If, by chance (combined with exemplary practice and much effort), an IT system is constructed with no possibility of failure behaviour, we can never know this.[1]

1 Partridge, *The Seductive Computer*, 9.

5.131 This poses a question for lawyers, experts and the courts: how the reliability of software should be reviewed in a court of law.

Challenging 'reliability'

5.132 When seeking to challenge the underlying software of a computer or computer-like device,[1] lawyers frequently have great difficulty in overcoming the presumption that a machine is working properly, although general assertions about the failure of software code are often made without providing any foundation for the allegations. This problem is compounded when a party refuses to deliver up relevant evidence, usually citing confidentiality as the reason for the refusal, and relying, directly or indirectly,[2] on the presumption that a computer is 'reliable'. In such circumstances, it is difficult to convince a judge to order the disclosure of relevant data.

1 Including machines controlled by software, often called 'robots'. For examples of people killed by machines controlled by software, see the following illustrative articles: Stephen S. Wu, *Summary of Selected Robotics Liability Cases* (19 October 2010), https://ftp.documation.com:8443/references/ABA10a/PDfs/2_5.pdf; Woodrow Barfield, 'Liability for autonomous and artificially intelligent robots' (2018) 9 Paladyn, J Behav Robot 193; Emilie C. Schwarza, 'Human vs. machine: a framework of responsibilities and duties of transnational corporations for respecting human rights in the use of artificial intelligence' (2019) 58 Colum J Transnat'l L 232. Robert N. Williams appears to have been the first person to be killed by a robot machine that was the subject of legal proceedings: *Williams v Litton Systems, Inc.*, 422 Mich. 796 (1985); *Williams v Litton Systems, Inc.*, 164 Mich.App. 195, 416 N.W.2d 704 (1987); *Williams v Unit Handling Systems Div. of Litton Systems, Inc.*, 433 Mich. 755, 449 N.W.2d 669 (1989), and in 1987 seven-year-old Barton Griffin was the first person to be killed because of a defect in a programmable read-only memory chip installed in a 2500 series Chevrolet pickup truck that caused the vehicle to stall. Another vehicle struck the pickup truck, killing the driver's grandson: *General Motors Corporation v Johnston*, 592 So.2d 1054 (1992).

2 The use of the word 'robust' is one such device, for which see Ladkin, 'Robustness of software'.

5.133 Yet, paradoxically, it is a well-known fact in the industry that software could hardly be said to be 'reliable', as noted by Steyn J in *Eurodynamic Systems Plc v General Automation Ltd*:

> The expert evidence convincingly showed that it is regarded as acceptable practice to supply computer programmes (including system software) that contain errors

and bugs. The basis of the practice is that, pursuant to his support obligation (free or chargeable as the case may be), the supplier will correct errors and bugs that prevent the product from being properly used.[1]

1 (6 September 1988, not reported), QBD, 1983 D 2804 at [5.a]; also see CL & P 1988, 5(2), 8.

5.134 Professor Matt Blaze reinforces this view:

> It is a regrettable (and yet time-tested) paradox that our digital systems have largely become *more* vulnerable over time, even as almost every other aspect of the technology has (often wildly) improved.
>
> ...
>
> Modern digital systems are so vulnerable for a simple reason: computer science does not yet know how to build complex, large-scale software that has reliably correct behaviour.[1] This problem has been known, and has been a central focus of computing research, since the dawn of programmable computing. As new technology allows us to build larger and more complex systems (and to connect them together over the internet), the problem of software correctness becomes exponentially more difficult.[2] [Footnote 2 is at this point, and is reproduced below.]
>
> Footnote 2:
>
> That is, the number of software defects in a system typically increases at a rate far greater than the amount of code added to it. So adding new features to a system that makes it twice as large generally has the effect of making [it] far more than twice as vulnerable. This is because each new software component or feature operates not just in isolation, but potentially interacts with everything else in the system, sometimes in unexpected ways that can be exploited. Therefore, smaller and simpler systems are almost always more secure and reliable, and best practices in security favor systems [that have] the most limited functionality possible.[3]

1 It should be noted that computer scientists have invented many ways to achieve this, and some companies use these methods to prove mathematically that their systems cannot fail at runtime – but the software will be running on a computer with unreliable hardware, other firmware and software and user interfaces, which might mean that the program might be 'right', but when interacting with the other components, can lead to a lethal failure. Also, we need to be aware that what is being proved is not that the systems do what is desired, but that the systems meet a formal statement of the requirements. The original requirements cannot by themselves be proved to be correct, or that the formal software requirements meet the constraints of the real world. There are limits to what formal methods can do, and those limits are not widely acknowledged. B. Littlewood and L. Strigini, 'Validation of ultrahigh dependability for software-based systems' (1993) 36(11) Communications of the ACM 69, http://openaccess.city.ac.uk/1251/1/CACMnov93.pdf.
2 It is not clear whether 'exponentially' means that the rate of growth is proportional to the amount present, or whether the word is used loosely to mean 'growing rapidly'.
3 Dr Matt Blaze, Testimony, 'Encryption Technology and Potential US Policy Responses' before the Subcommittee on Information Technology of the Committee on Oversight and Government Reform House of Representatives, 114 Congress 1st session, Wednesday, April 29, 2015 (Serial No. 114–143), https://www.govinfo.gov/content/pkg/CHRG-114hhrg25879/pdf/CHRG-114hhrg25879.pdf.

5.135 The late Professor Lawrence Bernstein and C. M. Yuhas also acknowledged this observation:

> Software developers know that their systems can exhibit unexpected, strange behaviour, including crashes or hangs, when small operational differences are introduced.[1] These may be the result of new data, execution of code in new

> sequences or exhaustion of some computer resource such as buffer space, memory, hash function overflow space or processor time.[2]

1 This is a consequence of discrete complexity, or digital complexity.
2 Lawrence Bernstein and C. M. Yuhas, 'Design constraints that make software trustworthy', *IEEE Reliability Society 2008 Annual Technology Report*, 3, https://rs.ieee.org/images/files/Publications/2008/2008-25.pdf; Ali Mili and Fairouz Tchier, *Software Testing Concepts and Operations* (John Wiley & Sons, Inc. 2015).

5.136 Finally, companies that write software code include a contract term in the software licence that makes it clear that writers of software code are not perfect. Here is an example:

> The Licensee acknowledges that software in general is not error free and agrees that the existence of such errors shall not constitute a breach of this Licence.

5.137 This section aims to provide a broad outline of the problems relating to computers and computer-like devices experienced by different industries, and to illustrate the importance of software and how there may be times when the output of a computer may not necessarily be 'reliable' and is therefore not to be trusted. Software code should be open to scrutiny, and should not necessarily share the benefit of a presumption of 'reliability' that is incapable of being effectively challenged.

5.138 One of the problems with understanding the role of the presumption is that people fail to distinguish software from computer systems. Computers are merely devices that are remarkable in that they can be turned to do many tasks rather than being limited to a single purpose. In order to perform a useful purpose, they must be instructed by software. A computer and its software together can be taken to form a *system*. No machine is 'reliable' or 'unreliable' in an absolute sense. Machines may be *more* or *less* reliable. The term 'reliable' in everyday use is an abbreviation of what in technical terms is 'reliable enough for the intended purpose'. All machines have some probability of failing, so none is 'reliable' in the sense that one can rely on it without any doubt, while many are reliable enough (their probability of failing to perform correctly at any one use is small enough) to be worth using. The problem with using the word 'reliable', as though reliability were a binary quality, is that we risk taking it to mean 'reliable enough' without allowing for the fact that what is 'enough' depends on the use to which we put the machine, or rather its outputs. For instance, a machine may be reliable enough to be worthwhile in everyday use, and yet not reliable enough to use as evidence in a specific case. The speedometer in a motor car is reliable enough to use as an aid for driving at reasonable speed, because this level of reliability is sufficient for the purpose. In such circumstances, precision is not necessary. Compare this to instruments in an aircraft: the same level of reliability could be catastrophic. It is not a matter of whether or not the instrument is 'reliable', but of 'how reliable' it is.

5.139 It follows that lay people are not aware of the inherent design faults, and trust their personal experience to reassure themselves that computers are 'reliable' machines. Yet lay users regularly experience problems with devices, which illustrates their failure to grasp that 'reliability' and software code are impossible to guarantee.[1]

1 David Harel, *Computers Ltd. What They Really Can't Do* (Oxford University Press, 2003); see also Neumann, *Computer Related Risks*, and his website, which is continually updated: http://www.csl.sri.com/users/neumann/insiderisks.html; see also the list of software failures on the web site of Nachum

Dershowitz, School of Computer Science, Tel Aviv University, http://www.cs.tau.ac.il/~nachumd/horror.html.

5.140 Lay people are not the only people to make this mistake. This is illustrated by the judicial claim that computers are 'reliable' because in current times their use is widespread. Villanueva JAD made just such an assertion without providing any evidence to sustain his claim that computers are 'presumed reliable' in the case of *Hahnemann University Hospital v Dudnick*:

> Clearly, the climate of the use of computers in the mid-1990's is substantially different from that of the 1970's. In the 1970's, computers were relatively new, were not universally used and had no established standard of reliability. Now, computers are universally used and accepted, have become part of everyday life and work and are presumed reliable.[1]

1 292 N.J.Super. 11, 678 A.2d 266 (N.J.Super.A.D. 1996), 268. See Ivars Peterson, *Fatal Defect: Chasing Killer Computer Bugs* (Random House 1996) to demonstrate the opposite.

5.141 This observation by Villanueva JAD was made in the same year as the failure of the software that caused the *Ariane 5* rocket to be destroyed shortly after take-off.

5.142 That computers are deemed to be 'reliable' because they are used more frequently now than when they were first developed is a poor substitute for a rigorous understanding of the nature of computers and their software.[1] However, it is accepted that long-term use can be an important element of justified trust in a software system. This comes about because there might be a long history of valuable and seemingly error-free use, but also because the long-term user typically gets to know the idiosyncrasies of the system.

1 That software is 'reliable' has been comprehensively demonstrated to be incorrect: Ladkin and others, 'The Law Commission presumption concerning the dependability of computer evidence'; Jackson, 'An approach to the judicial evaluation of evidence from computers and computer systems'.

Aviation

5.143 Errors in aviation software can have disastrous, or near disastrous, consequences. They can be caused by something as simple as bad coding. By way of example, consider the F-22A Raptor advanced tactical fighter, which entered service with the US Air Force in 2005. In February 2007, 12 of these aircraft were flying from Hickham AFB in Hawaii to Kadena AB on Okinawa. All of the aircraft experienced simultaneous and total software failure in their navigational console when their longitude shifted from 180 degrees West to 180 degrees East. The jets were accompanied by tanker planes, which meant the pilots in the tankers were able to guide the jets back to Hawaii. Major General Don Sheppard spoke about the problem on CNN on 24 February 2007. The relevant part of the transcript is set out below:

> Maj. Gen. Don Sheppard (ret.): ... At the international date line, whoops, all systems dumped and when I say all systems, I mean all systems, their navigation, part of their communications, their fuel systems. They were – they could have been in real trouble. They were with their tankers. The tankers – they tried to reset their systems, couldn't get them reset. The tankers brought them back to Hawaii. This could have been real serious. It certainly could have been real serious if the weather had been bad. It turned out OK. It was fixed in 48 hours. It

> was a computer glitch in the millions of lines of code, somebody made an error in a couple lines of the code and everything goes.
>
> [...]
>
> SHEPPERD: Absolutely. When you think of airplanes from the old days, with cables and that type of thing and direct connections between the sticks and the yolks [*sic*] and the controls, not that way anymore. Everything is by computer. When your computers go, your airplanes go. You have multiple systems. When they all dump at the same time, you can be in real trouble. Luckily this turned out OK.
>
> John Roberts, CNN anchor: What would have happened General Shepperd if these brand-new $120 million F-22s had been going into battle?
>
> SHEPPERD: You would have been in real trouble in the middle of combat. The good thing is that we found this out. Any time – before, you know, before we get into combat with an airplane like this. Any time you introduce a new airplane, you are going to find glitches and you are going to find things that go wrong. It happens in our civilian airliners. You just don't hear much about it but these things absolutely happen. And luckily this time we found out about it before combat. We got it fixed with tiger teams in about 48 hours and the airplanes were flying again, completed their deployment. But this could have been real serious in combat.
>
> ROBERTS: So basically you had these advanced air – not just superiority but air supremacy fighters that were in there, up there in the air, above the Pacific Ocean, not much more sophisticated than a little Cessna 152 only with a jet engine.
>
> SHEPPERD: You got it. They are on a 12 to 15-hour flight from Hawaii to Okinawa, but all their systems dumped. They needed help. Had they gotten separated from their tankers or had the weather been bad, they had no attitude reference. They had no communications or navigation. They would have turned around and probably could have found the Hawaiian Islands. But if the weather had been bad on approach, there could have been real trouble. Again, you get refueling from your tankers. You don't run – you don't get yourself where you run out of fuel. You always have enough fuel and refueling nine, 10, 11, 12 times on a flight like this where you can get somewhere to land. But again, attitude reference and navigation are essential as is communication. In this case all of that was affected. It was a serious problem.[1]

1 'F-22 Squadron Shot Down by the International Date Line', Defense Industry Daily, 1 March 2007, at http://www.defenseindustrydaily.com/f22-squadron-shot-down-by-the-international-date-line-03087/; Lewis Page, 'US superfighter software glitch fixed', The Register, 28 February 2007.

5.144 In practice, this means that most commercially produced software will have thousands of undetected defects.[1]

1 For software defects generally, see Brooks, *The Mythical Man-Month* and a discussion by Professor Les Hatton substantiates the broad range quoted here: *Some Notes on Software Failure* (Addison-Wesley Professional 2001). See also Nindel-Edwards and Steinke, 'Ethical issues in the software quality assurance function', article 6.

5.145 In conventional flight control, the flight control commands from the cockpit are conveyed mechanically through steel cables or pushrods, often servo-assisted, to hydraulic actuators which then physically move the aerodynamic control surfaces on the wings and tailplane. In 'fly-by-wire', the flight control commands are converted to electrical signals transmitted by wires to the control surface actuators (in some cases in modern fly-by-wire aircraft the actuators may also be electric). Flight control is completely intermediated by software code, so a more accurate description would now be 'fly-by-software-code'. Besides fly-by-wire, the autopilot and flight management systems of even conventionally controlled aircraft are software-based. The more reliable and functional the autopilot and flight management systems software have become, the more pilots have relied on them, even to the detriment of their piloting skills, as demonstrated by a number of accidents and ensuing loss of life. Accidents involving aircraft can exhibit a series of anomalous pilot–system interactions, and aviation regulations and investigators, with few exceptions, tend to assign the responsibility for the results of those interactions ultimately to the pilots.[1] This is so even in circumstances where it is clear that the software code and the system design are so faulty that a human being is not able to respond correctly – or with sufficient speed. In the case of American Airlines Flight 965 near Cali, Colombia, on 20 December 1995,[2] 151 passengers and all of the cabin crew members died in the crash. In this case, a significant error occurred, as explained by Highsmith DJ:

> American Airlines predicates its claims on Honeywell's role as supplier of the Flight Management Computer (FMC) used on Flight 965 and Jeppesen's role in furnishing the navigational database programmed into the FMC and the corresponding aviation charts. Without making any findings in this regard but simply reflecting the narrative contained in Judge Marcus' summary judgment opinion, the Court notes that, on the approach to Cali, the pilots entered 'R' into the FMC, anticipating (based on the aviation charts) that this cipher corresponded to a beacon designated as 'Rozo'. Instead, another beacon designated as 'Romeo' was activated. This resulted in a change of the aircraft's heading to the east, over the Andes mountains. When the pilots became aware of the aircraft's easterly swing, they turned back to the west, in the direction of the valley where the Cali airport is located. Sadly, since the aircraft had been descending during these directional changes, Flight 965 never made it back to the valley. It crashed into the side of a mountain.[3]

1 Bill Palmer, *Understanding Air France 447* (Print edition v1.05, 2013), 179 and *Safety Alert for Operators*, issued by the U.S. Department of Transportation, Federal Aviation Administration (SAFO 13002 1/4/13), https://www.faa.gov/other_visit/aviation_industry/airline_operators/airline_safety/safo/all_safos/media/2013/SAFO13002.pdf; Susan Carey, 'American Airlines flight delays continue as pilot iPad app glitch is fixed', *Wall Street Journal*, 29 April 2015, http://www.wsj.com/articles/american-airline-flight-delays-continue-as-pilot-ipad-app-glitch-is-fixed-1430335366; Alex Hern, 'App fail on iPad grounds "a few dozen" American Airlines flights', *The Guardian*, 29 April 2015, https://www.theguardian.com/technology/2015/apr/29/apple-ipad-fail-grounds-few-dozen-american-airline-flights.

2 *In Re Air Crash Near Cali, Colombia on December 20*, 24 F.Supp.2d 1340 (1998).

3 At 1342 (footnotes omitted).

5.146 The critical importance of verifying the design of aviation software based on industry standards was noted in the *Aviation Occurrence Investigation Final Report: In-flight upset 154 km west of Learmonth.*[1] In this case, a problem with the software controlling the aeroplane was the cause of the accident. In this investigation report, the authors cited text relating to software requirements from *Software Considerations in Airborne Systems and Equipment Certification,*[2] produced by the Radio Technical Commission for Aeronautics:

> DO-178A [now DO-178C] provided high-level guidance for the generation of software requirements, the verification that the resulting design met the requirements, and validation that the requirements were adequate. It also noted that for systems that performed certain critical and essential functions:

> ... it may not be possible to demonstrate an acceptably low level of software errors without the use of specific design techniques. These techniques, which may include monitoring, redundancy, functional partitioning or other concepts, will strongly influence the software development program, particularly the depth and quality of the verification and validation effort ...
>
> NOTE: It is appreciated that, with the current state of knowledge, the software disciplines described in this document may not, in themselves, be sufficient to ensure that the overall system safety and reliability targets have been achieved. This is particularly true for certain critical systems such as full authority fly-by-wire. In such cases it is accepted that other measures, usually within the system, in addition to a high level of software discipline may be necessary to achieve these safety objectives and demonstrate that they have been met.[3]

1 WA 7 October 2008 VH-QPA Airbus A330-303 (ATSB Transport Safety Report, AO-2008-070).
2 (DO-178A, SC-152, issued on 22 March 1985 and up-dated regularly), http://www.rtca.org.
3 At 2.3.5.

5.147 Perhaps it is not necessary to indicate that the Boeing 737 Max crashes that killed 346 people (189 on Lion Air Flight 610 and 157 on Ethiopian Airlines Flight 302), were, it appears, caused by a hardware–software interaction.[1] What is pertinent is that the problems originated in design changes that were apparently small and presumed to be unlikely to make any significant difference to the system's behaviour, and were intended to make the new system appear to the users like the old system.[2]

1 *Final Aircraft Accident Investigation Report, PT. Lion Mentari Airlines, Boeing 737-8 (MAX); PK-LQP 29 October 2018* (October 2019), http://knkt.dephub.go.id/knkt/ntsc_aviation/baru/2018%20-%20035%20-%20PK-LQP%20Final%20Report.pdf; *Aircraft Accident Investigation Bureau Interim Report on Accident to the B737-8 (MAX) Registered ET-AVJ operated by Ethiopian Airlines on 10 March 2019* (AI-01/19 9 March 2020), https://reports.aviation-safety.net/2019/20190310-0_B38M_ET-AVJ_Interim.pdf; a number of internal Boeing documents about this have been released, with a significant number of derogatory comments about this issue made by employees: https://archive.org/details/boeingemailsocr; the US House Committee on Transportation & Infrastructure provides a list of resources dealing with their investigation at https://transportation.house.gov/committee-activity/boeing-737-max-investigation; Gregory Travis, 'How the Boeing 737 Max disaster looks to a software developer', IEEE Spectrum, 18 April 2019, https://spectrum.ieee.org/aerospace/aviation/how-the-boeing-737-max-disaster-looks-to-a-software-developer; *Final Committee Report The Design, Development & Certification of the Boeing 737 MAX* (The House Committee on Transportation & Infrastructure, September 2020), https://transportation.house.gov/imo/media/doc/2020.09.15%20FINAL%20737%20MAX%20Report%20for%20Public%20Release.pdf.
2 Joint Authorities Technical Review, *Boeing 737 MAX Flight Control System Observations, Findings, and Recommendations* (11 October 2019), VI (item 4), XI (item 9), https://www.faa.gov/news/media/attachments/Final_JATR_Submittal_to_FAA_Oct_2019.pdf.

Financial products

5.148 In August 2006, the rating agency Moody's gave constant proportion debt obligations (CPDOs) an AAA rating, which was close to making an investment in a CPDO free of risk.[1] In comparison, a competing rating agency, Fitch, could not understand why such a high rating was given to such 'investments', because its own models put CPDOs at almost the grade of 'junk'.[2] It transpired that the software used by Moody's for the purpose of rating CPDOs had a number of faults. A fault was found in early 2008 that, when corrected, failed to give the AAA rating, increasing the likelihood of defaults. The rating committee failed to disclose the error to investors or clients, and although the error was eventually corrected, other changes were made to the code to ensure the AAA rating continued to be assigned.[3] A subsequent external investigation by the law firm Sullivan & Cromwell established that members of staff had engaged in conduct contrary to Moody's Code of Professional Conduct.[4] Moody's subsequently received a 'Wells Notice'[5] from the Securities and Exchange Commission (SEC) on 18 March 2011.[6] The Division of Enforcement of the SEC later issued a *Report of Investigation* into the matter.[7] In a section of the Report, there was an examination of the attitude of the people responsible for dealing with the software error. It is revealing, and it merits setting out in full:

> B. Rating Committee Conduct
>
> MIS subsequently held several internal rating committee meetings in France and the United Kingdom to address the coding error. MIS corrected the coding error on February 12, 2007, but made no changes to the outstanding credit ratings for CPDO notes at that time. Internal e-mails show that committee members were concerned about the impact on MIS's reputation if it revealed an error in the rating model. A January 24, 2007, e-mail from a rating committee member to the Team Managing Director chairing the committee stated:
>
>> In this particular case we seem to face an important reputation risk issue. To be fully honest this latter issue is so important that I would feel inclined at this stage to minimize ratings impact and accept unstressed parameters that are within possible ranges rather than even allow for the possibility of a hint that the model has a bug.
>
> On April 27, 2007, after additional analysis, the rating committee voted not to downgrade the affected credit ratings for the CPDO notes. The committee members felt that because the CPDO notes were generally performing well there would be no ostensible justification for downgrading the credit ratings, absent announcing the coding error. In declining to downgrade the credit ratings, the committee considered the following inappropriate non-credit related factors: (i) that downgrades could negatively affect Moody's reputation in light of ongoing negative media focus in Europe on Moody's Joint Default Analysis; (ii) that downgrades could impact investors who relied on the original ratings; and (iii) the desire not to validate the criticisms of Moody's ratings of CPDOs that had been made by a competitor and covered in the local media. The committee was comprised of senior level staff, including two Team Managing Directors, two Vice President-Senior Credit Officers, and a Vice President-Senior Analyst.

1 For the broader picture, see Charles W. Calomiris and Stephen H. Haber, *Fragile by Design: The Political Origins of Banking Crisis and Scarce Credit* (Princeton University Press 2014), 266–269.

2 The same scepticism was expressed by Richard Beales, Saskia Scholtes and Gillian Tett with Paul J. Davies, 'Failing grades? Why regulators fear credit rating agencies may be out of their depth' *Financial Times*, 17 May 2007, 13.

3 This was revealed by Sam Jones, Gillian Tett and Paul J. Davies, 'Moody's error gave top ratings to debt products' *Financial Times*, 20 May 2008.

4 Sam Jones, 'When junk was gold' *FT Weekend*, 18/19 October 2008, 16–22.

5 A 'Wells Notice' is a letter sent by a securities regulator to a prospective respondent, notifying him of the substance of charges that the regulator intends to bring against the respondent, and affording the respondent with the opportunity to submit a written statement to the ultimate decision maker.

6 Phil Wahba, 'UPDATE 2-Moody's says got Wells Notice from SEC', Reuters, 7 May 2010.

7 Release No. 62802/31 August 2012, https://www.sec.gov/litigation/investreport/34-62802.htm.

5.149 Because the rating committee met in France and the UK and not in the US, the SEC declined to take any further action, '[b]ecause of uncertainty regarding a jurisdictional nexus to the United States in this matter'.

5.150 Although the SEC declined to take action in this case, it did take action against AXA Rosenberg Group LLC, AXA Rosenberg Investment Management LLC and Barr Rosenberg Research Center LLC. In this instance, an employee discovered an error in the computer code of a quantitative investment model used to manage client portfolios. The employee brought the matter to the attention of senior management, but was told to keep quiet about the error and not to inform others about it. The error adversely affected 608 of 1,421 client portfolios managed by AXA Rosenberg Investment Management and caused US$216,806,864 in losses. Cease-and-desist proceedings were instituted and the respondents were jointly and severally ordered to pay a civil money penalty in the amount of US$25 million to the US Treasury.[1]

1 The order is available at https://www.sec.gov/litigation/admin/2011/33-9181.pdf.

5.151 Another example that might be considered to be mundane is that of software systems for the use of stockbrokers. Stockbrokers used to be regulated by the Financial Services Authority (FSA) (now by the Financial Conduct Authority), and were required to conduct their business in accordance with relevant legislation and the rules laid out by the FSA. Failure to follow the rules may have caused the FSA to take disciplinary action against the firm. In the case of *SAM Business Systems Limited v Hedley and Company (sued as a firm)*,[1] the partners of Hedley used to handle their stockbroking business with a system known as ANTAR, but late in 1999 they decided it might not work after the century date change, so they decided to buy a new product from SAM, a small software company whose only product was an item of software known as InterSet. SAM claimed this product was a ready-made package of software modules made by SAM for stockbrokers and others (such as banks) dealing in stocks and shares in administering their systems. Hedley agreed to buy the new system, but immediately after it went live, serious problems were apparent, many of which were fixed, some speedily. (The word 'fix' is the telling word here: a local fix within a large and complex piece of software often generates problems elsewhere.) Hedley continued to use InterSet, but problems persisted. Eventually, they decided to find another product for their purposes. In his judgment, Judge Bowsher QC discussed the issue of defaults in software:

> The point has frequently been made during the trial that InterSet works well elsewhere (and I have received evidence from stockbrokers, Hoodless Brennan to that effect) and accordingly it is said, if it did not work for Hedley's there must be something wrong with Hedley's method of working. That line of argument has prompted me to ask, (a) if it is a tried and tested system, why when supplied to Hedley's did it have admitted bugs? (b) what is the difference between a bug and a defect?[2]

1 [2002] EWHC 2733 (TCC), [2003] 1 All ER (Comm) 465, [2002] 12 WLUK 550, [2003] Masons CLR 11, (2003) 147 SJLB 57, [2003] CLY 3616.
2 [2002] EWHC 2733 (TCC) at [19].

5.152 The full nature of the problems encountered with this software that purported to be written for the specific purpose for which it was supplied merits setting out in full:

> To complete the history, I must mention a document produced at my request as Exhibit C2. During the evidence of Mr. Whitehouse, I asked for a copy of a timesheet to which he had referred. That is a timesheet of 'maintenance activity'

> for which no charge was made. That document had not been disclosed until I asked for it. It is a document of 10 pages. I have not counted each item, but there are about 35 items on each of the first 9 pages and 16 on the last page. According to the claimants, the hours worked amount to 785.25. The period of time covered by the document is from 4 January 2000 to 7 February, 2001. The majority of those items appear to be efforts to fix defects. The fact that no charge was made suggests that all items fall into that category. I am not going to go through all of that document, but I will take one example. On 12 January, 2001, there is an entry, 'Analysing the problems with Hedley contract report ... problem actually with contract form not the report'. On 15 January a temporary fix was prepared. On 15, 16 and 17 January over 17 hours are recorded working on this problem. Then on 17 January there is another entry, 'Attempting to find the reason for the intermittent bad contracts. Not found yet'. On 18 January, 2001, there is an entry, 'Attempting to find the reason for the intermittent bad contracts. The reason appears to be conflicting requirements of procedures. Needs deeper understanding of form'. There were then further entries for modifications to put the problem right on 19, 23, 24, 25 and 26 January, 2001. More work was done on the same problem on 5, 7, and 9 February, 2001. On 5 February, 2001, changes were made, 'To prevent contracts being saved where the values do not add up'. Through February, 2001 there was a series of calls to deal with a problem with split deals commission. In mid April, 2001 there was a problem with trial balances. It is quite clear from that document, produced only under pressure during the trial, as well as from all the other evidence to which I have referred, that InterSet as delivered to Hedley's was never in satisfactory working order.[1]

1 [2002] EWHC 2733 (TCC) at [128].

5.153 Two experts were appointed to give evidence in this case, and they signed an agreement which was, in fact, a schedule of defects alleged by Hedley with comments on each defect from SAM. This schedule of faults ran to 34 pages. Judge Bowsher QC offered some pertinent comments in relation to the attitude of the software supplier in this case:

> SAM, like some others in the computer industry seem to be set in the mindset that when there is a 'bug' the customer must pay for putting it right. Bugs in computer programmes are still inevitable, but they are defects and it is the supplier who has the responsibility for putting them right at the supplier's expense.[1]

1 [2002] EWHC 2733 (TCC) at [165].

Motor vehicles

5.154 Software can be manipulated to give whatever reading the writer wishes. Because software is presumed to be 'reliable', software that gives deliberate false data is also presumed to be 'reliable'. It is well known that traffic lights are now generally controlled by software code across a network, and the code can be written in such a way as to break the law. Stefano Arrighetti, an engineering student from Genoa, is reported to have developed the T-Redspeed traffic light system in Italy. The traffic lights were apparently programmed to remain on amber before turning to red for less than the time set out in regulations.[1]

1 Peter Popham, 'Smart traffic lights rigged to trap drivers' *The Independent* (30 January 2009); Jacqui Cheng, 'Italian red-light cameras rigged with shorter yellow lights', Ars Technica (2 March 2009), https://arstechnica.com/tech-policy/2009/02/italian-red-light-cameras-rigged-with-shorter-yellow-lights/.

5.155 The 'sudden unintended acceleration' incidents involving the unintended, unexpected and uncontrolled acceleration of modern vehicles with electronic controls raises the issue of the reliability of complex electronic vehicle systems.[1] Consider the prosecution of Ann Diggles, aged 82, who was found not guilty at Preston Crown Court (*R v Ann Diggles* T20157203 before Mr Justice Fraser) for causing death by dangerous driving and death by careless driving when her Nissan Qashqai hit and killed Julie Dean, aged 53, while she was attempting to park.[2] The prosecution's case was that the driving of Mrs Diggles caused the accident. The prosecution relied on the evidence from the motor car manufacturer, as reported by the BBC:[3]

> Takuma Nakamura, who is responsible for engine control systems development at Nissan, was asked by prosecutor Richard Archer: 'Is it possible, in your opinion, for a malfunction in an electronic throttle to cause sudden acceleration of the vehicle?'
>
> Mr Nakamura replied: 'I think that's impossible'.[4]

1 For a general outline of the case law in the USA, see Maria N. Maccone, 'Litigation concerning sudden unintended acceleration' 132 Am Jur Trials 305 (Originally published in 2013) (December 2020 Update); see also Philip Koopman, 'Practical experience report: automotive safety practices vs. accepted principles' Safecom 2018, http://safeautonomy.blogspot.com/2018/09/automotive-safety-practices-vs-accepted.html; Professor Koopman maintains a list of potentially deadly automotive software defects at https://betterembsw.blogspot.com/2018/09/potentially-deadly-automotive-software.html.

2 'Driver cleared over fatal Nissan Qashqai crash', BBC News, 7 February 2017, http://www.bbc.co.uk/news/uk-england-lancashire-38897681; 'Nissan cars "sped" without accelerator use, court hears', BBC News, 6 February 2017, http://www.bbc.co.uk/news/uk-england-lancashire-38885809; 'Driver who killed woman denies mistaking accelerator for brake', BBC News, 2 February 2017, http://www.bbc.co.uk/news/uk-england-lancashire-38846896.

3 We only have reports from the media to rely on.

4 'Nissan boss denies malfunction caused fatal crash', BBC News, 31 January 2017, http://www.bbc.co.uk/news/uk-england-lancashire-38814890.

5.156 The expert witness for the defence was Dr Antony F. Anderson CEng FIEE. Dr Anderson pointed out the following:

> A mechanical inspection of the vehicle was carried out. A Nissan garage, on the instruction of the police, downloaded diagnostic trouble codes. The police constable who witnessed the diagnostic testing took a screen shot with his camera that showed three trouble codes. Two of these were past codes of no significance, but one was a current U1000 trouble code. The U1000 code, as I understand it, signifies that there had been a CAN Bus malfunction lasting more than 2 seconds sometime in the ignition cycle during which the incident occurred. Mr Nakamura, the senior engineering manager from Nissan Japan, who was sent over to give evidence in the trial, implied that the trouble code was of no significance.[1]

1 Email communication with the author.

5.157 In addition to the evidence from Dr Anderson, two other women came forward at a late stage in the trial to give evidence that they had also had identical experiences. The evidence was that Mrs Diggles and the other two witnesses had their vehicles fully serviced in line with the manufacturer's recommendations.[1] The evidence put before the members of the jury is not readily available, which means it can only be observed that deaths and injuries appear to occur as a result of software failure. It would be of interest to know how the police and prosecution assessed the evidence, including the complexities between the software code and the mechanical and electronic systems.

1 Gabriella Swerling, '"Runaway car" driver cleared over road death' *The Times* (8 February 2017), 8.

5.158 Another prominent example involves Toyota and Lexus motor vehicles, some of which have involved deaths of drivers and their passengers.[1] Michael Barr, in giving expert evidence for the plaintiffs in the case of *Bookout v Toyota Motor Corporation*,[2] stated that:

> A. The Toyota's design actually they have an abysmal design, not just unreasonable in my view, but I use the word abysmal. This was actually the first chapter of my report I wrote because I couldn't believe what I was seeing.
>
> Toyota has a watchdog supervisor design that is incapable of ever detecting the death of a major task. That's its whole job. It doesn't do it. It's not designed to do it.
>
> It also, the thing it does in Toyota's design is lookout for CPU overload, and it doesn't even do that right. CPU overload is when there's too much work in a burst, a period of time to do all the tasks. If that happens for too long, the car can become dangerous because tasks not getting to use the CPU is like temporarily tasks dying.
>
> And in Toyota's watchdog you can have any overload going up to one and a half seconds, which at 60 miles an hour I calculated is about the length of a football field, you have any vehicle malfunction for up to a football field in length that's explained only because this watchdog design it [*sic*] bad, and because the processor is overloaded momentarily. And that should have been also a job of that watchdog supervisor. And that is one they tried to implement and they don't do it well.
>
> They also made a classic blunder, one that's taught by professor like at Dr. Koopman[3] to first year students in his imbedded systems class, which is, you don't dedicate a hardware timer on the main CPU to periodically kick the hardware on the watchdog, because that will keep functioning even though vast portions of the software and the tasks are not rubbing because these interrupts are a higher priority than the tasks.
>
> And so, that is a design that you – and I have spoken about that at many conferences, not doing it that way. And they do that.[4]

1 There are other examples. The members of a jury concluded that a cruise control malfunctioned on a Ford Aerostar vehicle in *Cole v Ford Motor Company*, 136 Or.App. 45, 900 P.2d 1059 (1995); for another Ford Aerostar vehicle case, in which the members of a jury concluded that a cruise control malfunctioned, see *Jarvis v Ford Motor Company*, 283 F.3d 33, 51 Fed.R.Serv.3d 1310 (2d Cir. 2002). Examples of conflicting evidence that is, on its face, inadequate to determine causation include: *Ford Motor Company v Stimpson*, 115 So. 3d 401 (Fla. 5th DCA 2013); *Belville v Ford Motor Company*, 919 F.3d 224 (2019) upholding the summary judgment decision and exclusion of expert testimony of plaintiffs in *Johnson v Ford Motor Company*, 310 F.Supp.3d 699 (2018) (consumers failed to establish that unintended acceleration of their vehicles was the result of the manufacturer's electronic throttle control system, granting summary judgment in favour of the defendant); *Kesse v Ford Motor Company*, 2020 WL 832363. See *Buck v Ford Motor Company*, 526 Fed.Appx. 603 (2013) where the plaintiff failed to produce adequate expert evidence and reliance on a report regarding unintended acceleration from the United Kingdom was not admitted into evidence.

2 The trial was held in the District Court of Oklahoma County State of Oklahoma before the Hon Patricia G. Parrish, District Judge; see also *In re Toyota Motor Corp. Unintended Acceleration Marketing, Sales Practices, and Products Liability Litigation*, 978 F.Supp.2d 1053, 92 Fed. R. Evid. Serv. 714, Prod.Liab.Rep. (CCH) P 19,244 (summary judgment granted regarding the claim by the plaintiff

of a manufacturing defect and negligence, denied motion for summary judgment as to the design defect claim and the failure to warn claim); transcript (not proofread) of the trial 14 October 2013 (Reported by Karen Twyford, RPR): examination and cross examination of Michael Barr, http://www.safetyresearch.net/Library/Bookout_v_Toyota_Barr_REDACTED.pdf.

3 Dr Koopman is an Associate Professor at Carnegie Mellon University, Department of Electrical and Computer Engineering.

4 Case No. CJ-2008-7969, at 70–71. Professor Philip Koopman also gave evidence in this case, and his assessment of the problem was similar to that of Mr Barr, for which see https://www.usna.edu/AcResearch/_files/documents/NASEC/2016/CYBER%20-%20Toyota%20Unintended%20Acceleration.pdf; https://users.ece.cmu.edu/~koopman/toyota/koopman-09-18-2014_toyota_slides.pdf.

5.159 Software in vehicles can also be manipulated to give the false assurance of regulatory compliance. In September 2015, the United States Environmental Protection Agency issued a notice of violation of the Clean Air Act to Volkswagen AG, Audi AG and Volkswagen Group of America, Inc.[1] The notice alleged that four-cylinder Volkswagen and Audi diesel cars manufactured in the years 2009–2015 included software that circumvented the emissions standards for some air pollutants. The State of California Air Resources Board had issued a separate In-Use Compliance letter to Volkswagen,[2] and the two agencies initiated investigations based on the allegations. A software algorithm on certain Volkswagen vehicles switched the full emissions controls on only when the car detected it was undergoing official emissions testing.[3] Thus the effectiveness of the emission control devices was greatly reduced during normal driving. This meant that motor vehicles met the emissions standards in the laboratory or testing station, but during normal operation the vehicles emitted nitrogen oxides, or NOx, at up to 40 times the standard. Over a one-year period of operation, the emission of this extra pollutant by Volkswagen was estimated to have resulted in 5 to 50 premature deaths.[4] The Department of Justice subsequently filed a complaint for alleged violations of the Clean Air Act.[5]

1 For details, see https://www.epa.gov/vw/learn-about-volkswagen-violations.

2 Letter from the Air Resources Board to Volkswagen AG, Audi AG, and Volkswagen Group of America, Inc dated 18 September 2015 reference number IUC.2015-007 (this has been archived and is no longer available on the Internet).

3 It has been identified as the EDC17 diesel ECU manufactured by Bosch, for which see Moritz Contag, Guo Li, Andre Pawlowski, Felix Domke, Kirill Levchenko, Thorsten Holz and Stefan Savage, 'How they did it: an analysis of emission defeat devices in modern automobiles', *2017 IEEE Symposium on Security and Privacy* (Institute of Electrical and Electronics Engineers 2017), 231–250. The authors indicate they found strong evidence that the defeat device was created by Bosch and enabled by Volkswagen. They also observed that the same device was installed in the Fiat 500X.

4 Lifang Hou, Kai Zhang, Moira A. Luthin and Andrea A. Baccarelli, 'Public health impact and economic costs of Volkswagen's lack of compliance with the United States' emission standards' (2016) 13(9) International Journal of Environmental Research and Public Health 891; Gregory J. Thompson, Daniel K. Carder, Marc C. Besch, Arvind Thiruvengadam and Hemanth K. Kappanna, *Final Report: In-Use Emissions Testing of Light-Duty Diesel Vehicles in the United States* (Center for Alternative Fuels, Engines & Emissions, Department of Mechanical & Aerospace Engineering, West Virginia University), 15 May 2014 http://www.eenews.net/assets/2015/09/21/document_cw_02.pdf.

5 Press release: 'United States files complaint against Volkswagen, Audi and Porsche for alleged Clean Air Act violations', Monday, 4 January 2016, https://www.justice.gov/opa/pr/united-states-files-complaint-against-volkswagen-audi-and-porsche-alleged-clean-air-act, including a link to the original Complaint; an amended Complaint was submitted on 7 June 2016 and is available at https://www.epa.gov/sites/production/files/2016-10/documents/amendedvw-cp.pdf.

5.160 Manufacturers of motor vehicles are rapidly increasing the amount of software in vehicles, partly with the aim of manufacturing autonomous vehicles.[1]

Semi-autonomous or fully autonomous vehicles will not provide the panacea that the industry constantly asserts. Vehicles controlled wholly or partially by software code will continue to cause accidents and kill and injure people.[2] Also, because the software in vehicles is open to being attacked, it is far from safe.[3]

1 Autonomous motor vehicles have been involved in numerous accidents, mainly because of software failures, and a number of people have been killed and injured by motor vehicles in 'autonomous' mode. Here is a sample list of articles and websites: Francesca M. Favarò, Nazanin Nader, Sky O. Eurich, Michelle Tripp and Naresh Varadaraju, 'Examining accident reports involving autonomous vehicles in California', PLoS One, 2017;12(9):e0184952, https://www.ncbi.nlm.nih.gov/pmc/articles/PMC5607180/; Song Wang and Zhixia Li, 'Exploring the mechanism of crashes with automated vehicles using statistical modeling approaches', PLoS One 2019; 14(3): e0214550, https://www.ncbi.nlm.nih.gov/pmc/articles/PMC6438496/; Đorđe Petrovića, Radomir Mijailovića and Dalibor Pešića, 'Traffic accidents with autonomous vehicles: type of collisions, manoeuvres and errors of conventional vehicles' drivers' (2020) 45 Transportation Research Procedia 161; for fatalities, see https://en.wikipedia.org/wiki/List_of_self-driving_car_fatalities (although this list does not correspond to the list of lives lost when relating to the Tesla motor case, for which see: https://www.tesladeaths.com/); for Uber, see https://en.wikipedia.org/wiki/Death_of_Elaine_Herzberg.

2 For instance, see NTSB, Preliminary Report, Highway HWY16FH018 (Josh Brown, Florida in Tesla Model S) https://www.ntsb.gov/investigations/AccidentReports/Pages/HWY16FH018-preliminary.aspx; NTSB, Preliminary Report, Highway HWY18MH010 (Uber car crash), https://www.ntsb.gov/investigations/AccidentReports/Reports/HWY18MH010-prelim.pdf.

3 Andrea Palanca, Eric Evenchick, Federico Maggi and Stefano Zanero, 'A stealth, selective, link-layer denial-of-service attack against automotive networks' in Michalis Polychronakis and Michael Meier (eds) *Detection of Intrusions and Malware, and Vulnerability Assessment* (DIMVA 2017, Lecture Notes in Computer Science, vol 10327, Springer); Roger Kemp, 'Autonomous vehicles – who will be liable for accidents?' (2018) 15 Digital Evidence and Electronic Signature Law Review 33; Michael Ellims, 'Brake systems: a mind of their own' (2021) 18 Digital Evidence and Electronic Signature Law Review 27; 'The braking system on Formula E cars is designed so that if the front brakes fail, the rear brake system is activated as a fail-safe. In this instance, an incorrect software parameter that meant the rear brake system didn't activate as intended and the fail-safe did not kick in. We have now corrected the software problem and demonstrated to the FIA's satisfaction that the matter has been resolved. As a result, the FIA will permit all Mercedes-powered cars to race this evening': Thomas Claburn, 'Incorrect software parameter sends Formula E's Edoardo Mortara to hospital: Brakes' fail-safe system failed', The Register, 1 March 2021, https://www.theregister.com/2021/03/01/formula_e_bug.

Emergency services

5.161 In 1992, the London Ambulance computer-aided dispatch system failed. A complex set of circumstances resulted in an effective failure of the dispatching system, which are set out in paragraph 1996 of the Report.[1] Apparently 'the computer system itself did not fail in a technical sense ... However, much of the design had fatal flaws that would, and did, cumulatively lead to all of the symptoms of systems failure'.[2] Among the contributing factors were 'exception messages' and 'requests for attention' which scrolled off the screen because of the large number of messages generated.[3] There is also a suggestion that one member of staff was not using the system as expected,[4] and the problems were compounded by 'a genuine failure of crews to press the correct status button owing to the nature and pressure of certain incidents'.[5] This was so even though the individuals who used the new system were from a skilled and trained pool of staff, namely ambulance crews and controllers. Other problems have occurred since.[6]

1 *Report of the Inquiry into the London Ambulance Service*, South West Thames Regional Health Authority (1993) – a scanned version is available at http://www0.cs.ucl.ac.uk/staff/A.Finkelstein/las.html; P. Mellor, 'CAD: Computer-aided disaster' (1994) 1(2) High Integrity Systems Journal 101;

Anthony Finkelstein and John Dowell, 'A comedy of errors: the London Ambulance Service case study' in *Proceedings of the 8th International Workshop on Software Specification & Design IWSSD-8*, (IEEE CS Press 1996), 2–4; Paul Beynon-Davies, 'Information systems "failure" and risk assessment: the case of the London Ambulance Service computer and despatch system' in G. Doukidid, B. Galliers, H. Kremar and F. Land (eds) *Proceedings of the 3rd European Conference on Information Systems*, Athens, 1–3 June 1995, 1153–1170; Paul Beynon-Davies, 'Human error and information systems failure: the case of the London Ambulance Service computer-aided despatch system project' (1999) 11 Interacting with Computers 699; D. Dalcher, 'Disaster in London: The LAS case study' 1999 Engineering of Computer-Based Systems 41.

2 *Report of the Inquiry into the London Ambulance Service*, para 1007(x).

3 *Report of the Inquiry into the London Ambulance Service*, paras 4012(c) and 4023.

4 *Report of the Inquiry into the London Ambulance Service*, para 4025.

5 *Report of the Inquiry into the London Ambulance Service*, para 4009(b).

6 Kelly Fiveash, 'London Ambulance Service downed by upgrade cockup', The Register (9 June 2011); Jon Ironmonger, 'Ambulance system failure "might have led to patient death"', BBC News (6 January 2017).

5.162 In 2014, an outage for 911 calls in the United States of America occurred because of a preventable software coding error in a 911 Emergency Call Management Center automated system in Englewood, Colorado, operated by Intrado, a subsidiary of West Corporation. This prevented non-PI-enabled long-distance assignments, which meant calls could not be routed to the appropriate destination.[1]

1 *April 2014 Multistate 911 Outage: Cause and Impact Report and Recommendations* (A Report of the Public Safety Homeland Security Bureau, Federal Communications Commission, October 2014, Public Safety Docket No. 14-72 PSHSB Case File Nos. 14-CCR-0001-0007), https://www.fcc.gov/document/april-2014-multistate-911-outage-report.

Medical

5.163 The widespread use of computer devices in the medical industry has also given rise to incidents where the reliability of devices and software has been called into question. The rules for approving medical devices leave a lot of scope for software failure. The device does not need new approval if it is 'substantially similar' to an existing approved device. This allows for errors to go unconsidered or for incremental changes to take the latest device far from the original design.[1] Most of the 'apps' promoted on smartphones are not licensed or inherited from an 'equivalent' device. Consider the 'Babylon health app' – a triage chatbot that is notoriously poor and not approved, but would pass the examination taken by final year doctors, as noted by Dr Margaret McCartney:

> Who's in charge of ensuring that this app [NHS 111 powered by Babylon app] is safe and fit for purpose?
>
> Knowing the staggering lack of publicly available robust testing that had accompanied the adult symptom checker app, I thought that perhaps Babylon might have done better with its paediatric one. What's Babylon's evidence? I don't know, for it replied with, 'we won't be responding to your enquiry'. The binary nature of the chatbot means that one thing that doesn't happen is history taking, in the medical sense ('Shut up, your patient is telling you the diagnosis'). It has a series of yes/no questions and short multiple choices.
>
> Who's in charge of ensuring that this app is safe and fit for purpose? The Medicines and Healthcare Products Regulatory Agency (MHRA) has said that it will ask Babylon to change the way it refers to the app as being 'certified as a medical device with the MHRA'. The MHRA says that, for class I devices such as

> this app, the manufacturer must register with the agency and self certify that the device meets the requirements of the regulations. The MHRA says that this process is purely administrative – the MHRA takes details of the types of devices manufactured, but it does not assess, certify, approve, or accredit devices as part of the CE (European Conformity) marking process.
>
> Who else could act? The Care Quality Commission has inspected Babylon, but it made no mention of the reliability, or not, of the app that it uses to direct people to and from general practice consultations. The General Medical Council regulates individual doctors, not clinical devices.
>
> We have many regulators but little proactivity, even for an app which – despite the small print warning us that it 'does not constitute medical advice, diagnosis, or treatment' – is being used as the front door into NHS care.[2]

1 For a general introduction that should be compulsory reading for all incoming ministers of health, see Martyn Thomas and Harold Thimbleby, *Computer Bugs in Hospitals: A New Killer* (Gresham College, 6 February 2018), https://www.gresham.ac.uk/lectures-and-events/computer-bugs-in-hospitals-a-new-killer; Dolores R. Wallace and D. Richard Kuhn, 'Failure modes in medical device software: an analysis of 15 years of recall data' (2001) 8(4) International Journal of Reliability, Quality and Safety Engineering 351; Homa Alemzadeh, Ravishankar K. Iyer, Zbigniew Kalbarczyk and Jai Raman, 'Analysis of safety-critical computer failures in medical devices' (2013 July/August) IEEE Security & Privacy, 14; Homa Alemzadeh, Jaishankar Raman, Nancy Leveson, Zbigniew Kalbarczyk and Ravishankar K. Iyer, 'Adverse events in robotic surgery: a retrospective study of 14 years of FDA data' (2016) 11(4) LPoS ONE 1, https://journals.plos.org/plosone/article?id=10.1371/journal.pone.0151470; Alessia Ferrarese, Giada Pozzi, Felice Borghi, Alessandra Marano, Paola Delbon, Bruno Amato, Michele Santangelo, Claudio Buccelli, Massimo Niola, Valter Martino and Emanuele Capasso, 'Malfunctions of robotic system in surgery: role and responsibility of surgeon in legal point of view' (2016) 11(1) Open Med (Wars) 286, https://www.ncbi.nlm.nih.gov/pmc/articles/PMC5329842/.

2 Margaret McCartney, 'AI in medicine must be rigorously tested', Thebmj, News and Views, 24 April 2018, https://www.bmj.com/content/361/bmj.k1752.

5.164 For instance, patients have been affected by an error in clinical IT software[1] and by the failure to timely correct an error,[2] and one study of a hospital computerized physician order entry system in the USA illustrated a number of errors that the system was supposed to resolve, such as an increased probability of prescribing errors. There were 12 flaws in the interface used by humans that reflected machine rules that in turn did not correspond to how work was organized or the usual behaviour of those using the system.[3] There is an increasing volume of articles on this topic,[4] and it would appear that some, and not all, of the problems were due to software defects,[5] but it is now very clear that software helps to kill people in hospitals.[6]

1 Alex Matthews-King, 'GPs told to review patients at risk as IT error miscalculates CV score in thousands', Pulse Today, 11 May 2016, https://www.pulsetoday.co.uk/news/clinical-areas/prescribing/gps-told-to-review-patients-at-risk-as-it-error-miscalculates-cv-score-in-thousands/.

2 *Singh v Edwards Lifesciences Corp.*, 151 Wash. App. 137, 210 P.3d 337 (2009) where the manufacturer of a heart monitor was aware of and had developed a fix for the software bug as early as 1998, but made a calculated business decision not to issue a recall or warning to any customers. Monitors were patched only when sent in for repair, and so the one used during Singh's operation had not been patched. The jury awarded Singh $31.75 million in compensatory damages plus an additional $8.35 million in punitive damages. The verdict was upheld on appeal.

3 Ross Koppel, Joshua P. Metlay, Abigail Cohen, Brian Abaluck, A. Russell Localio, Stephen E. Kimmel and Brian L. Strom, 'Role of computerized physician order entry systems in facilitating medication errors' (2005) 293(10 Journal of the American Medical Association 1197.

4 E. Alberdi, A. A. Povyakalo, L. Strigini and P. Ayton, 'Computer aided detection: risks and benefits for radiologists' decisions' in E. Samei and E. Krupinski (eds) *The Handbook of Medical Image Perception and Techniques* (Cambridge University Press 2009), 320–332.

5 Frances E. Zollers, Andrew McMullin, Sandra N. Hurd and Peter Shears, 'No more soft landings for software: liability for defects in an industry that has come of age' (2004) 21 Santa Clara High Tech. LJ 745; Sharona Hoffman and Andy Podgurski, 'E-health hazards: provider liability and electronic health record systems (2009) 24 Berkeley Tech LJ 1523; Paul T. Lee, Frankie Thompson and Harold Thimbleby, 'Analysis of infusion pump error logs and their significance for health care' (2012) 21(8) British Journal of Nursing (Intravenous Supplement) S12; Hon. John M. Curran and Mark A. Berman, 'Gremlins and glitches using electronic health records at trial' (2013) 85(4) New York State Bar Journal 20; Courtney L. Davenport, 'Dangers of electronic medical systems', (2013) 49(5) Trial: The National Legal Newsmagazine14; Timothy P. Blanchard and Margaret M. Manning, 'Electronic medical record documentation: inherent risks and inordinate hazards', in Alice G. Gosfield, (ed.), *Health Law Handbook* (Thompson Reuters 2016), 246–297; Jayanti Bhandari Neupane, Ram P. Neupane, Yuheng Luo, Wesley Y. Yoshida, Rui Sun and Philip G. Williams, 'Characterization of leptazolines A–D, polar oxazolines from the cyanobacterium leptolyngbya sp., reveals a glitch with the "Willoughby–Hoye" scripts for calculating NMR chemical shifts' (2019) 21 Org Lett 8449, where the authors discuss a flaw in software that could lead to incorrect conclusions; *Karam v Adirondack Neurosurgical Specialists, P.C.*, 93 A.D.3d 1260 (2012), 941 N.Y.S.2d 402, 2012 N.Y. Slip Op. 02182 (evidence pointed to error in software), motion for reargument or leave to appeal to the Court of Appeals denied, 96 A.D.3d 1513 (2012), 945 N.Y.S.2d 588, 2012 N.Y. Slip Op. 04645, motion for leave to appeal denied, 19 N.Y.3d 812 (2012), 976 N.E.2d 251, 951 N.Y.S.2d 722, 2012 N.Y. Slip Op. 83806.

6 Yong Y. Han, Joseph A. Carcillo, Shekhar T. Venkataraman, Robert S. B. Clark, R. Scott Watson, Trung C. Nguyen, Hülya Bayir and Richard A. Orr, 'Unexpected increased mortality after implementation of a commercially sold computerized physician order entry system' (2005) 116(6) Pediatrics1506; Harold Thimbleby, 'Ignorance of interaction programming is killing people', Interactions (September and October 2008), 52; Harold Thimbleby, *Fix IT: How to Solve the Problems of Digital Healthcare*(Oxford University Press 2021), open source at http://www.harold.thimbleby.net/rhbook/book.pdf.

The Post Office Horizon scandal

5.165 Between 2000 and 2019, the Post Office[1] operated a computerized accounting and electronic point of sale IT system called Horizon. This system was installed in its branch Post Offices around the country. It was not long before sub-postmasters and sub-postmistresses (SPMs) began experiencing balancing errors that they could not explain. Post Office employees did not attempt to find out why balance errors were occurring; they merely required the SPMs to make-up any shortfall from their own funds. The balancing errors ranged from small amounts to tens of thousands of pounds. Some SPMs would make up the shortfall, and some would not. The Post Office initiated a substantial number of prosecutions for theft and fraud (the Post Office itself is a prosecuting authority), relying on the presumption that computers are reliable.[2]

1 Post Office Limited is a private limited company registered in England and Wales, company number 02154540, incorporated on 13 August 1987. The Secretary of State for Business, Energy and Industrial Strategy holds a special share, and the rights attached to that special share are enshrined within the Post Office Limited Articles of Association.

2 The transcript of the trial of *Regina v Seema Misra*, T20090070, in the Crown Court at Guildford, Trial dates 11, 12, 13, 14, 15, 18, 19, 20, 21 October and 11 November 2010, His Honour Judge N. A. Stewart and a jury, was published in full in (2015) 12 Digital Evidence and Electronic Signature Law Review, Introduction 44, Documents Supplement; see also Tim McCormack, 'The Post Office Horizon system and Seema Misra' (2016) 13 Digital Evidence and Electronic Signature Law Review 133. In this case, the prosecuting barrister referred to the Horizon system being 'robust' – seemingly in an attempt to refer to the presumption that computers are reliable without actually committing to using the word 'reliable', for which see Ladkin, 'Robustness of software'; for a discussion of the evidence the Post Office ought to have disclosed before trial, see James Christie, 'The Post Office Horizon IT scandal and the presumption of the dependability of computer evidence' (2020) 17 Digital Evidence and Electronic Signature Law Review 49. The disclosure of relevant digital data was a live issue in this case. The defence made a number of requests for further disclosure of the computer system. This was refused four times: first application before Mr Recorder Bruce, 10 March 2010 (Day 1 Monday 11

October 2010, 3C; Judge's Ruling, Day 1 Monday 11 October 2010, 25, A–C); second application before HH Judge Critchlow, 7 May 2010 (Day 1 Monday 11 October 2010, 3G); third application before the trial judge (Day 1 Monday 11 October 2010, 15H–16H) and fourth application before the trial judge (Day 6, Monday 18 October 2010, 24H–25A) – on this precise point, see *Hamilton v Post Office Ltd* [2021] EWCA Crim 577 at [204].

5.166 In response to the failure of the Post Office to consider that SPMs were not defrauding or stealing from the Post Office, a group of ex-sub-postmasters and sub-postmistresses formed the Justice For Subpostmasters Alliance (JFSA)[1] in 2009 as the result of experiencing significant problems with how Post Office Limited dealt with apparent shortfalls in their accounts after the introduction of the Horizon IT system in 2000.[2] Following years of campaigning with the support of many MPs, in 2012 the Post Office appointed Second Sight Support Services Limited, a firm of independent forensic accountants, to investigate the claims being made about the Horizon system and the associated issues. On 8 July 2013, Second Sight published an Interim Report on its findings up until that date, which led to MPs raising questions with the Minister for Postal Affairs in the House of Commons on 9 July 2013.[3] The Interim Report demonstrated that there were issues that required further investigation, and in August 2013 an Initial Complaint Review and Mediation Scheme was established to investigate individual cases. The Scheme was open to both serving and ex-sub-postmasters and sub-postmistresses who had concerns relating to Horizon, and offered them an opportunity to have their cases independently reviewed and raised directly with the Post Office. A Working Group, comprising representatives from Second Sight, the Post Office and the JFSA, was established with an independent chair. The Scheme closed to applicants on 18 November 2013. During the 12 weeks it was open 150 applications were received. On 9 April 2015, the Post Office terminated the Scheme Working Group, and also terminated the contracts with Second Sight and the independent chairman. The draft of the Second Sight Report Part Two was due to be released to the Working Group on 10 April 2015, but the action of the Post Office prevented this from taking place. The second part of the Second Sight Report (version 2) eventually appeared on a journalists' website.

1 The Justice For Subpostmasters Alliance, https://www.jfsa.org.uk/.

2 The Post Office took civil action to recover monies on an account stated (for an explanation of 'account states' see Marshall below) by one of its former sub-postmasters, Mr Castleton: *Post Office Ltd v Castleton* [2007] EWHC 5 (QB), [2007] 1 WLUK 381. For a comprehensive assessment of this judgment, illustrating failure of the judge to accept that Mr Castleton was challenging the presumption that computers are reliable, see Paul Marshall, 'The harm that judges do – misunderstanding computer evidence: Mr Castleton's story' (2020) 17 Digital Evidence and Electronic Signature Law Review 25. In *Banks v Revenue & Customs* [2014] UKFTT 465 (TC), [2014] 5 WLUK 335, in response to the appellant's assertions that the online process for submitting tax forms was flawed, Revenue and Customs rejected the claim without providing any evidence, the members of the tribunal reporting, at [22], that 'HMRC says that it interrogated its computer system, and found no faults'. In addition, the members of the tribunal stated, at [28], in the absence of any evidence to make such an assessment, that 'It is equally difficult to envisage HMRC's systems failing in such a rudimentary way'.

3 Hansard, 9 July 2013, columns 198–209, https://publications.parliament.uk/pa/cm201314/cmhansrd/cm130709/debtext/130709-0002.htm#13070952000004.

5.167 In 2015, the law firm Freeths LLP agreed to represent those ex-sub-postmasters and sub-postmistresses who wanted to take part in any future legal action. Therium Group Holdings Limited funded the litigation.[1] A Group Litigation Order was subsequently made on 22 March 2017 by Senior Master Fontaine, and approved by the

President of the Queen's Bench Division. Procedural issues before the first trial were dealt with in the first judgment, *Bates v Post Office Ltd*,[2] and a second judgment dealt with a further application by the Post Office to strike out part of the claim in *Bates v Post Office Ltd (No 2)*.[3] It was anticipated that there would be four trials. In the event, only two trials have taken place.

1 Therium Group Holdings Limited, https://www.therium.com/.
2 [2017] EWHC 2844 (QB), [2017] 6 Costs LO 855, [2018] CLY 376.
3 [2018] EWHC 2698 (QB), [2018] 10 WLUK 291.

5.168 The first trial concerned, in the main, the contractual position between the Post Office and the sub-postmasters and sub-postmistresses. The judgment is in *Bates v Post Office Ltd (No. 3: Common Issues)*.[1] In this judgment, the judge included a comprehensive introduction to the issues generally between the parties at [2]–[43]. Orders in respect of costs of the Common Issues trial were determined in *Bates v Post Office Ltd (No. 5: Common Issues Costs)*.[2] The second trial, dealing with the Horizon software, took place between 11 March 2019 and 22 July 2019. During the course of this trial, the Post Office issued an application that the judge recuse himself as Managing Judge in this group litigation, and stop the Horizon Issues trial so that it could be recommenced at some later date before a replacement Managing Judge. That application was refused, for which see *Bates v Post Office Ltd (No. 4: Recusal Application)*.[3] Permission to appeal was refused by the single Lord Justice on 9 May 2019.[4] Between the end of the second trial and the judgment, the parties sought mediation. An agreement was reached on 11 December 2019.[5] The judge handed down his judgment in the second trial on 16 December 2019 – a comprehensive judgment that clearly indicated that the Horizon system had a significant number of software errors, including the ability of employees of Fujitsu to enter the computers of SPMs remotely and change data without the SPM being aware of what was happening.[6] When handing down his judgment, the judge indicated that he:

> [had] very grave concerns regarding the veracity of evidence given by Fujitsu employees in other courts in previous proceedings about the known existence of bugs, errors and defects in the Horizon system. These previous proceedings include the High Court in at least one civil case brought by the Post Office against a sub-postmaster and the Crown Court in a greater number of criminal cases, also brought by the Post Office against a number of sub-postmasters and sub-postmistresses.
>
> After careful consideration, I have therefore decided, in the interests of justice, to send the papers in the case to the Director of Public Prosecutions, Mr Max Hill QC, so he may consider whether the matter to which I refer should be the subject of any prosecution.[7]

1 [2019] EWHC 606 (QB), [2019] 3 WLUK 260.
2 [2019] EWHC 1373 (QB), [2019] 6 WLUK 80, [2019] Costs LR 857, [2019] CLY 431.
3 [2019] EWHC 871 (QB), [2019] 4 WLUK 150.
4 *Bates v Post Office Ltd* Case No: A1/2019/1387/PTA dated 22 November 2019. The approved judgment will be published in a future edition of the Digital Evidence and Electronic Signature Law Review.
5 Confidential settlement deed (10 December 2019) between the claimants in the action Bates v Post Office Limited, Post Office Limited and Freeths LLP, https://www.onepostoffice.co.uk/media/47518/20191210-glo-confidential-settlement-deed-executed-version-redacted_-003.pdf.
6 *Bates v Post Office Ltd (No 6: Horizon Issues) Rev 1* [2019] EWHC 3408 (QB), [2019] 12 WLUK 208; during this trial, the lead counsel for the Post Office, Anthony de Garr Robinson QC, repeatedly referred to the 'robustness' of the Horizon system and also cited statistics that were incorrect. For an analysis,

see the discussion in Parker, *Humble Pi* in (2019) 16 Book Reports, Digital Evidence and Electronic Signature Law Review 99–105.
7 Approved Proceedings sent to the author, High Court of Justice, Queen's Bench Division, No QB-2016-004710, 16 December 2019, to be published in the Digital Evidence and Electronic Signature Law Review in 2021.

5.169 In 2015, the Criminal Case Review Commission (CCRC) began reviewing claims of wrongful prosecution for offences such as theft and false accounting, caused, the complaints allege, as a result of problems with the Post Office's Horizon IT system. In 2020, the CCRC referred 47 Post Office cases on the abuse of process to the Court of Appeal,[1] and in October 2020 the government initiated a non-statutory inquiry into the Post Office's Horizon IT dispute led by Sir Wyn Williams.[2] The Court of Appeal Criminal Division heard the appeal of 42 appellants on 22, 23 and 24 March 2021 and handed down judgment on 23 April 2021 in which the appeals of 39 appellants were quashed.[3] The court also reached a rare determination: that the prosecutions were an affront to the conscience of the court.[4] In delivering the judgment of the court, Holroyde LJ noted that the Post Office constantly asserted that the Horizon system was 'reliable' [20] and [125], 'accurate and reliable' [68] or 'robust and reliable' [121]. He went on to say, at [137]:

> By representing Horizon as reliable, and refusing to countenance any suggestion to the contrary, POL [Post Office Limited] effectively sought to reverse the burden of proof: it treated what was no more than a shortfall shown by an unreliable accounting system as an incontrovertible loss, and proceeded as if it were for the accused to prove that no such loss had occurred. Denied any disclosure of material capable of undermining the prosecution case, defendants were inevitably unable to discharge that improper burden.

1 *R. v Hamilton* [2021] EWCA Crim 21, [2021] 1 WLUK 116, [2021] 1 Cr App R 17; 'The CCRC refers eight more Post Office cases for appeal – bringing total to 47 so far', 3 June 2020, https://ccrc.gov.uk/the-ccrc-refers-eight-more-post-office-cases-for-appeal-bringing-total-to-47-so-far/; 'CCRC to refer 39 Post Office cases on abuse of process argument', 26 March 2020, https://ccrc.gov.uk/ccrc-to-refer-39-post-office-cases-on-abuse-of-process-argument/; the Criminal Cases Review Commission's process for review of convictions relating to the Post Office and Horizon accounting system (Number 2020-0040, 3 March 2020), House of Commons Library, https://commonslibrary.parliament.uk/research-briefings/cdp-2020-0040/; for Scotland, see Reevel Alderson, 'Post Office scandal: Scottish probe into sub-postmasters' convictions', BBC Scotland, 30 September 2020, https://www.bbc.co.uk/news/uk-scotland-54339004.
2 https://www.gov.uk/government/publications/post-office-horizon-it-inquiry-2020; https://www.gov.uk/government/publications/post-office-horizon-it-inquiry-2020/terms-of-reference. The government converted the Inquiry into a statutory inquiry under the Inquiries Act 2005 on 1st June 2021, Statement UIN HCWS40, https://questions-statements.parliament.uk/written-statements/detail/2021-05-19/hcws40.
3 *Hamilton v Post Office Ltd* [2021] EWCA Crim 577, [2021] 4 WLUK 227.
4 *Hamilton v Post Office Ltd* [2021] EWCA Crim 577 at [66].

5.170 Not only was it factually incorrect that the Horizon system was reliable, but the failure to disclose relevant information meant:

> [the] defendants were inevitably unable to discharge that improper burden. As each prosecution proceeded to its successful conclusion the asserted reliability of Horizon was, on the face of it, reinforced. Defendants were prosecuted, convicted and sentenced on the basis that the Horizon data must be correct, and cash must therefore be missing, when in fact there could be no confidence as to that foundation.[1]

1 *Hamilton v Post Office Ltd* [2021] EWCA Crim 577 at [137].

Banking

5.171 The presumption that computers are reliable is particularly relevant with regard to banking. Banks across the world have introduced very complex systems and networks to control the flow of transactions, many of which are no longer under the sole control of the banks themselves. That a bank benefits from the presumption that its computers and networks, including the computers and networks it relies upon over which it has no direct control, were in order at the material time, puts an impossible burden on the customer. If a customer in dispute with his bank wants to challenge this presumption, he will require significant knowledge of the computers, systems and networks operated by the bank, how they work and where the vulnerabilities might lie, including the results of relevant audits, both internal and external – a task well beyond the majority of customers, including most lawyers without the benefit of expert advice, which in itself is difficult to obtain.

5.172 Issues regarding the reliability of banking systems manifested themselves in the problems in the UK in June and July 2012 with RBS, NatWest and Ulster banks.[1] On 19 June 2012, an important item of software known as CA-7 was updated. This software controls the batch processing systems that deal with retail banking transactions. It is used to automate large sequences of batch mainframe work, usually referred to as 'jobs'. The jobs take transactions from various places, such as ATM withdrawals, automatic salary payments and such like, so that accounts are credited and debited with the correct amounts by the next morning. The software initiates jobs, and when one job is finished, a new job will be initiated. Accounts are processed overnight when the mainframes are less busy, and finish by updating the master copy of the account in a system known as Caustic. It appears that the update made to CA-7 caused the files to run incorrectly or not to run at all for three nights. David Silverstone, delivery and solutions manager for NMQA, which provides automated testing software to a number of banks, is quoted to the effect that such problems can always be avoided if there is sufficient testing of the update before it is put into operational use.[2] Michael Allen, director of IT service management at Compuware, is reported to have said:

> The problem is that IT systems have become vastly more complex. Delivering an e-banking service could be reliant on 20 different IT systems. If even a small change is made to one of these systems, it can cause major problems for the whole banking service, which could be what's happened at NatWest. Finding the root cause of the problem is probably something NatWest is struggling with because of the complexity of the IT systems in any bank.[3]

1 For detailed information, the reader is directed to the Treasury Select Committee web page on the Parliament website.

2 Charles Arthur, 'How NatWest's IT meltdown developed', *The Guardian*, 25 June 2012.

3 Anna Leach, 'Natwest, RBS: When will bank glitch be fixed? Probably not today', The Register, 22 June 2012.

5.173 The complexity of the problem is highlighted in an article written by Hilary Osborne in *The Guardian* in 2014, in which the issues were explained:

> 'The banks do have a problem, but it's not a new problem, and it's not an easy problem to fix, which is why it's taking so long', says David Bannister, editor of Banking Technology magazine. 'In the old days these machines just had to run overnight in batch mode – it was like newspapers with just one edition – but

> now they have to deal with news that is being updated throughout the day. The users – us – are using internet banking, ATMs, we're spending money online. The reconciliation between what is going on in the background is the hard part, and the gulf is widening all the time.'
>
> Ben Wilson, associate director of financial services for techUK, says some of the 'legacy systems' at banks are 30–40 years old and were originally set up for branch banking, but 'then they needed to be ATM-focussed, then there was online banking, then mobile banking'. He says: 'Banks have bolted on these changes because it is cheaper and less risky than starting from scatch, but every time you bolt on a change it becomes more complex.'
>
> As well as new banking channels, systems are also tinkered with whenever regulatory changes are made, and when a product is withdrawn or changed.
>
> Jim McCall, managing director of the Unit, which works with banks and other companies on their mobile apps, says that while anyone now building a system from scratch would 'abstract out as much as possible so [different elements] are not as reliant on each other', the banks' systems often resemble a house of cards. 'If you make a change to a tiny bit of code on one thing it is like the butterfly flapping its wings far away and somewhere someone's mobile app stops working', he says.
>
> To make things more complicated, says Colin Privett, UK managing director of software firm Cast, new functions are usually 'written in different programming languages, on different machines, by different teams'. He adds: 'This prevents a single person/team from ever fully understanding the entire structure of a system. That is why when things do go wrong it can often take hours, or even days, to fix as teams scramble to find out where the problem lies.'[1]

1 Hilary Osborne, 'Why do bank IT systems keep failing?', *The Guardian*, 27 January 2014.

5.174 The effects of the CA-7 imbroglio were considerable. In some cases people were left homeless after the computer problems meant house purchases fell through; others were stranded abroad, unable to obtain access to funds which should have been in their account; wages and direct debits were not paid; and it is reported that one person spent the weekend in prison because the computer failure meant his bail money was not processed.[1] The problems continued into 2014.[2] In December 2014, the Royal Bank of Scotland Plc, National Westminster Bank Plc and Ulster Bank Ltd faced a combined financial penalty of £42 million by the Financial Conduct Authority for breaches of Principle 3 of the 'principles for businesses', forming part of 'the principles of good regulation', which requires a firm to take reasonable care to organize and control its affairs responsibly and effectively with adequate risk management systems,[3] and the Prudential Regulation Authority imposed a financial penalty of £14 million on the same banks for their failure to meet their obligations to have adequate systems and controls to identify and manage their exposure to IT risks.[4]

1 James Hall and Gordon Rayner, 'RBS computer failure condemns man to spend weekend in the cells', *The Telegraph*, 25 June 2012.
2 Emma Dunkley, 'RBS and NatWest to plough £1bn into digital upgrade' *Financial Times*, 28–29 June 2014, 18.
3 https://www.fca.org.uk/publication/final-notices/rbs-natwest-ulster-final-notice.pdf.
4 https://www.bankofengland.co.uk/-/media/boe/files/prudential-regulation/enforcement-notice/en201114.pdf?la=en&hash=7483F66E5533498680F8C2CD9F34CE9C10FD5EA8.

5.175 The problem of complexity and the difficulties in understanding and maintaining another banking system were emphasized in the report by Deloitte of the failure of the

Real-Time Gross Settlement (RTGS) system operated by the Bank of England in 2014.[1] The report stated:

> 133. During the 18 years since RTGS was first launched, the incremental changes have resulted in an increase in complexity and a system which is now more difficult to understand and maintain. In particular, the LSM and MIRS changes introduced additional functionality with an associated increase in complexity.
>
> 134. In combination with the ageing development language used to program RTGS, the result is a system which is more complex to support, heavily reliant on the skills and experience of the team to support it, and more susceptible to errors which take longer to diagnose. Therefore there is an increased risk of functional or configuration changes causing errors and if or when the system does fail it may take longer to resolve the issue.

1 Deloitte, *Independent Review of RTGS Outage on 20 October 2014* (23 March 2015), https://www.bankofengland.co.uk/-/media/boe/files/report/2015/independent-review-of-rtgs-outage-on-20-october-2014.pdf.

5.176 In this case, there was a design defect. The defect was mentioned at paragraph 151 of the report, but it had been redacted to such an extent that there was no meaningful text. The only information available is that a process known as 'Process A functionality' was changed in April 2014 and tested in May 2014 in preparation for the anticipated transfer of CHAPS members, and a design defect was introduced at this stage. This was the cause of the failure.[1]

1 Independent review of RTGS outage on 20 October 2014: Bank of England's response, https://www.bankofengland.co.uk/-/media/boe/files/report/2015/independent-review-of-rtgs-outage-on-20-october-2014-boes-response.pdf.

5.177 Other examples include Deutsche Bank AG, where a coding error caused Deutsche to reverse the buy/sell indicator for its CFD Equity Swaps in 2013. This meant it reported them inaccurately to the Financial Conduct Authority (FCA). The FCA imposed a financial penalty of £4,7818,800 on Deutsche for failing to provide accurate reports in accordance with the provisions of the Markets in Financial Instruments Directive.[1] In 2014, the Co-operative Bank identified that statements on a number of loans had been issued three days late because of a software error. Under the provisions of s 6 of the Consumer Credit Act 2006, which inserted s 77A into the Consumer Credit Act 1974, it is necessary to provide an annual statement to each borrower for a fixed-sum credit agreement, which should set out the amount borrowed, the money paid, the interest and the outstanding amount. If the creditor fails to provide the debtor with an annual statement, the creditor is not entitled to enforce the agreement during the period of the failure to comply, and the debtor is not liable to pay any interest during the period. The bank set aside £109.5 million to refund interest payments for this breach of the Act.[2]

1 https://www.fca.org.uk/publication/final-notices/deutsche-bank-ag-2015.pdf; Directive 2004/39/EC of the European Parliament and of the Council of 21 April 2004 on markets in financial instruments amending Council Directives 85/611/EEC and 93/6/EEC and Directive 2000/12/EC of the European Parliament and of the Council and repealing Council Directive 93/22/EEC, OJ L 145, 30.4.2004, p.1.

2 Adam Leyland and Beth Brooks, 'The Co-operative Bank's £400m costs bill caused by "programming error" ', *The Grocer*, 29 March 2014, at https://www.thegrocer.co.uk/the-co-operative-group/programming-error-to-blame-for-co-op-banks-400m-bill/356022.article; The Co-operative Bank plc, Annual Report and Accounts for 2013, 151 section 2(iv).

Interception of communications

5.178 In the half-yearly report in July 2015, the Report of the Interception of Communications Commissioner illustrated the effect that errors in software code had had on the interception of communications.[1] Although the number of technical errors were low in comparison to the overall number of requests made, nevertheless the effect such errors had on innocent parties was significant. In paragraph 5.28, it was indicated that eight out of ten errors made in relation to resolving IP addresses to individuals related to investigations into the sexual exploitation of children or cases where serious concerns were raised in relation to the welfare of a child.[2] The Commissioner commented, at paragraphs 5.29 and 5.37:

> Regrettably when errors occur in relation to the resolution of IP addresses the consequences are particularly acute. An IP address is often the only line of enquiry in a child protection case (so called 'single strand' intelligence), and it may be difficult for the police to corroborate the information further before taking action. Any police action taken erroneously in such cases, such as the search of an individual's house who is unconnected with the investigation or a delayed welfare check on an individual whose life is believed to be at risk, can have a devastating impact on the individuals concerned.
>
> ...
>
> 5.37 ... The eight technical system errors led to four warrants being executed at premises unconnected with the investigations and in one of these instances an individual was arrested. In another case the error delayed a welfare check on a child believed to be in crisis. In one instance a person unconnected with the investigation was visited by police. The majority of these errors resulted in communications data being obtained in relation to individuals who were unconnected with those investigations.

1 The Rt Hon Sir Anthony May, *Half-yearly Report of the Interception of Communications Commissioner* (July 2015, HC 308, SG/2015/105).
2 There is no suggestion from these examples that it was in error. The report may mean errors in resolving IP addresses in criminal investigations.

5.179 In his Report, the Commissioner said that the Crown Prosecution Service used funds provided by the government to work with vendors and the Home Office to develop secure disclosure systems – and although money has been spent on this issue, technical issues nevertheless continue to arise.[1] As a result of the disclosure of the technical errors, the Commissioner made a number of recommendations regarding technical system errors:

> 11 Ensure that the [Communication Service Provider] CSP secure disclosure systems are tested sufficiently prior to implementation and after significant updates or upgrades.
>
> 12 Ensure there is standardisation and as much consistency as possible in relation to the data entry requirements on the different CSP secure disclosure systems.
>
> 13 Requirement for [Single Point of Contact] SPoC to inform CSP immediately if an error is identified which might be the result of a technical system fault (even where the error has been classified as a recordable error).
>
> 14 Ensure that there are regular quality assurance audits of the CSP secure disclosure systems to identify any faults at an earlier stage.

15 Ensure that the CSPs and system vendors are aware of the potential significant consequences of system errors, that the public authorities are informed of any systems errors immediately and the errors are fixed at the earliest opportunity.[2]

1 At para 5.53.
2 At para 5.40.

5.180 Technical errors continue to be reported by successive Commissioners.[1]

1 The Rt Hon Sir Stanley Burnton, *Annual Report of the Interception of Communications Commissioner 2016* (December 2017, HC 297, SG/2017/77), Error Investigation numbers 22–27; The Rt Hon Lord Justice Fulford, *Annual Report of the Investigatory Powers Commissioner 2017* (January 2019, HC 1780, SG/2019/8), Error Investigation numbers 2, 19, 20, 23, and 24; The Rt Hon Sir Brian Leveson, *Annual Report of the Investigatory Powers Commissioner 2018* (March 2020, HC 67, SG/2020/8), Error Investigation numbers 16–22.

Most computer errors are either immediately detectable or result from input errors

5.181 Let us consider the proposition that most computer errors are either immediately detectable or result from errors in the data entered into the machines. The evidence is to the contrary: Mr Adams demonstrated that a third of software faults in a large IBM study took at least 5,000 execution years to appear for the first time (this was one of the largest studies of all time);[1] Professor Les Hatton and Andy Roberts conducted a study that demonstrated that seismic programs developed by oil companies were shown to have been used for many years even though they were defective;[2] and Nancy G. Leveson and Clark S. Turner demonstrated that between June 1985 and January 1987 the Therac-25 medical linear accelerator was involved in massive radiation overdoses, causing the deaths of six people, while others were seriously injured. The detailed investigations eventually indicated that the main cause of the deaths was software errors. Some of the lessons gleaned from the work by Nancy Leveson included the following: too much confidence was placed in the software, an assumption by lay people that software will not or cannot fail, and engineers ignoring software when analysing faults, because it was assumed the hardware was at fault, not the software.[3] In this respect, opinions have not changed since 1987.[4] When investigating sudden unintended acceleration in some of its motor cars in the US, Toyota did not include software engineers in its investigations, and incorrectly ruled out software as the cause of the resulting deaths and injuries.[5]

1 Edward N. Adams, 'Optimizing preventive service of software products' (1984) 28(1) IBM Journal of Research and Development 2.
2 Les Hatton and Andy Roberts, 'How accurate is scientific software?' (1994) 20(10) IEEE Transactions on Software Engineering 785.
3 'An investigation of the Therac-25 accidents' (1993) 26(7) Computer 18 (note the additional information in Nancy Leveson, *Software, System Safety and Computers* (Addison-Wesley 1995)); for descriptions of what some of the patients suffered, see Lee, *The Day the Phones Stopped*, chapter 1.
4 Simon Oxenham, 'Thousands of fMRI brain studies in doubt due to software flaws', *New Scientist*, 18 July 2016, https://www.newscientist.com/article/2097734-thousands-of-fmri-brain-studies-in-doubt-due-to-software-flaws/; Eklund and others, 'Cluster failure'.
5 Transcript (not proofread) of *Bookout v Toyota Motor Corporation Case* No. CJ-2008-7969 (Reported by Karen Twyford, RPR): examination and cross examination of Michael Barr 14 October 2013, 76–77, http://www.safetyresearch.net/Library/Bookout_v_Toyota_Barr_REDACTED.pdf.

5.182 Uncovering the faults in devices controlled by software used in medicine is now considered to be an important research area,[1] and in November 2000, 28 patients at the National Cancer Institute in Panama were given massive overdoses of gamma rays partly due to limitations of the computer program that guided use of a radiation therapy machine. A number of patients died.[2]

1 Kevin Fu, 'Trustworthy medical device software' (Appendix D, 97–118) in Theresa Wizemann (ed) *Public Health Effectiveness of the FDA 510(k) Clearance Process: Measuring Postmarket Performance and Other Select Topics: Workshop Report* (Food and Drug Administration 2011), https://www.ncbi.nlm.nih.gov/books/NBK209656/; see also Senate Hearing 112–92, United States Senate, Hearing on a Delicate Balance: FDA and the Reform of the Medical Device Approval Process, 13 April 2011, https://www.aging.senate.gov/hearings/a-delicate-balance-fda-and-the-reform-of-the-medical-device-approval-process.
2 Deborah Gage and John McCormick, *We Did Nothing Wrong: Case 109 A Dissection*, https://edisciplinas.usp.br/pluginfile.php/31797/mod_resource/content/1/casoCancerPanama.pdf; International Atomic Energy Agency, *Investigation of an Accidental Exposure of Radiotherapy Patients in Panama Report of a Team of Experts* (26 May–1 June 2001), https://www-pub.iaea.org/mtcd/publications/pdf/pub1114_scr.pdf; Cari Borrás, 'Overexposure of radiation therapy patients in Panama: problem recognition and follow-up measures' (2006) 20(2/3) Rev Panam Salud Publica/Pan Am J Public Health 173.

5.183 The observations by Professor Leveson will invariably remain relevant: the Toyota recall exercise in late 2009 and early 2010 serves to illustrate this point.[1] The US Congressional Committee on Energy and Commerce heard evidence on this matter, and a report by The National Highway Traffic Safety Administration and the National Aeronautics and Space Administration (NHTSA–NASA), which conducted a study into the problem entitled 'Study of unintended acceleration in Toyota vehicles', a revised version of which was published on 15 April 2011,[2] concluded that it was not proven that faulty software caused the problems, although it was accepted that just because no software faults could be found did not mean that software faults did not occur. The methods used to investigate this matter were challenged.[3]

1 A number of motor manufacturers are facing similar legal actions. It was known that sudden acceleration occurred in the 1980s and 1990s, for which see James Castelli, Carl Nash, Clarence Ditlow and Michael Pecht, *Sudden Acceleration: The Myth of the Driver Error* (University of Maryland, Calce EPSC Press 2003).
2 Available at http://www.nasa.gov/topics/nasalife/features/nesc-toyota-study.html.
3 For which see Michael Barr, 'Firmware forensics: best practices in embedded software source code discovery' (2011) 8 Digital Evidence and Electronic Signature Law Review 148. For an earlier article, see Joel Finch, 'Toyota sudden acceleration: a case study of the National Highway Traffic Safety Administration recalls for change' 22 Loy Consumer L Rev 472.

5.184 Civil proceedings were subsequently initiated by a number of people across the US. In *Bookout v Toyota Motor Corporation*,[1] Michael Barr, an expert in embedded software, gave evidence for the plaintiff regarding the software code in the relevant motor vehicles. He was also cross-examined about aspects of the NHTSA Report, among other issues. His evidence demonstrated that there were a significant number of errors in the software (referred to as 'bugs' in the transcript):

> Q. Did you find all the bugs in the software that you reviewed?
>
> A. Absolutely not.
>
> Q. Why not?
>
> A. Because there is a lot of bugs, and all indications are that there are many more. We haven't specifically gone out looking for bugs. The metrics, like the

> code complexity and a number of global variables, indicate the presence of large numbers of bugs. And just the overall style of the code is suggestive that there will be numerous more bugs that we haven't found yet.[2]

1 Case No. CJ-2008-7969. The trial was held in the District Court of Oklahoma, County State of Oklahoma before the Hon Patricia G. Parrish, District Judge.
2 Transcript (not proofread) of the trial 14 October 2013 before the Hon Patricia G. Parrish, District Judge (Reported by Karen Twyford, RPR): examination and cross examination of Michael Barr, 47–48, http://www.safetyresearch.net/Library/Bookout_v_Toyota_Barr_REDACTED.pdf.

5.185 He also demonstrated that motor cars are now largely run by software. In fact, motor cars have more software code than aircraft, and are prone to software recalls.[1] Drivers no longer have total control over their vehicles.[2] For instance, it was explained how the driver is no longer in direct control of the throttle:

> But the driver had always been directly in control of the air, which is directly related to how much power the engine has. When electronic throttle control comes in, you have software that is now responsible for all three of them at once. So you have a portion of the software, the job of which is to make the spark at the right time, inject the fuel at the right time and the right amount, and open the throttle a certain amount.
>
> ...
>
> The software in electronic throttle control is responsible for all three things, which means if the software malfunctions, it has control of the engine and can take you for a ride. What is of particular importance is that there is another part of the software that is looking at the driver controls, looking at the accelerator pedal and cruise control -- it is looking at more than that, but that is a simplification, that is appropriate right now -- so there is a part of the software looking at what the accelerator pedal position is, is it down, is it up, how much down. Then that is translating that into a calculated throttle angle. And then another part of the software is performing the sparking and the throttle control.[3]

1 Robert N. Charette, 'This car runs on code', IEEE Spectrum, 1 February 2009 http://spectrum.ieee.org/transportation/systems/this-car-runs-on-code; Jürgen Mössinger, 'Software in automotive systems publication' (2010) 27(2) IEEE Software 92; 'Today's car has the computing power of 20 modern PCs, features about 100 million lines of code, and processes up to 25 gigabytes of data per hour': *Connected Car, Automotive Value Chain Unbound* (McKinsey & Company, September 2014), 11. https://www.sas.com/images/landingpage/docs/3_McKinsey_John_Newman_Connected_Car_Report.pdf; James Scoltock, 'As vehicles become more reliant on software, the amount of code needed to run them is challenging OEMs and suppliers alike' *Eureka Magazine*, 1 February 2018, https://www.eurekamagazine.co.uk/design-engineering-features/technology/as-vehicles-become-more-reliant-on-software-the-amount-of-code-needed-to-run-them-is-challenging-oems-and-suppliers-alike/168096/.
2 For which see the prosecution of a driver in Switzerland driving a Tesla motor vehicle in 'Traffic-Aware Cruise Control' and 'Autosteer' mode: PEN 17 16 DIP, 30 May 2018, Regionalgericht Emmental-Oberaargau, Strafabteilung (Regional Court Emmental-Oberaargau, Criminal Division), translated by Thierry Burnens, (2020) 17 Digital Evidence and Electronic Signature Law Review 97.
3 Transcript of the trial of 14 October 2013, 53.

5.186 Mr Barr established that the motor vehicle had errors in the throttle system:

> A. So the first main conclusion is that the 2005 Camry electronic throttle control, the software is of unreasonable quality. It contains bugs, but that's not the only reason it is of unreasonable quality. And it's otherwise defective for a number of reasons. This includes bugs that when put together with the defects can cause unintended acceleration.

Q. As we go forward are you going to explain to us how those problems that you found will cause an unintended acceleration?

A. Yes.

Q. Then you mentioned the code quality metrics. What do you mean about that?

A. So the code complexity and the McCabe Code Complexity is one of the measures of that.[1] And the code complexity for Toyota's code is very high. There are a large number of functions that are overly complex. By the standard industry metrics some of them are untestable, meaning that it is so complicated a recipe that there is no way to develop a reliable test suite or test methodology to test all the possible things that can happen in it. Some of them are even so complex that they are what is called unmaintainable, which means that if you go in to fix a bug or to make a change, you're likely to create a new bug in the process. Just because your car has the latest version of the firmware – that is what we call embedded software – doesn't mean it is safer necessarily than the older one.[2]

1 McCabe Code Complexity has no sound theoretical basis. It is a rule of thumb. I owe this point to Dr Michael Ellims.
2 Transcript of the trial of 14 October 2013, 65–66.

5.187 Mr Barr stated his overall opinion in the following terms: 'ultimately my conclusion is that this Toyota electronic throttle control system is a cause of [unintended acceleration] software malfunction in this electronic throttle module, can cause unintended acceleration.'[1] The members of the jury found in favour of the plaintiffs, and awarded damages of US$1.5 million to each of the plaintiffs. The US Department of Justice subsequently concluded a criminal investigation into the Toyota Motor Company regarding the widespread incidents of unintended vehicle acceleration that caused panic for Toyota owners between 2009 and 2010. It was established with certainty that Toyota intentionally concealed information and misled the public about the safety issues behind these recalls.[2] It was alleged that Toyota made misleading public statements to consumers, gave inaccurate facts to Members of Congress and concealed the extent of problems that some consumers encountered from federal regulators. For instance, Betsy Benjaminson, a translator for Toyota, realized what she was translating was highly significant:

She began working on Toyota litigation in 2010. Before then, she'd been 'oblivious' to the events in the U.S., she says. Slowly she began to notice 'odd things' in documents she saw in connection with her role as translator. Revised press releases sometimes obscured important details, she says. Emails among engineers 'revealed facts that directly contradicted' Toyota's public statements.

Then it got worse. She read reports about runaway cars, including survivors' accounts of crashes that killed their companions. She was deeply affected. A 'tipping point' came when she read a document the company had prepared based on complaints filed with NHTSA. 'A summary of the injuries and deaths was attached', she recalls, 'and it was cynically titled "Souvenirs from NHTSA".' For her, that was it. 'At that moment,' she says, 'I knew something was really wrong inside the company.'[3]

1 Transcript of the trial of 14 October 2013, 67.
2 The literature on this topic in general merits further analysis, but is beyond the scope of this chapter: Suzanne M. Kirchhoff and David Randall Peterman, *Unintended Acceleration in Passenger Vehicles* (Congressional Research Service 7-5700, R41205, 26 April 2010); R. Graham Esdale Jr and Timothy R. Fiedler, 'Toyota's deadly secrets', 46-SEP Trial 16; Finch, 'Toyota sudden acceleration'; Molly S. O'Neill, 'Faulty cars or faulty drivers: the story of sudden acceleration and Ford Motor Company' (undated and

scanned images from an unidentified book), available at http://www.suddenacceleration.com/article-2/; Scott Elder and Travis Thompson, 'Recent development in automobile consumer class actions' 41-FALL Brief 44; Katherine Gardiner, 'Recent developments in automobile law' 47 Tort Trial & Ins Prac LJ 45; Joseph Gavin, 'Crash test dummies: what drives automobile safety in the United States?' (2012) 25 Loy Consumer L Rev 86; Maria N. Maccone, 'Litigation concerning sudden unintended acceleration' 132 Am Jur Trials 305; Qi Van Eikema Hommes, 'Review and Assessment of the ISO 26262 Draft Road Vehicle – Functional Safety' (SAE Technical Paper 2012-01-0025, 2012); David C. Vladeck, 'Machines without principals: liability rules and artificial intelligence' 89 Wash L Rev 117; Aaron Ezroj, 'Product liability after unintended acceleration: how automotive litigation has evolved' 26 Loy Consumer L Rev 470; Antony F. Anderson, 'Intermittent electrical contact resistance as a contributory factor in the loss of automobile speed control functional integrity' (2014) 2 IEEE Access 258; Antony F. Anderson, 'Case study: NHTSA's denial of Dr Raghavan's petition to investigate sudden acceleration in Toyota vehicles fitted with electronic throttles' (2016) 4 IEEE Access 1417.

3 David Hechler refers to Betsey Benjaminson, a translator who illustrated the mismatch in evidence when she informed the US authorities: 'Lost in translation?', 79, http://www.asbpe.org/blog/2014/07/28/david-hechler-wins-asbpes-2014-stephen-barr-award-for-article-on-toyotas-fatal-acceleration-problems/; the Crown Prince was having troubles with his vehicle, which the manufacturer took pains to resolve: David McNeil, 'Imperial Family's car woes sparked Toyota whistleblower', *The Japan Times*, 9 June 2013, http://www.japantimes.co.jp/news/2013/06/09/business/corporate-business/imperial-familys-car-woes-sparked-toyota-whistleblower/#.WJ14B-l4j8s.

5.188 In its settlement with the Department of Justice, Toyota admitted its wrongdoing in making such misleading statements in the Statement of Facts filed with the criminal information, and also admitted that it undertook these actions as an act of concealment as part of efforts to defend its brand. In consequence, Toyota paid a financial penalty of US$1.2 billion under the settlement.[1]

1 http://www.justice.gov/usao-sdny/programs/victim-witness-services/united-states-v-toyota-corporation.

Challenging the authenticity of digital data – trial within a trial

5.189 Laying the evidentiary foundations for the authenticity of electronic evidence is discussed elsewhere in this text, but if the authenticity of evidence is raised by one of the parties, it is appropriate to deal with it in a trial within a trial.[1] This will be a rare occurrence, as noted in *R. v Wayte (William Guy)*[2] by Bedlan J:

> It may be that in very rare cases, there will have to be a trial within a trial on the issue of the admissibility … but on such an issue, where the party producing the document and arguing for its admissibility contends that it is genuine … the issue will invariably be left to the jury.[3]

1 Rosemary Pattenden, 'Pre-verdict judicial fact-finding in criminal trials with juries' (2009) 29(1) Oxford Journal of Legal Studies 1.
2 [1982] 3 WLUK 247, (1982) 76 Cr App R 110, CA, Times, 24 March 1982, [1983] CLY 659.
3 (1982) 76 Cr App R 110 at 118.

5.190 In *R. v Stevenson (Ronald), R. v Hulse (Barry), R. v Whitney (Raymond)*,[1] Kilner Brown J was required to establish whether audio tapes were originals. After a lengthy and careful examination of the evidence held in a trial within a trial, it became clear that there was an opportunity for someone to have interfered with the original tape, and there was evidence that some interference might have taken place. Given the nature of the evidence before him, he said:

> Once the original is impugned and sufficient details as to certain peculiarities in the proffered evidence have been examined in court, and once the situation is reached that it is likely that the proffered evidence is not the original, is not the primary and best evidence, that seems to be to create a situation in which, whether on reasonable doubt or whether on a prima facie basis, the judge is left with no alternative but to reject the evidence.[2]

1 [1971] 1 WLR 1, [1971] 1 All ER 678, [1970] 10 WLUK 82, (1971) 55 Cr App R 171, (1971) 115 SJ 11, [1971] CLY 2264.
2 [1971] 1 WLR 1 at 3G.

5.191 In the case of *R v Robson (Bernard Jack), R v Harris (Gordon Federick)*,[1] the defence raised the issue of the admissibility of the evidence of 13 tape recordings. The judge had to consider whether, on the face of it, the tapes were authentic in the absence of the members of the jury. Shaw J heard evidence in a trial within a trial from a number of witnesses who gave evidence of the history of the tapes, from the actual process of recording to the time they were produced in court. He also listened to four experts called on behalf of the defence, whose examination of the tapes led them to question their originality and authenticity. The prosecution called a separate witness in rebuttal. After hearing the evidence, Shaw J decided that the tape recordings were originals and authentic, commenting that:

> My own view is that in considering that limited question [the primary issue of admissibility] the judge is required to do no more than to satisfy himself that a prima facie case or originality has been made out by evidence which defines and describes the provenance and history of the recording up to the moment of production in court.[2]

1 [1972] 1 WLR 651, [1972] 2 All ER 699, [1972] 3 WLUK 89, (1972) 56 Cr App R 450, [1972] Crim LR 316, (1972) 116 SJ 313, [1972] CLY 642.
2 [1972] 1 WLR 651 at 653H.

5.192 Professor Tapper expressed the view that this exercise should be conducted first by the judge, and if, on the balance of probabilities, the judge determines the evidence could go before the jury, it would then be necessary to cover the same ground again in the same way as any other question of fact that must be decided at trial.[1] On the standard of proof to be used by the judge, O'Connor LJ indicated the criminal standard of proof is to be used in the context of handwriting,[2] and in the case of *R v Minors (Craig), R v Harper (Giselle Gaile)*,[3] Steyn J, as he then was, set out the opinion of the Court of Appeal on this matter in relation to a computer printout:

> The course adopted by the judge in one of the two appeals before us prompts us to refer to the procedure which ought to be adopted in a case where there is a disputed issue as to the admissibility of a computer printout. It is clear that in such a case a judge ought to adopt the procedure of embarking on a trial within a trial.[4]

1 Colin Tapper, *Computer Law* (4th edn, Longman 1989), 370; see also Rosemary Pattenden, 'Authenticating "things" in English law: principles for adducing tangible evidence in common law jury trials' (2008) 12 E & P 273 and 'Pre-verdict judicial fact-finding in criminal trials with juries' (2009) 29 Oxford Journal of Legal Studies 1; in the context of s 69 Police and Criminal Evidence Act 1984, Professor Smith commented that during a trial within a trial, if a document is tendered by the prosecution, the standard is beyond reasonable doubt, and if tendered by the defence, the standard is presumably on the balance of probabilities: *R. v Shephard (Hilda)* [1993] Crim LR 295, 296.

2 *R. v Ewing (Terence Patrick)* [1983] QB 1039, [1983] 3 WLR 1, [1983] 2 All ER 645, [1983] 3 WLUK 125, (1983) 77 Cr App R 47, [1984] ECC 234, [1983] Crim LR 472, (1983) 127 SJ 390, Times, 15 March 1983, [1983] CLY 63.
3 [1989] 1 WLR 441, [1989] 1 All ER 208, [1988] 12 WLUK 161, (1989) 89 Cr App R 102, [1989] Crim LR 360, (1989) 133 SJ 420, [1989] CLY 546.
4 [1989] 1 WLR 441 at 448.

5.193 He went on to indicate that the judge should apply the ordinary standard of criminal proof in reaching a decision, and in the case of *R. v Neville*,[1] the members of the Court of Appeal also noted that trial judges 'should examine critically any suggestion that a prior computer malfunction has any relevance to the particular computer record tendered in evidence'.[2] The decision of the Court of Appeal in *R v Minors (Craig, R v Harper (Giselle Gaile)* to require a judge to apply the ordinary standard of criminal proof in reaching a decision when hearing evidence in a trial within a trial overrules the decision of Shaw J in *R v Robson (Bernard Jack), R v Harris (Gordon Federick)* (in which he reached an opinion that the standard was on a balance of probabilities[3]), although there is much to commend the view of Shaw J when he suggested that the prosecution need do no more than set up a prima facie case in favour of the authenticity of the evidence:

> It may be difficult if not impossible to draw the philosophical or theoretical boundary between matters going to admissibility and matters going properly to weight and cogency; but, as I have already said, it is simple enough to make a practical demarcation and set practical limits to an inquiry as to admissibility if the correct principle is that the prosecution are required to do no more than set up a prima facie case in favour of it. If they should do so, the questioned evidence remains subject to the more stringent test the jury must apply in the context of the whole case, namely, that they must be sure of the authenticity of that evidence before they take any account of its content.[4]

1 [1990] 11 WLUK 143, [1991] Crim LR 288, [1991] CLY 623.
2 [1991] Crim LR 288, 289.
3 [1972] 1 WLR 651 at 656C; this standard was agreed by counsel on both sides at 653E.
4 [1972] 1 WLR 651 at 655H–656A.

5.194 The standard that a judge must apply in determining the admissibility of a videotape was considered by Cameron JA in the Canadian case of *R v Penney*[1] before the Newfoundland and Labrador Court of Appeal in 2002. In this instance, the prosecution sought to adduce evidence of the killing of marine animals. The evidence comprised a video recording of the killing of a seal. The recording had been frequently switched on and off as the operator of the camera selected scenes to record. The recording was filmed in mini-digital format, transferred to Beta format and then to VHS format. Before the Crown took possession of the tape, it had been in the possession of a professional editing studio for several months. There was no attempt to provide for the security of or to restrict access to the tape. The Crown called the camera operator and the owner of the company for whom the camera operator worked to give evidence during the trial within a trial. The trial judge concluded that the witnesses were not credible and failed to tell the truth. He therefore refused to admit the video recording in any format. The Crown appealed to the summary appeal conviction court, which allowed the appeal. A subsequent appeal to the Newfoundland and Labrador Court of Appeal reversed the summary appeal conviction court decision and the decision of the trial judge was restored. Cameron JA addressed the issue of the standard that a trial judge should apply in determining the admissibility of videotape evidence, indicating that:

> The issue then is whether in making this finding the trial judge was usurping the role of the jury (or in this case the role of the judge at trial) or was properly carrying out the function of the judge on determination of the admissibility of hard evidence.[2]

1 (2002) 163 CCC (3d) 329.
2 (2002) 163 CCC (3d) 329 at [40].

5.195 He went on:

> [43] In my view, this consideration is really a matter of weighing prejudice against probative value, in much the same way that a trial judge must examine many other kinds of evidence.
>
> [44] It is the question of fairness and absence of any intention to mislead that is really at issue in this case. The trial judge on a *voir dire* must determine whether a videotape being offered in evidence has been edited in such a way as to distort the truth.

5.196 Reference was made to *R v Nikolovski*,[1] which established that where a videotape has not been altered or changed, and where it depicts the scene of a crime, then it becomes admissible and relevant evidence.[2] In *R v Bulldog*,[3] the members of the Court of Appeal of Alberta considered this issue, and emphasized that 'What matters with a recording, then, is not whether it was altered, but rather the degree of accuracy of its representation'.[4] In *R v Penney*, the judge addressed the problem of the falsification of evidence by pointing out that the members of a jury 'can be expected to have, if not experience with, knowledge of the possibilities for manipulating the content of photographs and videotapes', and concluded that the 'standard by which the trial judge is to determine the question is on the balance of probabilities'.[5]

1 (1996) 111 CCC (3d) 403, [1996] 3 SCR 1197 403.
2 In *R. v Andalib-Goortani*, 2014 ONSC 4690 (CanLII), the prosecution failed to establish the authenticity of a digital image obtained from the Internet: the metadata had been removed, and it was not possible to ascertain the provenance of the image.
3 2015 ABCA 251 (CanLII); 326 CCC (3d) 385; [2015] AJ No 813 (QL).
4 2015 ABCA 251 (CanLII) at [32].
5 (2002) 163 CCC (3d) 329.

5.197 If the standard of proof of a trial within a trial is the criminal standard, it can be argued that the prosecution is required to prove its case twice: once to the trial judge and a second time before the members of the jury. Arguably, the duty of the trial judge is to sift the evidence sufficiently to establish whether it is to go before the members of the jury in cases where the authenticity of the evidence is questioned by the defence.

A protocol for challenging software in devices and systems

5.198 Should it become the norm for the defence to challenge the authenticity of evidence in digital form, it is suggested that consideration might be given to the development of a protocol to deal with such challenges:

> (1) First, in criminal proceedings, the prosecution should be required to inform the trial judge and defence in advance that it intends to rely on the presumption.

> (2) Where the prosecution demonstrates reliance is warranted (with appropriate evidence), it will be for the defence to warn the trial judge that it will question the use of the presumption, in particular the authenticity of identified aspects of the evidence, and to set out the grounds upon which the challenge is made.[1]

1 To a certain extent this might be already happening, for which see Oriola Sallavaci, 'Streamlined reporting of forensic evidence in England and Wales: is it the way forward?' (2016) 20(3) E & P 235.

5.199 Such an approach would be entirely consistent with the trial management procedures set out in Part 3, rule 3.3(2)(c)(ii) of the Criminal Procedure Rules 2015 (as amended). If this first hurdle is overcome, then it will be for the trial judge to decide whether a trial within a trial is necessary, and if so, to set out the parameters, including the standard of proof, for which a ruling is required.

5.200 There is something missing in the suggestion noted above regarding criminal proceedings: there is no discussion regarding the sufficiency of the evidence the defence must adduce to persuade a judge to order appropriate disclosure.[1] Professor Imwinkelried has also considered this problem,[2] and has proposed a two-step process, the first part of which is:

> Faced with competing legitimate interests, a trial judge must attempt to strike a rational balance. In this context, the judge could do so by proceeding in two steps. First, a judge should assign to the accused seeking discovery the burden of showing that the facts of the instant prosecution exceed, or are at the margins of, the validation range of the empirical studies relied on by the prosecution. More specifically, the defendant must convince the judge that the available studies do not adequately address the effect of a specified, material variable or condition present in the instant case. The most clear-cut case would be a fact situation in which none of the available studies relied on by the prosecution experts tested the application of the technique to fact situations involving the condition.[3]

1 There are profound concerns relating to the disclosure (or discovery) of evidence in both civil and criminal proceedings. For the USA, see Matt Tusing, 'Machine-generated evidence', 43 No 1 The Reporter 13; Katherine Kwong, 'The algorithm says you did it: the use of black box algorithms to analyze complex DNA evidence' (2017) 31 Harv JL & Tech 275; Vera Eidelman, 'The First Amendment case for public access to secret algorithms used in criminal trials' (2018) 35 Ga St U L Rev 915; Sonia K. Katyal, 'The paradox of source code secrecy' (2019) 104 Cornell L Rev 1183; Rebecca Wexler, 'Life, liberty, and trade secrets: intellectual property in the criminal justice system' (2018) 70 Stan L Rev 1343, in which the author considers the history of the trade secret privilege, uncovering an interesting development where it was demonstrated that Wigmore was initially hostile to the privilege (at 1383), but his opinion later changed. He admitted in an aside that his brother had suffered loss relating to intellectual piracy (at 1385); Steven M. Bellovin, Matt Blaze, Susan Landau and Brian Owsley, 'Seeking the source: criminal defendants' constitutional right to source code' (2021) 17(1) Ohio State Tech LJ 38.
2 Edward J. Imwinkelried, 'Computer source code: a source of the growing controversy over the reliability of automated forensic techniques' (2017) 66 DePaul L Rev 97.
3 Imwinkelried, 'Computer source code', 128.

5.201 Professor Imwinkelried then indicates, at 128, that 'The judge should certainly not accept the ipse dixit assertion of the defense counsel that the omitted condition is material in the sense that its presence could affect the outcome of the test'. Providing the defence has met the burden of part one, the second part of the test provides as follows:

> Even then the judge should not automatically require the manufacturer to furnish the defense with a printout or electronic version of the source code. Instead, the judge could give the manufacturer a choice to: either (1) allow the defense to test the application of the program to a fact situation including the material condition or variable omitted from the validation studies, or (2) provide the defense with the source code.

5.202 Professor Imwinkelried points out, as 129, that:

> At the end of this first step, the judge is not licensing a fishing expedition of unlimited scope; rather, the judge is authorizing discovery designed to meet a discrete defense criticism of the state of the empirical record in order to determine whether the technique can be reliably applied to the facts in the pending case.

5.203 There are criticisms of this proposal. Professor Martyn Thomas has pointed out that an argument or proposal that depends on the outcome of testing to provide evidence of the correctness or of the specific, required reliability of some software is almost always based on erroneous or unverified assumptions.[1] At the very least, it should always be challenged by the following questions:

> (1) How many tests will be enough to satisfy the required threshold of confidence in the evidence?
>
> (2) How and on what assumptions will the applicant arrive at that number of tests?
>
> (3) What is the procedure to be used to test the software and to verify the test results?
>
> (4) On what assumptions can this be achieved within a practical period of time?

1 Email communication between the author and Professor Thomas CBE.

5.204 The answers to these questions will either reveal a fundamental flaw or provide the basis for challenging the assumptions. In addition, it is not clear how 'reliable' a court requires a forensic test to be. If a forensic system was known to be right more than half the time and randomly wrong otherwise, the question is whether a single positive result will pass the on-the-balance-of-probabilities requirement for a civil case.

5.205 As all judges are only too well aware, there is a danger that the trial judge may be seen to usurp the functions of the members of the jury in reaching preliminary decisions on authenticity when conducting a trial within a trial. Marshall J, in delivering the judgment of the Court of Appeal in the case of *R. v Ali (Maqsud), R. v Hussain (Ashiq)*,[1] indicated that conducting a trial within a trial should be a rare occurrence:

> In the view of this court the cases must be rare where the judge is justified in undertaking his own investigation into the weight of the evidence, which, subject to proper directions from the judge, is really the province of the jury, but the court sees that there can be cases – but they must be rare – where the issues of admissibility and weight can overlay each other.[2]

1 [1966] 1 QB 688, [1965] 3 WLR 229, [1965] 2 All ER 464, [1965] 4 WLUK 27, (1965) 49 Cr App R 230, (1965) 129 JP 396, (1965) 109 SJ 331, [1965] CLY 796.
2 [1966] 1 QB 688 at 703C.

5.206 This restricted view was reinforced by the comments in *R. v Stevenson (Ronald), R. v Hulse (Barry), R. v Whitney (Raymond)*[1] of Kilner Brown J:

> as a general rule it seems to me to be highly undesirable, and indeed wrong for such an investigation to take place before the judge. If it is regarded as a general practice it would lead to the ludicrous situation that in every case where an accused person said that the prosecution evidence is fabricated the judge would be called upon to usurp the functions of the jury.[2]

1 [1971] 1 WLR 1, [1971] 1 All ER 678, [1970] 10 WLUK 82, (1971) 55 Cr App R 171, (1971) 115 SJ 11, [1971] CLY 2264.
2 [1971] 1 WLR 1 at 4E.

5.207 Where the matter of authentication is raised, the trial judge is required to decide whether to conduct a trial within a trial. Where the decision is made to hold a trial within a trial, it will be useful for the judge to set out the scope of the hearing. In *R v Robson (Bernard Jack), R v Harris (Gordon Federick)*, Shaw J said that where such a hearing takes place, it should be defined narrowly.[1] This must be right.

1 [1972] 1 WLR 651 at 655H.

5.208 In respect of the costs of such an exercise, in *R. v Saward (Steven Kevin), R. v Bower (Steven Kevin), R. v Harrison (Keith)*,[1] the prosecution sought the admission of recordings of telephone conversations that were intercepted by the Dutch police and stored on a CD. The judge was invited to conduct a trial within a trial to determine whether or not the data recorded on the CD, transferred from a mainframe computer located in the Netherlands, was admissible in evidence as authentic, accurate and a reliable copy. The trial within a trial lasted for four days, and a number of witnesses, including British officers and a Dutch police officer, were called to give evidence. Lady Justice Hallett commented, at [44], on the costs of such an exercise:

> Given the evidence available to the Crown we also have reservations about the profitability of the four day exercise of putting the Crown to strict proof of the exhibit. All of those involved in the conduct of criminal trials must be aware by now of the constraints upon resources and we are far from persuaded that this was a proper use of limited resources.

1 [2005] EWCA Crim 3183, [2005] 11 WLUK 351.

5.209 The defence drew a number of errors in the CD recording to the attention of the trial judge, and it was only right that this issue should be considered.

5.210 When collecting electronic evidence, the investigator needs to pay careful attention to the process by which the evidence was obtained, and to demonstrate the provenance of the evidence. In *R. v Skinner (Philip)*,[1] the defence called into question evidence of screen images obtained by a police constable when conducting an investigation into indecent photographs of children. During the trial within a trial, the police officer gave evidence that he had a 'source' for the screen images. He admitted entering a website that he was not prepared to identify, and could only provide limited information about the provenance of the material he produced for the purposes of the investigation: namely, images that appeared on screen that were produced in the form of a printout. He refused to name or identify the website he had entered. It was held by the members of the Court of Appeal that the trial judge wrongly admitted the evidence. First, the members of the Court accepted that it was probable that the screen images were real evidence, because their content did not require any computer input, and likened the image to somebody switching on a television set. However, the printouts were not authenticated properly under the provisions of s 27 of the Criminal Justice Act 1988, and for that reason, the trial judge should not have admitted them. Second, there was no public interest immunity hearing to enable the judge to decide whether the prosecution need not disclose or need not give evidence as to the process by which the screen image reached the police officer, or in the absence of a proper explanation, how the screen image came to be on the police officer's computer. It was conceded that a public interest immunity hearing should have been requested, and in such circumstances the trial judge was wrong to admit the evidence.

1 [2005] EWCA Crim 1439, [2005] 5 WLUK 506, [2006] Crim LR 56.

Reintroduction of the common law presumption

5.211 The Law Commission proposed the repeal of s 69 of the Police and Criminal Evidence Act 1984 and a return to the common law presumption:

> In the absence of evidence to the contrary, the courts will presume that mechanical instruments were in order at the material time.[1]

1 Section 69 ceased to have any effect under s 60 of the Youth Justice and Criminal Evidence Act 1999, and s 69 was also repealed by Schedule 6; the Law Commission, *Evidence in Criminal Proceedings: Hearsay and Related Topics*, 13.13; Katie Quinn, 'Computer evidence in criminal proceedings: farewell to the ill-fated s.69 of the Police and Criminal Evidence Act 1984' (2001) 5(3) E & P 174; Amanda Hoey, 'Analysis of the Police and Criminal Evidence Act, s.69 – computer generated evidence' [1996] 1 Web JCLI.

5.212 The grounds for justification were set out in paragraphs 13.7 – 13.11, and are reproduced below with the references omitted:

> The problems with the present law
>
> 13.6 In the consultation paper we came to the conclusion that the present law was unsatisfactory, for five reasons.
>
> 13.7 First, section 69 fails to address the major causes of inaccuracy in computer evidence. As Professor Tapper has pointed out, 'most computer error is either immediately detectable or results from error in the data entered into the machine.'[1]
>
> 13.8 Secondly, advances in computer technology make it increasingly difficult to comply with section 69: it is becoming 'increasingly impractical to examine (and therefore certify) all the intricacies of computer operation'. These problems existed even before networking became common.[2]
>
> 13.9 A third problem lies in the difficulties confronting the *recipient* of a computer produced document who wishes to tender it in evidence: the recipient may be in no position to satisfy the court about the operation of the computer. It may well be that the recipient's opponent is better placed to do this.
>
> 13.10 Fourthly, it is illogical that section 69 applies where the document is tendered in evidence, but not where it is used by an expert in arriving at his or her conclusions, nor where a witness uses it to refresh his or her memory. If it is safe to admit evidence which relies on and incorporates the output from the computer, it is hard to see why that output should not itself be admissible; and

> conversely, if it is not safe to admit the output, it can hardly be safe for a witness to rely on it.
>
> 13.11 At the time of the publication of the consultation paper there was also a problem arising from the interpretation of section 69. It was held by the Divisional Court in *McKeown v DPP* that computer evidence is inadmissible if it cannot be proved that the computer was functioning properly – even though the malfunctioning of the computer had no effect on the accuracy of the material produced. Thus, in that case, computer evidence could not be relied on because there was a malfunction in the clock part of an Intoximeter machine, although it had no effect on the accuracy of the material part of the printout (the alcohol reading). On appeal, this interpretation has now been rejected by the House of Lords: only malfunctions that affect the way in which a computer processes, stores or retrieves the information used to generate the statement are relevant to section 69.

1 Ladkin and others, 'The Law Commission presumption concerning the dependability of computer evidence' (commented on this citation by the Law Commission, at 3: 'We were surprised to read Tapper's suggestion that the Tapper Condition categorises "most computer error", even allowing that he was writing in 1991. Reading the original paper, it seems to us as if Professor Tapper was not categorising "most computer error" in unqualified terms, but rather considering particular phenomena that are manifest in the use of one specific sort of IT system, namely systems commonly used for clerical work (maybe, more specifically, for legal-clerical work). The Tapper Condition does not appear to hold in general.'

2 It may be the case that computer technology made it increasingly difficult to comply with the provisions of s 69, but this is not an argument to presume that mechanical instruments were in order at the material time. Professor Les Hatton, in his article 'The chimera of software quality' 103, stated that:

> computer programs are fundamentally unquantifiable at the present stage of knowledge, and we must consider any proof based on them flawed until we can apply the same level of verification to a program as to a theorem.
>
> Scientific papers are peer reviewed with a long-standing and highly successful system. The computer programs we use today to produce those results generally fly somewhere off the peer-review radar. Even worse, scientists will swap their programs uncritically, passing on the virus of undiscovered software faults.

That the peer review process is successful is debatable – the scientific community itself has raised concerns about the various biases that afflict the selection and review processes of scientific papers and their eventual publication.

5.213 Curiously, the authors of the report did not produce any evidence to establish whether it is generally true in the absence of contrary evidence that 'mechanical instruments were in order at the material time'. There was no evidence to demonstrate that software code should benefit from this assertion. There was also no discussion of what is meant by 'in order'. This is an important issue, bearing in mind that the presumption is a presumption without the requirement of proof of a basic fact.[1] There was a great deal of technical material in the 1970s and 1980s to demonstrate that software errors might not be obvious. Indeed, in 1986 Professor Rudolph J. Peritz noted the following (footnotes omitted):

> [to] grant greater credibility to computerized records ... because they have not been touched by 'the hand of man' succumbs to two delusions. First, it is the hands and intellects of men and women that produce computers and the programs that guide them. To believe that the absence of direct physical contact means that records are untouched betrays a naive view of electronic data processing, one that ignores the centrality of humans to any computer system's functioning. Second, trustworthiness is equated with electronic processing and opposed to

> human reckoning ... It ignores, for example, the great dangers of traceless change and unauthorized access, as well as the benefits of having the proponent present evidence to prove systemic accuracy.
>
> ...
>
> Throughout law's intellectual history, scholars and jurists have sought methodological objectivity to justify legal decision making ... The jurisprudential lure of computer technology is a perceived absence of discretion. Once designed, built, and programmed, the machinery objectively executes the will of its creators, and thus is perceived as trustworthy. But closer scrutiny reveals, at best, a paradox of complete submission and complete autonomy. A computer performs relentlessly just as we have designed and programmed it, and in so doing, it is entirely independent of us. Computerized records also are treated as trustworthy for a second reason—because the technology is perceived as error-free. Moreover, even on those exceptional occasions of technological failure, we believe, a computer will still inform us that an error has occurred. In sum, we have come to believe that unacknowledged error and subjectivity are not only undesirable, but also indigenous to the human domain.
>
> But experience can teach us that such idealization of technology is a mirage that obfuscates the overlapping horizons of humans and computers, as well as their distinctive characteristics. In the human drama of litigation, better attention to the pragmatic jurisprudence of the Federal Rules of Evidence, as well as to the thoughtful practice recommended by the *Manual for Complex Litigation*, can help to dispel such harmful illusions. The concrete result of this attention will be the extension to the objecting party and to the court of a fair opportunity to evaluate the trustworthiness of all documents generated from computerized data.[2]

1 Quinn, 'Computer evidence in criminal proceedings', 182.

2 Rudolph J. Peritz, 'Computer data and reliability: a call for authentication of business records under the federal rules of evidence', 1001–1002; at the time of writing this article, Professor Peritz was a Visiting Associate Professor of Law at Benjamin N. Cardozo School of Law, and had worked with computers since 1962 as a programmer, operator, systems engineer and legal consultant. He was fully conversant with the errors regarding software code that occurred regularly.

5.214 In England and Wales, s 69 was subsequently repealed,[1] and a similar reform was adopted with respect to evidence in electronic form for civil proceedings with the passing of the Civil Evidence Act 1995. It is suggested that the presumption, as set out above, that 'mechanical instruments were in order at the material time' remains far too crude an assumption to apply to computers. The authors of the Law Commission Report cite excellent reasons as to why the criminal law might be amended, but the proponents of the presumption should establish what they mean by the term 'mechanical instruments were in order at the material time' when referring to computers or computer-like devices. A fundamental problem is caused by the fact that software errors can be present (in large numbers), but not observable in use until a specific situation is encountered.[2] For example, the 'Shellshock' vulnerability (CVE-2014-6271[3]) had been dormant since 1989 in a program called Bash, which was used in Unix systems for years.

1 By s 60 of the Youth Justice and Criminal Evidence Act 1999.

2 Stephen Castell, 'Computers trusted, and found wanting' (1993) 9(4) Computer Law and Security Report 155; Castell, 'Letter to the editor', 158 – the views expressed by Dr Castell, despite their age, remain valid; Student Comment, 'A reconsideration of the admissibility of computer-generated evidence' (1977) 126(1) University of Pennsylvania Law Review 425; George L. Paul, 'Systems of evidence in the age of complexity' (2014) 12(2) Ave Maria L Rev 173.

3 https://cve.mitre.org/cgi-bin/cvename.cgi?name=CVE-2014-6271.

5.215 Various challenges have been made in criminal proceedings as to the accuracy of speed measuring devices and breath analysis machines. Such devices rarely undergo a catastrophic failure, but they will drift from being accurate, which means a recalibration is necessary from time to time. Such devices continue to be the subject of challenge. This topic is not dealt with in any depth, because the aim of this chapter is to discuss the fragility of software code in particular, although the drift or wearing out of components can of itself be a cause of software error if the software was never designed to cope with the changes that occur in such circumstances.[1] With rare exceptions, such challenges have failed. For instance, in the case of *Darby (Yvonne Beatrice) v DPP*[2] the assertions of a police officer familiar with the use of such a device was held to be sufficient evidence to sustain the finding that the device was working correctly,[3] although where the legislation requires the date and time at which a specimen was provided to be printed on the printout and the date is incorrect, the machine is not considered to be capable of being 'reliable'.[4] This is supported by the comments of Kourakis and Blue JJ of the Supreme Court of South Australia in *Police v Bleeze*, who stated that 'an evidential basis for the presumption of accuracy of a scientific instrument, in a proper case, may be given by a person who, even though not a scientist with expertise in the machine's technology, is properly trained in its operation'.[5]

1 For the early history of case law, see 'The breathalyser' by A Magistrates' Clerk, (1970) 34 The Journal of Criminal Law 206, and for a later analysis, see C. E. Bazell, 'Challenging the breathalyser' (1988) 52 Journal of Criminal Law 177 and F. G. Davies, 'Challenging the accuracy of the breath-test device' (1988) 52 Journal of Criminal Law 280; Ian R. Coyle, David Field and Graham A. Starmer, 'An inconvenient truth: legal implications of errors in breath alcohol analysis arising from statistical uncertainty' (2010) 42(2) Australian Journal of Forensic Sciences 101; for a discussion based on the USA, including an indication of the technical problems relating to fixed speed cameras, see Steven A. Glazer, 'Those speed cameras are everywhere: automated speed monitoring law, enforcement, and physics in Maryland' (2012) 7(1) Journal of Business & Technology Law 1.

2 [1994] 10 WLUK 343, [1995] RTR 294, (1995) 159 JP 533 (DC), Times, 4 November 1994, [1994] CLY 674.

3 Extensive tests have indicated that many pieces of software widely used in science and engineering are not as accurate as imagined (thus affecting the accuracy of the output), and whether a police officer who has no knowledge of software code is capable of determining such a complex point is debatable: Les Hatton, 'The T experiments: errors in scientific software' (1997) 4(2) IEEE Computational Science & Engineering 27.

4 *Slender v Boothby* [1984] 11 WLUK 234, [1985] RTR 385, [1984] 149 JP 405, [1986] CLY 2951; 'The paradox of the reliable device' (1986) 50 Journal of Criminal Law 13–15.

5 [2012] SASCF 54 at [89]; for an earlier case with evidence from three witnesses, see *R v Ciantar; DPP v Ciantar* [2006] VSCA 263.

5.216 In New Zealand, Harvey J summarized the position regarding evidence of mechanical or technological devices in *R v Good*, although no evidence was proffered to substantiate the assumptions built into the presumption:

> (a) There is a presumption that mechanical instruments or technological devices function properly at the relevant time.
>
> (b) Judicial notice will be taken of the output of a notorious or well-known technology. Evidence of the way in which it works to establish that it is based on sound scientific principles is not required.
>
> (c) New or novel technologies will not receive judicial notice. Expert evidence is required to explain the operation of the technology and the scientific principles upon which it is based. Authority seems to suggest that problems have arisen when technologically based evidence has been adduced without undertaking the inquiry whether or not the technology is 'notorious' or requires expert evidence.

(d) There is no rule of law which says that the reliability of the device is a precondition to admissibility. In either situation set out in (a) or (b) above the evidence is admissible – it is for the fact finder to assess weight.

(e) In some cases the presumption of accuracy of a technological device will be created by statute. The manner in which the technology is operated may have an impact upon the weight to be attributed to its output.

(f) In some cases devices may, as a result of their own processes, create a record which is admissible. (*R v Spiby* (1990) 91 Cr App R 186, (1991) Crim LR 199).

(g) However, if there is human intervention in the performance of such processes either at the input, output or any intermediate stage, hearsay issues may arise, although in some cases exceptions to the hearsay rule may apply.

(h) Whether or not there is unfairness in the process of acquiring or dealing with the evidence is a recognized common law ground to test admissibility and may be available upon the facts of each case. That is a matter primarily of human behaviour and is not intrinsically part of the technology.[1]

1 [2005] DCR 804 at [70].

5.217 Proof that computers are presumed to work properly must rest with the proponent. The term 'computers' is used solely to reinforce the point that a computer or computer-like device is far more sophisticated than any pure mechanical machine, and such devices only work because a human being has written code to allow it to function. No evidence has been adduced to demonstrate the accuracy of such a presumption. One type of computer differs remarkably from another, and each will be controlled by software written by different people of varying degrees of competence to address problems of varying degrees of complexity and difficulty.[1]

1 For a discussion of software and the complex issues that affect devices used by the medical profession, see Sylvia Kierkegaard and Patrick Kierkegaard, 'Danger to public health: medical devices, toxicity, virus and fraud' (2013) 29 Computer Law and Security Review 13; Steven Hanna, Rolf Rolles, Andrés Molina-Markham, Pongsin Poosankam, Kevin Fu and Dawn Song, 'Take two software updates and see me in the morning: the case for software security evaluations of medical devices' in *Proceedings of the 2nd USENIX Conference on Health Security and Privacy* (USENIX Association Berkeley, California, 2011).

5.218 Thus the assertion that all computers are presumed to be working properly (whatever this means) cannot be right. It is to say that all motor cars, regardless of quality, are reliable – which they demonstrably are not (although it is acknowledged that most motor cars are generally reliable). In the view of George L. Paul, 'Just because businesses rely on faulty computer programs does not necessarily mean that courts should follow suit',[1] although in *People of the State of Colorado v Huhen* Vogt J considered that 'computer business records have a greater level of trustworthiness than an individually generated computer document'[2] without providing an authority, other than to quote from *Colorado Evidentiary Foundations*[3] that 'computers are so widely accepted and used that the proponent of computer evidence need not prove those two elements of the foundation'.

1 George L. Paul, *Foundations of Digital Evidence* (American Bar Association 2008), 129; *Gordon v Thorpe* [1985] 10 WLUK 38, [1986] RTR 358, [1986] Crim LR 61, [1986] CLY 2950, where two experts gave evidence of the accuracy or otherwise of a Lion Intoximeter 3000.
2 53 P.3d 735 (Colo.App. 2002) at 737.
3 Roxanne Bailin, Jim England, Pat Furman and Edward J. Imwinkelreid, *Colorado Evidentiary Foundations* (Michie 1997, with supplements), 736.

The statutory presumption

5.219 Mention might usefully be made of the powers conferred upon the Secretary of State by s 7(1)(a) of the Road Traffic Act 1988, by which a Minister may approve the use of breathalyser devices.[1] The view of the courts is illustrated in *Richardson v DPP*,[2] in which Stanley Burnton J noted that 'The device so approved is assumed to be an effective and sufficiently accurate device for the purposes of section 5(1)(a), and that is the end of the matter'.[3] The effect is to create a statutory presumption for breathalyser devices. He went on to indicate that if the device and software approved in 1998 had since changed, that was not relevant:

> On the face of it, therefore, it would seem that a device which did not include the Intoximeter EC/IR Gas Delivery System, by way of example, or the software version of which was not UK5.23, but some significantly different version, would not be an approved device. It does not follow from that that every modification to an Intoximeter takes it out of the approval. Far from it. The alteration must be such, in my judgment, that the description in the schedule to the order no longer applies to it.[4]

1 'Approval of breath test device' (1968) 32 The Journal of Criminal Law 255; 'Trying times for breath testers' (1969) 33 The Journal of Criminal Law 106; 'Proof of approval of "Alcotest" ' (1969) 33 The Journal of Criminal Law 168; 'Proof of approval by letter' (1969) 33 The Journal of Criminal Law 204; 'Judicial notice of Alcotest' (1970) 34 The Journal of Criminal Law 107.
2 [2003] EWHC 359 (Admin), [2003] 2 WLUK 596.
3 [2003] EWHC 359 (Admin) at [6].
4 [2003] EWHC 359 (Admin) at [9]; identical comments were made by Robert Goff LJ in *R v Skegness Magistrates' Court, Ex parte Cardy* [1985] RTR 49 at 61.

5.220 In *Fearnley v Director of Public Prosecutions*,[1] Mr Justice Field observed that:

> Whilst the defence statement purports to put the prosecution specifically to proof that the software was UK 5.23, this did not mean that the prosecution had specifically to prove this matter. This is because of the general presumption that flows from the fact that the machine was of a type that had been approved,[2] this being a presumption which in my view is plainly consistent with Article 6 ECHR. Thus, it was for the appellant to adduce some evidence that the software was otherwise than the specified software before the prosecution came under a burden to prove the software. At no stage did the appellant raise or adduce such evidence and therefore he can have no substantial complaint that the prosecution were allowed to provide specific proof of the software through the engineer's report.[3]

1 [2005] EWHC 1393 (Admin), [2005] 6 WLUK 191, (2005) 169 JP 450, (2005) 169 JPN 735, Times, 6 July 2005, [2005] CLY 729.
2 Illustrating a confusion between common law and statutory presumption.
3 [2005] EWHC 1393 (Admin) at [34].

5.221 In *Kemsley v DPP*,[1] Buxton LJ stated the opinion of the court on this matter:

> The statutory presumption as to approval of a particular device was conclusive as to the correctness of that device. That point does not now appear in this case, and should not appear in any case in the future.[2]

1 [2004] EWHC 278 (Admin), [2004] 2 WLUK 65, (2005) 169 JP 148, (2005) 169 JPN 239, [2005] CLY 874.
2 [2004] EWHC 278 (Admin) at [11].

5.222 In *DPP v Wood, DPP v McGillicuddy*,[1] Ouseley J indicated that if the breath test device is approved, it is therefore reliable: 'There is a common law presumption that the breath test device, if type approved, is reliable.'[2] Alternatively, where a device is weighted in favour of the accused, it is not an improper use of the device.[3] The same position is held in cases relating to speed measuring devices,[4] although if the road markings that are placed on the road to provide a scale for the digital device to measure speed are not the correct distance apart, the device will give a false reading.[5] This approach might be appropriate, given that the accused can agree to have a sample of blood taken, and at the same time a copy sample of the blood is provided to the accused. Analysis of the blood is more accurate, and the blood sample can thus be analysed by the police and independently by a person on behalf of the accused.[6] If this option is taken up by the accused, the evidence is more compelling, although consideration must be given to the deterioration of the blood sample.[7] Lord Hughes offered a further rationale in *Public Prosecution Service v McKee Public Prosecution Service*,[8] where the appellants had their fingerprints taken at the police station using an electronic device called Livescan. A match was subsequently made, which the Crown relied upon at trial. Livescan devices were in general use in Northern Ireland from 2006 and throughout the period 2007–2009 when statutory type approval was required by article 61(8B) of the Police and Criminal Evidence (Northern Ireland) Order 1989,[9] although approval was never granted. The appeal was dismissed. Of relevance in this context are the remarks by Lord Hughes:

> The control fingerprints taken from the appellants in the police station were not snapshots. The impressions which their fingers provided could be reproduced at any time afterwards, and would be the same. The accuracy of the Livescan readings, if disputed, could readily be checked independently by the appellants providing more samples, whether by ink and paper or by any other means, for examination by an independent expert.[10]

1 [2006] EWHC 32 (Admin), [2006] 1 WLUK 326, (2006) 170 JP 177, [2006] ACD 41, (2006) 170 JPN 273 (2006) 170 JPN 414, (2006) 156 NLJ 146, Times, 8 February 2006, [2006] CLY 951.

2 [2006] EWHC 32 (Admin) at [2]; also noted by Mr Justice Cresswell at [43] in *DPP v Brown (Andrew Earle), DPP v Teixeira (Jose)* [2001] EWHC Admin 931, [2001] 11 WLUK 426, (2002) 166 JP 1, [2002] RTR 23, Times, 3 December 2001, [2002] CLY 733.

3 *Ashton v DPP* [1995] 6 WLUK 298, (1996) 160 JP 336, [1998] RTR 45, Times, 14 July 1995, Independent, 10 July 1995, [1995] CLY 4416; for a discussion of other cases and the reverse burden of proof, see Ian Dennis, 'Reverse onuses and the presumption of innocence: in search of principle'(2005) Dec Crim LR 901; David Hamer, 'The presumption of innocence and reverse burdens: a balancing act' (2007) 66(1) CLJ 142; P. M. Callow, 'The drink-drive legislation and the breath-alcohol cases' (2009) 10 Crim LR 707.

4 Section 20 of the Road Traffic Offenders Act 1988 as amended; *Griffiths v DPP* [2007] EWHC 619 (Admin), [2007] 3 WLUK 572, [2007] RTR 44, [2007] CLY 3537.

5 Bill Gardner, 'Driver defeats speeding ticket with tape measure', *The Telegraph* (London, 15 December 2014) https://www.telegraph.co.uk/news/uknews/road-and-rail-transport/11294579/Driver-defeats-speeding-ticket-with-tape-measure.html.

6 Judges will not permit devices to be tested, and do not require the police to disclose details of the maintenance of machines. This leaves a defendant, when challenging the accuracy of a breath test device, the option of having their blood or urine tested, for which see *Hughes v McConnell* [1986] 1 All ER 268, [1985] 2 WLUK 235, [1985] RTR 244, [1985] CLY 3055, applying *Snelson v Thompson* [1984] 10 WLUK 254, [1985] RTR 220, [1985] CLY 3058.

7 As noted by Mr Justice Newman at [8] in *Dhaliwal v DPP* [2006] EWHC 1149 (Admin), [2006] 3 WLUK 459, also known as *R. (on the application of Dhaliwal) v DPP*; the position is similar in South Australia: *Police v Bleeze* [2012] SASCF 54, although the timing of the taking of the blood sample might be relevant, for which see *Evans v Benson* (1986) 46 SASR 317.

8 [2013] UKSC 32, [2013] 1 WLR 1611, [2013] 3 All ER 365, [2013] NI 133, [2013] 5 WLUK 542, [2013] 2 Cr App R 17, [2014] Crim LR 77, Times, 18 June 2013, [2013] CLY 3289, also known as *Public Prosecution Service of Northern Ireland v Elliott.*
9 1989 No. 1341 (NI 12); article 61(8B) was repealed by the Policing and Crime Act 2009 (s 26), ss 112(1)(2), 116(6), Sch 7 para 128(2), Sch 8 Pt 13.
10 [2013] UKSC 32 at [15].

5.223 Lord Hughes rejected the analogy between the Livescan device and speed guns and breathalysers. The latter device records an action that cannot be subsequently remeasured. Unlike a breath test, the digital data comprising the impressions of the fingerprints were reproducible, and further tests could be carried out. For this reason, it is argued, it is appropriate to expect the device to produce reliable evidence, which in turn infers that such devices have been investigated and approved by the relevant authorities.

5.224 In essence, this is what the defendants tried to achieve in *R v Skegness Magistrates' Court, Ex parte Cardy*.[1] In the absence of the right to obtain discovery as it was then called, solicitors for the accused sought to obtain relevant documents for the purpose of challenging the reliability of the Lion Intoximeter 3000 device by issuing witness summonses. Robert Goff LJ, as he then was, described the witness summonses as a means to obtain the discovery of documents, which was not permitted. Correct as this decision was, the judge commented on several occasions[2] that, in the judgment of the court, the documents that the defendants sought to obtain were not likely to be of material relevance, but failed to give any reason as to why such a conclusion was reached, given that some of the records that were requested included details of the microprocessor program and the standard operating procedures, which were highly relevant. The judge also indicated[3] that the court had been assured (it is not clear by whom) that the Home Office constantly monitored the device, and that if the devices were not reliable, the Secretary of State would not have approved their use.[4] In effect, the court was presuming the 'reliability' of such devices because the Secretary of State had so provided.

1 [1984] 12 WLUK 244, [1985] RTR 49, [1985] Crim LR 237, (1985) 82 LSG 929, [1985] CLY 3046; see also *R v Coventry Magistrates' Court Ex p. Perks* [1984] 7 WLUK 215, [1985] RTR 74, [1985] CLY 3051.
2 [1985] RTR 49 at 57F, 57J–K, 58B–C, 58J and 59A.
3 [1985] RTR 49 at 60J.
4 [1985] RTR 49 at 61F–G.

5.225 Where the defence is not given the opportunity to understand how such a device is constructed, and how new versions of software affect the accuracy of the device, defendants are not, it seems, permitted to obtain any evidence to challenge the 'reliability' or 'accuracy' of the machine. The failure to provide for the proper scrutiny of electronic evidence and the emphasis on relying on the assurances of the owner or user of the digital device means that the 'reliability' or 'accuracy' of these devices cannot be readily challenged in English courts.

Challenging the presumption

5.226 To sum up the thrust of this chapter, when considering the 'reliability' of computers, judges rarely take relevant expert advice or require lawyers appearing before them to cite the technical literature regarding the 'reliability' of computers. They reach their conclusions on this issue in the absence of relevant knowledge.[1] In essence, judges conclude that because a system or device appears to do what is expected of it, notwithstanding the opponent's challenge, they are satisfied that such systems or devices are 'reliable'.[2] In effect, the bench has incorrectly made the presumption into a legal presumption that reallocates the burden of proof on the party opposing the presumption. It is only if the party opposing the presumption succeeds that the relying party is required to discharge the legal burden in relation to the 'reliability' of the machine, and therefore the authenticity or integrity and the trustworthiness of the evidence.[3]

1 For instance, see Bryan H. Choi, 'Crashworthy code' 94 Wash L Rev 39.
2 By way of example, see the conclusion by Walsh J in *Her Majesty the Queen v Dennis James Oland*, 2015 NBQB 245.
3 For a consideration of this point, see Daniel Seng and Stephen Mason, 'Artificial intelligence and evidence' (2021) 33 SAcLJ 241.

5.227 It is possible to challenge the authenticity of electronic evidence in a number of ways, although many reported cases appear to indicate that a lawyer will do so on what might appear to be somewhat slender grounds,[1] and the judge will then have to determine whether to conduct a trial within a trial (if a criminal case) to receive evidence on the point. For instance, in *R. v Coultas (Kiera)*,[2] the accused was convicted of dangerous driving. Evidence from the defendant's mobile telephone indicated that she was probably writing a text message when she collided and killed the cyclist. Counsel for the defendant asserted, without any foundational evidence, that there was some fault in the network coverage that would demonstrate that the defendant was probably not writing a text message at the material time. Rix LJ accepted that if such an issue had been raised at an earlier stage in the proceedings, it would have been a matter for the Crown to cover, but there was nothing about this in the defence statement and the issue was not relevant at appeal.[3] In *The People v Lugashi*,[4] the defence argued that the prosecution had, in effect, to disprove the possibility of error before digital records of credit card fraud were admitted. Ortega J said that the 'proposed test incorrectly presumes computer data to be unreliable',[5] which does not follow. However, the appeal on this point was dismissed on a number of grounds, one of which was that the appellant did not challenge the accuracy of the information recorded in the printout.

1 Although a letter from the defence to the prosecution putting the validity of the information of a machine in issue is not sufficient in New Zealand: *Police v Scott* 30/5/97, HC Rotorua AP89/96 – a decision that must be right and probably would be followed in other jurisdictions.
2 [2008] EWCA Crim 3261, [2008] 9 WLUK 352.
3 [2008] EWCA Crim 3261 at [21].
4 205 Cal.App.3d 632 – Ortega J reviewed relevant case law up to the date of this judgment, 27 October 1988.
5 205 Cal.App.3d 632 at 640.

5.228 The problem for the lawyer making the challenge is that only the party in possession of the digital data has the ability to understand fully whether the computer or computers from which the evidence was extracted can be trusted. The authors of the Law Commission paper *Evidence in Criminal Proceedings: Hearsay and Related Topics* point out that a party might rely on evidence from a computer owned or controlled by a third party that is not a party to the proceedings. However, this should not prevent the party from making the challenge of providing a suitable foundation to justify most challenges. Reed and Angel indicate that there are two broad arguments that can be pursued:

> 1. Where the party adducing the evidence does so to prove the truth of the output, it may be that the other party will challenge the accuracy of the statement by proposing that the computer, or computer-like device, exhibited faults, errors or other forms of failure that might have affected the integrity and trustworthiness of the evidence, and thus its reliability. The reliability of the computer program that generated the record may be questioned. In addition, there might be a fault with the hardware.
>
> 2. The conduct of a third party (this phrase is meant to be construed widely to include any person who does not have the authority to alter how a computer or computer-like device operates, other than the way it is intended to operate) generated the faults, errors or other forms of failure that might have affected the integrity and trustworthiness of the evidence, and thus its reliability. For instance, this can include a claim that the records were altered, manipulated, or damaged between the time they were created and the time they appear in court as evidence, or the identity of the author may be in dispute: the person identified as being responsible for writing a document in the form of a word processing file may dispute they wrote the text, or it might be agreed that an act was carried out and recorded, but at issue could be whether the person alleged to have used their PIN, password or clicked the 'I accept' icon was the person that actually carried out the action.[1]

1 Chris Reed and John Angel, *The Law and Regulation of Information Technology* (6th edn, Oxford University Press 2007), 596; the following analysis closely follows that of Reed and Angel, and the author is indebted to them.

5.229 The first argument was considered in the case of *DPP v McKeown (Sharon), DPP v Jones (Christopher)*[1] over the inaccuracy of a clock in a Lion Intoximeter 3000[2] and whether the inaccuracy of the clock affected the facts relied upon as produced by the device, which was otherwise in working order. The court concluded that if there was a malfunction, it was only relevant if it affected the way in which the computer processed, stored or retrieved the information used to generate the statement tendered in evidence. This must be right. Regarding breathalyser cases, in *Director of Public Prosecutions (DPP) v Manchester and Salford Magistrates' Court*[3] Sir Brian Leveson P gave the judgment, and illustrated what the courts expected from the defence:

> [54] ... there must be a proper evidential basis for concluding that the material sought is reasonably capable of undermining the prosecution or of assisting the defence, or that it represents a reasonable line of enquiry to pursue.
>
> 55. ... It is not enough to say that the defence case is that the amount drunk would not put the defendant over the limit or anywhere near it, and therefore the machine must be unreliable. What the evidence needed to do, in order to provide a basis for such a disclosure order was to address two critical features.
>
> 56. The first requirement is the basis for contending how the device might produce a printout which, on its face, demonstrated that it was operating in proper fashion, but which could generate a very significantly false positive reading, where, on the defence case, the true reading would have been well below the prosecution limit. The second requirement is to identify how the material which was sought could assist to demonstrate how that might have happened. Those are the two issues which arise and which the expert evidence in support of disclosure should address. Unless that evidence is provided, the disclosure is irrelevant.

> 58. ... unless the disclosure application addresses the two questions which we have identified, this extensive disclosure would have to be given in every case in which a defendant alleged that his alcohol consumption had been too low to sustain a positive reading, and in effect proof of reliability would always be required and the presumption of accuracy would be displaced.

1 [1997] 1 WLR 295, [1997] 1 All ER 737, [1997] 2 WLUK 386, [1997] 2 Cr App R 155 (HL), (1997) 161 JP 356, [1997] RTR 162, [1997] Crim LR 522, (1997) 161 JPN 482, (1997) 147 NLJ 289, Times, 21 February 1997, Independent, 7 March 1997, [1997] CLY 1093; Philip Plowden, 'Garbage in, garbage out – the limits of s 69 of the PACE Act 1984' (1997) 61 Journal of Criminal Law 310; for an earlier case where the defence challenged the accuracy of the Intoximeter printout, see *Ashton v DPP*, [1995] 6 WLUK 298, (1996) 160 JP 336, [1998] RTR 45, Times, 14 July 1995, Independent, 10 July 1995, [1995] CLY 4416; 'Ashton v DPP' (1996) 60 Journal of Criminal Law 350.
2 The range of approved devices constantly alters, but the case law relating to older devices remains relevant. For a more detailed discussion, see the most up-to-date edition of *Wilkinson's Road Traffic Offences*, Sweet & Maxwell.
3 [2017] EWHC 3719 (Admin), [2019] WLR 2617, [2017] 7 WLUK 154 also known as *DPP v Manchester and Salford Magistrates' Court*; see also *DPP v Walsall Magistrates' Court* [2019] EWHC 3317 (Admin), [2019] 12 WLUK 61, [2020] RTR 14, [2020] Crim LR 335, [2020] ACD 21, [2020] 5 CL 43; Peter Hungerford-Welch, 'Disclosure: DPP v Walsall Magistrates' Court; DPP v Lincoln Magistrates' Court QBD (DC): Lord Burnett LCJ and May J: 5 December 2019; [2019] EWHC 3317 (Admin)' (2020) 4 Crim LR 335; for a speeding case regarding an approved measurement device, an LTi 20.20 Ultralyte 1000, with a Ranger system to make a video record of the use of the device and its results, see *R (on the application of DPP) v Crown Court at Caernarfon* [2019] EWHC 767 (Admin), [2019] 3 WLUK 830.

5.230 Where the evidential burden has been successfully raised to challenge an aspect of the digital data (whether it be its integrity or reliability),[1] then the persuasive burden will be on the party denying any error to prove the computer (normally the software), computer-like device or computer system is not at fault, thus demonstrating its reliability, integrity and trustworthiness and therefore the authenticity of the evidence tendered. One test is to determine how many important or critical updates of the software were made available and downloaded before the material time, and whether, if such updates were downloaded, they had a detrimental effect on the subsequent operation of the software. Claimants face a considerable problem with ATM cases because so much can go wrong, and it can be difficult to raise sufficient evidence to shift the burden: an outsider or a bank employee might have subverted the system, or a part of the system, or a hardware device forming part of the ATM network (or a cloned card is used) in such a way that money is stolen from the account of an individual.[2] In such circumstances, the electronic record adduced to prove the transaction may be perfectly reliable – what will be at issue is how the thief subverted the network to steal the money. In the case of *Marac Financial Services Ltd v Stewart*,[3] Master Kennedy-Grant observed:

> The use of computers for the recording of transactions on accounts such as the cash management account in this case is sufficiently well established for there to be a presumption of fact that such computers are accurate.[4]

1 As in *Young v Flint* [1986] 4 WLUK 218, [1987] RTR 300, [1988] CLY 3120, where the defence wished to cross-examine the witness respecting modifications made to the device to determine whether the machine ceased to be an approved device.
2 Ken Lindup, 'Technology and banking'; Roger Porkess and Stephen Mason, 'Looking at debit and credit card fraud' (2012) 34(3) Teaching Statistics 87.
3 [1993] 1 NZLR 86.

4 [1993] 1 NZLR 86, [40]. Examples of where banks have not been found to be fully in control of their systems include *Patty v Commonwealth Bank of Australia* [2000] FCA 1072, Industrial Relations Court of Australia VI-2542 of 1996; *United States of America v Bonallo*, 858 F.2d 1427 (9th Cir. 1988); *Kumar v Westpac Banking Corporation* [2001] FJHC 159; *Sefo v R* [2004] TOSC 51; *R v Clarke* [2005] QCA 483.

5.231 Master Kennedy-Grant did not provide any evidence to substantiate this statement.

'Working properly'

5.232 The Law Commission made comments about the presumption in *Evidence in Criminal Proceedings: Hearsay and Related Topics* at 13.14:

> Where a party sought to rely on the presumption, it would not need to lead evidence that the computer was working properly on the occasion in question unless there was evidence that it may not have been – in which case the party would have to prove that it was (beyond reasonable doubt in the case of the prosecution, and on the balance of probabilities in the case of the defence).

5.233 Three significant problems occur with the judicial comments on this topic: first, that there is no definition of what is meant by 'working properly'. A computer might be working 'properly' but not in the way an owner expects, and a third party can instruct a computer to do things that the owner neither authorizes nor is aware of. Second, it will not always be obvious whether the reliability of the evidence generated by a computer is immediately detectable without recourse to establishing whether there is a fault in the software code.

5.234 The third problem is that the presumption asserts something positive. The opposing party is required to raise a doubt in the absence of relevant evidence from the program or programs that are relied upon. In criminal proceedings, this has the unfair effect of undermining the presumption of innocence – subverting any article 6 rights under the European Convention of Human Rights and the Human Rights Act 1998 that the accused might have – and in civil proceedings the party challenging the presumption must convince a judge to order up the delivery of the relevant evidence, including software code, if the evidence is to be tested properly.

5.235 There is no authoritative judicial guidance in relation to the meaning of the words 'reliable', 'in order' or 'working properly' in the context of digital data. It is possible to refer to system reliability, interpreted broadly, as a measure of how a system matches the expectations of the user, but this view is problematic, because the expectations may be mistaken and can change arbitrarily, sometimes based on the user's experience. A more narrow definition is to define reliability in relation to the success with which a system provides the specified service.[1] Professor Randell and colleagues illustrate the conundrum: 'It is of course to be hoped that the reliance placed on a system will be commensurate with its reliability.' Herein lies the rub: 'Notions of reliance, therefore, can be as much bound up with psychological attitudes as with formal decisions regarding the requirement that a system is supposed to satisfy.'[2] The authors continue:

> In fact, the history of the development of computers has seen some fascinating interplay between reliance and reliability. The reliability of early computers caused relatively little reliance to be placed on the validity of their outputs, at

> least until appropriate checks had been performed. Even less reliance was placed on the continuity of their operation – lengthy and frequent periods of downtime were expected and tolerated. As reliability increased so did reliance, sometimes in fact outdistancing reliability so that additional efforts had to be made to reach previously unattained reliability levels. During this time computing systems were growing in size and functional capacity so that, although component reliability was being improved, the very complexity of systems was becoming a possible cause of unreliability, as well as a cause of misunderstandings between users and designers about system specification.[3]

1 Randell and others, 'Reliability issues in computing system design', 123.
2 Randell and others, 'Reliability issues in computing system design', 124.
3 Randell and others, 'Reliability issues in computing system design', 124. That IT projects invariably cost more than estimated, overrun and sometimes fail to be implemented is a notorious fact. A citation (or citations) is not necessary.

5.236 In considering a number of examples of reliability issues, Professor Randell indicates that the design of software is inextricably intertwined with the other factors that are responsible for the failure of computer projects:[1]

> reliability is a commodity whose provision involves costs, either direct, or arising from performance degradation. In theory, the design of any nontrivial computing system should involve careful calculations of trade-offs between reliability, performance, and cost. In practice the data and relationships which would be needed for such calculations in complex systems, are quite often unknown, particularly with regard to unreliability caused by residual design faults.[2]

1 For a more detailed treatment of the causes of the failure of projects, see Glass, *Software Runways*; Planning Report 02-3 The Economic Impacts of Inadequate Infrastructure for Software Testing, prepared by RTI for the National Institute of Standards & Technology (May 2002), https://www.nist.gov/system/files/documents/director/planning/report02-3.pdf; Charette, 'Why software fails', 42.
2 Randell and others, 'Reliability issues in computing system design', 127.

5.237 Linden pointed out that reliability 'means not freedom from errors and faults, but tolerance against them. Software need not be correct to be reliable',[1] and Denning indicated that although 'reliability, in the sense of error tolerance, has long been sought in operating system software, it has always been difficult to achieve'.[2] Responsible practice will often include processes such as the maintenance and review of defect records, and testing or requalification of an upgrade before it is distributed: these are some of the issues about which questions can be legitimately asked by a party in seeking to question the presumption of 'reliability'.

1 Peter J. Denning, 'Fault tolerant operating systems' 8(4) ACM Computing Services 359, 361.
2 Denning, 'Fault tolerant operating systems', 359.

Concluding remarks

5.238 It is proposed that the proponents of a presumption that computers and computer systems 'were in order at the material time' should state what is meant by such a proposition if it is to remain – if they are able to, given the notion that computers are 'reliable' has finally been exposed as erroneous.[1] In *Holt v Auckland City Council*, Richardson J observed the need to provide evidence to justify reliance:

> The results depend on the manner in which it is programmed. And there is no basis on which the Court could take judicial notice of the manner in which this equipment was programmed and maintained. Evidence was necessary to justify reliance on the computer print out.[2]

1 Ladkin and others, 'The Law Commission presumption concerning the dependability of computer evidence'; Ladkin, 'Robustness of software'; Jackson, 'An approach to the judicial evaluation of evidence from computers and computer systems'.
2 [1980] 2 NZLR 124 at 128 (35–40).

5.239 It does not appear that any thought has been given to demonstrating what the proposition means. The Law Commission specifically commented on the contrary argument made by David Ormerod, now Professor Ormerod, to their proposal to repeal s 69. Professor Ormerod 'contended that the common law presumption of regularity may not extend to cases in which computer evidence is central'.[1] This comment by Professor Ormerod must be right.

1 *Evidence in Criminal Proceedings: Hearsay and Related Topics* at 13.16.

5.240 In *Scott v Baker*,[1] Lord Parker CJ and his brother judges rejected the argument of the prosecution that there was a presumption that where an alcohol measuring device was used by the police, it therefore followed that the device was approved by the Secretary of State. The Law Commission agreed that this presumption must have been applicable to the Intoximeter cases, and yet noted that this had not been raised in previous cases. They then went on, at 13.17, to state (footnote omitted):

> It should also be noted that *Dillon* was concerned not with the presumption regarding machines but with the presumption of the regularity of official action. This latter presumption was the analogy on which the presumption for machines was originally based; but it is not a particularly close analogy, and the two presumptions are now clearly distinct.

1 [1969] 1 QB 659, [1968] 3 WLR 796, [1968] 2 All ER 993, [1968] 5 WLUK 42, (1968) 52 Cr App R 566, (1968) 132 JP 422, (1968) 112 SJ 425, [1968] CLY 3428; 'Divisional court cases breath tests: approval of Device *Scott v. Baker*' (1958) 32 The Journal of Criminal Law 151.

5.241 Professor Ormerod referred to *Dillon*[1] for the point that the prosecution is not entitled to rely on a presumption to establish facts central to an offence, and it is essential for the prosecution to prove, on the facts of *Dillon*, the lawfulness of the prisoner's detention by affirmative evidence.[2] In his article, Professor Ormerod argued that where evidence in digital form is fundamental, such as in bank frauds, it will be necessary to require specific proof of reliability. This proposition must be correct: the presumption on its own cannot bear the weight of proof beyond reasonable doubt.

1 *Dillon v R* [1982] AC 484, [1982] 2 WLR 538, [1982] 1 All ER 1017, [1982] 1 WLUK 749, (1982) 74 Cr App R 274, [1982] Crim LR 438, (1982) 126 SJ 117, [1982] CLY 547.
2 David Ormerod, 'Proposals for the admissibility of computer evidence' (1995) 6(4) Computers and Law 24.

5.242 In the absence of evidence that such a presumption can possibly apply to such complex objects as computers and computer systems, it is suggested that any presumption that a computer or computer-like machine is working properly be guided by considerations as to how 'correct operation', 'quality', 'reliability' and 'integrity' can be incorporated within the evaluation of the presumption.[1] It cannot be right to infer 'reliability' from reliance.

1 The *Model Law on Electronic Evidence* (Commonwealth Secretariat 2017) https://thecommonwealth.org/sites/default/files/key_reform_pdfs/P15370_7_ROL_Model_Bill_Electronic_Evidence_0.pdf also refers to 'reliability' at 2: 'The Group agreed that system reliability is the most sensible measurement', and article 7 and 7(a) provides for the presumption that the integrity of the electronic records system is working properly – as is normal with such pronouncements, no evidence was put forward to substantiate this assertion.

5.243 As it stands, the presumption places an evidential burden (in reality, as noted above, it is a legal burden) on the party opposing the presumption, as described by Tipping J: 'The accused must be able to point to a sufficient evidential foundation for the suggestion that the device was unreliable in the relevant sense, before being entitled to have the point considered by the jury. If there is such a foundation, the Crown must establish reliability beyond reasonable doubt'[1] and careful consideration ought to be given to the hurdle a party must overcome in order to meet the evidential burden. In this respect, the defence was correct to challenge the evidence of the CD which contained the intercepted recordings in *R. v Saward (Steven Kevin), R. v Bower (Steven Kevin), R. v Harrison (Keith)*,[2] because had the prosecution more thoroughly ensured the continuity of the evidence, it is possible the defence may not have had a legitimate objection. In *Scott v Otago Regional Council*, Heath J indicated that cross-examination of relevant points can be sufficient to put the point in issue, which must be right (although the cross-examination might more usefully have also considered questioning how many software updates were provided by the manufacturer of the product that corrected faults):

> No evidence was offered about the reliability of the computer and software used to establish that they were 'of a kind that ordinarily [do] what a party asserts [them] to have done'.[3] Mr Reeves offered no evidence that he had used the programme successfully in the past and had found it to be working normally. Nor was there any independent evidence to explain how the computer programme worked and what it could reliably be expected to do. In a prosecution such as this, Mr Andersen's cross-examination of Mr Reeves was sufficient to put the point in issue.[4]

1 *R v Livingstone* [2001] 1 NZLR 167 at [13].
2 [2005] EWCA Crim 3183, [2005] 11 WLUK 351.
3 Where the basic fact of the presumption is not satisfied, the presumption fails.
4 CRI 2008-412-17-20, High Court Dunedin, 3 November 2008, [2008] Your Environment 392; 31 TCL 48/8 at [33].

5.244 The Law Commission indirectly discussed 'reliability' at para 13.18, *Evidence in Criminal Proceedings: Hearsay and Related Topics*, but only by referring to the possibility of a 'malfunction'. The entire discussion seems to be predicated upon machines used to test the amount of alcohol a person has consumed, rather than the very much broader range of computers and computer-like devices that are in common use:

> Even where the presumption applies, it ceases to have any effect once evidence of malfunction has been adduced. The question is, what sort of evidence must the defence adduce, and how realistic is it to suppose that the defence will be able to adduce it without any knowledge of the working of the machine? On the one hand the concept of the evidential burden is a flexible one: a party cannot be required

> to produce more by way of evidence than one in his or her position could be expected to produce. It could therefore take very little for the presumption to be rebutted, if the party against whom the evidence was adduced could not be expected to produce more.

5.245 The comments by Lord Hoffmann in *DPP v McKeown (Sharon), DPP v Jones (Christopher)*,[1] in which he offered the opinion that 'It is notorious that one needs no expertise in electronics to be able to know whether a computer is working properly',[2] can be considered to be the extreme view that will not be shared by any computer experts – or indeed lay people. His comment is not merely dangerous but also vacuous. It is like saying that you do not need to know the chemistry of ink to know whether writing works. This is not relevant, because you can still write nonsense, regardless of the chemical properties of the ink. It is noticeable that paragraph 432 of the Explanatory Notes to the Criminal Justice Act 2003 indicated that, in respect of testimony under s 129(1):

> This section provides where a statement generated by a machine is based on information implanted into the machine by a human, the output of the device will only be admissible where it is proved that the information was accurate.

1 [1997] 1 WLR 295, [1997] 1 All ER 737, [1997] 2 WLUK 386, [1997] 2 Cr App R 155 (HL), (1997) 161 JP 356, [1997] RTR 162, [1997] Crim LR 522, (1997) 161 JPN 482, (1997) 147 NLJ 289, Times, 21 February 1997, Independent, 7 March 1997, [1997] CLY 1093.
2 [1997] 1 All ER 737 at 743b.

5.246 Here the emphasis is on the accuracy of the information as an input to the computer, not whether the computer was working consistently, or to put it another way, whether the system was not working in accordance with an expectation, or the ability of the computer to return generally verifiably correct results. The problem is that Lord Hoffmann considered the issue from the opposite perspective: an assumption that the computer is working properly because of what the user can see, not what an unknown third party does not want them to see, or attempts to prevent anyone from seeing and understanding what else the computer is doing without the knowledge of the owner or user.

5.247 As a matter of admissibility, it is necessary that proof that a computer, computer-like device or network (comprising many computers and modes of communication) was 'in order' at the material time – indeed, in England and Wales, s 129(2) of the Criminal Justice Act 2003 preserves the common law position:

> 129 Representations other than by a person
>
> (1) Where a representation of any fact—
>
> > (a) is made otherwise than by a person, but
> >
> > (b) depends for its accuracy on information supplied (directly or indirectly) by a person, the representation is not admissible in criminal proceedings as evidence of the fact unless it is proved that the information was accurate.
>
> (2) Subsection (1) does not affect the operation of the presumption that a mechanical device has been properly set or calibrated.[1]

1 Law Commission, Evidence in Criminal Proceedings: Hearsay and Related Topics (Law Com no 245) (19 June 1997), 7.50.

5.248 That software is notorious for being the subject of defects leads to a somewhat uneasy state of affairs. It cannot be right to presume that a machine (in particular a computer, computer-like device or network) was 'in order' (whatever that means) or 'reliable' at the material time. The proponents of the presumption have not provided any evidence to demonstrate the accuracy of this assertion. Evidence in digital form is not immune from being affected by the faults in software written by human beings. The use of the words 'operating properly' illustrates the misconceptions described in this chapter.

5.249 The lack of any evidence to support the proposition is especially relevant in the light of the underlying rationale of evidence. In *A Philosophy of Evidence Law: Justice in the Search for Truth*,[1] Professor Hock Lai Ho demonstrates that the finder of facts acts as a moral agent, and central to this is that the findings by a court must be justifiable, and meet the demands of rationality and ethics.[2] When read in the light of the unique characteristics of evidence in digital form, the rationale of the evidential process takes on an even more relevant role. This is because the factors and subsequent analysis have an added poignancy when taking into account the complexity of electronic evidence: the potential volumes of evidence, the difficulty of finding evidence, persuading the judge to order additional searches or to order the disclosure of relevant digital data, the ease with which electronic evidence can be destroyed, the costs of such exercises, the lawyer's lack of knowledge when dealing with this form of evidence and the presumption that computers are 'reliable' or 'working properly'. In this respect, the inadequacy of the procedure leading to trial brought about by an incomplete understanding and application of the presumption may cause unfairness.

1 Oxford University Press 2008.
2 Note the article by Louis Kaplow, 'Burden of proof' (2012) 121 Yale LJ 738, in which the author considers how robust the evidence ought to be in order to assign liability when the objective is to maximize social welfare.

5.250 The question is whether the presumption is to remain in its misunderstood form as a legal presumption. The failure of its proponents to provide evidence that the presumption has any basis in fact is a strong indication that it does not merit being in place, and any argument in favour of the proposition ought to clearly indicate why banking systems, manufacturers of motor vehicles, aircraft and medical devices – to name but a few – should be rewarded by such a presumption. In addition, the innumerable examples of the failure of software outlined in this chapter, and other failures that are constantly brought to our attention by the media, as well as the failures we witness ourselves in our everyday lives, act to challenge why software code should benefit from such a presumption. This is particularly so when evidence in digital form is more likely to bc open to challenge, as illustrated above.

5.251 In addition, considering that the presumption is only an evidential presumption, the bar for raising doubts about the reliability or otherwise of a computer, computer-like device or network must not be placed too high.[1] For instance, in *DPP v Wood, DPP v McGillicuddy* Ouseley J indicated (in respect of the Intoximeter EC/IR):

> The nature and degree of an alleged unreliability has to be such that it might be able to throw doubt on the excess in the reading to such an extent that the level of alcohol in the breath might have been below the level at which a prosecution would have been instituted.[2]

1 Sergey Bratus, Ashlyn Lembree and Anna Shubina, 'Software on the witness stand: what should it take for us to trust it?' in Alessandro Acquisti, Sean Smith and Ahmad-Reza Sadeghi (eds) *Trust and Trustworthy Computing: Proceedings of the Third International Conference*, TRUST 2010, Berlin, Germany, 21–23 June 2010 (Springer-Verlag 2010), 396–416.
2 [2006] EWHC 32 (Admin) at [36].

5.252 However, as indicated by Eric Van Buskirk and Vincent T. Liu:

> The Presumption of Reliability is difficult to rebut. Unless specific evidence is offered to show that the particular code at issue has demonstrable defects that are directly relevant to the evidence being offered up for admission, most courts will faithfully maintain the Presumption of Reliability. But because most code is closed source and heavily guarded, a party cannot audit it to review its quality. At the same time, however, source code audits are perhaps the best single way to discover defects.
>
> This difficulty gives rise to an important question: if a party cannot gain access to source code without evidence of a defect, but cannot get evidence of a defect without access to the source code, how is a party to rebut the Presumption? Rather than wrestle with, or even acknowledge, this conundrum, most courts simply presume that all code is reliable without sufficient analysis. (Footnotes omitted.) [1]

1 Van Buskirk and Liu, 'Digital evidence: challenging the presumption of reliability', 20.

5.253 This view is illustrated in the case of *State of Florida v Bastos*,[1] an appeal before the District Court of Appeal of Florida, Third District, where Cope J held that source code for an Intoxilyzer 5000 breath test machine used in the defendants' cases was not 'material' within the meaning of the provisions of the uniform law to secure the attendance of witnesses from within or outside a state in criminal proceedings. The judge went on to say:

> However, we cannot accept the proposition that simply because a piece of testing equipment is used in a criminal case, it follows that the source code for its computer must be turned over. There would need to be a particularized showing demonstrating that observed discrepancies in the operation of the machine necessitate access to the source code. We are unable to see that any such evidence was brought forth in the evidentiary hearing below.[2]

1 985 So.2d 37 (Fla.App. 3 Dist. 2008). In *State of North Carolina v Marino*, 747 S.E.2d 633 (N.C.App. 2013), the court refused to accept that the decisions of the Supreme Court in *Crawford v Washington*, 541 U.S. 36, 51, 124 S.Ct. 1354, 158 L.Ed.2d 177, 192 (2004), nor that the decision in *Melendez-Diaz v Massachusetts*, 557 U.S. 305, 310–11, 129 S.Ct. 2527, 174 L.Ed.2d 314, 321–22 (2009) stood for the proposition that a defendant had a right under the Sixth Amendment to examine the Intoximeter source code. But see *In re Commissioner of Public Safety v Underdahl*, 735 N.W.2d 706 (Minn. 2007) and *State of Minnesota v Underdahl*, 767 N.W.2d 677 (Minn. 2009), where it was held that an order that the Commissioner of Public Safety provide Mr Underdahl with an operational Intoxilyzer 5000EN instrument and the complete computer source code for the operation of the device was affirmed partly on the basis that the State had possession or control of computer source code for the purposes of discovery.
2 985 So.2d 37 (Fla.App. 3 Dist. 2008) at 43.

5.254 The party contesting the presumption will rarely be in a position to offer significant evidence to substantiate any challenge[1] because the party facing the challenge will generally (but not always) be in full control of the computer or computer systems that are the subject of the challenge.[2] Offering an explanation that is not reinforced with any evidence will not be sufficient, for which see *Burcham v Expedia, Inc.*,[3] and a theory that is 'incredible' should not require the court to consider the matter in any detail.[4] The lack of evidence for raising doubts about the presumption is not helpful, for which see *Public Prosecution Service v McGowan*.[5] From the perspective of criminal procedure, it must be right that the defence should give the prosecution advance notice that they intend to challenge the device, as suggested in *R. v Crown Prosecution Service Ex p. Spurrier*[6] by Newman J:

> As a matter of general rule, I can see no reason why the defence should not be taken to be required, of course on pain of paying the costs of an adjournment if that proves to be necessary, to give some notice in advance of the trial of the grounds upon which a claim that the device was defective will be advanced.[7]

1 For an interesting discussion that includes the burden in the context of authentication, see Rudolph J. Peritz, 'Computer data and reliability: a call for authentication of business records under the federal rules of evidence', 965–1002.
2 It is becoming increasingly common for organizations and individuals to rely on third parties to provide computing facilities through what is termed 'cloud computing' by the technical community; for a detailed explanation, see Stephen Mason and Esther George, 'Digital evidence and "cloud" computing' (2011) 27(5) Computer Law & Security Review 524.
3 2009 WL 586513.
4 For which see *Novak d/b/a PetsWarehouse.com v Tucows, Inc.*, 73 Fed. R. Evid. Serv. 331, 2007 WL 922306 affirmed *Novak v Tucows, Inc.*, 330 Fed.Appx. 204, 2009 WL 1262947.
5 [2008] NICA 13, [2009] NI 1.
6 [1999] 7 WLUK 431, (2000) 164 JP 369, [2000] RTR 60, Times, 12 August 1999, [1999] CLY 883, also known as *DPP v Spurrier*.
7 [2000] RTR 60, 68 item (6).

5.255 The evidence of relevant audits is also of significance, such as where John Rusnak forged trades in a Word document and an audit failed to indicate the forgery;[1] and where Nick Leeson forged data that was not noticed by audits.[2] The importance of audits was glaringly revealed in *A and others (Human Fertilisation and Embryology Act 2008)*.[3] Following Cobb J's judgment in *E (Assisted Reproduction: Parent), Re*,[4] the HFEA (Human Fertilisation and Embryology Authority) required all 109 licensed clinics to carry out an audit of their records. It transpired that 51 clinics (46 per cent) had discovered 'anomalies' in their records, including missing forms, forms completed or dated after treatment had begun, incorrectly completed, unsigned and not fully completed forms, forms with missing pages, and even forms completed by wrong persons.[5] Sir James Munby, President of the Family Division, had this to say:

> The picture thus revealed ... is alarming and shocking. This is, for very good reason, a medical sector which is subject to detailed statutory regulation and the oversight of a statutory regulator – the HFEA. The lamentable shortcomings in one clinic identified by Cobb J, which now have to be considered in the light of the deeply troubling picture revealed by the HFEA audit and by the facts of the cases before me, are, or should be, matters of great public concern. The picture revealed is one of what I do not shrink from describing as widespread incompetence across the sector on a scale which must raise questions as to the adequacy if not of the HFEA's regulation then of the extent of its regulatory powers.[6]

1 Siobhán Creaton and Conor O'Clery, *Panic at the Bank: How John Rusnak Lost AIB $691,000,000* (Gill & Macmillan 2002), 96–97.
2 Nick Leeson with Edward Whitley, *Rogue Trader* (Sphere 2013), 117, 120–121, 239; see also *Report of the Board of Banking Supervision Inquiry into the Circumstances of the Collapse of Barings*

(ordered by The House of Commons to be printed 18 July 1995) (HMSO 1995), chapters 9 and 10 and conclusions 13.4(b) and (c) at 232.
3 [2015] EWHC 2602 (Fam), [2016] 1 WLR 1325, [2016] 1 All ER 273, [2015] 9 WLUK 234, [2017] 1 FLR 366, [2015] 3 FCR 555, (2015) 146 BMLR 123, [2015] Fam Law 1333, [2016] CLY 928.
4 [2013] EWHC 1418 (Fam), [2013] 5 WLUK 682, [2013] 2 FLR 1357, [2013] 3 FCR 532, [2013] Fam Law 962, (2013) NLJ 163(7563) 19, [2014] CLY 1408, also known as *AB v CD*.
5 *A and others (Human Fertilisation And Embryology Act 2008)* [2015] EWHC 2602 (Fam), Sir James Munby P at [7].
6 [2015] EWHC 2602 (Fam) at [8].

5.256 In *Bates v Post Office Ltd (No 6: Horizon Issues) Rev 1*,[1] evidence was finally adduced regarding, and witnesses cross-examined upon, a Management Letter dated 27 March 2011 by Ernst & Young, providing, at [393] the following revealing information about the Horizon system:

> The main area we would encourage management focus on in the current year is improving the IT governance and control environment. Within the IT environment our audit work has again identified weaknesses mainly relating to the control environment operated by POL's third party IT suppliers. Our key recommendations can be summarised into the following four areas:
>
> Improve governance of outsourcing application management
>
> Improve segregation of duties within the manage change process
>
> Strengthen the change management process
>
> Strengthen the review of privileged access.

1 [2019] EWHC 3408 (QB), [2019] 12 WLUK 208.

5.257 Fraser J emphasized the last point: privileged access. It had been alleged for years that employees of Fujitsu had privileged access to the entire system, and could log into any computer connected to the Horizon system. The judge described the nature of the privileged access at [389]:[1]

> This entry was from Andy Beardmore, Senior Software and Solution Design Architect Application Services. The experts are agreed that the APPSUP role would, effectively, permit anyone who had that permission to do almost anything on Horizon. It was available to 3rd line support at SSC, the level at which Mr Roll was employed by Fujitsu. This PEAK further substantiates the evidence of Mr Roll and is consistent with it. APPSUP was described by Mr Parker as 'the more technically correct name for a type of privileged access to the BRDB'. It is a very powerful permission.

1 See also [423] in the Technical Appendix to the judgment.

5.258 Employees and officers from the Post Office repeatedly denied this was possible. Although Mr Richard Roll, previously employed by Fujitsu, gave evidence of the fact the employees of Fujitsu had such privileged access, the final disclosure of the audit by Ernst & Young acted to corroborate his evidence.

5.259 The banking cases also illustrate the nature of the problem,[1] as do the unintended acceleration cases. Crucially, in the US *Bookout* case, which was one of the high-profile unintended acceleration cases, Selna J ordered the disclosure of the software code.[2] The explanation for this might be because of two significant, and rather fortuitous, factors. When Jean Bookout was driving her 2005 Toyota Camry, it suddenly accelerated. She took action by pulling the parking brake. By so doing, the right rear tyre left a 100-foot skid mark, and the left tyre left a 50-foot skid mark. The vehicle continued to speed down a ramp, across the road, and came to rest with its nose in an embankment, injuring her and killing her passenger and best friend Barbara Schwarz. Before she died, Schwarz called her husband and said 'Jean couldn't get her car stopped. The car ran away with us. There's something wrong with the car.'[3] Both the skid marks and the telephone call by Barbara Schwarz undermined any suggestion that the acceleration was due to a physical problem in the cabin of the vehicle.

1 Gerwin Hayback, 'Civil law liability for unauthorized withdrawals at ATMs in Germany' (2009) 6 Digital Evidence and Electronic Signature Law Review 57; Mason, 'Debit cards, ATMs and negligence of the bank and customer', 163; Nuth, 'Unauthorized use of bank cards with or without the PIN; Mason, 'Electronic banking and how courts approach the evidence', 144.
2 United States of America, Central District of California, Case Protective Order *In re: Toyota Motor Corp. Unintended Acceleration Marketing, Sales Practices and Products Liability Litigation*, Case Number: 8:10ML2151 JVS (FMOx) (2018) 15 Digital Evidence and Electronic Signature Law Review 98.
3 Antony Anderson, 'Sudden acceleration, spaghetti software and trauma at the kitchen sink' (2014) Expert Witness Journal (no pagination), http://blog.copernicustechnology.com/wp-content/uploads/2014/05/Uncommanded-Acceleration-article.pdf; 'Sudden unintended acceleration redux: the unresolved issue' (2009) 6(3) The Safety Record, http://www.safetyresearch.net/blog/articles/sudden-unintended-acceleration; given that the *Bookout* case demonstrated the claims of the plaintiff, the decision of Carr J to exclude a number of important expert witnesses, while permitting the expert witness for Ford (an employee) to give evidence, is to be questioned in *Buck v Ford Motor Company*, 810 F.Supp.2d 815 (N.D.Ohio 2011).

5.260 As Professor Peritz pointed out in 1986:

> Computers provide an illusory basis for shortcircuiting traditional legal processes because they cannot be isolated from the people that build and run them. They simply cannot guarantee error-free processing.[1]

1 Peritz, 'Computer data and reliability', 1000; Lynda Crowley-Smith made the same point in 'The *Evidence Act* 1995 (Cth): should computer data be presumed accurate?' (1996) 22(1) Monash University Law Review 166.

5.261 This is why lawyers and members of the judiciary need to understand two significant issues about the world in which we live now, and our reliance on software code. First, the evidential presumption that software code is 'reliable' must be reconsidered – or more carefully understood. The rationale used by judges that software code is part of a 'notorious' class of machines, or that the operation of computers and other such devices are 'common knowledge', must be reversed. In his speech *Science and Law: Contrasts and Cooperation* before the Royal Society in London on 25 November 2015,[1] Lord Neuberger said that 'scientists and lawyers each search for and assess hard facts from which they can establish the truth',[2] yet lawyers and judges rely on 'common sense' when many 'well-established principles are positively contrary to common sense'.[3] Justifications around loose notions of 'notorious' or 'common knowledge' in respect of software programs is irrational. Justice should not be based on concepts with no basis in logic or science. It is necessary for lawyers and judges to take account of this element of irrationality that has been the law for far too long. To resolve the problem expeditiously, an appellate court could adjust the presumption by restricting it to mechanical instruments and instruments for which statutory presumptions exist. Thereafter, if it is treated as an evidential presumption instead of a legal presumption, it will be for the proponent to provide for the reliability (if the term 'reliability' is to be used) of the software. Evidence of reliability will not always be required. No doubt suitable procedural mechanisms can be put in place to allow a party to require relevant evidence of reliability where it is challenged.

1 https://www.supremecourt.uk/docs/speech-151124.pdf.
2 Lord Neuberger, *Science and Law: Contrasts and Cooperation*, [9].
3 Lord Neuberger, *Science and Law: Contrasts and Cooperation*, [13].

5.262 Second, judges should understand the necessity of requiring the disclosure of software code and relevant audits of systems, and determine whether security standards, if applied, have been applied properly.[1] This problem has been acknowledged by the European Court of Justice:

> In the context of disclosure of evidence, complex issues may arise concerning the disclosure of electronic data, which may constitute a certain mass of information in [the] hands of the prosecution. In such a case, an important safeguard in the sifting process is to ensure that the defence is provided with an opportunity to be involved in the laying-down of the criteria for determining what might be relevant for disclosure.[2]

1 Failures in banking systems used by millions of customers are demonstrated in Murdoch and others, 'How certification systems fail'.
2 *Guide on Article 6 of the European Convention on Human Rights, Right to a Fair Trial (Criminal Limb)* (31 August 2020), para 166.

5.263 A recent case in the State of New Jersey in the US illustrates that judges might have concluded that disclosure is essential.[1] in the case of *State of New Jersey v Pickett*,[2] the Superior Court of New Jersey, Appellate Division decided to permit the disclosure of the software code from a program called TrueAlle, described by Fasciale, PJAD for the court 'as software designed to address intricate interpretational challenges of testing low levels or complex mixtures of DNA'. The court agreed the criteria a judge should consider when deciding to permit disclosure or discovery of software code, at [284]:

> We hold that if the State chooses to utilize an expert who relies on novel probabilistic genotyping software to render DNA testimony, then defendant is entitled to access, under an appropriate protective order, to the software's source code and supporting software development and related documentation—including that pertaining to testing, design, bug reporting, change logs, and program requirements—to challenge the reliability of the software and science underlying that expert's testimony at a Frye hearing, provided defendant first satisfies the burden of demonstrating a particularized need for such discovery. To analyze whether that burden has been met, a trial judge should consider: (1) whether there is a rational basis for ordering a party to attempt to produce the information sought, including the extent to which proffered expert testimony supports the claim for disclosure; (2) the specificity of the information sought; (3) the available means of safeguarding the company's intellectual property, such as issuance of a protective order; and (4) any other relevant factors unique to the facts of the case. Defendant demonstrated particularized need and satisfied his burden.

1 See also *People v Williams*, 35 N.Y.3d 24 (2020), 147 N.E.3d 1131, 124 N.Y.S.3d 593, 2020 N.Y. Slip Op. 02123 (trial court abused its discretion in permitting the admission of low copy number DNS evidence without a Frye hearing (*Frye v United States*, 293 F. 1013 (D.C. Cir. 1923)).
2 466 N.J.Super. 270, 246 A.3d 279, followed in *United States v Ellis*, Slip Copy, 2021 WL 1600711.

5.264 A practical two-phase approach has been proposed:

Stage 1

(i) As a matter of procedure, disclosure should be given of:

(a) Known bugs in the system that have been reported, and the actions taken in response. This should include the disclosure of known error logs,[1] release notices,[2] change logs[3] and similar documents.

(b) The party's information security standards and processes. This should extend to cover logical access controls[4] (including emergency access), security vulnerability notifications[5] and security patches.[6]

(c) Relevant audits of systems and the management of the installation to provide assurance that suitable standards and processes have been implemented and complied with.

(d) Evidence of reliably managed records of error reports and system changes, including evidence to demonstrate that basic precautions, such as digital signatures, have been implemented to detect and limit accidental or deliberate corruption.

(ii) The disclosure set out above should be provided by a person authorised to do so by the party subject to the disclosure obligation. The party with the disclosure obligation should be required to undertake a reasonable and proportionate search for the documents and records in question. Disclosure should be supported by evidence confirming that a reasonable and proportionate search has been undertaken by a person with appropriate authority and knowledge, and that:

(a) The records disclosed are believed to be the records of the relevant standards, processes and audits, and of the known defects, security vulnerabilities, fixes and changes in the system.

(b) The party seeking to rely upon the evidence in question has taken reasonable steps to satisfy itself that access to the system is controlled in such a way that unauthorised and undetected amendment of system data, in a way that might affect the evidence in question, is prevented.[7]

(iii) The disclosure exercise should, where possible, be collaborative and co-operative between the parties, rather than adversarial. In particular:

(a) The parties should, if possible, seek to agree that the disclosed data is in a form that takes into account the ability of the party to whom the disclosure is made should be able to conveniently read/use it.

(b) It should not be required that the party challenging the reliability of the data relied upon should identify the particular issue to which the disclosure required to be given is alleged to go.

(iv) The documents under Stage 1 will be routinely kept and easily available for a bespoke system professionally developed and managed. The absence of such records will ordinarily suggest poor quality software/system management. For commercial-off-the-shelf software it should be enough to provide evidence of the particular version and release of the software and to disclose release documentation (usually publicly available from the supplier) for the relevant version and subsequent releases. (The latter will reveal errors in the version in question later found and corrected.) In either case, proportionate Stage 1 disclosure should not be onerous, and for a professionally managed system should be a straightforward exercise.

Stage 2

(i) If the limited disclosure under Stage 1 reveals any one or more of the following:

(a) a level of recorded defects or failures sufficiently high to provide grounds for questioning the reliability of the computer system from which the material is derived;

(b) that there exist records of specific defects or failures that provide grounds for questioning the evidence sought to be relied upon;

(c) that a person seeking to rely upon the evidence in question is not able to demonstrate that it has adequate control over the systems or data.

then the party seeking to rely upon the evidence produced by the computer system in question should be required to prove that none of the facts or matters identified under (a)–(c) above might affect the reliability of the material sought to be relied upon.

(ii) It is known that all large computer systems contain bugs, and that some of these may be 'small' bugs that reveal themselves rarely. This is true even for those systems that have been shown convincingly to be very reliable. It follows that, even in the case of such a reliable system, the court should have regard to the possibility that an apparent failure may be the consequence of a bug manifesting itself.[8] *Evidence of reliability is not evidence of the absence of software bugs.* The court should consider what degree of doubt remains in the context of all the other available evidence.[9]

1 Records of the errors that have been reported in a system and what action was taken. This should include evidence of testing after each system change to ensure that the same error has not been reintroduced.

2 Documentation of the changes that have been made in each new release of the software, including identifying all the known errors that have been corrected.

3 Records of every change that has been made to the software (containing information about what was changed, what was affected and what the results were, together with any resulting problems), including by whom, when and why it was done.

4 Organizational processes and software controls that ensure data and systems can be read, changed, created and deleted only by people who have been properly authorized and identified.

5 Notifications of a vulnerability in a software product that could allow unauthorized access to the system to compromise the integrity, availability or confidentiality of an organization's systems or data.

6 Software changes to correct security vulnerabilities, often made to software systems between releases of the software because an error has been detected that is too important to wait for a new system release to correct it.

7 The issue of remote access by a third party to Horizon branch terminals was a major issue in the Post Office *Bates* litigation. The fact that such access was possible was only conceded by the Post Office in January 2019. It had in fact been practised from early after the introduction of the Horizon system in 1999. Fraser J considered the issue to be of central importance, for which see *Bates v The Post Office Ltd (No 6: Horizon Issues) Rev 1* [2019] EWHC 3408 (QB) at [990] and [991] and *Hamilton v Post Office Ltd* [2021] EWCA Crim 577 at [49]. Until 2010 no records were kept by Fujitsu of such actions.

8 For which see Ladkin and others, 'The Law Commission presumption concerning the dependability of computer evidence'; Jackson, 'An approach to the judicial evaluation of evidence from computers and computer systems'.

9 Paul Marshall, James Christie, Peter Bernard Ladkin, Bev Littlewood, Stephen Mason, Martin Newby, Dr Jonathan Rogers, Harold Thimbleby and Martyn Thomas CBE, 'Recommendations for the probity of computer evidence', 24–25; see also *The Attorney General's Guidelines on Disclosure for Investigators, Prosecutors and Defence Practitioners* (2020) https://www.gov.uk/government/publications/attorney-generals-guidelines-on-disclosure-2020 (in force 31 December 2020) is a step in the right direction in respect of electronic material, for which see paras 54–57, and in which the overriding obligation to ensure a fair trial is stressed (para 55) .

5.265 The purpose of these recommendations is to ensure that the judicial process more fully comprehends the evidential reality of software code and 'digital systems', and helps to preserve fairness in legal proceedings.[1]

1 Colin Tapper, 'Judicial attitudes, aptitudes and abilities in the field of high technology' (1989) 15(3) and (4) Monash University Law Review 219, 228, where Professor Tapper considers the members of the House of Lords and Court of Appeal were unduly restrictive regarding the transient storage of a false password in *R v Gold (Stephen William), R v Schifreen (Robert Jonathan)* [1988] AC 1063, [1988] 2 WLR 984, [1988] 2 All ER 186, [1988] 4 WLUK 121, (1988) 87 Cr App R 257, (1988) 152 JP 445, [1988] Crim LR 437, (1988) 152 JPN 478, (1988) 85(19) LSG 38, (1988) 138 NLJ Rep 117, (1988) 132 SJ 624, [1988] CLY 787.

6

Authenticating electronic evidence

Luciana Duranti and Allison Stanfield

Authenticity and authentication

6.1 Authenticity is the quality of something that is what it purports to be. When referring to documentary materials, most definitions of authenticity refer to the fact that an entity, to be authentic, must have maintained not only its identity but also its integrity: that is, it must not have been corrupted or tampered with during the time between its creation and its use as a source of information or its submission as evidence.[1] While this concept, developed in an analogue world, is easily transferable to digital entities, the verification and consequent declaration of authenticity – that is, the authentication of digital entities – has proven to be problematic. This is one of the reasons why an increasing number of standards and scholarly papers discuss ways of ensuring the continuing and verifiable authenticity of digital materials.[2] For decades, courts and scholars have wrestled with the concept of authentication of digital evidence across various jurisdictions, and several notable judges have developed particular skills in understanding and applying the rules of evidence to digital evidence.

1 Heather MacNeil, 'Providing grounds for trust II: the findings of the Authenticity Task Force of InterPARES' (2002 January) 54 Archivaria 24.

2 Heather MacNeil, *Trusting Records: Legal, Historical and Diplomatic Perspectives* (Kluwer Academic Publishers 2000), xi; Livia Iacovino, *Recordkeeping, Ethics and Law* (Springer 2006), 41, for further comments about 'trustworthiness'. The standard of the Canadian Government Standards Board CGSB 74.32-2017, *Electronic Records as Documentary Evidence*, states that authenticity is the 'quality of an entity that it is what it purports to be and that is free from tampering or corruption', thereby adding the idea of integrity to that of identity. The standard of the Association of Records Managers and Administrators, BSR/ARMA 19-2019, *Policy Design for Managing Electronic Messages*, defines record authenticity as 'The sum of the qualities of a record that establish the origin, reliability, trustworthiness, and correctness of its content'. The InterPARES research project terminology database, on the basis of a shared understanding of researchers from more than forty countries and six continents, defines authenticity as 'The trustworthiness of a record as a record; i.e., the quality of a record that is what it purports to be and that is free from tampering or corruption', and authentication as a 'declaration of a record's authenticity at a specific point in time by a juridical person entrusted with the authority to make such a declaration (e.g., public officer, notary, certification authority)' Retrieved from https://interparestrust.org/terminology/term/authenticity and https://interparestrust.org/terminology/term/authentication.

6.2 Historically, in the classical world authenticity was linked to custody, as opposed to the characteristics of the object.[1] For example, in ancient Rome the *Tabularium*, guarded by the *quaestores*, had the custody of the records produced by the organs of the state to ensure the messages carried within those records remained intact, and users had access only to copies made by public scribes. The reason for such measures was that those records, mostly written on wax tablets, were as fragile as records in digital

Luciana Duranti and Allison Stanfield, 'Authenticating electronic evidence', in Stephen Mason and Daniel Seng (eds.), *Electronic Evidence and Electronic Signatures* (5th edn, University of London 2021) 236–278.

form, and as easy to change or delete. Thus, trusting the records involved trusting their custodians.[2]

1 There were exceptions for some public records, such as records exhibited for public consumption in public places, including laws which were written on bronze, and rolls of arms which were written on marble.
2 Luciana Duranti, 'Archives as a place' (1996) 24(2) Archives & Manuscripts 242.

6.3 In medieval times, with the loss of stable, trustworthy public bodies and the increasing use of media more durable than wax – wood or papyrus in the form of parchment and paper – trust moved from the custodian of the records to the records themselves, which had to be capable of being creditworthy on their own. Their formal characteristics and their status of transmission (i.e. their degree of perfection, from draft to original to copy) were fundamental to establishing their authenticity.[1]

1 Luciana Duranti, 'Medieval universities and archives' (1994–95) 38 Archivaria 37.

6.4 It was only in 1681, however, that a science was developed to assess the authenticity and authority of records, that is, to establish that they were what they purported to be, free from tampering or corruption, and capable of producing consequences. The science of diplomatics was developed by Dom Jean Mabillon to determine the identity and integrity of documents claimed to be diplomas of Merovingian kings, and their ability to demonstrate the land rights of the Benedictines of France.[1] Thus, diplomatics focused on both documentary form[2] and status of transmission, that is, the degree of perfection of a record.[3] It defined an original as a document imbued with three qualities: primitiveness, completeness and effectiveness. An original is the first complete document capable of reaching the effects that it intends to reach – the perfect document. Then it defined both a draft and a copy in relation to the original: a draft precedes the original, is made for purposes of correction and is not intended to have consequences, while a copy, which may be of a draft, an original or another copy, is made for purposes of either communication or security. There may be several generations of drafts and several types of copies, with different degrees of authority, as there may be multiple originals.[4]

1 See Luciana Duranti, 'Diplomatics: new uses for an old science' (1989) 28 Archivaria 12.
2 The form of a document is defined as the 'whole of the characteristics which can be separated from the determination of the particular subjects, persons, or places it is about'. Duranti, 'Diplomatics', 15.
3 The status of transmission of a record is shown in 'Ontology B': http://www.interpares.org/ip2/display_file.cfm?doc=ip2_ontology.pdf.
4 Duranti, 'Diplomatics', 18–21.

6.5 The science of diplomatics was the foundation of the law concerning evidence and proof in Europe, and was based on the fundamental assumption that the more authority a record has, the more believable is its content. As a consequence, the original was preferred to any other status of transmission, to the point that an *authenticum* was defined as 'an original instrument or writing; the original of a will or other instrument, as distinguished from a copy'.[1] If authenticity is by default attributed to the original for being the most authoritative status of transmission, then reliability of content is implied. Thus, the concepts of originality, authenticity and reliability were conflated and the 'best evidence' idea came into being. All of this has changed as the world has moved to the digital environment.

1 Henry Campbell Black, *Black's Law Dictionary*, Revised Fourth edn, 1968, s.v. 'authentic' and 'authentic act', 168.

An example: email

6.6 Emails can be stored in a number of different formats, depending upon the software that created them. For evidentiary purposes, it is important to obtain the item in the native format, the unmodified email message file, including its attachments, as this is the only way the identity and integrity of an email can be proven. Some older email repositories stored emails and attachments in a flat file structure which makes it difficult to retrieve and view them without specialist assistance.

6.7 Indeed, emails can be submitted as evidence for a number of purposes. The email, like all correspondence, may be offered to prove that the sender did, or did not,[1] communicate with another person or persons, in which case the communication, and not its content, may be called into evidence. It may be tendered to show the sender was at a particular location at a particular time, and this will be evidenced in the metadata showing the IP address of the computer from which the email was sent. If authenticity is still challenged, the sender of the email may have to give evidence of doing so. However, if the sender of the email denies having written it, then the party tendering the email will need to provide a wide array of circumstantial evidence in order to prove the identity of the sender.[2] This may be difficult unless the party tendering the email can show, on the balance of probabilities, that the purported sender did send the email.

1 See for example, *Greene v Associated Newspapers Limited* [2004] EWCA Civ 1462, [2005] QB 972, [2005] 3 WLR 281, [2005] 1 All ER 30, [2004] 11 WLUK 165, [2005] EMLR 10, (2004) 101(45) LSG 31, (2004) 148 SJLB 1318, Times, 10 November 2004, Independent, 9 November 2004, [2005] CLY 970.
2 By way of example, see *Takenaka (UK) Ltd and Corfe v Frankl* [2001] EWCA Civ 348, [2001] 3 WLUK 163, [2001] EBLR 40, [2001] CLY 1819 and *BSkyB Ltd v HP Enterprise Services UK Ltd (formerly t/a Electronic Data Systems Ltd)* [2010] EWHC 86 (TCC), [2010] 1 WLUK 491, [2010] BLR 267, 129 Con LR 147, [2010] 26 Const LJ 289, [2010] CILL 2841, [2010] CLY 3421.

6.8 Although public bodies and private corporations now use record-keeping systems, where records of all types are organized by function and activity, and which are designed according to requirements established by national and international standards, private people and small organizations tend to keep emails stored in the application used by the email client where it was generated or received.[1] Similarly, their electronic files, such as draft correspondence, spreadsheets, reports, PowerPoint presentations, drawings and so on, are stored in the applications where they are created, although this is now changing where these documents are saved and stored in cloud-based repositories. Sometimes these files are created using proprietary software, and stored in formats that can only be interpreted by that software, although open source software is increasingly used; however, there are now tools available that can obtain access to the content of proprietary files without the need to obtain the proprietary software.

1 For a detailed description of the characteristics of emails as digital entities, see Gianfranco Pontevolpe and Silvio Salza, *General Study 05 – Keeping and Preserving Email*, http://interpares.org/ip3/display_file.cfm?doc=ip3_italy_gs05a_final_report.pdf. See also Association of Records Managers and Administrators, BSR/ARMA 19-2019, *Policy Design for Managing Electronic Messages.*

Digital evidence compared to past paradigms

6.9 It is important to take into account the differences between analogue[1] and digital evidence when examining how the rules of evidence have been, and should be, applied to digital evidence. Indeed, 'evidence in digital form is paradigmatically different from pre-digital evidence which generally was inextricably associated with a medium be it paper, film, video, audiotape or some other fixed medium'.[2] It is true that, in January 2019, the Council of Europe adopted the 'Guidelines of the Committee of Ministers of the Council of Europe on electronic evidence[3] in civil and administrative proceedings',[4] which provide:

> Electronic evidence should be evaluated in the same way as other types of evidence, in particular regarding its admissibility, authenticity, accuracy and integrity.

1 Analogue is information written on physical material, such as a paper, parchment, stone, clay, film or certain types of magnetic audiotape and videotape (see CGSB 72.34-2017, 2).
2 Judge David Harvey, 'Digital evidence admissibility: some issues' (17 December 2019), https://papers.ssrn.com/sol3/papers.cfm?abstract_id=3505611.
3 In the context of this chapter, the expressions 'electronic evidence' and 'digital evidence' are used interchangeably, although 'electronic' refers to the storage and means of transmission of an entity and 'digital' to the discrete, binary values constituting it. See for example CGSB 74.34-2017, 3–4 'electronic record' and 'digital record'.
4 Guidelines of the Committee of Ministers of the Council of Europe on electronic evidence in civil and administrative proceedings (Adopted by the Committee of Ministers on 30 January 2019, at the 1335th meeting of the Ministers' Deputies), 30 January 2019, CM(2018)169-add1final, https://search.coe.int/cm/Pages/result_details.aspx?ObjectId=0900001680902e0c.

6.10 *Evaluating* electronic evidence in the same way as other types of evidence does not mean that they should be *dealt with* in the same way. Jokubauskas and Świerczyński[1] have, for instance, questioned whether those guidelines already require revision. The authors point out the increasing use of cloud computing, particularly as a cross-border technology, and the increasing popularity of emerging technologies such as blockchain and artificial intelligence tools. This suggests that there are gaps in the way the law deals with electronic evidence and these should be carefully examined by a careful comparison with analogue evidence.

1 Remigijus Jokubauskas and Marek Świerczyński, 'Is revision of the Council of Europe guidelines on electronic evidence already needed?', (2020) 16(1) Utrecht Law Review 13. DOI: http://doi.org/10.36633/ulr.525.

6.11 In the past, a document was understood as information affixed to an analogue medium[1] by means of a writing instrument or an apparatus for fixing data, images or sound, in a form that was both objectified and syntactic.[2] In legal proceedings, if a document is admitted into evidence, it generally contains information upon which one party wishes to rely as proof of an alleged fact.

1 'Analogue medium n., Physical material, such as paper, parchment, stone, clay, film or certain types of magnetic audio- and videotape, used for storage of data', http://www.interpares.org/ip2/display_file.cfm?doc=ip2_glossary.pdf&CFID=22025589&CFTOKEN=86498402.
2 Duranti, 'Diplomatics', 15. See also *R v Daye (Arthur John)* [1908] 2 KB 333 (KBD).

6.12 When a 'document' is not affixed to an analogue medium, but rather exists in an electronic form, the content, structure and form of a digital 'document' are not inextricably linked to one another, as is the case with information in analogue form. A digital document is composed of two parts: the *stored entity* (the digital component) and its *manifested entity* such as what appears on a computer screen or in other output form. These entities are vulnerable (easy to destroy, lose, corrupt, tamper with, or may become inaccessible if not protected), yet persistent (forever there, if not purposefully destroyed).[1] An electronic document also includes more information than is visible to the eye – the digital components may comprise information such as metadata and data about the structure of the document.

1 Luciana Duranti and Kenneth Thibodeau, 'The concept of record in interactive, experiential and dynamic environments: the view of InterPARES' (2006) 6(1) Archival Science13, http://www.interpares.org/ip2/display_file.cfm?doc=ip2_book_appendix_02.pdf.

6.13 For example, an email, if printed, looks like a paper document and appears complete because one can see the header lines. If the email is tendered through a witness who is the author of the email, without objection, then the paper version of the email may be perfectly adequate to prove its contents. However, the email as stored by the email client may contain additional information relevant to the issues in legal proceedings. Although there are four types of header lines – identity header lines (including thread headers), transmission header lines, security header lines and format/encoding header lines – only a small part of the header is typically displayed by email clients and is printable. Only if the email is accessed through special settings on the email client is it possible to see all the hidden information.

6.14 Some working groups have defined the main differences between paper (and other analogue media) and electronic documents. Among them, the most prominent is The Sedona Conference Working Group on Best Practices for Electronic Document Retention and Production (the Sedona Conference).[1] The Sedona Conference suggests that such differences can be broadly grouped into six categories: (a) metadata, (b) volume and duplicability, (c) persistence, (d) dynamic, changeable content, (e) environment dependence and obsolescence, and (f) dispersion and searchability.

1 The Sedona Conference, Electronic Document Retention and Production, Working Group 1 (2002).

Admissibility and authentication

6.15 To be admissible in legal proceedings, the potential evidence needs to be relevant to the facts at issue in the proceedings. If it is not relevant, it is not admissible. After the evidence is admitted, it is open to the opposing party to challenge it by contradicting, undermining or explaining it. The trier of fact then determines how much weight is to be given to the evidence, and makes a decision accordingly.

6.16 This does not prevent both parties and the court from accepting the authenticity of the evidence without proof.[1] Alternatively, one party may put the identity or integrity of digital documents in issue. In such a case the party adducing the evidence will also need to meet the requirement to provide suitable evidential foundations. For instance, in civil proceedings in England and Wales a party is deemed to admit the authenticity of a document disclosed under the provisions of the Civil Procedure Rules (CPR) Pt 31 unless notice is served that the party wishes the document to be proved at trial, as provided for by CPR 32.19. Notwithstanding the provisions of the CPR, the authenticity of documents is not, generally, challenged at such an early stage in the proceedings.[2] This is because neither party may be aware of the dispute over the authenticity of a document until during the trial, when it may be first raised by a witness during oral testimony.

1 For a number of early cases in the US where digital images from satellites were accepted by agreement, see Harald Ginzky, 'Satellite images as evidence in legal proceedings relating to the environment – a US perspective' (2000) VXXV(3) Air & Space Law 114, 116.
2 Although see *Gallaher International Ltd v Tlais Enterprises Ltd (Rev 1)* [2008] EWHC 804 (Comm), [2008] 4 WLUK 504, where Gallaher gave notice that it challenged the authenticity of a large number of the documents disclosed by Tlais, and required Tlais to prove them, at [586]. Clarke J considered that some documents were neither proved nor not proved at [630], that some were not proved at [685] and that some were not satisfactorily proved at [862].

6.17 Reported cases appear to indicate that a lawyer will merely assert that the authenticity, reliability or accuracy of the evidence is not to be trusted, and the court will then have to determine a suitable response to the allegation raised,[1] or a lawyer may fail to raise any specific objections as to the accuracy of the evidence.[2] For example, if an email, a web page, a social media post or any other form of digital evidence is admitted as evidence, the opposing party may challenge its reliability in order to reduce the weight to be given to the evidence by using witness testimony, certifications, forensic evidence and circumstantial evidence to do so.[3]

1 For instance, in *Noble Resources SA v Gross* [2009] EWHC 1435 (Comm), [2009] 6 WLUK 558, Mr Gross cast doubt over the reliability and (it seems) the authenticity of SMS messages, but the technical evidence demonstrated that it was not possible to alter an SMS message on a BlackBerry once it had been received or sent; note the discussion in relation to the printouts of records of telephone calls made by a mobile telephone in the case of *State v Navjot Sandhu* (2005) 11 SCC 600, 148–152.
2 *Olympic Insurance Company v H. D. Harrison, Inc.*, 418 F.2d 669 (5th Cir. 1969).
3 Micheál O'Floinn and David Ormerod, 'Social networking material as criminal evidence' [2012] Crim LR 486 for a discussion of the approach taken in the courts in England relating to data from social networking sites.

6.18 The way in which electronic evidence is adduced will affect the challenges as to its authenticity. Generally, evidence is adduced to assert or reinforce a positive position. For instance, it might provide reliable information,[1] act to confirm an alibi,[2] or where there is evidence from different devices and systems in combination (CCTV, automatic number plate recognition system and the use of mobile telephones[3] attributed to a particular person), act to corroborate and reinforce the evidence between the parties.[4] An example of the positive use of electronic evidence is the Application Transaction Counter on the chip of a debit card, which increases by one each time a transaction occurs, so that in the event of a disputed transaction, the counter on the card can be tested against the records maintained by the bank.[5] Another example of the positive use of electronic evidence can be found in the case of *City Park Co-operative Apartments Inc. v David Dubois.*[6] In this case, Spies J accepted that the code of an apartment entry–exit 'key' issued to the defendant contradicted the defendant's affidavit evidence that he had been denied access to his apartment. The management of the apartment was able to adduce in court evidence to show that this particular entry–exit 'key' was used 1,447 times in a six-month period, based on computer records of each entry or exit for the uniquely coded 'key' (which the judge questionably described as an 'electronic signature'). Nonetheless, the judge's meaning is clear: this was an example of electronic evidence demonstrating that the holder of a token had used the entry–exit 'key', thus showing that his affidavit evidence was incompatible with the electronic evidence.

1 *A (Death of a Baby), Re* [2011] EWHC 2754 (Fam), per Jackson J at [168].
2 *R. v Hallam (Sam)* [2012] EWCA Crim 1158, [2012] 5 WLUK 518.
3 In *R. v Hamilton* 2011 ONCA 399 the Ontario Court of Appeal held that evidence regarding cell tower records was factual evidence and not opinion evidence, and the court accepted evidence of three

employees rather than experts at [259]; see also *R. v Cyr* 2012 CarswellOnt 16386, 2012 ONCA 919, [2012] OJ No. 6148, 104 WCB (2d) 1033, 294 CCC (3d) 421, 300 OAC 111; these decisions have been criticized: Ken Chasse, 'Guilt by mobile phone tracking shouldn't make "evidence to the contrary" impossible', http://www.slaw.ca/2016/10/04/guilt-by-mobile-phone-tracking-shouldnt-make-evidence-to-the-contrary-impossible/.

4 *R. v Fagan (Taariq), R. Fergus (Michael)* [2012] EWCA Crim 2248, [2012] 9 WLUK 121. Note the discussion of a case in Switzerland where the absence of evidence that a mobile telephone that was switched on at the relevant time was the topic of a paper in considering probability and graphical probability models: Alex Biedermann and Joëlle Vuille, 'Digital evidence, "absence" of data and ambiguous patterns of reasoning' (2016) 16 Digital Investigation S86.

5 Jerzy Kosiński, 'A case of the customer attempting to claim their debit card was cloned' (2016) 13 Digital Evidence and Electronic Signature Law Review 167.

6 [2006] OJ No. 4428 (Sup. Ct.) (QL).

6.19 However, it is possible for digital data to prove a negative position (or perhaps be adduced as evidence of an inconsistent positive), a point made by Professor Tapper.[1] An example is a case where a number of customers of a bank report unauthorized ATM withdrawals, which will cause the bank to investigate whether an employee was responsible for the thefts. This happened in the case of *United States of America v Bonallo*,[2] where computer records had demonstrated that cash withdrawals were made when the defendant Bonallo was in the building. It transpired that the employee who assumed Bonallo's duties after his employment was terminated discovered a 'fraud program' in Bonallo's computer program library. This program was used to provide access to ATM computer files, and to allow him to alter transaction records, although it could have been used for legitimate purposes as well. This case not only illustrates the possibility of adducing evidence of an inconsistent positive, but also the care with which judges should approach assertions about 'reliable' computer systems and whether the business records exception ought to apply.

1 Colin Tapper, 'Evanescent evidence' (1993) 1(1) Intl J L & Info Tech35, 44–45; Beryl A. Howell and Brian M. Heberlig, 'The *Lamar Owens* case: how electronic evidence contributed to an acquittal in an explosive rape case' (2007) 24(12) The Computer & Internet Lawyer 1; *Alfano v LC Main, LLC*, 38 Misc.3d 1233(A) (2013) 969 N.Y.S.2d 801 (Table), 2013 WL 1111969 (N.Y.Sup.), 2013 N.Y. Slip Op. 50373(U) (a forensic computer examiner performed a forensic analysis of the metadata associated with the plaintiffs' photographs, concluding that the photographs were taken 12 days after the accident); Kashmir Hill, 'Fitbit data just undermined a woman's rape claim', Splinter (29 June 2015), https://splinternews.com/fitbit-data-just-undermined-a-womans-rape-claim-1793848735.

2 858 F.2d 1427 (9th Cir. 1988).

6.20 Although some jurisdictions deal with the issue of admissibility and authentication somewhat differently, it is clear that admissibility is a question of law for the judge and authenticity is a question of fact for the jury, or the judge alone if there is no jury.

6.21 For instance, in Australia, for evidence to be admissible, it must be relevant.[1] Authenticity is not a ground of admissibility pursuant to the Uniform Evidence Acts, so the issue does not arise when the court is considering objections to evidence.[2] When considering evidence such as social media screenshots or printouts, the judge will first determine whether, as a question of law, the evidence is relevant, and if it is, it will be admitted into evidence. The trier of fact will then determine whether the evidence is authentic. How the evidence is authenticated will depend upon the method of authentication used.[3] For example, Estcourt J posits that a proponent only has to 'prove' a document such as a screenshot or a photograph or printout of social media.[4] Estcourt J was referring to the decision of Perram J in *Australian Competition and Consumer Commission v Air New Zealand Ltd (No 1)*[5] in relation to business records. However, the judge was of the view that this approach applies equally to Facebook evidence. Estcourt J stated:[6]

> In a nutshell, when you tender a Facebook screenshot or printout no question of its authenticity arises as a threshold question. The only question at this stage is relevance. At no time does the judge as the judge of law determine that the document is or is not authentic because that is not a question for him or her. The question for the judge as the judge of law is only relevance. The question of authenticity is for him or her, after the document has been admitted into evidence, and that is for him or her as the judge of fact.

1 *Australian Competition and Consumer Commission v Air New Zealand Ltd (No 1)* [2012] FCA 1355 per Perram J at [92].
2 *Australian Competition and Consumer Commission v Air New Zealand Ltd (No 1)* [2012] FCA 1355 per Perram J at [92].
3 The Hon. Justice Stephen Estcourt AM, 'Social media as evidence', speech presented to New Technology and Trial Practice Workshop, Port Moresby, 18–20 March 2019, https://www.supremecourt.tas.gov.au/publications/speeches-articles/social-media-as-evidence/, at 8.
4 Estcourt, 'Social media as evidence'.
5 [2012] FCA 1355, (2012) 207 FCR 448.
6 This text, and the further text cited, is towards the end of Estcourt, 'Social media as evidence'.

6.22 Estcourt J goes on to say:

> As to the ultimate question of fact, if a person in his or her evidence denies that the post is his or hers, or claims that it is not genuine, then the issue will play out like any other disputed issue of fact. If the person denies he or she posted it, then that claim will be tested by cross-examination. 'Who had access to your account? How was your account hacked? Who knew your password? When was it hacked? What about the posts either side of that post?' If the tribunal is a judge alone, then he or she will decide the question of authenticity and the weight to be given to it.

6.23 In England and Wales, s 8 of the Civil Evidence Act 1995 provides that, where a statement contained in a document is admissible in civil proceedings, it may be 'authenticated in such manner as the court may approve'. As for criminal proceedings, the current position is now governed by s 133 of the Criminal Justice Act 2003, which provides as follows:

> 133 Proof of statements in documents
>
> Where a statement in a document is admissible as evidence in criminal proceedings, the statement may be proved by producing either–
>
> (a) the document, or
>
> (b) (whether or not the document exists) a copy of the document or of the material part of it, authenticated in whatever way the court may approve.

6.24 The Explanatory Notes to the Act states that s 133 'corresponds to the position under section 27 of the Criminal Justice Act 1988, whereby a statement in a document can be proved by producing either the original document or an authenticated copy' and continues: 'It is intended to cover all forms of copying including the use of imaging technology.'[1] Interestingly, the document must be an original or an authentic copy, which illustrates the need to pay careful attention to the means by which a document in digital form is authenticated before the court.[2] The use of imaging technology is also a mechanism for obtaining a copy of the original data, although the actual technology that is used to obtain an image of data may be challenged. The number of removes a copy may be from the original is dealt with indirectly by reference to the meaning of 'copy', which 'in relation to a document, means anything on to which information recorded in the document has been copied, by whatever means and whether directly or indirectly.'[3] This requires the trial judge to determine how a digital document is authenticated, which is why guidance on the mechanisms by which authenticity is tested after evidence is seized can be so important.[4] In essence, the move has been towards assessing the weight to be given to electronic evidence.

1 At paragraph 436.
2 O'Floinn and Ormerod, 'Social networking material as criminal evidence'.
3 Criminal Justice Act 2003, s 134(1) Interpretation of Chapter 2.
4 For which see article 4 of the Draft Convention on Electronic Evidence, which proposes five tests respecting evidence seized and subsequently submitted as evidence in legal proceedings: (2016) 13 Digital Evidence and Electronic Signature Law Review S1–S11, https://journals.sas.ac.uk/deeslr/article/view/2321.

6.25 The Court of Appeal's stance in *R. v O'Connor (Damien)*[1] has wider implications on the admissibility of electronic evidence beyond its own facts. The appellant and several others were accused of conspiring to import heroin and cocaine into the UK from Belgium. O'Connor was living in Belgium at the time. The prosecution relied upon telephone records provided by the Belgian police in relation to a mobile telephone used by the leader of the conspiracy, but there was no accompanying statement from the Belgian telephone provider. The court concluded that it was arguable that the records, which were produced by the Belgian authorities and handed to the prosecution, were not in fact statements made by a person. Hooper LJ went on to say, at [16]:

> and one concentrates on the person who interrogated the Belgium provider computer and obtained the data for the [alleged appellant's] phone, and if one assumes that in that respect a person is making a representation for the purposes of section 115 [of the Criminal Justice Act 2003], then the issue has to be whether it is admissible under section 117 [of the same Act as a business record exception to the hearsay rule]. The judge held that it was.

1 [2010] EWCA Crim 2287, [2010] 6 WLUK 467, Times, 19 July 2010, [2011] CLY 608.

6.26 In Canada, the Uniform Law Conference of Canada adopted in 1997 the text of a Uniform Electronic Evidence Act (Canada) that proposed a reform of the traditional common law evidentiary requirements in light of the characteristics of electronic materials submitted for admissibility as evidence.[1] The Uniform Electronic Evidence Act (Canada) subsequently became uniform law in Canada in the Canada Evidence Act (CEA) 1995, thereby prevailing in criminal proceedings anywhere in Canada.[2] Section 31.5 Canada Evidence Act provides:

> For the purpose of determining under any rule of law whether an electronic document is admissible, evidence may be presented in respect of any standard, procedure, usage or practice concerning the manner in which electronic documents are to be recorded or stored, having regard to the type of business, enterprise or endeavour that used, recorded or stored the electronic document and the nature and purpose of the electronic document.

1 See https://www.ulcc.ca/en/ and http://www.slaw.ca/2018/09/11/electronic-documents-in-civil-and-administrative-proceedings-uniform-rules/.
2 https://laws-lois.justice.gc.ca/eng/acts/c-5/.

6.27 Further, s 41.2 of the Act states that it does 'not modify any common law or statutory rule relating to the admissibility of records, except the rules relating to authentication and best evidence'. Section 41.3 goes on to provide that a 'person seeking to introduce an electronic record as evidence has the burden of proving its authenticity by evidence capable of supporting a finding that the electronic record is what the person claims it to be'. If evidence which is 'capable of demonstrating authenticity is adduced and not rebutted', it is still ultimately up to the trier of fact to determine whether or not the evidence is authentic, and to decide what weight, if any, is to be placed on that evidence.[1]

1 David Outerbridge and Ezra Siller, 'The admissibility of electronic evidence', https://www.lawinsider.com/documents/, at 10.

6.28 In summary, if a judge is satisfied, as a question of law, that evidence is admissible, it is then up to the trier of fact (judge or jury) to determine whether the evidence is authentic and what weight, if any, is to be given to the evidence. The judicial approach to authentication of digital data in legal proceedings is considered on a case-by-case basis. There are no judicial guidelines about the attributes or characteristics of digital data, and some commentators have provided guidance through the application of relevant case law in relation to different types of digital data, such as emails, websites, instant messages, text messages and photography.[1] Judges have to make judgments about the qualifications of the witnesses who appear before them, and interpret the nature of digital data in accordance with the evidence presented.

1 Steven Goode, 'The admissibility of electronic evidence' (2009) 29(1) Review of Litigation 1; Breanne M. Democko, 'Social media and the rules on authentication' (2012) 43 U Tol L Rev 367; Kenneth N. Rashbaum, Matthew F. Knouff and Dominique Murray, 'Admissibility of non-U.S. electronic evidence' (2012) XVIII Rich J J & Tech 9; Paul W. Grimm, Lisa Yurwit Bergstrom and Melissa M. O'Toole-Loureiro, 'Authentication of social media evidence' (2013) 36(3) American Journal of Trial Advocacy 433.

6.29 Two cases from the US and one from England and Wales serve to illustrate this point. In *State of New Jersey v Swed*,[1] the defendant was convicted of obtaining electricity without payment, and part of the evidence comprised computer printouts identifying the defendant as a customer with a registered address. The defendant contended that there was insufficient foundation for the admission of the printouts. In reaching its decision, the Appellate Division of the Superior Court of New Jersey applied the six foundational requirements set out in *Monarch Federal Savings & Loan Association v Gesner*:[2] personal knowledge on the part of the witness as to the act or event recorded was not necessary; the person called as a witness should be able to testify as to the type of computer used, the permanent nature of the record storage and how daily transactions were customarily recorded; the computer records were made in the ordinary course of business; the entries were made within a reasonable time after the transaction occurred; proof of the validity of the source of the information from which the entry was made was required; and the validity of the method used in obtaining the computer printout must be established. In each of these instances, the prosecution provided suitable evidence.

1 604 A.2d 978 (N.J.Super.A.D. 1992).
2 156 N.J.Super. 107, 383 A.2d 475 (Ch.Div. 1977).

6.30 In the criminal case of *R v Cochrane*,[1] McCowan LJ, Waterhouse and Brooke JJ set out the following guidance in relation to electronic evidence from mainframe computers:

> it was necessary that appropriate authoritative evidence should be called to describe the function and operation of the mainframe computer, including the extent to which it brought to bear information stored within it in order to validate a transaction and to enable an appropriate record to be made on the till roll. None of those matters were covered by any of the witnesses, and the judge had had to grapple with inadequate, and possibly, incorrect information ... The Crown had failed to adduce adequate evidence to enable the court to properly rule that the till rolls were admissible evidence; and in the absence of the till rolls the Crown's case could not be proved.

1 [1992] 6 WLUK 63, [1993] Crim LR 48 (CA), [1993] CLY 366.

6.31 In the context of the US, George L. Paul has indicated that 'the Federal Rules of Evidence do not contain a rule requiring informational records or other objects to be authentic. The requirement appears to be assumed',[1] and he indicates that authenticity is a *prerequisite*, because evidence must also be relevant. This observation must be considered to be accurate for most jurisdictions. In this part of the chapter, consideration is given to a number of jurisdictions and how judges have approached the authentication of digital data, to illustrate that comprehensive tests to demonstrate the authenticity of digital data are not necessary for every conceivable set of facts – an observation made by Erdmann J in *United States v Lubich* before the US Court of Appeals for the Armed Forces, in which he said 'There are numerous scenarios in which this issue will arise and we see no benefit in attempting to craft a "standard" test to analyze all computer data situations'.[2]

1 George L. Paul, *Foundations of Digital Evidence* (American Bar Association 2008), 39; George L. Paul, 'Systems of evidence in the age of complexity' (2014) 12(2) Ave Maria L Rev 173; for an earlier comment, see Rudolph J. Peritz, 'Computer data and reliability: a call for authentication of business records under the Federal Rules of Evidence' (1986) 80(4) Northwestern University Law Review 965.
2 72 M.J. 170 (2013) at 175 – the attorney for the appellant argued that the prosecution had failed to provide for the continuity of the evidence.

The best evidence rule

6.32 In order to circumvent forgery, the common law 'best evidence rule' established that original material be used whenever possible. This requires 'the party who claims to put the contents of a writing in evidence [to] produce [the original], or account for its absence'.[1] Each original must be attested by witnesses 'that it was sealed and delivered'[2] and it must be 'the best that the nature of the case will allow'.[3] The rule is traceable to the ancient method of trial by charter, where there could be no trial without the charter, and ultimately led to the requirement that original documents be produced in court.[4] The best evidence rule was thus based on the premise that no evidence other than the original was admissible unless secondary evidence, or proof other than the original, was admissible as an exception to this rule.

1 *R v Richard John Frankland* (1863) Le. & Ca. 276, 169 ER 1394.
2 *Doctor Leyfield's Case* (1572) 10 Co Rep 88, 77 ER 1057 at 9.
3 *Steyner v The Burgesses of Droitwich* (1700) Holt KB 290, 90 ER 1059; *Omychund v Barker* (1745) 1 Atk 21, 49, 26 ER 15 at 33.
4 Edmund M. Morgan, 'The jury and the exclusionary rules of evidence' (1937) 4 U Chi L Rev 247.

6.33 In the electronic environment, as originals do not exist other than for 'a nanosecond' when they are being made or received, the best evidence rule appears to be inapplicable. However, one can abide by the spirit of the law, rather than by its letter, by focusing on the primitiveness of the document, and on its completeness and effectiveness.

6.34 When a digital document is saved upon its creation or receipt, it is taken apart and separated into its digital components. When it is subsequently retrieved, and each time it is viewed, a copy is generated which, though not easily distinguishable from the original, is never identical to it, at least in regard to metadata, as the actions of closing, opening and navigating attach additional information to the document. Thus, although an original is generated when a document is first composed or received, upon closure it disappears and, as a consequence, there are no originals in the digital environment. As a further consequence, it is impossible to preserve digital entities: we can only preserve the ability to reproduce them from their digital components, or, in a database, regenerate them from content data, form data and composition data.[1]

1 Duranti and Thibodeau, 'The concept of record in interactive, experiential and dynamic environments'.

6.35 The fact that digital entities are capable of being reproduced in an almost identical fashion (at least to the human eye) poses the question of whether the original document rule is now redundant. Although this rule was abolished in the Uniform Evidence Acts in Australia, it still exists in some jurisdictions, such as Canada, and, without legislative acknowledgement of the true nature of digital evidence, courts may not be alerted to the need to consider that electronic documents that have the same formal presentation of the original can indeed be considered as having the same authority.[1]

1 In the digital environment it is important to distinguish formal presentation (that is what one sees on a screen and can print out) from technological presentation (the format of the document). Thus, a Word document and a PDF/A look the same on the screen (they have the same formal presentation) but their stored components are different. One important difference is that a Word document is changeable, but has metadata that can be examined, while a PDF/A is immutable, but has no metadata.

6.36 The absence of an original as the first complete and effective instantiation of a digital document does not mean that there is no one such instantiation capable of acting as an original, of having the authority and the force of an original, due to its degree of completeness: in the digital world, we refer to this as *integrity*. Likewise, the fact that every time a digital entity is recalled a new one is generated does not imply that the outcome cannot be what it purports to be, and that its content cannot be presumed reliable and accurate. This requires us to consider how the digital environment has separated the fundamental components of documentary trustworthiness that had flowed together in the seventeenth century: reliability, accuracy and authenticity.

Identity and integrity

6.37 Documentary authenticity in the digital environment is defined as the trustworthiness of a document – it is what it purports to be, untampered with and uncorrupted. Authenticity is based on the identity and integrity of a document.[1] The *identity* of a document refers to the attributes that uniquely characterize it and distinguish it from other documents. They include the names of the persons concurring in its creation (author, addressee, writer, originator, creator), its date(s) of creation (making, receipt, filing) and transmission, the matter or action in which it participates, the expression of its contextual relationships with other documents (classification code) and an indication of any attachment(s).

1 Heather MacNeil, 'Providing grounds for trust: developing conceptual requirements for the long-term preservation of authentic electronic records' (2000) 50 Archivaria 52; MacNeil, 'Providing grounds for trust II'.

6.38 *Integrity* refers to the quality of being complete and unaltered in all essential respects. We have never been fussy about it – consider a document that had holes, was burned on a side or where the ink passed through to the *verso* of it. In the analogue environment, the same definition of integrity was used with respect to data, documents, records and record systems. In the digital environment, integrity might refer to different things. It might refer to bitwise integrity, often identified with data integrity, which means that the data in the document are not modified either intentionally or accidentally, and that the original bits are in a complete and unaltered state from the time of capture, in that they have the exact and same order and value. In a digital entity, a small change in bits means a very different value is presented on the screen or action taken by a program or database (by way of example, 101 is a 5, 110 is 6 and 011 is a 3 – same bits, different order). Compromised bitwise integrity is revealed by digital signatures and emerging technologies such as blockchain.[1] Integrity might also refer to duplication. When we intentionally duplicate digital entities (rather than doing so in the act of accessing them), we either make a copy or take a forensic image. A copy is a selective duplicate in that you can only copy what you see. It rarely includes confirmation of completeness and provides an incomplete picture of the digital environment. A forensic image is a bit-for-bit copy of a storage medium and its content, including ambient data (such as snapshots of each open file), swap space (virtual memory, with passwords and encryption keys) and slack space (the unused space which contains deleted material).[2]

1 See the section on technological authentication below.

2 Ambient data refers to the data saved through the process of auto-save functions included with office productivity programs, which write temporary snapshots of an open file to the disk at set intervals. Swap space is the portion of the hard disk that the system uses as extension of its RAM during operation. It is termed as virtual memory in the Windows world. Forensic investigators recover significant ephemeral data such as password and encryption keys from swap space. Slack space refers to the space available on a cluster even after an active file is stored in some part of that cluster. This arises from the fact that space is allocated in fixed cluster sizes even if the file size is less than the cluster size. The data present in the remaining area of the cluster is not overwritten and reflects data about a past file that was using the cluster, and is called slack.

6.39 When digital material is duplicated either for forensic purposes or to be submitted as evidence, two principles must be respected: the Principle of Non-interference, which means that the method used to reproduce or recreate digital entities does not change them, and the Principle of Identifiable Interference, which means that, if the method used does alter the entities, the changes are identified and identifiable and that information is provided about who and what introduced the changes so that witnesses can testify as to them.

6.40 These conceptual changes affect authentication of digital entities. In the digital environment, we regard authentication as a declaration of authenticity at one point in time, based on either direct knowledge, material proof, inference or deduction.[1] Fundamentally, the conceptual basis for the authentication of digital material remains the same as for analogue material: a chain of legitimate custody for inferring authenticity; a digital continuity of evidence (also called chain of custody) to preserve information about the material and its changes, to show that specific data was in a particular state at a given date and time; a declaration of the author or a witness; and the affidavit of a digital evidence professional who bases his or her testimony on the trustworthiness of the system hosting the digital material, and on the procedures and processes controlling its maintenance and use. The latter is becoming increasingly relevant in some jurisdictions, such as Canada, where the idea was formally introduced in the late 1990s.[2]

1 Government of Canada Standards Board 72.34-2017, *Electronic Records as Documentary Evidence*, 3.
2 Luciana Duranti, Corinne Rogers and Anthony Sheppard, 'Electronic records and the law of evidence in Canada: the Uniform Electronic Evidence Act twelve years later' (2010) 70 Archivaria 95.

6.41 Thus, when considering digital evidence, an 'original' electronic document can no longer be equated with an 'authentic' electronic document.[1] Where a law such as the Uniform Electronic Evidence Act (Canada) shifts the focus from the best evidence rule, which is concerned with document integrity, to the authentication rule, which is concerned with its primitiveness, this is primarily due to the fact that computer-generated or computer-stored information may lack stability of form and content. Furthermore, there may be instances where, to assure its continued accessibility, a digital object is purposely migrated from one system to another and converted from one format to another to deal with technological obsolescence. It follows, therefore, that the ability to prove the authenticity of a digital object is not equal to proving that an 'original' exists. The issue is about trustworthiness, or the lack of it. Proving the authenticity of a digital object means providing sufficient evidence to convince an adjudicator that the object that has been retrieved is a faithful representation of what is claimed was the 'original', or a reliable representation of the object that was made by the originator or relied upon by the recipient and the user, or only the user.

1 Paul, *Foundations of Digital Evidence*, 48–49; Steven W. Teppler, 'Digital data as hearsay' (2009) 6 Digital Evidence and Electronic Signature Law Review 7, 9 n 18; Stephen Mason, 'Electronic evidence and the meaning of "original" ' (2009) 79 Amicus Curiae 26, http://sas-space.sas.ac.uk/2565/; Luciana Duranti and Corinne Rogers, 'Trust in digital records: an increasingly cloudy legal area' (2012) 28(5) Computer Law and Security Review 522, 527 with further references.

Reliability

6.42 Documentary *reliability* is defined as the trustworthiness of the content of a document as fact. Inferences can be drawn from factors such as competence (the authority and capacity) of the author, the completeness of the form and the control over the process of production of the document. On these bases, all public documents are considered reliable and so are all business records, which constitute an exception to the hearsay rule because of why they are generated and the process through which they are generated.[1] Reliability, however, does not imply accuracy.

1 Luciana Duranti, 'The concepts of reliability and authenticity and their implications' (1995) 39 Archivaria 5–10.

6.43 Documentary *accuracy* is defined as the correctness and precision of the data in the digital entity, based on the competence of the author and the controls on content recording and transmission. During transmission the data in a reliable document may change and the document may become inaccurate.[1]

1 See Ontology C, http://www.interpares.org/ip2/display_file.cfm?doc=ip2_ontology.pdf.

6.44 The concepts of integrity and reliability are also closely linked. For instance, in Canada, s 31.5 of the Canada Evidence Act provides as follows:

> For the purposes of subsection 31.2(1), in the absence of evidence to the contrary, the integrity of an electronic documents system by or in which an electronic document is recorded or stored is proven (a) by evidence capable of supporting a finding that at all material times the computer system or other similar device used by the electronic documents system was operating properly or, if it was not, the fact of its not operating properly did not affect the integrity of the electronic document and there are no other reasonable grounds to doubt the integrity of the electronic documents system.

6.45 The introduction of the Uniform Electronic Evidence Act (UEEA) provides that the integrity of the digital material submitted for admissibility could be inferred from the integrity of the electronic system in which the material is stored. Therefore, if a litigant offering an electronic record as evidence can show that the system producing or storing it operates in the way it is expected to, the output satisfies the evidentiary requirements, regardless of its form.

6.46 The Uniform Law Conference of Canada commentary for the UEEA states:

> This Act focuses on replacing the search for originality, proving the reliability of systems instead of that of individual records, and using standards to show systems reliability.

6.47 As a factor in determining the reliability of a system, s 6 of the Uniform Electronic Evidence Act (Canada) replaced the traditional identification of individual records by a witness, or other foundation evidence, with proof of compliance of the system with recognized records management standards, procedures, usages or practices.[1] Section 6 of the UEEA (Canada) provides:

> For the purpose of determining under any rule of law whether an electronic record is admissible, evidence may be presented [in any legal proceeding] in respect of any standard, procedure, usage or practice on how electronic records are to be recorded or stored, having regard to the type of business or endeavour that used, recorded or stored the electronic record and the nature and purpose of the electronic record.

1 Duranti and others, 'Electronic records and the law of evidence in Canada', 105.

6.48 Section 6 does not apply to data generated by computers without human intervention, which are not considered hearsay and are admissible as real evidence – the UEEA provides guidance on the authentication of such evidence by a witness qualified to explain how the device operates, which is all that is required for admissibility.[1] It only specifically applies to digital materials admissible as exceptions to the hearsay rule that need to be authenticated, or that are shown to constitute best evidence. Section 6 places great reliance on standards such as the Government of Canada Standard Board (CGSB) 72.34-2017, *Electronic Records as Documentary Evidence*, which specifies the characteristics of a system that operates in the way it is expected to and whose output will satisfy the evidentiary requirements, regardless of its form.[2] It is worth examining this standard in some detail.

1 Duranti and others, 'Electronic records and the law of evidence in Canada', 109.
2 Government of Canada Standard Board (CGSB) 72.34, 2017, *Electronic Records as Documentary Evidence. CAN/CGSB-72.34-2017,* 14–24, https://s3.amazonaws.com/tld-documents.llnassets.com/0014000/14461/chasse2.pdf.

6.49 In its introduction, the CGSB 72:34-2017 standard refers to s 6 of the UEEA as embedded in the Canada Evidence Act, as well as in most provincial and territorial Evidence Acts, encouraging the use of standards.[1] It states:

> 0.3 Use of this standard in legal proceedings
>
> In legal proceedings, this standard could inform the development of arguments about the definitions of the key phrases of the rules of admissibility for electronic records. These phrases are 'IT system integrity' and 'record integrity', as used in the electronic record provisions of the Evidence Acts, and records 'made in the usual and ordinary course of business' as used in the CEA.[2]

1 *Electronic Records as Documentary Evidence. CAN/CGSB-72.34-2017*, s2:iv.
2 *Electronic Records as Documentary Evidence. CAN/CGSB-72.34-2017*, s3:iv.

6.50 The standard defines an IT system as a 'set of one or more computers, associated software, peripherals, terminals, human operations, physical processes, information transfer means, that form an autonomous whole, capable of performing information processing and/or information transfer', and IT system integrity as 'proven capability of an IT system to perform its intended functions in an unimpaired manner, free from unauthorized manipulation, whether intentional or accidental, and the fact that it did so when the recorded information was generated and used'. It is important to know that this standard, like the legislation, focuses on the *integrity* of the system when discussing authentication, rather than on its reliability. The standard does consider reliability and defines it as the 'quality of a system that has been tested, subjected to peer review or publication, accepted within the relevant scientific community and whose known or potential error rate is acceptable', but only in relation to its recommendations on how organizations should manage their records.[1]

1 These definitions are in *Electronic Records as Documentary Evidence. CAN/CGSB-72.34-2017* at ss 3.36, 3.37 and 3.38, 5.

6.51 In s 5.2.2 the Standard states that 'the law of evidence provides that the best evidence rule can be satisfied by proof of the integrity of the records system, as in subs. 31.2(1)(a) of the CEA', and that 'such integrity is proven, in the absence of proof to the contrary, by evidence that: (a) the electronic records system was at all material times operating properly or, if it was not, the fact of its not operating properly did not affect the integrity of the electronic record, and there are no other reasonable grounds to doubt the integrity of the system. (e.g. subs. 31.3(a) of the CEA)'.[1]

1 *Electronic Records as Documentary Evidence. CAN/CGSB-72.34-2017*, s 5.2.2, 10.

6.52 In s 5.2.4 the Standard identifies the factors that can be used to prove the integrity of an organization's electronic records system. They include:

> (a) sources: the origin of the data in its electronic records is known;
>
> (b) contemporaneous recording: the electronic records are made or received or stored within a reasonable time after the events to which they relate, or stored within a reasonable time after they are received;
>
> (c) routine business data: the data within a record is of a type regularly supplied to the originating organisation, or created by it during its regular activities;
>
> (d) data entry: the data entry procedures are part of the usual and ordinary course of business of the organisation, and are carried out in compliance with the RM manual and IT system management guide (see 6.4 and 6.5);
>
> (e) standards: the organisation complies with applicable electronic records management standards (as per 6.3.2. b);
>
> (f) decision making: the organisation, when making decisions, relies upon the electronic records in its electronic records system;
>
> (g) software: the organisation's software reliably operates the electronic records system and processes its data;
>
> (h) system changes: a record of record system changes and alterations is kept;
>
> (i) privacy: the use of the data in the organisation's electronic records complies with the relevant Canadian, provincial and territorial privacy statutes governing the collection, use or disclosure of personal information, confidential commercial information, trade secrets, privileges or other confidential information; and
>
> (j) security: security procedures, such as protection against unauthorized access and disaster recovery plans, are used to guarantee the integrity of the electronic records system. [1]

1 *Electronic Records as Documentary Evidence. CAN/CGSB-72.34-2017*, 10–11.

6.53 Proof of these factors has to be provided by the organization's records management manual (s 6.4 of the Standard, 16–20) and the IT system management guide (s 6.5 of the Standard, 20–24). From the number of inferences that need to be made to establish authenticity and the requirements for system management, it is clear that *system security* is vital to authentication of the digital entities stored in the system.[1]

1 See *Denco Limited v Joinson* [1991] 1 WLR 330, [1992] 1 All ER 413, [1990] 11 WLUK 224, [1991] ICR 172, [1991] IRLR 63, Times, 22 November 1990, [1991] CLY 1679 where Wood J observed that the members of the industrial tribunal were 'extremely critical of the security arrangements made by the employers in connection with the use of the computer' ([1991] ICR 172 at 178).

6.54 The Canadian legislation recognizes that the authenticity of the digital evidence as created and stored within a computer system is tied to the integrity of the system. If there is evidence of the integrity of the computer system, which can be provided by a witness who has knowledge of such system and can attest that it was operating properly at the time the digital evidence was created or stored in it, the evidence can be authenticated. However, the evidence of system integrity can still be rebutted. If the party challenging the evidence convinces the judge that they have good reason for doing so, it will then be for the party adducing the digital evidence to demonstrate that such evidence is authentic and can be trusted.

6.55 While the rebuttable presumption works for a great number of cases, because it means that evidence can be admitted without challenge where required, reducing hearing time and, therefore, expense as a result, serious problems have followed when systems have been presumed – as opposed to proven, or declared by a knowledgeable witness – to be operating correctly (as has been the case in England[1]). Mason is of the view that the presumption of 'reliability' of computer evidence should be questioned, particularly in relation to software which is, and will continue to be, unreliable.[2] Mason points out that software is inherently complex and subject to change, whether in regard to the code, to the operating system or other components and other vulnerabilities, including being subject to 'hacking'. Likewise, Ladkin, Littlewood, Thimbleby and Thomas CBE[3] argue that it is a practical impossibility to develop such a system 'so that the correctness of every software operation is provable to the relevant standard in legal proceedings'.[4] The authors point out that most software contains defects at the rate of between 1 and 100 defects per 1,000 lines of source code.[5] As a result, software can be inherently unreliable; yet the presumption is quite the opposite. Although this presumption can be rebutted, this puts the onus, and, therefore, the expense, on the party who wishes to rebut the presumption. This fact has been highlighted in England by the case of *Bates v Post Office Ltd (No 6: Horizon Issues) Rev 1*[6] (the Horizon Software case), where a number of sub-postmasters and sub-postmistresses were prosecuted on the basis of the 'robustness' of the Horizon computer system, with some being imprisoned and others losing their life savings.

1 For which see the Post Office Horizon scandal in England and Wales, discussed in Chapter 5.
2 See Chapter 5.
3 Peter Bernard Ladkin, Bev Littlewood, Harold Thimbleby and Martyn Thomas CBE, 'The Law Commission presumption concerning the dependability of computer evidence' (2020) 17 Digital Evidence and Electronic Signature Law Review 1.
4 Ladkin and others, 'The Law Commission presumption', 1.
5 Ladkin and others, 'The Law Commission presumption', 2.
6 [2019] EWHC 3408 (QB), [2019] 12 WLUK 208.

6.56 In reviewing the presumption, Ladkin and others opined that inaccuracies in electronic evidence are as likely to result from errors in the computer software as from errors in the data.[1] They conclude there are three propositions that a court should consider when evaluating digital evidence:

> 1. A presumption that any particular computer system failure is not caused by software is not justified, even for software that has previously been shown to be very reliable.
>
> 2. Evidence of previous computer failure undermines a presumption of current proper function.
>
> 3. The fact that a class of failures has not happened before is not a reason for assuming it cannot occur.[2]

1 Ladkin and others, 'The Law Commission presumption', 4.
2 Ladkin and others, 'The Law Commission presumption', 9.

6.57 In *R v Cahill, R v Pugh*[1] two nurses in the UK National Health System (NHS) were charged with falsification of readings taken with blood glucometers which they operated to monitor patients' blood glucose levels. As a result of the incorrect glucose readings, a number of patients died. The glucometers had automatically taken a reading and uploaded them to a central database; police investigations showed that the manual readings taken by the nurses and written on paper did not correspond to any readings on the glucometers or on the database. The prosecution argued there were no problems with the equipment the nurses had used, and advanced the case that the nurses' manual records were fabricated. It turned out that the manual readings were taken by the nurses as workarounds to accommodate issues with the glucometer system. Nurses also used their staff ID because the glucometer software had difficulties reading the patients' ID. Such workarounds were accepted by the software, and meant a correct glucose reading was still obtained. However, the backend system had been configured to reject the data collected using the workarounds and store it separately for later 'fixing': these were subsequently ignored rather than being processed. Professor Thimbleby[2] was called as an expert witness to examine this evidence of the glucometer readings and database provided by the prosecution. He discovered 'that over 20 per cent of the database entries had an "error flag" set', which raised his suspicions and led him to conclude that the matter became 'a more complex story than the prosecution painted'.[3] The professor concluded that this indicated that 'nobody was paying much attention to the management of the database'.[4] He also criticized the way in which police had inexplicably converted the data from the database into Excel spreadsheets and copied them onto USB (Universal Serial Bus) drives rather than taking a forensic copy of the original database. Consequently, the court excluded the evidence relied on by the prosecution on the basis that it was unreliable and acquitted the nurses.[5] Professor Thimbleby summarized his experience by saying that 'the big picture is that nobody seems to be fully aware of the complexity and risks of IT. This results in lax legislation, lax regulation and lax procurement.'[6]

1 14 October 2014, Crown Court at Cardiff, T20141094 and T20141061 before HHJ Crowther QC, (2017) 14 Digital Evidence and Electronic Signature Law Review 67.
2 Harold Thimbleby, 'Misunderstanding IT: hospital cybersecurity and IT problems reach the courts' (2018) 15 Digital Evidence and Electronic Signatures Law Review 11.
3 Thimbleby, 'Misunderstanding IT',16.
4 Thimbleby, 'Misunderstanding IT',16–17.
5 14 October 2014, Crown Court at Cardiff, T20141094 and T20141061 before HHJ Crowther QC, (2017) 14 Digital Evidence and Electronic Signature Law Review 67.
6 Thimbleby, Misunderstanding IT', 23.

6.58 Reliability goes to the heart of authentication. Caruso and others sum up the problem as follows:

> Electronic evidence is typically authenticated by methods which are limited to analysis of computer coding to determine if the machine functions according to its code. Putting aside issues regarding the accessibility of that code,[1] and assuming the code is verifiable, the examples we have given earlier indicate that the proper functioning of the technology can be an incomplete answer to the authenticity of the electronic evidence produced.[2]

1 See Edward J. Imwinkelried, 'Computer source code: a source of the growing controversy over the reliability of automated forensic techniques' (2017) 66 DePaul Law Review 97; Professor Imwinkelried's suggestions are considered in Chapter 5.
2 David Caruso, Michael Legg and Jordan Phoustanis, 'The automation paradox in litigation: the inadequacy of procedure and evidence law to manage electronic evidence generated by the "Internet of Things" in civil disputes' (2019) 19 Macquarie Law Journal 157, 181.

6.59 This comment does make the point that the 'proper functioning of the technology', or reliability of the computer system as it is sometimes referred to, does not automatically prove that the evidence is authentic. Further, as demonstrated by the cases outlined above, it is not always easy to rebut the presumption of reliability.

Methods of authentication

6.60 Since the concept of an 'original' is no longer useful when dealing with digital evidence, a digital object has to be authenticated by verifying the claims associated with it, such as:

> 1. The organizational criteria demonstrating the provenance of the digital object, including the documentation pertaining to the continuity of custody (and the extent to which this documentation can be trusted), and the extent to which the custodians can be trusted.
>
> 2. When the object is examined forensically, its characteristics and content are consistent with the claims made about it and the record of its provenance (although the methods used may also be subject to challenge – for instance, how a computer is tested for reliability or consistency of output).
>
> 3. The forensic imaging techniques are appropriate when relying on the evidence from a personal computer.
>
> 4. Any signatures, seals and time stamps that may be attached to the object to help test the claims about consistency and provenance.

Self-authentication

6.61 Self-authentication allows a document to be authenticated without the need for external evidence and is proof of the particulars stated within. Self-authenticating evidence includes certified public or official records[1] such as certified copies of birth, marriage and death certificates. Some jurisdictions would go further and provide that such evidence fall within the exception to the rule against hearsay. If public or official records were to be admitted only through a witness who could attest to the document's creation and its authenticity, trials would take much longer and be more expensive. Many jurisdictions provide for rules of evidence to establish the authenticity of public documents.[2]

1 *Irish Society v Bishop of Derry & Raphoe* (1846) 12 Cl. & Fin. 641, 8 ER 1561.

2 For Australia, see s 155 of the Commonwealth Evidence Act 1995; for England and Wales, see s 9 of the Civil Evidence Act 1995; for Canada, see ss 24–26 the Canada Evidence Act 1995; for the USA, see the Federal Rules of Evidence, s 902(1), (2) – note that Rule 902(11) also provides that business records as 'records of a regularly conducted activity' may be self-certified as authentic. This rule has faced some criticism, for which see Paul W. Grimm, Daniel J. Capra and Gregory J. Joseph, 'Authenticating digital evidence' (2017) 69 Baylor L Rev 1, 40.

System authentication

6.62 Most public and private organizations keep their digital material in Electronic Documents and Records Management Systems (EDRMS). These systems are regulated by national and international standards, which are essential for assessing the reliability and integrity of the systems through which electronic evidence is created, stored and managed, as well as to determine whether such electronic evidence falls under the business records exception to the hearsay rule.[1] These standards share some fundamental requirements:

1. The system software should be able to present old materials as they originally appeared (backward compatible), and allow the sharing of materials easily with other systems (interoperable).

2. The software should have undergone theoretical or empirical testing and peer review; its error rate should be known; and it should have gained general acceptance within the scientific community (Daubert standard).[2]

3. The formats used should be non-proprietary, platform independent and uncompressed,[3] with freely available specifications (open format) and software whose source code is made (freely) available and can be modified (open source).

4. The results produced by using the system should be repeatable, objective and verifiable.

5. The specifications of the software must be maintained and available.

6. If the software is customized, the changes must be documented (including comments in the software code).

7. The construction of the whole system must be documented.

1 The established record-keeping standards are: in Europe, the Model requirements (Moreq) series of standards, https://moreq.info/; in the US, the Department of Defense 5015.2-2007 standard: https://www.esd.whs.mil/Portals/54/Documents/DD/issuances/dodm/501502std.pdf; in Canada, the CGSB 72.34-2017 standard: https://www.scc.ca/en/standardsdb/standards/28933; and internationally the International Council on Archives Requirements, ICA-Req standards: https://www.ica.org/en/ica-req (requires a username and password).

2 *Daubert v Merrell Dow Pharmaceuticals, Inc.*, 509 U.S. 579, 113 S.Ct. 2786. The Daubert rules are a generally accepted standard for records systems in the US: https://www.law.cornell.edu/wex/daubert_standard.

3 Note that the Moreq standard and Department of Defense 5015.2-2007 standard recognize the use of compression for archiving.

6.63 The integrity of any system, not only EDRMS, should be inferred from sufficient security measures[1] to prevent unauthorized or untracked access to the computers, networks, devices or storage; and stable physical devices that will ensure the values they were provided with should be maintained until changed with authorization. These devices include user names and permissions, passwords, firewalls and logs. While the first three are self-explanatory, the logs deserve a more detailed discussion, because they are an important part of the authentication of the system and the digital material stored in it. Logs are sets of files *automatically* created to track the actions taken, services run, or files accessed or modified, and the time, identity of the person undertaking the action and their location. They can be separated into:

1. Web logs (Client IP Address, Request Date/Time, Page Requested, HTTP Code, Bytes Sent, Browser Type, etc.).

2. Access logs (User account ID, User IP address, File Descriptor, Actions taken upon record, Unbind record, Closed connection).

3. Transaction logs (History of actions taken on a system to ensure Atomicity, Consistency, Isolation, Durability (ACID)[2]); Sequence number; Link to previous log; Transaction ID; Type; Updates, commits, aborts, completes).

4. Auditing Logs. They are increasing required by law to demonstrate the integrity of the system. If properly configured, and if their access is restricted, they can provide checks and balances, determine effective security policies, catch errors that occur, provide instantaneous notification of events, monitor many systems and devices through 'dashboards', help determine accountability

of people, provide the necessary snapshot for post-event reconstruction ('black-box'), and, if retained for a long enough time, have the capability to answer the Who-What-Where-When questions.

1 From a practical point of view, when organizations and individuals entrust their data, documents or records to cloud providers, it is not possible to verify the integrity of the data centres where the digital material is stored. Thus, it is only possible to examine the security measures agreed upon in the contract between provider and user, and make an inference of authenticity from these criteria. Contrary to common belief, security is usually higher in the cloud than in anyone's in-house repository, if the user is willing to pay for it. In fact, cloud providers have the ability to offer more complex and expensive technologies and centralized controls than would be available at any single organization. This means it is arguable that, in the cloud environment, security can be considered the equivalent of authenticity.

2 ACID (atomicity, consistency, isolation and durability) is an acronym and mnemonic device for learning and remembering the four primary attributes ensured to any transaction by a transaction manager (which is also called a transaction monitor). Atomicity: in a transaction involving two or more discrete pieces of information, either all of the pieces are committed or none are. Consistency: a transaction either creates a new and valid state of data, or, if any failure occurs, returns all data to its state before the transaction was started. Isolation: a transaction in process and not yet committed must remain isolated from any other transaction. Durability: committed data is saved by the system in such a way that, even in the event of a failure and system restart, the data is available in its correct state.

6.64 While any system can be authenticated on the basis of a thorough examination by an expert of the security measures mentioned above, EDRMS must be shown to protect documents from accidental loss or corruption as well as hardware and software obsolescence. This has more to do with management of the system and its contents than with technology. Thus, a witness who is knowledgeable of procedures and processes in the organization should be able to attest that the system is backed up at least once a day, using the best backup technique for the circumstances and ensuring that the backup system includes an audit trail. It should be noted that the purpose of the backup is to recover the system in case of failure, and backups are destroyed on a regular basis. Ideally, duplicates of documents should be maintained on additional hard drives. If they are stored on tapes or discs, it is necessary to refresh and upgrade them periodically. Considering that the integrity of the electronic system guarantees the trustworthiness of the documents stored in them, at least in Canada (and de facto also in the United States), it is important for organizations to eliminate dependence on specific hardware by transferring all its functionalities to the software (this is where IT departments can help); to plan for regular technology upgrades (keeping in mind the need for backward compatibility); to consider external storage for infrequently used documents; and, if documents are removed from the live system, to associate with it the system documentation and all the necessary information about the material to be able to maintain accessibility and to understand the content of the material itself.[1]

1 For the characteristics of EDRMS that ensure the trustworthiness of the records created and/or stored in them, see InterPARES 2 Project, *Creator Guidelines*, http://www.interpares.org/ip2/display_file.cfm?doc=ip2(pub)creator_guidelines_booklet.pdf.

Digital certification

6.65 Digital certification may be a way of proving the authenticity of evidence. However, such certification can only be as reliable as the method used to generate digital certificates, for example in a public key infrastructure where the certification authority, being the holder of the public key, is truly independent and capable of being verified.[1] The most significant issue with the authenticity certificates issued by certifying authorities is that they are usually valid for no longer than five years.[2]

1 See Chapter 7, 'Electronic signatures' for a detailed explanation of digital signatures.
2 See Hrvoje Stančić, 'Authentication', in Luciana Duranti and Corinne Rogers, (eds) *Trusting Records in the Cloud* (Facet Publishers and the Society of American Archivists 2019), 131–154. For a detailed technical explanation and how such systems fail, see Chapter 7, 'Electronic signatures'.

6.66 Other forms of digital certification include the use of checksums or of 'hash algorithms', such as MD5 or SHA-1, which, once generated, can be compared with those generated on later versions of the digital document to ascertain whether any changes have occurred to the document. These methods prove the bitwise integrity of the digital documents, and are one way to demonstrate the continuity of evidence and that the document has not been tampered with, if the metadata showing it is part of the checksum or the hash.

Digital forensics

6.67 If the evidence is collected in such a way that the continuity of evidence is not preserved from the time of collection until its presentation at trial, this may affect its admissibility or, if admitted, the weight that the court may attach to it. To obviate this challenge, a specialist 'science' known as computer forensics or digital forensics has evolved to assist the court. Digital forensics encompasses four elements: identification, preservation, analysis and presentation. Safeguards and methodologies used by digital evidence professionals must preserve evidence in a way that will withstand both judicial scrutiny and challenges raised by an opposing party, should the matter go to trial.[1]

1 This topic is discussed in detail in Chapter 9. See also Luciana Duranti, 'From digital diplomatics to digital records forensics' (2009) 68 Archivaria 39; Luciana Duranti and Barbara Endicott-Popovsky, 'Digital records forensics: a new science and academic program for forensic readiness' (2010) 5.2 Journal of Digital Forensics, Security and Law 45; and Luciana Duranti and Corinne Rogers, 'Memory forensics: integrating digital forensics with archival science for trusting records and data', *eForensics Magazine* (October 2013).

Extrinsic and circumstantial evidence

6.68 Circumstantial evidence is evidence of a fact from which the existence of the fact in issue may be inferred. Circumstantial evidence can be differentiated from direct evidence, which is evidence that directly supports an assertion. For example, circumstantial evidence would include testimony of a witness who saw a person leaving a murder scene carrying a blood-stained knife, but who did not actually see the person killing the deceased. With respect to digital evidence, circumstantial evidence can be necessary to prove, for example, that a person wrote a particular email, or placed a particular post on a social media site. Circumstantial evidence can be important, since some judges are reluctant to accept testimony from the recipient of messages as a sufficient basis for authentication.[1]

1 Elizabeth A. Flanagan, '#Guilty? Sublet v. State and the authentication of social media evidence in criminal proceedings' (2016) 61 Vill L R 287, 298.

6.69 Circumstantial evidence is particularly important when attempting to authenticate digital evidence, such as social media posts. The central issue with social media is that anyone can create a profile using a false name, and someone else might obtain access to another person's profile if they gain access to their username and password.[1]

1 Flanagan, '#Guilty? ', 301.

6.70 Grimm, Capra and Joseph note that the 'standard for establishing authenticity of digital evidence is the same mild standard as for traditional forms of evidence'.[1] For example, if the sender of an email denies having written the email, then the party tendering the email will need to provide a wide array of evidence to prove the identity of the sender. This may be difficult, unless the party tendering the email has circumstantial evidence to show the sender was at a particular place at a particular time and the balance of probabilities (for civil matters) is that she did send the email.

1 Paul W. Grimm, Daniel J. Capra and Gregory J. Joseph, 'Authenticating digital evidence', 5.

Judicial notice

6.71 Judicial notice may be taken of evidence where the facts are so notorious or well known that they cannot reasonably be doubted. Such evidence does not need to be admitted through a witness and can be admitted at the request of one party. Wigmore sums up the rule as follows:

> The object of this rule is to save time, labor, and expense in securing and introducing evidence on matters which are not ordinarily capable of dispute and are actually not bona fide disputed, and the tenor of which can safely be assumed from the tribunal's general knowledge or from slight research on its part ... It thus becomes a useful expedient for speeding trials and curing informalities.[1]

1 John Henry Wigmore, *A Pocket Code of the Rules of Evidence in Trials at Law* (Little, Brown & Co 1910), 2120.

6.72 The common law 'notorious instrument' presumption allows courts to presume that readings from scientific instruments are accurate. The courts, however, tend to be slow to recognize any newly developed scientific devices.[1] Once judicial notice has been taken of a fact, arguably no evidence in rebuttal is admissible.[2] However, some judges have been critical of judicial notice being taken of facts based on incorrect assumptions. Judge Harvey refers to the following passage made by Fogarty J in *Senior v Police*:

> The Court takes judicial notice that persons who use Facebook are very aware that the contents of Facebook are often communicated to persons beyond the 'friends' who use Facebook. When information is put on a Facebook page, to which hundreds of people have access, the persons putting the information on the page know that that information will likely extend way beyond the defined class of 'friends'. Very strong personal abuse directed at a former partner, placed on Facebook, read by a large number of friends, some of whom will inevitably have contact in the natural social network with the person being abused, is at the very least highly reckless.[3]

1 Harvey, 'Digital evidence admissibility: some issues'; this topic is dealt with more extensively in Chapter 5.
2 J. D. Heydon, *Cross on Evidence* (12th edn, LexisNexis 2020), 229.
3 [2013] NZHC 357.

6.73 Judge Harvey criticized this passage on the basis it relied on an incorrect assumption: it wrongly assumes that 'a person who posts to a network of friends is aware that publication is being made to the world', or that a posting will come to the attention of a particular person.[1] Judge Harvey says that, in his view, 'that cannot be assumed and should be the subject of proof' and that 'the sweeping assumption by Fogarty J couched in the concept of judicial notice, cannot be sustained and should be treated with extreme caution'. Further, given the lack of discussion and analysis of the facts or evidence that led to the assumption, Judge Harvey stated that 'in some respects, it creates a reversal of the burden of proof'. Importantly, Judge Harvey goes on to say:

> Working on the assumption that posting material on a Facebook page is automatically intended to be communicated to the 2 billion per month Facebook subscribers, a defendant then has the burden of proving that in fact this was not the case and evidence would have to be led that the various settings on the particular Facebook account did not permit this to take place. In reality the burden should be on the prosecution to exclude such a possibility.[2]

1 Harvey, 'Digital evidence admissibility: some issues', 13.
2 Harvey, 'Digital evidence admissibility: some issues', 13.

6.74 The fact recognized by judicial notice in *Senior v Police* was adopted in the later case of *S v S*,[1] where, in Judge Harvey's view, the incorrect generalization was extended to all social media platforms. Judge Harvey sums up the position as follows:

> The utilisation of digital technologies and the way that they are treated by lawyers and the Courts requires a rigorous approach and a journey into unfamiliar territory by both lawyers and judges.[2]

1 [2017] NZHC 1574.
2 Harvey, 'Digital evidence admissibility: some issues', 15.

6.75 In our view, Judge Harvey correctly sums up the position with respect to the assumptions made by courts and digital technology.

Digital evidence in archival systems

6.76 When the documentary material submitted as documentary evidence is in the custody of an archival institution, archival description (that is, inventories) acquires a primary authentication function. The authentication function of archival description is a collective attestation of the authenticity of the documents or records in an archival *fonds* (the Canadian expression 'archival *fonds*' is equivalent to 'archive' in British usage, and 'archives' in Australian and American usage) as well as of all their interrelationships; in other words, authenticity in their documentary context. Archival description provides a historical view of the records and of their transformations while maintaining the bond of their common provenance and destination. Archival description of permanent digital records relies on metadata as evidence about a record's identity and integrity, which is discussed in more detail below.

6.77 The authenticity of the documentary material of an organization can be presumed if such organization or the archival institution to which it transfers its records has a trusted digital repository. 'A trusted digital repository is one whose mission is to provide reliable, long-term access to managed digital resources to its designated community, now and in the future.'[1] Trusted Digital Repositories (TDR) are expensive and require professionals with specific and costly qualifications to operate them. There are few 'trusted' repositories that are 'trustworthy'. Regardless of certification, TDRs appear to be trusted only when they are in a trusted 'place of preservation' such as archives or a library.[2]

1 RLG-OCLC report *Trusted Digital Repositories: Attributes and Responsibilities*, 5, https://www.oclc.org/content/dam/research/activities/trustedrep/repositories.pdf.
2 Devan Ray Donaldson and Paul Conway, 'User conceptions of trustworthiness for digital archival documents' (2015) 66(12) Journal of the Association for Information Science and Technology 2427.

6.78 The two exemplary models of TDRs both come from research activities. The first was the Open Archival Information System (OAIS), created by the National Aeronautics and Space Administration (NASA), which became an ISO standard in 2003, revised in 2012 as ISO 14721:2012 and as Trusted Third Party Repository ISO 17068: 2012 and 2017.[1] The second was the Chain of Preservation Model generated by the InterPARES research project.[2]

1 Consultative Committee for Space Data System, *Reference Model for an Open Archival Information System (OAIS)*, (June 2021), https://public.ccsds.org/pubs/650x0m2.pdf.
2 Chain of Preservation Model: http://www.interpares.org/display_file.cfm?doc=ip2_COP_diagrams(complete).pdf.

6.79 The OAIS model was not developed by archival specialists, neither was it intended for archival institutions. Rather, it was conceived as a preservation system internal to an organization, such as NASA. It offers a conceptual framework for digital preservation that describes, in a technologically neutral manner, the activities and the information that are necessary for trustworthy preservation. Effectively, it has defined the universe of discourse for digital preservation in a variety of contexts around the world. It details the authorized custody services of a Trusted Third Party Repository (TTPR) in order to ensure provable authenticity of the clients' digital records and serve as a source of reliable evidence. It describes the services and processes to be provided by a TTPR for the clients' digital records during the retention period to ensure trust. It also details the criteria of 'trustworthiness' and the particular requirements of TTPR services, hardware and software systems, and management. Its limitation is that the authorized custody of the stored material is by way of an agreement between only the third party and the client.

6.80 The InterPARES project recognized that digital preservation requires a Chain of Preservation (COP) that ensures that digital records survive uncorrupted from creation through their migration from one system to another. The phrase 'Chain of Preservation' was chosen to indicate that all the activities to manage records throughout their existence are linked, as in a chain, and are interdependent. If a link in the chain fails, the chain cannot do its job. If certain actions are not undertaken on documentary evidence, its trustworthiness and preservation are imperilled. Any break in how digital information has been preserved could make it impossible to assert that what remains is what it should be.

6.81 The COP is realized by implementing controls that ensure that the requirements for preservation are satisfied throughout the life of the records. The COP is reflected, after the fact, in data that demonstrate that these requirements have been satisfied.

These are identity and integrity metadata. Identity metadata include, but are not limited to:

(1) Names of the persons concurring in the creation of the digital entity (e.g. author, writer, addressee, originator, creator, etc.);

(2) Date(s) and time(s) of issuing, transmission and receipt;

(3) The matter or action in which the entity participates;

(4) The expression of its relationship to other entities (e.g. classification code);

(5) Documentary form (e.g. report);

(6) Digital presentation (e.g. pdf);

(7) The indication of any attachment(s);

(8) Possible presence of digital signature; and

(9) Name of the person responsible for the business matter.

6.82 Integrity metadata include, but are not limited to:

(1) Name(s) of handling persons/offices over time;

(2) Name of person/office responsible for keeping the entity;

(3) Indication of annotations;

(4) Indication of technical changes;

(5) Indication of presence or removal of digital signature;

(6) Checksum;

(7) Time of planned removal from the system (migration);

(8) Time of transfer to a custodian (archives program or institution);

(9) Time of planned deletion; and

(10) Existence and location of duplicates outside the system.

6.83 Given the nature of digital material, the integrity of the digital environment is of greater concern than that of the identity metadata. If the server is stable, it is possible to be confident that the creator's records are what they purport to be, and therefore for all intents and purposes they can be presumed authentic.

6.84 By scrutinizing the digital records preservation practice in the context of the authenticity metadata listed above, it is possible to say that digital records authentication can be broken down into at least two tiers. The first, and most important, tier for the presumption of authenticity is to audit the integrity of the preservation system in which records are kept.[1] To date there are a number of ways metadata are included in this tier: the use of checksums, the conduct of visual inspection and the comparison with duplicated material in a parallel system. The checksum can be easily verified, whereas the comparison often goes undocumented. The second tier for the presumption of authenticity moves from audit of integrity to the verification of identity. Identity metadata are provided during the process of making, transmitting, receiving and storing the digital entity. The identity metadata rely on how the creator's system (for instance, an EDRMS) works to encapsulate the entirety of the state of the digital evidence as used by the creator in the ordinary course of business. Thus, to authenticate material that has been preserved in a system other than the one in which it was generated and/or received, it is necessary to authenticate all digital systems used over time to store such material and focus on the sum total of what can be said about the evidence from its creation to its preservation (and subsequent retrieval and use).

1 This is of course independent of the trustworthiness of the preserver. If the material submitted as evidence is preserved in a digital preservation system by a public archival institution, presumption of authenticity, until proof to the contrary, is a given.

Technological authentication

Digital signatures

6.85 The most common form of technological authentication for records is the secure digital signature. Such a signature acts to protect bitwise integrity, verifies a record's origin (part of its identity) and makes a record indisputable and incontestable (non-repudiation[1]). The digital signature has been given legal value mainly by legislative acts,[2] is enabled through complex and costly public-key infrastructures (PKI) and ensures authenticity of information across space (transmission from a person to another), though not through time. This is because it is subject to obsolescence, it compounds the problem of preservation, as it cannot be migrated with the record it is attached to, and the certificates linked to it have an expiry date. Archival science tells us that a digital signature has the function of a seal, in that it is attached to a document that is complete without it, rather than that of a signature, which is an essential part of a record, so it can be removed and substituted with metadata attesting to its presence at the time of transmission and receipt. This is largely the position taken by evidence law in common law countries. A detailed discussion of digital signatures and the challenges they present when the documents to which they are attached must be maintained for longer than 2–5 years can be found in Chapter 7.

1 For the meaning of 'non-repudiation' and its limits, see Chapter 7, Electronic signatures.
2 For a list, see 'World electronic signature legislation' (2019) 16 Digital Evidence and Electronic Signature Law Review 135, https://journals.sas.ac.uk/deeslr/article/view/5092.

Blockchain

6.86 The blockchain is a type of Distributed Ledger Technology (DLT), a concept referring to the maintenance of a decentralized data repository geographically spread across multiple sites, multiple countries and multiple organizations. The blockchain is the underlying technology that enables the virtual currency Bitcoin. It is a ledger – an information store that keeps a final and definitive (immutable) trace of transactions (their hash codes[1]). To operate, it relies upon a distributed network, given that all nodes and servers are equal, and on decentralized consensus, with no centre(s) and no single point of control or attack. The confirmed and validated sets of transactions are held in blocks, which are linked (chained) in a chain that is tamper-resistant and append-only. A blockchain starts with the genesis block, and each block contains, in addition to the hash of a predetermined number of documents, a hash of the prior block in the chain (referred to as the Merkle tree).

1 A hash code is computed from the base number using an algorithm. It is nearly impossible to derive without original data. It typically uses 128bit or greater algorithms, so 2^{128}. The hash code compresses bits of a message into a fixed-size value; thus, it is extremely difficult to come up with original records based on hash values. The common Hash functions are SHA-1 160 bit, RIPEMD-160 160bit and MD5 128 bit.

6.87 A blockchain can be used to confirm the integrity of a record kept elsewhere, in that a record existed or was created at a certain point in time, although not after it has been time-stamped and registered in the blockchain, and the sequence of records leading to it. It is not a system that records business records. It holds the hash of records, not the records themselves. Smart contracts, which are agreements between parties directly written into lines of code on a blockchain, are not yet recognized as records. The records must still be stored and managed off chain. This is good, because if they were in the blockchain, they would be immutable.

6.88 Immutability is the attraction of a blockchain: it is what ensures integrity, as nothing can be changed in a blockchain block or removed from a block. At the same time, this is the central problem of blockchain. In fact, with current records, that is records used in the present and active course of current business, any updating or correction of the wrong data, any form of privacy protection, any exercise of the right to be forgotten, any disposition of records that are no longer needed, any system upgrade, and in short any change in the record, would invalidate the blockchain. Where records are kept or identified for continuing and possibly long-term preservation, any transfer, migration or addition to the records of a preservation system would invalidate the blockchain.

6.89 The blockchain therefore presents a problem for authentication that goes beyond bit-wise integrity, in that any form of indirect or circumstantial authentication is not possible, because the hash on the blockchain does not allow for links to the hash of related records or the hash of metadata. If the metadata were embedded in each record at creation, the hash of such record would not allow for additions or changes, which is always necessary when carrying out any usual and ordinary business.

6.90 Further, handling the decentralized (and thus trans-jurisdictional) nature of the blockchain is complicated. At any given time, determining the author of a record, the owner and what law applies is difficult, especially when dealing with code in a situation where different participants in different jurisdictions control the necessary components of the transaction. An additional issue is presented by smart contracts, which lack both the equivalent of a signature and the date of the completion of an agreement. Thus, decentralization, the attractive aspect of blockchain that takes away central control and democratizes it, is a problem for authentication of data in digital form. This is because information processing happens on a complex technological stack in which different technical components may be in the custody of, and operated by, very different participants. Some components may be under the control of a single organization, others under the control of business partners who are members of a blockchain consortium, and still others under the control of unknown third-party contributors. An organization's records could be in the custody of thousands of independent legal entities or individuals over which the creators of the records exercise little or no control. The consensus mechanism, and other protocols or standards that determine how the blockchain operates, may not be within the decision-making purview of the creator (or the creator's designated records professional). These may be decided by remote (and even unknown) third party developers. In many cases, these protocols and standards are still unstable, and thus the reliability of the upload of organizational records to the blockchain could be very difficult to establish with any certainty.

Challenges to the authenticity of evidence in digital form

The cloud

6.91 Blanchette states that cloud computing has become a 'certain kind of *meta-infrastructure*' capable of unprecedented sustainable growth, where infrastructure is defined as 'the elements of the computing ecosystem that provide services *to applications*, in contrast to the applications that provide *services to users*'.[1] Countries are beginning to look at the cloud as a critical infrastructure, that is, an infrastructure that is vital to the functioning of their economy and society. It is therefore logical to expect that, in the future, IT systems, including record-keeping and preservation systems, will be more often than not in the cloud.

1 Jean-François Blanchette, 'Introduction' in Christopher S. Yoo and Jean-François Blanchette (eds) *Regulating the Cloud. Policy for Computing Infrastructure* (MIT Press 2015), 3, emphasis added.

6.92 When a user entrusts its data, documents or records to a cloud provider, and uses the provider's platform and application to generate additional data, the provider will create metadata related to the user's actions about data processing, management, and such like. While the user who creates content and stores that in the cloud owns that content, they do not own the metadata created by the provider. This means that as the user needs them to authenticate its material by demonstrating its integrity, the provisions of the contractual agreements between users and cloud providers will determine whether the user has the right to obtain access to and use the provider's metadata. Usually such agreements do not discuss ownership of metadata generated by providers and, as a consequence, authentication of material stored in a cloud environment cannot be easily supported with evidence of its integrity or the integrity of the system.[1]

1 For a discussion of contractual agreements for cloud services see Jessica Bushey, Marie Demoulin and Robert McLelland, 'Cloud service contracts: an issue of trust' (2015 June) 39(2) The Canadian Journal of Information and Library Science 128.

6.93 Cloud providers claim certain standards for the availability of services, such as retrieval and access to data. This involves making available the stored material and also implies the availability of the infrastructure, which facilitates the retrieval and readability of the data. But technical difficulties might slow discovery, access and authentication processes; these difficulties might create an issue when, for example, there are deadlines imposed by a judge. Could providers also claim certain standards for the reliability of their services? Reliability is the characteristic of behaving consistently with expectations. Data stored in the cloud has the characteristic of being redundant, which means that multiple copies exist in multiple places; thus, the issue arises as to consistency and accuracy of access: whether people obtaining access to different copies see the same thing. However, compliance is difficult to verify. The continuing transfer of data by the cloud provider from one data centre to another for retention purposes might involve the loss of authenticity. Where and how the data are stored and maintained may affect the quality of the documents and their ability to serve as evidence, especially in jurisdictions where the authenticity of the document is an inference made from the integrity of the system where the data reside. In a cloud environment, the data are constantly moved, and the provider's metadata, which reveals where the data were at any given time, may not be accessible, as mentioned above.

6.94 Contractual agreements with cloud providers do not generally specify how data, documents or records are maintained across changing technologies and data formats. They generally provide that users are responsible for backing up their data, including maintenance procedures such as proper storage, care, custody and data control as 'backup procedures'. Thus, it cannot be known how the data centres protect data from unauthorized access, use, alteration or destruction. And these issues have to be resolved before issues as to the authentication of cloud data can be addressed.

6.95 In a world where the integrity of a system is an inference made from its security, and the integrity of the data, documents or records is an inference one makes from the integrity of the system, security is the new authenticity, and authentication itself becomes an inference based on an assessment of security levels. Organizations enforce security with something they know (e.g. passwords), they own (e.g. tokens), or things which belong to the user (e.g., biometric measurements of eyes or fingerprints; private keys in a PKI environment). Cloud providers enforce security by means of encryption of data, in storage and during transmission, and should be in a position to produce audit trails and access logs, and capture, maintain and make available metadata associated with access, retrieval, use and management of the data, in addition to those linked to the data themselves. Unless a contract explicitly states so, comprehensive security measures may not be in place; but even if they are, security still relates directly to the matter of data location and cross-border data flow.

6.96 The cloud is the platform of choice for mobile applications and the data generated using them, as well as those created for use on smart devices. Records can be stored in data centres anywhere in the world and the location of the records is a criterion in determining the law that applies in case of litigation. But providers may not always know where the records are at any given time and they can subcontract some of their services to other providers in different countries.

6.97 If the material to be submitted as evidence has been retained for a long time, these issues are compounded. The same hardware and software will not remain in service for as long as the records must be preserved, and it is doubtful that the technologies replacing them will be compatible with the earlier ones. Providers may claim to follow the standards for preservation formats, but it is not possible to control compliance. Furthermore, if the provider ceases to exist, becomes insolvent or terminates one or more of its services (for breach, inactivity or convenience), the records will be deleted or inaccessible. This is the case with free services, since these do not have an established duration and providers may close users accounts unilaterally, require users to delete software and applications, and prevent them from obtaining access to the remaining data. When the data are given back to the user, it is not certain that it will be in a usable and interoperable format.

6.98 This all means that the authentication of data, documents or records created and stored in the cloud has to rely on circumstantial evidence, on testimony of witnesses, or on the existence of copies elsewhere. Otherwise, it has to rely on what is known about the security measures used by the provider and a presumption of authenticity, unless there is proof to the contrary.[1]

1 For an in-depth discussion of business records created and/or stored in the cloud environment, see Duranti and Rogers, *Trusting Records in the Cloud*.

The Internet of Things

6.99 Caruso and others[1] identify issues with authentication of Internet of Things (IoT) derived electronic evidence. Compared with traditional methods of authentication, they note that for IoT-derived evidence, there is 'the absence of human input in the ordinary functioning of the device'.[2] IoT is generating electronic evidence without human input and thus creating additional challenges for authentication. As the authors note:

> The absence of human input removes the IoT-derived evidence from the purview of the hearsay rule because the automation of recording eliminates the potential human foibles and infractions against which hearsay guards. The paradox is that this pathway to admissible use relies on the very divorce of the IoT from human input, monitoring or awareness that derogates from the capacity of the human-centric trial to authenticate IoT-derived electronic evidence. This derogation is likely to become more significant as future waves of autonomous technology decreasingly rely on human input; whilst humans increasingly rely on these technologies.[3]

1 Caruso and others, 'The automation paradox in litigation'; see also Anne Toomey McKenna, Amy C. Gaudion and Jenni L. Evans, 'The role of satellites and smart devices: data surprises and security, privacy, and regulatory challenges', (2019) 123 Penn St L Rev 591, and Marie-Helen Maras and Adam Scott Wandt, 'State of Ohio v Ross Compton: internet-enabled medical device data introduced as evidence of arson and insurance fraud', (2020) 24(3) E & P 321.
2 Caruso and others, 'The automation paradox in litigation', 176.
3 Caruso and others, 'The automation paradox in litigation', 177.

6.100 The Internet of Things comprises data collected by devices, which transmit such data to other devices including storage platforms. Such devices might include devices located in residences such as refrigerators, where the data generated are collected in a database for a variety of purposes, including garnering the 'lifestyle conditions and habits of the occupants of the residence'.[1] Such data collected without human input may be used in evidence, for example, to show the condition of the refrigerator where food poisoning is suspected or to monitor a patient's medication needs.[2] Likewise, wearable devices such as Fitbits collect all sorts of data that have been used in litigation as circumstantial evidence to prove the location of a person at a particular point in time.[3]

1 Caruso and others, 'The automation paradox in litigation', 159.
2 Caruso and others, 'The automation paradox in litigation', 164.
3 Nicole Chauriye, 'Wearable devices as admissible evidence: technology is killing our opportunity to lie' (2016) Cath U J L & Tech 495.

Digital preservation

6.101 The preservation of digital material is a continuous process that begins before data or documents or records[1] are created and the purpose of which is to transmit trustworthy (that is reliable, accurate and authentic) digital entities through time and across space.[2] Digital materials of a documentary nature (documents and records) consist of 'formal elements' that are shown on their face (address, date, salutation), metadata or attributes that demonstrate their identity and integrity, and digital components, that is, stored digital entities that require a specific preservation measure. Furthermore, they must have fixed form and stable content.

1 When discussing digital preservation, it is essential to keep in mind the difference among records (documents made or received in the course of activity as an instrument and by-product of it, and kept for the purposes of such activity), documents (information recorded on a medium, where information is a message meant for communication) and data (the smallest meaningful piece of information). When data is stored over the long term, we usually speak of curation, the cleaning of and adding value to data, rather than preservation. Digital preservation refers to documentary material, which includes documents and records (all records are documents, though not all documents are records, and not all records are 'business records'). In addition to the CGSB 74.34-2017, see Duranti and Thibodeau, 'The concept of record in interactive, experiential and dynamic environments'.

2 Luciana Duranti (ed), *The Long-term Preservation of Authentic Electronic Records: Findings of the InterPARES Project* (Archilab 2005); Luciana Duranti and Randy Preston (eds), *InterPARES 2: Interactive, Dynamic and Experiential Records* (ANAI 2008); Duranti and Rogers, 'Trust in digital records'.

6.102 Thus, when discussing preservation of digital documentary evidence, it is necessary to consider both the 'stored record' and the 'manifested record'. The stored record is composed of the digital component(s) used in re-producing it. This comprises the data to be processed in order to manifest the record (*content data* and *form data*) and the rules for processing the data, including those enabling variations (*composition data* – that is, data enabling any kind of structural change in the record). The manifested record is the visualization or instantiation of the record in a form suitable for presentation to a person or a system. Sometimes it does not have a corresponding stored record, but it is recreated from fixed content data when a user's action associates them with specific form data and composition data (for instance, a record produced from a relational database).

6.103 A documentary entity has a fixed form if its binary content is stored so that the message it conveys can be rendered with the same documentary presentation (or manifestation) it had on the screen when first saved (though it might have changed its stored presentation from, say, a MS Word document to pdf format). A documentary entity also has fixed form if the same content can be presented on the screen in several different manifestations but in a limited number of ways: in this case there would be a different documentary presentation of the same stored record with a fixed form (for instance, statistical data viewed as a pie chart, a bar chart or a table).

6.104 A documentary entity has stable content if the data and the message it conveys are unchanged and unchangeable, meaning that data cannot be overwritten, altered, deleted or added to. In the digital environment, the concept of 'bounded variability' is present when changes to the documentary presentation of a determined stable content are limited and controlled by fixed rules, so that the same query or interaction always generates the same result, and there are different views of different subsets of the same content, as required by the author or as a result of different operating systems or applications.

6.105 Digital documentary materials may be static, in that they do not provide possibilities for changing their content or form beyond opening, closing and navigating them (email, reports, sound recordings, motion video, snapshots of web pages), or interactive, in that they present variable content, form, or both, and the rules governing the content and form of presentation may be either fixed or variable.

6.106 Further, digital documentary evidence can be non-dynamic, in that the rules governing the presentation of content and form do not vary, and the content presented each time is selected from a fixed store of data (interactive web pages, online catalogues or inventories, records enabling performances – they are documents or records), or dynamic, in that the rules governing the presentation of content and form may vary (this is the case with, for instance, Geographic Information Systems or GIS, which contain only data[1]).

1 An example of a GIS is the VanMap of the City of Vancouver, which is used by all the city staff in order to make decisions. The data often does not exist anywhere else, especially in the correlated form shown on the GIS layers, and are consistently overwritten by new data flowing in from a variety of databases, without being saved, https://maps.vancouver.ca/portal/apps/sites/#/vanmap/.

6.107 Traditional preservation is defined as the whole of the principles, policies and strategies that control the activities designed to ensure the physical and technological stabilization and protection of intellectual content in materials (data, documents or records). Considering all the characteristics of digital material mentioned above, 'digital preservation' is defined as the process of maintaining digital materials during and across different generations of technology over time, irrespective of where they are stored.[1] This is because it is not possible to preserve digital material. It is only possible to preserve the ability to reproduce it in a reliable, accurate and authentic way. This means that, when obtaining access to digital documentary evidence that has been maintained for a period longer than the life of the system in which it exists at the time of submission, it is not sufficient to look at the integrity of such system, but it is also essential to assess the entire preservation plan from the creation of the documentary material in the original system through its entire cycle of maintenance and preservation across systems, keeping in mind the continuity of evidence through time.

1 InterPARES Trust, Terminology Database, https://interparestrust.org/terminology/term/digital%20preservation.

6.108 Thus, any organization, public or private, that intends to maintain its digital material in such a way that one day it can be used as documentary evidence and be authenticated, needs to develop plans for transfer to a trusted custodian (which can be an archives program within the organization or an external body with archival functions), enforce standardized procedures for implementing it, keep the oldest available logical format of any document that is moved to another IT system, eliminate duplicates while ensuring redundancy (all materials should be duplicated in a separate digital repository in another location), document all processing, and ensure that all transferred materials are authentic copies of the previous ones by keeping audit and transaction logs, in addition to the identity and integrity metadata.

Migration and format changes

6.109 When it comes to authentication of evidence preserved for the long term, judges and lawyers need to be aware of what activities are routinely carried out by the preserving organization to ensure the continuing integrity of the records, as well as the ability to verify them. Appropriately qualified witnesses should be able to attest that the organization has implemented the following:

1. A controlled process of migration of the records to the archives' technological environment (always keeping the records in the format in which they were acquired);
2. The accurate documentation of any change that the records undergo during such process and every time that the archives' technological environment is upgraded;
3. Privileges concerning the access, use and reproduction of the records within the archives; and
4. Procedures to prevent, discover and correct loss or corruption of records; to guarantee the continuing identity and integrity of the records against media deterioration and across technological changes though continuing conversion and migration; to assign responsibility for and means of authentication of individual records, when required; and to ensure redundancy, internally and remotely.

6.110 One of the major authentication challenges relates to formats and migration. Consideration should be given to verifying that the organization has selected preservation formats using accepted criteria, such as widespread adoption, non-proprietary origin, published specifications, interoperability (platform independence), and lack of compression or lossless compression. The most accepted standards for documentary evidence are PDF 1.4, which became PDF/A ISO 19005-1:2005; PDF 1.7, which became ISO 32000-1: 2008; PDF/A-2, which became ISO 19005-2:2011; and PDF/A-3, which became ISO 19005-3:2012.[1]

1 PDF/A disallows audio/video content, JavaScript, compression and encryption. It requires that all fonts be embedded, and uses XMP metadata rules with the ability to supply new metadata schema if needed. PDF/A-2 includes better PDF tagging, which improves accessibility for smaller file sizes. It permits the use of JPEG2000 image compression, and allows the attachment of other PDF/A files. PDF/A-3 has exactly the same functionalities as PDF/A-2 but with one major difference: instead of being able to only embed other PDF/A files, it can embed any kind of data stream. The 'hybrid archiving' approach of PDF/A-3 could provide the best of both worlds from an evidence and archival perspective. The static visual elements of the main display document present the record content with fixity. Any concern about integrity can be addressed with the embedding of the original bitstream of the source record itself. This format provides a faithful representation of the record, is similar to that of a printout and offers the option of comparing the best format to the native one. Other standards that are valid for evidentiary purposes are: for audio, WAVE (LPCM); for email, MBOX; for Raster Images, TIFF; and for video, FFV1/LPCM in MKV. See Archivematica Preservation Formats, https://www.archivematica.org/en/docs/archivematica-1.11/user-manual/preservation/preservation-planning/.

6.111 In consideration of the fact that migration of documentary material from an obsolescent system to a current or emerging technology always entails some degree of risk, expert witnesses should show that the required functionalities of the old format were maintained through migration to a new format. Useful tools to verify a migration that has respected professional standards are the Conversions Software Registry (NCSA – National Center for Supercomputing Applications, 'Conversions Software

Registry – Query Conversions') and the PRONOM's DROID (from The National Archives of the United Kingdom). It is important, when authenticating material older than the system in which it is stored, to gather all information about its migration history.[1]

1 For instance, see http://www.interpares.org/display_file.cfm?doc=ip2_file_formats(complete).pdf.

The business records exception to the rule against hearsay

The business records exception

6.112 Several exceptions to the rule against hearsay have been developed over time for documentary evidence, most notably for business records. The rule against hearsay ensures that out-of-court statements do not make their way into evidence as truth of the assertions made in such statements. In other words, for a statement to be relied upon, it must be tendered in evidence through the witness who made the statement. This rule was introduced in England in the 1500s;[1] however, it was not fully developed until the early 1700s.

1 John H. Wigmore, 'The history of the hearsay rule' (1904) 7 Harvard Law Review 437.

6.113 The rationale behind this exception has its origins in the bankers' books rule[1] where records entered into log books by bank employees could be relied upon as a record made at that point in time. This exception to the rule against hearsay is an important one when considering authentication of evidence, because the basis on which the law developed over centuries was that employees would literally enter records on paper within the binding of a book. The business records exception to the rule against hearsay essentially provides that, providing the record was generated in the ordinary course of business, someone with knowledge of the records, typically a senior member of the business, can give evidence which leads to the admission of the documents into evidence. This rule developed as a common-sense approach where employees leave businesses, only to have records tendered after their departure. In a matter involving documents over a lengthy period of time, it makes practical sense to have a person with knowledge of the business tender all documents, rather than several different people, many of whom may no longer work for the business.

1 This rule has its origins in the Bankers' Books Evidence Act 1879 (UK), which provided in s 3: 'Subject to the provisions of this Act, a copy of an entry in a banker's book shall in all legal proceedings be received as prima facie evidence of such entry, and of the matters, transactions, and accounts therein recorded.'

6.114 While not articulating the underlying rationale, Lord Phillips illustrated this assumption in *R v Horncastle (Michael Christopher)*:

> Business records are made admissible (by s.117 or, where a machine is involved, s.129) because, in the ordinary way, they are compiled by persons who are disinterested and, in the ordinary course of events, such statements are likely to be accurate; they are therefore admissible as evidence because *prima facie* they are reliable.[1]

1 [2009] UKSC 14 at [35].

6.115 The exclusionary rules of the common law were relaxed by the Bankers' Books Evidence Act 1879. This Act provided that copies of entries in bankers' books – that is, ledgers, day books, cash books, account books and all other books kept in the ordinary business of the bank – are considered prima facie evidence of the matters recorded,[1] subject to a number of requirements before they can be admitted into evidence. As Professor Tapper remarked, the primary purpose was to prevent the business from being disrupted by the need to produce the original books in court.[2] In 1938, the case of a prosecution at a Metropolitan Police Court was commented upon in the *Journal of Criminal Law*.[3] A bank clerk gave evidence, and produced a photograph of the document. The representative of the accused did not object to the way the evidence was presented, but the commentator on the case raised a number of issues of relevance, the first of which was that the photograph was secondary evidence of the original, which is correct. The commentator then proceeded to consider the rules by which evidence is admitted under the provisions of the Act. First, the provisions of s 5 were noted. Section 5 provides as follows:

> Verification of copy.
>
> A copy of an entry in a banker's book shall not be received in evidence under this Act unless it be further proved that the copy has been examined with the original entry and is correct.
>
> Such proof shall be given by some person who has examined the copy with the original entry, and may be given either orally or by an affidavit sworn before any commissioner or person authorised to take affidavits.

1 In *Job v Halifax PLC* (2009, unreported), Inglis J accepted printouts of records cut and pasted from log files as evidence of the matters recorded; the trial was held on 30 April 2009 in Nottingham County Court and judgment was delivered on 4 June 2009. The full transcript of the judgment is available, with a commentary by Alistair Kelman, in (2009) 6 Digital Evidence and Electronic Signature Law Review 235.

2 Colin Tapper, *Computer Law* (4th edn, Longman 1989), 407.

3 'Admissibility of a photograph of a banking account' (1938) 2(7) The Journal of Criminal Law 357.

6.116 It was pointed out that no such evidence was tendered in this case, and it was suggested that the photograph was admitted on the basis that 'the camera cannot lie' – which does not follow. Second, citing the comments by Smith LJ in *Hindson v Ashby*,[1] the bank clerk did not give evidence that he took the photograph that was produced, which meant that the image was no more than hearsay. The commentator distinguished the decision in *R v Tolson*[2] because the purpose of the photograph in *Tolson* was to identify the husband, who was accused of bigamy. In the case of the photograph of the bank account, it was claimed that a witness could not say whether the photograph was correct in every detail of that particular account. A further problem with admitting the photograph arose in the light of the provisions of s 4, which reads:

> Proof that book is a banker's book.
>
> A copy of an entry in a banker's book shall not be received in evidence under this Act unless it be first proved that the book was at the time of the making of the entry one of the ordinary books of the bank, and that the entry was made in the usual and ordinary course of business, and that the book is in the custody or control of the bank.
>
> Such proof may be given by a partner or officer of the bank, and may be given orally or by an affidavit sworn before any commissioner or person authorised to take affidavits.

1 [1896] 2 Ch 1 (CA) 21.
2 (1864) 4 F & F 103, 176 ER 488.

6.117 The commentator suggested that the photograph could not be admitted unless the photographer was an officer of the bank with the necessary knowledge about the books of the bank. Finally, the commentator offered the opinion that there would be no requirement for the photograph to be proved where the bank officer producing it had first checked it against the account to which it related, because the Act does not require the person who made the copy to be called as a witness.

6.118 The technology used by banks altered considerably during the twentieth century, but this did not prevent judges from providing a wide construction to the statute, as in the (criminal) case of *Barker v Wilson*.[1] The Divisional Court was requested to provide an opinion by way of case stated from North Yorkshire Justices sitting at York. The question was whether the justices reached the correct decision that microfilm was included within the definition of 'bankers' books' in accordance with s 9 of the Act. Bridge LJJ and Caulfield J were both of the opinion that this was correct. Caulfield J said:

> The justices came to the conclusion – and they put their conclusions in these terms: that they adopted some robust common sense – that section 9 does include microfilm, which is a modern process of producing banker's records. It is probable that no modern bank in this country now maintains the old-fashioned books which were maintained at the time of the passing of the 1879 Act and possibly maintained for many years after 1879.[2]

1 [1980] 1 WLR 884, [1980] 2 All ER 81, [1980] 2 WLUK 2, (1980) 70 Cr App R 283 (DC), [1980] Crim LR 373, (1980) 124 SJ 326, [1980] CLY 469.
2 (1980) 70 Cr App R 283 at 286.

6.119 Bridge LJ reinforced the point:

> The Bankers' Books Evidence Act 1879 was enacted with the practice of bankers in 1879 in mind. It must be construed in 1980 in relation to the practice of bankers as we now understand it. So construing the definition of 'bankers' book' it seems to me that clearly both phrases are apt to include any form of permanent record kept by the bank of transactions relating to the banks' business, made by any of the methods which modern technology makes available, including, in particular, microfilm.[1]

1 (1980) 70 Cr App R 283 at 287.

6.120 Professor Tapper commended the flexibility of the judiciary to amend a statutory rule in such circumstances.[1] Section 9 has been amended by various enactments, and the relevant section, s 9(2), now reads as follows:

> (2) Expressions in this Act relating to 'bankers' books' include ledgers, day books, cash books, account books and other records used in the ordinary business of the bank, whether those records are in written form or are kept on microfilm, magnetic tape or any other form of mechanical or electronic data retrieval mechanism.

1 Tapper, *Computer Law*, 408. See also the decision in *Victor Chandler International v Customs and Excise Commissioners* [2000] 1 WLR 1296, [2000] 2 All ER 315, [2000] 2 WLUK 990, [2001] LLR 401,

(2000) 97(11) LSG 36 (2000), 150 NLJ 341, (2000) 144 SJLB 127, Times, 8 March 2000, Independent, 10 March 2000, [2000] CLY 414, in which the Court of Appeal adopted an 'always speaking' construction to a statute, taking into account developments that had taken place since the provision was first enacted, even though it created a criminal offence.

6.121 Other statutory exceptions to the hearsay rule are covered in the standard practitioner texts on the subject.

6.122 Generally, business records should be accurate records, which are indeed more reliable than memory. However, business records in digital form are subject to manipulation from any number of sources and it is important to ascertain that the record-keeping system had a reasonable level of security around it before admitting them into evidence.

Authentication of digital business records

6.123 Documents in digital form can be forged as easily as, if not more easily than, documents in paper or other analogue form. The authenticity of digital data in legal proceedings has been considered on a case-by-case basis.[1] Email is one example of electronic documents that can be forged; however, this does not mean that every email needs to undergo an extensive authentication process to prove it is not a forgery.[2] In *R v Mawji (Rizwan)*,[3] evidence of a threat to kill included an email sent to the victim, which included the words 'I'm going to kill you'. The Court of Appeal rejected submissions that it was necessary to authenticate the email by showing the audit trail of where the email originated, because there was sufficient evidence to show that the email was written and sent by the appellant. The court said that the content of the email demonstrated its authenticity on the face of the totality of the evidence. If the email had been fabricated, why would somebody go to the length of forging the content of an email that was so obviously linked to the other evidence produced at the trial, the court asked.

1 For example, in *R v Cochrane* [1992] 6 WLUK 63, [1993] Crim LR 48 (CA), [1993] CLY 366, McCowan LJ, Waterhouse and Brooke JJ said that it was necessary for appropriate authoritative evidence to be called to describe the function and operation of a mainframe computer.
2 They were forged in *R. v Debnath (Anita)* [2005] EWCA Crim 3472, [2005] 12 WLUK 64, [2006] 2 Cr App R (S) 25, [2006] Crim LR 451, [2006] CLY 855; see also *Masood v Zahoor* [2008] EWHC 1034 (Ch), [2008] 5 WLUK 282; on appeal *Zahoor v Masood* [2009] EWCA Civ 650, [2010] 1 WLR 746, [2010] 1 All ER 888, [2009] 7 WLUK 101, [2009] CP Rep 44, [2010] Bus LR D12, [2010] CLY 424 where the trial judge reached the conclusion that both parties committed forgery and perjury.
3 [2003] EWCA Crim 3067, [2003] 10 WLUK 438.

6.124 At the hearing, it may be relevant to produce the analysis of the metadata of an email to show where it originated. The email header can prove that the email was sent and received and show it was not a forgery.[1] Use of IP addresses within emails, however, has limited utility as they cannot identify the person who drafted the email, but can only identify the person 'who has the contract with their ISP to have Internet access'.[2] Authenticating pages from the Internet can also be difficult because they alter frequently.[3]

1 *Greene v Associated Newspapers Ltd* [2004] EWCA Civ 1462, [2005] QB 972, [2005] 3 WLR 281, [2005] 1 All ER 30, [2004] 11 WLUK 165, [2005] EMLR 10, (2004) 101(45) LSG 31, (2004) 148 SJLB 1318, Times, 10 November 2004, Independent, 9 November 2004, [2005] CLY 970.

2 *Media CAT Limited v Adams* [2011] EWPCC 6, [2011] 2 WLUK 291, [2011] FSR 28, [2011] CLY 1945 ([2011] FSR 28 at [28] (Birss QCJ)).
3 *R. v Skinner (Philip)* [2005] EWCA Crim 1439, [2005] 5 WLUK 506, [2006] Crim LR 56.

6.125 Circumstantial evidence can be used to authenticate a document in digital format, and such circumstantial evidence includes a range of factors including, but not limited to, appearance and the contents of the document, the subject matter, witness testimony, and any distinctive features that indicate a nexus.

6.126 There have been a number of authorities in Australia that have considered the authentication of business records, and some confusion arose as to whether authenticity was a precondition to admissibility. Bryson J, in *National Australia Bank Ltd v Rusu*,[1] stated that documents would be relevant if they were shown to be authentic. In this case, the judge decided that the evidence of authenticity was lacking in the case before him. Bryson J's reasoning in *National Australia Bank Ltd v Rusu* was criticized by Stephen Odgers SC.[2] Odgers inferred that on Bryson J's approach, the court may not draw reasonable inferences from a document as to its authenticity. In *Lee v Minister for Immigration & Multicultural & Indigenous Affairs*,[3] Madgwick J took up Odgers' criticism. One of the arguments advanced by the applicant in that case was that the note was inadmissible as a business record, having regard to *National Australia Bank Ltd v Rusu*. Madgwick J described *National Australia Bank Ltd v Rusu* at [25] as a 'controversial NSW authority':

> In *Rusu*, his Honour may have meant no more than that there may be cases in which, as a matter of fact, no inference as to authenticity of a document may be properly drawn from the document itself. If he meant to say more than that, it is by no means clear to me that the way is open for a court to read some unexpressed limitation into a grant of power to courts: such grants are generally very liberally construed.

1 [1999] NSWSC 539, (1999) 47 NSWLR 309.
2 Stephen Odgers, *Uniform Evidence Law* (6th edn, Thomson Reuters 2004) 183.
3 [2002] FCAFC 305.

6.127 In *ASIC v Rich* Austin J examined the decision in *Rusu*. Austin J stated that:

> In the case of a business record, its authenticity may be proved, at the simplest, by the evidence of a person who satisfies two conditions: namely, first, that he or she participates in the conduct of the business; and secondly, that he or she compiled the document, or found it among the records of the business, or can recognise it as one of the records of the business.[1]

1 (2005) 216 ALR 320 at [99].

6.128 In referring to Bryson J's decision in *NAB v Rusu*, Austin J said that the judge did not have in mind proof of the authenticity of the business record 'by the evidence of a person unconnected with the business who has found the document among the records of the business or can recognise it as a business record'.

6.129 After reviewing the authorities,[1] Austin J considered authentication cannot be achieved solely by drawing inferences from the face of the document where there is no other evidence to indicate provenance. In his opinion, the other cases do not deny these propositions:

> for that would 'put the court entirely in the hands of whatever a document which a party chose to tender purported to be, subject to whatever opportunity another party had of overcoming its apparent effect'. On the other hand, it is important not to set the bar too high for the authentication of documents, because if too much is demanded, the authentication requirement will fight against the policy underlying the business records provisions which, as Hope JA remarked in Albrighton (at 548), is 'of great importance in the search for truth'. That policy recognises that any significant organisation depends for its efficiency upon the keeping of proper records, to be used and relied upon in the everyday carrying on of the activities of the business and therefore likely to be accurate, and 'likely to be a far more reliable source of truth than memory' (Albrighton, at 548–549 per Hope JA; see also Australian Law Reform Commission, Interim Report on Evidence (Report No 26, vol 1), at [709]). It is reflected in the terms of s 69, which makes hearsay representations in business records admissible without requiring evidence from their authors.[2]

1 See also *O'Meara v Dominican Fathers* [2003] ACTCA 24, *Albrighton v Royal Prince Alfred Hospital* (1980) 2 NSWLR 542.
2 (2005) 216 ALR 320 at [116].

6.130 In *Australian Competition and Consumer Commission v Air New Zealand Limited (No 1)*,[1] the court stated that if there is an issue regarding the authenticity of a document, it may still be admissible if it is relevant or arguably so. This is so, provided there is material from which its authenticity may reasonably be inferred. That material will include what may reasonably be inferred from the document itself. The process of determining whether or not documents are relevant is integral to the discovery process.

1 [2012] FCA 1355, (2012) 207 FCR 448, this decision was approved in *Federal Commissioner of Taxation v Cassaniti* [2018] FCAFC 212 and *Gregg v R* [2020] NSWCCA 245.

Conclusion

6.131 Authentication is about proving that something is what it purports to be. When seeking to prove the authenticity of digital material submitted as evidence, the traditional methods of authenticating paper and other forms of analogue evidence do not apply, because digital technology is a new and evolving paradigm and its products have characteristics quite different from those of evidence affixed to an analogue medium. Although traditional means of authentication, such as proof of the continuity of evidence and trustworthiness of the preserver, still have a role in assessing that an entity is what it claims to be, these criteria on their own are insufficient to demonstrate the authenticity of digital evidence. Even the term 'demonstrating' is at issue in the digital environment because, at most, authenticity may be 'inferred' from several factors rather than shown, due to the fact that digital material is perpetually being reproduced in the process of maintenance and use, and the entity under consideration is always new. The significant differences between authentication of analogue material and that of electronic evidence lie in three fundamental concepts: best evidence, system integrity and security, and the significant properties of the evidence.

6.132 The best evidence rule rose out of a concern that, when multiple instantiations of the same document exist, the most trustworthy and authoritative among them be submitted as evidence. In the analogue environment, this is the original, that is, the first complete document capable of reaching the purposes for which it was generated. Thus, the best evidence rule has been interpreted through time as a requirement to submit original documents when they existed, and to provide a rational explanation for their absence when only drafts or copies were available. In the digital environment, originals come into being when first received by an addressee or first saved to a system by an author, but in both cases, when the document is closed, it breaks into its digital components, and when it is opened a copy is generated. These copies that come into being every time digital documents are opened, navigated or, if interactive, reproduced from content data, form data and composition data, are never identical to the original or to each other, even when they may look so, because at the very minimum their metadata have changed. This does not mean that the best evidence rule is no longer applicable. It simply means that, rather than referring to the original document, it has to refer to the degree of integrity of the document, as proven either by technological authentication, the integrity of the system(s) where the document was created (made, received and managed) or stored over time, or the fixity and stability of the format in which it was created or preserved.

6.133 System integrity and security come into play in jurisdictions, such as Canada, where authentication is based on an inference made from the technological environment in which the potential evidence exists. Because of the vulnerability of digital material and the difficulty of establishing authenticity by examining the digital entity itself, its identity and integrity can be deduced from the system's requirements on access, use, management and such like. This implies that strict policies and procedures are in place for controlling not only all the documents in the system, but also any interaction with them within the system and from outside. Records management manuals and information technology guides are fundamental to establishing the integrity of a system. However, they exist only in public institutions and private organizations that have their own information and preservation systems subject to mandated standards of practice. When organizations and individuals entrust their data, documents or records to cloud providers, it is not possible to verify the integrity of servers in the data centres where the digital material is stored. Thus, it is only possible to examine the security measures agreed upon in the contract between provider and user and make an inference of authenticity from them.

6.134 The most significant properties of any item of electronic evidence are the attributes necessary to establish its identity and integrity through time. Some of these data are produced when a digital entity is generated (they contribute to establishing its identity), some during its use and management (they help to establish its integrity) and others are added after the entity is selected for permanent preservation in an archive to ensure that its authenticity remains verifiable over time. Some of these properties are metadata while others are logs, and several of them are not visible on the face of the document. These are attributes having different functions, the most significant of which for evidentiary purposes are: specifying the date a document is made or received and filed; identifying the names of the persons interacting with the document (author(s), addressee(s), other recipients, handling office); naming the form of the document (report, memo) and the action involved (contract, sentence, patent, application); indicating the format and other technological characteristics of the entity; naming the title of the document, its subject matter, or the action it embodies; indicating the relationships of the document to other documents (registry number, classification code, identification number); specifying whether the document was received with a digital seal or digital signature, or was encrypted; providing information about the technical context of the entity or the migration to a new system; describing rights and obligations such as copyright, usage and security restrictions; describing activities carried out on the entity over time and across technological changes, such as conversion or reproduction to ensure redundancy; documenting the structural relationships between or within digital entities, such as the linkage between pages in a website; and identifying the users of the entity (social tags, access logs, user search logs).

6.135 In conclusion, the fundamental difference between the authentication of analogue and electronic evidence is in the fact that, while analogue material can be authenticated on its face and only exceptionally is circumstantial or extrinsic evidence necessary, the authentication of digital material is always an inference based on extrinsic elements such as significant properties, and it relies on circumstantial evidence such as the integrity of the system hosting it, the policies and procedures controlling it, and the technology encrypting or securing the access to it.

7

Electronic signatures

Stephen Mason

The purpose of a signature

7.1 Legislation providing for electronic signatures has, essentially, been directed to provide for the authenticity of the person using the signature, although various statutes provide for additional uses, such as providing for the integrity of a message or document. Authentication can be the process by which a person or legal entity seeks to verify the validity or genuineness of a particular piece of information. Alternatively, it can mean the formal assertion of validity, such as the signing of a certificate: we authenticate what it certifies. In certain circumstances, there may also be a need to verify the identity of an individual or legal entity, although what is meant by 'identity' will also depend on the reason for ascertaining the identity. For example, with a cheque, the signature serves to link the name of the person printed on the cheque with the person who claims to have the authority to draw money from the account indicated on the cheque. In the past, the existence of the cheque guarantee card with a manuscript signature on the reverse served to reinforce the link between the card and the cheque, although the signature did not necessarily identify the person signing the cheque, even if the signature on the reverse of the cheque guarantee card matched the signature on the cheque. In cheque cases, the printed name on a cheque is not necessarily accepted as a form of signature, although it can contribute to authenticity. For instance, in *Ringham v Hackett*,[1] Lawton LJ considered the issue of authenticity in relation to a cheque with a name printed on it, and suggested that 'A printed name accompanied by a written signature was prima facie evidence that the cheque was being drawn on the account it purported to be drawn on',[2] although in the South African case of *Akasia Finance v Da Souza*,[3] Leveson J indicated, at 338 G–H, why he did not consider the name printed on the cheque could be a signature:

> At the foot of each cheque, where the signature of the drawer is normally to be found, appear the words, 'Domestic Homes (Pty) Ltd, Registration No 73/0541'. The words are printed and are plainly printed by machine.
>
> It is well known that for several years past banks have been issuing cheque books to their customers with the customer's name machine-printed thereon in the same space as the cheques in the present case. The printing is usually computer-controlled. This is done as part of a design to facilitate the modern banking system. Of importance is the fact that the printing is not done by the customer. It is therefore not the company's signature in the sense that, if put there by a person authorised by a corporate customer, it would constitute the company's signature or seal under the provisions of the Companies Act 61 of 1973.

1 [1980] 1 WLUK 323, (1980) 124 SJ 201, Times, 9 February 1980, [1980] CLY 158.
2 (1980) 124 SJ 201 at 202(a). In *Central Motors (Birmingham) v PA & SNP Wadsworth (trading as Pensagain)* [1982] 5 WLUK 265, [1983] CLY 6u, [1982] CAT 231, 28 May 1982; (1983) 133 NLJ 555, a

Stephen Mason, 'Electronic signatures', in Stephen Mason and Daniel Seng (eds.), *Electronic Evidence and Electronic Signatures* (5th edn, University of London 2021) 279–396.

second account holder was held jointly liable for a cheque that he did not sign under the provisions of the Bills of Exchange Act 1882.

3 1993 (2) SA 337 (W).

7.2 The function of a signature is generally determined by the nature and content of the document to which it is affixed.

7.3 It is thought that the act of a person fixing their name to a document is well understood by lawyers and non-lawyers alike. However, a consideration of the case law demonstrates the range of issues that have arisen in relation to what seems, at first glance, a relatively simple concept. The means by which judges have tested the validity of a signature has altered over time. From concentrating on the form a signature takes, judges went on to question its validity by considering the function the signature performs.[1] The analysis in the move from form to function applies equally to the analysis of electronic signatures. The perceptive comments from the sound dissenting judgment of Bell J in 1855 in the South African case of *Van Vuuren v Van Vuuren*,[2] at 121, provides a useful summary with which to begin:

> the expression 'to sign' a document has no strict legal or technical meaning different from the popular meaning, viz., to authenticate by that which stands for or is intended to represent the name of the person who is to authenticate. If you say to the most illiterate person 'Sign this paper', if he cannot write, he will put a cross to it, and if he do not know how to do this the most experienced man of business cannot tell him to do more. If the party have learned a little writing, or if rheumatism of hard labour have cramped the nerves of his hand, and you ask him to sign a document, he will put the initial capital letters of his Christian and surname, while he will not venture upon writing the other more minute and therefore more difficult to be executed letters of these names, and he will feel satisfied that he has 'signed'. If the man of business doubt this, and, seeing he can write so far as to be able to make the capital letters, think it will not be sufficient without the smaller letters, and insist upon his making them, should the party say he cannot, the lawyer will be content. On the other hand, should the party make the attempt and produce a scrawl more or less legible, so again the man of business will be content – whether the scrawl be legible or illegible, he will be satisfied that the man has 'signed'. Such is the popular and professional practice, and the decision of the Courts had been conformably to it.

1 Chris Reed, 'What is a signature?' (2000) 3 *Journal of Information, Law and Technology (JILT)*, http://www2.warwick.ac.uk/fac/soc/law/elj/jilt/2000_3/reed/.

2 2 Searle 116.

Dictionary definitions

7.4 The *Oxford English Dictionary* offers a number of definitions of the word 'signature' as a noun and a verb.[1] The earliest references relate to signatures of a public nature that are intended to have legal effect. The first definition of a signature as a noun is that of 'A writing prepared and presented to the Baron of Exchequer by a writer to the signet, as the ground of a royal grant to the person in whose name it is presented'. An illustration for 1534 refers to 'To pass with writings and signaturis to be subscrivit be the Kingis grace'. The remaining references for this entry also relate to royal signatures in the public domain. The second and third definitions continue with the same meaning. Item 2(a) is defined as 'The name (or special mark) of a person written with his or her own hand as an authentication of some document or writing', and is illustrated from Hollyband of 1580, referring to 'the signature or marke of a Notaries', with the next illustration from Coke dated 1633 referring to 'A bill superscribed with the signature or signe manuall, or royall hand of the King'. The third reference, item 2(b), 'The action of signing one's name, or of authenticating a document by doing so', is also illustrated by an early reference to Lord Keeper Williams from 1621: 'Some things wee must offer to the kings signature when the clarkes are not to bee found.' The law dictionaries vary in their treatment of the definition of 'signature'.[2]

1 *Oxford English Dictionary* (2nd edn on CD-ROM, version 4.0, 2009).
2 Bryan A. Gardner (ed), *Black's Law Dictionary* (11th edn, West Group 2019); Daniel Greenberg (ed), *Stroud's Judicial Dictionary of Words and Phrases* (11th edn, Sweet & Maxwell 2019); David Hay, *Words and Phrases Legally Defined* (5th edn, LexisNexis Butterworths 2018).

The manuscript signature

7.5 The epitome of a signature is the act of an individual writing their name in their own hand on a document, usually in the form of a manuscript signature.[1] More widely, it is the action of a person affixing a permanent imprint upon a document. In the world before the invention of electricity and computers, an imprint was required to have the characteristic of permanency because it was necessary to retain tangible evidence of intention. In addition, the parties to the document may consider it necessary to retain the evidence for a sufficient length of time in order to enforce any rights or obligations evidenced in the record.

1 Although the *tuğra* (a cipher or imperial monogram) of the Ottoman sultans that served as the signature of the sultan was drawn up by a court official and affixed to official documents. Over time, it was also carved on seals and stamped on coins, and artists illuminated later *tuğra*.

7.6 Before the development of the telegraph, a document would normally be considered something written onto a material, mainly paper. Although a number of people may be involved with the framing of a document and its subsequent manifestation in its final physical form, the document will have been created physically. Thus, if an instruction was passed from one party to another by means of the operators of semaphore, the sending operator could give evidence of the instructions received from the instructing party and the signals they used to transmit the message, and the receiving operator could give evidence of the signals they observed and noted down on paper. With the development of communications over the electric telegraph, the same principles would apply as with semaphore, but the electronic pulses of the telegraph would be interpreted in the light of the code used by the sending and receiving operators. The use of the telegraph meant that the message was encoded into electronic pulses, but the pulses were not stored. The receiving operator transferred the evidence of the message to a carrier. In contrast, software code transmits and stores the data in digital form, but the data are not visible to the human eye. A combination of the interpretation and use of hardware and software to make the data visible to the human are required.

7.7 In a world that relied on physical and permanent evidence of proof of intent, the requirement for an enduring record is understandable. While the legal consequences of a signature will differ when fixed to artefacts, such as items of pottery, paintings, sculpture and carvings on surfaces such as stone, marble, glass and wooden furniture, nevertheless a signature is capable of establishing the identity of the creator of the article and is also capable of authenticating the provenance of the object.[1]

1 The copy of a painting with a false signature painted on it with the intention of passing off the painting as by the genuine painter was determined to be a cheat at common law by Cockburn LCJ and his fellow judges in *Regina v Thomas Closs* (1858) LRCCR 460, Dears & B 460.

7.8 A document usually exists on a carrier, typically paper. The carrier is marked permanently with content, usually with ink, either in the form of handwriting or by means of a printing press. This process alters the carrier physically. The content imprinted on the carrier may include a range of information, depending on the nature of the document, including information about the person who created, issued or initiated the content. Over time, the carrier will include additional information as it is handled, including coffee or tea stains, scratches, additional content, fingerprints and DNA. Finally, a person or legal entity might sign the carrier with a signature. The reason for signing the document will depend on the nature of the document and the purpose for which the person is signing. When brought together, these components comprise the document in its entirety.[1]

1 For the meaning of a 'document', see Stephen Mason, 'Documents signed or executed with electronic signatures in English law' [2018] 34(4) Computer Law and Security Report 933.

Statutory definition of signature

7.9 There does not appear to be a statutory definition of the term 'signature', and Ashman J commented in 1892 in a case regarding probate that there was no judicial formula either:[1]

> Exactly what constitutes a signature has never been reduced to a judicial formula … The principle upon which these cases proceeded was that whatever the testator of grantor was shown to have intended as his signature was a valid signing, no matter how imperfect or unfinished or fantastical or illegible, or even false, the separate characters or symbols he used might be, when critically judged.

1 Mitchell J quoted these comments of Ashman J (whose decision was reversed) in *In re Plate's Estate*, 148 Pa. 55, 23 A. 1038.

7.10 The Interpretation Act 1978 does not provide a definition, although Professor Reed noted there were 15 statutory definitions of 'signature' or 'signing' in force in 1996, 11 of which adopted an identical or similar variation to the following: ' "signature" includes a facsimile of a signature by whatever process reproduced'.[1] This particular definition is sufficiently general to include a representation of a signature in electronic form. The most obvious example is that of a manuscript signature that is scanned and converted into digital form. Such a representation can be attached to a document produced on a computer, or it could be the image of the signature as sent and received by a facsimile machine. It is estimated that there are in the region of 40,000 references to the requirement for a manuscript signature.[2] However, whether a personal signature is required depends upon the wording of the statute or from the context of the requirement.[3] With respect to legislation, Professor Reed notes that the statutory provisions relating to the provision of a signature fall into three broad categories:

Where documents that have been signed are admissible in evidence, or create evidential presumptions. The evidential presumptions are either that the document is conclusive proof of its contents, or it is clear evidence of the facts set out in the document.

Where documents have to be signed for the purpose of authentication, either expressly or from the context of the requirement.

Where a signature is required to exercise a statutory power.[4]

1 Water Resources Act 1991 (c 57) Schedule 4, Part II, Proceedings of Flood Defence Committees, quoted in Chris Reed, *Digital Information Law: Electronic Documents and Requirement of Form* (Centre for Commercial Law Studies 1996) 225; table 5.1, 262–263 for the full list.

2 HC Official Report (6th series) col 41, 29 November 1999; note also Reed, *Digital Information Law*, 239 and n 41; Reed, 'What is a signature?', 3.1.2 and n 68.

3 Reed, *Digital Information Law*, 233–234 and nn 23 and 24.

4 Reed, *Digital Information Law*, 240–241. Professor Reed provides examples at 42–52.

The functions of a signature

7.11 A signature can serve a number of functions, each of which can have varying degrees of importance,[1] including complying with a legal requirement that something be signed.

1 Lon L. Fuller, 'Consideration and form' (1941) 42 Columbia Law Review 799 refers to the evidentiary, cautionary function and channelling functions; Ashbel G. Gulliver, 'Classification of gratuitous transfers (with Catherine J. Tilson)' (1941) 51 Yale Law Journal 1; John H. Langbein, 'Substantial compliance with the Wills Act' (1975) 88(3) Harvard Law Review 489; Mark Sneddon, 'Legislating to facilitate electronic signatures and records: exceptions, standards and the impact on the statute book' (1998) 21(2) University of New South Wales Law Journal 334 part 2 IIA (i)–(iv), http://www.austlii.edu.au/au/journals/UNSWLJ/1998/59.html; Adrian McCullagh, Peter Little and William Caelli, 'Electronic signatures: understand the past to develop the future' (1998) 21 University of New South Wales Law Journal 56; UNCITRAL Model Law on Electronic Commerce with Guide to Enactment 1996 with additional article 5 bis as adopted in 1998 (United Nations 1999) paras 48 and 53; UNCITRAL Model Law on Electronic Signatures with Guide to Enactment 2001 (United Nations 2002) para 29; *Promoting Confidence in Electronic Commerce: Legal Issues on International Use of Electronic Authentication and Signature Methods* (United Nations 2009) 1–8; for a similar overview of the same topic and discussion of the development of signatures, see Lorna Brazell, *Electronic Signatures and Identities Law and Regulation* (3rd edn, Sweet & Maxwell 2018) 2-001.

The primary evidential function

7.12 It is suggested that the primary purpose of a signature serves to provide admissible and reliable evidence that comprises the following elements:

(1) To provide tangible evidence that the signatory approves and adopts the contents of the document.

(2) In so doing, the signatory agrees that the content of the document is binding upon them and will have legal effect.

(3) Further, the signatory is reminded of the significance of the act and the need to act within the provisions of the document.

7.13 The nature of the act of signing differs between the application of a manuscript signature and the use of an electronic signature. This is because a manuscript signature, if authentic, is biologically linked to a specific individual, but cryptographic authentication systems bind signatures to individuals by way of software code and procedural mechanisms.

7.14 With electronic signatures, the person does not physically sign anything, but causes software to sign electronically using an untrustworthy machine for knowing what document has been signed[1] – even when using a biodynamic version of a manuscript signature. This is significant, because the act of signing using an electronic signature has a different symbolic meaning to that of a manuscript signature, and suggests a weaker sense of the involvement of the person in the process of signing, as noted by Professor Chou.[2]

1 Stephen Mason and Timothy S. Reiniger, '"Trust" between machines? Establishing identity between humans and software code, or whether you know it is a dog, and if so, which dog?' (2015) 21 Computer and Telecommunications Law Review 135.

2 Eileen Y. Chou, 'Paperless and soulless: e-signatures diminish the signer's presence and decrease acceptance' (2015) 6 Social Psychological and Personality Science 343. Professor Chou provides further citations.

Secondary evidential functions

7.15 A signature can also provide evidence of identification and proof of the following:

(1) The signature can authenticate the identity of the person signing the document. One example would be to reinforce the causal link between the signature and a name printed on a document, such as a name printed on a chequebook or credit card.

(2) The identity of a particular characteristic, or attribute, or status of the person such as a government minister or company director.

(3) Where a person signing acknowledges, verifies or witnesses the record, but does not necessarily agree to be bound by the content of the document.

(4) The existence of the document provides a record of the intent of the signatory, and, in turn, physical evidence of the originality and completeness of the document itself, including the time, date and place of the act of the affixing of the signature to the document.

(5) Where a person is a witness to the signing of a document, the signature of the witness can provide for the authenticity and the voluntary nature of the signature of a third party.

(6) It can demonstrate that the content of the document has not been altered subsequent to the affixing of the signature.

(7) A signature can provide evidence that the record is a true copy of another record.

(8) A signature can be used to confirm the receipt of something, or to obtain access to something.

Cautionary function

7.16 This function acts to reinforce the legal nature of the document, thereby encouraging the person affixing their signature that they should take care before committing themselves to the contents of the document.

Protective function

7.17 As a corollary to the cautionary function, the party receiving the document containing a manuscript signature recognizes that the other party affirms the content of the document and they have given their full attention to the content of the document. They can also be assured of the identity of the signatory, and are consequently in receipt of the proof of the source and contents of the document. This function is linked to the evidentiary function.[1]

1 Sneddon, 'Legislating to facilitate electronic signatures and records', Part 2 IIA (ii).

Channelling function

7.18 The formality of a manuscript signature helps to clarify the point at which a person recognizes the act has become legally significant. Also, the content of the document, by being recorded on a durable form, serves to concentrate the mind on the legally binding nature of the document, thus reducing the risks associated with oral recollections. This function is also linked to the evidentiary function.

Record-keeping function

7.19 Closely related to the evidentiary function, a document contained on a carrier manifest in physical form serves as a durable record of the terms of the agreement. It also enables governments to impose taxes on documents and permit audits based on the existence of documents having a physical existence.

Disputing a manuscript signature

Defences

7.20 A manuscript signature cannot be disputed unless the following defences can be established: the signature is a forgery;[1] the signature was conditional; the signature was obtained as a result of misrepresentation; the signature was obtained in such a circumstance that it was not the act of the person signing (*non est factum*); mental incapacity; mistake; where one party unilaterally added material terms to the writing after the other had signed the document; where the person signing the document did not realize the document they signed was a contractual document; by statute as being unreasonable or unfair. These defences are not dealt with in this chapter, other than a brief consideration of the disputes where a manuscript signature has been at issue. The reader is referred to the standard textbooks on the subject. It is well known that manuscript signatures can be and are forged. To prevent this problem, and to test both the validity and the effectiveness of a manuscript signature, some documents require the signature to be affixed in the presence of a witness or an authorized official, such as a notary.

1 In the case of *Brown v National Westminster Bank Ltd* [1964] 2 Lloyd's Rep 187, [1964] 6 WLUK 133, [1964] CLY 191, the bank paid sums of money on 329 cheques that were alleged to contain forged copies of Mrs Brown's signature. The bank admitted to paying out on 100 cheques that were forged, but put Mrs Brown to prove that the remaining cheques were forged. This was because the bank took measures, through the branch managers, to question Mrs Brown on a number of cheques that passed through her account. Mrs Brown failed to prove that she did not sign the remaining cheques. For similar facts in Australia, see *Tina Motors Pty. Ltd. v Australia and New Zealand Banking Group Ltd.* [1977] VR 205.

Evidence of the manuscript signature

7.21 Where a manuscript signature on a document is challenged, evidence will need to demonstrate the issues discussed below. It should be noted that the evidentiary burden is a factor in considering the precise nature of the signature. In the Canadian case of *Regina v Blumes*,[1] the signature on a vehicle registration document, issued by the Insurance Corporation of British Columbia, was challenged. It was alleged that the document was not admissible because it was not clear whether the signature was a manuscript signature, a rubber stamp or a facsimile signature. This document was afforded the presumption of regularity, which meant that a mere challenge was not sufficient to avoid the operation of regularity.

1 2002 BCPC 0045.

The identity of the person affixing the manuscript signature

7.22 Evidence will have to be adduced to show the signature affixed to the document is that of the signatory. In such cases, the signature in question will have to be compared to samples of the same signature. A signature may be forged or the signature could be that of the signatory, but they may have attempted to disguise their handwriting. Thus a handwriting analyst[1] will need to have two kinds of sample: 'request samples' which are produced for the examination and duplicate the material in question; and naturally occurring samples, made by the signatory without realizing the example will be examined. Two main factors can then be examined, the first being that of pictorial impression, which includes matters such as slope, size, margins, spacing and the position of the writing in relation to lines. Second, the construction of the letters can be examined, such as the direction in which the letter 'o' is formed, the way the letter 't' is crossed and the way in which the person has written letters that require more than one movement. Forgers tend to concentrate on the pictorial impression and fail to copy details of the way letters are constructed. Likewise, people trying to disguise their handwriting also concentrate on the pictorial impression, rather than changing the formation of their letters.

1 Recent research has demonstrated that the findings of experts across all forensic disciplines can be subject to bias as the result of cognitive factors, such that the same expert has reached the opposite conclusion with the same evidence, for which see Itiel D. Dror, Christophe Champod, Glenn Langenburg, David Charlton, Heloise Hunt and Robert Rosenthal, 'Cognitive issues of fingerprint analysis: inter- and intra-expert consistency and the effect of a "target" comparison' (2011) 208 Forensic Science International 10 and the references cited therein. Apparently the US Secret Service uses a software program called Forensic Information System for Handwriting (FISH) that enables document examiners to scan and digitize text writings such as threatening correspondence; for a claim of a forged signature on a facsimile transmission, see *Diya v Halifax Plc* [2009] EWCA Civ 183, [2009] 1 WLUK 245; for an electronic signature that was used without authority and a manuscript signature that was forged, see *Jones v Hamilton* [2017] EWHC 1065 (Ch), [2017] 5 WLUK 385.

7.23 Further analysis can be undertaken by considering the relative proportions of letters, the spaces between letters and pressure variations. The attributes of the instrument used to affix the signature to the document can also be considered, such as how smoothly the signature has been written, whether it is jagged or confident, whether there is a pause and where the instrument lifts off the surface. Further, the carrier itself can be examined, from the type of material used (physical properties, optical properties), any security features (watermarks), the printing process used (the use and identification of a photocopier, computer or printer) and other evidence such as perforations and microscopic analysis that might reveal imperfections that may link the carrier to the person. Further examination can include the comparison of typescript; impressions by means of Electrostatic Detection Apparatus; whether more than one type of material was used to affix information on the carrier; whether any alterations were made or entries obliterated, and the sequence in which intersecting lines have been written.

7.24 Where the party relying on the authenticity of the manuscript signature successfully demonstrates the similarity of the manuscript signature to the sample signatures, the evidential burden will then fall upon the alleged signatory to prove the signature was forged. Although this point was made in *Saunders v Anglia Building Society*[1] in relation to the defence where the signature was obtained in such circumstances that it was not the act of the person signing, the principle applies to a forged signature.

1 [1971] AC 1004, [1970] 3 WLR 1078, [1970] 3 All ER 961, [1970] 11 WLUK 45, (1971) 22 P & CR 300, (1970) 114 SJ 885, Times, 10 November 1970, [1971] CLY 1805; Dr Charles Y. C. Chew, 'Mistake in its variety of forms: the injustice of giving securities supporting financial institution debts on an error of judgement or without informed consent' (2017) 32(6) JIBLR 221.

Intention to authenticate and adopt the document

7.25 Where a person affixes their manuscript signature to a document, it must be shown that they intended to sign the document. The case of *L'Estrange v F Graucob Limited*,[1] which predates the modern legislation, serves to illustrate the point. In this case, Miss L'Estrange carried on the business of a café. The defendants manufactured and sold automatic slot machines. In early 1933, Miss L'Estrange agreed to buy an automatic slot machine for cigarettes for a total of £81 5*s* 6*d*, payable over 18 months. She signed a form, printed on brown paper, headed 'Sales Agreement'. This document included a number of contract terms written in very small print, one of which included 'This agreement contains all the terms and conditions under which I agree to purchase the machine specified above, and any express or implied condition, statement, or warranty, statutory or otherwise not stated herein is hereby excluded'. The machine was installed on 29 March 1933. However, it failed to work, and she eventually initiated an action in the county court to recover the payments she had made. Judgment was made in her favour. The decision was reversed in the Divisional Court because Miss L'Estrange had signed the written contract, and in doing so acknowledged that she was bound by the terms. There was no misrepresentation that induced her to sign. It was irrelevant that she did not read the contract or know its contents.[2]

1 [1934] 2 KB 394, [1934] 2 WLUK 22; J. R. Spencer, 'Signature, consent, and the rule in *L'Estrange v Graucob*' 32(1) CLJ 104, notes at 104 that this was not the first case in which the rule was laid down, although it was the case that made the rule famous; see *Parker v The South Eastern Railway Company* (1877) 2 CPD 416; *The Luna* [1920] P 22 and *Blay v Pollard and Morris* [1930] 1 KB 628.
2 This decision, and the discussion of a fourth defence, that the signatory did not agree to the term, is discussed in Spencer, 'Signature, consent, and the rule in *L'Estrange v Graucob*'.

7.26 This was not the case in *Pryor v Pryor*.[1] Anthony Pryor made a will on 5 November 1859. One of the attesting witnesses was his daughter. The testator wanted his daughter's husband to sign the will as a witness, but because it was not known when he would return, he asked his daughter to sign her husband's name instead of her own. She did so. Sir C Creswell refused to admit the will to probate because the subscription was not intended to represent her signature.

1 (1860) LJR 29 NS P, M & A 114.

7.27 Although a manuscript signature on a document may not be in dispute, the person signing the document may wish the other party to infer they had the authority to sign the document, as in the case of *Ringham v Hackett*.[1] The presumption may be rebutted by evidence. In this case, the name printed on the cheque in *Ringham* was that of a partnership, and the signature by one of the partners on the cheque was deemed to be sufficient evidence to intend the recipient to infer the cheque was drawn on the partnership. In the case of *Central Motors (Birmingham) v PA & SNP Wadsworth (trading as Pensagain)*,[2] Central Motors required a cheque for the payment for a motor car in the name of the firm. In accordance with this request, Mr Wadsworth gave Central Motors a cheque with his signature beneath the name of the firm, which was printed on the cheque, below that of the names of the defendants. It was held that by handing over a cheque signed in this way, Mr Wadsworth provided sufficient evidence from the circumstances to personally authenticate the document as being a cheque of the firm. By signing the cheque, Mr Wadsworth had the requisite intent to adopt the cheque as that of the firm.

1 [1980] 1 WLUK 323 (1980), 124 SJ 201, Times, 9 February 1980, [1980] CLY 158.
2 [1982] 5 WLUK 265, [1983] CLY 6u, [1982] CAT 231, 28 May 1982, (1983) 133 NLJ 555.

The electronic signature

7.28 An electronic signature can perform the same functions as a manuscript signature.[1] The difference is that the document to be signed does not exist as a physical object in the same way as the content of a document rendered on to a paper carrier, which means the quality and extent of the evidence to provide intent becomes vitally important in the event it is disputed that an electronic signature was affixed to a document or communication, was not bypassed by a third party,[2] or was affixed to the relevant document in a batch of documents.[3]

1 If there is a specific requirement for a handwritten signature, a laser signature is not acceptable, for which in the context of the law in Saudi Arabia, see *Golden Belt 1 Sukuk Company BSC(c) v BNP Paribas* [2017] WLR(D) 822, [2017] EWHC 3182 (Comm), [2018] 3 All ER 113, [2018] 1 All ER (Comm) 1126, [2018] Bus LR 816, [2017] 12 WLUK 159, [2018] 1 BCLC 385, [2018] CLY 1736.
2 *Sell Your Car With Us Ltd v Sareen* [2019] EWHC 2332 (Ch), [2019] 9 WLUK 397 [2019] BCC 1211, [2020] 1 CL 112.
3 *FHG Publications Ltd v Tee-Hillman* [2001] 11 WLUK 642, [2001] CLY 662, where a single Statement of Truth was sent accompanying a batch of proceedings to be issued.

7.29 When a manuscript signature is affixed to a physical carrier, two changes occur. First, the signature alters the carrier physically with the addition of a substance, such as ink, to the surface. Second, the signature increases the amount of information about the carrier, and thereby the document. An electronic signature, on the other hand, only tends to alter the information relating to the digital data, including the metadata that can include and be taken automatically from the originating application software or supplied by the person who originally created the record. As a result, a digital record will normally contain two main types of information: the content of the document and its internal structure, and the metadata, which describes the record and each of the constituent parts.

Forms of electronic signature

7.30 Electronic signatures are manifest in a variety of forms, all of which can demonstrate the intent of the signing party to authenticate the data. Unfortunately, the terms 'electronic signature' and 'digital signature' tend to be used interchangeably.[1] This creates confusion.[2] In essence, a digital signature is data appended to, or a cryptographic transformation of, a data unit that allows a recipient of the data to prove the source and integrity of the data unit. The digital signature mechanism defines two processes, that of the purported signing of a data unit by the person initiating the signature, which is a private action, and the verification of a signed data unit by using the procedures and information publicly available. A digital signature is a signature that is specifically based on asymmetric cryptography, coupled with a one-way hash function. It is a particular type of signature that is usually brought about by the use of a public key infrastructure[3] and is not a plain sequence of numbers.[4] It is often asserted that the digital signature provides a higher degree of certainty for the recipient. However, little attention is paid to illustrating the significant technical and legal obstacles to this assertion; that the verification process is opaque, or that a digital signature, as with other forms of signature, can be removed from a document in electronic form without trace,[5] and that a public key infrastructure provides for encryption, not the process of signing.

1 This is also pointed out in paragraph 2.2 of the Final Report of the European Electronic Signature Standardization Initiative Expert Team dated 20 July 1999 , and on page 16 of OECD, 'A Global Action Plan for Electronic Commerce Prepared by Business with Recommendations from Governments', 7–9 October 1998, Ottawa, Canada (Directorate for Science, Technology and Industry Steering Committee for the Preparation of the Ottawa Ministerial Conference, SG/EC(98)11/REV2); see also GUIDEC II, 'General Usage for International Digitally Ensured Commerce' for further discussion of the terms. GUIDEC II does not use the term 'electronic signature' but 'digital signature', thus adding to the confusion. In addition, the Draft Guide to Enactment of the UNCITRAL Model Law on Electronic Signatures, dated 12–23 March 2001 (A/CN.9/WG.IV/WP.88) also appears to refer to digital signatures and electronic signatures interchangeably: see paragraphs 31 to 62. Yet further confusion is rendered with the title of at least one legal textbook: D. Campbell (ed), *E-Commerce and the Law of Digital Signatures* (Oceana Publications 2005).

2 Also noted by Carlisle Adams and Steve Lloyd, *Understanding PKI Concepts, Standards, and Deployment Considerations* (2nd edn, Addison-Wesley 2002), 184–185.

3 See also paragraph 33 to UNCITRAL Model Law on Electronic Signatures, Guide to Enactment.

4 In *Ontario Workplace Safety and Insurance Appeals Tribunal* Decision No. 2877/07R 2008 ONWSIAT 3111 (CanLII), an NSR (a seven-digit number), where 'NSR' stands for 'no signature required', is incorrectly described as a digital signature. In *1475182 Ontario Inc. o/a Edges Contracting v Ghotbi* 2021 ONSC 3477 (CanLII), Boswell J incorrectly determined, at [50], that when text messages are exchanged without a name appearing at the end of the text message, that the unique telephone number linked to a cellular telephone, taken together with the International Mobile Equipment Identifier number 'provide, in effect, a digital signature on every message sent by the user of that particular device.'

5 Adrian McCullagh, William Caelli and Peter Little, 'Signature stripping: a digital dilemma' (2001) 1 Journal of Information, Law and Technology, http://www2.warwick.ac.uk/fac/soc/law/elj/jilt/2001_1/mccullagh.

7.31 By comparison, the term 'electronic signature' is anything in electronic form that can be used to demonstrate a signing entity intended their signature to have legal effect. An electronic signature, especially when defined in legislation, tends to represent a generic response to the concept of authentication, and is to be understood in such a context. A signature can be manifest in different forms,[1] and the term 'electronic signature' is used to reflect methods other than the use of a public key infrastructure to sign a message or document, such as the typing of a name on an electronic document, or the capture of the dynamics of a manuscript signature.

1 The use of 's/' instead of '/s/' when indicating the electronic signature of an attorney is irrelevant: Federal, 3rd Circuit, *Xu v Naqvi*, 537 Fed.Appx. 76 (2013), 112 A.F.T.R.2d 2013-6538, 2013-2 USTC P 50, 556.

7.32 For the sake of clarity, the term 'electronic signature' is used to denote the generic concept of a signature that is brought about by the use of a computer or computer-like device, and includes a digital signature as one form of electronic signature.[1] We should also be alert to new forms of electronic signature as they are developed and used.[2] However, this does not prevent the terms used to describe electronic signatures from adding to or increasing the confusion for failing to describe the form of electronic signature at issue. This is illustrated in the Zimbabwean case of *Tedco Mgmt Svcs (PVT) Ltd v Grain Marketing Board*,[3] in which an employee stole a total of $204,818.61 by adding the electronic signature of an authorized signatory to a series of cheques. The signatures were described as 'machine' signatures printed from the computer, which implies that the company caused authorized images of manuscript signatures to be scanned and stored on a computer.

1 In the British Columbia case of *Ghaed v Telus Communications Co.* 2013 Carswell BC 2727, 2013 BCSC 1675, [2013] BCWLD 8841, 234 ACWS (3d) 897, a digital signature is referred to, but it is debatable whether this particular form of signature was being used by Dr Ghaed, given his lack of technical knowledge.
2 Jillian Friedman, 'Signing your next deal with your Twitter @username: the legal uses of identity based cryptography' (2015) 13 Canadian Journal of Law and Technology 33.
3 1996 (1) ZLR 109 (SC).

Authority, delegation and ratification

7.33 A person can be delegated to sign a document, as in the Australian case of *Whittaker v Child Support Registrar*[1] where a person affixed the scanned electronic signature of another to a letter with authority.[2] In contrast, the New Zealand case of *Gong v Zhang*[3] provides an example of an electronic signature used without authority. When forms of electronic signature are placed on a hard drive in such a way that there is no mechanism to prevent others from using the electronic signature of another person, they are exposed to being used without authority, as in the Canadian case of *Adamo v College of Physicians and Surgeons of Ontario*,[4] where the electronic signature of another doctor was affixed to a falsified record without permission.[5]

1 [2010] FCA 43 (5 February 2010).
2 In *Athena Brands Ltd v Superdrug Stores Plc* [2019] EWHC 3503 (Comm), [2019] 12 WLUK 279, His Honour Judge David Cooke concluded that employees had the authority to bind their respective organizations in email exchanges.
3 [2014] NZHC 2838.
4 2007 CanLII 9873 (ON SCDC).
5 For allegations that a scanned image of a manuscript signature was 'photoshopped' on to documents, see *R&D Arts Inc. v Feld* 2013 Carswell BC 3153, 2013 BCSC 1896, [2013] BCWLD 9633, [2013] BCWLD 9767, 235 ACWS (3d) 501.

7.34 Depending on the facts, a person can ratify the signature. For instance, in a 2013 case the Supreme Court, New York County, New York concluded that where a personal assistant electronically signs a document for the purchase of property using dedicated electronic signature software without explicit authority, the signature is capable of being ratified by the principal.[1]

1 *In the Matter of an Article 75 Proceeding ADHY Investments Properties, LLC, Petitioner v Garrison Lifestyle Pierce Hill LLC*, 41 Misc.3d 1211(A), 980 N.Y.S.2d 274, 2013 N.Y. Slip Op. 51634(U).

Forged signatures

7.35 The use of electronic signatures can facilitate the smooth running of an organization, but undue pressure can be placed on employees who fail to act as they ought. This was illustrated in the Canadian case of *Re: Jade Truman Kaiser Mason*,[1] where Mr Mason affixed the electronic signature of a customer to electronic documents without their knowledge, although it is not clear what form the electronic signature took in this case.

1 2012 CanLII 42180 (CA MFDAC); 2012 CanLII 42181 (CA MFDAC).

7.36 An early case where the PIN to a corporate bank account was used without authority occurred in the Australian employment case of *H. Sayner and Joblink Plus Limited – re Termination of employment*,[1] where Joblink had an electronic transfer policy which stated that a member of the Board must enter a code into the system when transferring funds electronically. The codes were written on a piece of paper, placed in a sealed envelope and left with the Finance Manager to store in a safe location and to be opened in an emergency. The envelope had a direction written on the outside to the effect that the envelope was not to be opened except in an emergency. Ms Sayner used the corporate PIN to pay for a holiday for the then Finance Manager Mr Helanath Disanayake and his family to the Novotel Opal Cove Resort at Coffs Harbour using Joblink funds in the amount of A$2,241.50. This expenditure was improper and not approved by the Board.

1 PR950280 [2004] AIRC 748 (30 July 2004).

7.37 Other examples of forgery include the Australian case of *Salfinger v Niugini Mining (Australia) Pty Ltd (No 3)*,[1] which concerned the falsification of purported assignments, and *Re Macartney and Tax Agents' Board of Victoria*,[2] where the applicant obtained a copy of the letterhead of the firm he was working for, together with an electronic signature of one of the partners of the firm. He then forged a statement of employment using the letterhead and electronic signature of the partner.[3] A further example of a falsified electronic signature in the context of employment is provided in the British Columbia case of *Caravel Management Corp. v Roberts*,[4] where a senior employee used the electronic signature of an authorized signatory to steal.

1 [2007] FCA 1532 (8 October 2007).
2 [2008] AATA 210.
3 See also *Djordje Mitic v Eco Pro Australia Pty Ltd* [2009] AIRC 503 (26 May 2009) and *Williams Group Australia Pty Ltd v Crocker* [2015] NSWSC 1907, upheld on appeal *Williams Group Australia Pty Ltd v Crocker* [2016] NSWCA 265.
4 2014 CarswellBC 2249, 2014 BCSC 1419, [2014] BCWLD 6492, [2014] BCWLD 6586, [2014] BCWLD 6591, [2014] BCWLD 6594, 243 ACWS (3d) 766.

Evidence of intent to sign

7.38 An issue that can exercise the minds of the adjudicator is how to determine the actual act that constitutes the acceptance by the sender of the electronic signature, when the act occurred, and whether a person affixed their electronic signature in circumstances where they deny the signature was theirs.[1] In the case of a manuscript signature, the person furnishes evidence of their intent by physically writing on a carrier, and providing there is sufficient text to link the person to the document, the proof of intent is demonstrated.[2] The question of intent is illustrated in the New Zealand case of *MFT Properties Limited v Country Club Apartments Limited*,[3] which concerned negotiations by email. One email was signed 'Gary'. It was not in dispute that this referred to Mr Gary McNabb, the sole director of MFT. The issue was whether he was expressing a personal view during the course of negotiations or whether he was expressing an intention to bind MFT to the reduced rent it had been receiving. Woolford J concluded, at [39], that:

> The name 'Gary' sufficiently identifies Mr McNabb but I am of the view that it does not evidence his intention to bind MFT to the contents of the document.

1 Where a person denied the electronic signature was applied with their authority to a witness statement, see *Zurich Insurance Plc v Romaine* [2019] EWCA Civ 851, [2019] 1 WLR 5224, [2019] 5 WLUK 279, [2019] CLY 314.
2 For an example of the failure to prove an electronic signature, see the Californian case of *Rosas v Macy's, Inc.*, 2012 WL 3656274.
3 HC Auckland CIV-2010-404-005913 [2011] NZHC 422 (13 April 2011).

7.39 In the digital context, the moment of authentication may be when the person actually types in their name or adopts the signature text at the end of the email, or at the moment the signature is put in automatically when a new email is begun where the program is set up to include a signature at the end of the email.

The automatic inclusion of the signature

7.40 The problems with the automatic inclusion of the signature block in facsimile transmissions, email and SWIFT communications has caused some differences in opinion between judges.

Facsimile transmission

7.41 It is useful to consider the historical cases of facsimile transmission first. The practice of programming the machine to include automatically the name of the sender on the top or bottom of each page was challenged in the New York case of *Parma Tile Mosaic & Marble Co., Inc. v Estate of Fred Short, d/b/a Sime Construction Co.*[1] In this instance, it was held that the automatic imprinting by the facsimile machine of the name of the sender at the top of each page transmitted did not satisfy the requirement that writing shall be subscribed. The decision in this case remains arguable on the facts. Miller J reached the same conclusion in the New Zealand case of *Welsch v Gatchell*.[2] Having analysed a number of electronic signature cases, he said, at [63]:

> It follows from what I have said that a name written on a fax may amount to a signature. But a fax header printed using the machine's capacity to add writing to the document as it is copied and sent cannot serve as a signature unless, perhaps, there is evidence that is was specifically inserted for the transaction concerned. A fax header identifies the owner of the sending machine, the sending number and the time of despatch. There is no reason to suppose that it serves the added purpose of a signature, because every fax does not require a signature. And where the header is added automatically, it cannot qualify as a signature because

> it was not affixed to the particular writing with the intention that by adding his or her name the sender would adopt its contents.

1 155 Misc.2d 950, 590 N.Y.S.2d 1019 (Supp. 1992), motion for summary judgment affirmed, 209 A.D.2d 495, 619 N.Y.S.2d 628, reversed 663 N.E.2d 633 (N.Y. 1996), 640 N.Y.S.2d 477 (Ct.App. 1996), 87 N.Y.2D 524; this case was treated negatively in *Rosenfeld v Zerneck*, 776 N.Y.S.2d 458 (Sup. 2004), 4 Misc.3d 194.

2 [2007] NZHC 1898, [2009] 1 NZLR 241, (2007) 8 NZCPR 708, (2007) 5 NZ ConvC 194,549 (21 June 2007).

7.42 In this case, a contract for the sale of land was formed orally and by facsimile. The sale of land requires the adoption of the contract by way of a signature. The document was not signed, which means there was no evidence to demonstrate an intent to be bound by the transaction, because the name and number printed automatically only acted to identify the person sending and receiving the document.

Email

7.43 An identical legal question arises in the case of email. A human directs the software to include the signature block in an email when it is sent. There is little difference between manually typing a signature block into a series of emails and typing the block once and instructing a computer program to append it to future messages. The difference between an email program and a facsimile transmission is that to remove the information in a facsimile transmission would mean resetting the machine. In the case of an email (and depending on how the email client works), it is usually possible for a person to delete or amend the signature block when writing a new email or when replying to an email.

7.44 This issue arose in *Neocleous v Rees*,[1] where the claimant sought specific performance of an alleged contract of compromise that involved a disposition of an interest in land. The defendant contended that the contract failed to comply with the formalities required by s 2 of the Law of Property (Miscellaneous Provisions) Act 1989, and was therefore not enforceable. The issue was whether the signature included in the automatic footer of an email was sufficient to bind a party. The judge said that to suggest the text included in an email automatically should be ignored is incorrect. This is because the content of the footer was created and added to the software in a conscious action at some stage by a person. In addition, the sender knew their name was added to every email. It was also observed that the recipient of the email is not able to ascertain whether the footer was added because of an automatic rule or by the sender manually entering the content. When considered objectively, the judge concluded that the presence of the name in the footer indicated a clear intention to associate the sender with the email – and to authenticate or sign it. His Honour Judge Pearce concluded that the email was signed, as set out at [57]:

> In my judgment, no such difficulty arises if the email footer here is treated as being a sufficient act of signing:
>
> i) It is common ground that such a footer can only be present because of a conscious decision to insert the contents, albeit that that decision may have been made the subject of a general rule that automatically applied the contents in all cases. The recipient of such an email would therefore naturally conclude that the sender's details had been included as a means of identifying the sender with the contents of the email, since such a footer must have been added either as a result of a conscious decision in the particular case or a more general decision to add the footer in all cases.

> ii) The sender of the email is aware that their name is being applied as a footer. The recipient has no reason to think that the presence of the name as a signature is unknown to the sender.
>
> iii) The use of the words "*Many Thanks*" before the footer shows an intention to connect the name with the contents of the email.
>
> iv) The presence of the name and contact details is in the conventional style of a signature, at the end of the document. That contrasts with the name and contact address of Mr Hale, the person alleged to have signed the letter in *Firstpost*, whose name and address appeared above the text of the letter, in the conventional manner of inserting the addressee's details.

1 [2019] EWHC 2462 (Ch), [2019] 9 WLUK 295, [2020] 2 P & CR 4, [2020] 1 P & CR DG8.

7.45 Approaching the question from the point of view of how the technology is set up is one way of helping to determine this particular issue. Arguably, if an organization authorizes an employee to insert the name, address and contact details of the legal entity into an email program, then it must be appropriate for the organization to put recipients on notice that they can or cannot use this information as a form of signature, or to prove intent, or that the recipient cannot rely on such information to bind the company for any legal purpose. When reaching judgments on such issues, it cannot be correct to ignore the way the technology is set up and used.

SWIFT communications

7.46 In Singapore in 2003, Tay Yong Kwang JC held in the case of *Industrial & Commercial Bank Ltd v Banco Ambrosiano Veneto SpA*[1] that a message using an authentication code sent through the SWIFT (Society for Worldwide Interbank Financial Telecommunication) system has the legal effect of binding the sender bank according to its contents, and where a recipient bank undertakes further checks on credit standing or other aspects, this does not detract from the proposition. In England, Blair J reached the same conclusion in *WS Tankship II BV v The Kwangju Bank Ltd.*[2] A guarantee was issued by Kwangju Bank, but the guarantee was not signed. Even the words 'Kwangju Bank' did not appear on it; the bank was referred to as 'we' in the guarantee. The case for the bank was that the guarantee was therefore not signed and the bank was not bound. Blair J rejected this argument at [154], because the bank accepted that the guarantee was properly issued, fully authorized and intended the beneficiary to rely on it. In addition, it was sent by conventional means by way of the secure messaging system used between banks – that is, using a digital signature – and the words 'Kwangju Bank Ltd' were contained in the header to the SWIFT message. Blair J continued, at [155]:

> It is argued on behalf of Kwangju Bank that this is not text which it typed in, but an output message header, that is, text generated by the SWIFT messaging system. That may be correct, but the name appears, and in my opinion it is a sufficient signature for the purposes of the Statute of Frauds. The words 'Kwangju Bank Ltd' appear in the header, because the bank caused them to be there by sending the message. They were 'voluntarily affixed' in the words of the old cases (c.f. *J Pereira Fernandes SA v Mehta* [2006] 1WLR 1543 dealing with email addresses). Whether or not automatically generated by the system, and whether or not stated in whole, or abbreviated (in fact the name of the bank appeared here in complete form), this is in my judgment a sufficient signature for the purposes of the Statute of Frauds. The position is analogous to that considered by Christopher Clarke J

> in *Golden Ocean Group Ltd v Salgaocar Mining Industries Pvt Ltd* [2011] EWHC 56 (Comm) who at [103] observed that 'an email, the text of which begins "Paul/ Peter", may be regarded as signed by Peter because by that form of wording Peter signifies that he is addressing Paul and authenticates the content of the whole of what follows'. Therefore, I reject Kwangju Bank's submissions in this regard.

1 [2003] 1 SLR 221.
2 [2011] EWHC 3103 (Comm), [2011] 11 WLUK 729, [2012] CILL 3155.

7.47 One commentator who agrees with the decision in this case suggests it is arguable that the reasoning is wrong. Richard Bethell-Jones suggests that 'The automatic insertion of a name in a header is hardly something that any person (including a company) would regard as having the solemn authenticating properties of a "signature" '.[1] It is suggested that accepting this argument is to ignore the underlying rationale of the SWIFT system between banks.

1 Richard Bethell-Jones, 'Digital signatures and the statutory signature requirement', [2012] LMCLQ 184, 186.

Partial document with separate signature page

7.48 As technology is developed and used, so individuals will adjust their behaviour and adapt accordingly. It is undoubtedly the experience of many lawyers across the world that some clients will expect them to work at an impossibly fast pace when negotiating and entering into contractual relationships. The need for speed has increased significantly since the world became networked digitally. For this reason, contracts will be formed and real estate purchased solely relying on documents in digital form. In most cases, a document in digital form is a perfectly acceptable way of entering into legal relations. However, the digital environment often means that our concept of a 'document' has had to change.

7.49 Technically, there is only digital data, but for the purposes of this discussion, let us consider only documents on paper – thus we associate a contract as recorded on paper and signed with manuscript signatures on the relevant page. In developing the terms of a contract, the signature page is often left until the document is finished to the satisfaction of the parties. What then occurs will depend on the parties and the advice they receive from their lawyers. There are a number of options: the signature page is signed with the manuscript signature of each party who happen to be physically together; the signature page, containing a number of signatures for people across continents, is signed by each on a separate piece of paper and then scanned; perhaps each signatory appends a digital signature at different times to the document. Whatever method is used, it is highly likely that the document and the signature pages might well be separate documents.[1] In such circumstances, it then becomes necessary to undertake appropriate measures to prevent additional pages from being added to the agreement that have not been agreed, and for the signature pages, or signatures generally, to be properly associated with the agreement,[2] and for draft signature pages to be dealt with appropriately.[3] In Scotland, this particular issue is now dealt with by the Legal Writings (Counterparts and Delivery) (Scotland) Act 2015.[4]

1 Much as painters once signed the frame, not the painting, which makes attribution difficult, for which see Louise C. Matthew, 'The painter's presence: signatures in Venetian Renaissance pictures' (1998) 80(4) The Art Bulletin 616.

2 In the context of a lease, see *Garguilo v Gershinon and Brooks* [2012] EWLandRA 2011_0377 and *Gopaul v Naidoo* [2014] EWHC 2684 (QB), [2014] 7 WLUK 1132 regarding the redevelopment of two properties by conversion into six flats.
3 For draft signatures, see *Mercury Tax Group Ltd, R (on the application of) v HM Commissioners of Revenue & Customs* [2008] EWHC 2721 (Admin), [2009] STC 743, [2008] 11 WLUK 303, [2009] Lloyd's Rep FC 135, [2009] BTC 3, [2008] STI 2670, [2009] CLY 3928; Mason, 'Documents signed or executed with electronic signatures in English law'; Law Commission, *Electronic Execution of Documents* (Law Com No 386, HC 2624, 2019).
4 Hector MacQueen and Charles Garland, 'Signatures in Scots law: form, effect, and burden of proof' (2015) Juridical Review 107.

7.50 Signing a blank document cannot be correct in criminal matters. Morse J rejected an 'e-ticket' in the New York case of *People of the State of New York v Rose*,[1] where computer-generated simplified traffic information and supporting depositions were generated by a device. At the time, the e-ticket was 'signed' before any information was placed on the ticket. This meant the arresting officer was essentially signing a blank document.

1 11 Misc.3d 200 (2005), 805 N.Y.S.2d 506, 2005 N.Y. Slip Op. 25526.

The Electronic Communications Act 2000

7.51 In England and Wales,[1] the first draft of a bill, the Electronic Communications Bill, was published in July 1999. This Bill was withdrawn when it attracted a great deal of wrath regarding key escrow (which is now expressly excluded in the Act by s 14) and provisions that were later incorporated into the Regulation of Investigatory Powers Act 2000. The Electronic Communications Act received the royal assent on 25 May 2000, and extends to Northern Ireland.[2] Sections 7, 11 and 12 came into force on 25 July 2000 in accordance with the provisions of the Electronic Communications Act 2000 (Commencement No 1) Order 2000 (SI 2000/1798); s 4(2) was amended by s 82, Schedule 4(10) of the Regulation of Investigatory Powers Act 2000, s 15(1) was amended by s 406(1), Schedule 17(158) of the Communications Act 2003, and ss 11 and 12 were repealed by s 406(7), Schedule 19(1) of the Communications Act 2003. The Act was amended in 2016 by The Electronic Identification and Trust Services for Electronic Transactions Regulations 2016 (SI 2016/696),[3] and The Electronic Identification and Trust Services for Electronic Transactions (Amendment etc.) (EU Exit) Regulations 2019 (SI 2019/89).[4] The Explanatory Memorandum to the Statutory Instrument[5] makes an unsubstantiated assertion at paragraph 7.3, third bullet point, dealing with a qualified electronic signature:

> It is considered to be sufficiently secure to withstand repudiation in a court of law.

1 For a discussion of the topic in an international context, see Stephen Mason, 'International initiatives and electronic signatures' (2012) 27(2) Computer and Telecommunications Law Review 37.
2 Section 16(5).
3 Made on 30 June 2016; laid before Parliament 1 July 2016; into force on 22 July 2016.
4 Made on 22 January 2019, laid before Parliament 23 January 2019, coming into force in accordance with regulation 1 (that is, on exit day).
5 http://www.legislation.gov.uk/uksi/2019/89/pdfs/uksiem_20190089_en.pdf.

7.52 For the purposes of justice, the legal profession is supposed to base decisions on evidence. No evidence is offered for this bare claim, and the source and empirical basis of the assertion 'it is considered' is not provided. Furthermore, the discussion about computers and reliability in Chapter 5 is ignored. It is to be inferred that the government considers that this unproven declaration will be complied with in the same way as the presumption that a computer is reliable is also acted upon, in the absence of evidence and with lethargic indifference to the truth.

7.53 Unless there is a specific statutory requirement for a document to be signed, English law does not require any document to be signed to be both valid and effective. Thus, in many instances it was possible to sign a document with an electronic signature before the passing of the Act. The signature at the end of an email, as in the case of *Hall v Cognos Limited*,[1] was sufficient, providing the person signing the document intended to sign it and intended their signature to affect the authenticity of the document. If the identity of the person signing the document is in doubt, further evidence can be adduced to identify the person who affixed their signature to the document.

1 Hull Industrial Tribunal, 1997, Case No 1803325/97.

The definition of an electronic signature

7.54 The amended definition of an electronic signature[1] reads in s 7(2) as follows:

> (2) For the purposes of this section an electronic signature is so much of anything in electronic form as–
>
> (a) is incorporated into or otherwise logically associated with any electronic communication or electronic data; and
>
> (b) purports to be used by the individual creating it to sign.

1 Amended by The Electronic Identification and Trust Services for Electronic Transactions Regulations 2016 (SI 2016 No 696) (made on 30 June 2016; laid before Parliament 1 July 2016; in force on 22 July 2016).

7.55 An electronic communication is defined in s 15(1):[1]

> 'electronic communication' means a communication transmitted (whether from one person to another, from one device to another or from a person to a device or vice versa) –
>
> (a) by means of an electronic communications network; or
>
> (b) by other means but while in an electronic form;

1 As amended by s 406(1), Schedule 17(158) of the Communications Act 2003.

7.56 An electronic signature does not have the same characteristics as a manuscript signature, but it is the equivalent of a manuscript signature when it performs a similar function. The better view is to consider an electronic signature as a link between protocols of electronic devices that communicate via software, each with the other. The attention should be focused on the treatment of messages before they are transmitted and after they are received – the owner or user may not be aware that the computer cannot be trusted.

7.57 An electronic signature can be the equivalent of a manuscript signature where it performs a similar function, even though the two types of signature are conceptually different. The manuscript signature exists in the corporeal world and requires the physical application of matter to alter the surface of a carrier. An electronic signature can only be defined within the operational boundaries of the binary numbers used by computers.

The elements of an electronic signature

So much of anything in electronic form

7.58 This is a wide-ranging provision that should ensure new concepts yet to be invented are covered by the term 'electronic form'.

Incorporation or logical association

7.59 The first element, 'so much of anything in electronic form' must either be incorporated or logically associated with any electronic communication or electronic data. This part of the requirement differs slightly from article 3(10) of EU Regulation 910/2014,[1] which refers to 'attached to or logically associated with'. However, the meaning of the word 'attached' is defined as 'joined functionally', which implies a similarity to the meaning of 'incorporated', which in turn is defined as to 'be included as part of a whole' or 'embodied'.[2] This seems to be a semantic difference that does not affect meaning. The signature could be incorporated by reference to the way it is created. For instance, with a digital signature incorporation is possible when the software takes part of the plaintext and encrypts it (creating the message authentication code), so the recipient can check if the message has been altered. In effect, the message authentication code is a separate part of the message, but is also incorporated into the message by taking the message and encoding it. Alternatively, a biometric measurement can be attached to a message. This is where the biometric measurement, if used, must be logically associated with the message, otherwise it will not serve any function. Although the discussion above is predicated on particular methods of producing electronic signatures, the underlying principles are the same for all methods, including a name typed into an email or an email address, although the functions of an electronic signature may differ between products and methods.

1 Regulation (EU) No 910/2014 of the European Parliament and of the Council of 23 July 2014 on electronic identification and trust services for electronic transactions in the internal market and repealing Directive 1999/93/EC, OJ L257, 28.8.2014, 73; S. Mason, 'Electronic signatures and the EU legislation' (2020) 26(3) CTLR 73.
2 Oxford English Dictionary, 2nd edition on CD-ROM (v. 4.0).

Purports to be used by the individual creating it to sign

7.60 This revised sub-clause recognizes that it does not follow that where an electronic signature was affixed to data, the person whose signature it purports to be was the person who caused the signature to be affixed. In the context of the Act, the meaning of authenticity relates to the single issue of verifying the person or entity, as provided for in s 15(2):

> (2) In this Act–
>
> (a) references to the authenticity of any communication or data are references to any one or more of the following–

(i) whether the communication or data comes from a particular person or other source;

(ii) whether it is accurately timed and dated;

(iii) whether it is intended to have legal effect;

(b) references to the integrity of any communication or data are references to whether there has been any tampering with or other modification of the communication or data.

7.61 This definition relates to the evidential issues regarding the authentication of the communication or data. Where an electronic signature is in issue, whichever party has the burden of proof will be required to submit evidence in response to the guidance set out in s 15(2), together with any other extrinsic evidence that may be necessary to support the evidential burden.[1]

1 Nicholas Bohm and Stephen Mason, 'Electronic signatures and reliance' (2018, Summer) 110 Amicus Curiae The Journal of the Society for Advanced Legal Studies 1.

7.62 An electronic signature will have to be admissible before it can become legally effective.[1] In addition, it does not follow that the communication will have a legal effect unless it is intended to have such an effect,[2] and the provisions of s 7 do not address whether the signature is genuine. Section 7(1) of the Act provides for the admissibility of the electronic signature in two ways:

7(1) In any legal proceedings–

(a) an electronic signature incorporated into or logically associated with a particular electronic communication or particular electronic data, and

(b) the certification by any person of such a signature,

shall each be admissible in evidence in relation to any question as to the authenticity of the communication or data or as to the integrity of the communication or data.

1 Law Commission, *Electronic Commerce: Formal Requirements in Commercial Transactions Advice from the Law Commission* (2001), 3.27.
2 Section 15(2)(a)(iii).

7.63 First, an electronic signature is admissible under the provisions of s 7(1)(a) where it is incorporated into or logically associated with a particular electronic communication or data. Alternatively, in accordance with the provisions of s 7(1)(b), the authenticity or the integrity of the communication or data can be admissible where any person certifies the signature. The certificate would normally be provided by an entity such as a trusted third party, although it does not follow that such a certificate has to be provided by a trusted third party. For instance, it is perfectly possible for Bob to certify that Alice signed an email she sent when she typed her name at the bottom of the text. It seems, therefore, that if a recipient receives an electronic communication which is signed with an electronic signature, and the certifying certificate relating to the electronic signature can be verified, the communication in question is admissible in evidence, subject to the provisions of s 15(2) of the Act.[1]

1 It should be noted that all this evidence would have been admissible anyway, just as it has been in the past.

7.64 The certification by any person mentioned in s 7(1)(b) is satisfactory if the statement made includes the criteria set out in s 7(3), as follows:

> (3) For the purposes of this section an electronic signature incorporated into or associated with a particular electronic communication or particular electronic data is certified by any person if that person (whether before or after the making of the communication) has made a statement confirming that–
>
> (a) the signature,
>
> (b) a means of producing, communicating or verifying the signature, or
>
> (c) a procedure applied to the signature,
>
> is (either alone or in combination with other factors) a valid means of establishing the authenticity of the communication or data, the integrity of the communication or data, or both.

7.65 The person or organization certifying the electronic signature may need to certify before or after, or both before and after, sending the communication that the signature is authentic and the integrity of the data or communication is therefore not to be questioned. From a practical point of view, the certification process will probably occur before the sending of the communication, although there may be circumstances where the certification process can occur after the communication is sent. The actual certification will probably be an assertion, which ought to be substantiated by suitable evidence, by the person or organization certifying the signature that there is an association that links the verification key (if a digital signature) with an entity, and certifies that the use of the verification key is a valid way of verifying whether a private key issued to the person named was used in creating the signature. The link between the components of the key pair, if this were to be challenged, would have to be the subject of expert evidence. It is possible for a certificate in isolation to be sufficient in some instances. In all probability, where a party seeks to adduce evidence of a certificate as establishing the authenticity or integrity of the communication or message or both, additional evidence may be required. Hence the addition of the phrase 'alone or in combination with other factors' in s 7(3). It is the provision of this extrinsic evidence that is necessary to provide evidence of the user's identity.

7.66 From a practical point of view, it may be difficult to obtain such evidence if the communication in question is the subject of legal action years after it was sent. Even if such a certificate is accepted as evidence of the facts contained in the certificate, it will not link the act of signing with the individual or entity whose signature it is. Whether the certification is provided electronically or physically, it may have to be the subject of proof that part of the content of the certificate is acceptable as to the truth of the content, because the information relating to the subscribing party will be a hearsay statement in relation to any facts not within the knowledge of the certification service provider. It should be noted that the provisions of s 7 do not consider whether the signature is genuine, or if it demonstrates the necessary intent by the signing party. In dealing with admissibility, the section leaves the question of evidential weight to the adjudicator.

Liability of a certification service provider

7.67 The British government has set out the extent of the liability that a certification service provider faces when they issue a key pair that conforms to the criteria of an advanced electronic signature under the provisions of the Electronic Signatures Regulations 2002 (SI 2002/318), which came into force on 8 March 2002. The liability of a certification service provider is not dealt with in this text, but it is interesting to note that a certification service provider who issues a qualified certificate will be liable to the relying party unless it can be demonstrated that the provider was not negligent.[1] The burden of proof is reversed from the normal standard for negligence, where the person suffering loss is usually required to prove negligence. This leads to the possibility that organizations that decide to issue qualified certificates may seek an indemnity from the subscribing party against claims by a receiving party.

1 Regulations 4(1)(d) and 4(3)(d).

The power to modify legislation

7.68 There are many thousands of references in statutes and statutory instruments which require the use of paper or can be interpreted to require the use of paper, as well as the use of manuscript signatures. Amending such provisions with an overall catch-all clause was not possible, nor desirable. However, it is pertinent to observe a comment by the Law Commission in relation to this issue:

> While section 7 deals with admissibility, it does not provide that electronic signatures will satisfy a statutory signature requirement. It does not, therefore, assist in determining to what extent existing statutory signature requirements are capable of being satisfied electronically.[1]

1 Law Commission, *Electronic Commerce: Formal Requirements in Commercial Transactions Advice from the Law Commission* (2001), 3.27.

7.69 Power has been delegated to Ministers to modify, by order made by statutory instrument, the provisions of any enactment or subordinate legislation, or instruments made under such legislation, for which they are responsible. The authority granted to Ministers is provided by s 8(1). Ministers have the power to modify by statutory instrument the provisions of:[1]

> (a) any enactment or subordinate legislation, or
>
> (b) any scheme, licence, authorisation or approval issued, granted or given by or under any enactment or subordinate legislation, in such manner as he may think fit for the purpose of authorising or facilitating the use of electronic communications or electronic storage (instead of other forms of communication or storage) for any purpose mentioned in subsection (2).

1 By s 8(7), matters under the care and control of the Commissioners of the Inland Revenue or Customs and Excise are not included, because there are corresponding powers in s 132 of the Finance Act 1999 which have already been exercised by way of statutory instruments relating to electronic tax and VAT returns.

Limitation of powers

7.70 The power granted to the Minister is limited by the terms of s 8(3), where consideration must be given to the arrangements for record-keeping. Changes must not be made that make the new arrangements for record-keeping less satisfactory than before the changes were made. A further limitation is set out in s 8(6), which provides that an order 'shall not require the use of electronic communications or electronic storage for any purpose'. This subsection is qualified by s 8(6)(b), which permits a period of notice to expire before effect is given to a variation or withdrawal of an election or other decision.

Purposes for which modification can be made

7.71 Modification of an enactment can be made for the following purposes, by permitting the use of electronic means as follows:

> (a) The doing of things that may need to be evidenced in writing or where a document, notice or instrument is required.[1]
>
> (b) Alternative means of delivery where the post or other specified means of delivery is required.[2]
>
> (c) Where there is a requirement for a matter to be authorized by a person's signature or seal, or where it is required to be delivered as a deed or witnessed.[3]
>
> (d) Where a statement may be required to be made under oath or to be contained in a statutory declaration.[4]
>
> (e) Where records have to be kept, maintained or preserved in relation to any account, record, notice instrument or other document.[5]
>
> (f) The provision, production or publication relating to any information or other matter.[6]
>
> (g) The making of any payment.[7]

1 Section 8(2)(a).
2 Section 8(2)(b).
3 Section 8(2)(c).
4 Section 8(2)(d).
5 Section 8(2)(e).
6 Section 8(2)(f).
7 Section 8(2)(g).

The provisions a Minister may make

7.72 The Act provides the Minister with a power to provide for a range of issues when drafting a statutory instrument. The list is set out in s 8(4). The provisions of s 8(4)(g) cross refer to s 8(5). These two sections provide Ministers with the powers to determine such issues as matters relating to the legal presumption and the burden of proof. Section 8(4)(g) reads as follows:

> (g) provision, in relation to cases in which the use of electronic communications or electronic storage is so authorised, for the determination of any of the matters mentioned in subsection (5), or as to the manner in which they may be proved in legal proceedings.

7.73 Section 8(5) provides:

> (5) The matters referred to in subsection (4)(g) are–
>
> (a) whether a thing has been done using an electronic communication or electronic storage;
>
> (b) the time at which, or date on which, a thing done using any such communication or storage was done;
>
> (c) the place where a thing done using such communication or storage was done;

(d) the person by whom such a thing was done; and

(e) the contents, authenticity or integrity of any electronic data.

7.74 These two sections, taken together, indicate that a Minister has a great deal of control over how electronic communications are to be handled, and what presumptions will apply when using electronic communications. The combined effect of s 8(4) and s 8(5) permits a Minister to impose rebuttable or irrebuttable presumptions, with the potential for shifting the risks from the receiving party to the purported signing party. This has the potential for doing great injustice. Arguably, the power is wider than just replacing paper documents with an electronic equivalent. An example would be replacing the circulation of statutory accounts to shareholders by post or as attachments to an email, with an electronic notice of their availability at a nominated uniform resource locator.

7.75 The Electronic Communications Act 2000 has not altered the underlying flexibility of the meaning of a signature. An electronic signature does not have to be in the specific form of digital signature for it to be accepted as a signature. By typing a name on an electronic document, all the person needs to do is intend the name they type to act as a means of authentication, and intend the recipient to act upon the content of the document. The act of typing a name in this fashion comes within the provisions of s 7(2) of the Electronic Communications Act 2000, because the typed signature is incorporated with the content of the document for the purpose of establishing the authenticity of the communication.[1] No further requirements are necessary to make a typed signature admissible.

1 In *Golden Ocean Group Limited v Salgaocar Mining Industries PVT Ltd* [2011] EWHC 56 (Comm), [2011] 1 WLR 2575, [2011] 2 All ER (Comm) 95, [2011] 1 WLUK 356, [2011] 1 CLC 125, [2011] CILL 3022, [2011] CLY 3112, Mr Justice Christopher Clarke indicated at 103 that 'an email, the text of which begins "Paul/Peter", may be regarded as signed by Peter because by that form of wording Peter signifies that he is addressing Paul and authenticates the content of the whole of what follows'.

Regulation of Investigatory Powers Act 2000

7.76 The Regulation of Investigatory Powers Act 2000 (RIPA), which extends to Northern Ireland, received royal assent on 28 July 2000. For the purposes of this chapter, the powers relating to the disclosure of a key are relevant. The power to require disclosure is provided in s 49, but of importance is the meaning of a key. What constitutes a key is widely defined, and includes codes and passwords. The definition in s 56(1) is as follows:

> in relation to any electronic data, means any key, code, password, algorithm or other data the use of which (with or without other keys) –
>
> (a) allows access to the electronic data, or
>
> (b) facilitates the putting of data into an intelligible form

7.77 In the context of digital signatures, any person or organization that obtains and uses private keys should ensure the key is only suitable for the purposes of a digital signature, and it cannot be used for any other purpose.[1] If a key can be used for purposes other than a digital signature, it may be the subject of a s 49 notice. Also, it will be important to ensure keys used for digital signatures are stored separately from any other types of private key used for other purposes.

1 It is possible for encrypted data to be encoded in such a way that it can be decoded in two separate ways, one to reveal the secret message and the other to reveal an innocuous message, for which see Derrick Grover, 'Dual encryption and plausible deniability' (2004) 20 Computer Law & Security Report 37.

Possession of a key

7.78 A person has possession of a key in accordance with the provisions of s 56(2). A person may be deemed to have a key, even they do not have the key. The definition is as follows:

> References in this Part to a person's having information (including a key to protected information) in his possession include references–
>
> (a) to its being in the possession of a person who is under his control so far as that information is concerned;
>
> (b) to his having an immediate right of access to it, or an immediate right to have it transmitted or otherwise supplied to him; and
>
> (c) to its being, or being contained in, anything which he or a person under his control is entitled, in exercise of any statutory power and without otherwise taking possession of it, to detain, inspect or search.

7.79 This is a fairly important provision, because the officers of an organization, whatever the legal form the organization takes, are the ones responsible for the proper management of the private key.[1] This is because any s 49 notice will be served on an officer or senior manager. Control must, therefore, be exercised over the acquisition and use of private keys. For instance, a person at the highest level in an organization should be made responsible for this issue. Considerations on whether to use private keys will cover, but not be limited to:

> (1) Deciding if information sent electronically needs to be encrypted. If it does, whether there are more appropriate means of delivering the information to the intended recipient.
>
> (2) Deciding if documents or messages need to be digitally signed. If so, then the next question is whether a risk analysis has been conducted to determine the likely costs of resolving a dispute if a signature has been misused, bearing in mind the discussion elsewhere in this chapter relating to liability.
>
> (3) If private keys are to be used, whatever the purpose, sufficient consideration must be given to storage, access for appropriately authorized officers and employees, and the provision of checks and balances to provide for security.

1 Ross J. Anderson, *Security Engineering: A Guide to Building Dependable Distributed Systems* (2nd edn, Wiley 2008), ch 25 for a discussion on the principles involved in this process. (Professor Anderson was updating his book as this text was being updated. Some of his book will be available as open source at https://www.cl.cam.ac.uk/~rja14/book.html for a short period before the text is published. The entire book will be made available again as open source in 2023.)

Exclusion of electronic signatures

7.80 Where a key is used only for the purpose of generating a digital signature, it does not have to be disclosed in response to a notice, providing it has not been used for any other purpose.[1] It might be useful to recall that a key pair has more than the single function of producing a digital signature. The same key pair can be used to encrypt a message, depending on the algorithm used. An electronic signature is defined in s 56(2) as follows:

> anything in electronic form which–
>
> (a) is incorporated into or logically associated with, any electronic communication or other data;
>
> (b) is generated by the signatory or other source of the communication or data; and
>
> (c) is used for the purpose of facilitating, by means of a link between the signatory or other source and the communication or data, the establishment of the authenticity of the communication or data, the establishment of its integrity, or both;

1 Section 49(9).

7.81 This exemption may be less effective than it seems. In a commercial context, where more than one person may properly have access to a key, the person served with the notice may not be able to be sure that a key, despite being intended for signature purposes, has never been used to decrypt a message encrypted with the corresponding public key. Although it is arguably for the prosecution to prove that a key has been used for such a purpose, and is therefore subject to seizure, the mere assertion of this fact by the person demanding access to the key would place the recipient of the notice in a position of impossible difficulty in resisting the demand.

Electronic sound

7.82 It is possible to record sounds digitally when a person speaks to software code. In the USA, electronic signatures are defined by s 106(5) of the Electronic Signatures in Global and National Commerce Act, 106-229, which provides:

> Electronic signature. – The term 'electronic signature' means an electronic sound, symbol, or process, attached to or logically associated with a contract or other record and executed or adopted by a person with the intent to sign the record.

7.83 In the 2007 9th circuit case of *Shroyer v New Cingular Wireless Services, Inc.*,[1] a person indicated their assent, and thereby executed an electronic signature over the telephone, by selecting the answer 'Yes' in response to the statement 'You agree to the terms as stated in the Wireless Service Agreement and terms of service'. Although the judgment of the Court of Appeals did not explicitly indicate that this form of electronic signature is valid under the Act, nevertheless this decision is in keeping with the definition of electronic signature, and is a perfectly acceptable form of electronic signature.

1 498 F.3d 976.

7.84 In December 2007, the Court of Appeals in Kansas also reached a similar conclusion. In the case of *In the Matter of the Marriage of Takusagawa*,[1] the appellant argued that the provisions of the Kansas Statute of Frauds required a written signature where an agreement to the transfer of land was part of the divorce settlement. The trial judge approved the terms of an oral separation agreement on the final day of the hearing, and the details of the agreement were put on the record. Both parties stated under oath that what was recorded by the court was their understanding of the terms of the agreement. The transcript indicated that the judge asked the appellant 'Ma'am, is that your understanding of the agreement?' The appellant replied 'Yes'.[2] It is certain that the appellant did not affix her manuscript signature to any document. The issue was whether the oral response to a judge was a form of signature. Leben J, who wrote the judgment of the court, cited the 1921 decision of the Supreme Court of Kansas in *Whitlow v Board of Education*,[3] in which the members of the school board voted at a meeting to sell some land. When the appellant handed over her cheque in payment and to complete the transaction, the members of the board refused to complete the sale. The minutes of the meeting indicated that a motion to sell the land to Josephine Whitlow was made and passed, and that the members of the board authorized the president of the board to sign a deed in exchange for payment. The Supreme Court of Kansas rejected the argument of the school board that the Statute of Frauds prevented the agreement being enforced because the minutes of the board had not been signed. It was determined that the minutes as recorded by the clerk were an authentic record that the law required the board to keep. In this respect, the minutes constituted a sufficient memorandum of the contract to bind the board under the Statute of Frauds. In this instance, a signature was not necessary where a public record was maintained by law, which in turn provided authentication of the formation and terms of the contract. The members of the court considered that a properly certified transcript of a court hearing was superior to the minutes recorded by the clerk to the school board, and found that a signature was not necessary where 'a court transcript providing the terms of the agreement and the oral assent of the party to be charged with the agreement that has been fairly stated on the record of the proceeding'.[4]

1 38 Kan.App.2d 401, 166 P.3d 440.
2 38 Kan.App.2d 401 at 410.
3 108 Kan. 604, 196 P. 772.
4 38 Kan.App.2d 401 at 409.

7.85 However, the discussion did not end at this point. Leben J then went on to consider the provisions of the Uniform Electronic Transactions Act K. S. A. 2006 Supp 16-1601, on the assumption that the transcript of the agreement was recorded on equipment that required electricity to enable it to work. Based on this assumption, the judge then considered s 16-1602(f), (h) and (i), which reads as follows:

> (f) 'Electronic' means relating to technology having electrical, digital, magnetic, wireless, optical, electromagnetic or similar capabilities.
>
> ...
>
> (h) 'Electronic record' means a record created, generated, sent, communicated, received or stored by electronic means.
>
> (i) 'Electronic signature' means an electronic sound, symbol or process attached to or logically associated with a record and executed or adopted by a person with the intent to sign the record.

7.86 He concluded that where a party makes an oral statement in legal proceedings before a judge, and 'assuming that the court reporter's equipment was consistent with modern practice, it would appear that the electronic capture of Mieko's oral assent that this was the agreement would satisfy the Statute of Frauds. No more is needed to show that Mieko made or adopted the agreement'.[1] This line of reasoning is far from convincing,[2] and arguably stretches the meaning of electronic signature beyond the terms of the statute.[3]

1 38 Kan.App.2d 401 at 410.
2 This decision was distinguished by the Court of Appeals of Kansas in *Ronald L. Jones Charitable Trust v Sanders*, 284 P.3d 375 (2012), 2012 WL 3966557 and *In re Estate of McLeish*, 49 Kan.App.2d 246, 307 P.3d 221 (Kan.App. 2013).
3 The same could be argued if a will is recorded on tape, and not written down, as in the case of *In the Matter of the Estate of Reed v Buckley*, 672 P.2d 829 (Wyo. 1983); in *Franklin County Cooperative v MFC Services (A.A.L.)*, 441 So.2d 1376 (Miss. 1983) it was determined by the Supreme Court of Mississippi that the statement 'OK, we will take care of it' made over the telephone had the capacity of proving intent to enter a contract when the words are subsequently written down in a memorandum.

7.87 The final claim to support the thesis that both parties entered into a binding agreement in court is more convincing: that an oral settlement placed on the record and acknowledged by the parties in open court should be sufficient to satisfy the requirement of the Statute of Frauds, especially because the law in Kansas allowed for oral separation agreements in divorce proceedings, and such agreements can be incorporated into the decree of divorce if approved by the judge.

7.88 Where one party to a conversation records what is said without the knowledge of the other party or parties, it does not follow that promises made, including a statement that might be construed as an electronic signature, will be valid. In the case of *Sawyer v Mills*,[1] heard at appeal before the Supreme Court of Kentucky, Barbara Sawyer and her husband recorded a conversation with Mr Mills in which he made promises to make certain payments. Among other things, it was determined that any contract formed during this conversation was not enforceable under the provision of the Statute of Frauds. Further, the court considered that the agreement by Mr Mills did not constitute an electronic signature just because it was identifiable and was identified at trial as being his. In explaining this in giving the opinion of the court, Nobel J said, at 8:

> There must be intent to attach or logically associate the electronic signature to the agreement, that is, an intent to execute the contract. That was impossible here, because the medium on which the alleged agreement and electronic signature were recorded (the audio tape) was used surreptitiously. Mills did not know he was being recorded when he went to the Sawyers' art studio. Thus, Mills's identifiable voice on the tape, even if construed as an electronic signature, was procured without Mills's knowledge or intent, and would be tantamount to a forgery which cannot be used to demonstrate a valid contract.

1 Ky., 295 S.W.3d 79.

7.89 Although the comments made by Mr Mills were capable of being construed as an electronic signature, the text of the statute envisages more than a mere spoken assent that is recorded in secret. The statute requires the electronic equivalent of a signature, that is, an electronic sound, symbol or process that demonstrates an intention to enter the agreement. Furthermore, the parties put the agreement into writing. Mr Mills refused to sign the written contract. This refusal to sign by Mr Mills demonstrated that he did not intend to execute or adopt anything he said in the conversation.

The 'I accept' and 'wrap' methods of indicating intent

Click wrap

7.90 Clicking the 'I accept' or 'I agree' icon (also known as 'click wrap') to confirm the intention to enter a contract when buying goods or services electronically is now a very popular method of demonstrating intent. In the USA, the phrase 'wrap' has become common. The action of clicking an icon is capable of providing evidence of the process that is executed or adopted by the person clicking on the icon – that is, the user is required to undertake a positive activity.[1] This is certainly implied in the Canadian case of *Rudder v Microsoft Corp*,[2] and has been widely accepted in the USA.[3]

1 Although technically literate people are capable of installing software and bypassing the need to click on the 'I agree' icon, for which see *Aral v Earthlink, Inc.*, 134 Cal.App.4th 544 (2005), 36 Cal.Rptr.3d 229 (Cal. Ct. App. 2005) (determined by members of the Court of Appeal, Second District, Division, California, to be a contract of adhesion); where there is a succession of changes to the terms uploaded on to a website, it is incumbent on the issuer of such terms to ensure they retain evidence to prove when a person clicked to acknowledge that the new terms were received, as in the Maryland case of *Harold H. Huggins Realty, Inc., v FNC, INC.*, 575 F.Supp.2d 696; in *Rogers v Dell Computer Corporation*, 127 P.3d 560 (Okla. 2005), Dell failed to provide evidence to demonstrate where the contract was formed.
2 (1999) 2 CPR (4th) 474, 47 CCLT (2d) 168 (Ont Sup Ct), FSR (1996) 367. See also *Kanitz v Rogers Cable Inc.* (2002), 58 OR (3d) 299 (Sup Ct) and Barry Sookman, 'Browsewraps, fair dealing and Blacklock's Reporter v Canada: a critical commentary' (2017) 23(3) CTLR 55.
3 The following selected books and articles consider the US position: Nancy C. Kim, *Wrap Contracts: Foundations and Ramifications* (New York: Oxford University Press 2013); Simon Blount, *Electronic Contracts* (2nd edn, LexisNexis Butterworths Australia 2015); Rachel C. Anderson, 'Enforcement of contractual terms in clickwrap agreements: courts refusing to enforce forum selection and binding arbitration clauses'(2007) 3 Shidler J L Com & Tech 11; Robert Lee Dickens, 'Finding common ground in the world of electronic contracts: the consistency of legal reasoning in clickwrap cases' (2007) 11 Marq Intell Prop L Rev 379; Juliet M. Moringiello and William L. Reynolds, 'From Lord Coke to internet privacy: the past, present, and future of the law of electronic contracting' (2013) 72 Md L Rev 452; Erin Canino, 'The electronic "sign-in-wrap" contract: issues of notice and assent, the average internet user standard, and unconscionability' (2016) 50 UC Davis L Rev 535; Mark E. Budnitz, 'Touching, tapping, and talking: the formation of contracts in cyberspace' (2019) 43 Nova L Rev 235; Caterina Gardiner, 'Principles of internet contracting: illuminating the shadows' (2019) 48(4) CLWR 208 for a review of US and Irish cases.

7.91 For a 'click wrap' contract to be enforceable, it is necessary that the party to whom the contract is directed is notified that a contract exists, and that it is intended to apply to them. In the 9th circuit case of *Knutson v Sirius XM Radio, Inc.*,[1] Mr Knutson, in purchasing a motor vehicle from Toyota, was not aware that a trial subscription to Sirius XM satellite radio that accompanied the purchase of the vehicle also meant that Sirius intended him to be bound by the terms of a contract that he was not aware existed.

1 771 F.3d 559, 14 Cal. Daily Op. Serv. 12,769, 2014 Daily Journal D.A.R. 15,058.

7.92 In England and Wales, the Law Commission has suggested that this form of signature is the technological equivalent of a manuscript signature using a cross.[1] It is suggested that this analysis is sound. This analysis is also in keeping with the decisions made by judges over the past 200 years regarding the form that a manuscript signature may take.[2] In English law, the validity of the signature depends on the function it performs, not necessarily the form a signature takes. Even if the act of clicking on an icon to order goods or services is deemed to be less secure than that provided by a manuscript signature, it does not follow that the reliability of the signature will affect its validity. Should a dispute occur between a buyer and a seller where one of the issues relates to the pressing of the icon, and the parties fail to resolve the matter, they will have to contemplate taking legal action. Before the matter reaches court, both parties will have to pay particular attention to the quantity and quality of the evidence available to them. In all probability, the reliability of the signature will depend on the ability of one or both of the parties to adduce sufficient forensic evidence of a high enough quality to demonstrate that either the icon was clicked or it was not. Even if the relying party can prove that the icon was clicked, it will not follow that the purported buyer clicked it. The nexus between the action of clicking the icon and the identity of the person who purported to order the items may be difficult to resolve, bearing in mind the security risks associated with using the Internet.

1 Law Commission, *Electronic Commerce: Formal Requirements in Commercial Transactions Advice from the Law Commission* (2001), 3.37; see also 3.36 and 3.38.

2 For a historical consideration of the case law from every common law country relating to manuscript signatures, facsimile transmission and telegram up to 1990 (including an exhaustive treatment of the US) – invaluable in understanding electronic signatures and the various forms electronic signatures can take, and helpful in understanding how judges in common law jurisdictions adapted the meaning of a signature as technologies developed and people used them in ways that were not anticipated – see Stephen Mason, *The Signature: The Judicial Development of the Concept from the Thirteenth Century to the Age of the Facsimile Transmission* (Institute of Advanced Legal Studies for the SAS Humanities Digital Library, School of Advanced Study, University of London) (to be published in 2022).

7.93 Proof is central to the question. In the US case of *Kerr v Dillard Stores Services, Inc.*,[1] the issue was whether an employee had clicked the 'I accept' icon in respect of an arbitration agreement. In this instance, the employer required employees to consent to arbitration by executing the arbitration agreement by way of an intranet computer system. For months, the employee had made it clear that she did not wish to sign the arbitration agreement, and refused to do so. Evidence was given to demonstrate how easy it was for a supervisor to reset an employee's password: indeed, this is just what a supervisor did in front of the plaintiff when the plaintiff had failed to log on to find out when she was next on duty. On the same day that the supervisor logged on to change the plaintiff's password, the computer system sent an internal email to the plaintiff, indicating that the agreement had been 'signed'. The employee was adamant that she had not executed the agreement, and Vratil J concluded that it was unlikely that the plaintiff would not have spontaneously reversed her decision in front of the supervisor, and that the supervisor could have clicked on the 'I accept' icon as the plaintiff watched. The judge set out the problem:

> The problem with Dillard's position is that it did not have adequate procedures to maintain the security of intranet passwords, to restrict authorized access to the screen which permitted electronic execution of the arbitration agreement, to determine whether electronic signatures were genuine or to determine who opened individual emails. While the record establishes that Champlin and plaintiff were at the kiosk on April 28, it does not show that they were there at precisely 3:26:20 p.m. Therefore, it is not inconceivable Champlin or a supervisor logged on to plaintiff's account and executed the agreement. The Court recognizes that defendants' burden of proof is not absolute certainty, but merely a preponderance of the evidence. At the same time, Dillard's has not demonstrated the efficacy of its security procedures with regard to electronic

> signatures. Therefore, its version of events is no more likely true than plaintiff's. For these reasons, this case basically turns on the burden of proof. Dillard's has the burden of proof and its evidence that plaintiff executed the arbitration agreement is not persuasive. On this record, the Court cannot find that it is more likely than not true that plaintiff executed the electronic agreement to arbitrate.[2]

1 2009 WL 385863, 105 Fair Empl.Prac.Cas. (BNA) 1298, 92 Empl. Prac. Dec. P 43,483.
2 2009 WL 385863 at 5.

7.94 This case illustrates how important proof is in the context of digital evidence.

7.95 In passing, Professor Preston notes that 'wrap' contracts are now considered to be enforceable without further inquiry, and the trend among judges in the US demonstrates a 'circularity of judicial review: one court finds a new kind of contract enforceable, and other courts then assume enforceability because "everyone is doing it" without performing a thorough analysis of the earlier opinions and distinguishing the facts',[1] and cites Matheson CJ in the case of *Hancock v American Telephone & Telegraph Company, Inc.*,[2] where the judge states, at 1255, that 'Clickwrap agreements are increasingly common and "have routinely been upheld"'. New terms to describe the methods devised to enforce contract terms on websites include 'sign-in-wraps' and 'scrollwrap'.[3]

1 Cheryl B. Preston, '"Please note: you have waived everything": can notice redeem online contracts?' (2015) 64 American University Law Review 535,543, including the further citations noted in the article; see also Jeffrey H. Dasteela, 'Consumer click arbitration: a review of online consumer arbitration agreements' (2017) 9 YB On Arb & Mediation 1 .
2 701 F.3d 1248 (10th Cir. 2012).
3 New York: *Berkson v Gogo, LLC*, 97 F.Supp.3d 359 (2015).

7.96 In the Queensland case of *Harding v Brisbane City Council*,[1] the applicant used an online facility to appeal against a planning application. The person submitting the request was required to include details of a form of 'identification' as part of the submission process. Mr Harding typed in the number of his driving licence, but he made an error, and one of the numbers he typed in was incorrect. His application was rejected. At the appeal, the judge was required to determine, among other things, whether the input of an incorrect number merited the rejection of the submission. It did not. Robin QC DCJ held at [18] that:

> I think a common sense approach should be taken by which erroneous reproduction of more than a couple of digits (in the absence of special circumstances, such as the same number (exclusively) repeated – which may indicate some hardware or software malfunction) might be seen as creating some concern as to the signature, having regard to s 14(a) & (b) of the [Electronic Transactions (Queensland) Act 2001]; on a commonsense approach in the present context, one wrong digit does not create any real concern.

1 [2008] QPEC 75 (16 October 2008).

7.97 This discrepancy did not vitiate the submission as a properly made one. Interesting as the observation made by Robin QC DCJ is, that is the numbers identifying the driving licence constituted a 'signature', the judge was not correct. The signature comprised the act of clicking the 'accept' icon, and not the submission of the numbers identifying the driving licence.[1] The numbers identifying the driving licence acted as an additional item of evidence to demonstrate to the Council that the person making the submission was who they claimed to be, which is a different issue entirely.

1 The 'I accept' icon was accepted in *eBay International AG v Creative Festival Entertainment Pty Ltd* (ACN 098 183 281) [2006] FCA 1768.

Browse wrap

7.98 There is a category of electronic signatures commonly called 'browse wrap' agreements, although there is some controversy around how judges apply the distinction between 'click wrap' and 'browse wrap' in case law.[1] Judges have also had to deal with cases that look like 'browse wrap', but are 'click wrap',[2] and what can be described as hybrid cases,[3] as described in the case of *Fjeja v Facebook, Inc.*[4] by Holwell, J at 838:

> Facebook's Terms of Use are somewhat like a browsewrap agreement in that the terms are only visible via a hyperlink, but also somewhat like a clickwrap agreement in that the user must do something else – click 'Sign Up' – to assent to the hyperlinked terms. Yet, unlike some clickwrap agreements, the user can click to assent whether or not the user has been presented with the terms.

1 For the US, see: Monique C. M. Leahy, 'Litigation of internet "wrap" agreements' (2017) 150 Am Jur Trials 383; Cheryl B. Preston, 'How did we end up in a world where browsewraps are enforced even when they waive all consumer rights?' (2018) 45 Fla St U L Rev 1012; James Gibson, 'Boilerplate's false dichotomy' (2018) 106 Geo LJ 249; Kevin Conroy and John A. Shope, 'Look before you click: the enforceability of website and smartphone app terms and conditions' (2019) 63 B BJ 23. For the position in Canada, see Sookman, 'Browsewraps, fair dealing and Blacklock's Reporter v. Canada'; Theodore Milosevic, 'What makes a consumer? Mandatory arbitration clauses and free digital services in Canada' (2017) 75 UT Fac L Rev 9; see also Eliza Mik, 'Contracts governing the use of websites' 2016 Sing J Legal Stud 70. For the European Union, where clickwrap is acceptable in respect of Council Regulation (EC) No 44/2001 of 22 December 2000 on jurisdiction and the recognition and enforcement of judgments in civil and commercial matters, OJ L 12, 16.1.2001, 1–23, see *El Majdoub v CarsOnTheWeb.Deutschland GmbH* (C-322/14) EU:C:2015:3343, [2015] 1 WLR 3986, [2016] 1 All ER (Comm) 197, [2015] 5 WLUK 617, [2015] All ER (EC) 1073, [2015] CEC 1225, [2015] ILPr 32 and Andrew Dickinson and Johannes Ungerer, ' "Click wrapping" choice of court agreements in the Brussels I regime', L.M.C.L.Q. 2016, 1(Feb), 15–19.
2 California: *Savetsky v Pre-Paid Legal Services, Inc. d/b/a LegalShield*, 2015 WL 4593744 (previous hearing reported at 2015 WL 604767).
3 The Court of Appeals of Texas concluded the facts in *Hotels.com, L.P. v Canales*, 195 S.W.3d 147, 195 S.W.3d 147 (2006), which illustrated a similar hybrid approach. In this case, the terms did not apply to the main plaintiff because it entered a contract over the telephone, but the terms applied to those plaintiffs that had used the website.
4 841 F.Supp.2d 829 (2012).

7.99 In this case, the judge held that the user was bound by the terms and conditions, and said, at 839–840:

> The mechanics of the internet surely remain unfamiliar, even obtuse to many people. But it is not too much to expect that an internet user whose social networking was so prolific that losing Facebook access allegedly caused him mental anguish would understand that the hyperlinked phrase 'Terms of Use' is really a sign that says 'Click Here for Terms of Use'. So understood, at least for those to whom the internet is in an indispensable part of daily life, clicking the hyperlinked phrase is the 21st-century equivalent of turning over the cruise ticket. In both cases, the consumer is prompted to examine terms of sale that are located somewhere else. Whether or not the consumer bothers to look is irrelevant.

> …
>
> Here, Fteja was informed of the consequences of his assenting click and he was shown, immediately below, where to click to understand those consequences. That was enough.

7.100 'Browse wrap' agreements are where one party aims to impose terms of use or sale on another party where a visitor demonstrates assent by using the website.[1] The potential customer is not required to indicate acceptance of any terms by any positive action, but the user must have had actual or constructive knowledge of the terms and conditions for them to be effective.[2] This form of electronic signature comprises the process of using the website, thereby indicating knowledge of the relevant terms, although for such terms to be effective, or for constructive notice to apply, they must be conspicuous, intend to apply and the party with the burden of proof must demonstrate how a visitor is made aware of the terms. A party might fail because they cannot demonstrate a number of issues of relevance, such as that the agreement actually existed on its website at the material time, that any agreement applied to the actual product in dispute, or that the defendants agreed to its terms.[3]

1 Further reading: Uri Benoliela and Shmuel I. Becher, 'The duty to read the unreadable' (2019) 60 BC L Rev 2255; William Hurley, 'Failure of notice to terms in online contract formation: a solution that informs consumers of their obligations and rights' (2019) 14 Liberty U L Rev 249; Tal Kastner and Ethan J. Leib, 'Contract creep' (2019) 107 Geo LJ 1277; Budnitz, 'Touching, tapping, and talking'.
2 Or the product, if in Illinois: *Schafer v AT & T Wireless Services, Inc.*, 2005 WL 850459 (S.D.Ill.).
3 Florida: *IT Strategies Group, Inc. v The Allday Consulting Group, L.L.C.*, 975 F.Supp.2d 1267 (2013) where the plaintiff failed to demonstrate that the defendants had actual or constructive knowledge of its online user agreement and that they had assented to the terms of that agreement.

'I accept'

7.101 The first instance decision in the case of *Bassano v Toft*[1] is an example where the use of the 'I accept' icon was upheld in England under the provisions of the Consumer Credit Act 1974. It was argued by counsel for Mrs Bassano that the loan agreement was not executed by her in a manner that complied with the Act. Popplewell J disagreed, indicating, at [43], that:

> s61 of the Act requires the agreement to be signed in the prescribed form, and the form prescribed at the time was that required by The Consumer Credit (Agreements) Regulations 2010 (SI 2010 No 1014). The only relevant prescription was in regulation 4(3)(a), which provides that the signature must be in a space indicated in the document for that purpose and dated. Regulation 4(5) recognises that a regulated agreement may be concluded electronically by regulation 4(5), and that the document may contain 'information about the process or means of providing, communicating or verifying the signature to be made by the debtor'. There was therefore nothing in the Consumer Credit Act 1974 to suggest that regulated agreements were capable of being signed by an electronic signature; and I can see no reasons of policy why a signature should not be capable of being affixed and communicated electronically to an agreement regulated by the Act, just as it can for other documents which are required to be signed.

1 [2014] EWHC 377 (QB), [2014] 2 WLUK 800, [2014] ECC 144, [2014] CTLC 1177, [2014] Bus LR D99, [2014] CLY 273.

7.102 This type of conflicting evidence, coupled with a denial that the email communications were sent by the sender, occurred in Germany in the three cases of OLG Köln, 19 U 16/02, LG Konstanz, 2 O 141/01 A, and AG Erfurt, 28 C 2354/01.[1] The three individual defendants were asked to pay for items bought in Internet auctions. The winning bids were sent from email accounts where the user can write the email on the website of the provider of the address. Each of the defendants had access to the address by means of a password, but denied taking part in the bidding process. All three cases were dismissed, because the relying party failed to prove to the satisfaction of the courts that the defendants sent the declarations, which meant the plaintiff failed to prove that a contract had been concluded. By the same token, exactly the same problem may occur with the use of digital signatures. Whether a user denies clicking on an icon or using their private key to sign a document or message, the problem will be the same: proving that the sending party carried out the action. In this respect, the difference between a digital signature and clicking an icon is a narrow one.

1 Michael Knopp, Case Note, OLG Köln, Ur19 U 16/02; LG Konstanz, 2 O 141/01 A; AG Erfurt, 28 C 2354/01, (2005) 2 Digital Evidence and Electronic Signature Law Review 105; for a translation of Ur19 U 16/02, see Henriette Picot and Marlene Kast (2008) 5 Digital Evidence and Electronic Signature Law Review 108.

Personal Identification Number (PIN) and password

7.103 The PIN is possibly the oldest form of electronic signature,[1] and has become a very widely used form of authentication, especially to obtain access to a bank account through the use of an ATM (automated teller machine or automatic teller machine or automated banking machine or cash machine), or to confirm a transaction with a credit card or debit card.[2] Arguably, in the banking context, the PIN combines two functions. Before we consider these two functions, let us look at the requirements of the bank. The bank needs to satisfy itself that:

1. The card is legitimate (this is difficult to achieve, as the reports about fraud demonstrate), and
2. The card is in the possession of the customer to whom it was issued, or a person authorized by the customer to use the card.

1 In *United States of America v Miller*, 70 F.3d 1353 (D.C. Cir. 1995), Karen LeCraft Henderson J referred to the PIN at 1355 as acting 'as a sort of electronic signature authorizing an ATM to release available funds'.
2 The use of a PIN was explicitly recognized as a type of electronic signature by the Civil Chamber of the Supreme Court of Lithuania in its ruling in the case of *Ž.Š. v AB Lietuva taupomasis bankas*, civil case no. 3K-3-390/2002; for a case note, see S. Trofimovs (2008) 5 Digital Evidence and Electronic Signature Law Review 143, and for a translation, see Sergejs Trofimovs (2009) 6 Digital Evidence and Electronic Signature Law Review 255; for Austria, see case note, OGH Urteil vom 29.6.2000, 2 Ob 133/99v, Oberster Gerichtshof (Austrian Supreme Court) (2008) 5 Digital Evidence and Electronic Signature Law Review 141 and translation into English: OGH judgment of 29.06.2000, 2 Ob 133/99v – Liability for misuse of ATM cards, Oberste Gerichtshof (Supreme Court) (2009) 6 Digital Evidence and Electronic Signature Law Review 223.

7.104 If the bank satisfies itself that its computer systems are interacting with the card issued to the customer (which is not always the case), then the computer system requests the purported customer to undertake one further act to confirm they (or a person authorized by them) have physically inserted the card into the ATM, or the point of sale terminal, by keying in the correct PIN. Generally, if the computer systems receive positive results from both interactions, then the bank will permit the person at the ATM or the point of sale terminal to undertake whatever activity they are permitted to do within the terms of the mandate.

> 1. The first function of a PIN
>
> The first function of the PIN acts as a means of authentication. The PIN purports to demonstrate that the person who keyed in the PIN knew the correct PIN (there are some forms of attack that do not need the correct PIN – any combination of numbers will act to deceive the card issuer that the correct PIN has been keyed in).
>
> 2. The second function of a PIN
>
> Once the computer systems of the bank are satisfied that the card is legitimate and the PIN is the correct PIN of the customer, then the person at the ATM or the point of sale terminal can undertake any activity on the account that is permitted within the mandate and within the limitations of the technology.

7.105 The PIN, even though it is offered to the machine before a transaction is effected, acts as a signature to verify a payment or other form of transaction. This means that the presentation of a card to an ATM, and the input of a PIN, is similar to a cheque that is written out by the account holder, signed and then presented to the cashier at the bank. The customer completes the action necessary to request a payment in advance of the payment being made by the cashier, and then signs the cheque in the presence of the cashier – all before receiving acknowledgment that a transaction has been authorized. This means the PIN is a form of electronic signature.

7.106 It might be considered that the action of clicking the 'I accept' icon or box, or typing in a PIN, is merely a means by which the person agrees to conclude the contract, but the act is not that of appending their electronic signature. This analysis might be right, but we must recall that the digital world is different to the physical world. Conceptually, some of the forms of electronic signature may not strictly be considered 'signatures' in the physical world. Nevertheless, it is a convenient shorthand to refer to some forms of agreeing to enter a contract as an 'electronic signature' – at least we can all understand the meaning behind these words, even if the form is not quite what we expect.

7.107 Invariably, a claim by the user that they did not authorize one or more transactions conducted on the account will require the relying party – that is, the bank, with the burden of proof – to prove the account holder authorized the transaction. The fact that a withdrawal or other form of transaction took place may not be in issue, and in any event the bank can adduce the evidence under the relevant business records or the Bankers' Books exemptions. The burden remains the same,[1] whatever the technology used.[2]

1 In Cormac Herley, P. C. van Oorschot and Andrew S. Patrick, 'Passwords: if we're so smart, why are we still using them?', in Roger Dingledine and Phillipe Golle (eds), *Financial Cryptography and Data Security, 13th International Conference, FC 2009, Accra Beach, Barbados, February 23–26, 2009* (Springer 2009), https://www.microsoft.com/en-us/research/publication/passwords-if-were-so-smart-why-are-we-still-using-them/?from=http%3A%2F%2Fresearch.microsoft.com%2Fpubs%2F80199%2Ffc09.pdf, the statement that 'users become responsible for all approved transactions where authorization relied on a correct PIN' is incorrect. Whatever the form of technology

that is used, the relying party has the burden of proof. The bank must prove that it had the mandate of the customer to undertake an action on the account, regardless of the nature of the technology. Although it was held in the South African case of *Diners Club SA (Pty) Ltd v Singh* 2004 (3) SA 630 (D) that a contract term by which the customer was liable, irrespective of who used the PIN, was not against public policy; compare this to the Japanese decision by the Supreme Court in *Taro Kono (an alias) v The Shinwa Bank, Ltd* 8 April 2003, MINSHU Vol. 57 No 4 at 337, Hanrei-Times No 1121 at 96, discussed with other Japanese authorities and the effect of the Depositor Protection Act 2005 by Hironao Kaneko, 'How bank depositors are protected in Japan' (2011) 8 Digital Evidence and Electronic Signatures Review 92. For a comparative analysis of the contractual tension between the liability of a bank and the liability of the customer generally, see Sandra Booysen, 'Consumer protection and the court's role in shaping the bank-customer contract' (2019) 135 (Jul) LQR 437.

2 Maryke Silalahi Nuth, 'Unauthorized use of bank cards with or without the PIN: a lost case for the customer?' (2012) 9 Digital Evidence and Electronic Signature Law Review 95; case translation: Norway, Journal number 04-016794TVI-TRON, *Bernt Petter Jørgensen v DnB NOR Bank ASA by the Chairman of the Board* (Trondheim District Court, 24 September 2004) (2012) 9 Digital Evidence and Electronic Signature Law Review 117; case translation: Republic of Turkey, case number: 2009/11485, judgment number: 2011/4033, by Av. Burcu Orhan Holmgren (2012) 9 Digital Evidence and Electronic Signature Law Review 124.

7.108 The central concern is usually whether it was the customer or somebody else who was responsible for withdrawals made from the customer's account using the correct PIN or password. Judges across the globe have had to address numerous problems that have arisen in connection with the use of the PIN in personal banking. Issues include:

(1) Whether it was the customer or a third party without authority who used the PIN (the debate might be that the technology does not need the correct PIN)[1] – by way of example, cases that illustrate this issue are recorded in the USA,[2] Germany,[3] Nigeria,[4] Papua New Guinea,[5] and England and Wales.[6]

(2) Responsibility for the PIN sent by the bank through the postal service falling into the wrong hands and leading to the unauthorized use of the PIN in banking transactions, causing loss to the customer.[7]

(3) Transactions that occur with the authority of the user, but the user may dispute the amount they authorized, as in the Danish case of U.2000.1853V, where, at a restaurant with late-night opening hours, A authorized two Dankort card payments as he swiped his debit card through one of N's card terminals, entered his PIN and agreed the amount that appeared on the display. The court was satisfied that one of the payments was erroneously accepted in the sum of DKK 10,500 instead of DKK 105. N was therefore ordered to pay back the difference. The court accepted, as a starting point, that when the appellant entered his PIN and approved an amount in the sum of DKK 10,500, the appellant made a binding payment to the respondent. However, that action did not rule out that it could be proved that payment of a higher amount was made by mistake.[8]

1 Steven J. Murdoch, 'Reliability of chip & pin evidence in banking disputes' (2009) 6 Digital Evidence and Electronic Signature Law Review 98; Roger Porkess and Stephen Mason, 'Looking at debit and credit card fraud' (2012 Autumn) 34(3) Teaching Statistics 87 (also translated into German: Betrug mit Kundenkarten und Kreditkarten, Stochastik in der Schule (2014) 34(2), S. 15).

2 For a number of early cases in the US, see *Judd v Citibank*, N.Y.City Civ.Ct., 435 N.Y.S.2d 210; *Feldman v Citibank, N.A.; Pickman v Citibank, N.A.*, N.Y.City Civ.Ct., 443 N.Y.S.2d 43; *Ognibene v Citibank, N.A.*, N.Y.City Civ.Ct., 446 N.Y.S.2d 845; see also *State of New York, by Abrams v Citibank, N.A.*, 537 F.Supp. 1192 (1982); in *Porter v Citibank, N.A.*, 123 Misc.2d 28, 472 N.Y.S.2d 582 (N.Y.City Civ.Ct. 1984), where the customer used their card but no money was dispensed, employees of the bank testified that on average cash machines were out of balance once or twice a week.

3 5 October 2004, XI ZR 210/03, published BGHZ 160, 308–321 Bundesgerichtshof (Federal Court of Justice); for a translation and commentaries by Michael Eßer and Thomas Kritter, see (2009) 6 Digital

Evidence and Electronic Signature Law Review 248; it has been demonstrated that any PIN can be used to obtain money from an ATM, with no need for the thief to have the correct PIN, for which see Steven J. Murdoch, Saar Drimer, Ross Anderson and Mike Bond, 'Chip and PIN is broken', 2010 IEEE Symposium on Security and Privacy, http://www.cl.cam.ac.uk/~sjm217/papers/oakland10chipbroken.pdf (this was awarded the Best Practical Paper).

4 *Geoffrey Amano v United Bank for Africa (UBA) PLC*, Suit No: PHC/257/2011, reported in (2013) 3 SLP (Section on Legal Practice) Law Journal 114; *Benjamin Agi v Access Bank PLC* (2014) BNLR 23 discussed by Timothy Tion, 'Electronic evidence in Nigeria' (2014) 11 Digital Evidence and Electronic Signature Law Review 76; for an example of members of staff stealing from ATMs, see Timothy Tion, 'Another method of stealing cash from ATMs' (2017) 14 Digital Evidence and Electronic Signature Law Review 13.

5 *Roni v Kagure* [2004] PGDC 1, DC84 (1 January 2004).

6 *Job v Halifax PLC* (not reported) Case number 7BQ00307 (2009) 6 Digital Evidence and Electronic Signature Law Review 235; *Shojibur Rahman v Barclays Bank PLC*, commentary by Stephen Mason and Nicholas Bohm (2013) 10 Digital Evidence and Electronic Signature Law Review 169; *Shojibur Rahman v Barclays Bank PLC* (on appeal from the judgment of Her Honour District Judge Millard dated 24 October 2012), commentary by Stephen Mason and Nicholas Bohm (2013) 10 Digital Evidence and Electronic Signature Law Review 175.

7 Court of First Instance of Athens constituted by a single judge 5526/1999; for a translation into English, see Anastasia Fylla, Case note – Greece (2007) 4 Digital Evidence and Electronic Signature Law Review 89.

8 For a full report of this case, see (2007) 4 Digital Evidence and Electronic Signature Law Review 98.

7.109 Of interest is a decision that accepts the proposition that the unique number issued by a bank can be a signature. In the New Jersey case of *Spevack, Cameron & Boyd v National Community Bank of New Jersey*,[1] the unique account number assigned by a bank to a depositor was determined to be as complete a signature as the depositor's written or printed name. Bilder J (retired and temporarily assigned on recall) observed, at 1169, that a signature may take many forms, and there was no reason why a bank account number could not be one of them:

> In this computer age the use of numbers as a means of identification has become pervasive. Indeed, numbers are more readily recognized and handled than signatures. The 'signature' used by Homequity was its account number at Midlantic, the bank in which it deposited the check. That 'signature' accurately identified the payee and the funds were properly credited to the payee's account. In fact, had Homequity written a name without the account number, the bank would have had to look up the number that corresponded with the same. In keeping with the electronic age, it is the numbers which have the primary significance.

1 677 A.2d 1168 (N.J.Super.A.D. 1996), 291 N.J.Super. 577. Note the 1844 New York case of *Brown v The Butchers & Drovers' Bank*, 6 Hill 443, 41 Am.Dec. 755 where a person writing '1. 2. 8.' on the back of a bill of exchange as a substitute for his name served to endorse the bill.

7.110 The problems with the PIN and banking applications represent an ever-changing struggle between clever thieves who implement new strategies to steal and the banks in overcoming the threats as they are discovered.[1]

1 Mason and Reiniger, '"Trust" between machines?'; Stephen Mason, 'Electronic banking and how courts approach the evidence' (2013) 29 Computer Law and Security Review 144; Stephen Mason, 'Debit cards, ATMs and negligence of the bank and customer' (2012) 27 Butterworths Journal of International Banking and Financial Law 163; Stephen Mason, 'UK credit card fraud: the scale of the problem' (2012) 6 e-Finance & Payments Law & Policy 14.

7.111 As to the use of passwords as a form of electronic signature, in England and Wales Companies House relies on a six-character alphanumeric 'Authentication Code' which it describes as the 'equivalent of a company officer's signature'.[1] The password, which can be changed by the user, will only be sent out by Companies House by post to the company's registered office. Likewise, electronic tax returns to HM Revenue & Customs go through a government gateway, which involves identity and security checks including a unique taxpayer reference number, a password and an activation code, thereby removing the need for a signature.[2]

1 https://www.gov.uk/guidance/company-authentication-codes-for-online-filing.
2 Confirmed in *Creative Eye Photography LLP Helipix LLP v The Commissioners for Her Majesty's Revenue & Customs* [2017] UKFTT 399 (TC), [2017] 5 WLUK 213 at [27], a decision of the First-tier Tribunal Tax Chamber.

7.112 In *Niche Generics Ltd v European Commission (T-701/14)*,[1] an application was made for an annulment of a decision by the Commission that a settlement agreement entered into by the applicant constituted a restriction on competition. An issue arose as to whether a defence had been filed by the Commission, it being a requirement in article 3(1) of the Rules of Procedure of the General Court of 2 May 1991, that '[t]he original of every pleading must be signed by the party's agent or lawyer'. However, the Rules also provided a mechanism by which certain criteria could be put in place to satisfy that requirement. A decision by the General Court on the lodging and service of procedural documents by means of e-Curia was made on 14 September 2011[2] in these terms in article 3:

> A procedural document lodged by means of e-Curia shall be deemed to be the original of that document for the purposes of the first subparagraph of Article 43(1) of the Rules of Procedure where the representative's user identification and password have been used to effect that lodgement. Such identification shall constitute the signature of the document concerned.

1 Also known as Perindopril, Re, Servier, Re EU:T:2018:921, [2018] 12 WLUK 705, [2019] 4 CMLR 15.
2 Decision of the General Court of 14 September 2011 on the lodging and service of procedural documents by means of e-Curia, OJ C 289, 1.10.2011, 9.

7.113 The argument as to any failure to file a defence was rejected. The procedural decision and overall decision of the General Court in *Niche Generics* demonstrates the fact that a user identification and password are capable of amounting to an electronic signature in that context. It is easy to see how that concept could be expanded in relation to passwords actually being a component of an electronic signature.

Typing a name into an electronic document

7.114 The use of electronic signatures predates any form of legislation, and in the latter decade of the twentieth century adjudicators found themselves applying well-established legal principles to new technologies when presented in the form of electronic signatures, just as judges in the nineteenth century were confronted with the increasing use of printing, typewriting and telegrams: all, it must be said, without the need for special legislation to be enacted. The early case law in which electronic signatures appeared demonstrated the flexibility of the common law,[1] although this form of electronic signature is not uniformly accepted in all jurisdictions,[2] and some judges in common law jurisdictions have failed to demonstrate flexibility.[3]

1 The first example appears to be *Wilkens v Iowa Insurance Commissioner* 457 N.W.2d 1 (Iowa App. 1990), where an agent countersigned insurance policies by typing his name into the document on the computer; see also *Doherty v Registry of Motor Vehicles*, No 97/CV0050 (Suffolk, SS Massachusetts District Court, May 28, 1997), http://www.loundy.com/CASES/Doherty_v_RMV.html, where an email was signed by the typewritten name of the officer; electronic signatures are used routinely in traffic offences, for which see the Canadian cases of *R v Eged*, 2009 BCPC 180 (CanLII) and *City of London v Caza*, 2010 ONSC 1548 (CanLII) by way of example.
2 For instance, see the following case translations from Denmark: U.2001.252Ø (request for dissolution; Bankruptcy Court; signature; sufficiency of electronic signature with name typed on document) and U.2001.1980/1H (request for dissolution; Bankruptcy Court; requirement for manuscript signature; sufficiency of electronic signature with name typed on document) (2009) 6 Digital Evidence and Electronic Signature Law Review 232.
3 In the Australian case of *Philip Laming v TicketXpress Pty Ltd* PR941462 [2003] AIRC 1503 (3 December 2003), Hamilton, Deputy President of the Australian Industrial Relations Commission indicated, incorrectly, at [2] that 'Emails do not contain signatures, even electronic signatures, and the only readily identifiable marking may be the email address'.

7.115 Typing a name into a document such as an email is a valid method of signing a document,[1] as established in *Orton v Collins*,[2] where the word 'Putsmans' was deliberately typed in an email after the customary salutation 'Yours faithfully'. Mr Peter Prescott QC, sitting as a Deputy Judge, said, at [21]:

> I have no doubt that its purpose would be recognized throughout the profession. Anyone would think: 'Putsmans are signing off on this document'. It was intended to signify that document was being sent out with the authority of the defendants' legal representative.

1 For additional examples, see China: *Beijing Han-Hua-Kai-Jie Technology development Ltd. v Chen Hong* (2018) Zhe 0192 (2007) 4 Digital Evidence and Electronic Law Review 96 (employment); France: Case number 235784 from the Conseil d'Etat, Elections municipales de la Commune d'Entre-Deux-Monts dated 28 December 2001 (2004) 1 Digital Evidence and Electronic Law Review 81; Case number 00-46467 from the Cour de Cassation, chambre civile 2, Sté Chalets Boisson c/ M. X. dated 30 April 2003 (2004) 1 Digital Evidence and Electronic Law Review 82; Germany: OLG Köln, 19 U 16/02; LG Konstanz, 2 O 141/01 A; AG Erfurt, 28C 2354/01 (2005) 2 Digital Evidence and Electronic Law Review 105; Ur19 U 16/02, OLG Köln, 6 September 2002 (2008) 5 Digital Evidence and Electronic Law Review 108; 12 U 34/07, Court of Appeal Berlin (Kammergericht Berlin), 30 August 2007 (2008) 5 Digital Evidence and Electronic Law Review 110 (all contracts); Italy: Tribunale sez. V, Milano, 18/10/2016, n. 11402 (2019) 16 Digital Evidence and Electronic Law Review 90 (contract); Slovenia: I Up 505/2003, The Supreme Court of the Republic of Slovenia (2007) 4 Digital Evidence and Electronic Law Review 97 (procedure). For a name in a text message, see China: *Yang Chunning v Han Ying* (2005) hai min chu zi NO.4670, Beijing Hai Dian District People's Court (2008) 5 Digital Evidence and Electronic Law Review 103 and Denmark: U.2001.252Ø (2009) 6 Digital Evidence and Electronic Law Review 232; U.2001.1980/1H (2009) 6 Digital Evidence and Electronic Law Review 234.
2 [2007] EWHC 803 (Ch), [2007] 1 WLR 2953, [2007] 3 All ER 863, [2007] 4 WLUK 353, [2007] 2 EGLR 147, (2007) 151 SJLB 608, [2007] NPC 49, [2007] CLY 488; *Green (Liquidator of Stealth Construction Ltd) v Ireland* [2011] EWHC 1305 (Ch), [2011] 5 WLUK 588, [2012] 1 BCLC 297, [2011] BPIR 1173, [2011] CLY 1875 where it was accepted that typing a name into an email is sufficient for the purposes of s 2 Law of Property (Miscellaneous Provisions) Act 1989; *Lindsay v O'Loughnane* [2010] EWHC 529 (QB), [2010] 3 WLUK 515, [2012] BCC 153.

7.116 The main area of contention is to argue whether an email or series of emails constitutes the necessary evidence that an agreement has been reached.

Acts by a lawyer as agent

7.117 An agent, with the appropriate authority, remains capable of binding their principal digitally, just as in the physical world. That this applies to attorneys is illustrated in the Tennessee case of *Waddle v Elrod*,[1] where the Supreme Court determined that the emails exchanged between counsel with their name typed at the bottom of the email satisfied the signature requirement of the Statute of Frauds. The same principle applies in New Zealand.[2]

1 367 S.W.3d 217 (2012).
2 *Cox v Coughlan* [2014] NZHC 164 (14 February 2014).

Interest in real property

7.118 In *Faulks v Cameron*,[1] the Supreme Court of the Northern Territory in Australia applied the provisions of s 9 of the Electronic Transactions (Northern Territory) Act 2000 (NT) to the name typed at the bottom of the email. Acting Master Young concluded, at 64:

> I am satisfied that the printed signature on the defendant's emails identifies him and indicates his approval of the information communicated, that the method was as reliable as was appropriate and that the plaintiff consented to the method. I am satisfied that the agreement is 'signed' for the purposes of s45(2).

1 [2004] 32 Fam LR 417, [2004] NTSC 61; see also *Kavia Holdings Pty Limited v Suntrack Holdings Pty Limited* [2011] NSWSC 716.

Loan of money

7.119 In the New South Wales case of *Stuart v Hishon*,[1] Ms Hishon loaned money to Mr Stuart and subsequently initiated proceedings to recover A$28,216.17 plus interest, being the outstanding and unpaid balance of monies owing to her pursuant to the loan of A$83,760.87 made by Ms Hishon to him in July 1996. Prior to the litigation, a series of email correspondence occurred between the parties regarding the payment of the loan, and Mr Stuart ended each email with 'Tom'. Counsel for Mr Stuart argued that it was necessary to provide evidence to establish that Mr Stuart placed the printed name on his email intending it to be an acknowledgment of the debt, and that no such evidence existed. Harrison J did not accept this argument, stating, at [34], that 'Mr Stuart typed his name on the foot of the email. He signed it by doing so. It would be an almost lethal assault on common sense to take any other view.'

1 [2013] NSWSC 766.

7.120 In China, in the court of first instance case of *Yang Chunning v Han Ying*,[1] Mr Yang claimed that the defendant Miss Han asked to borrow RMB 11,000 from him. Yang agreed to lend the money to Miss Han, but she failed to return the money. As evidence, Mr Yang exhibited several text messages sent from Miss Han's mobile telephone about the loan. It was confirmed that the messages were transmitted from Miss Han's mobile telephone number. In this case, the judge supported the plaintiff's claim based on the evidence of the mobile telephone message between the parties. The court judged that these messages, as a form of electronic text according to the Electronic Signature Law,[2] could serve as evidence to support Mr Yang's claim.

1 (2005) hai min chu zi NO.4670, Beijing Hai Dian District People's Court; for a translation into English of this case, see (2008) 5 Digital Evidence and Electronic Signature Law Review 103.

2 Electronic Signatures Law of the People's Republic of China of 2004 (amended by Electronic Signatures Law of the People's Republic of China of 2015 (Order No. 24 of the President of the People's Republic of China, promulgated on and effective since 4 April 2015).

7.121 In the Texas case of *Parks v Seybold*[1] before the Court of Appeals, the Gaming Management Corporation executed a note payable to Scott Seybold in the amount of US$10,000, plus 15 per cent interest. Clyde Parks wrote the note by hand, and he signed it in his capacity as vice-president of the corporation. The corporation ceased to exist, and Mr Seybold sought full payment on the note. The parties subsequently exchanged a number of emails, and the court agreed with the trial judge that the emails constituted writing, and the inclusion of the words 'Thank you, Clyde' above an automatic signature block served to demonstrate that Parks had signed the emails.

1 2015 WL 4481768; John G. Browning, 'No ink, no problems? A look at the validity of email signatures as contracts' (2017) 80 Tex BJ 772 ; George L. Blum, 'Use of e-mails to establish enforceable contracts' (2017) 32 ALR 7th Art 6.

Employment

7.122 In England and Wales, the first case of this nature occurred in the Industrial Tribunal case of *Hall v Cognos Limited.*[1] Cognos employed Mr Hall as a sales executive under the terms of the Standard Employment Agreement used by Cognos. He was provided with a motor car for business and personal use. Mr Hall was reimbursed for all reasonable expenses incurred for travel, accommodation and other costs in accordance with the relevant policy, which the chairman determined was incorporated into the contract. The policy stated that all expenses over six months old would not be paid. Mr Hall failed to submit any travel expenses between 1 December 1995 and 3 June 1996. By January 1997 Mr Hall wanted his expenses to be paid. A series of emails was exchanged on 15 January between Mr Hall, Sarah McGoun (of HR) and Keith Schroeder, Mr Hall's line manager. Mr Hall asked if he could submit a late expenses claim to Ms McGoun. Ms McGoun in turn referred Mr Hall to Keith Schroeder, and Mr Schroeder, in response to the question as to 'whether [the late submission] is OK with you?' replied, 'Yes, it is OK.' Mr Hall subsequently submitted his expenses, although he did not provide all the necessary forms immediately. He also inflated his claims. His employers refused to make any payment and dismissed him.

1 Industrial Tribunal Case No 1803325/97.

7.123 Counsel for Cognos argued that because an email was not in writing and signed, the exchange of emails did not have any effect on the terms of the employment agreement. Mr C. T. Grazin, the chairman sitting on his own, declined to accept this proposition, attractive as it appeared to him. He held that the emails were in writing and signed once they were printed out. Despite there being no reference or discussion to any relevant case law or the statutory definitions of 'writing' and 'document,' the chairman concluded at 5:

> I am satisfied than an email is 'in writing and signed by the parties' once it is printed out. The position might (it is not necessary to make any finding on this point) be different if the email was only retained temporarily on the computer's hard disk storage system. The documents that were, however, produced from the computer are clearly in writing and bear the signatures of both 'Sarah' and 'Keith'. The fact that those signatures are printed, rather than hand-written, is not in my view material. For those reasons, I reject Mr Pym's submission that the relevant

email messages are incapable, as a matter of law, of having any modifying effect on the specific contract between the parties.

7.124 A further argument put forward on behalf of Cognos was that Mr Schroeder did not have the authority to respond to Mr Hall's request, nor was he authorized to agree to it. This was rejected on the basis that, as Mr Hall's line manager, Mr Schroeder was vested with the appropriate authority to deal with such a request, and as a result, Mr Hall could rely on Mr Schroeder's response. This meant Mr Schroeder's response acted to bind Cognos. As a result, the exchange of emails between Mr Hall and his line manager acted to vary the policy, and Cognos was obliged to pay Mr Hall his reasonable expenses.

Contract

7.125 The members of the Court of Appeal Civil Division in *Nicholas Prestige Homes v Neal*[1] did not concern themselves with the question of the signature in emails in this particular case. It was concluded that a contract was formed with the exchange of emails regarding the commission on a sale of property. By implication, the names typed at the end of the email, 'Marc Taylor' and 'Sally', were construed as valid signatures.[2]

1 [2010] EWCA Civ 1552, [2010] WLUK 9, (2010) 107(48) LSG 14.

2 An exchange of emails constituted an agreement in *Bieber v Teathers Ltd (In Liquidation)* [2014] EWHC 4205 (Ch), [2014] 12 WLUK 408, [2015] CILL 3609, and as with *Nicholas Prestige Homes v Neal*, the nature of the signatures was not considered. In *Temple, Re* 2012 CarswellOnt 2817, 2012 ONSC 376, [2012] O.J. No. 856, 109 O.R. (3d) 374, 214 A.C.W.S. (3d) 609, 75 C.B.R. (5th) 312, Newbould J determined that a name on an email was a sufficient signature within the requirements of the Limitations Act, 2002, S.O. 2002, c. 24 (Ontario), but the judge did not indicate where the name was placed, whether it as at the end of the email or the name as part of the email address, in *Toronto Common Elements Condo. Corp. No. 2041 v Toronto Standard Condo. Corp. No. 2051*, 2015 ONSC 4245 (CanLII), Corbett J refused to accept an email was signed, but failed to indicate whether a name appeared in the body of the email, and if a name was included in the body of the email, where the name was placed, whether it as at the end of the email or if a name formed part of the email address. In *Lev v Serebrennikov* 2016 ONSC 2093 (CanLII), Pattillo J accepted an email was signed, but did not clarify where the name was placed, whether it as at the end of the email or the name as part of the email address, although by inference, the judge was probably referring to the name that formed part of the email address.

7.126 Whether a signature contained in an email constitutes a valid contract in Israel was considered by Noa Grossman J in *Computer Sky Edv v Prime Medical Company Ltd.*[1] It was held that a contract that was signed through email correspondence is valid. In essence, the reasoning of the decision was as follows: negotiations are carried out today through electronic communications; an offer, a request for an offer and the reception of an offer can all be performed via email correspondence; the correspondence as a whole is what creates the actual agreement; unlike a printed contract that incorporates the parties' will into one document, a contract reached by way of reciprocating electronic communications is a mosaic of all the parties' communications.

1 Tel Aviv Peace Court Civil Case 29488/04 (4 August 2005, unpublished decision).

7.127 Two rulings of the Lithuanian courts, in the Court of Appeal[1] and in the Supreme Court of Lithuania,[2] accepted email communications (typed by the person who appends their name at the end) as evidence in civil proceedings, although it is not certain whether names written in the emails will be accepted as a form of electronic signature.

1 10 April 2006, case no. 2A- 95/2006.

2 6 March 2006, case no. 3K-3-169/2006.

7.128 In Scotland, the nature of the electronic signature was not specifically at issue in *Baillie Estates Ltd v Du Pont (UK) Ltd*,[1] where Hodge L concluded that an exchange of emails constituted a valid contract, notwithstanding the apparent informality of the content of the emails exchanged, because the exchange demonstrated an agreement to enter into a contract. By inference, it is possible to observe that the name typed at the bottom of each email constituted an electronic signature.

1 2009 GWD 25–399, [2009] ScotCS CSOH_95, [2009] CSOH 95.

7.129 A contract in South Africa can be varied by an exchange of emails that includes the name of the person sending the email where their name appears in the email, as in the case of *Spring Forest Trading v Wilberry*,[1] where the parties agreed to cancel a contract by exchange of emails. Cachalia JA said, at [28]:

> The typewritten names of the parties at the foot of the emails, which were used to identify the users, constitute 'data' that is logically associated with the data in the body of the emails, as envisaged in the definition of an 'electronic signature'. They therefore satisfy the requirement of a signature and had the effect of authenticating the information contained in the emails.

1 (725/13) [2014] ZASCA 178, 2015 (2) SA 118 (SCA) (21 November 2014).

7.130 This finding is also consistent with the approach taken by the courts in South Africa, as noted by the judge at [26]:

> The approach of the courts to signatures has therefore been pragmatic, not formalistic. They look to whether the method of the signature used fulfils the function of a signature – to authenticate the identity of the signatory – rather than insist on the form of the signature used.

Guarantees and debt

7.131 That email correspondence is used extensively for business has become a fact that judges now take for granted. An exchange of emails occurred in respect of a debt claimed in two amounts, one of A$33,884.02 and the other of A$2,859.14, in respect of two different companies in a case before the Federal Circuit Court of Australia in *Austral-Asia Freight Pty Ltd v Turner*.[1] Hartnett J concluded, at [30], that there was an objectively manifested intention to be legally bound, that it was conveyed in sufficient writing, and that the name typed at the end of the emails constituted a signature for the purposes of s 126 of the Instruments Act 1958 (Vic). In New Zealand, in the case of *Sanson v Parval Marketing Limited*,[2] upheld on appeal under *Gachot v Sanson*,[3] it was accepted that the first name of a person typed into an email is capable of forming part of the evidence to demonstrate the assignment of a guarantee.

1 [2013] FCCA 298 (2013), 2013 WL 2253153; Dane Weber, 'Tech neutrality in Australian signature law' (2015) 24 JL Inf & Sci 101.
2 [2008] NZHC 87 (11 February 2008).
3 [2009] NZCA (CA95/2008) 86; Barry Allen, 'The validity of informal guarantees' (2013) 13 Otago L Rev 57.

Public administration, the judiciary and the police

7.132 In *Badre v Court of Florence, Italy*,[1] an extradition order was made in enforcement of a European Arrest Warrant. The electronic signature on the certificate issued by the

Serious Organised Crime Agency was challenged because, it was argued, it was not subscribed with a physical signature in ink, but with an electronic signature in the form of letters and a number: 'GW (200820)'. There was no other dispute about the content of the certificate. It was accepted that in all other respects the document produced was a proper certificate. The certificate was issued under the provisions of s 2(7) and (8) of the Extradition Act 2003. The purpose of the certificate is to assert the authority to issue an arrest warrant under the Act. Counsel for the appellant submitted that the provision of a proper certificate under s 2 of the Act is a precursor to the validity of the warrant and the subsequent jurisdiction of the court. When a certificate is issued, the requested person may be lawfully arrested. The powers of the court follow on from such an arrest. If the arrest cannot be shown to be lawful, the court has no jurisdiction. Mr Summers argued that a machine purported to issue the certificate in this case. McCombe LJ rejected this argument, indicating that it seemed clear that the designated authority provided the certificate. The official causing the certificate to be issued used their initials GW and an identifying code as a means of authentication. The electronic form of the signature on the certificate did not act to detract from the validity of it. The judge then went on to observe, at [16], that a manuscript signature would be preferable:

> It is perhaps unfortunate that the electronic age has produced more haste and less speed, because it has thrown up this technical argument where none existed before. It must surely be the easiest task in the world to produce a signature in ink, or at least the full name and designation of the individual certifying and perhaps an official stamp or rubric confirming that that individual does indeed certify the contents of the document to lend some additional force of authority to the certificate that is being produced. I would hope that SOCA would consider either reverting to the old practice of producing these certificates, properly signed by a real person, in the form that was actually used in an earlier warrant in this case (subsequently withdrawn); or at least better identifying the individual making the certification on the face of the document.

1 [2014] EWHC 614 (Admin), [2014] 3 WLUK 250, [2014] ACD 933.

7.133 An identical point was taken in *The Queen on the Application of Neculai Jugan v Deta Court of First Instance, Romania*,[1] where a certificate was issued pursuant to s 2(7) of the Extradition Act 2003. It was dated 28 May 2013, and below the date were the words 'Signed LT' in type, and underneath that '#101782'. The appellant contended that this was not a valid signature, which meant that an essential procedural requirement had not been made out. This argument was rejected on the basis that a witness gave written evidence confirming the signature and the authenticity of the certificate.

1 [2014] EWHC 460 (Admin), [2014] 2 WLUK 261.

7.134 Many police forces in the United Kingdom now use digital systems to implement and record decisions, as in the case from Scotland of *HM Advocate v Purves*,[1] as explained by Maciver S at [7]:

> I found from that evidence that the procedure within Lothian and Borders Police is that the applications from various officers for directed surveillance are dealt with by a secure online system which meets that Force's requirements in respect of security and accessibility. A password system is used which means that only selected and appropriate individuals can access the system and once authorization has been given by a detective superintendent the authorization cannot be altered. The applying officer makes his application by typing the grounds for his request in his online

> application and that is read on screen by a detective superintendent or superior rank who, having considered the application, either grants or refuses authorization. If authorization is granted as in this case, the reasons for authorization are typed personally by the superintendent and thus entered into the secure system.

1 2009 GWD 30-479, [2009] HCJ 2, 2009 SLT 969, [2009] ScotHC HCJ_2, 2010 SCL 88.

7.135 In this instance, the solicitor advocate for the first accused argued that the authorization for directed surveillance granted by the police superintendent in terms of the Regulation of Investigatory Powers (Scotland) Act 2000 was not in writing until it was printed off, and it could not therefore be a valid authorization until that time, and that when it was printed off, it did not have the signature of the authorizing superintendent and was also defective on that account. The Sheriff rejected both arguments. As a matter of general principle, he dismissed the first argument at [11]:

> I found on a simple basis of commonsense and reality, that it must be accepted and understood that in every phase of life, society has moved forward, and specifically in this connection has moved on from only producing documents in pen and ink, and that the development is normal and acceptable. I did not find it an acceptable or reasonable argument that an online document which had not yet been printed off but which had been typed and was viewable on a screen was not to be regarded as being 'in writing'. I came to the view that such a document, having been prepared in this case by Detective Superintendent Doneghan personally by depressing the keys on his personal computer and by the use of a secure system, was in fact a written document and was preserved for future use within Lothian and Borders Police online system. I consider it to be a flawed argument to suggest that that document could not be regarded as a written document until it was actually printed off and could be held in the hand for reading purposes.

7.136 Regarding the issue of whether the authorization was signed, there is no requirement for the document to be signed under the provisions of the statute, so it follows that the authorization was valid.[1]

1 For an electronic facsimile in Scotland, see *Scrimgeour-Wedderburn v Procurator Fiscal, Kirkcaldy* [2019] HCJAC 57.

Statute of Frauds

7.137 Email is a particularly useful means of communicating and negotiating the terms of contracts. Aside from the question as to whether the content of an exchange of emails is sufficient to demonstrate the formation of a contract, one of the issues is whether the exchange of electronic communications was signed, and if so, whether the emails were sufficiently signed under the relevant Statute of Frauds, or whether the signatures in an exchange of emails between the parties clearly identified the parties. In Canada, an electronic signature in an email was held to constitute a signature under the Statute of Frauds 1677.[1] In England and Wales, Clarke J considered that a series of emails was capable of constituting writing under the Statute of Frauds in *Golden Ocean Group Limited v Salgaocar Mining Industries PVT Ltd*,[2] and said, at [103], that 'an email, the text of which begins "Paul/Peter", may be regarded as signed by Peter because by that form of wording Peter signifies that he is addressing Paul and authenticates the content of the whole of what follows'. On appeal before the Civil Division of the Court of Appeal,[3] Tomlinson LJ saw no reason why a series of emails ought to be excluded from the Statute of Frauds. He said, at [22]:

> I can see no reason why the contract of guarantee so identified should not be regarded as an agreement in writing for the purposes of the Statute ... I can see no objection in principle to reference to a sequence of negotiating emails or other documents of the sort which is commonplace in ship chartering and ship sale and purchase. Whether the pattern of contract negotiation and formation habitually adopted in other areas of commercial life presents difficulty in adoption of the same approach must await examination when the problem arises. Nothing I have said is intended to discourage the obviously sensible practice of incorporating a guarantee either in a readily identifiable self-standing document or otherwise providing for it as part of the terms of a formally executed document. The Statute must however, if possible, be construed in a manner which accommodates accepted contemporary business practice. The present case is not concerned with prescribing best or prudent practice. It is concerned with ensuring, so far as is possible, that the adoption of usual and accepted practice cannot be used as a vehicle for injustice by permitting parties to break promises which are supported by consideration and upon which reliance has been placed.

1 *Leoppky v Meston* 2008 ABQB 45 (CanLII).
2 [2011] EWHC 56 (Comm), [2011] 1 WLR 2575, [2011] 2 All ER (Comm) 95, [2011] 1 WLUK 356, [2011] 1 CLC 125, [2011] CILL 3022, [2011] CLY 3112.
3 *Golden Ocean Group Ltd v Salgaocar Mining Industries PVT Ltd* [2012] EWCA Civ 265, [2012] 1 WLR 3674, [2012] 3 All ER 842, [2012] 2 All ER (Comm) 978, [2012] 1 Lloyd's Rep 542, [2012] 3 WLUK 313, [2012] 1 CLC 479, [2012] CILL 3161, (2012) 162 NLJ 425, [2012] CLY 3047.

7.138 The court dismissed the arguments that the name 'Guy' at the end of the email was not a signature, and no more than a salutation, and one typed in a 'matey' or familiar fashion, or in the alternative, if it was a signature, it was only the signature of a communication and not appropriate or effective to authenticate a contract of guarantee. The court considered that the name was typed in a manner that indicated that it was intended to authenticate the document, and agreed that an electronic signature is sufficient and that a first name, initials or a nickname will suffice.

Wills

7.139 There are circumstances when a will has been considered for probate as a result of being written on a computer, and it is conceivable that a court may be required to consider the content of an email that is clearly testamentary in character – perhaps an email sent by a serviceman or woman while on active duty.[1]

1 Jeremy Malcolm, a lawyer in Australia, signed his will using digital signatures; see Angus Kidman, 'Australian makes digital will', ZDNet Australia, 20 January 2004, http://www.zdnet.com/article/australian-makes-digital-will/, (2004) 1 Digital Evidence and Electronic Signature Law Review 90; Michael Cameron Wood-Bodley, 'Wills, data messages, and the Electronic Communications and Transactions Act' (2004) 21 The South African Law Journal 526; Law Commission, *Making a Will* (Consultation Paper 231, 2017), ch 6 on electronic wills – the Law Commission has yet to finalize its recommendations at the time of writing.

7.140 An early example of a will prepared in digital form is the Quebec case of *Rioux v Coulombe*,[1] where the police found a note after the testator committed suicide on 4 May 1996 that led to the discovery of a diskette, with the following text written by hand on the label: 'Ceci est mon testament/Jacqueline Rioux/1er février 1996' ('This is my will/Jacqueline Rioux/1 February 1996'). A single electronic file was stored on the disk, comprising directions of a testamentary nature. There was no signature in the document. The file had been last saved on 16 April 1996 at 10:25 am. On the same day, the testator wrote in her diary that she had made a will on her computer, bearing the date 1 February 1996. Michaud, greffier (master) of the Quebec Superior Court, decided that the text did not meet the requirements of article 726 of the Code civil du Québec requiring a holograph testament.[2] However, he found the electronic will to be valid under the dispensing power of Quebec. In so doing, he failed to address any of the evidential issues that arose out of the circumstances.[3] Such matters were covered in the South African case of *Macdonald v The Master*,[4] where the deceased committed suicide on or about 14 December 2000 and left in his own handwriting four notes dated 13 December 2000 on a bedside table next to the bed on which he was lying. One of the notes read as follows:

> I, Malcom Scott MacDonald, ID 5609065240106, do hereby declare that my last will and testament can be found on my PC at IBM under directory C:/WINDOWS/ MYSTUFF/MYWILL/PERSONAL.

1 1996 CarswellQue 1226, 19 ETR (2d) 201, JE 97-263, EYB 1996–87749.

2 Brown J considered the meaning of the word 'holograph' in detail in the case of *In the Matter of the Estate of Reed v Buckley*, 672 P.2d 829 (Wyo. 1983) at 831–832, and reached the logical conclusion that a tape recording could not be considered to be a piece of writing. It follows that a will drafted using digital data cannot be a holographic will.

3 Nicholas Kasirer, 'From written record to memory in the law of wills' (1997–8) 29 Ottawa Law Review 39, suggested, at 44, that the Master was somewhat perfunctory in deciding that the diskette and the text recorded on it did not constitute a holographic will, missing the opportunity of testing the elasticity of the ordinary rules of form, and he went on to discuss the evidential problems that were not addressed (44–48).

4 2002 (5) SA 64; Michael Cameron Wood-Bodley, '*Macdonald v The Master*: computer files and the "rescue provision" of the Wills Act: notes' (2004 January) 21(1) South African Law Journal34; Sizwe Snail and Nicholas Hall, 'Electronic wills in South Africa' (2010) 7 Digital Evidence and Electronic Signature Law Review 67; see also Juliet Brook, 'Succession: to dispense or not to dispense? A comparison of dispensing powers and their judicial application' (2019) 1 PCB 9.

7.141 The deceased was employed as a senior IT specialist with IBM Global Services. The evidence before the court was that the personal computer allocated to the deceased was controlled by a password that only the deceased knew. Each employee with a personal computer at IBM was required to change their password every month, to record the password on a piece of paper, seal it in an envelope and hand it over to an employee whose job was to safeguard the passwords by keeping them in a locked facility. Only three senior members of staff had the right to request the password. Mr Dimmick, the Professional Development Manager, had a right to obtain the password. On 14 December 2000 he obtained access to the computer and printed the contents on to paper. The document purported to be the deceased's last will and testament. It was handed to his widow and the file was then deleted. The document had the following heading: LAST WILL AND TESTAMENT FROM MALCOLM SCOTT MACDONALD. The first paragraph read:

> I, the undersigned, Malcolm Scott Macdonald (ID 5609065240106), divorced, do hereby revoke all wills, codicils and other testamentary acts heretofore made by me and declare the following to be my last will and testament.

7.142 The document then appointed an executor and set out the disposition of the deceased's property, but it was neither dated nor signed by any witnesses or the deceased. The Master refused to accept the will, because it failed to comply with the provisions of the Wills Act 34 of 1964, s 2(1)(a), in that it is necessary for a will to be in writing, signed and attested by two competent witnesses, and the testator must initial every page. Hattingh J set out the requirements necessary for the will to be accepted at 70 F–G:

> In order to be successful with their application under this section, the applicants must, on a balance of probabilities, establish:
>
> (a) the documents, annexures A and F were drafted by the deceased;
>
> (b) that the deceased had died since the drafting of the documents; and
>
> (c) the documents were intended by the deceased to be his will.

7.143 It was necessary to decide whether the requirements of s 2(3) had been satisfied. It reads:

> If a court is satisfied that a document or the amendment of a document drafted or executed by a person who has died since the drafting or execution thereof, was intended to be his will or an amendment of his will, the court shall order the Master to accept that document, or that document as amended, for the purpose of the Administration of Estates Act, 1965 (Act No. 66 of 1965), as a will, although it does not comply with all the formalities for the execution or amendment of wills referred to in subsection (1).

7.144 Hattingh J commented that the legislature introduced s 2(3) with the intention of eliminating injustice and inequity where a person failed to comply with the formalities set out in s 2(1). It was necessary to determine whether the deceased drafted the documents. Of the two approaches that could be adopted (the document must be drafted in the deceased's handwriting, or the document may be typed by the deceased or even dictated by the deceased), the judge adopted the liberal approach, commenting at 71A–B that:

> The retention of the formal requirements of s2(1) and the peremptory nature of s2(3) do not justify a strict interpretation of s2(3). Not only is this inconsistent with the very purpose of s2(3), namely to prevent the last wishes of a testator from being nullified by a non-compliance with technical formalities, but it also does not take cognizance of the realities of the technological world we live in.[1]

1 Hattingh J gave detailed reasons for trusting the digital data and the surrounding circumstances at 71G–J.

7.145 The second point, that the deceased had died since the drafting of the documents, was accepted, as was the third point, that the testator intended the draft will to be his last will and testament. Hattingh J usefully set out the factors at 72C–G that were of importance in reaching his decision:

> (a) the documents are a clear indication of the deceased's intention that they should be regarded as his will and testament;
>
> (b) the documents are not preliminary sketches or notes for discussion with an attorney or anybody else to draft a will, but his final wishes;
>
> (c) there is no element of suspicion of fraud attached to the documents and their reproduction;
>
> (d) there is no suspicion that there could have been any tampering with the computer or the documents;

(e) not only did the documents exist on the computer, but there was indeed clear reference by the testator to these specific documents in his notes;

(f) there was a clear indication by the deceased where this document could be found on his computer;

(g) only the deceased had access, by way of secret password, to put the documents on the computer;

(h) only the deceased could have typed the said documents;

(i) they could only be extracted upon the instructions of the deceased in his own handwriting and only with the deceased's own secret code.

7.146 In this case, Hattingh J concluded, at 721–J, that s 2(3) called 'for an approach which promotes an extensive or flexible interpretation. This is also in accordance with the spirit of the technological age. ' Although the testator did not sign his name in the document, it could be argued that the password served a similar function.

7.147 In the Saskatchewan case of *Buckmeyer Estate (Re)*,[1] the executor proffered three documents for admission to probate: a will dated 5 May 2007, an email dated 23 August 2007 and an amendment to the will dated 27 August 2007. The will was properly proven. The issue to be determined was whether the email and the amendment were testamentary documents and whether s 37 of The Wills Act, 1996, S.S. 1996 c. W-14.1 applied. The email was from the deceased, John Buckmeyer, to the executor (johnbuckmeyer@hotmail.com to dave.gibson@sasktel.net). The subject was 'John's arrangements'. The email consisted of two pages. It was accepted that he wrote the email and that it contained his electronic signature. The content indicated that he was very sick and in his last days, and stated that he wanted to give the executor more information and express his wishes clearly before he died. The deceased listed his credit accounts, gave a direction with respect to his cremation, where his ashes were to be sent and directions with respect to funeral services. Ottenbreit J considered the provisions of the Electronic Information and Documents Act 2000, S.S. 2000 c. E-7.22 in respect of the electronic signature in the email. The judge, it is respectfully suggested, correctly indicated that the issue was whether the content of the email complied with the provisions of the Wills Act. The issue was whether the content of the email constituted a disposition intended to take effect on death, reflecting testamentary intention, as an essential element for a clause to be considered testamentary is the disposal of property. In this instance, Ottenbreit J decided that the purpose of the email was to provide additional information to the executor in carrying out his duties. It was not a testamentary document and therefore not admitted to probate.

1 2008 SKQB 260 (CanLII).

7.148 There have been a number of cases in Australia where wills have been made only in electronic form. Aside from deciding whether the electronic will is valid, the judges have also had to decide whether a will is signed where the deceased typed their name into the document. In the case of *In the will of Mark Edwin Trethewey*,[1] Beach J concluded that typing the name at the foot of the document was the equivalent of a signature in the circumstances of the case.[2]

1 [2002] VSC 83 (14 March 2002).

2 Other cases from Australia include: Queensland: *Mellino v Wnuk* [2013] QSC 336, where the deceased recorded his testament on to a DVD before taking his own life; *Re Yu* [2013] QSC 322, where

shortly before the deceased took his own life he created a series of documents on his iPhone, typing his name at the end of the document in a place where on a paper document a signature would appear, followed by the date, and a repetition of his address; *Re Nichol; Nichol v Nichol* [2017] QSC 220, where the deceased created a text message stating a testamentary intention on his mobile telephone without sending it shortly before he took his own life, signing it 'MRN190162Q', which matched the deceased's initials and date of birth, 19 January 1962; but see *Mahlo v Hehir* [2011] QSC 243, where McMurdo J concluded that he was not satisfied that Dr Mahlo intended that an electronic document should form her will, because she knew that in writing a new will, she had to do more than type or modify a document upon her computer. She understood that she also had to sign it; New South Wales: *Alan Yazbek v Ghosn Yazbek* [2012] NSWSC 594, where a Microsoft Word document, Will.doc, was completed by the deceased on 14 July 2009 and was found in his laptop computer after his death; *Re Estate of Wai Fun Chan, Deceased* [2015] NSWSC 1107, where the deceased made a will by video; *The Estate of Roger Christopher Currie, late of Balmain* [2015] NSWSC 1098, where a will written by the deceased in a computer file, ending 'Signed by the writer Roger Christopher Currie on this day Wednesday, 1 April 2009', was granted probate; South Australia, In the *Estate of Wilden (Deceased)* [2015] SASC 9, where the deceased left two items of a testamentary nature, a DVD containing a video recording of the deceased and a typed document signed by the deceased but not witnessed. For a useful discussion of the case law in the USA, see David Horton, 'Tomorrow's inheritance: the frontiers of estate planning formalism' (2017) 58 BC. Rev 539 and David Horton, 'Wills without signatures' (2019) 99 BUL Rev 1623. In 2007, the Borgarting lagmannsrett (Court of Appeal for the region near Oslo) in Norway was required to determine whether an electronic copy of a testament that was lost could be admitted into probate in the case of LB-2006-27667, for which see Jon Bing, translation and commentary (2008) 5 Digital Evidence and Electronic Signature Law Review 134.

Constitution of a legal entity

7.149 In *Islamic Council of South Australia Inc v Australian Federation of Islamic Councils Inc*,[1] Brereton J observed at [22] that the constitution of the organization did not explicitly require that a request be signed, but went on to observe that 'if it were necessary that it be formally signed, the word "Ramzi" was subscribed to the email with the intent of authenticating the communications, and constitutes a signature notwithstanding that it appears in typewritten and not handwritten form'.

1 [2009] NSWSC 211.

Amending boilerplate contractual terms

7.150 The findings in the above cases, especially those cases that revolve around the exchange of emails, are significant. Even if the Industrial Tribunal decision of *Hall v Cognos Limited* from England and Wales is not binding on any court, it remains a good decision. This is partly because the form of the document is irrelevant. First, the effect the case law should have on the advice that a lawyer gives their clients is highly pertinent, whether dealing with commercial contracts, employment contracts or any other form of relationship that it is possible to create or vary in writing. Consider, by way of example, a standard clause added to most contracts in the following terms:

> The contract shall not be altered unless done so in writing and signed by both parties.

7.151 If the words 'in writing and signed' remain as a standard element in such a clause, it will leave open the probability that contracts, no matter how long they have taken to negotiate, or their apparent length, are susceptible to being varied by an exchange of emails, perhaps between two fairly junior employees, or a person posing as an employee using the company email address.[1] This may well occur because most organizations have now lost control of their means of communication, because all, or virtually all, employees in some sectors have the ability to communicate with the outside world by means of email and other forms of technology, contrary to the position before the introduction of such facilities. This problem will be mitigated to a certain extent in contracts that provide a list of nominated personnel within each organization who have the authority to agree alterations and variations. In such circumstances, if a junior employee agrees an alteration without reference to those who are authorized to agree such changes, any dispute will centre on what, if any, authority was vested in the junior employee, and whether their actions acted to bind the organization. From the point of view of the organization, it is imperative to ensure that its employees are made aware of the effect that a promise can have if made by exchange of email. To mitigate this problem, it may be wise to establish whether the parties are content for a contract to be altered by exchange of emails, and if not, to include an amended version of the standard clause, such as:

> The contract shall not be altered unless done so in writing on paper and signed with the manuscript signature of both parties.

1 As occurred in *CSX Transportation, Inc. v Recovery Express, Inc.*, 415 F.Supp.2d 6 (D.Mass. 2006).

7.152 The *Hall v Cognos Limited* case illustrates the ease by which a contract can be varied, as does *C&S Associates UK Ltd v Enterprise Insurance Company Plc*,[1] the Ohio case of *In re National Century Financial Enterprises, Inc., Amedisys, Inc., v JP Morgan Chase Manhattan Bank, as Trustees*[2] and the New York case of *Stevens v Publicis, S.A.*[3] A further point centres on whether the use of email is appropriate and reasonable in the circumstances. Whether the use of email is a reasonable means of communication between two parties, or any number of parties, will depend on a range of factors, as indicated by Marrero DJ in *Bazak International Corp. v Tarrant Apparel Group*,[4] where he commented, at 387–388:

> Nonetheless, whether email is an appropriate and reasonably expected form of communication between the two particular parties before the court is a question of fact. Here, the issue's resolution requires a factual inquiry into trade usage and course of dealing ... Neither party directly addresses whether email is an appropriate method of communication in the re-sale trade generally or in Tarrant and Bazak's particular relationship. Yet later email correspondence from Tarrant to Bazak (the 'GMAC email') provides evidence in light of which a reasonable jury could find that the parties did accept email as an appropriate form of communication.

1 [2015] EWHC 3757 (Comm), [2015] 12 WLUK 703.
2 310 B.R. 580 (Bkrtcy.S.D.Ohio 2004).
3 50 A.D.3d 253, 854 N.T.S.2d 690, 2008 N.Y. Slip Op. 02880.
4 378 F.Supp.2d 37758 (S.D.N.Y. 2015).

7.153 This view corresponds with that expounded in *Campbell v General Dynamics Government Systems Corporation*,[1] although this issue was never debated with other forms of communication, such as the use of telegrams or telex.[2]

1 321 F.Supp.2d 142 (D.Mass. 2004), affirmed 407 F.3d 546 (1st Cir. 2005).
2 The position is reinforced in the case of *Basis Technology Corporation v Amazon.com, Inc.*, 71 Mass. App.Ct. 29, 878 N.E.2d 952 (Mass.App.Ct. 2008).

The name in an email address

7.154 The name in an email address is capable of identifying a person. This is particularly so where an email address in an organization, whether public or private, is allocated by setting out the name of the person followed by the domain name of the organization. There are other variations that can be used, such as when an email address describes the office or function of the person, rather than their name. However, even this, if allocated to a single person, can also function to identify an individual. The link between the prefix of the email address and the person responsible for sending the email can be problematic: for instance, the sender may be able to choose the first part, and may decide to adopt letters or numbers or a combination of letters and numbers with a view to obfuscating their identity. Further, the sender might hide the true email address. If it was not obvious who the sender was, and if correspondence ensues and a dispute occurs, it will be a matter of establishing what, if any, evidence there is pertaining to the source of the relevant emails as a preliminary point. It has been held in a number of jurisdictions that the name in an email address, or the combination of the name and the domain name in an email address can be a form of electronic signature.

Limitation Act 1969 (NSW)

7.155 The case of *McGuren v Simpson*[1] raised the issue as to whether correspondence by email was capable of constituting an acknowledgement that was in writing and signed for the purposes of the Limitation Act 1969 (NSW). Mr Simpson and Ms McGuren were in a relationship between 1992 and 2000. Mr Simpson received a cheque for A$23,000 when he was in prison in November 1993 in respect of a claim for damages for personal injuries he suffered in a motor vehicle accident. He endorsed the cheque in favour of Ms McGuren's sister to enable her to bank the cheque in her account on behalf of Ms McGuren (Ms McGuren did not want to pay the cheque into her own account as it would have affected the state benefits she was receiving at the time). Mr Simpson claimed that the defendant used the money almost entirely for her own purposes and he sought recovery of the money from Ms McGuren. Ms McGuren asserted that she used the money in accordance with his instructions and with his approval. Mr Simpson's main item of evidence was in the form of an email sent to him by Ms McGuren. It read in part:

> Date: Wed, 29 Sep 1999 14 16.20+1000
>
> To: "Rob – yahoo"<Robert-john-simpson@yahoo.com.au>
>
> From: "McGuren, Kim" Kim.Mcguran@air.gov.au
>
> I am going to try and book a cab for 6pm at childcare does that suit you?
>
> It probably won't turn up but I may as well book it. So, what do you want to do: split up, – go to counselling or – just blame each other for every thing since everything is obviously the other persons fault, for the rest of our lives? Yes, I spent the money and I shouldn't have and yes, you have been violent and you shouldn't have so what now??

1 [2004] NSWSC 35.

7.156 Master Harrison dealt with an appeal from a Local Court Magistrate, and the main issue to determine was whether Mr Simpson's cause of action was statute barred under s 14 of the Limitation Act 1969 (NSW). The time limit is extended under the provisions of s 54 where the person against whom the cause of action lies confirms the cause of action by acknowledging it to the person who holds the action, providing the acknowledgment is in writing and signed by the maker. Mr Simpson's case was that Ms McGuren acknowledged the cause of action in the email she sent when she wrote the words 'Yes, I spent the money and I shouldn't have'. The Magistrate had previously determined that the email was an electronic communication within the meaning of s 9(1) of the Electronic Transaction Act 2000 (NSW). However, the Act was not in force at the time the email was sent, which meant the provisions of the Act did not apply to the email, hence the Magistrate's decision was incorrect. Master Harrison dealt with the problem in the context of the common law. First, he concluded that the email constituted a written document. In so doing, he noted the expansive approach taken in other jurisdictions [at 20], and decided to construe the Act to take into account the changes in technology [at 21], a view taken by judges in England and Wales and the USA in the nineteenth century: 'It is my view that ... section 54 of the Act ought to be read to accommodate technological change and that, accordingly, the email sent by the plaintiff constitutes a written document'. Second, he agreed with the decision of the Magistrate, that the email address was a signature for the purpose of s 54(4) of the Limitation Act 1969 (NSW), at [22]:

> As Ms McGuren's name appears in the email and she expressly acknowledges in the email as an authenticated expression of a prior agreement, the email is recognisable as a note of a concluded agreement. Accordingly, the Magistrate was correct at law to conclude that Ms McGuren signed the email and that the requirements of s 54(4) of the Act were met. It was open to the Magistrate to find that Ms McGuren acknowledged the claim and she has admitted her legal liability to pay Mr Simpson that which he seeks to recover.

Statute of Frauds

7.157 The question arose in the English case of *J Pereira Fernandes SA v Mehta*[1] whether the name forming part of an email address could be construed as a signature. J Pereira Fernandes SA is a Portuguese company that supplied bedding products in July 2002 to Bedcare (UK) Limited,[2] a company of which Mr Mehta was a director. Bedcare failed to pay for the products it had received, and was wound up on a Petition by J Pereira Fernandes SA by an Order made on 7 March 2005. The cause of the appeal before His Honour Judge Pelling QC, sitting as a judge of the Chancery Division, related to the presentation of a winding up petition by J Pereira Fernandes SA on 12 January 2005. On 20 February 2005 an email was sent from the email address 'Nelmehta@aol.com' to Ian Simpson & Co, solicitors acting for J Pereira Fernandes SA.[3] Mr Mehta's name was not typed at the end of the email. On 9 November 2005, District Judge Harrison gave summary judgment to J Pereira Fernandes SA in the sum of £24,985.53 and ordered Mr Mehta to pay the costs of the claim, which were summarily assessed in the sum of £1,080.00. Mr Mehta was subsequently given permission to appeal by Holman J on 20 February 2006. The email contained the following text:

> I would be grateful if you could kindly consider the following.
>
> If the hearing of the Petition can be adjourned for a period of 7 days subject to the following:

a. A Personal Guarantee to be given in the amount of £25,000 in favour of your client – together with a list of my personal assets provided to you by my solicitor

b. A repayment schedule to be redrawn over a period of six months with a payment of £5,000.00 drawn from my personal funds to be made before the adjourned hearing

I am also prepared to give a company undertaking not to sell market or dispose of any company assets without prior consent from your client pending the signing of the Personal Guarantee.

1 [2006] EWHC 813 (Ch), [2006] 1 WLR 1543, [2006] 2 All ER 891, [2006] 1 All ER (Comm) 885, [2006] 2 Lloyd's Rep 244, [2006] 4 WLUK 182, [2006] Info. TLR 203, Times, 16 May 2006, [2006] CLY 774, also known as *Metha v J Pereira Fernandes SA*.

2 A search on the website of Companies House for Bedcare (UK) Limited does not reveal any results, and there are no results for a person by the name of Nilesh Mehta associated with a legal entity known as Bedcare (UK) Limited.

3 In the reports, it is said that Mr Mehta caused one of his members of staff to send the email. The email was sent on Tuesday 20 February 2005 at 20:30. It was subsequently confirmed in May 2006 to Ian Simpson & Co by the Insolvency Service in Manchester that no employee or salary records were recorded as being delivered up for Bedcare (UK) Limited (information provided by Ian Simpson & Co to the author).

7.158 The email address that appeared on this particular email also appeared on other emails sent to Ian Simpson & Co by Mr Mehta, which included his name typed at the end of the email. There were two matters of relevance to consider: whether the email could be considered a sufficient note or memorandum, and if so, whether it was signed by the party charged, that is, or on behalf of Mr Mehta. The email was a rare example of a document that is brought into the purview of s 4 of the Statute of Frauds 1677.[1] This is because s 4 now only applies to contracts of guarantee, and the content of this email provided a guarantee, in that Mr Mehta offered to personally cover debts owed by the company. Section 4 reads:

> Noe action shall be brought ... whereby to charge the defendant upon any speciall promise to answere for the debt default or miscarriages of another person ... unlesse the agreement upon which such action shall be brought or some memorandum or note thereof shall be in writeing and signed by the partie to be charged therewith or some other person thereunto by him lawfully authorised.[2]

1 For a history of the Statute, see W. S. Holdsworth, *A History of English Law Volume VI* (Methuen & Co 1924), 379–97, who considered that the Statute was out of date when he wrote this text, at 396: 'the prevailing feeling both in the legal and the commercial world is, and has for a long time been, that these clauses have outlived their usefulness, and are quite out of place amid the changed legal and commercial conditions of to-day.'; E. Rabel, 'The Statute of Frauds and comparative legal history' (1947) 63 Law Quarterly Review 174, in which he concluded, at 187, 'The case against the Statute of Frauds has been proved time and again by outstanding authorities, even before the Sixth Interim Report of the English Law Revision Committee of 1937 solemnly pronounced sentence for repeal. An examination of the historical background on which the Statute arose can but support the views expressed by the Revision Committee and the conclusion that the Statute essentially belongs to distant times, far removed from the conditions of modern life'; Lord Wright, *Legal Essays and Addresses* (Cambridge University Press 1939), 226; for a discussion of the purpose and additional sources of criticism, see Graham S. McBain, 'Legislative comment abolishing the Statute of Frauds 1677 section 4' (2010) 5 Journal of Business Law 420, who concluded, at 433: 'When dealing with ancient legislation it is easy to develop a visceral fear akin to that of Vitalstatistix in the Asterix cartoons. He has only one fear: he is afraid that the sky may fall on his head tomorrow. However, as he always says, tomorrow never comes. If s.4 is repealed, one would assert that the legal sky will not fall: the number of oral guarantees given will not increase,

nor the amount of litigation concerning them. And there is no reason to believe that, in the case of oral guarantees giving rise to litigation, the English judiciary will fail to be vigilant in detecting perjury.'

2 *Halsbury's Statutes of England and Wales Volume 11(1)* (4th edn, 2010 reissue), 7; Chronological Table of the Statutes Part 1 (HMSO).

7.159 Harrison DJ, in giving summary judgment, considered that the email did amount to a note or memorandum of guarantee, although he did not explicitly comment on whether the names in the email address could amount to a signature. Judge Pelling QC agreed with Harrison DJ on this point, and also held the email to be a note or memorandum that brought it within s 4 of the statute. He commented on the purpose of the statute as follows at [16]:

> The purpose of the statute of frauds is to protect people from being held liable on informal communications because they may be made without sufficient consideration or expressed ambiguously or because such a communication might be fraudulently alleged against the party to be charged. That being so, the logic underlying the authorities I have referred to would appear to be that where (as in this case) there is an offer in writing made by the party to be bound which contains the essential terms of what is offered *and* the party to be bound accepts that his offer has been accepted unconditionally, albeit orally, there is a sufficient note or memorandum to satisfy s 4.

7.160 The second question to consider was whether the email had been signed. Solicitors for J Pereira Fernandes SA already had a number of emails from Mr Mehta in which he included his name typed at the bottom of the text. In this respect, the evidence of a number of communications from the same address demonstrated that they were authentic. Mr Mehta did not dispute that the email was sent.

7.161 The evidence upon which a decision could be made in *Fernandes* was more substantial than the evidence that Prakash J (as she then was) dealt with in *SM Integrated Transware Ltd v Schenker Singapore (Pte) Ltd*.[1] In this instance, Judge Pelling QC took the view that the email address was similar to an automatically generated name and facsimile number of the sender of a facsimile transmission, although his comments, at [19], noted that a human being had to type the data into the software:

> As is well known to anyone who uses email on a regular basis, what is relied upon is not inserted by the sender of the email in any active sense. It is inserted automatically. My knowledge of the technicalities of email is not sufficiently detailed to enable me to know whether it is inserted by the ISP with whom the sender or the recipient has his email account. However, I accept Mr Aslett's submission that as a matter of obvious inference, if it is inserted by the latter it can only be from information supplied by the former. Mr Mehta suggested that the address was inserted by his employee. I do not see how this could be so and certainly Mr Mehta was not able to give me a coherent explanation of how that might be so. It is possible that Mr Mehta's employee was authorised to use Mr Mehta's e mail account remotely but, even if that is so, I do not see how that can impact on any of the issues I have to resolve since it is not in dispute that the email was sent on the instructions of Mr Mehta and the method by which the sender address came to be inserted would not be affected even if that was the position.

1 [2005] 2 SLR 651, [2005] SGHC 58.

7.162 That such information is considered in judgments to be 'automatic' illustrates a misunderstanding. A human being has to put the information into the machine. The facsimile number of the sender is put into the machine by a person, as is the name in an email address or the 'signature block' of an email.

7.163 Counsel for J Pereira Fernandes SA submitted that the intent to sign was not relevant, and mentioned *Elpis Maritime Co. Ltd. v Marti Chartering Co. Inc.*,[1] which had different facts to the case in point, and also emphasized the decision in *Evans v Hoare*,[2] where the name and address were relied upon to serve as a signature. However, the judge pointed out that in *Evans v Hoare*, Cave J considered, at 597, that the place of the signature was not relevant: 'Whether the name occurs in the body of the memorandum, or at the beginning, or at the end, if it is intended for a signature there is a memorandum of the agreement within the meaning of the statute.' Judge Pelling QC then went on to indicate that the name of the party to be bound must be intended as a signature. In reaching this conclusion, the judge did not refer to the comments made by Cave J (at 597–598, (reference omitted)) after the text he quoted, which are highly significant:

> In the present case it is true that the name of the defendants occurs in the agreement; but it is suggested on behalf of the defendants that it was only put in to shew who the persons were to whom the letter was addressed. The answer is that there is the name, and it was inserted by the defendants' agent in a contract which was undoubtedly intended by the defendants to be binding on the plaintiff; and, therefore, the fact that it is only in the form of an address is immaterial. A case was referred to in the argument, *Schneider v Norris*, in which a printed bill-head was held to amount to a signature within the meaning of the statute. That is a stronger case than the present. The printed heading there was not put into the document for the purpose of constituting a memorandum of the contract; but it was so used with the assent of the party sought to be charged, and it therefore was held to have the effect of a signature. This shews that it is unimportant how the name came to be inserted in the document.

1 [1992] 1 AC 21, [1991] 3 WLR 330, [1991] 3 All ER 758, [1991] 2 Lloyd's Rep 311, [1991] 7 WLUK 297, (1991) 141 NLJ 1109, (1991) 135 SJLB 100, [1992] CLY 3931.
2 [1892] 1 QB 593, (1892) 66 LTRep NS 345.

7.164 The judge considered that the approach he took was supported by the decision in *Caton v Caton*.[1] The facts in this case might be compared to the decision in the case decided by the Master of the Rolls, *De Biel v Thomson*,[2] and subsequently affirmed by the Lord Chancellor and reaffirmed upon further appeal, *Hammersley v De Biel, an infant, by Blake*,[3] where an extremely vague promise, the evidence of which was very tenuous, was upheld under the Statute of Frauds.

1 (1867) LR 2 HL 127.
2 3 Beav. 469.
3 [1845] 12 Clark & Finnelly 45, 8 ER 1312.

7.165 Earlier cases on the physical position of the signature also emphasizes the need to consider the intent behind the signature, as commented on by the Lord Chief Baron in *Stokes v Moore*.[1] In *Ogilvie v Foljambe*,[2] a letter written by the plaintiff relating to the sale of a lease situated in Grosvenor Place began 'Mr Ogilvie has the pleasure to acquaint Mr Foljambe ...' In this instance, Sir William Grant MR held the name governed all that followed in the letter. In *Holmes v Mackrell*,[3] a promissory note written in the hand of the defendant with his name written on top, but not signed at the end, was held to be a sufficient signature for the document. In his judgment at 796, Crowder J intimated why this issue was of some importance:

> In the case of a note written in the third person, the name at the commencement serves to authenticate the document just as well as a formal signature at the foot of it. If, then, the signature is sufficient, what does the defendant say here? In effect he says, – 'I have given two promissory notes for 510*l*., and I am now liable upon them'. That is a plain and deliberate and unconditional acknowledgment of a debt, and it is clear from the case of *Tanner v Smart*, 6 B. & C. 603, 9 D. R. 549, and the authorities which have followed it, that, where there is an absolute and unconditional acknowledgment of an existing debt, a promise to pay is to be inferred. It seems to me that the acknowledgment here is one from which a promise to pay must necessarily be inferred.

1 (1786) 1 Cox 219, 29 ER 1137.
2 (1817) 3 Mer 53, 36 ER 21.
3 (1858) 3 CB (NS) 789, 140 ER 953.

7.166 It appears that judges, when dealing with cases where a promise was made that affected an innocent party, and the person making the promise subsequently sought to avoid being held to their promise by arguing a technical point that the promise was not signed, thus making it unenforceable, were generally not willing to allow the person making the promise to succeed on such a technicality. Two of the most notable English cases, *Lobb and Knight v Stanley*[1] and *Tourret v Cripps*,[2] neither of which was cited or discussed in *Fernandes*, illustrates that similar situations had arisen in the past, and lawyers and judges have previously been required to deal with similar factual situations as in *Fernandes*. In *Lobb*, Stanley, a certified bankrupt, gave a written promise signed by him after his bankruptcy. Three undated letters were produced, one of which read 'Mr Stanley begs to inform Mr Lobb ...' It was considered sufficient that he began the text with his name, and his name governed the promise that followed.[3] In *Tourret v Cripps*,[4] Mr R. L. Cripps wrote in his own hand on a sheet of memorandum paper an offer to lease parts of 14 and 15 Mortimer Street, Cavendish Square. The memorandum was not signed by him, but contained, at its head, the words 'From Richd. L Cripps' and his address. Tourret, who initiated an action against Cripps for specific performance, accepted the offer. His printed name served as a signature to hold him to the promise he made.

1 (1844) 5 QB 574, 114 ER 1366.
2 (1879) 48 L J Ch 567, 27 WR 706.
3 This case was specifically mentioned by Phipson, where a 'signature under the Statute of Frauds may be by surname only' (S. L. Phipson, *The Law of Evidence* (6th edn, Sweet and Maxwell 1921), 516).
4 (1879) 48 L J Ch 567, 27 WR 706. These cases were reviewed by Buckley J in *Hucklesby v Hook* 82 LT 117.

7.167 Judge Pelling QC considered the automatic insertion of an email address at [28] and [29] (original emphasis):

> However, that is not the issue in this case. Here the issue is whether the automatic insertion of a person's email address after the document has been transmitted by either the sending and/or receiving ISP constitutes a signature for the purposes of s 4.

> 29. In my judgment the inclusion of an email address in such circumstances is a clear example of the inclusion of a name which is incidental in the sense identified by Lord Westbury in the absence of evidence of a contrary intention. Its appearance divorced from the main body of the text of the message emphasizes this to be so. Absent evidence to the contrary, in my view it is not possible to hold that the automatic insertion of an e mail address is, to use Cave J's language, '*intended for a signature*'. To conclude that the automatic insertion of an email address in the circumstances I have described constituted a signature for the purposes of s 4 would I think undermine or potentially undermine what I understand to be the Act's purpose, would be contrary to the underlying principle to be derived from the cases to which I have referred and would have widespread and wholly unintended legal and commercial effects. In those circumstances, I conclude that the e mail referred to at [3] above did not bear a signature sufficient to satisfy the requirements of s 4.

7.168 In this particular instance, the judge made observations about the technicalities of email in the absence of expert evidence, as did Lyberopoulos J, the president of the court in the Greek case 1327/2001 – Payment Order.[1] It seems that the judge assumed that the ISP adds the email address to the document.[2] He then concluded, in the absence of any relevant technical evidence, that the email address could not, therefore, be intended as a signature. It is suggested that this approach is arguable. It is possible to distinguish the decision by Hall VC in *Tourret v Cripps*[3] on the basis that Cripps wrote the content by hand. That decision must be correct, taking into account the handwritten text, the printed words 'From Richd. L Cripps', and the address printed on the paper. Hall VC might have speculated as to the purpose of having stationery printed, and whether each time a letter or note is sent, the use of the information printed on the letter was sufficient evidence to demonstrate an intent to sign. In this instance, as in other cases, the judge looked to the entire document for evidence to indicate intent, and taking into account the message written on the letter, together with the name printed on the top of the stationery, Hall VC considered that this was sufficient to hold the man to his promise. However, to distinguish *Tourret* from *Fernandes* in this way is far from satisfactory. This is because the facts in *Tourret* comprised a mix of text written by hand with pre-printed text. With networked communications, such a mix is impossible. The very nature of networked communications means that content must be typed – or cut and pasted – so to argue that the decision in *Tourret* is significantly different because of the addition of text written by hand cannot be right.

1 English translation by Michael G. Rachavelias, Case Translation – Greece (2006) 3 Digital Evidence and Electronic Signature Law Review 104; Georgia Skouma, Case Note (2004) 1 Digital Evidence and Electronic Signature Law Review 83.

2 In *Golden Ocean Group Limited v Salgaocar Mining Industries PVT Ltd* [2011] EWHC 56 (Comm), Mr Justice Christopher Clarke indicated, at [103], that 'There is authority that the insertion of a person's email address by an internet service provider after the document has been transmitted is, absent evidence to the contrary, incidental'.

3 (1879) 48 L J Ch 567, 27 WR 706. These cases were reviewed by Buckley J in *Hucklesby v Hook* 82 LT 117.

7.169 Also, Judge Pelling QC did not consider the email as a complete document. The problem with his analysis is that the information contained in the 'From', 'To', 'Sent' and 'Subject' part of the email cannot be disconnected from the body. The information is neither separate when presented visually on a screen, nor when printed out on paper. In addition, the source code (usually hidden) is also an integral part of the email, and this set of metadata is of considerable evidential value, as argued by the applicant in the pleadings in the case of Tribunale Mondovì, 7 giugno 2004, n. 375 (decr.), *Giur. It. 2005, 1026.*[1] Further, should the method used to cause an email address to be attached to a particular email be of relevance, then other factors ought to be considered, including the mechanism by which the application software brings the disparate objects together to permit the user to view the email on screen, because each object will be in a different storage location on the computer.

1 For a translation of the pleadings, see Gian Paulo Coppola, Case Note (2007) 4 Digital Evidence and Electronic Signature Law Review 86.

7.170 A similar issue relating to email correspondence confronted Phelan J in the Canadian case of *Dursol-Fabrik Otto Durst GmbH & Co. c. Dursol North America Inc.*,[1] decided after the decision by Judge Pelling QC, in proceedings for contempt of court where the defendant and his company were the subject of a number of orders prohibiting the marketing and selling of goods. One of the issues to determine was whether the defendant, Robert Scott, used email correspondence to market and sell products. In his evidence, he claimed he was ignorant of two email addresses in issue and how the signature that appeared at the end of emails worked. The evidence indicated he sent out emails that identified him in his corporate capacity. In this case, the court heard appropriate technical evidence as well as the evidence from the defendant. The judge did not believe the defendant because his evidence was both contradictory and inconsistent. In reaching his decision, the judge made some interesting and highly pertinent remarks at 56 about the use of email and the practical aspects of using email that bear repeating:

> Even if one accepted Scott's explanation, which I do not, he was a business man who used computers constantly to transact business. He took no steps to deal with his address and signature. In today's world such ignorance, or, more importantly, the refusal to secure the technical assistance to deal with these types of matters, is not acceptable. Scott exhibited recklessness and a complete disregard for the obligations he had under this Court's Orders.

1 2006 FC 1115.

7.171 The technical evidence demonstrated that, contrary to the defendant's assertions, he could see the default signature he set up, thus contradicting his claim that he was not aware his signature appeared at the end of the email. Further, it was also established that the defendant had a number of different email addresses, and had the option of using whichever address he chose when sending and responding to correspondence. The judge rejected the contention that the defendant's claimed lack of knowledge of email addresses and signatures was a mitigating factor in disobeying a court order.

7.172 One further point might be usefully considered, and that is the purpose of the email address, which is of the utmost significance. The address acts to ensure the communication reaches the person it is addressed to; otherwise, an email address, even if different by one letter, number or dot, is unforgiving. It will not reach its destination, unlike a letter sent by way of post, where a human being can extract information from the envelope and use their knowledge to effect delivery of an envelope incorrectly addressed. It is also suggested that the 'From' address is also used with the intent to identify the sender (it being the function of the 'reply-to' address to indicate where, by default, a reply will be sent). If it follows that the 'From' line of an email acts to designate the sender, then the act of signature is the irrevocable dispatch of the email. Additional technical evidence may be adduced to demonstrate a connection to the person who sent, or caused to be sent, a document in electronic form, taking into account all of the data associated with the document, including the metadata, client software and any other technical information that may not be obvious on the face of the document as presented on the screen to a recipient without further exploration of the technical attributes of the software. In this respect, it is difficult to see how the email address can be considered to have merely appeared or is incidental: it is a crucial element of the document.[1]

1 On the face of it, the email address, if correct, appears to contain all the information required to deliver it to the intended recipient. However, that is not always the case, as illustrated by Tim McCormack in 'Electronic delivery' (2018) 15 Digital Evidence and Electronic Signature Law Review 70, where he considers this precise problem in *Edgbaston Golf Club Ltd v Revenue and Customs (VAT – REPAYMENTS: Vat – repayments)* [2018] UKFTT 189 (TC), [2018] 4 WLUK 30, [2018] STI 834.

7.173 It is the action of clicking the 'send' icon, or causing an agent to click the 'send' icon, that is the act of authentication. This view accords with the comments offered in the Law Commission Report,[1] where it is suggested that the clicking of an icon probably constitutes the technological equivalent of signing with mark, and is therefore a signature. Further, the action of clicking the 'send' icon tends to be the irrevocable dispatch of the communication (although if the person is quick enough, they may, depending on the software, stop the software from sending the email), and can be similar to, or the equivalent of, the act of writing a manuscript signature or affixing a stamp to a document. In this respect, the information contained in the email address serves the same function as the use of headed notepaper in *Tourret v Cripps*. Cripps took a sheet of headed notepaper and wrote a promise on the paper. In *J Pereira Fernandes SA v Mehta*, Mehta either himself or through an agent, caused an email to be written (or the contents cut and pasted) that contained a promise. Instead of taking out a physical piece of notepaper and writing on it, he or his agent used a machine, namely a computer. The information contained in the email address served the same purpose as the name and address on the notepaper used by Cripps. Conceptually, there is no difference between the two: the cases are merely separated by time and the technology – that is, Mehta did not add any content by writing by hand. Prakash J gave her reasons for accepting the name in an email address based upon the same principle in *SM Integrated Transware Ltd v Schenker Singapore (Pte) Ltd*[2] at 92:

> There is no doubt that at the time he sent them out, he intended the recipients of the various messages to know that they had come from him. Despite that, he did not find it necessary to identify himself as the sender by appending his name at the end of any of the emails whether the messages were sent to his colleagues or to third parties like Mr Heng. I can only infer that his omission to type in his name was due to his knowledge that his name appeared at the head of every message next to his email address so clearly that there could be no doubt that he was intended to be identified as the sender of such message.

1 Law Commission, *Electronic Commerce: Formal Requirements in Commercial Transactions Advice from the Law Commission* (2001), 3.37–3.38.
2 [2005] 2 SLR 651, [2005] SGHC 58.

7.174 In analysing this case, Professor Ter Kah Lang indicated that the judge only addressed the identification function of the email address, not the intent to authenticate. Had the judge considered authentication, Professor Ter Kah Lang suggests that the conclusion might have been different.[1] Simon Blount also agrees with this analysis. However, he suggests that if Tan was saying that he did not need to sign his emails because he knew his name was already part of the email address, the decision may be correct, although in such case the author then intends to be bound by every word sent in the email.[2]

1 Ter Kah Leng, 'Have you signed your electronic contract?' (2011) 27 Computer Law & Security Review 75, 77.
2 Simon Blount, *Electronic Contracts* (2nd edn, LexisNexis Butterworths 2015), 35.

7.175 In *J Pereira Fernandes SA v Mehta*, Judge Pelling QC mentioned the Electronic Communications Act 2000, but no consideration was given to the provisions of s 7,[1] or whether s 7 applied to the facts of this case. Arguably, an email address is brought within the ambit of the Act as a form of electronic signature. First, the question is whether the email address can be considered a signature for the purposes of the Act, and the provisions of s 7(2)(a) have to be considered. As discussed above, an email will not arrive at its destination without a correct address, and if a person sending an email wishes the person receiving the email to reply, they must also use an accurate 'reply-to' email address, otherwise the recipient will not be able to respond. It is suggested above that there is a purpose for including a name or other form of description (such as the use of a title in lieu of a name) in the address of an email: to identify the sender. Also, technically, an email includes the various addresses in the email. Without an address, there would be no purpose in sending or receiving email correspondence. If the email address is not logically incorporated into the body of the text to be sent, the content will not be sent or received. To relate the email address to the provisions of s 7(2), it is necessary to consider the elements of an electronic signature:

> 'So much of anything in electronic form': This is such a wide-ranging provision that the address associated with an email must come with the term, just as the hidden metadata must also come within the term. Without the email address, the email could not be sent and received.
>
> 'Incorporation or logical association for the purpose of establishing authenticity or integrity': The thing in electronic form must be incorporated or logically associated with the communication or data for the purpose of being used to establish the authenticity or the integrity of the communication or data, or both. For the thing to be an electronic signature, it must be affixed to the data for a purpose: that is, to authenticate the communication or data or provide for the identity of the communication or data.

1 The judge stated, at [30], that it was his understanding that the Electronic Communications Act 2000 was enacted to give effect to Directive 2000/31/EC on certain legal aspects of information society services, in particular electronic commerce, in the Internal Market (Directive on electronic commerce) (OJ L 187/1, 17.7.2000). The aim of the Act was to implement the provisions of the now repealed Directive 1999/93/EC of the European Parliament and of the Council of 13 December 1999 on a Community framework for electronic signatures, OJ L 13, 19.01.2000, 12, as set out in Note 19 of the Explanatory Notes to the Act.

7.176 An email address clearly comes within the requirements of this provision: it is in electronic form, and the name in the email address is included for the purpose of establishing the authenticity of the content. If the name were a nickname or pseudonym, rather than a proper name or part of a proper name, the same conclusion would apply, based on the previous decisions at common law. If it is accepted that the email address, or the name of the person in an email address, can be considered an electronic signature, it can be admitted into evidence under the provisions of s 7(1).[1]

1 Judge Pelling QC expressed the view, at [30], that typing a name into the main body of an email can constitute an electronic signature, which is correct.

7.177 Finally, the Law Commission considered the nature of the evidence required to demonstrate the intent to authenticate. An objective test was proposed:

> 3.29 Because signatures affect many areas of personal and commercial life, it is essential that the courts develop a straight-forward approach. We believe this should be by way of a purely objective test: namely, would the conduct of the signatory indicate an authenticating intention to a reasonable person? This approach is consistent with the authorities, flexible and would, over time, produce the greatest certainty.[1]

1 Law Commission, *Electronic Commerce: Formal Requirements in Commercial Transactions Advice from the Law Commission.*

7.178 It is suggested that this test cannot be right, because an objective test would need to be based on an analysis of the surrounding circumstances, including the technology, and the average person using the technology probably varies widely in terms of their technical understanding and ability, partly because the technology changes so rapidly. It was suggested that a subjective test is more appropriate.[1] This is the view taken by Flemming DJP in the South African case of *Chisnall and Chisnall v Sturgeon and Sturgeon*,[2] where he held that the signing of a contract for the sale of an erf (a legal term for a plot of land in Namibia, South Africa) was achieved by a mark or marks with the function of making the document an act of the signer, and of signifying assent to the content of the document. He indicated, at 645F, that 'An enquiry concerning assent must, of course, not be into what the signatory subjectively planned but what his acts signify to the other party'. This is what the English authorities have also held up to this point. A subjective test will allow a judge to consider both the surrounding circumstances and what was in the mind of the sender at the moment they are deemed to sign. If the facts of *J Pereira Fernandes SA v Mehta* are considered in this light, the conclusion must be that the email in question was signed. The surrounding circumstances in this case, as in *SM Integrated Transware Ltd v Schenker Singapore (Pte) Ltd*, were as follows:

> (1) The email was from Mr Mehta.
>
> (2) Mr Mehta knew that his email address would appear in the email, which went to show that it came from him; it also enabled the recipient to respond; as a result, the email address was his unique mark.
>
> (3) There was a course of correspondence between the parties by email.
>
> (4) The email contained a promise made by Mr Mehta or under his authority.
>
> (5) Mr Mehta admitted the email was sent, which indicated that he adopted the content of the email.

1 The subjective test is proposed by Mr Pépin Aslett, counsel for J Pereira Fernandes SA, Nicholas Bohm and the author.
2 1993 (2) SA 642 (W).

7.179 In this case, Prakash J had a great deal of evidence to demonstrate that the name in the email address could be construed as an electronic signature.

7.180 In summary, it is suggested that the requirement for a signature is not dependent and should not be limited by technology, and this is borne out by the case law from the past.[1] Lawyers and judges have been required to consider how new technologies affect the underlying legal principles. The decisions reached in the past remain relevant: the conclusion was, and remains, that any form of mark, whatever the technology used, has the capacity to demonstrate intent, and this should be no different when considering electronic signatures. Taking this into account, the decision by Judge Pelling QC is open to question. In addition, the judge suggested, in reaching his decision, that to conclude otherwise would lead to 'widespread and wholly unintended legal and commercial effects'. Arguably, this decision has led to the opposite: there is now uncertainty, especially among lay people who cannot be expected to understand that this decision refers only to s 4 of the Statute of Frauds, and only to guarantees. This decision is incompatible with the previous decisions on identical facts, albeit in applying the legal principles to different technologies, and sends a signal out that implies that a person may no longer be held to their promise for the lack of typing their name into the body of an email.[2] Notwithstanding this observation, this decision is generally accepted as being correct, sometimes with no discussion,[3] and sometimes with some discussion but without covering much of the case law discussed above.[4] Professor Ter Kah Lang set out the issue: that there is a fundamental distinction between identifying the sender by means of the pre-printed letterhead, and the intent of the signatory to adopt the name as authenticating the document.[5] Miller J commented on this point in *Welsch v Gatchell*[6] at [75], although arguments could abound if one party specifies that a particular type of electronic signature is required:

> An electronic signature will not prove adequate unless the Court is satisfied that its insertion was intended to signify adoption of the electronic note or memorandum of which it forms part or with which it is otherwise associated. That suggests that it would be prudent for those who wish to rely on an electronic writing and signature to warn the party to be charged that the writing is a contract that will bind that party when he or she attaches an electronic signature to it, and to specify what form of electronic signature is required.

1 In *Mercury Tax Group Ltd, R (on the application of) v HM Commissioners of Revenue & Customs* [2008] EWHC 2721 (Admin), [2009] STC 743, [2008] 11 WLUK 303, [2009] Lloyd's Rep FC 135, [2009] BTC 3, [2008] STI 2670, [2009] CLY 3928 the signature pages of a trust deed, an option agreement and a sale/purchase agreement were signed some time before the final versions were complete, and were then attached, without the consent of those who signed the pages, to final versions that were different to the draft versions; see also Emma Walton, 'Guidance on the execution of documents at "virtual" signings following the *Mercury* case' (2009) 24 Butterworths Journal of International Banking and Financial Law 327.

2 Judges in both the High Court and Court of Appeal (Civil Division) took a different view where it appears there was no signature in the case of *Decouvreur v Jordan* [1987] 1 WLUK 115, Times, 25 May 1987, [1987] CLY 1842; an appeal was dismissed before a court comprising Fox and Nourse LJJ and Sir Denys Buckley, where judgment for the plaintiff had been given by Mr Justice Farquharson in the sum of £15,000 on a claim against the second defendant under a contract of guarantee. The report states that 'Any writing by which the guarantor of a debt could be identified in a memorandum of the guarantee and which showed an intention to adopt the guarantee sufficed as a signature for the purposes of the Statute of Frauds 1677'. See Clive Freedman and Jake Hardy, 'J Pereira Fernandes SA v Mehta: a 21st-century email meets a 17th century statute' (2007) 21 Computer Law & Security Report 77.

3 Brazell, *Electronic Signatures and Identities Law and Regulation*, 2-017; The Hon Mrs Justice Geraldine Andrews and Richard Millett, *Law of Guarantees* (7th edn, Sweet & Maxwell 2015), 82; MacQueen and Garland, 'Signatures in Scots law'.
4 Leng, 'Have you signed your electronic contract?'; Blount, *Electronic Contracts*.
5 Leng, 'Have you signed your electronic contract?', 79.
6 [2007] NZHC 1898, [2009] 1 NZLR 241, (2007) 8 NZCPR 708, (2007) 5 NZ ConvC 194,549 (21 June 2007).

7.181 Whether the name typed into an email can satisfy the provisions of s 4 of the Statute of Frauds is open to debate. What is disappointing is the lack of consideration of the decisions by senior judges from the nineteenth century when faced with identical facts in slightly different formats. The common law is supposed to be based on precedent, yet pertinent decisions by senior judges have either been missed or ignored in this debate.

Legal fees arrangement

7.182 In Israel, Hagai Brenner J determined, in a claim for legal fees in the case of *Atias v Salfan Ltd*,[1] that there was no basis for the defendant's claim that a legal fees agreement between her and the plaintiff was not signed. The plaintiff sent an email to the defendant in which he summarized their joint understanding of the legal fees. The defendant confirmed that understanding in a reply message, and used an expression that literally translates as 'No problem'. A legal fees agreement is not required to be in writing (although this is recommended) and the email correspondence between the two parties was determined to be sufficient proof of the existence of the agreement. In the absence of any other information, such as whether the defendant also signed her name in the reply email, it may be inferred that Hagai Brenner J reached the decision based on the email address of the defendant.

1 Tel Aviv Peace Court Civil Case 24210/06 (5 July 2006, unpublished decision).

Civil Law Act

7.183 In Singapore, whether the name in an email address could be an electronic signature was raised in the case *SM Integrated Transware* of *Ltd v Schenker Singapore (Pte) Ltd*.[1] In this instance, Prakash J determined that it was possible for an email address to be a form of electronic signature for the purposes of s 6(d) of the Civil Law Act (Cap 43, 1994 Rev Ed). In this case, SM Integrated entered into negotiations to provide warehousing space and logistics services to Schenker. Schenker intended to enter a contract with a third party to handle dangerous goods, which in turn meant Schenker needed more storage facilities than it actually had. SM Integrated and Schenker prepared a draft agreement by way of meetings and the exchange of email correspondence, the content of which included reference to the transaction and the terms of the draft agreement. The agreement was never signed. Schenker subsequently failed to enter a contract with the third party, and because it no longer required the additional storage space, it declined to sign the draft agreement. SM Integrated initiated an action for damages suffered as a result of the alleged repudiation of the proposed lease, claiming that a combination of the draft agreement and the correspondence by email relating to the terms of the agreement demonstrated that an agreement had been formed. Schenker took the view that there was no contract because the negotiations failed to produce a final agreement, but even if a valid contract existed, it did not satisfy the requirements of the Electronic Transactions Act 1998 (Cap 88 of 1999), in that it was neither in writing nor signed.

1 [2005] 2 SLR 651, [2005] SGHC 58; Ter Kah Leng, 'Concluding leases by email' (2005) 21 Computer Law & Security Report 423; Bryan Tan, 'SM Integrated Transware Pte Ltd v Schenker Singapore (Pte) Ltd [(2005)] SGHC 58' (2005) 2 Digital Evidence and Electronic Signature Law Review 112; Daniel Seng, 'The Singapore Electronic Transactions Act and the Hong Kong Electronic Transactions Ordinance' (2008) 5 Digital Evidence and Electronic Signature Law Review 7.

7.184 The arguments put forward by Schenker were not accepted. In her reasons for judgment, Prakash J gave careful consideration to the issue of whether or not the correspondence by email that passed between the parties was capable of satisfying the Statute of Frauds requirements of s 6(d) of the Civil Law Act (Cap 43, 1994 Rev Ed).

7.185 Counsel for Schenker argued that the signature and writing requirements regarding this particular type of contract were not capable of being satisfied electronically because of the provisions of s 4(1)(d) of the Electronic Transactions Act 1998 (as it was then), which stated that the Act does not apply to 'any contract for the sale or other disposition of immovable property, or any interest in such property'. This argument was also rejected.

7.186 In reaching a decision on this matter, it was reasonable to consider the position at common law and by construing the provisions of s 6(d) Civil Law Act 1994, not by 'blindly relying on s4(1)(d) of the ETA'.[1] It was also held that the communications exchanged by email were in writing.[2] Apart from the legal basis of the decision that the emails were in writing, Prakash J, at [81], took a realistic and sound approach by making it clear that, despite the claim that the emails did not constitute writing, the facts did not correspond to such a contention.

1 [2005] 2 SLR 651, paragraph 76.
2 [2005] 2 SLR 651, paragraphs 77–85.

7.187 Arguments that email and other documents created in digital form do not constitute 'writing' are disingenuous. The law is often derided for not responding to the development of new technologies, yet the comments made by judges in the nineteenth century indicated they were perfectly willing and able to apply legal principles to new forms of technology. It is widely recognized that digital data is the mainstay of many businesses and governments across the world, and to suggest that evidence from such sources is not admissible because it is not a 'writing' is bordering on the preposterous.

7.188 Mr Tan did not append his name at the bottom of the email, so the only evidence of a signature comprised the content of the heading: 'From "Tan Tian Tye"<tian-tye.tan@schenker.com>.' The name in the email address was considered a signature, and in reaching this conclusion, Prakash J referred to the Massachusetts case of *Shattuck v Klotzbach*,[1] and the seventh circuit case of *Cloud Corporation v Hasbro, Inc.*[2] In her judgment, Prakash J provided a clear exposition of the underlying principles that were established in the English and American courts in the nineteenth century:

> 91. I am satisfied that the common law does not require handwritten signatures for the purpose of satisfying the signature requirements of s 6(d) of the CLA. A typewritten or printed form is sufficient. In my view, no real distinction can be drawn between a typewritten form and a signature that has been typed onto an email and forwarded with the email to the intended recipient of that message.

> 92. One minor difficulty in this case is that Mr Tan did not append his name at the bottom of any of his email messages. All his email messages, however, including the message dated 4 February 2003 and sent to Ms Yong, had, near the start thereof, a line reading '**From**: "Tan Tian Tye" <tian-tye.tan @schenker.com>'. Mr Tan confirmed in court that he had sent out those messages. There is no doubt that at the time he sent them out, he intended the recipients of the various messages to know that they had come from him. Despite that, he did not find it necessary to identify himself as the sender by appending his name at the end of any of the emails whether the messages were sent to his colleagues or to third parties like Mr Heng. I can only infer that his omission to type in his name was due to his knowledge that his name appeared at the head of every message next to his email address so clearly that there could be no doubt that he was intended to be identified as the sender of such message. Therefore, I hold that the signature requirement of s6(d) is satisfied by the inscription of Mr Tan's name next to his email address at the top of the email of 4 February 2003.
>
> 93. I recognize that one person's email facility can, in some cases, be accessed by a third party who can then send out messages which purport to be authentic messages from the owner of that email address. If that happened, the owner of the address would be entitled to dispute the authenticity of the messages purportedly sent by him. That is not the case here. Further, such dispute would be as to the person who initiated the message and would not be decided on the basis of whether the message bore a signature.

1 14 Mass. L. Rptr 360, 2001 WL 1839720 (Mass. Super.).
2 314 F.3d 289 (7th Cir. 2002).

7.189 In the same year, Lai Kew Chai J referred to the decision of Judith Prakash J in the bankruptcy proceedings of *Wee Soon Kim Anthony v Lim Chor Pee*.[1] Although the judge did not have to consider the email correspondence in this case, having determined that the exchange did not form a valid agreement because there was no meeting of the minds, nevertheless he commented, at [39], that he considered the exchange of email correspondence was likely to satisfy the written record and signature requirements of s 111 of the Legal Profession Act (Cap 161, 2001 Rev Ed).[2]

1 [2005] 4 SLR 367, [2005] SGHC 159.
2 Note also *Singh Chiranjeev v Joseph Mathew* [2008] SGHC 222, [2009] 2 SLR 73.

7.190 It can be safely concluded that whether an email address is capable of constituting a form of electronic signature will depend on the facts of each case.[1]

1 For other examples regarding a name in an email address: Greece – 32/2011, translation and commentary by Michael G. Rachavelias (2014) 11 Digital Evidence and Electronic Signature Law Review 174 (assignment; validity; status of electronic document; email address; evidential weight); Payment Order 5845/2013, translation by Michael G. Rachavelias (2014) 11 Digital Evidence and Electronic Signature Law Review 177 (debt; electronic document; email; email address; burden of proof; forgery); Court Decision No. 1963/2004 (2005) 2 Digital Evidence and Electronic Signature Law Review 107 (notification procedure); Italy, Tribunale Mondovì, 7 giugno 2004, n. 375 (decr.), Giur. It. 2005, 1026 (2007) 4 Digital Evidence and Electronic Signature Law Review 86 (email acknowledging debt).

A manuscript signature that has been scanned

7.191 A variation of the biodynamic version of a manuscript signature is where a manuscript signature is scanned[1] from the paper carrier and transformed into digital form, which makes it very easy to use by the recipient for the purposes of forgery. The files containing the representation of the signature can then be attached to a document. This version of a signature is used widely in commerce, especially when marketing materials are sent through the postal system and addressed to hundreds of thousands, if not millions, of addresses. It could be argued that when sending a document by facsimile transmission the recipient of the document has in their possession this version of the manuscript signature: the entire document is scanned and transmitted, together with the content. Arguably, this is the form of signature that was discussed in the case of *Re a debtor (No 2021 of 1995), Ex p, Inland Revenue Commissioners v The debtor; Re a debtor (No 2022 of 1995), Ex, Inland Revenue Commissioners v The debtor*[2] where a completed form of proxy was sent by facsimile transmission. Although the report does not clearly state the proxy form, as transmitted, contained the manuscript signature of the relevant official from the Commissioners of Inland Revenue, it can be inferred that a manuscript signature had been appended to the original form of proxy that was sent by facsimile transmission. Laddie J offered an opinion in relation to this point at 351f–g:

> For example, it is possible to instruct a printing machine to print a signature by electronic signal sent over a network or via a modem. Similarly, it is now possible with standard personal computer equipment and readily available popular word processing software to compose, say, a letter on a computer screen, incorporate within it the author's signature which has been scanned into the computer and is stored in electronic form, and to send the whole document including the signature by fax modem to a remote fax. The fax received at the remote station may well be the only hard copy of the document. It seems to me that such a document has been 'signed' by the author.

1 By way of example, scanned signatures were relied upon in the following cases in England and Wales (this list is not exhaustive): *National Bank Trust v Yurov* [2020] EWHC 100 (Comm), [2020] 1 WLUK 148; *TFS Stores Ltd v The Designer Retail Outlet Centres (Mansfield) General Partner Ltd* [2019] EWHC 1363 (Ch), [2019] Bus LR 1970, [2019] 6 WLUK 10, [2020] 1 P & CR 6, [2019] L & TR 26, [2019] CLY 1697; *Rotam Agrochemical Company Ltd v GAT Microencapsulation GMBH* [2018] EWHC 2765 (Comm), [2018] 10 WLUK 406; *FSHC Group Holdings Ltd v Barclays Bank Plc* [2018] EWHC 1558 (Ch), [2018] 6 WLUK 448; *Chartwell Estate Agents Ltd v Fergies Properties SA* [2014] EWHC 1567 (QB), [2014] 5 WLUK 471.

2 [1996] 2 All ER 345, [1995] 11 WLUK 290, [1996] BCC 189, [1996] 1 BCLC 538, [1996] BPIR 398, [1996] CLY 3469.

7.192 This observation must be correct. Providing the sending party intended the recipient to accept such a signature as a method of authentication and to act upon the content of the document transmitted, the method used to transmit the signature remains merely a method by which the document or message is communicated. The means of communication used should not affect the legal consequences that follow the delivery and subsequent receipt of the document.[1]

1 For a discussion of cases involving scanned images of manuscript signatures in Belgium, see Johan Vandendriessche, 'An overview of some recent case law in Belgium in relation to electronic signature' (2010) 7 Digital Evidence and Electronic Signature Law Review 90.

Mortgage redemption

7.193 In 2006 a registration judge in Denmark refused to cancel a mortgage because the signatures on the documentation were not manuscript signatures. The Danish

Western High Court upheld this decision in case U.2006.1341V. The facts were that a mortgage bank N delivered a mortgage for the purpose of cancellation. The scanned signatures of A and B were affixed to the cancellation endorsement. By a notice circulated to all judicial districts, N had authorized A and B to jointly endorse the mortgage by means of scanned manuscript signatures. The endorsements were added or attached to the original mortgage. The registration judge refused to cancel the mortgage because the signatures were not added by means of a manuscript signature in accordance with s 9(1) of the Danish Registration of Property Act. The Danish Western High Court upheld this decision, and took the view that under s 261(2) of the Danish Administration of Justice Act, the endorsement must be signed, and in accordance with established case law, pleadings must be available in their original form, and photocopies or facsimiles are therefore not sufficient. In addition, the registry took the view that, on grounds of due process, manuscript signatures are still required on documents to be registered (or cancelled), and that any change of this state of the law should, if necessary, be clarified by the legislature in the same way as the provisions on digital signatures.[1]

1 For a case report, see (2007) 4 Digital Evidence and Electronic Signature Law Review 99.

Writing

7.194 In a case before the German Federal Supreme Court (Bundesgerichtshof), file number XI ZB 40/06, NJW 2006, 3784 regarding §130 Zivilprozessordnung (ZPO) (the German code of civil procedure), it was held that a scanned manuscript signature is not sufficient to be qualified as 'in writing' under §130(6) ZPO if the signature is printed on a document and then sent by facsimile transmission. This ruling appears to prevent the admission into evidence of a document twice removed from the source. First, the signature is scanned and then printed on the document, then the document is sent on by means of facsimile transmission. As an item of evidence, such a document might be highly suspect in the absence of a clear acknowledgment by the person whose signature it is that they were entirely responsible for the entire process or they authorized another person to produce the document and transmit it, and they adopted the content of the document as their own.

Employment

7.195 In France, the case of Cour de Cassation, soc., 17 mai 2006, 04-46706[1] also considered the legal effect of a scanned signature. In this instance, an employee of the Association of La Réunion Marine Park was dismissed on 27 January 2002. A claim for unfair dismissal was issued. The only relevant issue for present purposes was that the dismissal letter had not been signed, but took the form of a letter bearing a signature that had been scanned. On 25 May 2004 the Court of Appeal of Saint-Denis de la Réunion held that a scanned manuscript signature did not constitute an electronic signature, as defined by article 1316–4 of the French Civil Code, but nevertheless considered that the dismissal letter had been validly signed. Upon appeal to the Cour de Cassation, the supreme French civil court, the employee argued that the Court of Appeal should have decided that the dismissal letter was not admissible, as the Court of Appeal had found the signature had been rendered into digital form earlier. On this point, the Cour de Cassation held that the fact that the signature had been put into digital form on the dismissal letter might affect the formal process of the dismissal procedure, but did not in itself deprive the dismissal of substantive justifiable grounds. The Cour de Cassation appeared to leave open the question of whether or not the electronic signature did affect the dismissal procedure. In this instance, the Cour de Cassation held that there were justifiable substantive grounds for the dismissal.

1 The decision in French is available at http://www.legifrance.gouv.fr/.

Biodynamic version of a manuscript signature

7.196 There are products available that permit a person to produce a biodynamic version of their manuscript signature.[1] For instance, some delivery companies use hand-held devices that require the recipient of an item of post or parcel to sign on a screen acknowledging receipt of the mail, and some banks use similar methods to provide a signature when using a debit or credit card.

1 Such a system was relied upon in *Sell Your Car With Us Ltd v Sareen* [2019] EWHC 2332 (Ch), [2019] 9 WLUK 397, [2019] BCC 1211, [2020] 1 CL 112; see also *Fitzpatrick v AIG Europe* (unreported) 1 July 2015, Jenkinson DJ, where the judge considered an electronic signature made with a proprietary product on a witness statement to be valid, for which see Gordon Exall, 'Electronic signature of witness statements: is it valid? A first instance decision', https://www.civillitigationbrief.com/2015/07/02/electronic-signature-of-witness-statements-is-it-valid-a-first-instance-decision/.

7.197 Another method of obtaining a digital version of a manuscript signature is where a person can write their manuscript signature by using a special pen and pad. The signature is reproduced on the computer screen, and a series of measurements record the behaviour of the person as they perform the action. The measurements include the speed, rhythm, pattern, habit, stroke sequence and dynamics that are unique to the individual at the time they write their signature.[1] The subsequent electronic file can then be attached to any document in electronic form to provide a measurement of a signature represented in graphic form on the screen. While it appears that this concept might be usefully applied in the electronic environment, the drawbacks are as significant as for any other form of generating electronic signatures, including linking the evidence in a coherent fashion to prove a person signed a particular document,[2] and problems relating to the protection of personal data.[3]

1 Such a device seems to be used by the Queensland Police Services, for which see *Bismark v Queensland Police Service District Court of Queensland* [2014] QDC 152 2014, WL 8104519 in which such a device is used by the appellant.

2 The nature of the evidence was discussed by Chin DJ in *Labajo v Best Buy Stores, L.P.*, 478 F.Supp.2d 523 (S.D.N.Y. 2007) at 530, although this report was in respect of a motion for judgment on the pleadings and before discovery, so the defendants would have had the opportunity of obtaining more coherent evidence for the trial; Fangjun Luan, Shiliang Ma, Kaidong Cheng and Xianfeng Dong, 'On-line handwritten signature verification algorithm based on time sequence' (2005) 1 International Journal of Information and Systems Sciences 229; Ricardo P. Gonçalves, Alexandre B. Augusto and Manuel E. Correia, 'Time/space based biometric handwritten signature verification', *10th Iberian Conference on Information Systems and Technologies (CISTI), 2015* (IEEE 2015), 743–748.

3 Anderson, *Security Engineering*, 15.9 for an indication about what can go wrong with biometric systems, and Jan Grijpink, 'Biometrics and privacy' (2001) 17 Computer Law and Security Report 154.

Electoral register

7.198 In Australia, the Electoral Commissioner rejected the biodynamic version of a manuscript signature (biodynamic signature) in the case of *Getup Ltd v Electoral*

Commissioner[1] prior to the Australian election in August 2010. Ms Trevitt used her biodynamic signature to enrol as a voter over the Internet before the election took place. Lawyers for the Commissioner wrote to Ms Trevitt, indicating 'that the electronic signature on the claim form was not sufficient'.[2] Her attempt to register her vote was rejected. The main point at issue was whether the form of signature used was appropriate, in accordance with the provisions of s 10(1)(b) of the Electronic Transactions Act 1999 (Cth). Perram J considered s 10(1)(a) and (b), and whether this Act applied to the Commonwealth Electoral Act 1918 (Cth).

1 [2010] FCA 869 (13 August 2010).
2 [2010] FCA 869 (13 August 2010) at [8].

7.199 Ms Trevitt affixed her electronic signature to the form with a biodynamic signature. It was argued by counsel for the Commissioner that it was for the Commissioner to form an opinion about the reliability of the method in accordance with the purpose. The judge did not agree with this argument. He set out his reasoning at 14–15:

> The provision does not mention anyone forming an opinion. In particular, because s 10(1)(b) is pitched at a very high level of generality it understandably eschews identifying any of the parties to the communication at all. Even assuming the provision should be read as requiring someone to hold an opinion it is silent as to whether it is to be held by the sender or the recipient or both. Further, as Mr Kirk, who appeared with Ms Rao for the applicants, pointed out, the breadth of the requirement that the issue be considered in light of all of the relevant circumstances bespoke the possibility that not all of the circumstances might be known to the participants to the communication. Such a view of the provision counted against it being read as requiring the formation of an opinion by one or other of the persons involved in its application.
>
> 15. I do not see a way around those concerns. To accede to the notion that s 10(1)(b) required the Commissioner to form an opinion would involve, so it seems to me, an intolerably strained construction of its plain words. Further, it would be a construction which necessarily identified the recipient as the person whose opinion mattered. That reading of s 10(1)(b) might have very serious consequences in a range of cases yet to come and about which nothing can be known. In those circumstances, I do not read s 10(1)(b) in a manner for which the Commissioner contends. This has the consequence that the provision sets a standard which, in this instance, is to be ascertained and applied by the Court.

7.200 Perram J then considered the nature of the evidence, the possibility of forgery and the fact that the Commissioner accepted other forms of signature (whether they were sent by facsimile transmission and scanned versions of manuscript signatures), and concluded, at 17 that:

> In that circumstance, I cannot accept the slightly pixelated nature of Ms Trevitt's signature rendered it unreliable for the Commissioner's purposes, not at least while he continues to accept faxed or emailed claim forms.

7.201 This particular point, the abstract reliability test, refers to article 9(3) of the United Nations Convention on the Use of Electronic Communications in International Contracts. If not understood, the abstract reliability test could increase the risks of invalidity after the event, where the form of signature had never posed problems of authentication previously.[1]

1 The provision of the abstract reliability test merits further observations, for which see John D. Gregory, 'Must e-signatures be reliable?' (2013) 10 Digital Evidence and Electronic Signature Law Review 67.

Contract formation

7.202 At issue in the US case of *American Family Life Assurance Company of Columbus v Biles*[1] was whether the signature of the late David Biles was a forgery. The method used by Mr Biles to apply his signature to a life insurance policy was by way of a proprietary biodynamic version of his manuscript signature, using a pad and computer. Of interest was the approach taken by the two document examiners in the case. Robert G. Foley gave evidence for the plaintiff,[2] and William J. Flynn gave evidence for the defendant.[3] Mr Foley compared the photocopies presented to him by the plaintiff of the images of two signatures affixed to the document. Mr Flynn, in contrast, examined the data files used to create the images representing the electronic signature. One of the reasons for the hearings was an application to strike out the affidavit of Robert G. Foley on the basis that his examination was not appropriate, given that he ought to have examined the data files. Lee DJ ordered a *Daubert*[4] hearing to determine whether to agree to exclude Mr Foley's evidence.[5] At the subsequent hearing, the defendants sought to exclude the evidence of Mr Flynn. After hearing the evidence, the judge concluded that the challenge to Mr Foley's reliability was well taken, because his opinion was not based on the examination of the best evidence available.[6] The implication is that when electronic signatures of this nature are challenged, it is important to ensure the adjudicator is aware of the need for the examination of the digital data, and that a comparison of the images produced by the digital data alone is not appropriate.[7]

1 2011 WL 4014463 (S.D.Miss.) and 2011 WL 5325622 (S.D.Miss.).

2 *American Family Life Assurance Company of Columbus v Biles*, 2011 WL 5835356 (S.D.Miss.) (affidavit of Robert G. Foley); *American Family Life Assurance Company of Columbus v Biles*, 2011 WL 7909386 (S.D.Miss.) (supplemental affidavit of Robert G. Foley).

3 *American Family Life Assurance Company of Columbus v Biles*, 2011 WL 5835357 (S.D.Miss.) (affidavit of William J. Flynn).

4 *Daubert v Merrell Dow Pharmaceuticals*, 509 U.S. 579 (1993).

5 *American Family Life Assurance Company of Columbus v Biles*, 2011 WL 4014463 2011 (S.D.Miss.).

6 *American Family Life Assurance Company of Columbus v Biles*, 2011 WL 5325622 (S.D.Miss.); *American Family Life Assurance Company of Columbus v Glenda C. Biles, Individually, Natural Mother of David Biles, Deceased, and Administratrix of Estate of David Biles, Deceased*, 714 F.3d 887 (5th Cir. 2013) (appeal on the enforcement of the arbitration agreement).

7 Heidi H. Harralson, 'Forensic document examination of electronically captured signatures' (2012) 9 Digital Evidence and Electronic Signature Law Review 67; for the failure to adduce relevant evidence of a signature, see a case from the Court of Appeals of North Carolina, *Meadlock v American Family Life Assurance Company of Columbus*, 221 N.C.App. 669, 729 S.E.2d 127 (Table), 2012 WL 2891079.

Digital signatures

Technical overview of digital signatures

7.203 Cryptography is the method of hiding the contents of a message, as used from ancient times to the present. Encryption (or enciphering) is the process by which a plaintext (or cleartext) message is disguised sufficiently to hide the substance of the content. As well as ordinary text, a plaintext message can be a stream of binary digits, a text file, a bitmap, a recording of sound in digital format, audio images of a video or film and any other information formed into digital bits. When a message has been encrypted, it is known as ciphertext or a cryptogram. The opposite procedure, that of turning the ciphertext back into plaintext, is called decryption (or deciphering).[1] In essence, contemporary cryptographic systems change one set of symbols that have meaning (binary data) into a second set of symbols that have no meaning, by means of a mathematical process. Cryptography is usually required to undertake a number of functions, the most important of which is authenticity rather than secrecy. These functions are discussed below.

(1) Authenticity: When sending or receiving information or placing an order, both parties need to have assurance of the origin of the message. The aim is to corroborate the identity of the software that sent the data. The identity of a person cannot be corroborated, because a person is not part of the communications process – the process only involves communications between software.

(2) Integrity: It is helpful to demonstrate the integrity of the message, because it is important to know if the content of the message has been tampered with.

(3) Honesty: To provide an assurance, to the extent that is technically possible, that demonstrates that the software emanates from a known source, such that the purported sender has been honest about the actions that have been caused to be undertaken. The purpose is an attempt to bind human users to specific actions in such a way that if they deny taking the action, they either demonstrate an intention to deceive, or they have been negligent in failing to secure the use of their private key adequately. This is called 'non-repudiation' in the security industry. There are different types of non-repudiation: non-repudiation of origin, which prevents the entity that sent the message or document from denying that they sent it, and non-repudiation of receipt, where an entity cannot deny they have received a message or document. Other types of non-repudiation include non-repudiation of creation, non-repudiation of delivery and non-repudiation of approval.[2]

(4) Confidentiality: Another purpose is to provide for the confidentiality of a document. In the digital environment, cryptography is used as a substitute for a manuscript signature, and is often described as a digital signature. To understand how a document can be signed with a digital signature, it is necessary to be aware of how cryptography works, for which see the discussion below.

1 Encipher and decipher are terms used in the ISO 7498-2 standard.
2 Adams and Lloyd, *Understanding PKI Concepts*, 51.

Algorithms and keys

7.204 The plaintext of a message is encrypted and decrypted by the use of a cryptographic algorithm (also called a cipher). There tend to be two related functions, one for encryption and another for decryption. In most instances, the secrecy of the algorithm will not matter, because modern cryptography uses a key. However, it is possible to have what is called a restricted algorithm, because the security of the algorithm is based on ensuring the way it works is kept a secret. There are drawbacks to the use of restricted algorithms. If a user leaves the group that shares the algorithm, or should the secret be revealed for any reason, then the algorithm must be changed. Further, there is no quality control or standardization, which means these algorithms can be easy to break. By using a key, a strong algorithm does not need to be secret and can be used by millions of users. As a result, there is no need to constantly develop new algorithms. A key can comprise a number of values. This range of values is called a keyspace. A key can be used to encrypt and decrypt a message, or there can be two separate keys, one to encrypt a message and another for decrypting the message. To complete the picture, a cryptosystem comprises an algorithm, all possible messages, all possible cryptograms and all possible keys.

Control of the key

7.205 To decrypt the ciphertext, the recipient needs to know both the decryption algorithm and the decryption key. The way a key is controlled, managed and distributed is crucial. This is why the principle laid down by Auguste Kerckhoffs von Niuewenhof remains a fundamental rule of cryptanalysis: the security of a cryptosystem must depend on keeping the key secret.[1] This issue is discussed more fully when considering the weaknesses relating to cryptosystems.

1 Auguste Kerckhoffs, 'La Cryptographie militaire' (1983) 9 Journal des Sciences Militaires 5, although this principle applied to a time when all systems were symmetric.

Disguising the message

7.206 There are two types of mathematical families that permit a message to be disguised: symmetric cryptographic systems and asymmetric cryptographic systems.

Conventional or symmetric cryptographic systems

7.207 As the name infers, the encryption key can be computed from the decryption key, and the decryption key can be computed from the encryption key. In practice, these two keys are often identical when used in symmetric systems. The symmetric system is also referred to as secret-key algorithms, single-key algorithms, one-key algorithms or shared key ciphers. Two people can use the same system to send and receive encrypted messages to each other and both the sender and the receiver must agree on the key before they can communicate. This system can have very long keys, which means a message can be very secure. The effectiveness of this system depends on the key, and is suitable for closed user groups where there is a strong element of mutual trust between the users, such as banks, the military and intelligence agencies. However, a disadvantage is that the key must be kept secure and secret. Two people must have the key to communicate. If encrypted messages are to pass between large numbers of people, a large number of keys will have to be distributed. The security of the system depends on those people with access to the keys ensuring they are kept secure and secret. Also, from the point of view of managing the keys, it is important for pairs of users to have different keys to reduce the risks of compromise when large numbers of people share a key.

7.208 Some symmetric algorithms work on the plaintext, one digit at a time. These are called stream ciphers. Others work in groups of digits on the plaintext. The groups of digits are called blocks, and the algorithms are called block algorithms or block ciphers. How an algorithm and the cipher work is important, because of their strengths and weaknesses. If an algorithm or cipher is easy to attack, then an application should not use it, and if losses occur because of the failure of either, then a successful legal action may be possible because it could be argued that the system was designed and possibly implemented negligently.

7.209 Sending a message that has been encrypted provides for the security of the content only. It does not attribute the message to the source from which the message was sent. It is possible for an interceptor to intercept the message and send a substitute message in place of the original message. If a forger sends the message, the recipient will not be aware that the sender of the message has used the key improperly. Authentication seeks to corroborate the integrity of the message and authenticity of the sender. There are two types of authentication.

> (1) One-way authentication is where one party is authenticated to another party, such as a person using an ATM when they wish to withdraw cash or make a deposit. The user identifies themselves by using their PIN, and the card is authenticated cryptographically.
>
> (2) Two-way authentication, where both parties to a message seek to verify the attribution of data that purports to identify each other or the message or both, such as virtual private networks.

7.210 The process of authentication also uses a secret key. This is called the message authentication code or data authentication code. This mechanism can provide authentication without the need for secrecy. In symmetric cryptographic systems, the aim is for the originator and the legitimate recipient to be the only two entities that can create or check the message authentication code. Here is an example of how the message authentication code can work:[1]

> Alice sends a message in plaintext to Bob. The software on the computer that Alice uses encrypts the message by using a block algorithm or cipher. All of the ciphertext blocks are then discarded with the exception of the last block. The last block is the message authentication code. (Note: if Alice wants to provide for both the integrity and the privacy of the message, the message can also be encrypted again.)
>
> Bob receives the message. The software on his computer computes what the message authentication code should have been. If Eve intercepted and altered the message, Bob will realise this, because the incorrect plaintext is re-encrypted, producing an incorrect message authentication code. If the plaintext has been altered, the ciphertext blocks will be different, especially the last ciphertext block. If the plaintext has not been altered, the re-encrypted plaintext will not have changed, and Bob can be sure that Alice has sent the plaintext message.

1 Alice, Bob, Carol, Dave and interloper Eve are used widely in cryptology. See 'The Alice and Bob after dinner speech' given at the Zürich Seminar, April 1984 by John Gordon by invitation of Professor John Massey, http://web.mit.edu/jemorris/humor/alice-and-bob.

7.211 However, this does not prevent Eve from listening in to Alice when she sends the message to Bob. Eve can then record every message, together with the message authentication code. Alternatively, she can delete the message sent by Alice, repeat old messages or change the order in which the messages are sent. Thus the message authentication code needs to include a scheme by which each message is numbered sequentially.

Asymmetric cryptographic systems (Public key)

7.212 Using a symmetric cryptographic system with large numbers of users is difficult. Keys cannot be distributed over the open communications network, so they have to be distributed in other ways. When a member leaves the group, all the other members have to redistribute new keys. Thus, assuming a separate key is used for each pair in a group, and if there are 10 people as members of the group, 45 different keys will be required. The development of the asymmetric cryptographic system, or public key,[1] helps to resolve this problem. With this system, keys only have one purpose: one key to encrypt and one key to decrypt. Given a large enough key, the decryption key cannot be calculated from the encryption key within a useful length of time (perhaps several centuries). The algorithms used in the system are commonly called 'public key' because the encryption key is usually made public. Anybody can use the encryption key to encrypt a plaintext message, but only the person with the decryption key that corresponds to the encryption key can decrypt the message. The encryption key is called the public key or public encryption key, and the decryption key is called the private key, secret key or private decryption key. The system can work in two ways, as indicated below.

1 The concept of public key cryptography was invented twice during the twentieth century. First, by James H. Ellis, Clifford Cocks and Malcolm J. Williamson at British Intelligence GCHQ, whose work remained classified until December 1997. Second, two researchers at Stanford University, Whitfield Diffie and Martin Hellman, proposed the concept in 1976. Development of the principles can also be attributed to Ralph C. Merkle, Ronald L. Rivest, Adi Shamir and Leonard A. Adleman.

7.213 An individual creates and controls their own public key The user can generate a pair of keys using what is called a trapdoor one-way function, containing the mathematical equivalent of a secret trapdoor. For the purposes of understanding the concept, this algorithm is easy to compute in one direction and difficult to compute in the opposite direction, unless you know the secret.[1] Sending a message using public key cryptography can be described as follows:

> Alice and Bob decide to exchange messages that are encrypted.
>
> Alice generates her own public and private keys using the software on her computer. Although she keeps the private key secret, she gives Bob her public key.
>
> Bob writes his message and encrypts it using Alice's public key. He sends it to Alice.
>
> Alice decrypts Bob's message using her private key.

1 It has yet to be proven that a mathematical function can have a one-way function, for which see Fred Piper, Simon Blake-Wilson and John Mitchell, *Digital Signatures: Security & Controls* (Information Systems Audit and Control Foundation 1999), 16.

7.214 This method of encrypting and decrypting messages means that private keys do not have to be distributed. The private key should always be under the direct control of the owner. If the private key was distributed, there is no way of asserting a signature is yours, because you could always claim the other person who received your key executed the signature.

7.215 In addition, it is possible for Alice to place her public key in a public database. The protocol then looks like this:

> Bob goes to the database and obtains Alice's public key.
>
> Bob writes Alice a message and uses her public key to encrypt the message. Bob then sends the message to her.
>
> Alice decrypts the message using her private key upon receipt.

7.216 There can be problems in relation to the methods by which an individual creates and controls their own keys, as in *Maughan v Wilmot*,[1] where the husband created his own digital signature to attach to emails.

1 [2016] EWHC 29 (Fam), [2016] 1 WLR 2200, [2016] 1 WLUK 90, [2016] 2 FLR 1349, [2016] Fam Law 307, [2016] CLY 316.

7.217 Authenticating a signature using public key cryptography The underlying rationale of public key cryptography is that a message can be attributed to a particular entity. First, Alice can use a key generation algorithm to generate a key pair: a private signing key and the public signature verification key, or she can use her existing key pair. She then publishes her public key on a database. Thereafter, the example continues:

> Alice writes a message and wants to send it to Bob with her digital signature. The software on her computer computes a digital signature from her private key and the content of the message.
>
> Alice sends her message and the digital signature to Bob. The signature may be, but does not need to be, separate from the message.[1] The signature operates in the same way as a message authentication code.
>
> Upon receipt of the message, Bob uses Alice's public key to verify that the corresponding private key signed the message.

1 This can be important, for which see Nicholas Bohm, 'Watch what you sign!' (2006) 3 Digital Evidence and Electronic Signature Law Review, 45.

7.218 However, given this scenario, it is generally noted in the technical literature that Bob cannot be sure that the public key in the database is that of Alice. This means this mechanism does not resolve the issue of identifying the sender of the message. A person could generate their own public and private keys, post the public key on a database and claim it belongs to Alice. Bob might think he is sending messages to Alice, but in fact his message might be posted to an interceptor. In addition, the interceptor could use their own private key to send messages to Bob, which he would assume came from Alice. There is a further problem with this method of adding a signature to a message, which in turn is inherent in any system that uses cryptography in the electronic environment to create a signature. The signature is not computed by Alice, but by the software on her computer. Thus there is no direct evidence to show Alice appended the signature to the message. This is, naturally, an identical problem with all forms of electronic signature and communication over networked communications – for instance, the same point can be made about the origin of an email. The recipient cannot be certain that an email comes from the purported source, yet the vast majority of emails that are sent and received are trusted. This is because the correspondents either know each other in the physical world, or even if they have not met, then they become familiar with each other in the virtual world by way of an exchange of correspondence and other signs, such as looking at websites and asking others who are trusted to indicate whether the person they have yet to meet is indeed the person they claim to be.

Public key infrastructure

7.219 The concept of the public key infrastructure (PKI) tries to resolve this problem by linking a public key to a named individual or legal entity.[1] The notion behind a public key infrastructure is to have organizations called trusted intermediaries, trusted third parties, trust service providers or certification authorities that act to certify the connection between a person and their public key. In theory, the trusted third party guarantees the authenticity of the public key by issuing an individual identity certificate (usually abbreviated to 'certificate'), which binds a name string to a public key. This in turn seeks to create a link between the provision of a key and the identity of the natural person or legal entity to which the key has been issued. It should be emphasized that, when using a public key infrastructure, users should aim to continue to generate their own key pairs. Where a third party generates the key pair on behalf of a user, the degree of security exercised over the key pair is reduced.

1 For the flaws in PKI, see Carl Ellison, 'Improvements on conventional PKI wisdom', *Proceedings of the 1st Annual PKI Research Workshop* (NIST 2002), https://users.ece.cmu.edu/~adrian/731-sp04/readings/ellison-PKI-wisdom.pdf.

7.220 The certification authority issues an individual identity certificate, which includes the following characteristics: data identifying the certification authority, data identifying the subscriber that includes the subscriber's public key, and that it is signed with the Certification Authority's private key. The individual identity certificate may also contain other information, such as the level of inquiry carried out before issuing the certificate.

7.221 To acquire such a certificate, Alice will provide the certification authority with a copy of her public key and proof of her identity. The degree of proof of identity will differ, depending on the level of liability Alice wants to cover. When Alice sends a message to Bob, she also sends him a copy of her certificate. Alternatively, when she publishes her verification key, she publishes the certificate. The software on Bob's computer will decrypt the message according to the key he has been given. It will then be for Bob in most circumstances to undertake his own due diligence, perhaps by checking the certificate revocation list to ensure the public key has not been revoked or has expired, or sending an email to Alice (or contacting her by telephone) to confirm that she sent the communication. If Bob does not act to verify the information contained in the certificate, but contacts Alice directly, his due diligence will not involve the organization that issues the certificate.

Difficulties with public key infrastructure

7.222 The rationale behind the public key infrastructure is this: when a certification authority issues a certificate, it bases the issuance of the certificate on its Certificate Practice Statement and terms of trade. A contractual relationship is formed between the certification authority and the customer who buys the certificate. While the certificate purports to verify the identity of an individual person or legal entity, it is the merchant or person receiving the certificate who relies on the content of the certificate. The logic is as follows:[1]

> (1) The individual or entity provides the certification authority with sufficient evidence acceptable to the certification authority or registration authority to demonstrate that they are who they say they are. Depending on the level of the certificate obtained, this information could be the name, address and the number of a driving licence. For certificates that will support high value transactions, the

person or entity seeking a certificate may be required to provide more robust evidence, including physically appearing before a notary public.

(2) The certification authority provides the user with a certificate.

(3) The individual or entity is then given a keyholder's name.

(4) The keyholder is the person or entity that obtained the certificate.

(5) This is all the recipient needs to know.

1 Carl Ellison and Bruce Schneier, 'Ten risks of PKI: what you're not being told about public key infrastructure' (2000) 16 Computer Security Journal 1; for two responses to this article, see Ben Laurie, 'Seven and a half non-risks of PKI: what you shouldn't be told about public key infrastructure', https://groups.google.com/forum/#!topic/jyu.ohjelmointi.coderpunks/PtWHnFue9Zk and Aram Pérez, 'Response to "Ten risks of PKI"', https://sites.google.com/site/aramperez/home/10-risks-of-pki; 'PKI Assessment Guidelines', C.4.2 'Attribution presumptions in digital signature statutes'.

7.223 There are a number of flaws with this logic. For instance, John Smith of York may wish to enter a contract with a company who is not aware of his identity. The company cannot distinguish, when it looks at the certificate, how many John Smiths live in York and whether this particular John Smith is the person identified with the certificate. Unless the certificate provides the company with a unique identifier for this particular John Smith (which they may or may not provide), and the company wishes to confirm John Smith's identity, it must consider other ways of doing so. The certification authority generally does not share a secret with the person to whom it issues a certificate, although there must be a method by which the certification authority can verify the identity of the person to whom it issues a certificate. Some certification authorities use the information collected by a credit bureau to verify the identity of the applicant. This means the identification verification process can be based on the accuracy of the data collected by the credit bureau – bearing in mind the focus of a credit bureau is on creditworthiness – and their effectiveness in keeping the information up to date and secret. Another issue is whether the recipient of the electronic signature trusts the originator's certification authority. If a certification authority were to undertake to positively identify a subscribing party, the information that might be needed to satisfy the recipient may be so extensive that few individuals or legal entities would consider subscribing for such a certificate.[1] In conclusion, a certification authority provides a very narrow promise when issuing a certifying certificate. It does not appear that certification authorities seek first to establish the identity of a person and then go on to verify that identity. It is important to understand that verification is not the same as identification.[2]

1 For a useful discussion, see Carl Ellison, 'Improvements on conventional PKI wisdom', *Proceedings of the 1st Annual PKI Research Workshop* (NIST 2002), 165–75, https://users.ece.cmu.edu/~adrian/731-sp04/readings/ellison-PKI-wisdom.pdf; Nicholas Bohm and Stephen Mason, 'Identity and its verification' (2010) 26 Computer Law & Security Review 43.

2 Jan Grijpink and Corien Prins, 'Digital anonymity on the internet' (2001) 17 Computer Law and Security Report 379, 381(a).

7.224 The purported advantage to the relying party of using the 'standard model' public key infrastructure digital signature is not that the signature provides greater security, but arises from persuading the subscribing party that because it is apparently more secure, the user takes responsibility for every use of the private key, whoever does so. It must be emphasized, however, that the greater security of the mechanism does not, in fact, offer the subscribing party any protection against attacks, such as the theft of the key or the failure of software such that the software signs something other than what is presented on the screen. The industry implies that the system has a 'non-repudiation' property, and it is this property that justifies the imposition of a non-repudiation term on the subscribing party. This cannot be right, because if the system genuinely possessed a non-repudiation property, it would not be necessary to impose such a term. Given that digital signatures in a public key infrastructure do not possess such a property, and the inability to create false digital signatures is based on complex theoretic assumptions,[1] the acceptance of such a term invariably involves an acceptance of risk by the user. However, the nature and extent of the risk is not made clear, and it is highly improbable that ordinary users will have the knowledge, skills and resources to manage such a risk.[2]

1 Birgit Pfitzmann, 'Fail-stop signatures: principles and applications', in *Proceedings of the Eighth World Conference on Computer Security, Audit and Control* (Elsevier 1991), 125–134; Birgit Pfitzmann, *Digital Signature Schemes: General Framework and Fail-Stop Signatures* (Springer 1996).
2 Audun Jøsang and Bander AlFayyadh, 'Robust WYSIWYS: a method for ensuring that what you see is what you sign', in Ljiljana Brankovic and Mirka Miller (eds), *Proceedings of the Sixth Australasian Conference on Information security – Volume 81* (Australian Computer Society 2008), 53–58; Bohm, 'Watch what you sign!'; Don Davis, 'Compliance defects in public-key cryptography', *Proceedings of the Sixth USENIX UNIX Security Symposium* (San Jose, CA, 1996).

Authenticating the sender

7.225 There are various methods of obtaining sufficient evidence to demonstrate, with a degree of probability, that an electronic signature came from the person it purports to have been sent by. The aim is to gather sufficient evidence to be assured that the person sending the signature is the person they claim. Attempts are made, using various mechanisms, to obtain information from a combination of the following:[1]

Proof by knowledge: what the person knows.

Proof by possession: what the person owns.

Proof by characteristics: what the person is.

1 For an analysis of the strengths and weaknesses of each, see Richard E. Smith, *Authentication from Passwords to Public Keys* (Addison-Wesley 2002), 1.6.

7.226 When combined, the techniques relating to authentication can provide a higher level of authentication than a single method. In many instances, the method by which a person seeks to authenticate themselves is through a combination of hardware and software. A software component can retrieve and verify passwords. A token, such as a smart card, can be placed in a slot in a computer or in a separate 'reader'. However, both methods are vulnerable to attacks.[1] Identification can also be achieved by using a biometric measurement.

1 Saar Drimer, Steven J. Murdoch and Ross Anderson, 'Optimised to fail: card readers for online banking', in Roger Dingledine and Phillipe Golle (eds), *Financial Cryptography and Data Security, 13th International Conference, FC 2009, Accra Beach, Barbados, February 23–26, 2009* (Springer 2009), 184–200; Bohm and Mason, 'Identity and its verification'.

The ideal attributes of a signature in electronic form

7.227 Whether a signature is in manuscript or electronic form, the purpose for affixing the signature will not alter. However, when a signature is in electronic form, more considerations will apply. While it is abundantly clear that a manuscript signature can be forged, or can be transferred from one piece of paper to another,[1] or that documents can be altered after they have been signed, digital signatures can help to resist attacks of these kinds. The requirements of a digital signature are set out below:

(1) The signature must be authentic. In this respect the method ought, ideally, to provide for the authentication of the origin of the data and the integrity of the message.

(2) Ideally, there ought to be a technical method in place that prevents the person appending the signature to the document from claiming later that they did not sign it. This is virtually impossible to achieve in the electronic environment. Care must be taken to distinguish between the degree of probability that a system can be designed to prevent a person from making such a claim, and any suggestion of a presumption that purports to bind the user to a signature that is verified.[2]

(3) The signature should not be capable of being forged, in that the private key is secure.

(4) Where a signature is added to a message that comprises a legal act, the signature and its link to the relevant document should remain verifiable for as long as it is of legal importance.

(5) The signature cannot be reused.

(6) The document that has been signed cannot be altered without rendering the signature unverifiable.[3]

1 For examples where the cutting and pasting of manuscript signatures have been upheld in the USA, see Iowa: *Ferguson v Stilwill*, 224 N.W.2d 11, where the signature of the Illinois Secretary of State, cut from an instrument and attached to a certificate of conviction, was sufficient in the absence of evidence to show the act of pasting was not authorized (1974); Maine: *Richardson v Bachelder*, 19 Me. 82, 1841 WL 932 (Me.), 1 App. 82, where an attorney affixed the signature of the magistrate, which was physically on a slip of paper, to the writ, and the writ was held to be properly issued, the magistrate having recognized and adopted it.

2 For an analysis of the means by which a computer can be affected by malicious software, see Daniel Bilar, 'Known knowns, known unknowns and unknown unknowns: anti-virus issues, malicious software and internet attacks for non-technical audiences' (2009) 6 Digital Evidence and Electronic Signature Law Review 123.

3 Bruce Schneier, *Applied Cryptography* (2nd edn, Wiley 1996), 2.6.

7.228 In the digital environment, it is considered technically possible to achieve all of these attributes – in theory[1] – but it must be emphasized that the connection between the human and the machine cannot be bridged, and the technology is fallible.[2] Practical problems, which are discussed below, continue to exist with the implementation of a digital signature. However, the essential functions set out above can, largely, be met by the application of cryptography to the formation of a digital signature. As with manuscript signatures, there are always risks attached to the use of any form of electronic signature, and the user, whether a sending party or a receiving party, should make themselves aware of the risks before using any form of electronic signature for high value transactions.

1 Javier Lopez, Rolf Oppliger and Günther Pernu, 'Why have public key infrastructures failed so far?' (2005) 15 Internet Research 544.

2 Adam L. Young and Moti Yung, *Malicious Cryptography: Exposing Cryptovirology* (Wiley 2004).

7.229 There is one further meaning that an electronic signature cannot, without education and training, provide. This is the addition of what is termed 'social meaning', or what can also be described as the 'significance of the act'. A ceremony is attached to the signing of a document, and when a person affixes their manuscript signature to a document, the importance of the act is reinforced by the physical nature of the act, because 'People intuitively understand that they are legally responsible for the documents to which they attach their autographs'.[1] The function of attaching an electronic signature to a document or message is not understood in the same way as the use of manuscript signatures, partly because the signature can be applied to the document without any action by the individual to whom the signature is attributed, or even without their knowledge.[2]

1 Jos Dumortier, Patrick Van Eecke and Ilse Anné, *The Legal Aspects of Digital Signatures* (Interdisciplinary Centre for Law & Information Technology, Katholieke Universiteit Leuven, 1998), 77.
2 Eileen Y. Chou, 'Paperless and soulless: e-signatures diminish the signer's presence and decrease acceptance' (2015) 6 Social Psychological and Personality Science 343.

Methods of authentication

Authentication using secret codes

7.230 Secret codes or passwords have been used for some time, especially in banking. The code usually consists of a combination of digits or characters or both. The principle is based on ensuring the code is unique and only known to the user and the issuer. There is a shared secret between the two parties. The user identifies themselves by using the code, and if the code is correct, the issuer assumes the person entering a transaction is the person to whom the code is assigned.[1] Secret codes tend to be most appropriate when used in a closed community, as opposed to the open structure of the Internet, because a secret code cannot guarantee the identity of the person using the code. However, it should be noted that the evidence of a shared secret will not necessarily be sufficient to satisfy the relying party that an authorized user used the code. Evidence of the procedures and systems used by the relying party will not be sufficient to prove to a third party, such as a court, that it was the user that added the code. It is posited that a secret code cannot be considered strictly as a signature, because the code tends only to be used for the single characteristic of authenticating the user,[2] but two courts have decided otherwise, with respect correctly, given the facts.[3]

1 See United States District Court, Southern District of New York: *Banco del Austro, S.A., v Wells Fargo Bank, N.A.*, 215 F.Supp.3d 302, 90 UCC Rep.Serv.2d 1292; Salvatore Scanio, 'Interbank liability for fraudulent transfers via SWIFT: Banco del Austro, S.A. v. Wells Fargo. Bank, N.A.', (2017) 36(12) Banking & Fin Services Pol'y Rep 8; on the 2016 hack of the computers at Bangladesh Bank, the central bank of the country of Bangladesh, see Julie Anderson Hill, 'SWIFT bank heists and Article 4A' (2018) 22 J Consumer & Com L 25, and Geoff White and Jean H. Lee, 'The Lazarus heist: How North Korea almost pulled off a billion-dollar hack' (this is the story of the hack taken from 'The Lazarus Heist', a series of 11 programmes on BBC News World Service, broadcast in April 2021), https://www.bbc.co.uk/news/stories-57520169.
2 Anderson, *Security Engineering*, 10.4 for a study of the problems relating to ATMs; Dumortier and others, *The Legal Aspects of Digital Signatures*, 60–63.
3 *Standard Bank London Ltd v Bank of Tokyo Ltd* [1995] 2 Lloyd's Rep 169, [1995] 3 WLUK 182, [1995] CLC 496, [1998] Mason's CLR Rep 126, Times, 15 April 1995, [1995] CLY 397 and *Industrial & Commercial Bank Ltd v Banco Ambrosiano Veneto SpA* [2003] 1 SLR 221, where a message using an authentication code sent through the SWIFT (Society for Worldwide Interbank Financial Telecommunication) system had the legal effect of binding the sender bank according to its contents, and where a recipient bank undertook further checks on credit standing or other aspects, this did not detract from this proposition.

Authentication using biometric measurements

7.231 Using a biometric measurement is the method by which it is possible to authenticate an individual through the measurement of physical characteristics.

A biometric measurement has the ability to identify a person because the image is reduced to digital form. Such a measurement represents a unique characteristic of that individual, but it cannot be a secret. Human characteristics comprise a number of attributes, some of which lend themselves to being measured:

(1) Appearance, such as height, weight, colour of skin, hair and eyes, visible physical markings, gender, facial hair, wearing of spectacles.

(2) Social behavioural traits, including voice recognition, style of speech, visible handicaps.

(3) Natural physiography, such as iris patterns, retinal scan, fingerprint or thumbprint verification, capillary patterns in earlobes, two or three dimensional facial recognition, vein check and hand geometry, DNA patterns.

(4) Bio-dynamics, such as signature verification and the dynamics when using the keys on a keyboard.[1]

1 Anderson, *Security Engineering*, ch. 15.

7.232 There are significant difficulties with the use of biometric measurements, including the range of tolerances to reduce false negatives and increase false positives, or vice versa. The manufacturer of the device usually sets the tolerances, and a great many devices do not work as claimed.[1]

1 Anderson, *Security Engineering*, ch. 15.

Fingerprints

7.233 Most fingerprint systems use optical or capacitive sensors for capturing the details of a fingerprint, such as branching and end points of the ridges. An optical sensor detects differences in reflection, while capacitive sensors detect differences in capacitance. Other systems use thermal sensors and ultrasound sensors. The process can be described thus: the image of the fingerprint is captured, features are then extracted from the image, and they are stored as templates on a database. Some systems encrypt templates and only manage the compressed images. Although widely used, there are problems associated with fingerprint scanners. Such systems can be undermined in a number of ways:

(1) A person can be forced to press their finger against a scanner by a criminal.[1]

(2) An impostor can use their own fingerprint and challenge the false rejection rate and false acceptance rate. Fingerprints tend to be categorized as 'loops', 'whorls' and 'arches', among other descriptions. If the impostor knows the category of the registered fingerprint and has a pattern similar to that of the registered one, there is a possibility that the scanner may not reject the false fingerprint.

(3) A person may have their finger cut off, so a criminal can use the severed finger to defeat the scanning device.[2] This can be avoided where a device also gauges the temperature of the finger.

(4) The use of an artificial clone of the original fingerprint, where a fingerprint is copied by making a mould of the registered fingerprint. Such copies are cheap to replicate and seem to be effective against many fingerprint devices.[3]

(5) Other attacks will work, depending on the nature of the fingerprint system, such as making a noise or flashing a light against the scanner. Other techniques that can cause the scanner to stop working within the tolerances to the environment include heating up, cooling down, changing the humidity, and hitting or causing the scanner to vibrate.

1 The police in Norway now have the power to force a finger or thumb on to a screen to unlock it, for which see Ingvild Bruce, 'Forced biometric authentication – on a recent amendment in the Norwegian Code of Criminal Procedure' (2017) 14 Digital Evidence and Electronic Signature Law Review 26.
2 See the example of Mr Kumaran, who had the tip of his index finger chopped off by thieves because the security system installed in his S-Class Mercedes Benz utilized the measurements of both the index fingers and thumbs of the owner. The immobilizer system caused the engine in the vehicle to cut out after a few minutes unless the owner pressed their finger or thumb on to the sensor: Jonathan Kent, 'Malaysia car thieves steal finger', BBC News Kuala Lumpur, 31 March 2005, http://news.bbc.co.uk/1/hi/world/asia-pacific/4396831.stm).
3 Tsutomu Matsumoto, Hiroyuki Matsumoto, Koji Yamada and Satoshi Hoshino, 'Impact of artificial "gummy" fingers on fingerprint systems', Paper prepared for Proceedings of SPIE Vol 4677 Optical Security and Counterfeit Deterrence Techniques IV, 24–25 January 2002, http://cryptome.org/gummy.htm; note the comments on tests run by others as a result of this research in Anderson, *Security Engineering*, 15.5; see also David Chek Ling Ngo, Andrew Beng Jin Teoh and Jiankun Hu (eds), *Biometric Security* (Cambridge Scholars Publishing 2015). It is becoming possible to use machine learning to create false fingerprints: Philip Bontrager, Aditi Roy, Julian Togelius, Nasir Memon and Arun Ross, 'DeepMasterPrints: Generating MasterPrints for Dictionary Attacks via Latent Variable Evolution' in *Proceedings of IEEE International Conference on Biometrics: Theory, Applications and Systems (BTAS)* (Los Angeles, USA,October 2018), https://arxiv.org/pdf/1705.07386.pdf.

7.234 Regardless of how easy it may be to defeat fingerprint reading systems, they seem to be most effective when used as a deterrence factor, especially in reducing false claims by people on state benefits.[1]

1 Anderson, *Security Engineering*, 15.9.

7.235 In summary, it is possible to use a measurement of a biometric characteristic to authenticate an individual, but the use of such a measurement can only be effective in a closed system. There are many problems associated with the use of biometric measurements in an open system that have yet to be resolved.

Types of infrastructure for asymmetric cryptographic systems

7.236 There are a number of methods that provide for the signing of electronic documents by means of a digital signature. The discussion in this chapter will focus on the issues relating to the provision of key pairs that are provided and maintained by commercial organizations. However, it is to be noted that key pairs generated and used by individuals using any form of digital signature will also be subject to many of the issues discussed below.

7.237 The type of structure will affect the nature and extent of the legal liability that participants are exposed to. This in turn will determine how participants manage their legal liability. The two categories are:

> (1) A closed environment, where there is only one domain for all communications. This domain can be located in a single place for a single enterprise, or comprise a collection of enterprises, each of which operates under the same set of technical and operational procedures. One example may be a multinational company that operates in several jurisdictions and maintains an intra-company domain across the world. Another example may be a group of end users (both sending and receiving parties) that enter a network with one or more certification authorities by which liability is allocated according to agreed contractual terms between the parties. IdenTrust and Bolero are examples of such networks.[1]

(2) An open environment, where a sender enters into an agreement with a certification authority to provide a certificate for a verification key, and where the receiving parties are not known by either the sending party or certification authority in advance. The role of trusted third parties, also called certification authorities, is to provide certificates that link the identity of the owner to the public key.[2] These bodies can be public or private, licensed or unlicensed. Whether a certification authority is in the hands of a public or private body, and whether is it licensed or unlicensed, it must be trustworthy.

1 IdenTrust: http://www.identrust.com; Bolero: http://www.bolero.net.

2 Certification authorities issue certificates linked to a monetary value to limit liability on the certificate. When submitting documents to a court, it would hardly seem necessary to link the digital signature to the monetary value placed on the certificate, because the content of the document is the item of value, and the court does not rely on the monetary value of the certificate to accept documents electronically. This issue arose in the German case of FG Münster 11 K 990/05 F (Electronically signed statement of claim – On the interpretation of the term 'monetary limitation') before the Finance Court of Münster in Westphalia on 23 March 2006, which dismissed the claim because the corresponding signature certificate contained a monetary limitation of €100. This decision caused some consternation in Germany, for which see Martin Eßer, 'Case note – Germany' (2006) 3 Digital Evidence and Electronic Signature Law Review 111. The Federal Finance Court (Bundesfinanzhof) subsequently heard the appeal to this decision, and it was held that if such a signature contained a monetary restriction that restricts the kind of transactions it can be used for, the restriction does not impair the validity of the signature for the purposes of legal appeals: File number XI R 22/06; BB 2007, 92 (leading record only, otherwise not published); Martin Eßer, 'Case note Germany, 19 February 2009, IV R 97/06' (2009) 6 Digital Evidence and Electronic Signature Law Review 278.

Management of the key and certificate

7.238 The foundation of the public key infrastructure rests on asymmetric cryptography, with a public and private key pair. The public key is usually distributed in the form of a certificate, while the private key is a separate item with its own distinct structure that should be protected from being disclosed to unauthorized third parties when it is transported, used and stored. Once a person subscribes to a digital signature, a range of issues that are referred to as life-cycle management, among other terms, must be addressed. Regardless of the name given to the process, procedures and processes must be in place to create the certificate and key pair, verify the identity of the applicant, distribute the certificate and cancel the certificate at the end of its period of validity or before, should it be compromised. The quality of software, design of the network and management of the security system all affect the way the keys and certificate are managed and stored. This is important, because a digital signature is not computed by the user, but by software. The software on a computer will carry out the task on the instructions of a user, but the software is not in a position to identify whether the instructions come from a legitimate user or the signals from unauthorized malicious software that has successfully embedded itself in the user's computer.

Identifying an applicant

7.239 It should be recalled that an individual could generate their own public and private key pair, using software on their computer. The individual then provides the certification authority with evidence of their identity. The type of evidence and degree of proof will depend on the nature of the type of certifying certificate required. In any event, the identity of the person or entity must be bound to the public key. When confirming the identity of a person or legal entity, a certification authority will tend to be expected to comply with the requirements from a recognized body.[1]

1 For an overview, see Piper and others, *Digital Signatures*, ch 5 and Adams and Lloyd, *Understanding PKI Concepts*, Part II.

7.240 The European Patent Office sets out the rules regarding electronic signatures and authentication in Decision of the President of the EPO dated 26 February 2009 concerning the electronic filing of documents.[1] In *ERICSSON/Electronic filing of appeals T1427/09*,[2] an electronic signature was affixed to the electronic filing of an appeal, but not in the correct name. This was an application for an appeal against the decision of the examining division, sent on 9 March 2009, refusing European patent application 01962282.8. The notice of appeal and the statement setting out the grounds of appeal in this case were filed electronically on 11 May 2009 and 17 June 2009 respectively. The notice of appeal dated 11 May 2009 included the name of Mr Friedrich Kühn, a European Patent Attorney. There was no manuscript signature. The electronic filing of this document was certified by a signature authentication showing that both the sender certificate and the signer certificate underlying the filing were issued to I. Elfving. Mr Kühn provided a manuscript signature to the statement setting out the grounds of appeal dated 17 June 2009. The electronic filing of this statement was certified by a signature authentication showing that both the sender certificate and the signer certificate underlying the filing were issued to R. Ahlund. The reference to a 'sender certificate' and a 'signer certificate' appears to indicate that a digital signature was affixed to the notice. In Decision of the President of the EPO dated 26 February 2009 concerning the electronic filing of documents,[3] article 8(2) provides that the authenticity of documents filed in appeal proceedings are to be confirmed by the use of an enhanced electronic signature of a person authorized to act in the proceedings in question. Neither I. Elfving nor R. Ahlund were authorized to act in the proceedings. As a result, the notice of appeal and the statement setting out the grounds of appeal were deemed not to be signed. The appellant was therefore invited to file signed copies of the documents within two months in accordance with Rule 50(3) of the European Patent Convention.

1 [2009] OJ EPO 182.
2 [2009] 11 WLUK 365, [2010] EPOR 22.
3 [2009] OJ EPO 182.

The certificate

7.241 When the certification authority has verified the identity of the individual or entity to their satisfaction, they will issue a certificate. This is a software record that affirms the connection of a public key to an identified person or corporate entity. It does not follow that a certification authority will undertake this task. There are a number of reasons for this. First, the cost of developing a suitable administrative infrastructure with the relevant expertise will be expensive. It may not, therefore, be possible to justify the cost in commercial terms. Second, there are a number of organizations that already have the relevant expertise, such as banks and credit reference agencies. While the database these organizations use may be imperfect, nevertheless it makes sound economic sense not to replicate a service that already exists. This usually means there is an added layer of contact where a certification authority issues a certificate. First, the registration authority will take steps to verify the identity of the person or legal entity seeking a certificate. Upon confirmation of identity by the registration authority, the certification authority will then issue a certificate. Thus an additional layer of complexity is added to the mix surrounding the link between the person or legal entity seeking a certificate and the subsequent granting of the certificate.

7.242 The next point to ponder is the entity that generates the registration authority's key. Whoever generates the registration authority's key will also be involved in the contractual matrix. In all probability, a contractual relationship will exist between the certification authority and the registration authority, and the contract will provide for the liability and warranties between each entity. Where liability will fall in the event of a dispute will depend on the particular circumstances of the case.

The generation of the key pair belonging to the subscribing party

7.243 It is good practice for the subscribing party to generate their own key pair. Where the subscribing party generates a key pair, there is, theoretically, less of a risk of the private key being compromised. However, many subscribing parties will not have the software to generate their own key pair. This means a third party will be requested to generate a key pair on their behalf. There are two aspects to this that demonstrate a level of vulnerability that may be undesirable. The party generating the key pair will have to be trusted not to compromise the key, and the key pair will be vulnerable to attack or compromise when transported to the user.[1]

1 Adams and Lloyd, *Understanding PKI Concepts*, 92–94; Piper and Murphy, *Cryptography*, 109–110.

Validating the public key

7.244 Either the certification authority or the registration authority should carry out checks that the public key is actually that of the applicant, and that the applicant has the corresponding private key. The check is simple: it needs to be determined whether the subscriber can make a signature that can be verified by the public key. If carried out, such a check can protect both the subscribing party and the authority that undertakes the task, because it can ensure the subscribing party has submitted the correct key and the authority can demonstrate it undertook care to investigate and verify for itself that the public key was that of the applicant, thus making sure it did not certify an incorrect or invalid key.

Distributing certification authority keys

7.245 Individuals or entities wishing to use the public keys of different organizations or individuals may well have to visit each certificate authority to obtain the relevant public key. One mechanism is to have a hierarchy of certification authorities, where higher-level authorities certify low-level authorities. In this case, the prospective user needs to verify the highest level certificate first, usually called a root certification authority, then to check the trail and validity of every authority certificate that leads to the certificate the user wants to trust or use.[1] When a person buys a computer, there are a number of certificates already installed in their browsers. As a result, the user, without realizing it, 'trusts' whoever uploaded the software to the computer to include the appropriate authorities' certificates.[2] The certificates can be deleted and new ones added, if the user knows how to do this. If the user does not update their browser, the certificates will eventually expire and produce sometimes rather obscure error messages when signatures are verified. In addition, unless the user is aware of the complexities of the hierarchy of certification authorities, it is possible for a malicious party to insert a fraudulent certificate into a chain of certificates, and appear to be trusted.[3]

1 Adams and Lloyd, *Understanding PKI Concepts*, 132–145 for a detailed discussion; Piper and others, *Digital Signatures*, 37–38.
2 Mason and Reiniger, '"Trust" between machines?'
3 Niels Ferguson, Bruce Schneier and Tadayoshi Kohno, *Cryptography Engineering: Design Principles and Practical Applications* (Wiley 2010), 18.3.1 for an example of where a software fault had the capacity to undermine the security of an entire system; for further examples, especially of Secure Socket Layer (SSL) certificates, see http://wiki.cacert.org/Risk/History; *Carbanak APT: The Great Bank Robbery* (v 2.1, Kaspersky 2015), https://media.kasperskycontenthub.com/wp-content/uploads/sites/43/2018/03/08064518/Carbanak_APT_eng.pdf.

Revocation of a certificate

7.246 The certificate is used to bind the name of a person or entity to their public key. However, just as with physical seals, there may be many reasons for revoking a certificate (or seal) before the expiry date. In the past, the owner of the seal would put notices up in such public places as churches and markets, warning people not to rely on the seal.[1] In the digital age, such notices are placed over the Internet. The reasons for revoking a certificate include, but are not limited to:

(1) The user is aware that the private key corresponding to the certificate has been lost or compromised.

(2) The certificate holder asks for the certificate to be revoked.

(3) The certification authority revokes a certificate where the holder breaches a term of the agreement.

(4) The certificate was issued in error.

1 As described by Wills J in *The Staple of England v The Governor and Company of the Bank of England* (1888) 21 QBD 160 at 167.

7.247 There are a range of technical solutions to providing public knowledge of certificates that have been revoked, but the most well known is the certificate revocation list.[1] A certification revocation list is a signed data structure that contains a list of those certificates that have been revoked. Where a list exists, there are a number of important issues that must be addressed:

(1) The difference in time between the command to revoke the certificate and the last time the certificate was used.

(2) The reliability of the revocation procedure; in other words, whether it can be relied upon to provide a definitive answer that can be trusted (in addition, the accuracy of the clocks that determine the time the revocation was actually uploaded to the certification revocation list – whether it was the certification authority time or the relying party time, and at whose risk – for instance the relying party deliberately sets their clock at a different time to confuse the evidence).

(3) The number of revocation commands that the revocation system can handle at any one time.[2]

1 Adams and Lloyd, *Understanding PKI Concepts*, 107–126.
2 Niels Ferguson and others, *Cryptography Engineering*, 19.8.

7.248 If a certification authority does not have a revocation list, the person seeking to determine whether to rely on a certificate needs to know how they can establish whether a key has been revoked or compromised.

Expiry of keys

7.249 Certificates have a fixed period of validity, in the same way that a royal seal matrix had, and they expire in due course. One technical question relates to how the life of the key is computed. Ellison and Schneier contend that the key has a 'theft lifetime' as a function of the vulnerability of the subsystem that stores the key. Other factors that should also be taken into account include the threat of physical and network exposure to attacks and how attractive the key is to an attacker.[1] In any event, there are three options available when a certificate expires: (1) no action is taken; (2) the certificate is renewed and the same public key is placed into a new certificate with a new period of validity, (3) a new pair of public and private keys are generated and a new certificate is generated to provide for a certificate update.[2]

1 Ellison and Schneier, 'Ten risks of PKI'.
2 Adams and Lloyd, *Understanding PKI Concepts*, 101–102.

The duties of a user

7.250 There are a number of points that people or organizations that use private keys should be aware of, as set out below.

> (1) Management of private keys
>
> The user must manage their private keys effectively and take measures that are appropriate to prevent the unauthorized use of the keys, and to protect them securely against any other form of attack, such as theft or misuse by a third party that gains access to the system by way of malicious software or other method. This duty is included in some electronic signature legislation.
>
> (2) Storage of private keys after expiry
>
> When deciding whether to use private keys, their use should be carefully monitored, because different types of algorithm are used for different purposes. Thus in the United Kingdom, consideration must be given to the possibility that a private key may be the subject of a s 49 notice under the Regulation of Investigatory Powers Act 2000, and to the safe storage of keys that have expired.
>
> (3) Disposal of equipment with private keys
>
> Particular care should be taken when disposing of the hardware that contains the private keys.

Internal management of a certification authority

7.251 The internal management of a certification authority, which the individual user may not be familiar with, can affect the trust to be placed in the certificates issued. Such issues include, but are not limited to, the following:

> (1) The level and extent of the checks made on employees.
>
> (2) How to verify the identity of the employees who control the keys.
>
> (3) Policies on how keys are stored.

(4) The mechanisms in place to verify that the relevant policies are followed.

(5) Whether the internal management of the certificate system is properly carried out.

(6) The level and extent of any insurance cover may also have a bearing on the suitability of different types of certificate issued.

Barriers to the use of the public key infrastructure

7.252 There are a variety of problems that affect those vendors that offer digital signature services. For instance:

(1) There is no standard in the industry relating to the provision of a directory service. A number of models exist and competing standards are under consideration, as well as the development of proprietary solutions.

(2) Vendors do not implement some functions, and when they are implemented, they may be implemented in a different manner to another vendor. This leads to problems with interoperability between the systems of different vendors.[1]

(3) The performance of the repository service where the certificate revocation lists are held may be a problem. At present there are a limited number of vendors that operate a public key infrastructure, and the numbers of people using those that are available are in the minority. Whether the systems in place are capable of expanding with greater use in the future is open to debate.

(4) The number of people that have any knowledge of public key cryptography is small. The numbers of personnel required are not limited to administrative personnel, but include people in senior positions who can develop the relevant policy documents, such as certification practice statements and interdomain interoperability agreements. The public key infrastructure strategy must also be considered and documented.[2]

1 Paweł Krawczyk, 'When the EU qualified electronic signature becomes an information services preventer' (2010) 7 Digital Evidence and Electronic Signature Law Review 7.

2 Adams and Lloyd, *Understanding PKI Concepts*, ch 25.

7.253 In addition, there are weaknesses that can affect the use of the signature, including the fact the data to be signed can be modified; a personal identity number can be obtained; the person affixing a signature might sign different data than intended; and an attacker can interfere with the software code as it is communicated between component parts. In essence, the signatory has to have trust in the writer of the software that it will work as intended.[1]

1 Adrian Spalka, Armin B. Cremers and Hanno Langweg, 'Trojan horse attacks on software for electronic signatures' (2002) 26 Informatica 191; Hanno Langweg, *Malware Attacks on Electronic Signatures Revisited* (2006), ftp://ftp.cryptopro.ru/pub/TrustedPass/110519/Theory/_hanno_research_gi06p.pdf; 'Attacks on PDF Signatures', https://www.pdf-insecurity.org/signature/signature.html; Fabian Ising and Vladislav Mladenov, *How to Break PDFs: Breaking PDF Encryption and PDF Signatures*, https://media.ccc.de/v/36c3-10832-how_to_break_pdfs; Christian Mainka, Vladislav Mladenov and Simon Rohlmann, 'Shadow attacks: hiding and replacing content in signed PDFs', Network and Distributed Systems Security (NDSS) Symposium 21–25 February 2021, (Virtual), https://www.ndss-symposium.org/wp-content/uploads/ndss2021_1B-4_24117_paper.pdf.

Risks associated with the use of digital signatures

Issuing a certificate to an impostor

7.254 A number of certification authorities have issued false SSL (Secure Socket Layer) certificates that support the security of websites.[1] The issuing of false certificates illustrates the weakness of how certificates are created and issued, and also how important the certificates are in relation to the operation of the Internet. It is not known whether false certificates have been issued that are associated with digital signatures that are used by people or legal entities. The 2001 example of VeriSign issuing two Class 3 Software Publisher certificates incorrectly has been cited in previous editions of *Electronic Signatures in Law* (now incorporated into this text) by way of example.[2] A more significant incident occurred in 2011, when DigiNotar B.V., a Dutch certificate authority owned by VASCO Data Security International, Inc, was placed into voluntary bankruptcy as a result of the discovery that the company had issued several hundred fraudulent certificates.[3] The company also issued certificates for the PKIoverheid program on behalf of the government in the Netherlands. A hacker obtained access to the DigiNotar computer systems and issued an unknown number of false certificates. On 2 September 2011, after being informed of the results of the investigation of the DigiNotar systems by Fox-IT, the Dutch government stopped trusting certificates issued by DigiNotar[4] and regained control over the company's intermediate certificate to manage an orderly transition, replacing untrusted certificates with new ones from another provider.[5] The fact that false certificates have been issued illustrates the weaknesses inherent in the trust placed in software code[6] – because it is software code that controls the entire edifice of everything digital – and it is imperative for lawyers to more fully understand the technical issues by adopting a realistically sceptical approach to understanding the nature of software.[7]

1 For the risks generally, see Piper and others, *Digital Signatures*, ch 4; Ferguson and others, *Cryptography Engineering*, ch 19; Doowon Kim, Bum Jun Kwon and Tudor Dumitras, 'Certified malware: measuring breaches of trust in the windows code-signing PKI', in *CCS '17: Proceedings of the 2017 ACM SIGSAC Conference on Computer and Communications Security* (Association for Computing Machinery 2017), 1435–1448, https://dl.acm.org/doi/10.1145/3133956.3133958. See the CAcert Wiki for a list of fraudulent certificates that have been issued (the aim of this website is to maintain a list of attacks with reasonably authoritative references): http://wiki.cacert.org/Risk/History.

2 The 'VeriSign security alert fraud detected in Authenticode signing certificates', 22 March 2000, is no longer available, nor is Gregory L. Guerin, 'Microsoft, VeriSign, and certification revocation'; the CERT Advisory is also no longer available; for the Microsoft Security Bulletin MS01-017, see https://docs.microsoft.com/en-us/security-updates/securitybulletins/2001/ms01-017; US Department of Energy Computer Incident Advisory Capability, L-062: Erroneous Verisign-Issued Digital Certificates for Microsoft; Ferdinand Gomes, 'Security Alert: Fraudulent Digital Certificates' (SANS Institute 2003), https://www.sans.org/reading-room/whitepapers/certificates/security-alert-fraudulent-digital-certificates-679.

3 The bankruptcy of DigiNotar B.V. is set out in Form 10-K submitted by VASCO Data Security International, Inc. to the US Securities and Exchange Commission on 10 March 2017, https://s24.q4cdn.com/314592314/files/doc_financials/2016/q4/VASCODataSecurityInternational_10K_20170310.pdf.

4 *Factsheet: Fraudulently Issued Security Certificate Discovered*, 5 September 2011, version 2.2 (no longer available); *Black Tulip Report of the Investigation into the DigiNotar Certificate Authority Breach* (Fox-IT BV, PR-110202, 13 August 2012, version 1.0), https://www.researchgate.net/publication/269333601_Black_Tulip_Report_of_the_investigation_into_the_DigiNotar_Certificate_Authority_breach.

5 *Overheid zegt vertrouwen in de certificaten van Diginotar op, Nieuwsbericht* (3 September 2011) (no longer available).
6 Mason and Reiniger, ' "Trust" between machines?'
7 Note the comments by Nico van Eijk in 'The DigiNotar case: internet security is no abstract matter' (2013) 23 Computers & Law 21.

Certificate revocation list

7.255 There are two technical issues that affect the ability to download a suitably recent certificate revocation list: how the certification authority tells you where to obtain the relevant certificate revocation list, and whether your computer carries out the functions you require. There are many different ways to obtain a certificate revocation list, and because there is no standard within the industry, no one method is mandatory.[1] Regardless of the method used, the significant issues for every recipient, which they may not be aware of, are as follows:

> (1) The certificate revocation list should be digitally signed by the certificate authority using its root certificate to prevent a certificate revocation list from being forged.
>
> (2) The certificate revocation list is dated by the certification authority, which means that every certificate revocation list expires.
>
> (3) Every certificate revocation list has a higher sequence than the one issued previously, to prevent forgery.
>
> (4) The person wishing to check a particular certificate must know where to find a suitably recent certificate revocation list.
>
> (5) The certificate revocation list must be able to be obtained by a relying party.
>
> (6) The contents of the certificate revocation list must be authenticated.

1 Adams and Lloyd, *Understanding PKI Concepts*, 107–126.

7.256 Any duty that is to be imposed on a certification authority should take into account the complexity of these issues. If Microsoft designed the software to take a user to the address where the certificate revocation list existed only if the address was provided by the certification authority with the certificate, then establishing the responsibility for passing on this knowledge to a recipient will be a necessary prerequisite to any possible defence by a certification authority. In the VeriSign case, it did not issue Class 3 Software Publisher certificates with an address for the certificate revocation list. This appears to mean that, at the time of the incident, the user of the relevant Microsoft software was not able to retrieve the certificate revocation list of a given certifying certificate issued by VeriSign and Guerin concluded that Microsoft did not have software that had a working revocation infrastructure. Microsoft did not agree with this analysis, and published a rebuttal that is no longer available,[1] to which Guerin rebutted the points raised by Microsoft in his article, which is also no longer available. The report located on the US Department of Energy Computer Incident Advisory Capability website, referring to 'L-062: Erroneous Verisign-Issued Digital Certificates for Microsoft' no longer appears to be available. However, if a vendor of software such as Microsoft did not have a working revocation infrastructure in place in the past, then it could be argued that past certificates can hardly be said to be reliable. This means the evidential weight to be given to a certificate must be considered against these practical problems, otherwise the evidence may be so poor as to make the concept of a certificate irrelevant. Arguably, a court should take such practical issues into account when deciding whether a duty of care should be imposed on a certification authority.

1 Microsoft published 'Response to inaccurate Crypto-Gram article on VeriSign certificates' at https://docs.microsoft.com/en-us/previous-versions/tn-archive/cc751324(v=technet.10)?redirectedfrom=MSDN.

7.257 Depending on how it is used, a public key infrastructure has its uses.[1] However, it is very important to be clear about what a digital signature can and cannot do.

1 Ferguson and others, *Cryptography Engineering*, at 19.9, 'So what is a PKI good for?'. The authors conclude that 'there are few advantages to PKIs'.

What a digital signature is capable of doing

7.258 The uses to which cryptography can be put within a public key infrastructure include demonstrating the integrity of the message and providing for the confidentiality of a document, although using digital signatures within a public key infrastructure will not act to correct human behaviour.[1] A public key infrastructure is only capable of making a link between a public key and a claimed identity. A digital signature only authenticates that a certain private key was used to create the relevant digital signature.

1 Davis, 'Compliance defects in public-key cryptography', paragraph 1; Adams and Lloyd, *Understanding PKI Concepts*, ch 14 for a useful and more detailed discussion; Bernard Reynis and Ugo Bechini, 'European civil law notaries ready to launch international digital deeds' (2007) 4 Digital Evidence and Electronic Signature Law Review 14; Joan Decker, 'The e-notarization initiative, Pennsylvania, USA' (2008) 5 Digital Evidence and Electronic Signature Law Review 73; Timothy S. Reiniger, 'The proposed international e-identity assurance standard for electronic notarization' (2008) 5 Digital Evidence and Electronic Signature Law Review 78; this article is followed by the text of 'The draft International Electronic Notarization Assurance Standard' (2008) 5 Digital Evidence and Electronic Signature Law Review 81.

What no form of electronic signature is capable of doing

7.259 A digital signature can provide for the authenticity of information. It binds key pairs with names. The recipient of a message or document with which a digital signature is associated can confirm the binding of the verification key with the name of the person whose private key has been used. But the recipient cannot determine whether the sending party authorized the use of the digital signature: this is also true of any other form of electronic signature. The private key of a digital signature is protected by a password or passphrase. The most important point to be aware of is this: *the private key of a digital signature is only as good as the password that protects it*. This means that when the password is inserted into a computer to provide access to the private key of a digital signature, it proves any of the following:

> (1) The person to whom the private key was issued might have been the person that inserted this information into the software, and therefore the recipient can infer that the private key of the digital signature is capable of proving that the person to whom the private key was issued was physically at the keyboard at the time of the session; or
>
> (2) a person (perhaps the owner of the private key or her secretary) instructed the software to retain the password information in the computer memory, so that any person (*whether they were sitting in front of the computer or whether they*

obtained control of the computer remotely) who obtains access to the private key can use the password, which in turn does not prove that the person to whom the private key was issued is physically at the keyboard at the time of the session (the recipient of the correspondence is not to know whether it was the person whose key it was, or her secretary, or an impostor), although it can be concluded that the use of the password proved the computer stored this information; or

(3) that a person (whether the owner of the key, their secretary or an imposter) who used the password actually knew the password.

7.260 The recipient relies on one small item to persuade them that the sender is the person whom they claim to be: the password that enables the sender to cause a computer to affix the private key of a digital signature to the document. In reality, reliance rests on the quality of the digital evidence[1] that ties a presumed identity to a presumed act, and in turn the integrity of the password, the software code and the security in place to protect the password and private key. The problems with passwords are so well known that Dan Geer merely stated the obvious in a talk at the UNC Charlotte Cyber Security Symposium in 2013: 'Everyone in this room knows how and why passwords are a problem.'[2]

1 Bearing in mind that computers and networks are not secure, for which see in the legal context, R. R. Jueneman and R. J. Robertson, Jr, 'Biometrics and digital signatures in electronic commerce' (2008) 38 Jurimetrics Journal 427; note also the further technical problems in P. Švéda and V. Matyáš Jr, 'Digital signatures and electronic documents: a cautionary tale revisited' (2004) 5 Upgrade 35.
2 Dan Geer, 'Tradeoffs in cyber security', a talk at the UNC Charlotte Cyber Security Symposium (2013), 9 October 2013, http://geer.tinho.net/geer.uncc.9x13.txt; see also Joseph Bonneau and Ekaterina Shutova, 'Linguistic properties of multi-word passphrases', in Jim Blythe (ed) *Financial Cryptography and Data Security Volume 7398* (Springer 2012), 1–12; Joseph Bonneau, Cormac Herley, Paul C. van Oorschot and Frank Stajano, *The Quest to Replace Passwords: a Framework for Comparative Evaluation of Web Authentication Schemes* (University of Cambridge Computer Laboratory Technical Report 817, 2012), https://www.cl.cam.ac.uk/techreports/UCAM-CL-TR-817.pdf; Dan Goodwin, 'Anatomy of a hack: how crackers ransack passwords like "qeadzcwrsfxv1331"', arstechnica, 21 May 2013, http://arstechnica.com/security/2013/05/how-crackers-make-minced-meat-out-of-your-passwords/; Andrey Belenko and Dmitry Sklyarov, '"Secure password managers" and "military-grade encryption" on smartphones: oh, really?', (n.d.), http://www.elcomsoft.co.uk/WP/BH-EU-2012-WP.pdf.

7.261 It is generally recognized that the password is an exceedingly weak mechanism, as indicated by P. C. van Oorschot and Julie Thorpe:

> The ubiquitous use of textual passwords for user authentication has a well-known weakness: users tend to choose passwords with predictable characteristics, related to how easy they are to remember. This often means passwords which have 'meaning' to the user. Unfortunately, many of these 'higher probability' passwords fall into a tiny subset of the full password space. Although its boundaries vary depending on its exact definition and the probabilities involved, we refer to this smaller subset as the probable password space.
>
> Ideally, users would choose passwords equi-probably from a large subset of the overall password space, to increase the cost of a dictionary attack, i.e., a brute-force guessing attack involving candidate guesses from a prioritized list of 'likely passwords'. If a password scheme's probability distribution is non-uniform, its entropy is reduced. [1]

1 P. C. van Oorschot and Julie Thorpe, 'On the security of graphical password schemes', Technical Report TR-05-11, http://service.scs.carleton.ca/sites/default/files/tr/TR-05-11.pdf. There is a considerable amount of material on this topic, together with the associated subject of memory and the

human need to write down complex passwords (which could have a bearing on whether a human can be made liable for writing down passwords that the vendor or bank insists must be long and difficult to remember), for which see the following short list of more recent references, all of which in turn refer to other sources: Kirsi Helkala and Nils Kalstad Svendsen, 'The security and memorability of passwords generated by using an association element and a personal factor', in Peeter Laund (ed) *Information Security Technology for Applications, Lecture Notes in Computer Science, Volume 7161* (Springer 2012), 114–130; Joseph Bonneau, 'Guessing human-chosen secrets' (University of Cambridge Computer Laboratory Technical Report 819, 2012); Joseph Bonneau and Sören Preibusch, 'The password thicket: technical and market failures in human authentication on the web', *Ninth Workshop on the Economics of Information Security* (WEIS 2010), http://www.jbonneau.com/publications.html and http://preibusch.de/publications/password_market/; Wendy Moncur and Grégory Leplâtre, 'PINs, passwords and human memory' (2009) 6 Digital Evidence and Electronic Signature Law Review 116; Martin A. Conway and Emily A. Holmes, *Guidelines on Memory and the Law: Recommendations from the Scientific Study of Human Memory* (The British Psychological Society Research Board 2008, revised 2010), https://www.academia.edu/2326108/Guidelines_On_Memory_And_The_Law_Recommendations_From_The_Scientific_Study_Of_Human_Memory; Mark L. Howe and Lauren M. Knott, 'The fallibility of memory in judicial processes: lessons from the past and their modern consequences' (2015) 23(5) Memory 633, https://www.ncbi.nlm.nih.gov/pmc/articles/PMC4409058/; Herley and others, 'Passwords' (the authors report that transactions by way of a PIN reverse the burden of proof, but this is not correct).

7.262 The weaknesses are also explored by Petr Švéda and Václav Matyáš Jr.[1] The authors illustrate, at paragraph 3, that when a person has the private key of a digital signature on their computer, the user or owner 'cannot be sure that no further signature processes will be executed in the background when using his private key', and they make the point in paragraph 4 that 'It is very hard to build a system or an application that does not compromise its security. There are a lot of potential problems – e.g., it can be misused, one of the components can fail, as well as the signing application, keys stored on hard disk or in memory are vulnerable'. They go on to indicate, at 4.1:

> At the time of writing, we know of no technology that can make a hardware device fully resistant to penetration by a skilled and determined attacker from a powerful organization. A lot of experts believe that absolute protection will remain unattainable. So the total cost of breaking a hardware device has to be much more than the value of stored and protected information.

1 Švéda and Matyáš, 'Digital signatures and electronic documents'; Peter A. Loscocco, Stephen D. Smalley, Patrick A. Muckelbauer, Ruth C. Taylor, S. Jeff Turner and John F. Farrell, 'The inevitability of failure: the flawed assumption of security in modern computing environments', in *21st National Information Systems Security Conference: Building the Information Security Bridge to the 21st Century* (National Institute of Standards and Technology 1998), 303–314, https://babel.hathitrust.org/cgi/pt?id=coo.31924083977813&view=1up&seq=5 – the individual paper is available at https://www.cs.utah.edu/flux/fluke/html/inevit-abs.html; Dan Goodin, 'Once seen as bulletproof, 11 million+ Ashley Madison passwords already cracked', arstechnica, 10 September 2015, https://arstechnica.com/information-technology/2015/09/once-seen-as-bulletproof-11-million-ashley-madison-passwords-already-cracked/.

7.263 Smart cards are also vulnerable, as the authors point out at 4.2 (reference omitted):[1]

> A smart card is a simple and inexpensive security module. It consists of multiple components combined with a single chip that uses external power supply and clock. When a card is used as a personalized trusted device it generates a key pair locally, stores the private key locally, and only publishes the corresponding public key. The biggest problem with smart cards is that they lack a direct

> communication channel to the user. None of current available smart cards has a really trustworthy user interface. The user is completely dependent on potentially untrusted devices to get some information about his transactions. For example if the personal computer to which the smart card has been connected is compromised, it might ask the smart card to sign a completely different message to that which the user sees.
>
> Many successful attacks have occurred because smart cards were exposed to more sophisticated attackers than designers anticipated ... The smart card without trustworthy user interface is a typical example of an architectural error. Many attacks are also possible due to protocol and application programming interface failures.

1 Klaus Schmeh, *Cryptography and Public Key Infrastructure on the Internet* (Wiley 2001), has a different view, although acknowledges attacks are possible (15.2.3).

7.264 In summary, it is necessary to ensure the person receiving data signed with the private key of a digital signature understands the difference between trusting the signature and trusting the owner of the signature.

The weakest link

7.265 Although this chapter has emphasized the reliance placed upon the activities of certification authorities and other participants in the public key infrastructure (registration authorities, directory services listing public keys, certification revocation list services, time stamping, to name but a few), comparatively little discussion has been given to the weakest link in the chain of a digital signature. If Bob wants Alice to use a digital signature to authenticate her messages, he has to persuade Alice that it is essential that when he receives a message or document from her, he can be completely assured, whether he decides to become a verifying party or not, that it was Alice, and only Alice, who caused the digital signature to be affixed to the document or message. He therefore has to persuade Alice that she must take good care of her private key, such that she accepts the risk of being held responsible for unauthorized use of it by others. If Alice asks, not without reason, 'What's in it for me?', there seems to be no answer. Whether Bob decides to undertake the sometimes gargantuan task of carrying out the verification procedure or not, if he cannot satisfy himself that Alice kept her private key absolutely safe, he cannot be sure that Alice affixed the digital signature to the message. So he will try to insist that Alice carries the blame anyway.

7.266 In any event, the recipient of a digital signature can be certain that:

> The person (whomsoever they might be) who keyed in the password that protects the private key of the digital signature, knew the password.

7.267 Or in the alternative, the recipient of a digital signature can be certain that:

> The person who caused the private key to be attached to an email or document called up the private key and clicked on the 'password' icon (they did not need to know the password) because the software was instructed to remember the password.

7.268 There seems to be an unquestioning reliance on the use of digital signatures that has no bearing on the risks associated with the use of the technology. This reliance is also manifest in the assumption made that a digital signature proves the person whose signature it is, and was the person that caused the computer to affix the signature to the document, as in the Portuguese case of (Evora) Ac. RE 13-12-2005 (R.982/2005), in which an email was sent with a digital signature attached. In this instance, it was determined that the digital signature served to authenticate the document, and guaranteed the identity of the sender and the integrity of the message. While a digital signature is capable of identifying the sender, it cannot guarantee that the sender caused the digital signature to be affixed to the message. The most important point to be aware of is this: the private key of a digital signature is only as good as the password that protects it and any additional mechanism used to protect the private key, as Richard E. Smith has pointed out:

> Public key cryptography succeeds only as long as a private key's owner can keep it under control – always available when needed but never disclosed to anyone else. [1]

1 Richard E. Smith, *Authentication: From Passwords to Public Keys* (Addison-Wesley 2002), 431.

7.269 It will be argued by some that the private key to a digital signature can be secured by a combination of a password and the biometric measurement of a fingerprint, for instance. This 'solution' relies on the technology (secret) of the biometric scanner that is chosen to fulfil this role, and does not take into account the various methods by which the mechanism can be compromised.

7.270 A digital signature is not linked to the person creating it: the unique link is made with the private key, not the user. Nobody is capable of committing a private key to memory[1] because it is far too complicated, which is why passwords are used to protect the key. Below is an example of a private key in TXT format (2048 bits), by way of example:

privateExponent:

5c:a2:77:1b:6a:45:0c:af:e4:aa:c3:91:b2:7e:ab:ea:ec:27:14:25:6a:2a:67:d8:c
e:25:1a:e4:09:11:f2:31:10:b1:43:c9:dd:d7:a7:13:d7:14:21:91:c5:15:27:ff:cd
:8d:64:d5:e5:3e:64:48:a2:95:ec:d9:3f:75:8e:22:d9:11:42:90:c3:e9:fb:de:3d:
ba:69:d4:db:b5:eb:84:68:f1:92:ad:36:71:04:b4:4a:f6:03:2f:5f:6c:ac:b0:ed:30
:5a:89:94:c8:82:ea:55:eb:62:e8:09:0b:d0:d2:40:b8:a7:2e:70:71:aa:59:58:14:2
1:ae:20:d6:16:84:d2:29:5c:9b:a7:56:50:3a:10:0b:c6:70:2b:97:dd:f8:fa:73:74:2
2:5f:d6:ce:0d:75:45:8a:61:5d:86:25:cb:ad:19:06:fe:8e:a4:f9:0d:35:2a:02:04:9
3:ec:df:0c:db:ca:f0:8c:ae:a7:54:c2:37:a1:11:7b:9f:40:54:a4:fd:31:a4:f9:ee:60:3
c:8f:3b:0e:b1:e2:10:6d:f0:36:50:63:27:6e:cc:85:c1:5d:10:4a:36:23:5d:bf:c7:ee
:9b:af:3f:e6:49:47:c6:9e:b8:00:b0:d9:d2:de:07:46:43:14:2f:de:7c:51:57:a5:8d
:4b:13:04:54:25:3b:d5[2]

1 'Guidelines on memory and the law recommendations from the scientific study of human memory'; Howe and Knott, 'The fallibility of memory in judicial processes'.

2 This example is from Symeon (Simos) Xenitellis, 'The open-source PKI book: a guide to PKIs and open-source implementations' and quoted under GNU Free Documentation License, Version 1.3, 3 November 2008, published by the Free Software Foundation: http://ospkibook.sourceforge.net/docs/OSPKI-2.4.7/OSPKI-html/sample-key-components.htm. For an example of a private key in PEM format, see http://ospkibook.sourceforge.net/docs/OSPKI-2.4.7/OSPKI-html/sample-priv-key.htm. I am grateful to Arnis Paršovs and Alan Liddle for explaining that it is only necessary to memorize this part.

7.271 This means that private keys are retained on a computer, disk or smart card. It is not possible to create an electronic signature that can be uniquely linked to the signatory, and it remains the case that passwords have to be relied upon to secure the private key of a digital signature.

The burden of managing the private key

7.272 The user of a digital signature is expected to keep their private key secure. Failure to do so will mean a mischievous member of staff or a malicious third party can append a digital signature to a document or message for nefarious purposes. The management of the private key acts to underpin the efficacy of a digital signature. Some of the issues to which a recipient must give consideration include those set out below.

Bypassing passwords

7.273 Depending on the nature of the application software on any given computer or system, where a user has set their security setting to 'High' they will have to enter their password every time they wish to enter their private key to affix the private key of a digital signature to a document or message. Where the security setting is set to the default, 'Low', the messages will be automatically signed without any further intervention by the user. Given this scenario, any person with access to a computer or device containing a digital signature in a powered-up state will be able to send messages or documents with a digital signature affixed.

7.274 A busy person might find it inconvenient to enter their password every time they wish to use their private key to affix a digital signature to a document or message. An alternative is for the user to retain their private key in memory during the login session. If a user keeps the private key in memory, this exposes the key to being stolen. Examples include leaving the computer unattended, thus permitting a third party to take sufficient action to steal the key. Alternatively, if the private key is on a laptop computer and the laptop computer is stolen, it may be possible for the thief to obtain access to the private key. Further, malicious software has been developed to steal passwords and private keys.[1] Finally, even if the private key is stored on an encrypted smart card, it must be used with a computer to sign a message or document, and the computer may have been maliciously programmed to sign a document or message other than the one the user intends to sign.[2]

1 Swati Khandelwal, 'Symantec API flaws reportedly let attackers steal private SSL keys and certificates', The Hacker News, 28 March 2017, https://thehackernews.com/2017/03/symantec-ssl-certificates.html; 'How cybercrime exploits digital certificates', 28 July 2014, https://resources.infosecinstitute.com/cybercrime-exploits-digital-certificates/.

2 See Young and Yung, *Malicious Cryptography* for further examples of how the technology can be used for malicious purposes; note the discussion on this issue by Markus Rückert and Dominique Schröder, 'Security of verifiably encrypted signatures', in *Pairing-Based Cryptography – Pairing 2009, Lecture Notes In Computer Science Volume 5671* (Springer 2009), 17–34.

Quality of passwords

7.275 There are a number of issues surrounding the question of passwords, as noted above, and they are well documented. The entire edifice of the public key infrastructure and the security of the private key rests to a very large extent on the quality of the password used to protect it, and attempts are made to replace passwords.[1] Most of us prefer to use passwords that are easy to remember, which in turn makes a password easy to guess and vulnerable to attack. If the user does not have effective control over the quality of the passwords used,[2] the system will be vulnerable to an offline guessing attack.[3]

1 Bonneau and others, *The Quest to Replace Passwords.*
2 Kresimir Solic, Hrvoje Ocevcic and Damir Blazevic, 'Survey on password quality and confidentiality' (2015) 56 Automatika 69.
3 Davis, 'Compliance defects in public-key cryptography'; Heiko Roßnagel and Jan Zibuschka, 'Integrating qualified electronic signatures with password legacy systems' (2007) 4 Digital Evidence and Electronic Signature Law Review 7.

7.276 If a recipient of a digital signature intends to rely on the purported authority of the signature, they have a range of options:

(1) To rely on the signature without taking any affirmative action. In some jurisdictions, the electronic signature legislation lays down a duty on the recipient to verify the signature, although the duty is invariably set at a high level of generality. It is conceivable that judges will take into account the arrangements between the sender and recipient before reaching a conclusive judgment. For instance, if a recipient relied on a digital signature attached to a high-value contract, a court may well consider it is appropriate in the circumstances that a recipient takes reasonable steps to authenticate and verify the digital signature, and to ensure the sending party duly authorized it.

(2) To rely on the signature after undertaking steps to verify and authenticate the various certificates in the chain (that is, assuming the recipient has a trusted copy of the public key of the Root Certification Authority), and checking the authenticity and reliability of any time stamps (the time the time stamp is generated should not be independent of the time the digital signature data is generated),[1] thus becoming a verifying party. Should a dispute occur, one of the questions that will need to be addressed is to what extent the actions taken by the verifying party were adequate in the circumstances of the case, including their state of knowledge at the time.

(3) Ignore the infrastructure surrounding the use of the digital signature, and require the sending party to confirm their intentions by an alternative method, or to confirm, using another medium (such as letter, facsimile transmission or telephone) that the communication was sent by them.

1 Jeff Stapleton, Paul Doyle and Steven Teppler, 'The digital signature paradox' (an updated version of a paper of the same name that was originally published in the *Proceedings of the 2005 IEEE Workshop on Information Assurance and Security*), http://docplayer.net/10585603-The-digital-signature-paradox.html.

7.277 As a result of the foregoing discussion, it becomes clear that public key cryptography is more suitable for server-to-server security, rather than for use on a desktop.

Evidence and digital signatures

7.278 Should an electronic signature become the subject of a dispute, the normal considerations will apply regarding the submission of evidence into legal proceedings, including any rules relating to the authentication of the evidence, the weight to be given to the evidence and whether it is necessary to help the adjudicator in reaching a decision by providing for expert witnesses. The following discussion aims to alert the reader to some of the issues that might arise in relation to digital signatures in particular.

The evidence forming a digital signature

7.279 A certificate is issued with a digital signature,[1] which is a signed data structure that binds a public key to an identity. This certificate will purport to bind the public key to the information contained in the certificate. The subscribing party provides some of the information contained in the certificate, which may or may not be verified by the certification authority, and the certification authority is responsible for the remaining information. The subscriber will have a pair of keys, private and public. The key pairs may be generated by the keying material available to the subscribing party in their computer, by a registration authority, by the certification authority or by a trusted third party key generation facility.

1 The use of the word 'certificate' is shorthand for an individual identity certificate.

7.280 Individuals can create their own private and public key pairs, or key-generating organizations can undertake this task. The creation and certification processes are distinct. The same issues discussed here will apply to keys not certified by a third party, with the added complication that the level of authenticity may be lower because proving who the public key belonged to might be more difficult for any person wishing to rely on an uncertified key. How the key pair is generated may also be problematic if there is evidence that the software used to generate key pairs has flaws, such as being liable to generate weak keys.

7.281 A recipient can go through a list of checks to assure themselves that the certificate links the sending party to the document or message that was signed. To trust the certificate sent by Alice, Bob must check all of the certificates back to the root or foundation certificate. Only by checking back to the foundation certificate can Bob determine whether he can trust the public key in Alice's certificate in relation to the purpose for which he will use it. The certificate attached to the message or document and the corresponding public key can only be trusted if every certificate and their corresponding keys in the path from the foundation key to Alice's key can be trusted. There are two phases to this exercise:

> (1) Constructing the path, which requires Bob to bring together all the relevant certificates to form a complete path. This process may be complicated and time-consuming, because there may be a number of certification authorities in the chain, all of which have cross-certified their respective certificates. The assumption is that Bob can retrieve all of the certificates he needs to scrutinize them and put the chain of certificates together in a logical sequence. Bob must also check the issuing certificate of each of the certification authorities in the chain against a certificate revocation list.
>
> (2) Validating the path, where Bob must decide whether the path between each certificate is valid. This involves undertaking the mathematical computation to verify each digital signature; checking the validity period of each certificate for date of expiry; making sure each certificate has not been revoked, by checking the relevant certification revocation list; and then considering other issues such as the policies that apply to the certificate, any restrictions on the use of the key and if there are any other constraints on the use of the certificate.[1]

1 Adams and Lloyd, *Understanding PKI Concepts, Standards, and Deployment Considerations*, 147–149.

7.282 Once Bob has checked and validated the certificates and certificate path, he must then carry out the following checks:

> (1) Establishing the integrity of the certificate by ensuring the digital signature on the certificate is properly verified.
>
> (2) Checking the certificate validity period to ensure it is valid on the date and the time Bob intends to rely on it.
>
> (3) Checking the certificate has not been revoked. There are various methods to implement a certificate revocation list with a number of variations, including, but not limited to, certificate revocation lists (which is a signed data structure that contains a list of revoked certificates) and certification authority revocation lists, used to revoke the public key certificates of certification authorities and online certificate status protocol, which is a protocol that permits Bob to receive a response to his request for information.
>
> (4) Checking Alice has used the certificate in accordance with the constraints set out in the certificate, including the relevant agreements and certification policies.

7.283 As a result, when determining the nature of the evidence, it is necessary to ascertain the source of the information and the uses to which the relevant document is put. It is worth recalling the nature of the promise made to a receiving party when a sending party affixes a digital signature to a document or message:

> Bob receives a message digitally signed by Alice with Alice's digital signature certificate attached. Alice's public key is incorporated into the certificate. The certificate purports to bind Alice's name with her public key, and in turn the certificate purports to assure Bob that the message was signed using a key verifiable by a key certified in a certificate issued to Alice.

7.284 The nature of this promise is well illustrated by the following comment from the Select Committee on Trade and Industry, Seventh Report, House of Commons Session 1998–99, paragraph 12:

> Written signatures are tightly associated with people and weakly associated with documents, whilst digital signatures are tightly bound to documents and weakly bound to individuals (or identities).

7.285 The crucial point to remember is that a digital signature does not, of itself, provide evidence that the sending party actually caused the private key of the digital signature to be affixed to the message or document. This proposition is relevant in respect of any form of electronic signature. Where a certification authority is involved within the framework of a public key infrastructure, all the certification authority can do is give evidence about how the certificate was formed, where the information was obtained, and if they verified the information, what methods were used to verify the information. Thus a certification authority can give evidence as to the formation of the certificate, but the certificate cannot be adduced as evidence of the truth of the facts stated within it.

'Non-repudiation'

7.286 By way of an introduction, the term 'non-repudiation' has become part of the vocabulary of digital signatures. This is a dangerous expression, and one that lawyers should take particular care in understanding. It does not mean the system for non-repudiation is perfect, although some technical authors (and lawyers and academics[1]) continue to assert that digital signatures are better than they actually are. By way of example, Klaus Schmeh incorrectly states that:

> The purpose of a digital signature is to ensure non-repudiation. This means that Alice cannot contest her completed signature in retrospect. When all is said and done, a digital signature is an excellent way of meeting this requirement.[2]

1 'Data encryption' (The Parliamentary Office of Science and Technology, no. 270, October 2006), incorrectly states at 2 that digital signatures 'can also be used for non-repudiation: if a party digitally signs an electronic document, they cannot later deny this'; Rouhshi Low and Ernest Foo, 'The susceptibility of digital signatures to fraud in the National Electronic Conveyancing System: an analysis' (2009) 17 Australian Property Law Journal 303 incorrectly comments, at 307, that 'When the recipient receives the coded summary and the certificate, the recipient can use the CA's public key to verify the CA's signature on the certificate. If that is successful, the recipient can have confidence that the sender's public key is what it purports to be, that is, the sender's public key actually did come from the sender'; Raymond Wacks, *Privacy: A Very Short Introduction* (Oxford University Press 2010) incorrectly states at 25–26 that 'The advantage of a public key system is that if you are able to decrypt the message, you know that it could only have been created by the sender'; Michael Bromby, 'Identification, trust and privacy: how biometrics can aid certification of digital signatures' (2010) 24 International Review of Law, Computers & Technology 133 incorrectly states at 135: 'Parties involved in such an electronic communication cannot deny their involvement subsequently'; Arne Tauber, Peter Kustor and Bernhard Karning, 'Cross-border certified electronic mailing: a European perspective' (2013) 29 Computer Law & Security Review 28, in which the authors fail to indicate the issues relating to 'non-repudiation'.

2 Schmeh, *Cryptography and Public Key Infrastructure*, 16.1.1.

7.287 Francisco Jordan-Fernádez and Jordi Buch i Tarrats assert:

> The most important benefit electronic signatures brings to e-commerce and all electronic transactional systems is that they cannot be repudiated. This service provides evidentiary value that proves that the data has been created by a specific entity and has not been altered since the date of its creation, thereby guaranteeing its irrefutability.[1]

1 'Electronic signature today: a manufacturer's viewpoint' (2004) 5 Upgrade 23, 24. See also an early paper by Roger Clarke, 'Conventional public key infrastructure: an artefact ill-fitted to the needs of the information society', prepared for submission to the 'IS in the Information Society' track of the European Conference on Information Systems (ECIS 2001), Bled, Slovenia, 27–29 June 2001, http://www.rogerclarke.com/II/PKIMisFit.html.

7.288 Professor Sorge states:

> The private key, which is to be kept secret, is used by the signatory to sign messages; signatures can be verified with the corresponding public key. Successful verification of a digital signature guarantees integrity and authenticity of the corresponding message. Non-repudiation is also achieved, i.e. it can be proven that the message was signed by the signatory.[1]

1 Christoph Sorge, 'The legal classification of identity-based signatures' (2014) 30 Computer Law & Security Review 126, 126.

7.289 None of these statements is correct.

7.290 When engineers use the term non-repudiation in an engineering sense, they mean that there is a degree of probability or certainty that the protocol can demonstrate that one item of software communicated with another item of software, or to put it another way, 'Nonrepudiation provides proof of the integrity and origin of data that can be verified by a third party'.[1] Many technicians assert that non-repudiation is a fact: that is, once the software proves that a message or document was sent and received, it follows that a human being caused the message to be sent. Such an assertion is not logical and is misleading. This reasoning is often extended from the engineering domain into the legal domain, by asserting that if the system can demonstrate that one item of software communicated with another item of software, that is, that digital data comprising a message or document was sent or received, it is for the purported sender to demonstrate that they caused it to be sent – or to prove they did not cause it to be sent. The purpose of the concept is to bind users to specific actions in such a way that if they deny taking the action, they either demonstrate an intention to deceive, or they have been negligent in failing to secure the use of their private key adequately. The use of the term is inherently misleading. The logic is as follows:

> It is proven that certain items of software communicated, each with the other. (A message was sent from Alice's computer to Bob's computer, and Alice's private key was affixed to the communication.)
>
> It follows that the purported sender caused the software to communicate. (Ergo, Alice affixed the private key to the message.)

1 United States General Accounting Office, Report to the Chairman, Subcommittee on Government Efficiency, Financial Management and Intergovernmental Relations, Committee on Government Reform, House of Representatives, 'Information security: advances and remaining challenges to adoption of public key infrastructure technology', GAO-01-277, 2001, 18.

7.291 The purpose of the term non-repudiation is to provide for causation, which it cannot. It is generally assumed that non-repudiation has a legal effect: that is, a person cannot deny causing the software to send a message or document. However, a signature can be challenged for a number of reasons. The most pertinent is where the purported sender claims that they did not cause the electronic signature to be affixed to the message or document, as in the case of Dara O'Reilly, whose digital signature was used on two occasions in India in a complex property transaction. He denied using the digital signature.[1] In effect, there is a claim that the signature is a forgery. In such circumstances, the fact that a message or document was sent might not be at issue. The dispute often turns on whether the sender caused the signature to be affixed to the message or document.[2] In such instances, it is for the party relying on the signature to prove the message or document was sent, and that the purported sender caused their electronic signature to be affixed.

1 Dearbhail McDonald, 'Sean Quinn aide at centre of mystery over $90m asset', *Irish Independent*, 23 August 2012, http://www.independent.ie/business/irish/sean-quinn-aide-at-centre-of-mystery-over-90m-asset-26889961.html.

2 For the cases where private keys were used without the authority or authorization of the person to whom the private key was linked, see the banking cases from the Russian Federation: Olga I. Kudryavtseva, 'Russia', in Stephen Mason (ed), *International Electronic Evidence* (British Institute of International and Comparative Law 2008); Olga I. Kudryavtseva, 'The use of electronic digital signatures in banking relationships in the Russian Federation' (2008) 5 Digital Evidence and Electronic

Signature Law Review 51; Resolution of the Federal Arbitration Court of Moscow Region of 5 November 2003 N КГ-А 40/8531-03-П(2008) 5 Digital Evidence and Electronic Signature Law Review 149; Alex Dolzhich, 'Digital evidence and e-signature in the Russian Federation: a change in trend' (2009) 6 Digital Evidence and Electronic Signature Law Review 181.

7.292 Other examples where the signature may be in dispute are where the sender accepts the message or document was sent with an electronic signature, but the signature was obtained as a result of unconscionable conduct by a party to a transaction, fraud instigated by a third party or undue influence exerted by a third party, among other reasons recognized in law. It will be for the adjudicator to determine whether a particular argument is credible. That the sender caused the signature to be affixed to a message or document may not be in issue.

7.293 It is important to ensure that the technical meaning of non-repudiation does not override the need to restrain the meaning within a legal context. Where engineers use the term, it should not be understood that they are using it in a legal context, despite a general misunderstanding in the view of some engineers that the term should have a legal meaning. Even where the evidence demonstrates that a message or document was sent or received with an electronic signature affixed, it does not follow that the message was sent by the person whose username or password (or both username and password) was used at the material time, nor that it was signed by them. Carl Ellison of Intel Laboratories in his paper 'Improvements on conventional PKI wisdom' has dismissed these arguments by technicians about non-repudiation.[1] The comments in paragraph 3.4.3 entitled 'Not Achievable' demonstrate the vacuity of the link between evidence that software has communicated with software, and the assertion that such evidence is therefore proof that a particular person caused a machine to undertake a particular action:

> The main problem with the theory of non-repudiation is that it is not technically achievable. That is, the intention is to bind a human being to a digitally signed document. With a holographic signature on a paper document, the human's hand came in contact with the paper of the document. With a digital signature there is machinery between the human and the signed document: at least a keyboard, software (to display the document and to drive the signature process) and a key storage and use facility (e.g., a smart card).
>
> No one has demonstrated, in the normal computer for home or office use, the prevention of introduction of hostile software. To the contrary, we have seen a steady increase in such incursions over the years.
>
> There are secure facilities for key storage and use, but no mechanism that an average home or small business user would choose to buy has been proved secure.
>
> Meanwhile, computers are not restricted to isolated rooms with card access entry, raised floors, guards outside the glass walls, etc., that they might have been in the 1970s when much of this thinking about public key cryptography had its nascence. Computers are not only everywhere; they are unprotected to a continually increasing degree. Therefore, even if the computer has no hostile software and its private key is kept in a truly secure facility, access to the keyboard of that computer is not limited to the person certified to be associated with that private key.
>
> What might make this process of non-repudiation work would be hardware that would serve as a witness to a signature, providing tamper-proof evidence of

> the actions of a human being (e.g., through videotape), of what that human was reading and of the human's positive action to assent to the displayed document. Such a log of human behavior could then be presented in court to prove the claim of non-repudiation.
>
> Of course, if such hardware were available, then we would not need digital signatures, much less the assumption of non-repudiation on digital signatures.

1 First Annual PKI Research Workshop – April 2002, https://users.ece.cmu.edu/~adrian/731-sp04/readings/ellison-PKI-wisdom.pdf.

7.294 This point is also considered in a slightly different way by Niels Ferguson, Bruce Schneier and Tadayoshi Kohno:

> In theory, a PKI should provide you with nonrepudiation. Once Alice has signed a message with her key, she should not be able to later deny that she signed the message. A key server system can never provide this; the central server has access to the same key that Alice uses and can therefore forge an arbitrary message to make it look as if Alice sent it. In real life, nonrepudiation doesn't work because people cannot store their secret keys sufficiently well. If Alice wants to deny that she signed a message, she is simply going to claim that a virus infected her machine and stole her private key. [1]

1 Ferguson and others, *Cryptography Engineering*, 19.9, bullet point 3.

7.295 In 2000, Carl Ellison and Bruce Schneier wrote on the same topic:

> Alice's digital signature does not prove that Alice signed the message, only that her private key did. When writing about non-repudiation, cryptographic theorists often ignore a messy detail that lies between Alice and her key: her computer. If her computer were appropriately infected, the malicious code could use her key to sign documents without her knowledge or permission. Even if she needed to give explicit approval for each signature (for example, via a fingerprint scanner), the malicious code could wait until she approved a signature and sign its own message instead of hers. If the private key is not in tamper-resistant hardware, the malicious code can steal the key as soon as it's used.
>
> While it's legitimate to ignore such details in cryptographic research literature, it is just plain wrong to assume that real computer systems implement the theoretical ideal. Our computers may contain viruses. They may be accessible to passers-by who could plant malicious code or manually sign messages with our keys. Should we then need to deny some signature, we would have the burden of proving the negative – that we didn't make the signature in question against the presumption that we did. [1]

1 Carl Ellison and Bruce Schneier, 'Risks of PKI: e-commerce' (2000) 43 Communications of the ACM 152.

7.296 Where the party whose private key is used denies they caused the private key to be affixed to the data, it is for the party relying on the signature to prove the signing party caused the private key to sign the data. The burden of proof will depend on the pleadings and what presumptions, if any, apply.

7.297 The term 'cryptographic non-repudiation' means being able to prove that where a digital signature verifies a public key, then the associated private key made that signature: it does not prove that the person whose private key is used caused the private key to make the signature.[1] However, non-repudiation is of no benefit without a secure time-stamping service to demonstrate that a particular event occurred at a given time and date, or that a specific item of data existed before a specific date. This technical meaning of the term has begun to be used in a legal sense by vendors of the public key infrastructure, which in turn has tended to confuse legislators.[2]

1 Adams and Lloyd, *Understanding PKI Concepts*, 32–33, 51–53; Dr Catharina Candolin, a Policy advisor at NATO HQ (Emerging Security Challenges Division/Cyber Defence), demonstrated confusion in her PhD dissertation, 'Securing military decision making in a network-centric environment' (TKK Dissertations 20 Helsinki University of Technology, 20 December 2005), where, at 59 and 104, it is stated that the sender cannot deny having sent the packet, and at 77, the technical meaning of non-repudiation is correctly indicated: 'that is, a malicious node cannot deny having created the IP packets.'
2 Bruce Schneier, *Secrets & Lies: Digital Security in a Networked World* (Wiley 2000), 235, and Adrian McCullagh and William Caelli, 'Non-repudiation in the digital environment', https://firstmonday.org/ojs/index.php/fm/article/view/778/687.

Certifying certificates

7.298 Regardless of the technical meaning of the term 'non-repudiation', there are a number of problems that affect the reliability of systems that are used to affix digital signatures to an electronic communication:

(1) A confusing design on the screen, which can lead a user to activate the signing function without knowing the significance others attach to the signature.

(2) The software application may be set up to send a receipt, but this does not necessarily indicate to the recipient that the sender sent the receipt. This also raises the question as to whether the receipt is authentic.

(3) A design flaw in the public key infrastructure.

(4) The open nature of the Internet, which means hackers could insert malicious software into computers that can be designed to steal private keys or replay the keystrokes of the user, thereby obtaining the passwords used to obtain access to a private key.

7.299 The general rule with respect to signed documents is this: a person is normally bound by their signature to a document, even if they fail to read and understand the content. Where a party relies on a signed document and wishes to enforce it against the signing party, the relying party must prove the signature is that of the signing party, or that the signing party authorized the document. This is so where the signing party claims they did not sign the document, or if they did sign the document, that they did so under duress or because of the fraud of a third party. It is not for the signing party to prove that they did not authorize the document or sign it.

7.300 A person has a defence where they have been misled into signing a document that is essentially different to that which they intended to sign, a state of affairs that has usually, but not always, been induced by a fraud perpetrated upon the party signing the document.[1] However, this does not mean that a person should fail to exercise care when they affix their signature to a document in the absence of a fundamental mistake as to the content of the document. This occurred in *Saunders v Anglia Building Society*,[2] where Mrs Gallie signed what she understood was a deed of gift of her house to her nephew, but it was, in fact, a deed of assignment to a third party. Mrs Gallie raised the defence that she thought the effect of the document was to give her house to her nephew, but in fact it assigned her rights to a fraudulent third party. The members of the House of Lords agreed that the identity of the person to whom the house was assigned did not make the deed totally different in character to the document Mrs Gallie intended to sign, and her defence failed. Lord Hodson offered the following observations at 1019(E) respecting the use of a signature:

> Want of care on the part of the person who signs a document which he afterwards seeks to disown is relevant. The burden of proving non est factum is on the party disowning his signature; this includes proof that he or she took care. There is no burden on the opposite party to prove want of care. The word 'negligence' in this connection does not involve the proposition that want of care is irrelevant unless there can be found a specific duty to the opposite party to take care.

1 In *United Dominions Trust Ltd v Western* [1976] QB 513, [1976] 2 WLR 64, [1975] 3 All ER 1017, [1975] 10 WLUK 88, (1975) 119 SJ 792, Times, 28 October 1975, [1976] CLY 339 a party signed a blank hire-purchase proposal form, and the dealer inserted incorrect figures before sending it to the finance company.

2 [1971] AC 1004, [1970] 3 WLR 1078, [1970] 3 All ER 961, [1970] 11 WLUK 45, (1971) 22 P & CR 300, (1970) 114 SJ 885, Times, 10 November 1970, [1971] CLY 1805.

7.301 In his judgment, Viscount Dilhorne agreed with the comments made by Lord Hodson, and commented, at 1023(E):

> In every case the person who signs the document must exercise reasonable care, and what amounts to reasonable care will depend on the circumstances of the case and the nature of the document which it is thought is being signed. It is reasonable to expect that more care should be exercised if the document is thought to be of an important character than if it is not.

The burden of proof

7.302 A person has total control over the use of their manuscript signature, and the legal rules that apply to manuscript signatures reflect this physical reality. However, once the accepted form of the signature changes, it may be considered appropriate, depending on the nature of the transaction, for the legal rules that apply to the new form of signature to reflect the different range of risks associated with the new manifestation of signature. Consider the example of Charles Goodman, the solicitor who used a rubber stamp to sign a letter that accompanied his bill of costs.[1] Although the control of the rubber stamp was not the subject of judicial comment, Evershed MR noted at 554, that Mr Goodman 'kept the stamp locked up in his own room so as to be available only for his own use'. Although neither Mr Goodman's actions nor the comment by Evershed MR make an explicit point about taking reasonable care of the rubber stamp, nevertheless the implication that the rubber stamp should be kept safe is obvious. It is clear that Mr Goodman took reasonable care to ensure only he had access to the rubber stamp, and the observation by Evershed MR implied that this made the use of the rubber stamp acceptable as a method of authenticating documents. If Evershed MR had considered the matter further, he might have reached the conclusion that there is a reasonable expectation in circumstances where a person decides to use a rubber stamp as a form of signature that they can be expected, as a rule of law, to provide for the security of the use of the signature, and to take appropriate steps to guard against its use by unauthorized persons.

1 *Goodman v J Eban Limited* [1954] 1 QB 550, [1954] 2 WLR 581, [1954] 1 All ER 763, [1954] 3 WLUK 22, (1954) 98 SJ 214, [1954] CLY 3173.

7.303 Williams J discussed this point in the case of *Robb v The Pennsylvania Co. for Insurance on Lives and Granting Annuities*,[1] discussed below. The matter of the security of a rubber stamp was also mentioned briefly in *British Estate Investment Society Ltd v Jackson (H M Inspector of Taxes)*,[2] where an Additional Commissioner regularly used a rubber stamp to sign significant volumes of documents. In his judgment, Danckwerts J mentioned the measures taken in the office to provide for the prevention of unauthorized use of the rubber stamp.[3] Once again, there is no explicit mention of the need for a signing party to provide for the security of the rubber stamp and to protect it against misuse. However, the action of the signing party in providing for the security of the rubber stamp suggests that, even without a rule of law requiring them to take steps to secure the rubber stamp, they took such precautions because the nature of the instrument thus created permits others to use a recognized means of identifying and authenticating a document:

> (1) The evidence from Charles Goodman in *Goodman v J Eban Limited* and of the Additional Commissioner in *British Estate Investment Society Ltd v Jackson (H M Inspector of Taxes)* demonstrates that when the signing party acquired a rubber stamp as a means of affixing their signature to a document, they took appropriate precautions to safeguard it from misuse and theft.
>
> (2) The comments by Evershed MR[4] and Danckwerts J[5] imply that the authorized use of the rubber stamp rested on the care the signing party took of the item, and because the security of the rubber stamp was assured, the signature affixed to the document by the rubber stamp was authentic and therefore valid.
>
> (3) In the event the recipient doubts the authenticity of the signature, they can undertake their own form of due diligence to verify its authenticity and validity. This point was made by Romer LJ at 564 in *Goodman v J Eban Limited*, where he pointed out that 'If in fact his clients entertained any doubt as to the authenticity of the letter, nothing could be easier than to ask him, by telephone or letter, to confirm it'. While the point made by Romer LJ is an explicit instruction as to what action the recipient could take, the comment was not necessarily meant to form a legal rule.

1 40 W.N.C. 129, 3 Pa.Super. 254, 1897 WL 3989 (Pa.Super. 1897), affirmed by186 Pa. 456, 40 A. 969, for dissenting opinion, see 186 Pa. 456, 41 A. 49.
2 (1954–1958) 37 Tax Cas 79, [1956] TR 397, 35 ATC 413, 50 R & IT 33.
3 (1954–1958) 37 Tax Cas 79 at 87.
4 *Goodman v J Eban Limited* [1954] 1 QB 550 at 554.
5 *British Estate Investment Society Ltd v Jackson (H M Inspector of Taxes)* (1954–1958) 37 Tax Cas 79 at 87.

7.304 Although none of the comments made by the judges in these two cases are sufficient to form a rule of law in relation to such matters, nevertheless they recognized that where technology is used to provide a substitute for so physical an act as the affixing of a manuscript signature to a document, new considerations relating to the presumptions that should apply to alternative methods of applying a signature must be considered.

7.305 In light of the decision of Waller J in *Standard Bank London Ltd v Bank of Tokyo Ltd*,[1] it appears that this train of thought may have already been adopted in England and Wales. In this case, the Bank of Tokyo in Kuala Lumpur arranged for three tested telexes to be sent to Standard, containing a secret code confirming and authenticating the authorized signatory of three letters of credit with a total face value of US$19.8 million, and confirming that the Bank of Tokyo accepted all responsibilities and liabilities under those letters of credit. Evidence was adduced to indicate that banks not only used this system with confidence, but also used it to avoid arguments about authority. In this instance, the tested telexes were sent fraudulently.

1 [1995] 2 Lloyd's Rep 169, [1995] 3 WLUK 182, [1995] CLC 496, [1998] Mason's CLR Rep 126, Times, 15 April 1995, [1995] CLY 397.

7.306 The main thrust of the Bank of Tokyo's case was this: because they could establish that a thief must have been working in their tested telex department, Standard could only rely upon the apparent authority of the tested telexes. As a result, it argued that there was a lower test to establish the lack of apparent authority. Waller J disagreed with this argument at 502C, because the issue was not reliance on apparent authority:

> Standard rely first on a general representation by BOT that if a telex comes by tested telex that telex will be duly authorised by BOT (that representation on any view is authorised);
>
> second they rely on the use of the tested telex mechanism itself as representing that the telex is authorised as the previous representation stated that it would be; and
>
> thirdly they rely on the statement in the telex as being the authorised statement of BOT.

7.307 The Bank of Tokyo was found liable for negligent misrepresentation because the tested telexes could not have been sent without negligence on the bank's part. Whether Standard had a duty to inquire into the authenticity of the tested telexes depended on the circumstances of each case.[1] Tested telexes contain codes or tests which are secret between the sender and the recipient. This allows the recipient to accept without question that the telex was sent by and with the authority of the sender. The tested telexes in this instance were sent through other banks, because the Bank of Tokyo in Kuala Lumpur did not have a means of directly authenticating telexes between itself and Standard. By sending tested telexes, banks intend the receiving bank to act on the content without further instructions. This means the receiving bank requires the sending bank to confirm the person signing the document is an authorized signatory, verify the signatory is authorized to sign the particular document, and provide sufficient evidence to satisfy the recipient that the sending bank authorized the sending of the telex.

1 [1995] CLC 496 at 501H.

7.308 Superficially, there is a similarity between the circumstances of this case and the public key infrastructure, where the authentication process has to go through so many channels.[1] However, there is a distinction between a tested telex produced in a bank and the public key infrastructure. The authority of a telex is reliant upon internal systems within the bank.[2] No third party is involved in identifying the sender of the telex or authenticating the codes or text sent. In addition, the tested telex is sent through other banks over apparently secure lines of communication. Conversely, the public key infrastructure operates over the Internet, which was designed to be open and is, therefore, insecure. The link between the identity and authentication of a user of an electronic signature is not as cohesive as that between such trusted parties as banks. There are significantly more links, which neither party has control over, in the chain between the sending party and receiving party of an electronic signature. As a result, it can be argued that there is a distinction between what can be termed a 'secure or closed communication system' and an 'open communications system'. Clearly the burden of proving that an electronic signature was used without authority must be borne by either the user or the relying party. In this instance, Waller J took the view that the sender was in full control of the environment in which the tested telex was sent, and decided that the burden should fall on the sender.

1 See also Jean-François Blanchette, *Burdens of Proof: Cryptographic Culture and Evidence Law in the Age of Electronic Documents* (MIT Press 2012) – 'This book is not about the burden of proof or the law relating to electronic evidence. The reader must look to legal text books on electronic evidence to understand burdens of proof and the law relating to electronic evidence. However, it is a useful text in discussing the technical issues and policy decisions behind the use of technology that has an effect on electronic evidence.' Book Report, (2012) 9 Digital Evidence and Electronic Signature Law Review 181; for a similar broad introduction by the same author, see 'The digital signature dilemma', Annales des Télécommunications (May/June 2006), 908.

2 A message using an authentication code sent through the SWIFT system has the legal effect of binding the sender bank according to its contents: *Industrial & Commercial Bank Ltd v Banco Ambrosiano Veneto SpA* [2003] 1 SLR 221.

7.309 In the context of an open insecure network, however, different criteria, based upon the protection of the consumer, might be applied by the courts.

The recipient's procedural and due diligence burden

7.310 Whether it is for the user of an electronic signature to bear such a burden is debatable. If it is accepted that the recipient is required to establish whether they can rely on the certificate in all the circumstances, they may be required to provide any or all of the evidence discussed above in relation to verifying the integrity of a certificate, depending on the nature of the challenge. Providing the recipient has carried out all the relevant checks required, it is possible to argue that it has discharged what can be described as a procedural and due diligence burden and has become a verifying party.

The sending party: the burden of proof of security and integrity

7.311 Once the recipient, if required so to do, has satisfied a judge that it has discharged the procedural and due diligence burden, the user will need to address the issue of the security and integrity of their computer or system, among other topics of relevance in the circumstances. This can be described as the burden of proof of security and integrity, which comprises both a persuasive burden (or burden of proof on the pleadings) and the evidential burden of adducing evidence. In discussing this aspect, it is useful to compare identical problems that have exercised the minds of people in the past, and what mechanisms were put in place to provide for the integrity of the method of proving intent.

7.312 The use of a seal became so common by the fourteenth century in England that consideration had to be given to provide for additional evidence, other than the impression of a seal affixed to the document, that the seal impression was not a forgery or added without authority. The sovereign might have a number of seals for different purposes: a signet for the secretary; a privy seal, which was in between the secretary and the Chancellor; the great seal, controlled by the Chancellor to authenticate the most formal of acts; and a finger ring, later called a privy signet, for the personal affairs of the monarch.[1] Care was taken to destroy seal matrices in a public ceremony, as occurred when Edward III ascended the throne and had the great seal used by his father and grandfather broken into tiny pieces in his presence.[2] However, the physical object of the impression of a seal can be undermined, just as any other form of authentication. For instance, the seal itself might be forged,[3] or the seal of a dead person used, as in the case of Hannibal when he forged letters in the name of the dead Roman consul Marcellus after removing the signet ring from his body.[4] In England, it was an offence to forge the royal seal. By the Statute of Edward III, counterfeiting the great and privy seals were treasonable offences, and one man who forged the seal of Henry II was only saved from being hanged by the king's mercy.[5] At common law it was a felony and regarded as a capital offence, and there are three medieval cases of this nature.

1 Patricia M. Barnes and L. C. Hector, *Guide to Seals in the Public Record Office* (2nd edn, HMSO 1968), 8; P. Chaplais, *English Diplomatic Practice in the Middle Ages* (Hambledon and London 2003), 97–98.
2 P. D. A. Harvey and Andrew McGuinness, *A Guide to British Medieval Seals* (University of Toronto Press 1996), 34.
3 T. F. Tout, 'Mediæval forgers and forgeries' (1919) Bulletin of the John Rylands Library 208 describes how a medieval forger might be clever enough to cut the wax or lead of a seal into two thin slices, introduce a new attachment of parchment, silk or leather, and affix it to a new document, then heat the sides to fasten the seal together for a second time.
4 Chaplais, *English Diplomatic Practice*, 6.
5 Harvey and McGuinness, *A Guide to British Medieval Seals*, 33, 98–99.

7.313 A person could challenge a document where the incorrect seal had been used, or the right seal was attached to the wrong document. As seals became more common, the other issue was the degree of forgery for ordinary seals.[1] There is evidence illustrating that people took their seal very seriously. In 1190, for instance, Adam, son of Peter de Birkin, broke his seal and replaced it. He went to the length of repeating a grant he had previously made to the abbey of Rievaulx.[2] There then developed a means of countersigning the main seal with the use of a secret seal as a counter-seal to one of the great seals. The great seal would be in the possession and under the control of the officer of state, and the secret seal in the possession of the owner, thus providing a double-check to the authenticity of the document, because the second seal may be imprinted on to the great seal, providing two seal impressions on the same seal. The concerns for the security of the seal were sometimes carried to what seems like extraordinary lengths, but were probably routine. In 1214 the chapter seal of Salisbury cathedral was in the care of two cannons, but by 1353 it was kept in a chest with three locks, and was only used in the presence of all three cannons, each of whom held a key. By the Statute of Acton Burnell in 1283, debts could be registered before the mayor, who issued a recognisance with a special seal supplied by the crown. However, in 1285 the Statute of Merchants amended the previous statute and ordered that the seal must be contained in two parts, the larger to be retained by the mayor and the smaller to be retained by the clerk – indicating, in the opinion of one scholar, that there had probably been a scandal.[3] In the late thirteenth century, the seal of the corporation of Winchester was placed in a box with three locks and the keys retained by two counsellors and one ordinary person, and this box in turn was itself kept in a chest with two keys, held by one counsellor and one other person.[4]

1 For an example of a Chinese seal in the context of documentary letters of credit, see *Deutsche Bank AG, London Branch v CIMB Bank Berhad* [2017] EWHC 3380 (Comm), [2018] 2 Lloyd's Rep 510, [2017] 12 WLUK 407, [2019] CLY 631.
2 Barnes and Hector, *Guide to Seals in the Public Record Office*, 29–30.
3 T. F. T. Plucknett, *Legislation of Edward I* (Clarendon 1949), 140, quoted in Harvey and McGuinness, *A Guide to British medieval Seals*, 111.
4 Harvey and McGuinness, *A Guide to British Medieval Seals*, 58–62, 98–99.

7.314 Conceptually, there is little difference between the seal matrix and a rubber stamp, and the nature of the security in place to prevent unauthorized use is identical. In this respect, the 1897 Pennsylvania case of *Robb v The Pennsylvania Co. for Insurance on Lives and Granting Annuities*[1] is highly instructive. This case predates the use of electronic signatures in any form by 100 years, yet the difference in time does not diminish the issues, even if they were articulated with different concepts and language by the judges at the time. In this case, money had been paid out on two cheques signed with the facsimile signature of the bank depositor by means of a rubber stamp. Mr Robb did not authorize either cheque.

1 40 W.N.C. 129, 3 Pa.Super. 254, 1897 WL 3989 (Pa.Super. 1897), affirmed by 186 Pa. 456, 40 A. 969; for a dissenting opinion, see 186 Pa. 456, 41 A. 49.

7.315 In 1893 Mr Robb, as the president of a commercial corporation, had occasion to send out a large number of invitations to a banquet. To save himself the trouble of signing each invitation, he had a rubber stamp made with a facsimile of his signature. After retiring, he rented a private office, and with the rent came the services of an office boy. He employed the boy on various errands, including sending him to the bank to draw money on cheques. It can be inferred from the report that he used the rubber stamp to sign cheques. He kept the rubber stamp in a compartment inside a fireproof safe. He locked the compartment and put the key to the compartment in a drawer in the safe, behind some papers, and covered it up. He then locked the drawer, and placed the key into an unlocked drawer in the safe. He then locked the safe, and put the key in a little box, which he put in a wooden drawer or box, and this was kept on top of another safe. The plaintiff surmised that the office boy had watched his moves at some time in the past. The majority of the judges found that Mr Robb was not negligent in the use of the rubber stamp. The basis of their decision centred on whether he was negligent in failing to exercise care in preventing the rubber stamp from falling into the wrong hands. Rice PJ rejected the proposition that Mr Robb was bound to keep the stamp in a place that prevented any person from obtaining it without authority. However, no attempt was made by the majority judges to explain how the bank was in a position to challenge the signature, given that the signature was identical each time the rubber stamp was used, with the exception that the impression will vary in quality depending on the amount of ink used and the pressure applied to the stamp as the signature is affixed to the cheque. The majority held that the bank was liable for the cheques. Williams J wrote an elegant dissenting judgment that raises the modern issues, using different language, but germane nevertheless, with which Sterrett CJ concurred. Williams J argued that it was for the bank, relying on the signature, to prove it was genuine. The image of the signature was genuine, but Mr Robb had neither applied it nor authorized the signature to be applied to the cheque. In this respect, it was a forgery, and in the words of Wills J in *The Staple of England v The Governor and Company of the Bank of England*:

> A forgery can give no title, and those that rely upon it must be able to shew some extraneous ground – such as that of estoppel – why they should be entitled to act upon it.[1]

1 (1887) 21 QBD 160 at 166.

7.316 In *The Staple of England*, the bank was held liable for failing to make proper enquiries as to title where the company gave the safekeeping of the Company seal to their clerk (a solicitor), and the clerk, without authority, affixed the seal to a power of attorney that enabled him to sell funds of the Company for his own benefit. The seal and the rubber stamp have the same problem: the need to prevent unauthorized use. Although the use of rubber stamps was not new at the time of this case, nevertheless Mr Robb failed to notify the bank that he was using a mechanical reproduction of his manuscript signature. Arguably, if the bank had been made aware of this practice, as suggested by Williams J, it might have refused to honour such cheques, or if it accepted them, the bank might have taken additional care to ensure with each cheque that he had affixed the signature with the intention of signing it.

7.317 There is a difference of degree between securing a physical object such as a rubber stamp and a digital signature, but in the event of a dispute, it follows that it is the holder of the certificate and private key who is in the best position to prove that the security in place was adequate, such that the certificate and private key could not be used improperly.

7.318 If the user wishes to argue their security was so poor that an unauthorized third party could have gained access to the system to send an electronic communication with an electronic signature attached without authority, the user will undoubtedly be admitting breach of contract with the vendor from whom they obtained the certifying certificate. They are also probably admitting they were negligent. This is the central conundrum any user of a digital signature faces.

7.319 The flexible nature of the need to implement suitable precautions relating to securing a seal was recognized by Wills J, and in a prescient comment in *The Staple of England*, he indicated at 168 that:

> The precautions which appear to be natural in one century may appear pedantic and unnecessary in another ... there can be no inflexible and unvarying rule of law as to that which is essentially a mixed question of fact and law.

Burden of proof – the jitsuin

7.320 Since the eighth century, a similar system of authentication to that of the electronic signature has existed in the physical world, by which a signing party deposits an imprint of their mark with a trusted third party, and relying parties can rest assured that when the mark is used, they can rely on the authentication of the person by the mark. This is the *jitsuin* (original seal) of Japan. Other seals include the *ginko-in* (bank seal) for banking purposes, and *mitome-in* (approval seal) for use in everyday circumstances, such as signing for a delivery of post. The seal is called an *insho*, and the word *inkan* describes the impression of the seal. The purpose of a name seal is to confirm a person's intention to enter a transaction and to act as a form of identification. The use of *mitome-in* in Japan is so much part of everyday life that foreigners, although they are permitted in some situations to use a manuscript signature instead of a name seal, are advised to obtain such a seal if they are going to remain in the country for any length of time.[1]

1 For a further explanation, see G. P. McAlinn (ed), *Japanese Business Law* (Wolters Kluwer 2007), 202–204.

7.321 *Jitsuin* are used instead of manuscript signatures to execute important documents. For instance, the Jitsuin Seal Registration Certificate is required as an attachment to the document of application for the transfer of registration in the real property registry at the Legal Affairs Bureau. The importance attached to the Jitsuin Seal Registration Certificate under Japanese Law is such that the transfer of the registration is essential for the perfection of the transfer of title of a real property. The *jitsuin* is endowed with a legal presumption that is founded partly on the common understanding that a name seal either cannot be forged, or is difficult to forge, and partly on a very long history of use.

Registering a jitsuin

7.322 *Jitsuin* are required to conform to specific criteria:

> (1) The name on the seal must conform to the registered name; the seal must have a border surrounding the name (and the border must not be missing or chipped); machine-made, mass-produced seals are not acceptable; the seal must be made of a material that cannot be altered easily, and the diameter must be greater than 8 mm square but smaller than 25 mm square.
>
> (2) Only the owner of a seal or a representative can apply to register a *jitsuin*, and the applicant has to be over the age of 15 years.
>
> (3) A *jitsuin* must be registered at the offices of the local government, whether village, town or city.

7.323 Upon application for a registered seal (*jitsuin*) and Seal Registration Certificate (*inkan toroku shomeisho*), some local offices will send the applicant a letter of verification for the purpose of confirming the identity of the person applying. Alternatively, the usual range of documents will be required to be produced when the applicant attends the office. The registration takes place when the applicant attends the office with their seal, during which their identity is checked. Where a representative registers the seal, they will be required to provide a Letter of Attorney or a Letter of Advice Giving Right of Representation, which must be signed and sealed by the owner of the seal. After registering the seal, the applicant is given a Seal Registration Card (*inkan torokusho*, a plastic card) rather than a Seal Registration Certificate.

The Seal Registration Certificate

7.324 The Seal Registration Certificate includes the following information: an impression of the registered seal; the name of the seal holder; the date of birth of the seal holder; the gender of the seal holder; the address of the seal holder. The registration of the *jitsuin* is tied to a particular geographical locality, so if the seal holder moves to another part of Japan or leaves Japan for good, the seal registration becomes null and void, and a new registration process must be undertaken at the new location. Where a *jitsuin* is lost, the process is to attend the office that issued the Seal Registration

Certificate and initiate the procedure to delete the registration. There is no procedure to notify relying parties that the *jitsuin* has been stolen or lost.

The legal presumption of the Seal Registration Certificate

7.325 A Seal Registration Certificate proves the seal holder has adopted the impression of the seal that is recorded in the Certificate. The Civil Procedure Law provides for a legal presumption relating to the authenticity of a private document, as follows: 'A private document shall be presumed to be authentically executed if it bears the signature or seal of the principal or his representative.'[1] It appears that this presumption is rebuttable and the following discussion is restricted to private documents, and does not include government documents.[2] For this presumption to operate, the party bearing the burden of proof is required to prove that the registered owner of the seal intended to affix an impression of their seal on the document. This intention may itself be presumed if the relying party proves that the seal impressed on the document and the impression of the adopted seal held by the owner is the same. However, the relying party must also prove that the signing party has in fact adopted the seal. This fact is proved by using the Seal Registration Certificate, because the Seal Registration Certificate bears the adopted seal and the name of the signing party, thus it is easy for the relying party to prove that the signing party adopted the seal.[3] Once it is established that the signing party intended to affix an impression of their seal by operation of this presumption, the presumption under the Civil Procedure Law takes effect, and the document in question is presumed to be authentically executed.

1 Civil Procedure Law (Law No 109 of 1998) article 228(4).
2 Civil Procedure Law (Law No 109 of 1998) article 228, 228(2) and 228(3).
3 This chain of presumption is reinforced by the provisions of Civil Procedure Law (Law No 109 of 1998) article 229, which states: 'The authenticity of execution of documents may also be proved by a comparison of a specimen of handwriting or seal impression'.

7.326 This explanation demonstrates that there are two levels of presumption, a process known as the 'Two Phase Presumption'. It involves the following steps.

> If the impression of the seal and the adopted seal held by the signing party are the same, then it is presumed that:
>
> The signing party intended to affix the seal impression, which in turn creates the presumption that:
> The document bearing the seal impression was authentically executed.

7.327 It is to be noted that there is no statutory requirement of due diligence in order to utilize this presumption.

Rebutting the presumption

7.328 The owner of the seal can rebut these presumptions. However, it is difficult to effectively prove that the document was not authentically executed, which is tantamount to trying to prove a negative. Recently, this presumption has been found to pose problems in an age when it is very easy to forge name seals with the availability of advanced technology. This problem reached national importance following a series of thefts from deposit accounts held in banks using forged or stolen seals. The problem is partly explained by Matsushita Shuli:

> Door-picking artist quietly breaks and enters victim's house and nicks bank account passbook. The passbook, especially old ones, usually carries the seal image on the first page. The joker scans this image and prints it on the withdrawal slip with color printer. The bank teller accepts this slip and passbook as authentic, and victim's account will be emptied. Sometimes, the scanned digital image goes to hanko carving machine, too.
>
> The real cause of trouble: It's the stamped image of one's hanko that is stored in the databases of government offices, banks and other public institutions. Not the particulars of physical hanko itself! And any image can be flawlessly reproduced in this era of digital processing. QED.[1]

1 Obtaining information about this problem in the English language is difficult; but see Mayumi Negishi, 'Security concerns jeopardize future of age-old tradition of "hanko" seals', *The Japan Times*, undated, https://www.japantimes.co.jp/news/2004/01/14/business/security-concerns-jeopardize-future-of-age-old-tradition-of-hanko-seals/#.XrFKZhOYWSy. The most recent news item is Terrie Lloyd, 'Huge local fraud case, ebiz in Japan', 20 April 2010, Japan.Inc, https://www.japaninc.com/tt562_huge-local-fraud-case.

7.329 The *jitsuin* and the Seal Registration Certificate have been a very effective method of providing for the authenticity and intention of a person when entering into a legally binding agreement as a trusted third party undertakes to certify the nexus between the applicant and the *jitsuin*. The presumption worked well in a society where the accurate copying of name seals was difficult for the would-be thief.[1] However, with the advent of modern means of duplication, a tension has arisen between the assurance that an individual can prove their identity and thereby authenticate a document with the use of a Seal Registration Certificate in combination with a *jitsuin*, and the failure to require the relying party to take steps to authenticate the identity of the person who claims the name seal is their adopted *jitsuin*. The Seal Registration Certificate proves the seal holder has adopted the impression of the seal that is recorded in the Certificate. In modern Japan, the failure to balance the presumption that accompanies the use of a *jitsuin* with an accompanying duty to take steps to require the person using the name seal to provide the certificate of authenticity has meant ordinary consumers suffer the loss. This is an example where advances in technology have caused problems in a system of authentication that has worked well over an extended period of time in Japanese history. While a change to the law will not follow immediately, when a change does occur, a cultural shift will also have to take place, in which the relying party will have to take reasonable steps to verify the signing party.

1 Noriko Kawawa, 'The Japanese law on unauthorized on-line credit card and banking transactions: are current legal principles with respect to unauthorized transactions adequate to protect consumers against information technology crimes in contemporary society?' (2013) 10 Digital Evidence and Electronic Signature Law Review 71, for a general overview of the position in Japan.

Burden of proof – summary

7.330 In the context of electronic signatures, and digital signatures in particular, there is a clear lesson to be understood. In the physical world where the signature-creation device is difficult to replicate accurately, a tri-part method of providing assurance can be very effective. The owner of the Japanese seal provides evidence of their identity to satisfy a nominated authority sufficiently for the authority to create a certificate to link the seal to the owner. The authority retains the evidence of the link, and the relying party can rest assured that the person with the seal, if authenticated with a certificate, is who they say they are. The flaw in this model, in an age when a name seal is easy to duplicate, is that it fails to impose a duty on the relying party to undertake sufficient due diligence to satisfy themselves that the holder of the seal is the person whose name seal is registered.

7.331 The use of a rubber stamp as a form of signature has similar properties to the name seal, but without the properties of the *jitsuin*. In the cases of *Goodman v J Eban Limited*[1] and *British Estate Investment Society Ltd v Jackson (H M Inspector of Taxes)*,[2] the respective recipients of the stamped documents did not question the authenticity of the stamped signature but sought to challenge the form of the signature. The underlying assumptions about the security of a rubber stamp were not fully articulated; that is, the owner of such a stamp is expected to keep it secure and prevent any unauthorized use. If the recipient was in any doubt as to the authenticity of the document signed with a rubber stamp, they could always take steps to verify the integrity of the document. While observations about security were made by the judges in passing and did not lay down a rule of law, nevertheless they represent underlying assumptions about the risks to be attached to the use of a means of providing authentication to a document which may not always be under the control of the owner, at least in cases where the means in question are adopted for the convenience and advantage of the user rather than the recipient.

1 [1954] 1 QB 550, [1954] 2 WLR 581, [1954] 1 All ER 763, [1954] 3 WLUK 22, (1954) 98 SJ 214, [1954] CLY 3173.
2 (1954–1958) 37 Tax Cas 79, [1956] TR 397, 35 ATC 413, 50 R & IT 33.

7.332 The risks for the participants when using electronic signatures is, to a certain extent, similar to that of the *jitsuin* and rubber stamp, depending on the type of electronic signature used. In the context of the digital signature, the trusted third party allocates the risks and responsibilities. In general, a subscribing party or receiving party that relies on such technology is either fully aware of the limitations associated with the use of a digital signature, or they have no concept of the issues, and they use a digital signature in ignorance of the risks they may face if their reliance were to be tested. Statute provides that where a trusted third party with a contractual relationship with its customer (a bank) debits the account of a customer with the payment of a cheque the customer did not sign, the bank has no authority to take the money and therefore must credit the account with the amount charged.[1] The allocation of risk with the *jitsuin* is under threat because of the ease by which a name seal can now be forged.

1 Bills of Exchange Act 1882 s 24; Directive 2007/64/EC of the European Parliament and of the Council of 13 November 2007 on payment services in the internal market amending Directives 97/7/EC, 2002/65/EC, 2005/60/EC and 2006/48/EC and repealing Directive 97/5/EC (Text with EEA relevance) OJ L 319, 5.12.2007, 1–36, implemented by The Payment Services Regulations 2009 (SI 209/2009) as amended by The Payment Services (Amendment) Regulations 2009 (SI 2475/2009).

7.333 It was judges during the nineteenth century who created the protection for those customers who affixed their manuscript signature to a cheque and politicians codified this rule.[1] While it will be important to take into account the suggestion made by Romer LJ in *Goodman v J Eban Limited*[2] that the recipient of a document stamped with a rubber stamp can take action to authenticate the document, the action and effort required to check that the writer of a letter intended to affix their signature by means of a rubber stamp is far less than the magnitude of the task facing a recipient of, in particular, a digital signature. The terms and content of the certification practice policies of the certification authorities demonstrate the complexity of the task faced by a recipient if they are expected to verify a digital signature.

1 Nicholas Bohm, Ian Brown and Brian Gladman, 'Electronic commerce: who carries the risk of fraud?' (2000) 3 Journal of Information, Law and Technology, paragraph 2, https://warwick.ac.uk/fac/soc/law/elj/jilt/2000_3/bohm.

2 [1954] 1 QB 550 at 564.

8

Encrypted data

Alisdair Gillespie, Jessica Shurson and Stephen Mason

8.1 Any discussion about electronic evidence in the digital era must now include reference to encryption. This is an increasingly important issue for law enforcement authorities where criminals use strong encryption to thwart the legitimate investigation of officers.[1] It is important to note at the outset that encryption itself is neutral. It is used for legitimate as well as prohibited reasons. Indeed, e-commerce as we know it could not exist without encryption, since it is encryption that makes purchasing on the Internet or a mobile device safe, without fear that our payment details can be intercepted during transmission. However, in this chapter we will be primarily concerned with those who use encryption to hide material.

1 Although it is difficult to identify how widespread the use is. Within England and Wales, it seems relatively uncommon, with the Investigatory Powers Commissioner reporting only 66 approvals for a notice under the Regulation of Investigatory Powers Act (RIPA) 2000, s 49 being granted in 2018: *Annual Report of the Investigatory Powers Act 2018* HC 67 (2000), 81.

Encryption

8.2 Encryption is a form of cryptography. It is about disguising the contents of a message or file. Encryption (or enciphering) is the process by which a plaintext (or cleartext) message is disguised sufficiently to hide the substance of the content. As well as ordinary text, a plaintext message can be a stream of binary digits, a text file, a bitmap, a recording of sound in digital form, audio images of a video or film, or any other information. When a message has been encrypted, it is known as ciphertext. The opposite procedure – that of turning the ciphertext back into plaintext – is called decryption (or deciphering). An encryption scheme usually uses a 'key' to encrypt and decrypt the message. Data that is encrypted properly can be virtually impossible to decrypt. It is an art that has been practised for thousands of years,[1] but digital technology has revolutionized it. By way of example, consider the message 'The Eagle is Alive'. The difficulty with transmitting a message in plaintext is that anybody who sees the message knows its content. They may not, of course, know its meaning, but often the actual content of the message is problematic (for instance if the message is a photograph, then you may not want people to see the image). Encryption turns the message into a code that hides the meaning. So, for example, the message 'The Eagle is Alive' may be shown as 'WEK85%LSc43*4lzqnc782'. If someone obtains that message, she will have no idea what this means. Indeed, she will not even know how many characters are in the original message. As digital media, including pictures and sound files, are simply binary data, it means that anything can be encrypted, with the encrypted binary file appearing to have completely random data. A more detailed technical description of encryption is provided in Chapter 1.

1 A useful history can be found in Donald Davies 'A brief history of cryptography' (1997) 2(2) Information Security Technical Report 14.

Alisdair Gillespie, Jessica Shurson and Stephen Mason, 'Encrypted data', in Stephen Mason and Daniel Seng (eds.), *Electronic Evidence and Electronic Signatures* (5th edn, University of London 2021) 397–428.

Methods to obtain encrypted data

8.3 As noted, to decrypt encrypted text and render it into plaintext requires a key. In complex environments this could be an algorithm, complex data, a dongle (a physical device with a computer chip contained within it) or even biometric measurements,[1] but in most instances it is a code or password. All forms of keys are recognized in the statute that regulates the exercise of investigatory powers to acquire the means by which encrypted electronic data may be decrypted or opened.[2] For the purposes of this chapter, we will be restricting our analysis to passwords, because they are the most common key used in personal encryption.

1 Biometric measurements may be secure in many instances, but they are spectacularly unhelpful when information is being hidden from law enforcement authorities, because the police will have the power to take photographs and potentially pictures of one's iris, for example. For the position in Norway, see Ingvild Bruce, 'Forced biometric authentication – on a recent amendment in the Norwegian Code of Criminal Procedure' (2017) 14 Digital Evidence and Electronic Signature Law Review 26.
2 RIPA 2000, s 56(1).

Breaking the encryption without obtaining the key

8.4 It is not always necessary to use the key to convert the encrypted material into plaintext. Some examples include:

(1) Exploit a known flaw in the encryption scheme.[1] This is also known as a 'vulnerability attack', where the implementation of the encryption or password protection used is flawed and susceptible to programmatic compromise.[2]

(2) Obtain access to the plaintext when in use. Some law enforcement authorities have been known to gain rapid entry into a suspect's house when they know that the device is being used, because the contents of the device will be in an unlocked state as plaintext. Providing the device is not allowed to go into sleep mode or lock, then the contents can be freely viewed and copied.

(3) Use covertly installed keylogging software to record the suspect entering the password into the computer.[3]

(4) Locate a separate plaintext version of the encrypted data.[4]

1 Derek Kortepeter, 'Modern cryptographic methods: their flaws, their subsequent solutions, and their outside threats' TechGenix, 27 June 2016, http://techgenix.com/modern-cryptography-methods/; Casey Chin, '13-year-old encryption bugs still haunt apps and IoT' Wired, 8 July 2019, https://www.wired.com/story/rsa-encryption-signature-validation-flaws/.
2 In *R v Kelly (Lee Paul)* [2013] EWCA Crim 1893, [2018] 7 WLUK 478, the Court of Appeal upheld the decision of a judge to withhold the technique used to circumvent encryption on a mobile telephone. While the court noted that there must always be a fair trial, it also stated that 'there is an important public interest in not disclosing information which would jeopardize the effective prevention and detection of crime', at [33].
3 *U.S. v Scarfo* 180 F.Supp.2d 572 (D.N.J. 2001). While this may not tell you who depressed the keys (thus proving who had control), it would provide access to the encrypted material, which, by itself, is likely to assist the wider investigation. See also Giuseppe Vaciago and David Silva Ramalho, 'Online searches and online surveillance: the use of Trojans and other types of malware as means of obtaining evidence in criminal proceedings' (2016) 13 Digital Evidence and Electronic Signature Law Review 88.
4 Officials were able to examine draft copies of a ransom note automatically saved by word processing software on the suspect's computer in *Commonwealth of Pennsylvania v Copenhefer*, 526 Pa. 555, 587 A.2d 1353 (Pa. 1991), abrogated on sentence by *Commonwealth of Pennsylvania v Rizzuto*, 777 A.2d 1069 (Pa. 2001).

8.5 Most encryption programs are extensively tested, which means that vulnerabilities are rare. Installing keylogging software is difficult in the era of multiple devices, high-quality firewalls and anti-virus software; the installation of such software by authorities may itself also be illegal. The era of solid-state memory and cloud storage means that encryption can be near-instantaneous. While entering a house requires a legal warrant, it is also high-risk because if a drive is removed, or a connection to the cloud is broken, the plaintext contents can be programmed to be immediately encrypted. Thus, in many instances there is insufficient time to gain entry before the suspect can do any of these things.

Obtaining the key

8.6 A more productive way of breaking the encryption is to identify the key. Let us assume that the police wish to obtain the key from a person they suspect of committing a crime, whose documents are protected by encryption. The police could obtain it in the following ways:

(1) The suspect could voluntarily provide the password.

(2) The password might be written down. People frequently write down passwords (so they do not forget), which is remarkably helpful for those trying to find them.

(3) It is possible to use intelligence, including profiling, to guess what the password is, operating on the basis that the password may be something memorable about that person, such as a name or date of birth.[1]

(4) The use of decryption tools to break the encryption, including brute-force attacks. Software will allow, for example, every word in the dictionary to be tried as the password. A 'brute-force attack' will use powerful computers to try every possible combination of a key.[2] The difficulty with this method is that complex keys and long keys are almost impossible to break in this way.

(5) The suspect may be compelled to surrender the key.

1 For instance, United States border agents successfully guessed that Michelle Lopez used her date of birth as a password: in *United States v Lopez*, 2016 WL 7370030 (S.D. Cal. Dec. 20, 2016). In *Rollo (William) v HM Advocate* 1997 JC 23, 1997 SLT 958, 1996 SCCR 874, [1996] 9 WLUK 194, [1997] CLY 5753, the police succeeded in gaining access to an encrypted part of a Memomaster notebook by trying a number of combinations, one of which – the appellant's date of birth – was successful. See Ian Grigg and Peter Gutmann, 'The curse of cryptography numerology' (2011) 9(3) IEEE Security & Privacy 70 for a brief foray into the failure of everything but the cryptography.

2 In *R v ADJ* [2005] VSCA 102 the defendant claimed that he could not recall the password, and suggested possible alternatives, none of which were correct, so the police used password-cracking software that took over four months to identify the password. The encrypted partition revealed a large quantity of abusive images of children.

8.7 The fifth option – compulsion – has two possible alternatives. The first is torture, which is illegal in most countries, or the second is through a legal requirement to comply. Usually, this is backed by penal sanction. It is this latter method which has begun to be adopted by countries, although subject to dissenting opinions.

Compelling disclosure in England and Wales

8.8 England and Wales became one of the first jurisdictions to (controversially) introduce specific powers to allow the police to compel the disclosure of a password. The powers are set out in Part III of the Regulation of Investigatory Powers Act 2000 (RIPA). Alongside RIPA, a Code of Practice is issued under the authority of the Act.[1] The latest version was published in 2018.[2] The Code expands on the rules and procedures set out in RIPA 2000, providing greater certainty to investigators, judges and suspects in understanding how the disclosure powers under the Act will be exercised.

1 RIPA 2000, s 71(4). The Codes of Practice are released as statutory instruments and, therefore, have the force of secondary legislation.
2 Investigation of Protected Electronic Information: Revised Code of Practice (Home Office 2018).

Protected information

8.9 At the heart of the RIPA provisions is the concept of 'protected information'. This is defined in s 56(1) as:

> any electronic data which, without the key to the data–
>
> (a) cannot, or cannot readily be accessed; or
>
> (b) cannot, or cannot readily be put into an intelligible form.

8.10 Encrypted data would be the most obvious example of 'protected information', although the provisions in RIPA are wider than this.[1] There are three powers contained in RIPA 2000 that relate to protected information:

> 1. The power to require disclosure of protected information in an intelligible form.[2]
>
> 2. The power to require disclosure of the means to either obtain access to protected information, or render the protected information into plaintext.[3]
>
> 3. The power to attach a secrecy provision to any disclosure requirement (a 'tipping off' provision).[4]

1 In *R v Spencer (Jeffrey)* [2019] EWCA Crim 2240, [2019] 12 WLUK 246, the appellant had been convicted under RIPA s 53 for not providing the PIN to unlock two mobile telephones in his possession. A disclosure notice under s 49 had been presented to the appellant, who declined to provide the codes.
2 RIPA 2000, s 49.
3 RIPA 2000, s 49 when read in conjunction with s 50(3).
4 RIPA 2000, s 54.

8.11 These powers are considered below. While the first two will lead to the disclosure of information in an intelligible form, the first differs in that it does not technically require the surrendering of the key. It suffices that the person produces the data in an intelligible form. Thus, for example, if there were other documents that were encrypted that were not relevant to the crime, the police would not see them. However, in many instances it is unlikely that the police would be content with an assurance that other documents are not relevant and, instead, they will require the key to be disclosed, which will either provide access or allow the encrypted material to be rendered intelligible. In essence, the difference is who does the decryption. In the first scenario it is the suspect, whereas in the second scenario it will be the relevant investigator, or a nominated person.

Notice requiring disclosure

8.12 Where a suspect does not voluntarily provide her key, or where the police are unable to identify the key using the techniques discussed above, they may seek to serve a notice requiring disclosure of either the information sought or the key. The police can only do so with the permission of the National Technical Assistance Centre (NTAC).[1] NTAC is a government unit that became part of GCHQ (Government Communications Headquarters) in 2006, and has specialist officers dedicated to decrypting ciphertext, including through brute-force attacks and other technical solutions. NTAC will determine whether the encryption is known to NTAC and can be circumvented without the need to invoke RIPA 2000. Where they cannot, NTAC will determine whether the case is appropriate for application for a notice under s 49.

1 Investigation of Protected Electronic Information: Revised Code of Practice, [3.9].

8.13 The power to require disclosure applies where protected electronic information comes into the possession of an officer[1] as a result of exercising a statutory power[2] or by other lawful means.[3] In order to serve such a notice, s 49(2) provides that a person who has been authorized to give permission must have reasonable grounds to believe:

(1) the suspect has the protected information in his possession;

(2) the imposition is necessary for a specified purpose;

(3) the imposition is proportionate; and

(4) it is not reasonably practicable to obtain the information in any other way.

1 A police officer, an officer of Customs and Excise or a member of the intelligence services.
2 For example, the police have the right to search any premises occupied or controlled by a person who has been arrested for an indictable offence (Police and Criminal Evidence Act (PACE) 1984, s 18).
3 For example, a constable has exercised a search warrant: PACE 1984, s 8.

8.14 The person who is authorized to give permission is a circuit judge or a district judge (Magistrates' Court).[1] Judicial permission recognizes the sensitivities of compelling the disclosure of protected information and provides reassurance that there is independent scrutiny on the grounds set out above. However, it should be remembered that the judge need only have reasonable grounds to believe the criteria is met, and this is a relatively low threshold.[2] The purposes mentioned above include the interests of national security, the purpose of preventing or detecting crime and the interests of the economic well-being of the United Kingdom.[3] It is notable that it is crime, and not *serious* crime, which is a threshold required for some types of investigatory powers.[4]

1 RIPA 2000, Schedule 2, paragraph 1(1).
2 It is less than the civil and criminal standards of proof. It requires that there is some evidential basis to believe that something *might* be true, as distinct from more likely than not to be true (civil standard) or sure to be true (criminal standard).
3 RIPA 2000, s 49(3).
4 Intrusive surveillance (surveillance that takes place in residential premises or a private vehicle) will only be authorized if, among other things, it is for the prevention or detection of serious crime – see RIPA 2000, s 32(3)(b).

8.15 Proportionality is a concept that is now well understood by the courts. Proportionality is best thought of as requiring 'reasonableness between the objective sought and the means used to achieve that end'.[1] It requires a balance to be struck, ensuring that a measure is not disproportionate to the aim. It requires an examination of alternatives, but does not necessarily require that the least intrusive method always be chosen.[2] The Code of Practice suggests several aspects of proportionality that the judge should consider:

- The extent of the proposed interference with privacy against what is sought to be achieved;
- How and why the methods to be adopted will cause the least possible interference to the subject and others;
- Whether the activity is an appropriate use of the legislation and is a reasonable way, having considered all reasonable alternatives, of obtaining the necessary result;
- What other methods, as appropriate, were either not implemented or have been employed but which were assessed as insufficient to fulfil operational objectives without the use of the proposed conduct.[3]

1 *Halsbury's Laws* (5th edn, 2018), vol 61A, para 17.
2 *R (on the application of Corner House Research) v Director of the Serious Fraud Office* [2008] UKHL 60, [2009] 1 AC 756, [2008] 3 WLR 568, [2008] 4 All ER 927, [2008] 7 WLUK 921, [2008] Lloyd's Rep FC 537, [2009] Crim LR 46, (2008) 158 NLJ 1149, (2008) 152(32) SJLB 29, Times, 31 July 2008, [2008] CLY 1661.
3 Investigation of Protected Electronic Information: Revised Code of Practice, [3.41], bullet points in the original.

8.16 The last bullet point realistically does not add much more than the final requirement contained in the Act – that it is not reasonably practicable to obtain the information by other means. It is somewhat strange that it is included on the face of the legislation given that the consideration of alternatives is an important part of proportionality. However, its inclusion perhaps reflects the view that Parliament expects the alternatives to be seriously considered, with a s 49 notice being issued only where there is no real alternative.

Possession of a key

8.17 A person having possession of information or a key to protected information, is defined in s 56(2), RIPA 2000, as follows:

> References in this Part to a person's having information (including a key to protected information) in his possession include references–
>
> (a) to its being in the possession of a person who is under his control so far as that information is concerned;
>
> (b) to his having an immediate right of access to it, or an immediate right to have it transmitted or otherwise supplied to him; and
>
> (c) to its being, or being contained in, anything which he or a person under his control is entitled, in exercise of any statutory power and without otherwise taking possession of it, to detain, inspect or search.

8.18 Three different scenarios exist under this definition:

(i) a person may possess a key if it is under his control, or

(ii) if he has an immediate right of access to it, or an immediate right to have it transmitted or supplied to him, or

> (iii) if he (or a person under his control) is entitled, in exercise of any statutory power and without taking possession of it, to detain, inspect or search the thing which contains the key.

8.19 In the second and third scenarios, a person may be deemed to have a key, although he does not have the key himself. This is a fairly important provision, because the managerial officers of an organization, whatever the legal form the organization takes, are the ones responsible for the proper management of the private key, rather than the operational staff members.[1] Where the relevant ciphertext is to be found on a company's device, it would therefore make sense to serve the s 49 notice on an officer or senior manager of the organization, because she will have the power to order compliance by another.

1 Ross Anderson, *Security Engineering: A Guide to Building Dependable Distributed Systems* (2nd edn, John Wiley & Sons 2008) para 3.7.4 for a discussion on the principles involved in this process. (Professor Anderson was updating his book as this text was being updated. Some of his book will be available as open source at https://www.cl.cam.ac.uk/~rja14/book.html for a short period before the text is published. The entire book will be made available again as open source in 2023.)

Form of the notice

8.20 The form a disclosure notice is set out in s 49(4), RIPA 2000. It must, among other things, describe the protected information to which the notice relates;[1] specify the grounds upon which the disclosure is believed to be necessary;[2] specify the time by which the notice is to be complied with,[3] which must allow a reasonable period for compliance, depending on the circumstances of the case;[4] and specify the disclosure required and the form and manner in which it is to be made.[5] Where there is a cost to complying with a s 49 notice, s 52 provides for the Secretary of State to make an appropriate contribution towards such costs, although it is the investigating authority that ultimately bears the burden of paying these.[6]

1 RIPA 2000, s 49(4)(b).
2 RIPA 2000, s 49(4)(c).
3 RIPA 2000, s 49(4)(f).
4 RIPA 2000, s 49(4) proviso.
5 RIPA 2000, s 49(4)(g).
6 Investigation of Protected Electronic Information: Revised Code of Practice, 4.4.

Disclosure of protected information and keys

8.21 Where a person is served with a s 49 notice requiring the disclosure of protected information in an intelligible form, she may ether provide the key or use it to render the encrypted material into an intelligible form,[1] unless the notice states that she must surrender the key. The Code of Practice specifically notes that rendering into an intelligible form means returning the data to the state that it was in before encryption was applied, even if this means that there is other protection that might prevent someone from reading it immediately.[2] Consider an example:

> S has a Word Document that is protected by a password. To further enhance security, S uses encryption technology on the document. The police secure permission from a judge to serve a s 49 notice. S can either remove the encryption, or supply the key to do so. However, the s 49 notice may not require him to provide the password to the Word Document.[3]

1 RIPA 2000, s 50(1).
2 Investigation of Protected Electronic Information: Revised Code of Practice, [3.16].
3 Other legal powers may do so, but in any event, computer forensic programs may be able to read the data in such a file once it has ceased to be encrypted. This will depend on the version of the Word Document (which use different types of password protections) and the complexity of the password used.

8.22 There may be times when the person to whom the notice is directed does not have the key, or cannot gain access to the key. In such instances, she must give up what keys she actually has, although she does not have to disclose every key she has in her possession.[1] It follows that where a notice is to be served on a body corporate or a firm and it is obvious that more than one person may be in possession of the key, the notice should be directed to a senior officer, partner or senior employee.[2] However, where it is considered that the circumstances are such that the purpose of the notice would be defeated if it were to be served on the most appropriate person (for instance, she may be the subject of an investigation), then the notice may be served on another individual.[3]

1 RIPA 2000, s 50(3) and the effects of s 50(4), (5) and (6). See also s 50(7) and (8).
2 RIPA 2000, s 49(5) and (6).
3 RIPA 2000, s 49(7).

8.23 An exception is created as regards the disclosure of keys that are used for generating electronic signatures. Section 56(1) RIPA 2000 defines an 'electronic signature' as:

> anything in electronic form which
>
> (a) is incorporated into or logically associated with, any electronic communication or other data;
>
> (b) is generated by the signatory or other source of the communication or data; and
>
> (c) is used for the purpose of facilitating, by means of a link between the signatory or other source and the communication or data, the establishment of the authenticity of the communication or data, the establishment of its integrity, or both.

8.24 Where a key is used only for this purpose, it does not have to be disclosed in response to a notice, provided it has in fact not been used for any other purpose.[1] It might be useful to recall that a key pair has more than the single function of producing an electronic signature. The same key pair can be used to encrypt a message, depending on the algorithm used.

1 RIPA 2000, s 49(9).

8.25 However, this exemption may be narrower than it seems. In a commercial context, where more than one person may properly have access to a key, the person served with the notice may not be able to be sure that a key, despite being intended for signature purposes, has never been used to decrypt a message encrypted with the corresponding public key (there is no disclosure obligation if the key 'has not in fact been used for any ... purpose [other than that of generating electronic signatures]').[1] Although it will be for the prosecution to prove that a key has been used for such a purpose (that does not involve generating electronic signatures and is therefore subject to seizure), the mere assertion of this fact by the person demanding access to the key would place the recipient of the notice in a difficult position to prove a negative in resisting the demand.

1 RIPA 2000, s 49(9)(b).

Failure to comply with a notice

8.26 Where a person knowingly fails to make the disclosure required by the notice, he commits a criminal offence.[1] Section 53(2) sets out an important presumption of possession of the key:

> In proceedings against any person for an offence under this section, if it is shown that that person was in possession of a key to any protected information at any time before the time of the giving of the section 49 notice, that person shall be taken for the purposes of those proceedings to have continued to be in possession of that key at all subsequent times, unless it is shown that the key was not in his possession after the giving of the notice and before the time by which he was required to disclose it.

1 RIPA 2000, s 53(1).

8.27 An evidential burden is placed on the recipient. This requires her to adduce 'sufficient evidence of the fact ... to raise an issue'.[1] This does not mean she needs to prove that it was not in her possession. Instead, she must adduce some evidence (including through cross-examination) to show that it is not just a hypothetical argument.[2] Once such evidence is adduced, the prosecution must disprove the assertion beyond all reasonable doubt.[3]

1 RIPA 2000, s 53(3)(a).
2 Ultimately it is for a judge to decide, as a matter of law, whether sufficient evidence has been adduced: see, by implication, *Bratty v Attorney-General for Northern Ireland* [1963] AC 386, [1961] 3 WLR 965, [1961] 3 All ER 523, [1961] 10 WLUK 5, (1962) 46 Cr App R 1 (1961) 105 SJ 865, [1961] CLY 1839.
3 RIPA 2000, s 53(3)(b).

8.28 A defence exists where a person can show that 'it was not reasonably practicable for him to make the disclosure required by virtue of the giving of the section 49 notice before the time by which she was required, in accordance with that notice, to make it' but only if '[he] did make the disclosure as soon after that time as it was reasonably practicable for him to do'.[1] Unlike the presumption of possession of the key, this imposes a legal burden on the defence. Thus, the defendant must prove, on the balance of probabilities, that it was not reasonably practicable to disclose the key or data in the time frame required. It only applies if she subsequently makes disclosure and that this was when it was reasonably practicable to do. Accordingly, it would not assist those who continue to refuse to disclose the key.

1 RIPA 2000, s 53(4).

8.29 A person who honestly does not know the key, or cannot remember it, would not commit the offence, as she must *knowingly* refuse to surrender the key. If she does not remember the key, then she cannot surrender it. Whether it is credible that she has forgotten it is a matter of fact for the jury. In many instances, forensic data will be important here. While forensic software cannot say what is in an encrypted file, they can often tell when it was last viewed. If a person has been viewing the encrypted data just before the notice under s 49 is served, it is unlikely that a jury would consider it feasible that she has now forgotten the key.

Sentencing

8.30 The offence under s 53 is triable either in the Magistrates' Court or the Crown Court. The penalty depends on what it is believed the encrypted data contains. Where it is a case of 'national security' or 'child indecency', the maximum penalty on conviction is five years' imprisonment;[1] otherwise it is two years' imprisonment.[2] A case is a 'national security case' if the application made under s 49 stated that the case was 'in the interests of national security'.[3] Similarly, a case is a 'child indecency case' if it was stated in the s 49 application that the applicant believed the suspect was involved in the taking, making, distribution or possession of indecent photographs of a child.[4]

1 RIPA 2000, s 53(5), s 53(5A)(a).
2 RIPA 2000, s 53(5), s 53(5A)(b).
3 RIPA 2000, s 53(5B).
4 RIPA 2000, s 53(6), (7).

8.31 It should be remembered that the threshold for applications under s 49 is reasonable belief. Accordingly, a suspect is at risk of the higher sentence purely because a judge is satisfied that there is reasonable belief that the encrypted material poses a threat to national security or consists of indecent photographs of children. Reasonable belief is a low threshold and is significantly below the standard of proof ordinarily required for higher sentences. For example, where there is a dispute between the prosecution and defence over the circumstances of a guilty plea, the matter is normally resolved in a 'Newton Hearing',[1] where the prosecution must prove its version of the facts to the ordinary criminal standard.[2]

1 *R. v Newton (Robert John)* [1982] 12 WLUK 57, (1983) 77 Cr App R 13, (1982) 4 Cr App R (S) 388, [1983] Crim LR 198, [1983] CLY 815.
2 *R. v Ahmed (Nabil)* [1984] 12 WLUK 43, (1985) 80 Cr App R 295, (1984) 6 Cr App R (S) 391, [1985] Crim LR 250, [1985] CLY 828.

8.32 At issue might be whether the lower threshold can be justified. At first sight it would seem difficult to do so. However, the point of s 53 is that the police cannot decrypt data without the cooperation of the defendant. If they could prove, to the criminal standard, that the encrypted folder contained, for example, indecent images of children, then they would not need to serve a s 49 notice in the first place. While it may be difficult to justify the full criminal standard, it might be possible for the prosecution to prove a lower standard, for example on the balance of probabilities, through, for example, circumstantial evidence (email messages, IP traces etc.) that indicates the contents of the encrypted material.[1] Presumably, the higher penalty can only be used where it is not known what the contents are. Consider an example:

> The police believe that S is storing indecent photographs of children on an encrypted memory stick. They serve a s 49 notice, which S refuses to comply

with. After proceedings under s 53 have begun, NTAC manages to gain access to the memory stick and discover that it does contain pornographic pictures, but of adults.

1 The facts of *Greater Manchester Police v Andrews* [2011] EWHC 1966 (Admin), [2011] 5 WLUK 614, [2012] ACD 18, which will be examined later, would be a good example of this. Indecent photographs of a child were found on an unencrypted laptop. Two encrypted memory sticks were discovered alongside the computer. It could be argued that it is more likely than not (civil burden) that these sticks contained more illegal images.

8.33 The Crown Prosecution Service (CPS) may still wish to proceed with the prosecution under s 53 because the suspect has failed to comply with the s 49 notice. A literal reading of s 53 would mean that S is liable for up to five years' imprisonment, because the grounds for seeking the notice will have included reasonable grounds for believing that S was hiding indecent photographs of children. As this is now known not to be true, S can only be sentenced to a maximum of two years' imprisonment. For this reason, the courts adopt a strict approach to s 53 cases. In *R. v Cutler (Barry George)*[1] the Court of Appeal held:

> [A s 53 offence is] a very serious offence because it interferes with the administration of justice and it prevents the prosecuting authorities and the police finding out what offences someone has committed.[2]

1 [2011] EWCA Crim 2781, [2011] 10 WLUK 732.
2 [2011] EWCA Crim 2781 at [35].

8.34 This is an important point. Encryption puts evidence beyond the reach of law enforcement authorities and prosecutors. It means the full extent of the criminality cannot be ascertained, and the courts must consider this seriously. If s 53 is proven, it is a deliberate attempt to try and conceal evidence from the competent authorities, and this must merit harsh sanctions.

8.35 The seriousness of the offence is perhaps reflected in the comments of the Court of Appeal in *R v Padellec (Pierre)*.[1] The appellant entered a plea of guilty to an offence under s 53. He came to the attention of the police as a possible acquaintance of a person known to be involved in the trafficking of children. His computer (which included an encrypted folder) was recovered, and while no indecent images of children were found, search terms relating to indecent photographs were found. The appellant alleged that he purchased the encrypted device in Belgium and had no knowledge of the key. Following negotiations, a basis for the plea was tendered and accepted by the Crown. This was as follows:

> 1. The defendant accepts that he did not provide passwords as requested.
>
> 2. He did not do so because he knew he had used wiping software to remove evidence of a small number of images, which he accepts were indecent.
>
> 3. The defendant had accessed these images during the currency of internet browsing. The defendant will assert that the content of these images did not depict images of very young children. He cannot state the ages. The images did not contain scenes of sexual or any other type of violence to children.[2]

1 [2012] EWCA Crim 1956, [2012] 6 WLUK 651.
2 [2012] EWCA Crim 1956 at [6].

8.36 The importance of the third basis of plea is that it states the defendant did not obtain access to the images of the very worst forms of indecent photographs of children, and which would lead to more severe sentencing.[1] The judge accepted the plea, but suggested that he did so with reluctance. The Court of Appeal was scathing about the basis of plea. In giving judgment, Collins J said:

> It seems to us that in a case such as this, it is entirely wrong for a basis of plea to be accepted, either by the prosecution or ultimately by the judge. What it does is to enable the defendant in question to identify, to his advantage, what was or was not on the computer and to get a lesser sentence than otherwise might be appropriate. That is to enable him to dictate, wrongly, what the situation is. The whole point of requiring access is so that it can be seen what was, in fact, there. We express hope that in a situation that arose in this case, there will never again be a basis of plea accepted which is based on keeping the contents secret and the defendant saying, to his advantage, what was or was not contained.[2]

1 At the time of this decision, the sentencing for possession of indecent photographs was subject to the definitive sentencing guideline of 2007. This created five categories of seriousness. The basis of plea would ensure that it did not fall within the highest category or contain any aggravating factors. The guideline was replaced in 2013, but the changes are irrelevant to this decision.
2 [2012] EWCA Crim 1956 at [11].

8.37 If the defendant had not viewed, or stored, images that constituted the most serious examples of indecent photographs of children, then he could have proved this by allowing access to the device. Instead, the prosecution (and the judge) decided that the defendant could admit that he had looked at illegal content but could also keep the details of this illegality secret. The Court of Appeal, quite rightly, considered this an affront to justice. They stated, correctly, that in the absence of an explanation, an assumption of the worst-case basis should be made and the person be sentenced accordingly. To avoid this, the defendant could simply provide access to the images to allow their proper classification. This does not breach the presumption of innocence as the offence itself relates solely to the provision of indecent photographs of children. The defendant conceded this. Sentencing is separate to ascertaining guilt, and it must be right that it is appropriate for the court to take into consideration the refusal to show the images to the court.

Obligations of secrecy and tipping off

8.38 There is a power to attach a secrecy provision to any disclosure requirement.[1] This will require the person to whom the notice is given, and every other person who becomes aware of its contents, to keep the giving of the notice, its contents and the things undertaken in responding to it, a secret.[2] Breach of this requirement is punishable by a maximum of five years' imprisonment,[3] which is a heavier sentence than that which can be imposed on someone under s 53, save where it is a national security or child indecency case. Several defences exist to this offence, including:

(1) the disclosure was effected entirely by the operation of software designed to indicate when a key to protected information has ceased to be secure, and it was not reasonably practicable to prevent this;[4]

(2) that the disclosure was made by or to a professional legal adviser as part of giving legal advice as to the provisions of Part III of RIPA. The disclosure must have been by or to the client or a representative of the client;[5]

(3) that the disclosure was made by a legal adviser in contemplation of any legal proceedings;[6]

(4) that the disclosure was made to a judicial commissioner, or someone authorized by a commissioner;[7]

(5) that the recipient neither knew, nor had reasonable grounds to suspect, that the notice contained a secrecy requirement.[8]

1 RIPA 2000, s 54.
2 RIPA 2000, s 54(1).
3 RIPA 2000, s 54(4).
4 RIPA 2000, s 54(5).
5 RIPA 2000, s 54(6).
6 RIPA 2000, s 54(7).
7 RIPA 2000, s 54(9).
8 RIPA 2000, s 54(10).

8.39 In all cases, a legal burden is placed on the defence: it must prove the salient facts on the balance of probabilities. Where the defence is that a disclosure has been made to, or by, a professional legal adviser, the defence does not apply where the purpose of the disclosure is to further any criminal purpose.[1]

1 RIPA 2000, s 54(8).

8.40 It should be noted, however, that the effectiveness of the 'tipping off' offence is debatable. It might be possible for a person to sign off her email correspondence with a disclaimer, such as 'I will always explain why I revoke a key, unless the UK government prevents me using the RIP Act 2000'. Using this qualification, let us assume that a correspondent revokes a key. If the correspondent is asked for the reason and she replies that she cannot give one, it is doubtful if she can be convicted of the offence of tipping off, though this is exactly what she has done. There is no suggestion that a disclosed key cannot lawfully be revoked.

Circumventing the procedure

8.41 It has been held, albeit in a first-instance Magistrates' Court decision, that RIPA 2000 is the only way that the authorities can compel access to encrypted data. Lauri Love is a UK citizen who was a member of the Anonymous hacker collective.[1] He was accused of hacking into US government sites and stealing information.[2] The US government requested his extradition and the National Crime Agency (NCA) arrested him, exercising a warrant to seize his computers. The computers were found to be encrypted, and a notice under RIPA 2000 s 49 was served, requiring him to disclose either the key or render the information intelligible. He declined to do so. The USA sought his extradition, but this was ultimately refused by the English courts, in part because of his mental health, but also because he could be tried for the offences in England and Wales.[3] To date, no criminal proceedings have been brought against him.

1 An interesting discussion about Anonymous is to be found in Gabriella Coleman, *Hacker, Hoaxer, Whistleblower, Spy: The Many Faces of Anonymous* (Verso Books 2015).

2 *Love v United States* [2018] EWHC 172 (Admin), [2018] 1 WLR 2889, [2018] 2 All ER 911, [2018] 2 WLUK 89, [2018] Lloyd's Rep FC 217, [2018] ACD 33, [2018] CLY 988.

3 The Computer Misuse Act 1990 allows a person to be tried for hacking where the victim was outside the territory of England and Wales. To date, no prosecution has been brought against Love.

8.42 Love applied to the Magistrates' Court to have his computer equipment returned.[1] The court declined to order its return unless he provided a detailed list of the contents of the computer, something he has refused to do. The NCA made an application that Love be directed to provide the keys to the encryption.[2] The district judge, however, held that this was not a proper use of the court's jurisdiction. The judge held that RIPA 2000 provided the statutory procedure to secure access to encrypted data. The decision of the district judge was undoubtedly the correct one. In essence, the NCA was seeking to use civil proceedings to gain access to the key, rather than rely on RIPA 2000. Had the application succeeded, the NCA could have sought to use contempt of court proceedings to require compliance with the direction, which could ultimately have led to the imprisonment of Love. However, as the judge noted, the correct avenue to enforce s 49 is to bring a prosecution for non-compliance under s 53.

1 Police (Property) Act 1897, s 1.
2 The application being made in pursuance of the Magistrates' Court Rules 1981/552, r 3A(2) and the Criminal Procedure (Amendment) Rules 2016/120.

8.43 While Love defeated the application, a strange impasse now exists, because his application under the Police (Property) Act 1897 was also rejected. He refused to discuss what was encrypted, hence the district judge held that its continued seizure was required. The police have the right to retain seized material to prevent it from being concealed, lost, damaged, altered or destroyed.[1] Not unreasonably, it was thought there was reason to believe that Love may seek to destroy any incriminating evidence contained on the machine should it be returned to him.

1 Criminal Justice and Police Act 2001, s 56.

8.44 The reluctance to prosecute Love is somewhat puzzling since, on the face of it, it appears that Love did breach s 49. For whatever reason, the NCA has chosen not to prosecute. As Love refuses to comply, the NCA are left with computers that they cannot obtain access to (although presumably NTAC is trying to override the encryption) and Love is allowed to ignore the requirement to surrender the encrypted information. This demonstrates that while it is often said that RIPA compels the disclosure of encryption keys, technically it does not. Ultimately, all the legislation can do is to ensure that those who refuse to disclose the key or render information intelligible can be punished. The encrypted material, however, remains beyond reach.

The privilege against self-incrimination

8.45 Compelling someone to provide a key has proven to be controversial. In most cases, the key is a password, and this password might have been thought of by the suspect, although random password generators are also used. It has been suggested that compelling the disclosure of the key infringes the common law privilege that someone cannot be compelled to incriminate herself. It is the fact that the password is the product of one's mind, and can only be released through testimony, that raises this argument. A key could be something physical, including another piece of code, a biometric measurement or, for example, a dongle (a piece of technology usually including a chip). Requiring a person to hand over, for example, a dongle to unlock the encryption would not necessarily breach the privilege,[1] because the key is invariably a self-produced password. The remainder of this chapter will explore how compelling the production of the key interferes with the privilege of self-incrimination in three jurisdictions: England and Wales, the USA[2] and Belgium.[3] The position in Canada is considered in brief.

1 It would be an object that was created independently and is not the testimony of an individual: see *Saunders v United Kingdom* [1996] 12 WLUK 363, [1997] BCC 872, [1998] 1 BCLC 362, (1997) 23 EHRR 213, Times, 18 December 1996, Independent, 14 January 1997, [1997] CLY 2816.
2 For these purposes, federal law will be considered.
3 For France, see Décision n° 2018-696 QPC du 30 mars 2018, Le Conseil constitutionnel (Constitutional Court). Translated by Pauline Martin (2018) 15 Digital Evidence and Electronic Signature Law Review 92.

England and Wales

8.46 While the privilege of self-incrimination has long been a creature of the common law,[1] it is also considered to be a fundamental part of article 6 of the European Convention on Human Rights (ECHR).[2] The Human Rights Act 1998 requires public authorities, including the police and the judiciary, to act in a way compatible with the ECHR,[3] and the courts must take account of the jurisprudence of the European Court of Human Rights.[4]

1 An excellent history of the privilege is found in Andrew Choo, *The Privilege against Self-Incrimination and Criminal Justice* (Hart Publishing 2014).
2 *Funke v France (A/256-A)* [1993] 2 WLUK 374, [1993] 1 CML 897, (1993) 16 EHRR 297, [1994] CLY 2431; *Saunders v United Kingdom* [1996] 12 WLUK 363, [1997] BCC 872, [1998] 1 BCLC 362, (1997) 23 EHRR 213, Times, 18 December 1996, Independent, 14 January 1997, [1997] CLY 2816.
3 Human Rights Act 1998, s 6(1).
4 Human Rights Act 1998, s 2(1); Rosemary Pattenden, 'Privilege against self-incrimination' (2009) 13(1) E. & P. 69.

8.47 The first case to challenge the compatibility of Part III of RIPA was *R v S (F) and A (S)*.[1] A third party (H) was made the subject of a control order under the Prevention of Terrorism Act 2005. S, A and H conspired to circumvent this control order by allowing H to move houses. This occurred, but shortly afterwards the police detected his presence. When the police arrived, H and S were in different rooms. S was alone in a room with a laptop. The password to an encrypted file was partly entered. S was arrested, and his premises searched, but nothing that contravened terrorism laws was found. However, the police could not examine the laptop due to the encryption. Later, A was arrested and a laptop was seized from him. Again, there was an encrypted folder on it, and the police were unable to gain access to the laptop.

1 [2008] EWCA Crim 2177, [2009] 1 WLR 1489, [2009] 1 All ER 716, [2008] 10 WLUK 197, [2009] 1 Cr App R 18, [2009] Crim LR 191, (2008) 158 NLJ 1459, Times, 15 October 2008, [2008] CLY 711.

8.48 Neither A nor S made any comments during their interviews and did not voluntarily disclose the passwords that would unlock the encryption. Both were served with a notice under s 49 of RIPA 2000. Neither complied, and they were prosecuted under s 53. They both entered a plea of not guilty and sought a stay of prosecution, alleging that the notices themselves were incompatible with the privilege against self-incrimination and article 6 of the ECHR. The judge at first instance refused the stay, and A and S appealed to the Court of Appeal.

8.49 The members of the Court of Appeal noted that the submissions of all parties were premised on the basis that incriminating evidence would be discovered if the laptops were examined without encryption.[1] There was no evidence of this, but the appellants conceded that incriminating material may be discovered. The members of the Court of Appeal noted that under both domestic and European jurisprudence, the privilege against self-incrimination was not absolute, and that there were several statutory provisions that overrode it. Thus, the first question was whether the privilege applied in these circumstances. It was held by the judge at first instance that the key was something held independent of the will of the suspect. If that was true, then the privilege against self-incrimination would ordinarily not apply.[2] The Court of Appeal held:

> On analysis, the key which provides access to protected data, like the data itself, exists separately from each defendant's 'will'. Even if it is true that each created his own key, once created the key to the data remains independent of the defendant's 'will' even when it is retained only in his memory, at any rate until it is changed.[3]

1 [2008] EWCA Crim 2177 at [14].
2 [2008] EWCA Crim 2177 at [18].
3 [2008] EWCA Crim 2177 at [20].

8.50 The logic behind this argument is that while the password may initially have been the product of the defendant's mind, it has an independent status once used. If the password was guessed or identified, then the encryption would unlock irrespective of whether the defendant willed it or not. They also noted that the key is neutral. It is not by itself either exculpatory or incriminating – it is simply a piece of information. However, if the contents are incriminating, then knowledge of the key could in itself be incriminating. The court provided the example of an encrypted folder containing indecent photographs of children.[1] The fact that a person knows the key – and this would be shown through complying with the s 49 notice – could be used by the prosecution to show that the offender was in possession of the photographs.[2] Of course, that depends on the facts. Where the substantive offence does not rely on control, then the possession of the key may not be incriminating.

1 [2008] EWCA Crim 2177 at [21].
2 Possession in the context of indecent photographs of children includes showing that the offender is in control of the material: see *R. v Porter (Ross Warwick)* [2006] EWCA Crim 560, [2006] 1 WLR 2633, [2007] 2 All ER 625, [2006] 3 WLUK 471, [2006] 2 Cr App R 25, [2006] Crim LR 748, (2006) 103(4) LSG 28, Times, 21 June 2006, [2006] CLY 858). Having the ability to unlock the encrypted folder is unquestionably control.

8.51 Ultimately, the Court of Appeal conceded that s 49 could interfere with the privilege of self-incrimination, but noted that it would only do so if the evidence that is being shielded by encryption is itself incriminating. However, the court opined that material unquestionably exists independent of the will of the individual and, therefore, there is no question of it being protected by the privilege. Thus, the only argument that could be put forward is that it is unfair for that evidence to be put before the court due to the circumstances in which it was found (through complying with s 49).[1] That being the case, the Court of Appeal held that such matters could be dealt by the trial judge under the discretionary power to exclude prosecution evidence.[2]

1 *R v S (F) and A (S)* [2008] EWCA Crim 2177 at [24].
2 PACE 1984, s 78.

8.52 The decision in *S and A* has not been universally welcomed. This is partly because the logic of the Court of Appeal stretches credibility. Roberts in the *Criminal Law Review* observed that an encryption key, unless documented, is an 'intangible "psychological fact", that is to say, it is information which exists only in the suspect's memory and that of any other person who might "know" it'.[1] The Court of Appeal would argue that this is not true because the key does exist – it is recorded and used within the encryption algorithm that is unlocked by the password. However, for all practical purposes, it is not. There is a very small chance that the password can be discovered by any other means. Indeed, if the police were able to identify the password other than through compelling the suspect to testify, there would be no need to issue a s 49 notice. As was noted above, it is almost impossible to guess a key when encryption is used properly due to the potentially vast number of possible combinations. Therefore, while in theory the key is independent of the will of the accused, it is, for all practical purposes, a psychological fact and, therefore, probably within the privilege. However, Roberts' later point is perhaps the more salient. He notes that it does not matter whether privilege was or was not engaged because, following *Brown v Stott*,[2] English law recognizes the privilege can be set aside by statute where it is proportionate to do so.[3] Given the facts of the case, the national security implications would inevitably mean that displacement was undoubtedly proportionate.

1 Andrew J. Roberts, 'Evidence: privilege against self-incrimination – key to encrypted material' [2009] Crim LR 191, 192. In 1993, Professor Tapper observed that the increased use of computers will lead to the position that we recess 'to the earlier period where information reposed only in the brains of those who were party to it, and had no material form': Colin Tapper, 'Evanescent evidence' (1993) 1(1) Intl J L & Info Tech 35, 40.
2 [2003] 1 AC 681, [2001] 2 WLR 817, [2001] 2 All ER 97, 2001 SC (PC) 43, 2001 SLT 59, 2001 SCCR 62, [2000] 12 WLUK 108, [2001] RTR 11, [2001] HRLR 9, 11 BHRC 179, (2001) 3 LGLR 24, (2001) 145 SJLB 100, 2000 GWD 40-1513, Times, 6 December 2000, Independent, 7 February 2001, [2001] CLY 6319; Roisin Pillay, 'Self-incrimination and Article 6: the decision of the Privy Council in Procurator Fiscal v. Brown' (2001) 1 EHRLR 78; Roger Masterman, 'Taking the Strasbourg jurisprudence into account: developing a "municipal law of human rights" under the Human Rights Act' (2005) 54(4) ICLQ 907–1; Mark Berger, 'Compelled self-reporting and the principle against compelled self incrimination: some comparative perspectives' (2006) 1 EHLR 25; John Jackson, 'Re-conceptualizing the right of silence as an effective fair trial standard' (2009) 58(4) ICLQ 835; Hamish Stewart, 'The privilege against self-incrimination: reconsidering Redmayne's rethinking' (2016) 20(2) E & P 95.
3 The leading examination on the application of the privilege of self-incrimination is Choo, *The Privilege against Self-Incrimination and Criminal Justice*.

8.53 The issues were further rehearsed in *Greater Manchester Police v Andrews*.[1] Rather than proceedings under s 53, this was an appeal from the refusal of the circuit judge to authorize a s 49 notice being served. Andrews had previous convictions for the sexual abuse of children, and was the subject of a Sexual Offences Prevention Order. Police arrested him on suspicion of breaching this order, and seized a computer and two memory sticks. Indecent photographs of children were found on the computer, but the memory sticks were encrypted. This meant that they could not be viewed. Andrews refused to provide the passwords or software used to encrypt the devices. The police applied for permission to serve a s 49 notice, but this was refused. The judge stated that requiring Andrews to reveal the key infringed his privilege against self-incrimination, because there was no independent evidence to show that he knew what the key was.[2] The judge sought to use these facts to distinguish this case from *R v S (F) and A (S)*.[3] The Court of Appeal was unimpressed with the logic of the judge. They noted that as the devices were unquestionably found in his possession, that it was not unreasonable to believe that he might know of the existence of the encryption and its key.[4] The court did not disagree that the privilege might be invoked, and noted once more that the privilege applied only in a limited way (repeating that the key was, in essence, neutral and it simply provided access to non-privileged material that was itself incriminating), and that English law allowed it to be displaced where it was proportionate to do so.[5]

1 [2011] EWHC 1966 (Admin), [2011] 5 WLUK 614, [2012] ACD 18.
2 [2011] EWHC 1966 (Admin) at [18]–[19].
3 [2008] EWCA Crim 2177, [2009] 1 WLR 1489, [2009] 1 All ER 716, [2008] 10 WLUK 197, [2009] 1 Cr App R 18, [2009] Crim LR 191, (2008) 158 NLJ 1459, Times, 15 October 2008, [2008] CLY 711.
4 *Greater Manchester Police v Andrews* [2011] EWHC 1966 (Admin) at [21].
5 [2011] EWHC 1966 (Admin) at [27].

8.54 Section 49 has not been challenged again, and so the legal position now seems relatively settled. As noted at the beginning of this chapter, the power is not exercised particularly frequently. This suggests that the police are only using it where they suspect that encryption is shielding serious criminality. That being the case, it is likely the courts would consider it proportionate that the privilege against self-incrimination is set aside, as they did in *R v S and F*.

The USA

8.55 The position in England and Wales can be usefully contrasted with the approach taken in the USA, where the Fifth Amendment protects the privilege against self-incrimination.

The Fifth Amendment privilege against self-incrimination

8.56 One of the first cases in the USA to deal with this issue was also cited in *R v S (F) and A (S)*[1] to illustrate the point that knowledge of the password might be relevant to the privilege against self-incrimination. The case of *In re Grand Jury Subpoena to Sebastien Boucher*[2] involved facts arising out of the search of a laptop at the US border with Canada. On 17 December 2006, Boucher and his father entered the US from Canada. A customs and border protection officer found a laptop computer in the vehicle they were travelling in. He opened the computer and switched it on without entering a password. He searched the various files in the computer and discovered approximately 40,000 images, some of which appeared to be pornographic, based on the names of the files. Boucher was asked if any of the files contained abusive images of children, to which he responded that he was not certain. The officer continued to search the files and noticed some files with names that suggested images of a minor engaging in sexually explicit conduct. He then requested the help of another officer, who determined that a number of files contained abusive images of children. Boucher was then read his *Miranda* rights. He told the second officer that he downloaded pornographic files and indicated that he did not intentionally download images of a minor engaging in sexually explicit conduct and deleted any such images when he came across them. Boucher was given access to the laptop and navigated to the Z drive, to which he obtained access by inserting a password. The second officer did not see Boucher do this. Boucher was subsequently arrested and his laptop was seized. After obtaining a search warrant, the government discovered that the Z drive was encrypted and the investigating authorities could not open the Z drive. A grand jury subpoena was issued for Boucher, directing him to 'provide all documents, whether in electronic or paper form, reflecting any passwords used or associated with' his seized computer.[3]

1 *R v S (F) and A (S)* [2008] EWCA Crim 2177, [2009] 1 WLR 1489, [2009] 1 All ER 716, [2008] 10 WLUK 197, [2009] 1 Cr App R 18, [2009] Crim LR 191, (2008) 158 NLJ 1459, Times, 15 October 2008, [2008] CLY 711.
2 2009 WL 424718 (D.Vt.), reversing and remanding 2007 WL 4246473 (Maj. Ct. D.Vt.).
3 2007 WL 4246473 (D.Vt.) at [2].

8.57 Boucher moved to quash the subpoena because, he alleged, it violated his right not to incriminate himself under the provisions of the Fifth Amendment. Whether the privilege against self-incrimination applied in this instance depended on whether the subpoena sought testimonial communication. Both parties agreed that the contents of the laptop computer were not covered by the Fifth Amendment because they were voluntarily prepared and not testimonial in nature. The magistrate court held that requiring Boucher to enter the password would disclose both that he knew the password and that he had control over the files on the encrypted drive.[1] The magistrate therefore concluded that the Fifth Amendment prevented the government from compelling Boucher to provide the password on the basis that it would compel him to display the contents of his mind and thereby incriminate himself.[2] The government appealed this decision,[3] arguing that it was already aware of the existence and location of the information during the border examination (when the officer viewed the contents of some of the Z drive files, and ascertained that they could consist of images or videos of a minor engaging in sexually explicit conduct). On appeal, the district court agreed. The court held that requiring Boucher to 'provid[e] access to the unencrypted Z drive "adds little or nothing to the sum total of the Government's information" about the existence and location of files that may contain incriminating information', and therefore this did not constitute 'compelled testimonial communication' and did not breach Boucher's Fifth Amendment right against self-incrimination.[4]

1 2007 WL 4246473 (D.Vt.) at [3].
2 2007 WL 4246473 (D.Vt.) at [6].
3 *In re Grand Jury Subpoena to Sebatien Boucher*, 2009 WL 424718 (D.Vt.).
4 *In re Grand Jury Subpoena to Sebastien Boucher*, 2009 WL 424718 (D.Vt.) at [2]–[3]. For more discussion in the US context and reference to other articles, see Aaron M. Clemens, 'No computer exception to the constitution: the Fifth Amendment protects against compelled production of an encrypted document or private key' (2004) 8(1) UCLA Journal of Law and Technology 1; Andrew J. Ungberg, 'Protecting privacy through a responsible decryption policy' (2009) 22(2) Harv J L & Tech 537; John Duong, 'The intersection of the Fourth and Fifth Amendments in the context of encrypted personal data at the border' (2009) 2(1) Drexel Law Review 313; David Colarusso, 'Heads in the cloud, A coming storm: the interplay of cloud computing, encryption, and the Fifth Amendment's protection against self-incrimination' (2011) 17(1) Boston University Journal of Science and Technology Law 69; Adam M. Gershowitz, 'Password protected? Can a password save your cell phone from a search incident to arrest?' (2011) 96(4) Iowa L Rev 1125; Susan W. Brenner, 'The Fifth Amendment, cell phones and search incident: a response to password protected?' (2011) 96 Iowa L Rev Bulletin 78; Michael Wachtel, 'Give me your password because Congress can say so: an analysis of Fifth Amendment protection afforded individuals regarding compelled production of encrypted data and possible solutions to the problem of getting data from someone's mind' (2013) 14 U Pitt J Tech & Policy 44; Andrew T. Winkler, 'Password protection and self-incrimination: applying the Fifth Amendment privilege in the technological era' (2013) 39(2) Rutgers Computer & Tech LJ 194; David Rassoul Rangaviz, 'Compelled decryption & state constitutional protection against self-incrimination' (2020) 57(1) American Criminal Law Review 157; Rafita Ahlam, 'Apple, the government, and you: security and privacy implications of the global encryption debate' (2021) 44(3) Fordham Int'l LJ 771; Orin S. Kerr, 'Decryption originalism: the lessons of Burr' (2021) 134(3) Harv L Rev 905.

8.58 The *Boucher* case is illustrative of compelled decryption cases in the US. A defendant's Fifth Amendment privilege against self-incrimination is implicated when the police require a suspect to enter a passcode to unlock an encrypted device, such as a telephone or computer. United States courts tend to agree that the act of entering a passcode is testimonial, which activates the privilege against self-incrimination; however, this privilege is not available if the police can show that the testimony would be considered a 'foregone conclusion'.

8.59 This rule is based on the 'act of production' doctrine from *Fisher v United States*,[1] which was developed in the context of producing documents pursuant to a subpoena. The Supreme Court in *Fisher* held that the Fifth Amendment privilege against self-incrimination was implicated when the government compelled a suspect to produce documents when the act is both testimonial and incriminating.[2] The act of production is neither testimonial nor incriminating, however, when it 'adds little or nothing to the sum total of the Government's information' and is therefore a 'foregone conclusion'.[3]

1 425 U.S. 391 (1976), 96 S.Ct. 1569 (1976).
2 425 U.S. 391 (1976) at 409–410.
3 425 U.S. 391 (1976) at 411.

8.60 Courts have adopted and applied the act of production doctrine and its foregone conclusion exception to cases of compelled decryption. Courts differ, however, on how the foregone conclusion exception should be applied on two primary fronts. First, courts differ on whether the police must show that they already have knowledge that the suspect knows his passcode, or whether the police must show that they already have knowledge of the encrypted content of the device.[1] In other words, courts differ on what constitutes the 'testimony' that must be a foregone conclusion. Second, courts differ on the burden of proof of this foregone conclusion: some courts have required the police to show clear and convincing evidence,[2] some have required proof beyond a reasonable doubt,[3] some have required a showing of facts with reasonable particularity,[4] and still others seem to gloss over the standard required entirely. This section will survey some of the more influential cases, noting that these jurisprudential splits can only be resolved by the US Supreme Court.

1 Compare *United States v Apple MacPro Computer*, 851 F.3d 238 (3rd Cir. 2017) (in dicta clarifies that the government must only show that they have knowledge that the suspect knows the passcode or owns the device) to *In re Grand Jury Subpoena Duces Tecum Dated March 25, 2011*, 670 F.3d 1335 (11th Cir. 2012) (requires the government to show that they have knowledge of the encrypted content of the device).
2 *United States v Spencer*, 2018 WL 1964588 (N.D. Cal. 2018).
3 *Commonwealth v Jones*, 117 N.E.3d 702 (Mass. 2019), 481 Mass. 540 (Sup.Jud.Ct. 2019). It is worth noting that this court found that the Massachusetts State Constitution required a showing of the foregone conclusion beyond a reasonable doubt. State courts in the US may interpret their state constitutions to be more protective of individual rights than the federal US Constitution. The US Constitution is considered to guarantee the minimum amount of rights protection, which the states may strengthen through their own constitutions. Further, the court in *Commonwealth v Jones* does not bind any courts outside the State of Massachusetts.
4 *In the Matter of the Search of a Residence in Aptos, California 95003*, 2018 WL 1400401 (N.D. Cal. 2018). This Magistrate Judge's decision was overturned by the District Court in *United States v Spencer*, 2018 WL 1964588 (N.D. Cal. 2018). The *Spencer* Court clarified that the reasonable particularity standard was a substantive standard that 'helps to ensure that any testimony at issue really is a "foregone conclusion"'. In the case of a determination concerning whether a suspect is capable of decrypting a device, it is a binary question – either he can or he cannot – rather than something that

must be described by the government with reasonable particularity. Therefore, the correct evidentiary standard is clear and convincing evidence. See also *In the Matter of the Decryption of a Seized Data Storage System*, 2013 WL 12327372 (E.D. Wis. 2013) (holding that the government must show the foregone conclusion with reasonable particularity). Arguably, the reasonable particularity standard only makes sense when the government must show its knowledge of the contents of a device, which is why it was also used by the court in *In re Grand Jury Subpoena Duces Tecum Dated March 25, 2011*, 670 F.3d 1335 (11th Cir. 2012).

8.61 In the case of *In re Grand Jury Subpoena Duces Tecum Dated March 25, 2011*,[1] law enforcement agents began an investigation in March 2010 of an individual suspected of using a YouTube.com account for sharing explicit materials involving underage girls. During the course of their investigation, officers obtained several Internet protocol (IP) addresses from which the individual had obtained access to the Internet. Three of the addresses were subsequently traced to hotels. A review of the register in each hotel revealed a common name registered at the hotel at the relevant time, being that of one Doe. Doe was found at a hotel in California, and the police applied for and obtained a warrant to search his room. Seven items were seized, including two laptops and five external hard drives. Examiners from the Federal Bureau of Investigation analysed the digital media but could not obtain access to some parts of the hard drives because they were encrypted with a software program called TrueCrypt.

1 670 F.3d 1335 (11th Cir. 2012).

8.62 Doe refused to provide the passwords to enable the government to open and view the encrypted data, and he also refused to decrypt the data. As a result, he was served with a subpoena duces tecum, requiring him to appear before a grand jury and produce the plaintext of the encrypted files located on the hard drives of his laptop computers and the five external hard drives. Federal prosecutors offered him immunity for the act of decrypting the computer but reserved the right to use any evidence it found on the computer against him.[1] When he appeared before the grand Jury, Doe invoked his Fifth Amendment privilege against self-incrimination to not reveal the plaintext. During the hearing, the forensic examiner testified that he could obtain access to some parts of the hard drives, but he could not know for certain whether there might be data on the encrypted part of the hard drive – indeed, he accepted there might not be any data in the encrypted part of the drives. The district court determined that Doe's failure to decrypt the relevant parts of the hard drives amounted to contempt of court and committed him to custody.

1 670 F.3d 1335 at 1350.

8.63 On appeal, the Eleventh Circuit Court of Appeals reversed the district court decision and held that the decryption and production of the hard drives was a testimonial act, and thus the defendant could assert his Fifth Amendment privilege against self-incrimination. The court reasoned:

> the decryption and production of the hard drives would require the use of the contents of Doe's mind and could not be fairly characterized as a physical act that would be nontestimonial in nature. We conclude that the decryption and production would be tantamount to testimony by Doe of his knowledge of the existence and location of potentially incriminating files; of his possession, control, and access to the encrypted portions of the drives; and of his capability to decrypt the files.

> We are unpersuaded by the Government's derivation of the key/combination analogy in arguing that Doe's production of the unencrypted files would be nothing more than a physical nontestimonial transfer. The Government attempts to avoid the analogy by arguing that it does not seek the combination or the key, but rather the contents. This argument badly misses the mark.' [1]

1 670 F.3d 1335 at 1346.

8.64 Further, the 'foregone conclusion' exception was not available to the government because it failed to show that it had knowledge of the contents of the defendant's device. The court noted that:

> nothing in the record before us reveals that the Government knows whether any files existed and are located on the hard drives; what's more, nothing in the record illustrates that the Government knows with reasonable particularity that Doe is even capable of accessing the encrypted portions of the drives.[1]

1 670 F.3d 1335 at 1346.

8.65 In this regard, *In re Grand Jury* is distinguishable from *Boucher* in that the government was aware of what was on Boucher's computer because of his own actions in displaying them to the officers.[1]

1 For a more detailed discussion of this case, see Hanni Fakhoury, Esq., 'A combination or a key? The Fifth Amendment and privilege against compelled decryption' (2012) 9 Digital Evidence and Electronic Signature Law Review 81.

8.66 While there is wide agreement that the act of production doctrine and foregone conclusion exception apply to cases of compelled decryption, courts differ on what constitutes the testimony that must be a foregone conclusion. The *In re Grand Jury* court required the government to show that the contents of the suspect's device would be a foregone conclusion. Interestingly, the *Boucher* court, while not explicit in its analysis about what testimony must be proven, found that the government knew both the contents of the device and that the suspect could decrypt the device. The Third Circuit Court of Appeals considered a similar case, although it would go on to provide detailed guidance of what type of testimony must be shown to be a foregone conclusion – and in so doing, diverged from the Eleventh Circuit in this regard.

8.67 In 2017, the Third Circuit considered the case of *United States of America v Apple MacPro Computer*[1] in which the suspect Doe refused to decrypt hard drives that were obtained by police pursuant to a valid search warrant. Along with the hard drives, police also seized a mobile telephone and a MacPro computer. The police were able to bypass the encryption on the MacPro computer and found evidence that Doe had downloaded photographic files constituting images of a minor engaging in sexually explicit conduct. The police suspected that the files themselves were stored on the separate encrypted hard drives that Doe refused to decrypt. Doe argued that the act of decryption would violate his Fifth Amendment privilege against self-incrimination.

1 851 F.3d 238 (3rd Cir. 2017).

8.68 The Third Circuit followed the Eleventh Circuit's legal reasoning that the act of production and foregone conclusion rules applied to the compelled decryption of devices. Unlike the facts of the case before the Eleventh Circuit, however, the Third

Circuit found that the testimony sought by the government from Doe was a foregone conclusion. The court reasoned: 'the Government has provided evidence to show both that files exist on the encrypted portions of the devices and that Doe can access them.'[1] Among other reasons, the evidence to support this assertion was: the encrypted devices were found at Doe's residence and he did not dispute his ownership of them, analysts found evidence on the MacPro computer that the user had visited groups that had titles used in child exploitation and had downloaded images known through hashing to be images of a minor engaging in sexually explicit conduct, and Doe's sister had witnessed Doe unlock the hard drives to view images and videos of a minor engaging in sexually explicit conduct.[2] Based on these and similar facts, the magistrate had found that the testimony would be a foregone conclusion. The district court and the Third Circuit Court of Appeals both affirmed that conclusion.

1 851 F.3d 238 at 248.
2 851 F.3d 238 at 248.

8.69 Due to the overwhelming amount of proof against Doe, it could be difficult to ascertain whether the Third Circuit requirement that the testimony must be shown to be a foregone conclusion is simply the passcode or ownership of the devices, or the contents of the device. The Third Circuit had evidence in that case that Doe owned the devices and had decrypted the devices previously, and that the government knew the contents of the devices, all of which qualified as a foregone conclusion. Helpfully, the court added a footnote, that although dictum, is persuasive authority for future cases in the Third Circuit:

> It is important to note that we are not concluding that the Government's knowledge of the content of the devices is necessarily the correct focus of the 'foregone conclusion' inquiry in the context of a compelled decryption order. Instead, a very sound argument can be made that the foregone conclusion doctrine properly focuses on whether the Government already knows the testimony that is implicit in the act of production. In this case, the fact known to the government that is implicit in the act of providing the password for the devices is 'I, John Doe, know the password for these devices'. Based upon the testimony presented at the contempt proceeding, that fact is a foregone conclusion. However, because our review is limited to plain error, and no plain error was committed by the District Court in finding that the Government established that the contents of the encrypted hard drives are known to it, we need not decide here that the inquiry can be limited to the question of whether Doe's knowledge of the password itself is sufficient to support application of the foregone conclusion doctrine.[1]

1 851 F.3d 238 at 248, n 7.

8.70 Other cases have cited this dictum by the Third Circuit Court of Appeals in *Apple MacPro Computer* to hold that the government need only show that the suspect's knowledge of the passcode is a foregone conclusion.[1] This is consistent with an unpublished opinion of the Fourth Circuit Court of Appeals in *United States of America v Gavegnano*,[2] in which the appellant was convicted of receipt and possession of abusive images of children stored on a laptop computer owned by the government and issued to him for the purposes of his work. One of the grounds of appeal was based on the Fifth Amendment, in that he gave the password of the laptop computer to the prosecuting authorities after meeting with his lawyer. The Fourth Circuit rejected his claim, on the basis that 'Any self-incriminating testimony that he may have provided by revealing the password was already a "foregone conclusion" because the Government independently proved that Gavegnano was the sole user and possessor of the computer'.[3]

1 *State of Oregon v Pittman*, 452 P.3d 1011 (Or.App. 2020); *Commonwealth v Jones*, 117 N.E.3d 702 (Mass. 2019), 481 Mass. 540 (Sup.Jud.Ct. 2019); *State of Missouri v Johnson*, 576 S.W.3d 205 (Mo.App. W.D. 2019); *State of New Jersey v Andrews*, 197 A.3d 200 (N.J.Super.A.D. 2018); *United States v Spencer*, 2018 WL 1964588 (N.D. Cal. 2018); *State of Florida v Stahl*, 206 So.3d 124 (Fla.App. 2 Dist. 2016) at 136; *U.S. v Fricosu*, 841 F.Supp.2d 1232 (D.Colo. 2012).
2 305 Fed.Appx. 954 (4th Cir. 2009), 2009 WL 106370.
3 305 Fed.Appx. 954 (4th Cir. 2009) at 956.

8.71 Nonetheless, other courts have chosen to follow the approach set out by the Eleventh Circuit that requires the government to show, with reasonable particularity, that the contents of the device are a foregone conclusion.[1] In adopting this approach, the district court *In the Matter of the Search of a Residence in Oakland, California* explicitly rejected the notion that an encrypted device, in this case a telephone, was akin to a safe and that the government's demand for a passcode is merely the same as compelling a suspect to enter a passcode to open a safe, much like the use of a key.[2] The court reasoned that '[t]oday's mobile phones are not comparable to other storage equipment, be it physical or digital, and are entitled to greater privacy protection'. Quoting the US Supreme Court's opinion in *Riley v California*, the District Court considered that a search of a telephone 'would typically expose to the government far more than the most exhaustive search of a house'.[3] Given the primary split between the Eleventh Circuit Court of Appeals and the Third and Fourth Circuit Courts of Appeals, it is possible that the US Supreme Court will, at some time in the future, be asked to clarify the scope of the act of production doctrine and the foregone conclusion exception in the context of compelled decryption of devices by the use of passcodes.[4] Likewise, courts seem to be split on the issue of whether a forced use of biometric measurements constitutes 'testimony' such that the Fifth Amendment privilege against self-incrimination will apply.

1 *In the Matter of the Search of a Residence in Oakland, California*, 354 F.Supp.3d 1010 (N.D. Cal. 2019); *Seo v State*, 109 N.E.3d 418 (Ind.App. 2018), transfer granted and opinion vacated on other grounds, see *Eunjoo Seo v State*, 148 N.E.3d 952 (2019); *Securities and Exchange Commission v Huang*, 2015 WL 5611644 (E.D. Pa. 2015).
2 354 F.Supp.3d 1010 at 1017.
3 354 F.Supp.3d 1010 (quoting *Riley v California*, 573 U.S. 373 (2014), 134 S.Ct. 2473 (2014)).
4 It is beyond the scope of this chapter to discuss the correct approach. For a thorough exploration of these issues, consult Orin Kerr, 'Compelled decryption and the privilege against self-incrimination' (2018) 97 Texas L Rev 767, and Laurent Sacharoff, 'What am I really saying when I open my smartphone? A response to Orin S. Kerr' (2019) 97 Texas L Rev Online 63.

8.72 There are several Federal District Courts[1] and at least one State Supreme Court[2] that have found that compelling the suspect to unlock a device, usually a telephone, with a biometric measurement such as a fingerprint or face, does not constitute testimony such that the privilege against self-incrimination is implicated. As the District Court of Idaho reasoned in the case of *In the Matter of the Search of: a White Google Pixel 3 XL Cellphone in a black incipio case*, 'the Government agents will pick the fingers to be pressed on the Touch ID sensor, [and so] there is no need to engage in the thought process of the subject at all in effectuating the seizure'.[3] The court in that case compared this act to other compelled displays of physical features that have been allowed by the US Supreme Court, including, 'putting on a shirt to see whether it fits the defendant; providing a blood sample to test for alcohol content; submitting to the taking of fingerprints or photographs; providing a voice exemplar; and providing a handwriting exemplar'.[4]

1 *In the Matter of the Search Warrant Application for the Cellular Telephone in United States v Barrera*, 415 F.Supp.3d 832 (N.D.Ill. 2019); *In the Matter of the Search of: a White Google Pixel 3 XL Cellphone in a Black Incipio Case*, 398 F.Supp.3d 785 (D.Idaho 2019); *Matter of Search of [Redacted] Washington, District of Columbia*, 317 F.Supp.3d 523 (D.D.C. 2018).
2 *State of Minnesota v Diamond*, 905 N.W.2d 870 (Minn. 2018).
3 398 F.Supp.3d 785 at [13]; for Illinois, see *In the Matter of the Search Warrant Application for the cellular telephone in United States v Barrera*, 415 F.Supp.3d 832 (N.D.Ill. 2019).
4 398 F.Supp.3d 785 at [10–12] (internal citations omitted).

8.73 Other courts disagree, however. In *United States v Wright*, a federal district court in Nevada held:

> First, a biometric feature is functionally the same as a passcode, and because telling a law enforcement officer your passcode would be testimonial, so too must the compelled use of your biometric feature to unlock a device. Second, unlocking a phone with your face equates to testimony that you have unlocked the phone before, and thus you have some level of control over the phone.[1]

1 431 F.Supp.3d 1175 (D.Nev. 2020) (citing *In the Matter of the Search of a Residence in Oakland, California*, 354 F.Supp.3d 1010 (N.D. Cal. 2019)) (internal citations omitted).

8.74 Another Federal District Court in Illinois agreed, and cited the Eleventh Circuit opinion in the case of *In re Grand Jury Subpoena Duces Tecum Dated March 25, 2011* to support its holding that 'the connection of a fingerprint to the electronic sources that may hold contraband ... does explicitly or implicitly relate a factual assertion or disclose information'.[1] The court rejected the government's claim that the Fifth Amendment does not apply to the compulsion to submit to fingerprinting, stating:

> We do not believe that a simple analogy that equates the limited protection afforded a fingerprint for identification purposes to forced fingerprinting to unlock an Apple electronic device that potentially contains some of the most intimate details of an individual's life (and potentially provides direct access to contraband) is supported by Fifth Amendment jurisprudence.[2]

1 *In re Application for a Search Warrant*, 236 F.Supp.3d 1066 (N.D.Ill. 2017) at 1073.
2 236 F.Supp.3d 1066 at 1073–1074.

8.75 Similar to the issue of forced decryption through use of passcodes, the testimonial nature of biometric features used for decryption needs clarification from a higher court.

Bypassing the Fifth Amendment by compelling the assistance of third parties

8.76 Given the limitations of the cases noted above regarding compelled decryption by suspects, governments increasingly seek to compel third party intermediaries, usually technology companies or communications service providers, to provide plaintext data to law enforcement authorities. Perhaps the most famous example of the US government attempting to compel a third party intermediary to decrypt a device is the litigation over an Apple iPhone seized by the FBI in *Government's ex parte application for order compelling Apple Inc. to assist agents in search*[1] before the district court of the Central

District of California. The US government seized an iPhone 5C believed to have belonged to Syed Rizwan Farook, an alleged terrorist who perpetrated an attack which killed 14 people and injured 22 others in San Bernandino, California. The iPhone was protected by a passcode. Later generation iPhones have their contents encrypted by default, and the passcode acts as the password. Thus, without the password, the FBI was unable to obtain access to the contents of the device. It is also possible to set the iPhone to auto-erase the contents of the telephone if a set number of incorrect passcodes is entered.

1 *In the Matter of the Search of an Apple Iphone Seized During the Execution of a Search Warrant on a Black Lexus IS300, California License Plate 35KGD203*, 2016 WL 618401 (C.D. Cal. 16 February 2016).

8.77 Given these obstacles, the government sought an order under the All Writs Act[1] requiring Apple to assist the FBI in circumventing the encryption.[2] Contrary to what was reported in most media, the order did not require Apple to break the encryption, but rather Apple was ordered to provide reasonable technical assistance in bypassing or disabling the auto-erase function, enabling the FBI to submit unlimited passcodes to the device for electronic testing and ensuring that the device would not purposefully introduce any additional delay between passcode attempts, essentially enabling a brute-force attack.[3] Apple resisted the imposition of the order, arguing that to do so would hand unparalleled powers to the government, which would render data privacy laws meaningless. They argued that any process they put in place could be exploited by others, which meant that the privacy of all its customers would be put at risk.[4] Ultimately, the FBI were able to obtain access to the device with the help of an unnamed third party, and the litigation was discontinued.[5]

1 28 U.S. Code § 1651.
2 2016 WL 618401 (C.D. Cal. 16 February 2016).
3 2016 WL 618401 (C.D. Cal. 16 February 2016), Order 2.
4 Tim Cook, 'A message to our customers' (Apple, Inc, 16 February 2016), http://www.apple.com/customer-letter/.
5 Rob Crilly, 'FBI finds method to hack gunman's iPhone without Apple's help', http://www.telegraph.co.uk/technology/2016/03/29/fbi-finds-method-to-hack-gunmans-iphone-without-apples-help0/.

8.78 In a similar case,[1] the government sought an order before a New York court requiring Apple to bypass the passcode security on an Apple device on the basis that such an order would assist in the execution of a search warrant previously issued by the court. The court denied the government's motion, on the basis that the government had failed to establish that the All Writs Act permitted the relief it sought, partly because Congress had considered legislation that would achieve the same result but had not adopted it. The judge also noted that a court, when deciding whether to take such discretionary action, was required to consider three additional factors:

> 1. the closeness of the relationship between the person or entity to whom the proposed writ is directed and the matter over which the court has jurisdiction;
>
> 2. the reasonableness of the burden to be imposed on the writ's subject; and
>
> 3. the necessity of the requested writ to aid the court's jurisdiction (which does replicate the second statutory element, despite the overlapping language).[2]

1 *In re Order requiring Apple, Inc, to assist in the execution of a search warrant issued by this Court*, 2015 WL 5920207 (E.D.N.Y. 2015); *In re Apple, Inc.*, 149 F.Supp.3d 341 (E.D.N.Y. 2016).
2 *In re Apple, Inc.*, 149 F.Supp.3d 341 (E.D.N.Y. 2016) at 351.

8.79 The court said that even if the statute did apply, all three discretionary factors weighed against the issuing of the requested writ, and that the application would be denied as a matter of discretion, even if it is available as a matter of law.

8.80 These cases brought renewed attention to the encryption debates between law enforcement authorities who seek lawful access to plaintext data and the information and communication technology (ICT) companies who implement encryption by default for security purposes. In addition to security concerns, these companies also benefit from encryption by shifting control to the user, which limits the abilities of the companies to cooperate with the government. ICT companies can also benefit from appearing to champion user privacy, especially after the Snowden revelations in 2013.[1] After these revelations, both Apple and Google announced they would begin encrypting devices by default.[2] Around the same time, James Comey, then Director of the FBI, articulated concerns about the growing use of encryption:

> Unfortunately, the law hasn't kept pace with technology, and this disconnect has created a significant public safety problem. We call it 'Going Dark', and what it means is this: Those charged with protecting our people aren't always able to access the evidence we need to prosecute crime and prevent terrorism even with lawful authority. We have the legal authority to intercept and access communications and information pursuant to court order, but we often lack the technical ability to do so.[3]

1 https://en.wikipedia.org/wiki/Edward_Snowden.
2 'Don't panic: making progress on the going dark debate' (Berkman Center for Internet & Society, Harvard University 2016) 10, https://cyber.harvard.edu/pubrelease/dont-panic/Dont_Panic_Making_Progress_on_Going_Dark_Debate.pdf.
3 James B. Comey, Federal Bureau of Investigation Director, 'Going dark: are technology, privacy, and public safety on a collision course?', speech delivered to the Brookings Institution (2014), https://www.fbi.gov/news/speeches/going-dark-are-technology-privacy-and-public-safety-on-a-collision-course.

8.81 To solve this 'going dark' problem, Reitinger argues that 'permitting law enforcement to compel the production of keys when necessary, with judicial supervision as appropriate, is a minimal accommodation to the need for public security in a world in which criminals have an increasing array of sophisticated tools at their disposal'.[1] It is difficult to think of any other aspect of evidence where a suspect is allowed to wilfully hide evidence of his criminality from law enforcement and for this to be condoned by the criminal justice system. Using encryption, a person can hide thousands of abusive images of children on a device. They could obtain access to them every day but, if they took appropriate precautions,[2] law enforcement authorities would find it almost impossible to prove that the offence has taken place.[3] That is not in the interest of society. This is a point made by Orenstein MJ of New York in his concluding remarks in one of the cases involving Apple:

> How best to balance those interests is a matter of critical importance to our society, and the need for an answer becomes more pressing daily, as the tide of technological advance flows ever farther past the boundaries of what seemed possible even a few decades ago. But that debate must happen today, and it must take place among legislators who are equipped to consider the technological and cultural realities of a world their predecessors could not begin to conceive.[4]

1 Phillip R. Reitinger, 'Compelled production of plaintext and keys' (1996) U Chi Legal F 206, fn omitted.

2 Deleting caches, recent document lists, etc.
3 Keylogging software would only work if a single device was used to obtain access to the material (or the software would be required to be placed on each device) and if a regular Internet connection was used. Covert surveillance (cameras) could be installed to show the material being viewed, but law enforcement authorities would need to know which room the device was located in, and it could be difficult to obtain authorization to do so, depending on the level of intrusion this could cause (for example, if it was on a tablet, it may be necessary to have devices in each room, which could be construed a gross invasion of privacy).
4 *In re Apple, Inc.*, 149 F.Supp.3d 341, 376 (E.D.N.Y. 2016) at 376.

8.82 Jim Baker, former general counsel for the FBI, was responsible for leading the government efforts to compel Apple to decrypt the iPhone in the San Bernandino case in 2016.[1] In 2019 Baker wrote that his opinion on encryption had changed in light of the serious cybersecurity threats facing the US:

> *All public safety officials should think of the protecting of the cybersecurity of the United States as an essential part of their core mission to protect the American people and uphold the Constitution.* And they should be doing so even if there will be real and painful costs associated with such a cybersecurity-forward orientation. The stakes are too high and our current cybersecurity situation too grave to adopt a different approach.
>
> ...
>
> In light of the serious nature of this profound and overarching [cybersecurity] threat, and in order to execute fully their responsibility to protect the nation from catastrophic attack and ensure the continuing operation of basic societal institutions, public safety officials should embrace encryption.[2]

1 The telephone was eventually 'unlocked' by the Australian company Azimuth: Ellen Nakashima and Reed Albergotti, 'The FBI wanted to unlock the San Bernardino shooter's iPhone. It turned to a little-known Australian firm' *The Washington Post*, 14 April 2021, https://www.washingtonpost.com/technology/2021/04/14/azimuth-san-bernardino-apple-iphone-fbi/.
2 Jim Baker, 'Rethinking encryption' Lawfare (22 October 2019), https://www.lawfareblog.com/rethinking-encryption (original emphasis).

8.83 Baker's remarks illustrate how the encryption debate has turned in recent years from the 'false dichotomy' between security and privacy to a discussion of competing security interests.[1] ICT companies and computer scientists argue that encryption is necessary to protect users from criminals, while law enforcement authorities argue that encryption protects criminals from detection and prosecution. In reality, encryption does both. Privacy advocates and computer scientists argue that criminals will always find a way to communicate anonymously and that measures designed to allow governments to have access to keys or back doors will do more harm to regular users of these technologies.[2] Computer scientists in particular have raised alarms that any government proposals for 'exceptional access' to encrypted systems are 'unworkable in practice, raise enormous legal and ethical questions, and would undo progress on security at a time when Internet vulnerabilities are causing extreme economic harm'.[3] These same computer scientists concluded a report analysing law enforcement proposals for exceptional access with the following observations:

> This report's analysis of law enforcement demands for exceptional access to private communications and data shows that such access will open doors through which criminals and malicious nation-states can attack the very individuals law enforcement seeks to defend. The costs would be substantial, the damage to innovation severe, and the consequences to economic growth difficult to predict.[4]

1 Professor Susan Landau sets out the arguments about encryption very clearly in her book: *Listening In: Cybersecurity in an Insecure Age* (Yale University Press 2017); Encryption Working Group, Carnegie Endowment for International Peace, Center for Information on Technology Policy, Princeton University, 'Moving the encryption policy conversation forward' (September 2019) 3, https://carnegieendowment.org/files/EWG_Encryption_Policy.pdf.
2 For more on this debate, see the essay series at Daniel J. Weitzner, 'Perspectives on encryption and surveillance', Lawfare, 29 November 2018, https://www.lawfareblog.com/perspectives-encryption-and-surveillance; for a historical perspective, see Danielle Kehl, Andi Wilson and Kevin Bankston, 'Doomed to repeat history? Lessons from the crypto wars of the 1990s' (2015), https://static.newamerica.org/attachments/3407-doomed-to-repeat-history-lessons-from-the-crypto-wars-of-the-1990s/Crypto%20Wars_ReDo.7cb491837ac541709797bdf868d37f52.pdf.
3 Harold Abelson, Ross Anderson, Steven M. Bellovin, Josh Benaloh, Matt Blaze, Whitfield Diffie, John Gilmore, Matthew Green, Susan Landau, Peter G. Neumann, Ronald L. Rivest, Jeffrey I. Schiller, Bruce Schneier, Michael A. Specter and Daniel J. Weitzner, 'Keys under doormats: mandating insecurity by requiring government access to all data and communications' [2015] Journal of Cybersecurity 1, https://academic.oup.com/cybersecurity/article-lookup/doi/10.1093/cybsec/tyv009.
4 Abelson and others, 'Keys under doormats', 24–25.

8.84 However, the Encryption Working Group, funded by the Carnegie Endowment for International Peace and comprising former government officials, business representatives, privacy advocates, law enforcement authorities and computer scientists in the US, believe that 'more common ground is attainable' if the discussion between participants focuses on the individual 'component parts' within the larger umbrella of encryption policy.[1] For example, while encryption for data in transit may raise many of the issues that concerned the computer scientists cited above, 'some forms of access to encrypted information, such as access to data at rest on mobile phones' may be possible.[2] By debating specific types of encryption, data and devices, it may be possible to find a sensible middle ground approach which allows for law enforcement authorities to obtain access to decrypted data without endangering cybersecurity or privacy.[3]

1 Encryption Working Group, Carnegie Endowment for International Peace, Center for Information on Technology Policy, Princeton University, 'Moving the encryption policy conversation forward' (September 2019) 4, https://carnegieendowment.org/files/EWG_Encryption_Policy.pdf.
2 Encryption Working Group, Carnegie Endowment for International Peace, 'Moving the encryption policy conversation forward', 17.
3 Similarly, UK officials at GCHQ have advocated for cooperation and collaboration given the lack of straightforward solutions in the security versus security debate. Ian Levy and Crispin Robinson, 'Principles for a more informed exceptional access debate', Lawfare, 29 November 2018, https://www.lawfareblog.com/principles-more-informed-exceptional-access-debate.

Canada

8.85 Another perspective to this debate is added by the decision of the Canadian court in *R. v Beauchamp*.[1] In this case, an unusual application was brought. Rather than the law enforcement agency seeking access to encrypted data, the defence sought an order to require the Crown to disclose a copy of encrypted files located on a hard drive that had been seized by the police. The Crown had not been able to decrypt the files, and as a result had no knowledge of the data that was encrypted. It was agreed that the encrypted information was both potentially inculpatory and potentially exculpatory for the accused parties. The Crown submitted that the encrypted information was beyond its control, and although it was arguably in its possession, it was not in a format that the Crown was able to view. The judge concluded that the Crown was in partial possession and control of the hard drives, but it had no knowledge of the information in the encrypted files. Smith J analysed the position as follows:

> The seizure by the police of the hard drives containing encrypted information is similar to the seizure of a locked safe which the police cannot open, containing documents which include both inculpatory and exculpatory evidence. The police or Crown would clearly be in possession or control of the safe, but if they did not have the key or combination and were unable to break the safe open, then they would not have knowledge of the contents of the safe. In this case, the Crown's control of the contents of the safe, which are known to one accused but not to the Crown, is not complete, as the Crown needs the key or combination, or in this case the password, in order to access the documents in the safe. The unique feature of this case is that the accused ... has the key or password, which is necessary to complete the possession or control of the information in the safe.[2]

1 2008 CarswellOnt 2756, [2008] OJ No 1347, 171 CRR (2d) 358, 58 CR (6th) 177, 77 WCB (2d) 177; for further cases in Canada, see *R. v Burke* 2013 CarswellOnt 8417, 2013 ONCA 424, [2013] OJ No 2920, 107 WCB (2d) 662, 285 CRR (2d) 6, 298 CCC (3d) 396, 307 OAC 171; *R. v M.* 2012 CarswellMan 256, 2012 MBQB 141, [2012] MJ No 174, 101 WCB (2d) 168, 279 Man R (2d) 80, 93 CR (6th) 155; *R. v Stemberger* 2012 CarswellOnt 492, 2012 ONCJ 31, [2012] OJ No 221, 100 WCB (2d) 20, 254 CRR (2d) 1; see also Lex Gill, 'Law, metaphor, and the encrypted machine' (2018) 55 Osgoode Hall LJ 440; Steven Penney and Dylan Gibbs, 'Law enforcement access to encrypted data: legislative responses and the *Charter*' (2017) 63 McGill LJ 201 (2017).

2 2008 CarswellOnt 2756 at [40].

8.86 For these reasons, the application for disclosure of a copy of the encrypted files in the hard drives was refused, although the judge indicated that the applicants could, at their option, obtain disclosure of the contents if they provided the password or key to the Crown, and the Crown would then review the material. Had the application been allowed, it would have created an untenable situation. The state would have provided a file that only one party (the defence) could view. The defence would presumably extract the exculpatory evidence without giving the Crown sight of the inculpatory evidence. It is suggested that this decision struck the correct balance, which is to enable the defence to disclose the key so that both parties will have access to the plaintext material.

Belgium

8.87 The Court of Cassation in Belgium[1] has held that Belgian law can require a criminal suspect to disclose their mobile telephone passcode without violating their right to remain silent and to not incriminate oneself, provided the investigating authority can show that the mobile telephone was detected without coercion and that the suspect knows the passcode 'without reasonable doubt'.[2] The Belgian Court interpreted the right to not incriminate oneself as guaranteed by the ECHR, the International Covenant on Civil and Political Rights, and Directive (EU) 2016/343 of 9 March 2016 on the strengthening of certain aspects of the presumption of innocence and of the right to be present at the trial in criminal proceedings.[3] The court found that the qualified right against self-incrimination would not prevent authorities from gathering evidence that exists 'independently of the will of the person who has knowledge of' the passcode.[4] It held that 'the main purpose of the right not to incriminate oneself is to safeguard the right to a fair trial by excluding false statements made under duress'.[5] Because the passcode remains unchanged regardless of whether it is communicated, the court determined that '[t]here is no risk of unreliable evidence'.[6]

1 The authors thank Professor Dr Joachim Meese, Faculty of Law, Universiteit Antwerpen, Belgium and lawyer at the bar of Ghent, Belgium for his review of this section on Belgium.
2 *Attorney General at the Court of Appeal of Ghent v M A*, 4 februari 2020 P.19.1086.N, Hof van Cassatie, tweede kamer (Court of Cassation, second chamber), English translation in (2020) 17 Digital Evidence and Electronic Signature Law Review 94. For comments on this decision, see C. Conings and R. De Keersmaecker, 'To save but not too safe: hoogste Belgische rechters zien geen graten in het decryptiebevel voor de verdachte' (2020) 3 Tijdschrift voor Strafrecht 163 and F. Koning, 'Droit au silence et à ne pas s'incriminer: Quo Vadis?' (2020) 6807 Journal des Tribunaux 204.
3 OJ L 65, 11.3.2016, 1.
4 *Attorney General v M A*, 4 februari 2020 P.19.1086.N, Hof van Cassatie, tweede kamer (Court of Cassation, second chamber), English translation in (2020) 17 Digital Evidence and Electronic Signature Law Review, 95–96.
5 *Attorney General v M A*, 4 februari 2020 P.19.1086.N, Hof van Cassatie, 3.
6 *Attorney General v M A*, 4 februari 2020 P.19.1086.N, Hof van Cassatie, 3.

8.88 The court found that the passcode is thus akin to the communication of biometric data, which is a permissible derogation from the right to not incriminate oneself. Even if the passcode reveals information that is subjected to substantial criminal sanctions, the communication of the passcode itself only relates to accessing an 'already discovered IT system'.[1] Thus, the compelled decryption of a telephone passcode did not violate the suspect's right to remain silent.

1 *Attorney General v M A*, 4 februari 2020 P.19.1086.N, Hof van Cassatie, 3.

Concluding observations

8.89 Encryption is a fundamental part of modern cybersecurity. Good quality encryption provides reassurance to users that sensitive information can be securely stored. However, it is obvious that a criminal can also use encryption to hide his actions. More than this, encryption allows material to be hidden from everyone else, but remain accessible to the possessor of the cryptographic key. Throughout history, people have hidden files or objects that they do not want law enforcement authorities to find. However, that invariably affects the ability of the owner to use the files or objects. For example, a person could send photographs or physical records out of the jurisdiction where no mutual legal assistance treaty exists. This will keep the data away from investigators, but the owners will not be able to view the photographs or records themselves. Encryption, however, means that the possessor of the key can easily open a file and, for example, look at illegal material at will, while preventing law enforcement authorities from knowing what is being looked at.

8.90 The philosophical basis around the right to self-incrimination is of fundamental importance in any criminal justice system. The difficulty is in establishing a balance between the right not to incriminate oneself when accused by the state, and the rights of victims and society to liberty and security. This is a difficult balance to achieve,[1] and in this chapter we have described how various jurisdictions have approached this problem.

1 For a different perspective, see Phillip Rogaway, 'The moral character of cryptographic work', Cryptology ePrint Archive, Report 2015/1162, http://web.cs.ucdavis.edu/~rogaway/papers/moral.html.

8.91 The balance between the competing security interests implicated by encryption will require continued scrutiny from courts and lawmakers as encryption technologies advance.[1] These issues will continue to affect criminal investigations into a wide variety of criminal conduct.[2] While the cases explored in this chapter mostly involved criminal offences concerning child sexual abuse materials, law enforcement authorities need to obtain access to encrypted evidence in offences ranging from cybercrime and organized crime to routine investigations into theft, assault and homicide. Thus, we can expect the law concerning access to encrypted data to continue to develop and evolve.

1 Quantum cryptography and computing are expected to revolutionize encryption in the coming decades. This may result in unbreakable encryption and likewise the capability to break all existing encryption keys. See Ian Walden, ' "The sky is falling!" – responses to the "going dark" problem' (2018) 34 Computer Law & Security Review 901, 906.

2 Support for end-to-end encryption increases if child safety can be protected. While this is useful for privacy, it also presents risks to child safety and means abuse can go unnoticed online. The following papers set out new research and analysis about the implications of end-to-end encryption for child protection: National Society for the Prevention of Cruelty to Children, 'End-to-end encryption: understanding the impacts for child safety online (April 2021); National Society for the Prevention of Cruelty to Children, 'Private messaging and the rollout of end-to-end encryption: the implications for child protection' (April 2021), both at https://www.nspcc.org.uk/about-us/news-opinion/2021/adults-support-encryption-if-children-safety-protected/; also see Derek Johnson, Erin Faulkner, Georgia Meredith and Tim J. Wilson, 'Police functional adaptation to the digital or post digital age: discussions with cybercrime experts' (2020) 84(5) Journal of Criminal Law 427; Tim J. Wilson, 'Collaborative justice and harm reduction in cyberspace: policing indecent child images' (2020) 84(5) Journal of Criminal Law 474.

9

Proof: the technical collection and examination of electronic evidence

Nigel Wilson, Andrew Sheldon, Hein Dries, Burkhard Schafer and Stephen Mason

9.1 This chapter addresses the challenges and methodologies associated with proving a fact with electronic evidence, and considers the measures relating to the accreditation of those performing a digital forensic analysis, together with the validation of the technologies, systems and methodologies used. It looks at how and why the correct handling, preserving and analysing of electronic evidence are critical steps in an investigation process to ensure reliability of proof. It explains how the probative value of the evidence can be affected and its reliability compromised when critical procedures or measures are not followed. It further describes the use of automation and technology solutions to enhance the efficiency of investigations, and the controls used to ensure the accuracy and forensic reliability of such investigations.

9.2 All electronic evidence exists, at its most basic level, in binary form. The Binary Digit ('bit'), which represents a logical state with one of two possible digits, is typically represented as a single digit in a binary number as either 0 or 1. These bits are in turn organized in a larger group of 8 bits called a byte. A byte can be used to represent letters of the alphabet and other characters. For example, the byte comprising the 8-bit sequence 01000001 may represent the letter 'A' in a word processing system, but could represent something entirely different in a video processing application. Interpretation is, therefore, relative to context and determined by the software used to interpret it. Such representation and interpretation is achieved by using multiple processing and storage layers within a digital system such as a computer, mobile telephone, GPS device or media player, etc. These processing layers include hardware such as processing chips, digital cameras and networks, operating systems such as Windows, Linux, iOS and Android, application software such as word processors, email, web browsers, messaging clients and media players, and data storage such as hard disks, memory cards and cloud environments.

9.3 Thus, when proving a fact using electronic evidence, what an individual may witness on the output such as the screen is the result of multiple phases of digital processing and interpretation performed by software. The risk is that any processing phase may be subject to error. Similarly, when specialist digital forensic software is used to preserve and present electronic evidence, it does so using a programmatic interpretation of the bits and bytes it finds, and this also may be subject to error or wrongful assumptions about the meaning of the data.

9.4 For these reasons, proof, as it applies to electronic evidence, requires more than simple reproduction of data. The process of adducing evidence and determining

Nigel Wilson, Andrew Sheldon, Hein Dries, Burkhard Schafer and Stephen Mason, 'Proof: the technical collection and examination of electronic evidence', in Stephen Mason and Daniel Seng (eds.), *Electronic Evidence and Electronic Signatures* (5th edn, University of London 2021) 429–487.

proof relies on the systems used and the training and experience of the people creating and using them. Both people and systems need to meet significant accreditation and demanding validation to demonstrate that all such interpretations of data have been performed accurately. This is partly because of the unique nature of electronic evidence: it is extremely volatile and subject to being altered with ease, even by the simple act of switching a computer on or off.[1]

1 Graeme B. Bell and Richard Boddington, 'Solid state drives: the beginning of the end for current practice in digital forensic recovery?' (2010) 5(3) Journal of Digital Forensics, Security and Law 1; Michael Wei, Laura M. Grupp, Frederick E. Spada and Steven Swanson, 'Reliability erasing data from flash-based solid state drives', *Proceedings of the 9th USENIX Conference on File and Storage Technologies* (USENIX Association Berkeley, CA, 2011).

Accreditation of the digital forensics discipline

9.5 By their nature, investigations and examinations of electronic evidence are relatively new compared to other more established forms of forensic analysis such as fingerprinting, DNA analysis, toxicology and ballistics. Broadly speaking, electronic or digital (the terms are used interchangeably) investigations are concerned with the gathering, preservation and analysis of relevant digital data to provide both evidence and intelligence to assist with criminal investigations[1] and prosecutions, and with civil and regulatory matters and proceedings.

1 The evidence of digital systems can also help reconstruct what happened in an incident, for which see Mario Piccinelli and Paolo Gubian, 'Modern ships Voyage Data Recorders: a forensics perspective on the Costa Concordia shipwreck' (2013) 10 Digital Investigation S41.

9.6 Forensic analysis of electronic evidence draws from diverse disciplines such as electrical and electronic engineering and computer science, and includes sub-disciplines such as computer forensics, network forensics, cloud forensics, data analysis, audio and video analysis and analysis of mobile devices. Accreditation has been strongly supported from within the diverse digital forensics discipline. In the USA, the American Society of Crime Laboratory Directors/Laboratory Accreditation Board (ASCLD/LAB) formally accredited digital forensics as a discipline in 2003 together with four sub-disciplines: computer forensics, audio analysis, video analysis and image analysis. In 2016 the ASCLD/LAB was acquired by the American National Standards Institute-American Society for Quality (ANSI-ASQ) National Accreditation Board (ANAB) and the four sub-disciplines were merged into a single discipline known as digital evidence forensics.[1] There are similar specialist advisory groups in Australia and New Zealand.[2] In the United Kingdom, the Forensic Science Regulator was established in 2008, and included digital forensics as a specialist group. In April 2020 the Forensic Science Regulator produced updated Codes of Practice and Conduct (issue 5) across the entire forensic industry, including for digital forensics.[3]

1 https://anab.ansi.org/about-anab; Hong Guo and Junlei Huo, 'Review of the accreditation of digital forensics in China' (2018) 3 Forensic Sciences Research 194, who note that over 70 forensic inspection and laboratories in the US are ANAB accredited. Fred Cohen, *Digital Forensic Evidence Examination* (4th edn, Fred Cohen & Associates 2012); Eoghan Casey, *Digital Evidence and Computer Crime Forensic Science, Computers and the Internet* (3rd edn, Academic Press 2011) 1; Alastair Irons and Anastasia Konstadopoulou, 'Professionalism in digital forensics' (2007) 4 Digital Evidence and Electronic Signature Law Review 45; Simson Garfinkel, Paul Farrell, Vassil Roussev and George Dinolt, 'Bringing science to digital forensics with standardized forensic corpora' (2009) 6 Digital Investigation S2; Yinghua Guo, Jill Slay and Jason Beckett, 'Validation and verification of computer forensic software

tools—Searching Function' (2009) 6 Digital Investigation S12; Simson L. Garfinkel 'Digital forensics research: the next 10 years' (2010) 7 Digital Investigation S64; Jason Beckett and Jill Slay, 'Scientific underpinnings and background to standards and accreditation in digital forensics' (2011) 8 Digital Investigation 114.

2 Australia New Zealand Policing Advisory Agency, http://www.anzpaa.org.au/forensic-science/forensic-sciences/forensic-groups; Australian Forensic Science Society, http://anzfss.org/about/; National Association of Testing Authorities, https://www.nata.com.au/.

3 The Forensic Science Regulator, Codes of Practice and Conduct (FSR-C-100, Issue 5, 2020), https://assets.publishing.service.gov.uk/government/uploads/system/uploads/attachment_data/file/880708/Codes_of_Practice_and_Conduct_-_Issue_5.pdf; the Nederlands Register Gerechtelijk Deskundigen (Netherlands Register of Court Experts) undertook a similar process in 2018, see https://lrgd.nl.

9.7 Although formal academic certification of practitioners in various disciplines and accreditation of digital forensic processes are relatively common among the digital forensic community, there is, at the time of writing, a noticeable absence of such accreditation for the process of 'cloud forensics' and other evidence obtained online or through, for example, social media. In this regard, rather than qualifications to use commercial tools, academic qualifications that teach fundamental principles of preservation, continuity, critical thinking and verification can be applied to 'cloud' forensics. However, there are a number of significant and unique challenges when dealing with data obtained online, not least of which is the fact that potential evidence held by a service provider may not be preserved in the normal manner when creating an image or snapshot of the target storage or computer platform. To this end, frameworks[1] are being developed for cloud forensics evidence collection and analysis using security information and event management that draw upon research by the National Institute of Standards and Technology (NIST),[2] specifically the NIST Cloud Computing Forensic Science Working Group.

1 Muhammad Irfan, Haider Abbas, Yunchuan Sun, Anam Sajid and Maruf Pasha, 'A framework for cloud forensics evidence collection and analysis using security information and event management', Security Comm. Networks (2016), 9:3790-3807, https://onlinelibrary.wiley.com/doi/pdf/10.1002/sec.1538; https://doi.org/10.1002/sec.1538.

2 Martin Herman, Michaela Iorga, Ahsen Michael Salim, Robert H. Jackson, Mark R. Hurst, Ross Leo, Richard Lee, Nancy M. Landreville, Anand Kumar Mishra, Yien Wang and Rodrigo Sardinas, NIST Cloud Computing Forensic Science Challenges (NISTIR 8006, August 2020), https:doi.org/10.6028/NIST.IR.8006.

Guidelines for handling digital evidence

9.8 Along with the benefits of consistency and uniformity arising from accreditation, numerous guidelines have been produced, premised on uniformity and standardization of procedures that are relevant to the collection and handling of electronic evidence. In 1995 the International Organization on Computer Evidence was established to provide international law enforcement authorities with a forum to facilitate the exchange of information relating to computer crime investigations and other issues relating to digital forensic investigations.[1] This organization, together with several other UK authorities, including the Association of Chief Police Officers (ACPO) and the National High-Tech Crime Unit, have produced a number of guidelines for the investigation and examination of electronic evidence within a criminal context. Although various sets of guidelines have, in the main, been produced specifically for criminal investigations, nevertheless the guidelines are also of significant help to practitioners and lawyers in civil matters.[2]

1 See also N. Dudley-Gough, 'Digital forensic certification board' (2006) 3(1) Digital Investigation 7; Amber Schroader and N. Dudley-Gough, 'The Institute of Computer Forensic Professionals' (2006) 3(1) Digital Investigation 9; note also the European Informatics Data Exchange Framework for Court and Evidence, a project running for 32 months (March 2014–October 2016), http://www.evidenceproject.eu.
2 Casey, *Digital Evidence*, 230, indicates that the most mature and practical guidelines are those produced by ACPO.

9.9 In April 2020 the UK Forensic Science Regulator published an informational guidance document entitled Legal Obligations Issue 8.[1] This provides a relatively high-level overview of the obligations placed on expert witnesses in the Criminal Justice System in England and Wales. Contemporary guidelines include documents from Australia and New Zealand,[2] the United Kingdom,[3] the USA,[4] Europe,[5] Asia[6] and ISO/IEC Standards.[7] Likewise, INTERPOL has also established the Global Guidelines in relation to Digital Forensics Laboratories.[8]

1 Forensic Science Regulator Legal Obligations (FSR-I-400, Issue 8, 2020), https://www.gov.uk/government/publications/legal-obligations-issue-8.
2 Australia and New Zealand Guidelines for Digital Imaging Processes (2013, ANZPAA), https://www.anzpaa.org.au/ArticleDocuments/180/2013%20Australia%20and%20New%20Zealand%20Guidelines%20for%20Digital%20Imaging%20Processes.pdf.aspx.
3 UK ACPO Good Practice Guide for Digital Evidence, https://www.digital-detective.net/digital-forensics-documents/ACPO_Good_Practice_Guide_for_Digital_Evidence_v5.pdf.
4 National Institute of Justice, Forensic Examination of Digital Evidence: A Guide for Law Enforcement, US Department of Justice, 2004, https://www.ncjrs.gov/pdffiles1/nij/199408.pdf.
5 European Union, European Anti-Fraud Office, Guidelines on Digital Forensic Procedures for OLAF Staff, 2016, https://ec.europa.eu/anti-fraud/sites/antifraud/files/guidelines_en.pdf.
6 For example, see China – Ministry of Public Security of the People's Republic of China (2019) *Rules on Collection of Electronic Data by Public Security Bureau when Handling Criminal Cases* and (2016) *Rules on Electronic Data Collection, Extraction and Review in Criminal Cases.*
7 ISO/IEC 27037:2012 [ISO/IEC 27037:2012] 'Information technology — Security techniques — Guidelines for identification, collection, acquisition and preservation of digital evidence' (confirmed in 2018), https://www.iso.org/standard/44381.html.
8 INTERPOL, 2019 Global Guidelines by INTERPOL for Digital Forensics Laboratories, https://www.interpol.int/content/download/13501/file/INTERPOL_DFL_GlobalGuidelinesDigitalForensicsLaboratory.pdf.

Handling electronic evidence

9.10 As with any other form of evidence, there are a number of discrete elements that accompany the collection and handling of digital evidence. It is suggested that a digital evidence professional should, ideally, undertake her duties against the highest standards that are propounded by her peers, regardless of whether she is assisting in a criminal or civil matter. In *Bilta (UK) Limited (in Liquidation) v Nazir*,[1] Lewison J indicated that he did not consider it an automatic requirement that parties to civil proceedings have to subject hard drives to forensic discovery techniques. It is debatable whether it is wise not to subject hard drives to forensic search techniques, as demonstrated in the case of *In the matter of Stanford International Bank Limited (in liquidation), Fundora v Hamilton-Smith*.[2] This was an application for the discharge of the appointed Joint Official Liquidators of Stanford International Bank Limited and other parties on the basis that, among other reasons, they destroyed digital data and employed improper practices in relation to computer and electronic data.[3] The precise matters in dispute were as follows:

> The matters which tell [*sic*] to be considered can be narrowed down to the following: (a) three servers at the Montreal office of SIB were not imaged and not copied, (b) four desktops and laptops were not imaged but were securely erased, (c) the email servers and Blackberry enterprise servers were not imaged; (d) the IT specialists did not appear to have been instructed by the Liquidators to search for, collect and image the Blackberrys and data sticks.[4]

1 [2010] EWHC 1086 (Ch), [2010] Bus LR 1634, [2010] 2 Lloyd's Rep 29, [2010] 5 WLUK 368, [2010] CLY 420.

2 2–3 March and 8 June 2010, Claim Number ANUHCV2009/0149 Eastern Caribbean Supreme Court in the High Court of Justice Antigua and Barbuda; the judgment is available at http://www.eccourts.org/wp-content/files_mf/1358795765_magicfields_pdf_file_upload_1_1.pdf and the Court of Appeal decision is available at http://www.eccourts.org/wp-content/files_mf/1358779099_magicfields_pdf_file_upload_1_1.pdf; see also *Stanford International Bank Ltd (In Receivership), Re* [2010] EWCA Civ 137, [2011] Ch 33, [2010] 3 WLR 941, [2010] Bus LR 1270, [2010] 2 WLUK 712, [2011] BCC 211, [2010] Lloyd's Rep FC 357, [2010] BPIR 679, [2010] CLY 1873, also known as *Serious Fraud Office v Wastell, Janvey v Wastell, Stanford International Bank Ltd v Director of the Serious Fraud Office.*

3 Discussed at [44]–[115] of the judgment.

4 At [50] of the judgment.

9.11 After considering the relevant ACPO guidelines at the material time, Thomas J decided that the action of the Joint Official Liquidators was not in accordance with standard forensic practice, and in so doing, they acted improperly. To this extent, the various guidelines put forward as best practices provide sound advice and guidance when dealing with electronic evidence, and if followed, they can serve to counter allegations that the evidence has not been gathered or dealt with properly.

9.12 In *Khodorkovskiy and Lebedev v Russia*,[1] a case before the European Court of Human Rights, the defence raised a number of important issues challenging the electronic evidence sought to be admitted that related to the volatile and mutable nature of such evidence. It alleged, among other things, that the hard drives that were seized had not been properly packed and sealed, so it was possible to add information to them while the drives were in the possession of the General Prosecutor of the Russian Federation,[2] as the investigators discovered more files on the drives than there were on the same drives when examined by the experts,[3] that the drives and the list of files discovered by the prosecution were not attached by the General Prosecutor to the case materials, and that there was no evidence that documented the continuity of the evidence.[4] In concluding that these deficiencies were not relevant, the court said:

> Possible discrepancies in the documents describing the amount of data contained on the hard drives, inaccuracies as to the exact location of the computer servers, and other defects complained of may have various explanations. The Court cannot detect any manifest flaw in the process of seizing and examining the hard drives which would make the information obtained from them unfit for use at the trial.[5]

1 11082/06 and 13772/05 – [2013] ECHR 747 (25 July 2013).

2 11082/06 and 13772/05 – [2013] ECHR 747 (25 July 2013) at [72]. When examining the hard drives seized during the searches of 9 October 2003, the investigators discovered 4,939 more files on the drives than those examined by the experts: 11082/06 and 13772/05 – [2013] ECHR 747 (25 July 2013) at [181].

3 11082/06 and 13772/05 – [2013] ECHR 747 (25 July 2013) at [679].

4 11082/06 and 13772/05 – [2013] ECHR 747 (25 July 2013) at [678].

5 11082/06 and 13772/05 – [2013] ECHR 747 (25 July 2013) at [702].

9.13 In our opinion, this decision fails to emphasize the importance of professional digital forensics when seizing data in digital form. From a technical perspective, a hash value, calculated on site upon taking a forensic image of the hard drives that have been seized (or, if this is impossible, shortly thereafter), could have easily served as proof of the evidence having been untouched since it was first acquired (provided that the hash was kept securely or communicated to the defence or suspect at an early stage). However, there was no indication that the court relied upon, or the defence proffered, such evidence in support of such a conclusion.

9.14 Notwithstanding the preference for an original forensic image, or a demonstration of full and complete provenance, together with contemporaneous notes beginning from the source of the evidence, it may still be possible to prove the authenticity of certain types of digital evidence beyond doubt. One example of such a method is the examination of email messages which are downloaded to a USB drive. In such circumstances, it may not be possible to establish direct continuity from the computer or server on which the original email messages were created or transmitted before they were downloaded to the USB drive. Neither is it possible to obtain a forensic image of the senders' or receivers' computers. Therefore, the authenticity of the email messages and any attachments may be called into question. However, if an email message contains a DKIM[1] (Domain Keys Identified Mail) signature, it is possible to establish beyond doubt that the message and any attachment is authentic and has not been modified since it was sent, regardless of how it has been handled since.[2] This is because DKIM is one of the authentication methods used by mailbox providers to determine that an email was sent from a particular email account.[3]

1 Internet Engineering Task Force (IETF) RFC 6376 – Domain Keys Identified Mail (DKIM), https://tools.ietf.org/html/rfc6376. Updated by RFCs 8301, 8463, 8553 and 8616.

2 Organizations wishing to sign mail by way of DKIM will first generate two cryptographic keys. One of the keys is kept private and available to the sending server for the signing of mail, and the other is made public in the DNS (Domain Name System) for use by receiving domains in attempts to validate the signature. By using this cryptographic key exchange and the same validation mechanisms used by the original sender's domain, it is possible to revalidate the content of the email message using the original sender domain cryptographic DKIM keys to recalculate the DKIM signature. If the DKIM signature can be reverified, not only is the content of the email message submitted for examination identical to the original message sent, including any attachments, but it also confirms the date and time of transmission, the subject line and the sender and recipient email addresses. An email message with a successfully revalidated DKIM signature can be considered to have similar veracity to a forensic image of the message.

3 Even this need not be true. It depends very much on how users and senders are authenticated and how relaying is allowed on the system involved. DKIM is merely a pipeline: everything that goes in one end comes out the other signed.

9.15 However, in other cases the application of cryptographic hashing or other cryptographically sound acquisition techniques is difficult, if not impossible. Increasingly, evidence procured from large computing platforms and cloud services will require testing by digital evidence professionals.[1] Another way to prove the data is to rely on a third party – such as the service provider – that controls the storage of data. This means that rather than relying on an operating procedure for acquiring evidence, the provenance and trustworthiness of the provider become relevant.

1 An example is a case where Facebook was asked to provide the IP address of the poster of what is called 'revenge porn' (sexually explicit material typically posted after a break-up or end of a relationship). For an example see 'Facebook ordered by Dutch court to identify revenge porn

publisher', *The Guardian*, 26 June 2015, https://www.theguardian.com/technology/2015/jun/26/facebook-ordered-by-dutch-court-to-identify-revenge-porn-publisher and 'Facebook to give access to two revenge porn investigators', *NL Times*, 6 November 2015, https://nltimes.nl/2015/11/06/facebook-give-access-two-revenge-porn-investigators.

Identifying electronic evidence

9.16 The first sign that something is wrong may be in the form of electronic evidence. For instance, a security administrator in a bank might consider an investigation necessary when the intrusion detection system sets off an alarm, or where the email logs indicate that a particular member of staff is receiving an excessive number of emails during the course of a day or over an extended period. The case of *Miseroy v Barclays Bank plc*[1] is illustrative. In July 2002 a formal investigation was initiated because an employee of Barclaycard appeared to be receiving a disproportionate number of emails during the day. The audit of the emails sent and received by three employees showed that one Mr Miseroy, who was with the Fraud Prevention Department, had sent a significant number of emails. As a result, he was also included in the investigation. After a series of investigatory meetings, it was concluded that Mr Miseroy had abused the email facilities by sending out an unwarranted number of personal emails, in breach of the Group IT Security Policies regarding the use of corporate email facilities. Some of the emails he sent out included content that was derogatory, offensive and sexist, which Mr Miseroy admitted was not appropriate. The investigations also showed emails exchanged between him and a manager in a different department, in which Mr Miseroy had arranged to pass cannabis to that manager. It was also determined that Mr Miseroy disclosed confidential information regarding Barclay's operations and customers. Mr Miseroy was summarily dismissed for gross misconduct, and the members of the tribunal accepted that his dismissal was within the range of reasonable responses of a reasonable employer in relation to the circumstances of the case.

1 (Case No 1201894/2002) (18 March 2003, unreported) Bedford employment tribunal.

9.17 Such a case, where the source and reliability of evidence that something is wrong needs to be assessed, will require an investigation into the facts. At such an early stage, the actions of the investigator may inadvertently change the electronic evidence itself. For instance, in the case of *Aston Investments Limited v OJSC Russian Aluminium (Rusal)*,[1] the actions of the IT administrators caused important files and information to be removed, and subsequent forensic examination ran into difficulties because of the unintended changes made to the system. This is why it is essential to have an appropriate procedure in place to deal with the way an investigation is initiated and conducted, whether by way of civil proceedings, where there is an obligation for each party to disclose documents relating to matters in question under the Civil Procedure Rules,[2] or in criminal matters, where the relevant investigating authorities have both common law and statutory powers to search and seize evidence. In the criminal context, investigating police officers will be expected to have conducted themselves in accordance with recognized guides for their jurisdiction. In the United Kingdom, ACPO[3] has produced the *ACPO Good Practice Guide for Digital Evidence* (ACPO Guide).[4] The ACPO Guide sets out the four main phases for handling electronic evidence – collection, examination, analysis and reporting – and concentrates on the collection phase. A digital evidence professional should consider adopting the practices for the four phases of his investigations. With the advent of forensic triage techniques, these four phases may be augmented with an initial 'assessment' or 'triage selection' phase.

1 [2006] EWHC 2545 (Comm), [2007] 1 All ER (Comm) 857, [2007] 1 Lloyd's Rep 311, [2006] 10 WLUK 470, [2006] 2 CLC 739, [2006] Info TLR 269, Times, 31 October 2006, [2007] CLY 684.
2 For a discussion of some flaws in the legal and forensic process, see Vlasti Broucek, Paul Turner and Sandra Frings, 'Music piracy, universities and the Australian Federal Court: Issues for forensic computing specialists' (2005) 21(1) Computer Law & Security Report 30.
3 ACPO was replaced in 2015 by a new body, the National Police Chiefs' Council. This was set up under a police collaboration agreement under the provisions of s 22A of the Police Act 1996. The acronym ACPO will continue to be used in this chapter, because the current version of the guidelines predated the formation of the National Police Chiefs' Council.
4 (March 2012, v5), http://library.college.police.uk/docs/acpo/digital-evidence-2012.pdf.

9.18 While the following discussion concentrates on matters relating to electronic evidence in the context of a criminal investigation, the reader will readily acknowledge the relevance of the discussion in the context of a civil matter when undertaking work in the disclosure phase of a civil action.[1]

1 The tension between forensics and investigations is discussed, among other things, in Monique Mattei Ferraro and Andrew Russell, 'Current issues confronting well-established computer-assisted child exploitation and computer crime task forces' (2004) 1(1) Digital Investigation 7.

Gathering electronic evidence

9.19 Once it has been established that it is necessary to seize or gather evidence in digital form, a further set of procedures should be in place to guide the digital evidence professional with respect to the scene or information itself, including the identification and seizure or acquisition of the evidence as necessary.[1] Where a physical crime scene is involved, it is now a well-established practice that the scene should be photographed, or even recorded by video, and the layout of the hardware recorded in relation to the scene. The investigator then needs to determine what, if any, physical evidence, such as computers, printers, computer mice or facsimile machines, should be retained (the ACPO Guide provides a list of the types of hardware and storage devices that are susceptible to being retained).[2] It is important to not permit anybody to disturb the hardware or the network, or work on any computer. It is also advisable that the police officers engaged in searching for digital evidence be properly trained.[3]

1 For a brief discussion about gathering evidence and issues surrounding personal privacy, see María Verónica Péez Asinari, 'Legal constraints for the protection of privacy and personal data in electronic evidence handling' (2004) 18(2) International Review of Law, Computers & Technology 231.
2 Brian Carrier and Eugene H. Spafford, 'Getting physical with the digital evidence process' (2003) 2(2) International Journal of Digital Evidence.
3 Although Harvey J in the District Court, Manakau in Canada, ruled that digital evidence was not necessarily rendered inadmissible because the accuracy of the data might have been jeopardized where a police officer, with full knowledge of the relevant guidelines, chose to ignore them. In this instance, during the search of premises a police officer switched on a computer and took 45 minutes to search various files stored on it: *R v Good* [2005] DCR 804. For problems when investigating mainframes and very large systems, see Matthew Pemble, 'Investigating around mainframes and other high-end systems: the revenge of big iron' (2004) 1(2) Digital Investigation 90.

9.20 The problem with digital evidence is the ease by which the data can be altered or destroyed. Digital devices are volatile instruments. For instance, the random access memory in a computer will contain a great deal of information relating to the state of the computer, such as the processes that are running, whether the computer is connected to the Internet and what file systems are being used. When a computer is switched off, a large part of this volatile data is immediately and irretrievably lost. Depending on the circumstances of the case being investigated, it may be very important to retain such data before the computer is switched off or simply unplugged from the electricity supply. This question is becoming increasingly important because of the ready availability of encryption utilities that are easy to use, and the increasing availability of low-cost hard disks that include whole disk encryption as a matter of course. The preservation of a forensic copy of a computer system's RAM may be the only way of gaining investigative access to the contents of a target device whose content is encrypted with complex keys.[1] Indeed, there may be occasions when great care should be taken when arresting suspects physically at a computer, because it is possible that they might switch off the computer and disrupt or delete any incriminating files before any preventative action can be taken, as in the case of Aleksei Kostap. He was arrested by members of the Serious and Organised Crime Agency, who attached handcuffs to him, but with his hands in front of his body. According to a press report, he managed to take action that caused certain databases to be deleted. It was thought the databases might have contained records of the gang's activities. Apparently, while handcuffed, Kostap also acted to initiate the use of intricate layers of encryption on various computer systems, which experts were not able to decrypt.[2] In addition, new developments in the methods used to store data on storage devices may cause problems in the future. Graeme B. Bell and Richard Boddington have demonstrated that:

> Evidence stored on modern internal primary storage devices can be subject to a process we label 'self-corrosion'. What is meant by this is that even in the absence of computer instructions, a modern solid-state storage device can permanently destroy evidence to a quite remarkable degree, during a short space of time, in a manner that a magnetic hard drive would not. Here, the phenomenon of solid-state drive (SSD) self-corrosion is proven to exist through experimentation using real world consumer hardware in an experimentally reproducible environment.[3]

1 Casey, *Digital Evidence*, 478.
2 Tom Espiner, 'Jailed ID thieves thwart cops with crypto', ZEDNet UK (19 December 2006).
3 'Solid state drives'; Ravi Kant Chaurasia and Priyanka Sharma, 'Solid state drive (SSD) forensics analysis: a new challenge' (2017) 2(6) International Journal of Scientific Research in Computer Science, Engineering and Information Technology 1; Ravi Kant Chaurasia and Priyanka Sharma, 'Solid state drive (SSD) forensics analysis: a new challenge' (2017) 2(6) International Journal of Scientific Research in Computer Science, Engineering and Information Technology 1081; Shiva Sai Ram Marupudi, 'Solid state drive: new challenge for forensic investigation' (2017) 30 Culminating Projects in Information Assurance, https://repository.stcloudstate.edu/msia_etds/30.

9.21 The authors provide the observations in this chapter for the guidance and assistance of professionals involved in facilitating the proof of digital evidence.

9.22 While it may be convenient to consider preservation of 'cloud storage' as analogous to preservation of data on a hard disk in a computer, this is not the case. Cloud service providers make computing infrastructure available as virtualized components that can be connected using virtualized networking infrastructure. It is usually possible, given enough privileges, to quickly preserve the state and contents of a virtual machine, its volatile memory and any block storage attached to it. But that is not the whole picture. In such virtualized environments, data of material relevance such as access and event logs may be available only to the members of staff of the service provider. Therefore, identifying and preserving the contents of volatile data and attached storage accessible to the victim(s) or suspect(s) but failing to have the service provider preserve all relevant system, access and event logs would be to miss the most important facts about the evidence and thus potentially undermine the ability to prove the case.

Gathering of data following legal retention or reporting obligations

9.23 In other cases, metadata and logs are retained by service providers who follow a legal requirement. This is often the case for identifying information such as IP addresses, telephone numbers and related subscriber information, and in the UK this was extended to data on sites visited on the Internet.[1] Where such legal obligations exist, other safeguards will typically apply, and an assumption can be made about the accuracy of the data that is provided by a service provider. Such data, and the process of access and acquisition or reporting, are often subject to different legislative requirements such as privacy legislation, safeguards and obligations set out in telecommunications legislation or data retention regimes.[2] In such cases, the probative value and admissibility will increasingly depend on the reliability of the service provider. In some cases, special accreditations or security checks are required for members of staff who work with this data or analyse it. In other cases, the related infrastructure is subject to audit requirements.

1 Investigatory Powers Act 2016, s 62(7) reads: 'In this Act "internet connection record" means communications data which – (a) may be used to identify, or assist in identifying, a telecommunications service to which a communication is transmitted by means of a telecommunication system for the purpose of obtaining access to, or running, a computer file or computer program, and (b) comprises data generated or processed by a telecommunications operator in the process of supplying the telecommunications service to the sender of the communication (whether or not a person)'.

2 The legal basis of data retention can affect an investigation, in particular the attribution of an IP address. It appears that the Court of Justice of the European Union understands this position, but up to this point in time has invalidated a number of data protection regimes, which has caused considerable uncertainty for investigators, for which see Joined Cases C-203/15, *Tele2 Sverige*, and C-698/15, *Tom Watson and Others;* as well as currently pending cases: C-623/17 – A request for a preliminary ruling by the Investigatory Powers Tribunal of the UK concerning data retention in terrorism cases. C-520/18, a request for a preliminary ruling by the Belgian Constitutional Court concerns the questions concerning the admissibility of a general data retention scheme; and lastly Cases C-511/18 and C-512/18, both requests for a preliminary ruling of the French Conseil d'Etat which concern the legal framework for data retention for criminal investigations and for data retention for intelligence services.

Internet of Things data and sensors

9.24 A wide variety of sensors can be found at crime scenes, depending on how many devices are connected to the Internet. Due to the increasing number of sensors, a wide array of Internet of Things (IoT) devices is becoming available and may contain evidence which can assist in the proof of a crime. The analysis of this data, which is sometimes also present at service providers (located 'in the cloud'), can present a unique set of problems.

9.25 Location data, health data and other types of sensor may not be easy to interpret and will often require contextual analysis and interpretation. For example, location data may be important in the investigation of a murder that is alleged to have occurred in a park at a certain hour. The presence of data recorded within a personal device at the north entrance, and then again at the south entrance of the park within ten minutes of each other, may, at first sight, be indicative of a suspect's presence at the crime scene. However, it may also be indicative of a loved one slowly driving around half the park by car, in ten minutes, to see if the victim is to be found. The accuracy, measurement interval and behaviour of the services involved (which may, for example, store the closest destination, such as the park entrance gates) and evidence from other sensors (such as the connections to the car radio and navigation by way of wireless technologies like Bluetooth) may serve as corroborating evidence of such a defence.[1] Each of the available sensors in modern-day IoT devices has its own accuracy, measurement interval and data storage mechanisms, and, therefore, evidential value. A detailed knowledge of and access to significant testing facilities is needed to stay abreast of developments in this field and in order to understand the behaviour of devices in the IoT ecosystem.[2]

1 By way of example relating to the accuracy of mobile telephone locations, see Matthew Tart, Iain Brodie, Nicholas Gleed and James Matthews, 'Historic cell site analysis – overview of principles and survey methodologies' (2012) 8(3–4) Digital Investigation 185; R. P. Coutts and H. Selby, 'Problems with cell phone evidence tendered to "prove" the location of a person at a point in time' (2016) 13 Digital Evidence and Electronic Signature Law Review 76; Reg Coutts and Hugh Selby, '"Mobile ping data" – metadata for tracking' (2017) 14 Digital Evidence and Electronic Signature Law Review 22; Matthew Tart, Sue Pope, David Baldwin and Robert Bird, 'Cell site analysis: roles and interpretation' (2019) 59(5) Science & Justice 558; Matthew Tart, 'Opinion evidence in cell site analysis' (2020) 60(4) Science & Justice 363; in *R. v Turner (Andrew Neil)* [2020] EWCA Crim 1241, [2020] 9 WLUK 308, where a mobile telephone analyst provided evidence that was tantamount to expert evidence in which the members of a jury were presented with the appearance of cell site analysis, and then invited to infer facts without any knowledge of the technical knowledge required to substantiate any conclusions – this was wrongly upheld by the Court of Appeal. On similar facts, a differently composed Court of Appeal determined the position correctly in *R. v Calland (Sean Thomas)* [2017] EWCA Crim 2308, [2017] 12 WLUK 706.

2 Compare, for example: M. J. Sorell and K. Hovhannisyan, 'Arkangel: investigation of children's tracking smartwatch ecosystem. Forensic value and privacy implications', in *Proceedings of the 4th Interdisciplinary Cyber Research Workshop 2018*, Tallinn University of Technology, 60–62; M. DeVries and M. J. Sorell, 'Biometric profiling of wearable devices for medical monitoring and authentication' in *Proceedings of the 4th Interdisciplinary Cyber Research Workshop 2018*, Tallinn University of Technology, 46–48; Ibrahim Baggili, Jeff Oduru, Kyle Anthony, Frank Breitinger and Glenn Mcgee, 'Watch what you wear: preliminary forensic analysis of smart watches', *2015 10th International Conference on Availability, Reliability and Security*, IEEE Explore (2015) 10.1109/ARES.2015.39.

Gathering data through network searches

9.26 The initiation of advanced encryption has significantly decreased the value of evidence gathered from traditional police powers, such as lawfully authorized interception. The advent of end-to-end encryption has led to the introduction, in many countries, of the power to conduct remote searches. These include the use – or exploitation – of software vulnerabilities in order to gain access to the systems involved. The evidence obtained through this method is difficult to evaluate, because it is typically obtained in an end user device without the user being aware of the fact that the device was deliberately being made use of. While it may be assumed that law enforcement authorities may be the only parties with legitimate access to a device, other third parties may also have authorized access. Attribution of any data and evidence found on the device is therefore more difficult, due to the existence of such an exploitable vulnerability. The value of this type of evidence can be improved where corroboration of the evidence is sought, and obtained, through other sources.

Copying electronic evidence

9.27 The process of acquiring, copying and handling electronic evidence should be carried out to the highest standards, regardless of whether the source is a hard disk, mobile device or cloud-based resources. Several commonly applied best practices and principles are relevant to this process and the four principles of handling computer-based electronic evidence as set out in the ACPO Guide illustrate the importance of the data collection phase of this process:[1]

> Principle 1: No action taken by law enforcement agencies, persons employed within those agencies or their agents should change data which may subsequently be relied upon in court.
>
> Principle 2: In circumstances where a person finds it necessary to access original data, that person must be competent to do so and be able to give evidence explaining the relevance and the implications of their actions.
>
> Principle 3: An audit trail or other record of all processes applied to digital evidence should be created and preserved. An independent third party should be able to examine those processes and achieve the same result.
>
> Principle 4: The person in charge of the investigation has overall responsibility for ensuring that the law and these principles are adhered to.

1 See Casey, *Digital Evidence*, 471 for a further discussion of documentation and a sample preservation form.

9.28 The problem of what types of electronic evidence and hardware to seize and retain can be compounded where a computer or an entire system of computers is linked to a network, and the sources of electronic evidence exist in a number of separate geographical locations. In such circumstances, and before taking any action, it will be necessary to ascertain whether it is possible or feasible to shut the network down. In most instances, this will not be an option. The investigators will need to be aware of the range of original data that might be required, should they be presented with such a situation. This will include establishing the topology of the network that is to be investigated for the data, especially if a system administrator will not cooperate. For instance, it will probably be necessary to establish the number of computers on a network, and the various types of network connection such as the Internet, cellular data networks and wireless connections that are available on the network. In the case of cloud-based resources where the user is not cooperative or unaware of the investigation, it will be necessary to engage with the cloud service provider's team to obtain the required information and, with the appropriate authorities, gain access to the data of interest.

9.29 Professor Casey posits two empirical laws of electronic evidence collection that ought to be high on the agenda:

> Empirical Law of Digital Evidence Collection and Preservation 1: If you only make one copy of digital evidence, that evidence will be damaged or completely lost.
>
> Empirical Law of Digital Evidence Collection and Preservation 2: A forensic acquisition should contain at least the data that is accessible to a regular user of the computer.[1]

1 Casey, *Digital Evidence*, 481.

9.30 To ensure a complete copy of a disk is obtained, Professor Casey recommends taking a bitstream copy of the electronic evidence.[1] As a result, the copy will include information that will normally enable a digital evidence professional to reconstruct deleted files, depending on the storage technology that was used. In circumstances where the volume of digital data is so large or its storage is so complex that copying it in its entirety is not possible,[2] it is generally accepted that copies of selected data may be made, provided the data that is copied can be shown to be an accurate and an exact duplicate of the data that is the subject of copying, frequently referred to as 'first in time evidence'. Many methods exist for achieving this, including the use of proprietary 'logical evidence file formats' of common forensic tools.

1 Casey, *Digital Evidence*, 482. A bitstream copy or image is a 'sector-by-sector' or 'bit-by-bit' copy of a computer's hard drive. In non-technical terms, a bitstream image is a set of files which also preserves latent data. The image can be used to create an exact copy of a hard drive. A bitstream image is readable by most tools that the digital forensics professional will use.
2 This is reflected in the *Supplementary Attorney General's Guidelines On Disclosure: Digitally Stored Material* (14 July 2011), para 12.

9.31 In addition to Professor Casey's empirical laws of electronic evidence collection, there are two fundamental principles to be observed by a digital evidence professional when copying electronic evidence:

> (i) The process of making the image should not alter the first in time evidence. This means that appropriate steps should be taken to ensure that the process used to take the image should not write any data to the original medium.
>
> (ii) The process of copying data should produce an exact copy of the first in time evidence. Such a reproduction should allow the specialist to investigate the files in the way that they existed on the original medium.[1]

1 Troy Larson, 'The other side of civil discovery: disclosure and production of electronic records', in Eoghan Casey (ed), *Handbook of Computer Crime Investigation: Forensic Tools and Technology* (Academic 2007), 35.

9.32 To ensure the first in time evidence and the copy are the same, the data should undergo a hashing process, described below. The reason for establishing hash values for data, including the time and date stamps of each file, is that this information will serve as a reference for checking the authenticity or veracity of the files after they have been copied.

9.33 The quality of digital files that are copied can be crucial. In the case of *The Gates Rubber Company v Bando Chemical Industries Limited*,[1] Schlatter MJ commented on the evidence of two digital evidence experts. The judge was impressed by the 'credentials, experience and knowledge' of Bando's expert Wedig, and indicated in his decision that he relied on his opinions. As Gates failed to obtain an expert in a timely fashion, much less weight was placed on its expert.[2] Gates' expert Voorhees also failed to undertake appropriate measures to secure the first in time evidence. Schlatter MJ's judgment is quoted more fully to illustrate this point:

> Gates argued that Voorhees did an adequate job of copying the Denver computer. Wedig persuaded me, however, that Voorhees lost, or failed to capture, important information because of an inadequate effort. In using Norton's Unerase, Voorhees unnecessarily copied this program onto the Denver computer first, and thereby overwrote 7 to 8 percent of the hard drive before commencing his efforts to copy the contents.

> Wedig noted that information which is introduced into a computer is distributed, in a random manner, to space which is not being used, or to space which contains a deleted file and is therefore available for use. To use Norton's Unerase, it was unnecessary for Voorhees to copy it onto the hard drive of the Denver computer. By doing so, however, the program obliterated, at random, 7 to 8 percent of the information which would otherwise have been available. No one can ever know what items were overwritten by the Unerase program.
>
> Additionally, Voorhees did not obtain the creation dates of certain of the files which overwrote deleted files. This information would have assisted in determining the deletion date of some files. If a deleted file has been overwritten by a file which was created prior to the Gates litigation, for example, Bando would be relieved of suspicion as to that file. Thus, failure to obtain the creation dates of files represented a failure to preserve evidence which would have been important to Bando in its efforts to resist Gates' motions for default judgment.
>
> Wedig pointed out that Voorhees should have done an 'image backup' of the hard drive, which would have collected every piece of information on the hard drive, whether the information was allocated as a file or not. Instead, Voorhees did a 'file by file' backup, which copies only existing, nondeleted files on the hard drive. The technology for an image backup was available at the time of these events, though rarely used by anyone. Wedig testified that Gates was collecting evidence for judicial purposes; therefore, Gates had a duty to utilize the method which would yield the most complete and accurate results. I agree with Wedig. In these circumstances, Gates failed to preserve evidence in the most appropriate manner. Gates' failure to obtain an image backup of the computer is a factor which I have weighed against Gates as I considered a number of the claims which Gates has asserted.[3]

1 167 F.R.D. 90 (D.Colo. 1996).
2 167 F.R.D. 90 (D.Colo. 1996) at 111(a).
3 167 F.R.D. 90 (D.Colo. 1996) at 112(a) and (b).

9.34 Although the tools and techniques used by digital evidence professionals are constantly changing and improving, the comments made by the judge in this case illustrate a very clear point: when electronic evidence is copied, the techniques that are used ought to comply with the highest possible standards for the evidence to have any probative value in legal proceedings. However, it must be emphasized that there will be occasions when the investigator is faced with a unique situation such that she can only apply her knowledge to the best of her ability in seizing data in as forensic a way as possible. One example would be a live banking system. The system might be stored on hundreds of servers in a data centre that is the size of a football field, and the data will be changing every second. No existing guidelines cover such an eventuality, which is why the investigator must make decisions based on principles of good practice.[1]

1 For a sample imaging procedure, see Larson, 'The other side of civil discovery', 36–37; Barbara Guttman, James R. Lyle and Richard Ayers, 'Ten years of computer forensic tool testing' (2011) 8 Digital Evidence and Electronic Signature Law Review 139.

9.35 An examination of the surrounding area of the scene, including any materials that are likely to be relevant to disclosure or a criminal investigation, is also important. For instance, in the case of *R. v Pecciarich*[1] the police seized a number of documents, catalogues and a scrapbook of newspaper articles concerning trials of sexual assault and proposed legislation dealing with abusive images of children. In this instance, the material constituted real evidence. It was also considered, as Sparrow J determined, to be circumstantial evidence to support the allegations that Pecciarich distributed abusive digital images of children, which were found on his computer and hardware devices. The relevance of materials found at the scene, including fingerprints and DNA samples taken directly from hardware devices, may become more obvious once the digital evidence professional has examined the electronic evidence in detail.

1 1995 CarswellOnt 504, [1995] OJ No 2238, 22 OR (3d) 748, 26 WCB (2d) 603.

Forensic triage

9.36 Preceding the investigation and examination of electronic evidence by digital evidence professionals is a technique known as 'forensic triage',[1] which has received considerable attention within the forensic practitioner and law enforcement communities. Digital forensic triage is the term used to cover a range of processes, methodologies, software and hardware that can be used to enable people to prioritize their digital forensic investigations more effectively. Forensic triage is not suitable for every case. Users with appropriate training must use it in conjunction with appropriate risk assessment. Indeed, there are direct comparisons to be drawn in this regard with law enforcement processes and the medical profession. Applying the triage process, a police officer, trained in the use of a breath test meter, can use such a device to make informed decisions about a driver suspected of being intoxicated. The officer does not need to be an expert in the science embodied in the device but, instead, simply needs to be appropriately trained to configure, use and interpret the results it provides, and decide how best to take the investigation forward.

1 Marcus K. Rogers, James Goldman, Rick Mislan, Timothy Wedge and Steve Debrota, 'Computer forensics field triage process model' (2006) 1(2) Journal of Digital Forensics, Security and Law 19.

9.37 The UK Defence Science and Technology Laboratory has reviewed various digital forensic triage methods: software, hardware and processes. These evaluations, although often focused on establishing if individual tools meet the claims made by the publishers, also test the effectiveness of the technology to preserve the integrity of the target media, to correctly identify specific digital artefacts and to produce results using other forensic techniques that would withstand scrutiny. The outcomes of these independent tests are made available to police and other authorities under various classification restrictions, allowing them to form opinions about the suitability of each tool for the given scenarios.

9.38 Digital forensic triage technologies and methods are in their infancy,[1] and must take account of the need for appropriate training and accreditation. Similarly, suitable risk assessment is required in order to minimize the omission of relevant data. It could be argued that by not performing a full forensic examination of every piece of digital media found, vital evidence may be lost. An important consideration when employing digital triage techniques is the need to balance the rapid identification of material of interest and the consequence of stopping further analysis, in the knowledge that such a process may fail to identify exculpatory material or material of more significance.[2] Through the use of manual and automated techniques, digital forensics triage techniques have the potential for beneficial or non-degrading applications in a wide range of digital forensics matters, particularly those that require classification such as abusive images of children (from which the digital triage process originated)[3] through to copyright matters.[4]

1 Dr Faye Mitchell, 'The use of artificial intelligence in digital forensics: an introduction' (2010) 7 Digital Evidence and Electronic Signature Law Review 35.
2 Vacius Jusas, Darius Birvinskas and Elvar Gahramanov, 'Methods and tools of digital triage in forensic context: survey and future directions' (2017) 9(4) Symmetry 1, 49.
3 Jusas, Birvinskas and Gahramanov, 'Methods and tools of digital triage in forensic context: survey and future directions', 51.
4 David McLelland and Fabio Marturana, 'A digital forensics triage methodology based on feature manipulation techniques', 1st IEEE International Workshop on Secure Networking and Forensic Computing (SNFC2014), ICC2014, Sydney, Australia.

9.39 In the context of cloud computing, forensic triage techniques may be highly effective and appropriate, and can use the functionality of the cloud environment to standardize and automate a method of deployment. For instance, Amazon Web Services[1] suggest a programmatic use of triage as part of an automated incident response methodology. The inclusion of forensic controls such as hashing and comprehensive audit logging are available as standard options when such tasks are performed. Once such techniques and capabilities have been provisioned by practitioners with the appropriate skills and knowledge, any user with appropriate credentials can use them.

1 AWS Security Incident Response Guide published June 2020 by Amazon Web Services, https://d1.awsstatic.com/whitepapers/aws_security_incident_response.pdf.

Preserving electronic evidence

Validating digital data

9.40 Electronic evidence in particular needs to be validated if it is to have any probative value. A digital evidence professional will typically need to copy the contents from a number of disks or storage devices. To prove that the electronic evidence has not been altered from its source copy, it is necessary to put in place checks and balances to prove that the duplicate evidence is identical to its source. A method used to prove the integrity of source data at the time the evidence was collected is known as electronic fingerprinting or 'hashing'.[1] The electronic fingerprint uses a cryptographic technique that is capable of being associated with a single file, a floppy disk or the entire contents of a hard drive. A digital evidence professional should use software tools that are relevant to the task.[2] Such software tools will invariably incorporate a program that causes a checksum operation called a hash function to be applied to the source file or disk that is being copied. When a hash function is applied to digital data, the result is called a hash value as it is calculated against the content of the data. The hash function is a one-way function, and is the mathematical equivalent of a secret trapdoor. For the purposes of understanding the concept, this algorithm is easy to compute in one direction and difficult to compute in the opposite direction.[3] The hash function is used to verify that a source file or the copy of a file has not changed. If the file has been altered in any way, their hash values will not be the same, and the investigator will be alerted to the discrepancy.

1 Ovie Carroll and Mark Krotoski, 'Using "digital fingerprints" (or hash values) for investigations and cases involving electronic evidence' (2014) 62 US Attorney's Bulletin 44.
2 This is not what occurred in *State of Connecticut v Julie Amero* (Docket number CR-04-93292; Superior Court, New London Judicial District at Norwich, GA 21; 3, 4 and 5 January 2007) – for a

detailed analysis of this case, see Stephen Mason (gen ed), *International Electronic Evidence* (British Institute of International and Comparative Law 2008), xxxvi–lxxv; compare with the actions of the digital evidence professional David Hendricks in *Krause v State*, 243 S.W.3d 95 (Tex.App. 2007), 2007 WL 2004940.

3 It has yet to be proven that a mathematical function can have a one-way function: see Fred Piper, Simon Blake-Wilson and John Mitchell, *Digital Signatures Security & Controls* (Information Systems Audit and Control Foundation 1999), 16.

Hash collisions

9.41 There are many possible hashing algorithms that can be used to establish forensic veracity. For many years the MD5 (Message Digest 5) algorithm was used, but research conducted by Xiaoyun Wang and Hongbo Yu showed that it was possible to create two files with different content that produced the same MD5 value.[1] The implications of this possibility quickly led to some debate in the forensic community. One common interpretation was that MD5 could no longer be trusted because an analyst might wrongly identify an innocent file as a known file (the identification issue) or deliberately modify a file and change its hash value back to the original (the verification issue). Another hypothesis was that a suspect could make all his bad files have the hash values of known system files, thereby avoiding detection. While theoretically possible, it is practically very difficult to achieve an MD5 hash collision, and doing so requires considerable computational time for files larger than a few hundred bytes. According to Stephens and others:

> It is important to note that the hash value shared by the two different files is a result of the collision construction process. We cannot target a given hash value, and produce a (meaningful) input bit string hashing to that given value. In cryptographic terms: our attack is an attack on collision resistance, not on preimage or second preimage resistance. This implies that both colliding files have to be specially prepared by the attacker ... Existing files with a known hash that have not been prepared in this way are not vulnerable.[2]

1 Xiaoyun Wang and Hongbo Yu, 'How to break MD5 and other hash functions', http://merlot.usc.edu/csac-f06/papers/Wang05a.pdf; Arjen Lenstra, Xiaoyun Wang and Benne de Weger, *Colliding X.509 Certificates* (version 1.0, 1 March 2005), http://eprint.iacr.org/2005/067.pdf; the earliest research is Hans Dobbertin, 'The status of MD5 after a recent attack' (1996) 2(2) RSA Laboratories' CryptoBytes 1, 3–6.

2 Marc Stevens, Arjen K. Lenstra and Benne de Weger, 'Vulnerability of software integrity and code signing applications to chosen-prefix collisions for MD5' (30 November 2007), http://www.win.tue.nl/hashclash/SoftIntCodeSign/.

9.42 In mathematical terms, an MD5 hash is 128 bits wide and therefore the probability of two files having the same MD5 value is 2^{-128}. Put another way, the probability of finding two files with the same MD5 value is one in just over $3x10^{-39}$. That is once in 340 billion, billion, billion, billion comparisons. By contrast, an SHA-1 hash is 160 bits wide and so the probabilities decrease to once in every $6.8x10^{-49}$ comparisons. In other words, in realistic terms it is very hard to produce a 'doctored copy' of a larger digital evidence set that has the exact same MD5 or SHA-1 hash value as the 'original' while still being 'believable'. However, it is not impossible, as the recent practical technique for generating an SHA-1 collision for PDF documents has demonstrated. It took the equivalent processing power of 6,500 years of single-CPU computations and 110 years of single-GPU computations, but resulted in a (believable) 'doctored copy' with a hash that was equal to a known original.[1]

1 Marc Stevens, Elie Bursztein, Pierre Karpman, Ange Albertini and Yarik Markov, 'The first collision for full SHA-1' (27 February 2017), https://shattered.io/static/shattered.pdf; John Leyden, Thomas Claburn and Chris Williams, '"First ever" SHA-1 hash collision calculated. All it took were five clever brains ... and 6,610 years of processor time', The Register, 23 February 2017.

9.43 The result of this debate is that, although the chance of an MD5 or SHA-1 collision is remote, best practice suggests creating two hash values for every file or forensic image when used for comparison. If only a single hash algorithm is used, SHA-256 would be better than MD5 or SHA-1. Using both MD5 and SHA-1 instead of a single SHA-256 is mathematically more robust. Further logic for this approach is the fact that although there are no national or international standards that require SHA-256 in digital forensics, its use instead of MD5/SHA-1 would immediately render all global child sexual exploitation image databases, which use MD5 and SHA-1 values, unusable. Furthermore, MD5 and SHA-1 are still used and accepted by every law enforcement authority worldwide to perform the three essential forensic functions: to identify known indecent images, to exclude known files such as those in the National Software Reference Library hash keeper list and to verify that files have not been changed. In the light of the recent successful collision attack of SHA-1, this practice may need to be reviewed. It is therefore advisable to retain first in time copies of any files that are to be identified in order to be able to recalculate hashes as algorithms become deprecated and new ones are introduced. For the purpose of detecting changes using digital signatures, SHA-1 and MD5 should be considered unreliable and deprecated as usage of SHA-1 began to be phased out in the technology community in 2017.[1] Since digital signatures are usually only valid for a limited time period, this is less of a problem, although even with MD5, issues have been identified since at least 2004, and they still persist.[2]

1 Google Security Blog, 'Announcing the first SHA1 collision', 23 February 2017, https://security.googleblog.com/2017/02/announcing-first-sha1-collision.html.
2 Xiaoyun Wang, Denggou Feng, Xuejia Lai and Hongbo Yu, 'Collisions for hash functions MD4, MD5, HAVAL-128 and RIPEMD', Cryptology ePrint Archive Report 2004/199, 16 August 2004, Institute of Software, Chinese Academy of Sciences, https://eprint.iacr.org/2004/199.pdf; Fahmida Y. Rashid, 'Oracle to Java devs: stop signing JAR files with MD5', InfoWorld, 19 January 2017, http://www.infoworld.com/article/3159186/security/oracle-to-java-devs-stop-signing-jar-files-with-md5.html.

Fuzzy logic and uncertainty

9.44 Hashing technology, although useful in cases where absolute certainty is required, is not the best way to recognize pre-existing material – especially in relation to images, video and sound recordings. Child abuse imagery, for example, is often 'marketed' using different logos present inside the image. While the majority of the content is unaltered, the mere addition of a logo will invalidate any hash value that was previously calculated. For this reason, numerous technologies exist that do not rely on establishing an exact match (by way of a file hash), but rather are capable of comparing content to establish the proximity of a file to the content of a known previous copy of the material sought. These filtering algorithms usually provide an indication at a preset level of certainty, of the fact that material matches a previously observed copy. The result is a percentage of likeness, rather than an exact match (which is what is achieved by file hashes).[1] Note that the results from these algorithms, contrary to hashes, are therefore less usable as a single source of evidence. However, due to the increased use of online filtering,[2] their acceptance is likely to increase.

1 Well-known technologies include Microsoft's PhotoDNA, used for identifying altered image material, and the Sift algorithm, used, for example, through technology applied by Facebook to filter illegal uploads.
2 For example, see articles 15 and 17 of the Directive (EU) 2019/790 of the European Parliament and of the Council of 17 April 2019 on copyright and related rights in the Digital Single Market and amending Directives 96/9/EC and 2001/29/EC OJ L 130, 17.5.2019, 92–125 requiring such filters for copyright purposes on larger sharing platforms.

The continuity of custody

9.45 For those professionals experienced in criminal matters, the concept of the continuity of custody (also known as the chain of evidence) is well established. However, the continuity of custody, in both civil and criminal matters, should be considered very carefully with respect to electronic evidence. The reason for taking particular care with electronic evidence is because it is easy to alter. It is necessary to demonstrate the integrity of the evidence and to show that it cannot have been tampered with after being seized or copied. There is another reason for being meticulous about ensuring the continuity of electronic evidence and that its custody is correctly recorded: in a case involving a number of items of hardware and more than one computer, it will be necessary to ensure that there is a clear link between the hardware and the electronic evidence copied from the hardware. In this respect, the record should address such issues as who collected the evidence, how and where it was collected, the name of the person who took possession of the evidence, how and where it was stored, the protection afforded to the evidence while in storage and the names of the people who removed the evidence from storage, including the reasons for removing the evidence from storage.[1] Due to the increased use of online storage and services, access and custody of records may also be of relevance in the phases before they become evidence in a legal matter or dispute, especially in cases where applying cryptographic safeguards is less practical.

1 Warren G. Kruse II and Jay G. Heiser, *Computer Forensics Incident Response Essentials* (Addison-Wesley 2002), 6–11.

Transporting and storing electronic evidence

9.46 Consideration should be given to the methods by which any hardware and digital evidence is transported and stored.[1] Computers need to be protected from accidentally booting up, and consideration should be taken to ensure that hardware is clearly marked to prevent people from using the equipment unwittingly. Loose hard drives, modems, keyboards and other such materials should be placed in anti-static or aerated bags to prevent them from being damaged or their data being corrupted. Storage conditions should be appropriate. Hardware and electronic evidence should be protected from dirt, humidity, fluids, extremes of temperature and strong magnetic fields. It is possible for data to be rendered unreadable if the storage media upon which the electronic evidence is contained are stored in a damp office or overheated vehicle. In many forensic storage facilities, special data safes protect evidence from fire risk. These safes are designed to withstand heat, and keep digital media at an acceptable temperature for longer periods of time during a fire.

1 Philip Turner, 'Unification of digital evidence from disparate sources (Digital Evidence Bag)' (2005) 2(3) Digital Investigation 223.

9.47 More recently, the availability of sophisticated file storage and server systems has resulted in systems that can store and manage data as 'objects', directed and controlled by policies with corresponding automated move, copy, delete and replication functions. In many cases these systems are also distributed geographically, providing better failover (the ability to automatically switch to a reliable backup system) and availability. While these features should not adversely affect the evidential veracity of stored data, it is essential for meeting evidential continuity that comprehensive access controls and audit logs are maintained at all times. Furthermore, the geographically dispersed storage of data may increasingly lead to questions of jurisdiction.

Cloud computing and online services

9.48 In the same vein, evidence is increasingly stored on publicly accessible, network-based services. Both cloud computing (the use of, often shared or virtualized, computing or storage resources available through the Internet) and the online delivery of services (software, infrastructure or platform as a service) are rapidly becoming more popular. Forensic investigation of these sources of evidence is inherently complex,[1] and is likely to force forensic standards involving the concept of 'original evidence' or 'first in time evidence' to become outdated or impracticable. In consequence, cloud forensics is emerging as a new aspect of computer forensics.[2]

1 Eoghan Casey, 'Cloud computing and digital forensics' (2012) 9(2) Digital Investigation 69; M. Taylor, J. Haggerty, D. Gresty and R. Hegarty, 'Digital evidence in cloud computing systems' (2010) 26(3) Computer Law & Security Review 304.
2 Stephen Mason and Esther George, 'Digital evidence and "cloud" computing' (2011) 27(5) Computer Law & Security Review 524; Ian Walden, 'Law enforcement access in a cloud environment', Legal Studies Research Paper No 74/2011, http://papers.ssrn.com/sol3/papers.cfm?abstract_id=1781067; Giuseppe Vaciago, 'Remote forensics and cloud computing: an Italian and European legal overview' (2011) 8 Digital Evidence and Electronic Signature Law Review 124.

9.49 At the same time, the use of free or low-cost 'cloud storage' adds a challenging complication to the process of preserving digital evidence. At the heart of this technology is the concept that a user can upload and store data and software applications to 'the cloud', which can then be accessed from anywhere using any device with an Internet connection. In reality, such 'cloud storage' can consist of many thousands (or tens of thousands) of mass storage devices (arrays of high capacity hard disks) located in many different physical locations, all connected to a storage management system software via the Internet. It is often the case that, in order to ensure that users' data is available at all times and to protect them from loss such as disk failure or interruptions in network connectivity, many copies of the users' data are spread across many redundant storage nodes that are physically and geographically separated from one another. Furthermore, many unrelated users share the same cloud storage facilities. In these 'multi-tenanted' systems, the management of such data is essentially automatic and controlled by the storage management system software rather than human managers. The implications for forensic preservation of such data may not be readily apparent.[1] It follows that because of the geographically distributed nature of such systems, issues of legal jurisdiction may also arise when seeking to preserve or obtain the data with the cooperation of the cloud operators.

1 For a general overview of some of the issues, see the entire issue of IAnewsletter, (2011) 14(1), entitled 'Cyber forensics in the cloud', https://www.csiac.org/wp-content/uploads/2016/02/Vol14_No1.pdf.

9.50 One method of securing access to such data is to request that the user provides details of her account to enable suitably authorized investigators to log into the relevant account and forensically copy all pertinent data to disk, or, more efficiently, copy from the user's 'cloud' to a storage location on a 'forensic cloud'. The forensic process should include the creation of hash values (discussed above) for every file or object and the use of automatic or manual logging of each action to create a contemporaneous note for all actions undertaken. Additionally, it may be prudent, with the appropriate legal authorization, to change the access credentials of the original storage in order to prevent any deliberate or inadvertent changes from being made to it.[1] In such circumstances, principles 2 and 3 of the ACPO should be considered:

> Principle 2: In circumstances where a person finds it necessary to access original data, that person must be competent to do so and be able to give evidence explaining the relevance and the implications of their actions.
>
> Principle 3: An audit trail or other record of all processes applied to digital evidence should be created and preserved. An independent third party should be able to examine those processes and achieve the same result.

1 For example, see the powers of preservation prescribed by the Convention on Cybercrime ETS No.185 (Budapest, 23/11/2001), articles 16 (domestic) and 29 (preservation in view of international cooperation).

9.51 Furthermore, reasonable precautions must be taken to ensure that any changes are kept to a minimum, the changes are noted and recorded, and the person conducting the acquisition process is fully aware of the effect of her actions. For those occasions when permission to obtain access to the data from the suspect is not forthcoming, it is then essential, if possible, to preserve a copy of the volatile memory in the computer (that has access to the data), so that it is possible to search for any remaining data relating to the account.

9.52 Data can be deleted on a remote server or cloud storage before it can be secured.[1] In such complex scenarios as described above, the role of forensic triage becomes increasingly important, because it allows the investigators to evaluate the scene contemporaneously, and to identify the data, seek the appropriate authority to search and seize the data (if such an order or warrant has not been obtained, or if the order or warrant under which the search is being conducted does not cover the materials that have been found) and secure the online data before anybody who might be under suspicion (or their accomplices) gets the opportunity to destroy it remotely. It is in such circumstances that conducting a preliminary risk assessment is essential to success.

1 For a discussion of the complexities of recovering data from modern operating systems and file systems, see Geoff H. Fellows, 'The joys of complexity and the deleted file' (2005) 2(2) Digital Investigation 89.

9.53 Throughout this phase of any investigation, the emphasis will be on the digital evidence professional to make informed decisions as to what data or equipment to seize and retain in any given set of circumstances.[1] Depending on the circumstances of the case, consideration has to be given to the possibility that the person at the centre of the investigation might be framed for personal or political reasons.[2] It will also be necessary to give reasons for seizing and retaining the property, and it will be essential to ensure that the entire procedure is properly documented. The documentation relating to electronic evidence is important. Standard operating procedures such as those described in the ACPO Guide, as noted above, should be followed. A record should be kept of every item seized, every action performed that may affect electronic data on every item, and exhibit labels should be attached to every physical item retrieved.

1 The prosecution failed to analyse the evidence from the family computer effectively in the case of the death of Casey Marie Anthony in 2011, for which see Craig Wilson, 'Digital evidence discrepancies – Casey Anthony trial, 11 July 2011', http://www.digital-detective.net/digital-evidence-discrepancies-casey-anthony-trial/; Tony Pipitone, 'Cops, prosecutors botched Casey Anthony evidence', Clickorlando.com, 28 November 2012, http://www.clickorlando.com/news/cops-prosecutors-botched-casey-anthony-evidence; Jose Baez and Peter Golenbock, *Presumed Guilty: Casey Anthony: The Inside Story* (BenBella Books, updated edition, 2013), 46, 180–183, 211, 346–348, 365, 368–371, 400, 426–428; Jess Ashton and Lisa Pulitzer, *Imperfect Justice: Prosecuting Casey Anthony* (William Morrow 2011), 105, 239, 277, 291–292, 298, 315.
2 John Leyden, 'Child abuse frame-up backfires on stalker', The Register, 6 April 2010, in which Ilkka Karttunen broke into the Essex home of a woman he wanted to be with, downloaded abusive images of children on to her computer, then stole the hard drive and sent it into the police with a note identifying the owner; for a similar example, see 'Handyman jailed for planting porn on boss's computer', BBC News London, 23 September 2010.

9.54 There are occasions when the physical hardware cannot be seized, because it is too large, it is not physically located in the jurisdiction or even in a single jurisdiction, or where seizing it would cause an organization to cease functioning. In such circumstances, the electronic evidence will have to be copied. As a result, greater care must be exercised when such electronic evidence is retrieved and copied for the first time. The range of electronic evidence that might need to be copied will include audit trails, data logs (for applications, Internet access[1] and firewall traffic, to name a few), biometric data, metadata from applications, file systems,[2] intrusion detection reports and contents of databases and files. Given the nature of the evidence to be copied, the integrity of the evidence that is copied and its subsequent history becomes paramount.[3] Data pertaining to the integrity of these copies and their creation should be retained wherever possible.

1 For an interesting discussion, see Dr Richard Clayton, 'Online traceability: who did that? Technical expert report on collecting robust evidence of copyright infringement through peer-to-peer filesharing' (Consumer Focus 2012), http://www.cl.cam.ac.uk/~rnc1/Online-traceability.pdf.
2 Florian Buchholz and Eugene Spafford, 'On the role of file system metadata in digital forensics' (2004) 1(4) Digital Investigation 298.
3 The volume of digital evidence is causing problems in respect of the methodologies around the collection of evidence, as discussed in the US context by Erin E. Kenneally and Christopher L. T. Brown, 'Risk sensitive digital evidence collection' (2005) 2(2) Digital Investigation 101; Simon Attfield and Ann Blandford, 'E-disclosure viewed as "sensemaking" with computers: the challenge of "frames"' (2008) 5 Digital Evidence and Electronic Signature Law Review 62; Daniel R. Rizzolo, 'Legal privilege and the high cost of electronic discovery in the United States: should we be thinking like lawyers?' (2009) 6 Digital Evidence and Electronic Signature Law Review 139.

9.55 Another way of dealing with this challenge is to request the cooperation of the service provider to retrieve evidence from its systems. This, however, often leads to jurisdictional issues. Thus, the need for better guidance on the issues arising out of cloud computing is becoming clearer. The Council of Europe has established a working group to address this issue and explore solutions in relation to access for criminal justice purposes to evidence stored on servers in the cloud and in foreign jurisdictions, including through the process of mutual legal assistance.[1] The preparation of a second

Additional Protocol to the Budapest Convention on Cybercrime seeks to urgently address the need for solutions 'for a more efficient criminal justice response to cybercrime and other crime involving electronic evidence in accordance with data protection and other safeguards'.[2] The shared nature of many of the services involved also creates significant issues surrounding the privacy aspects of the enhanced jurisdiction proposed. Furthermore, direct access to such data raises questions regarding the safeguards that need to be applied before such access is permitted.[3]

1 http://www.coe.int/en/web/cybercrime/ceg.
2 Chair, Cybercrime Convention (T-CY), Preparation of the 2nd Additional Protocol to the Budapest Convention on Cybercrime – State of Play, (23 June 2019), 4; first complete draft text of the 2nd Additional Protocol to the Convention on Cybercrime on enhanced cooperation and disclosure of electronic evidence (Draft Protocol, v2, 12 April 2021), https://rm.coe.int/2nd-additional-protocol-budapest-convention-en/1680a2219c.
3 See https://www.eff.org/deeplinks/2019/11/council-europe-shouldnt-throw-out-our-privacy-rights-just-speed-police-access.

Analysis of electronic evidence

9.56 A digital evidence professional is not only required to obtain and copy electronic evidence that has a high probative value, but must also provide an analysis of that evidence. The analysis of the evidence will involve reviewing the content of the data and the attributes of the data. This exercise may also include, but will not be limited to, looking for and recovering deleted files and other data that may be hidden on the disk, checking logs for activity and checking unallocated and slack space or unallocated space[1] for residual data. Failure to assess the electronic evidence can lead to false assumptions, as in the case of *Liser v Smith*.[2] The facts of the case were not in dispute. The victim was shot after leaving work on the night of 5 May 2000. By Monday 8 May, it was known that the victim's bank card had been used to withdraw US$200 from a Bank of America branch about 20 minutes after the murder, approximately one mile from where the body was found. According to the electronic evidence, the withdrawal occurred at 1.47 am on 6 May. The Bank of America ATM also had a video surveillance tape, which was subsequently retrieved by the police.

1 Slack space is a part of a block or cluster of a filesystem that is used for another file, but that is not entirely overwritten by it. The block may then contain remnants of the file that was previously there. Unallocated space consists of blocks or clusters of the filesystem that were once used for a file but, upon deletion of that file, are no longer referenced in the filesystem's allocation table. They will contain the original content of the file until they are (fully) overwritten.
2 254 F.Supp.2d 89 (D.D.C. 2003).

9.57 The bank manager informed the police that there would be a discrepancy of up to 15 minutes between the time indicated on the surveillance tape and the actual time of the withdrawal. When the tape was viewed, there was no ATM activity recorded at 1.47 am. The closest transaction that occurred was at 1.52 am, when a black male wearing a white t-shirt (the accused Jason Liser) was recorded as standing before the machine. While the evidence seemed to lead to the conclusion that Liser as the man recorded at 1.52 am was one of the killers, the evidence contained on the surveillance video did not warrant such an assumption. Other pictures from the videotape showed black males other than Liser using the ATM at 1.56 am and 2.05 am, and a black female using the machine at 2.04 am. Copies of these pictures were provided to the court. All of them were grainy and poorly photocopied. However, of relevance was that both of the men in question appeared, like Liser, to have been wearing white t-shirts and to be relatively young.

9.58 In August 2000, about three months after the murder, the police decided to put out a press release and a copy of the photograph of the man recorded as standing at the ATM at 1.52 am. Liser was subsequently recognized and arrested for the murder. He was held for less than a week, because the police decided, at this late point in time, to carry out an experiment at the aforesaid ATM machine and its video surveillance facilities. The result of the experiment led the police to conclude that the discrepancy was greater than the 15-minute gap the bank had stated. Liser was subsequently released. It is instructive to note the comments made in the Memorandum Opinion by the judge:

> While this issue is a close one, the Court is not ready to conclude that it was objectively reasonable under the circumstances of this investigation for the police to rely solely on the bank's representations about the time discrepancy without attempting to verify that information by empirical (or other) means. The crucial point here is that this was not a fast moving investigation in which the officers were called upon to make snap judgments based on limited information. Far from it. Detective Smith had the surveillance tapes within a week after the murder; at that early date he had been told by the branch manager that the time on the tape could be off by up to fifteen minutes ... Plaintiff was not, however, arrested until August, three months later. During this lengthy interval, neither Detective Smith nor anyone on his team made any further attempt to verify the estimation about the length of the gap. They had no further contact with anyone at Bank of America, especially its security personnel, who might have had more accurate information about the camera's timer ... They did not inspect the camera itself. Nor did they attempt [to] use the ATM themselves to compare real time against tape time.
>
> In short, despite the fact that the tape was their central lead as to the identity of the murderer, the investigators did nothing to pin down exactly how far off the video clock was, at least not before plaintiff was arrested. [Footnote 3: The fact that the police finally sought to verify the information – and quickly and readily learned that it was inaccurate – *after* Liser's arrest certainly does not help their cause. That such an [*sic*] simple test was not done in the three months preceding the arrest, and if done would have cast serious doubt on the propriety of that arrest, suggests an investigative sloppiness that at least casts doubt on whether the initial arrest was actually supported by probable cause.] Instead, Detective Smith and his team chose to rely solely on a single, untested statement from the bank manager. Such reliance might well have been unassailable had the investigators been making an on-the-spot determination as to whether probable cause existed to arrest plaintiff in the first frantic days after the murder. But in the circumstances of the deliberate, slowly unfolding investigation that ensued, during which the officers should have had ample time to pursue leads and to check facts, their failure to verify the length of the gap on the video stands in a rather different light. Their conduct appears more sloppy than reasoned, the product of carelessness rather than craft. The Court is thus unable to say with certainty that this crucial mistake was ultimately a permissible one, or that prudent investigators would necessarily have conducted themselves as defendants did here.[1]

1 United States District Court for the District of Columbia No 00-2325 (ESH) 26 March 2003 before Ellen Segal Huvelle DJ, at 11–12.

9.59 Compare this case with the murder of Denise Mansfield, who was found bound and strangled in her home on 29 June 2002. It was thought that she had been dead since 22 June. The police investigation centred on a surveillance camera that recorded images of people using an ATM, owned by the Sun Trust Bank. This ATM was used to withdraw US$200 from the victim's bank account at 2.30 pm on 22 June, using her debit card. Three women (Virginia Shelton, her daughter Shirley and one of her daughter's friends, Jennifer Starkey) were subsequently arrested. They were identified as using the machine between 2.28 pm and 2.33 pm the same day. The women did not dispute using this particular ATM. They were subsequently released after three weeks. After they were arrested, it came to light that it was assumed the clocks on the transaction computer and the ATM were synchronized. This was not correct. The women had used the ATM earlier than the time stamp on the video recording. It was reported that police officers had these records in their possession on the day they arrested the women, but it was not clear if they had examined the records before making the arrests. It was not until the father of one of the women obtained a copy of the relevant records that the women were released.[1]

1 Ruben Castaneda, 'Mistaken arrests leave Pr. George's murder unsolved', washingtonpost.com, 22 June 2003, https://www.washingtonpost.com/archive/politics/2003/06/22/mistaken-arrests-leave-pr-georges-murder-unsolved/8e6257de-22c6-4e73-894f-0e71f7ad9b2c/.

9.60 Both *Liser v Smith* and the Mansfield murder cases are good examples of the failure to fully test the electronic evidence, in particular, the time. No clock is accurate. This can be important in terms of assessing evidence in digital form.[1] In the legal context, Lord Hoffman observed, in *DPP v McKeown (Sharon), DPP v Jones (Christopher)*[2] that 'The clock, although no doubt physically in the same box as the computer, is something which supplies information to the computer rather than being part of the processing mechanism'.[3] It might have been correct that the clock was one hour out because of the difference in time zones, but clocks in computers are not always accurate. Clocks on facsimile machines may also be far from accurate, and so the following comments by Burton J (President) in *Woodward v Abbey National plc (No 2), J P Garrett Electrical Limited v Cotton*[4] that imply that the data recorded by the logs at the offices of the Employment Appeals Tribunal are accurate as a matter of 'common sense' cannot be correct:

> [I]t must make common sense to accept the accuracy, as I believe there to be, of the record of receipt in the fax log of the [Employment Appeals Tribunal (EAT)], and not to accept either uncertain evidence about the accuracy of the sender's machine or some kind of speculation as to electronic receipt short of the record in the EAT fax log.[5]

1 The first voice in the play *Under Milk Wood* by Dylan Thomas, referred to 'slow clocks, quick clocks' at [60], and the narrator in *The Time Regulation Institute* by Ahmet Hamdi Tanpınar (Penguin Classics 2014), translated by Maureen Freely and Alexander Dawe, [11], tells the reader that 'Everyone knows that a watch or clock is either fast or slow. For timepieces, there is no third state.' Dr John C. Taylor invented, designed and gave the Corpus Chronophage to Corpus Christi College in Cambridge, England. It is a mechanical clock designed to demonstrate the principle of relative time, doing the unexpected, and is only accurate once every five minutes. The Chief Scientist for Time Services at the US Naval Observatory, Dr Demetrios Matsakis, is responsible for precise time determination and the management of time dissemination. To achieve this, there is a USNO Master Clock that is in turn based on a system of a number of independently operating cesium atomic clocks and hydrogen master clocks, all of which automatically compare with each other, so that rate does not change by more than

about 100 *picoseconds* (0.000 000 000 1 seconds) per day: https://www.usno.navy.mil/USNO/time/master-clock/precise-time-and-the-usno-master-clock.

2 [1997] 1 WLR 295, [1997] 1 All ER 737, [1997] 2 WLUK 386, [1997] 2 Cr App R 155 (HL), (1997) 161 JP 356, [1997] RTR 162, [1997] Crim LR 522, (1997) 161 JPN 482, (1997) 147 NLJ 289, Times, 21 February 1997, Independent, 7 March 1997, [1997] CLY 1093.

3 [1997] 1 All ER 737 at 754d.

4 [2005] 4 All ER 1346, [2005] 7 WLUK 814, [2005] ICR 1702, [2005] IRLR 782, [2005] CLY 1244.

5 [2005] IRLR 782, [14]. See his further comment on both cases in *Woodward v Abbey National plc, J P Garrett Electrical Limited v Cotton* (26 July 2005, unreported) (UKEATPA/0534/05/SM and UKEATPA/0030/05/DZM), and similar comments on the same point in *Clark v Midland Packaging Limited* [2005] 2 All ER 266, [2005] 2 WLUK 317, [2014] CLY 1057, also known as *Midland Packaging Limited v Clark*. In *R v Good* [2005] DCR 804 the clock in the computer was running 42 minutes and 30 seconds behind the actual time.

9.61 A more realistic comment on the accuracy or otherwise of clocks was made by Smart AJ in the case of *R v Ross Magoulias*,[1] where the identity of the appellant centred on the recordings made by an ATM and a security video:

> It is a notorious matter of fact that reliable clocks or timing devices may show slightly different times. A clock may gain or lose ever so slightly, and it may be some days before the difference becomes noticeable. When setting a clock or timing device there might be a very small error. Perhaps the clock from which the timing device is set is slightly astray. It is exceedingly well known that the timing of differing clocks needs to be synchronised if pinpoint accuracy is required. It is beyond argument that both [the victim] and the appellant attended the service station on 7 July 2001. She can be seen on the video tape for about three minutes (18.37.18 to 18.40.25 according to the video tape timing device). That cannot be disputed. Nor can it be disputed that the appellant attended at the ATM and withdrew $50 (18.40.59 according to the ATM timing device). As earlier pointed out there was no direct evidence available to the jury that the timing mechanisms were not synchronised. If there had been the video tape would have recorded a person (the appellant) withdrawing $50 from the appellant's account at 18.40.59 (bank record time). The video does not show anybody near the ATM at that time. Thus there was no room for any presumption to operate in any useful way.[2]

1 [2003] NSWCCA 143, 2003 WL 21208345.

2 [2003] NSWCCA 143 at [41].

9.62 A clock can also help reveal the truth when somebody attempts to alter electronic evidence. In the case of Shaun Richards, who was caught speeding on 1 June 2009, Richards attempted to prove his innocence by driving the same route (without speeding) in January 2010 and used his satellite navigation data (whose date he had doctored on his computer to 1 June 2009) as proof of his innocence. However, he had forgotten about the clock change from British Summer Time to Greenwich Mean Time, which meant that there was a one hour difference in the time for the doctored data. After this was discovered, Richards was imprisoned for four months for perverting the course of justice.[1]

1 'Devon driving instructor jailed for sat-nav speed fraud' BBC News Devon, 13 January 2011.

9.63 There may be occasions where, in the absence of proof, an intelligent assumption that comments recorded on a document have a certain meaning might be accepted by an adjudicator, even when it is possible that the comments are capable of other meanings. In particular, the failure to offer an explanation to rebut the assumed meaning of the content of a digital document submitted in evidence may lead to a finding against the party adducing the evidence, as in *Hedrich v Standard Bank London Limited*.[1] The case concerned a wasted costs order, which was based on breach of the duty owed by a solicitor to the court to perform his duty as an officer of the court in promoting the cause of justice. Ward LJ took particular care in assessing the conflicting evidence, because of the complexity of the facts. The bank sought to have its costs paid by the claimants' solicitors, Messrs Zimmers. The bank was required to establish a strong prima facie case to succeed, and as part of its case, it sought to prove Zimmers were in receipt of an email on a date before Zimmers claimed that they had actual sight of the evidence. The bank relied on the following relevant text of that email:

> No virus found in this incoming message.
>
> Checked by AVG Free Edition.
>
> Version: 7.1.362/Virus Database: 267.12.8/162-Release Date: 05/11/2005.[2]

1 [2008] EWCA Civ 905, [2008] 7 WLUK 916, [2009] PNLR 3, [2009] CLY 386.
2 [2008] EWCA Civ 905 at [70].

9.64 In the absence of evidence from a digital evidence professional, the inference the bank sought to draw from this information was that Zimmers received notification of this particular email in May 2005, to counter the claim that Zimmers did not see it until the trial was under way in December 2005. This was highly relevant, because the bank was asking the court to order Zimmers to pay costs of £342,917.08. In meeting this argument, the barrister for Zimmers, Graeme McPherson QC, conducted some research on the Internet for an alternative explanation for the printed date of 11 May 2005. Ward LJ accepted the following offered explanation, although there was no evidence of the truth of it:

> Mr McPherson's researches [*sic*] on the internet gave him an alternative explanation. He told us that the first line showed, as it states, that no virus had been detected. The second line indicates that the means of checking was by the AVG Free Edition, which is a free virus detection software programme marketed as AVG. The third line identifies the version of AVG's software and the crucial date upon which the Bank relies is simply, as is stated on the e-mail, the date of the release of that particular version of the software. We have no evidence that this is the true explanation: we only have Mr McPherson's word that his researches [*sic*] on the internet produced that answer. It may have been a moment of inspiration by counsel but for my part it has a compelling ring of truth and I have no reason to think that it is unreliable. It destroys that part of the Bank's case.'[1]

1 [2008] EWCA Civ 905 at [71].

9.65 It would have been wise of the bank to establish the meaning of this information, because of the evidential hurdle required to prove its case. It would not have taken a digital evidence professional long to have established whether the information proved the date was the date of the release of that particular version of the software or not. It might have been for the court to ask the parties to seek an opinion on this issue before reaching a conclusion, but given the nature of the proceedings, in particular the rule that where there is room for doubt, the respondent lawyers are entitled to the benefit of it, it is not surprising that the court did not let the matter continue any further, and accepted the alternative explanation.[1]

1 There was a similar point raised in *State of Connecticut v Julie Amero*, but the digital evidence professional for the prosecution failed to even consider looking for malicious software: Stephen Mason, *International Electronic Evidence*, xxxvi–lxxv.

9.66 A further observation of relevance is that, in itself, the electronic evidence may not be conclusive. The case of *Mogford v Secretary of State for Education and Skills*[1] illustrates this point. Mr Mogford appealed against a decision of the Secretary of State for Education and Skills to include his name in the list maintained under the provisions of the Education (Restriction of Employment) Regulations 2000 (SI 2000/ 2419) that prevented him from being employed as a teacher under the provisions of regulation 5(1)(c). The Secretary of State made this decision because abusive images of children, text files, emails relating to this material and bookmarks with links to websites containing abusive images of children had been found on Mogford's computer. Mogford denied that he was responsible for this material. The members of the Tribunal were satisfied that the Secretary of State proved on a balance of probabilities that either Mogford was solely responsible for the materials found on the computer, or that he participated with others in obtaining this material, and he knew that it was on his machine. The reasons given included:

> (1) Inconsistencies in Mogford's evidence. He frequently changed his story. He told the interview team that he was visiting his girlfriend on the weekend 25–27 April 1997, then changed his story before the members of the Tribunal, indicating that three people had stayed at his house that weekend. Mogford also said in the interview that one RS had helped set up his Internet link. In evidence to the Tribunal, RS denied this. And Mogford gave evidence to the effect that one P set up the Internet for him.
>
> (2) There was no attempt to find P, or indeed either of the other two friends whom Mogford claimed were with him that weekend. That he failed to take steps to ask his friends to corroborate his story was held by the members of the Tribunal as being consistent with the fact that his version of events was not credible.

1 [2002] EWCST 11(PC) (26 June 2002).

9.67 Consideration was also given to the timing of the file system activity, especially those that occurred close to midnight of 27 April 1997 that showed access to a series of websites depicting abusive images of children, and the members of the Tribunal carefully examined the evidence presented by the digital evidence professional who sought to link access to such websites to Mogford. The electronic evidence showed that Mogford had created a spreadsheet that contained details of earnings from private lessons, and this spreadsheet was closed down at 00.28 on 27 April 1997. Mogford denied that he had closed down this spreadsheet, claiming that he had opened his spreadsheet at some other time earlier, had failed to close it down, and someone else had shut down his computer, thereby closing the spreadsheet in the process. The members of the Tribunal articulated the importance of this item of evidence and the explanation offered by Mogford as follows:

> It is our interpretation of the evidence that Mr M must have been using the computer at this time, either alone or with someone else, surfing the net and finding child pornography sites and text messages, and therefore when closing down the computer his spreadsheet would have been closed. The spreadsheet would have been of no interest to his friends, and he himself said in evidence that it was unlikely that he would have opened the spreadsheet and left it for a couple

of days. We can only infer that he was working on the spreadsheet earlier that evening or the previous day.[1]

1 [2002] EWCST 11(PC) (26 June 2002) at [25].

9.68 The observations noted above illustrate the importance of understanding the nature of digital data.[1] The aim should be to test the accuracy of the evidence and to ask if the conclusions are correct, rather than making decisions based on an imperfect analysis of the available evidence. It should never be assumed that because evidence is in electronic form, that it must therefore be correct and impervious to being tested to prove whether it is accurate or false. The important point to note is that questions of the accuracy and quality, together with the nature and quantum, of electronic evidence are contextual.

1 The British Computer Society Expert Panels: Legal Affairs Expert Panel Submission to the Criminal Courts Review (March 2000), http://www.computerevidence.co.uk/Papers/LJAuld/BCSComputerEvidenceSubmission.htm.

Tools

9.69 A digital evidence professional will not only, ideally, require an in-depth knowledge of the operating system she is to investigate, but will also need to use a number of proprietary tools in the performance of the investigation and analysis of digital evidence. The types of tool to be used will depend on the operating system being examined and whether the investigation is of networks, hand-held devices, embedded systems or wireless networks.[1] Due to their technicality, the reader is encouraged to become familiar with the technology and techniques by referring to appropriate practitioner texts,[2] including those discussing their limitations.[3] The tools used can, naturally, be the subject of cross-examination, and the underlying scientific methodology and structure of such tools can also be questioned.[4] In this section, the aim is to illustrate why and how tools are used in the context of the Windows operating system, partly because it is so widely used.

1 W. Jansen and R. Ayers, 'An overview and analysis of PDA forensic tools' (2005) 2(2) Digital Investigation 120.
2 Brian Carrier, 'Defining digital forensic examination and analysis tools using abstraction layers' and James R. Lyle, 'NIST CFTT: testing disk imaging tools' (2003) 1(4) International Journal of Digital Evidence; A. D. Irons, P. Stephens and R. I. Ferguson, 'Digital investigation as a distinct discipline: a pedagogic perspective' (2009) 6(1–2) Digital Investigation 82; Bradley Schatz, *Digital Evidence: Representation and Assurance*, PhD submitted to the Information Security Institute, Faculty of Information Technology, Queensland University of Technology (October 2007), http://eprints.qut.edu.au/16507/1/Bradley_Schatz_Thesis.pdf.
3 For instance, see SWGDE (Scientific Working Group on Digital Evidence), *Establishing Confidence in Digital Forensic Results by Error Mitigation Analysis* (1.5, 5 February 2015).
4 Erin Kenneally, 'Gatekeeping out of the box: open source software as a mechanism to assess reliability for digital evidence' (2001) 6 (13) Virginia Journal of Law and Technology 1; Eric Van Buskirk and Vincent T. Liu, 'Digital evidence: challenging the presumption of reliability' (2006) 1 Journal of Digital Forensic Practice 19; Lei Pan and Lynn M. Batten, 'Robust performance testing for digital forensic tools' (2009) 6(1–2) Digital Investigation 71; SWGDE Recommended Guidelines for Validation Testing, Version 1.1 (January 2009); Fred Cohen, Julie Lowrie and Charles Preston, 'The state of the science of digital evidence examination', in Gilbert Peterson and Sujeet Shenoi (eds) *Advances in Digital Forensics VII*, 7th IFIP WG 11.9 International Conference on Digital Forensics, Orlando, FL, USA, 31 January–2 February 2011 (Springer 2011); *Computer Forensic Tool Testing Handbook* (National Institute of Standards and Technology 2012); Jeremy Leighton John, *Digital Forensics and Preservation* (Digital Preservation Coalition 2012).

9.70 Automated tools are necessary to perform a forensic examination of a computer economically. However, the digital evidence professional should understand the process used by the tool to perform the relevant tasks. This is because it may be necessary to explain the process to a court, or the specialist may be required to carry out the analysis without the aid of a tool, because the use of a tool in any given situation may not be appropriate. These are issues that lawyers may well need to take cognizance of in the future.[1] For instance, it is not clear that practitioners themselves are familiar with some tools, and may question the worth of early versions.[2] This is because it seems that such tools are tested informally, rather than formally proven to be correct. It has therefore been suggested that such tools should be tested formally.[3] In an effort to enhance the veracity of evidence adduced from a forensic examination, it is becoming common practice within forensic laboratories to use what is known as 'dual tool' verification techniques. Simply put, an analyst will perform an examination using one piece of forensic software and, where data of potential relevance is identified, will use a second tool, produced by a different vendor, to perform the same examination and compare the results. If they match, more weight can be given to the accuracy of the data. However, it must be emphasized that such techniques are not a replacement for critical thinking or experimentation.[4]

1 For an example of where tools were the topic of judicial scrutiny in Australia, see *Bevan v The State of Western Australia* [2010] WASCA 101, (2010) 202 A Crim R 27 and *Bevan v The State of Western Australia* [2012] WASCA 153, 2012 WL 3298167. These cases are discussed in more detail in Chapter 5 on the presumption that computers are 'reliable'.

2 Eoghan Casey, 'Network traffic as a source of evidence: tool strengths, weaknesses, and future needs' (2004) 1(1) Digital Investigation 28.

3 Lyle, 'NIST CFTT: testing disk imaging tools'; Matthew Gerber and John Leeson, 'Formalization of computer input and output: the Hadley model' (2004) 1(2) Digital Investigation 214; Ibrahim M. Baggili and Richard Mislan, 'Mobile phone forensics tool testing: a database driven approach' (2007) 6(2) International Journal of Digital Evidence; David Byers and Nahid Shahmehri, 'A systematic evaluation of disk imaging in EnCase 6.8 and Li En 6.1' (2009) 6(1–2) Digital Investigation 61; SWGDE Recommended Guidelines for Validation Testing, Version 2.0 (5 September 2014).

4 See also Eoghan Casey, 'The increasing need for automation and validation in digital forensics' (2011) 7(3–4) Digital Investigation 103; Joshua I. James and Pavel Gladyshev, *Challenges with Automation in Digital Forensic Investigations* (Digital Forensic Investigation Research Group University College Dublin), http://arxiv.org/pdf/1303.4498.pdf; mistakes were made in the case of Casey Marie Anthony in 2011, and one tool that was used did not give correct results, although once the designer was aware of the error, he informed the police immediately: Craig Wilson, 'Digital evidence discrepancies – Casey Anthony trial, 11 July 2011'; Pipitone, 'Cops, prosecutors botched Casey Anthony evidence'; Baez and Golenbock, *Presumed Guilty*; Ashton and Pulitzer, *Imperfect Justice*; Ivar Friheim, 'Practical use of a dual tool verification in computer forensics', 2016, UCD Dublin (minor thesis).

9.71 It should also be noted that software in forensic tools is far from impartial or infallible.[1] Indeed, the users of forensic tools may themselves not be aware that some tools do not carry out as detailed an examination as they think. Jonathan Zdziarsk commented on a problem encountered with forensic tools in his 2014 blog post 'An example of forensic science at its worst: US v. Brig. Gen. Jeffrey Sinclair':

> I worked from a physical image dump created by a commercial forensics tool, and three reports from various tools which, as it would turn out, appeared to be misreporting (or at best 'under explaining') at least some of data that the case would later hinge on. What the tools didn't report turned out to be much more interesting than what they did ... As my findings would later reflect, the commercial tools that had been used to initially evaluate the evidence on the device had either misreported key evidence, or failed to acknowledge its existence

> entirely ... All you need to know from a technical perspective is right here: some of the types of information that these commercial tools were (and likely still are) misreporting is significant. Evidence and timestamps of a device erasure event. Evidence of a backup restore event. Application usage dates. Application deletion events and timestamps. File access times. This, and many other types of artifacts are often either completely overlooked by numerous commercially sold, expensive-as-hell tools, or in the case of at least one tool – seemingly made up data. All of these came into play in this case.[2]

1 Stephanie J. Lacambra, Jeanna Matthews and Kit Walsh, 'Opening the black box: defendant's right to confront forensic software' (2018) Champion 28, https://www.eff.org/files/2018/07/30/champion_article_-_lacambra_forensic_software_may_2018_07102018.pdf.

2 https://www.zdziarski.com/blog/?p=3717. This remains the case in 2021, and is one reason to undertake verification with more than one tool – but it is also true that most commercial telephone tools do not identify or under-report data present on the device.

Copying the hard drive

9.72 Before obtaining access to a computer, it is essential that the investigator is familiar with the underlying operating systems, file systems and applications. By understanding the file systems, the digital evidence professional will be aware of how information is arranged, which in turn enables her to determine where information can be hidden, and how such information can be recovered and analysed. In order to establish answers to questions such as 'Who might have had access to a computer or system?', 'Which files would they have been able to look at?' and 'Was it possible for an unauthorized outsider to obtain access to the computer from the Internet?', the digital evidence professional should understand the nature of user accounts and profiles, and the control mechanism that determines which files a user is permitted to access upon logging into a system.

9.73 To acquire the data on a hard disk installed in a computer, an investigator will, in most cases, prefer to remove the hard disk from the computer and attach it to a specialist 'write-protected' interface that is attached, in turn, to an 'imaging' device capable of copying the forensic image stored on the media on to a previously cleaned (and verified as clean) storage device. Such interfaces are commonly referred to as 'write blockers', and the imaging capability may be performed by specifically designed imaging hardware or by a standard computer running imaging software. However, in some circumstances removal of the hard disk from a computer may not be possible or advisable, in which case it is common to leave the hard disk installed in the host computer and obtain access to it using the procedures described in the following paragraphs.

9.74 To avoid altering any evidence on a computer, it is necessary to bypass the operating system. When the power supply is switched on, the basic input and output system (BIOS) will carry out a power-on self-test (POST) before looking for the operating system. After the BIOS is activated and before the POST test has completed its cycle, it is possible to interrupt the process. Most computers are programmed to expect the operating system to be found on a floppy disk, hard disk, compact disc or a device attached to the Universal Serial Bus (USB). As a result, the system looks at these locations in the order set out in something called the Complementary Metal

Oxide Silicon (CMOS) configuration tool. The CMOS chip retains the date, time, hard drive parameters and other details relating to configuration while the main power is switched off. By looking at the CMOS tool between the POST test and the computer being fully powered up, the digital evidence professional is able to determine where the computer will look for the operating system: for instance, a floppy disk, a hard disk or a compact disc. With this knowledge, the investigator is able to pre-empt the search for the operating system on the computer and provide an alternate operating system from another disk. It is common for this alternative operating system to be a variant of the Linux operating system that is designed to allow storage devices to be viewed in 'Read Only' mode. By interrupting the normal boot-up process in this way, the evidence on the hard drive remains intact and unaltered, thereby permitting the content to be copied in the state it was in when the computer was switched off. Various techniques and tools (such as an evidence acquisition boot disk) can be used to intercept this process, and the precise technique depends on the circumstances of each case.

9.75 Once the computer is booted from a suitable tool, the program can then do a sector-by-sector copy of the electronic evidence. Some tools will acquire the data and undertake an integrity check at regular intervals. There is some technical discussion about whether the tools that undertake these tasks do take an exact copy of the disk, even though all of the information is copied from the disk. One of the reasons for this is that data may be arranged in a different manner in a proprietary file format. Professor Casey suggests this is not as important as ensuring that the integrity of the evidence is maintained, which must be correct. In addition, he also suggests that at least two copies be made with different tools.[1] From a practical point of view, this may not always be possible because of time constraints and the absence of storage media.

1 Casey, *Digital Evidence*, 480.

9.76 A number of the forensic imaging tools, such as Encase and FTK, have used the expression 'Logical Evidence Files' which, instead of being an image of an entire hard disk, are copies of specific data accessible in the devices' file systems (that is, the contents of a specific directory or directories). This technique has significant advantages where it is impractical to image an entire drive due to the amount of data required to be copied or because of time constraints. It should be noted that file hashing and image hashing techniques are still used to ensure the integrity of the data that is collected.[1]

1 Michael Cohen, Simson Garfinkel and Bradley Schatz, 'Extending the advanced forensic format to accommodate multiple data sources, logical evidence, arbitrary information and forensic workflow' (2009) 6(1) Digital Investigation S57; Da-Yu Kao, Shiuh-Jeng Wang and Frank Fu-Yuan Huang, 'SoTE: strategy of Triple-E on solving Trojan defense in cyber-crime cases' (2010) 26(1) Computer Law & Security Review 52.

Viewing the data

9.77 When the electronic evidence has been copied, the data can be viewed in raw format (examining the contents of the file in binary, hexadecimal or another format that displays the literal file contents as expressed in bits) or logically (using a viewer or program suitable for processing the file at hand). It is usually necessary to view the data through a tool; human beings need the binary code, which resides on a disk or in a disk image, to be interpreted before the data can be viewed and interrogated in a sensible manner. In many tools for viewing raw data, the data can be viewed in hexadecimal form on one side of the screen and in plaintext (ASCII or Unicode) on the other side of the screen. Depending on the tool used, the data can be examined and analysed. For instance, a tool can recover slack space and compare files to determine if there are any differences to be observed.[1] Viewing data in logical view enables the user to examine it as represented by the file system. This way of looking at the data permits the user to analyse it in a different way, but it does not show the underlying information that is visible when using the physical method. Both forms of viewing data have their limitations, and it is also important to be aware that data can be misinterpreted. There is some debate about the best way of examining digital evidence, but the emphasis should be on verifying the accuracy of the evidence by using different tools.

1 Note also that the volume of images that need to be reviewed and searched are increasing, and tools are being developed for this purpose: Paul Sanderson, 'Mass image classification' (2006) 3(4) Digital Investigation 190.

Recovering data

9.78 An increasing number of people delete the content of their hard drives in computers in anticipation of legal action or after legal action has begun.[1] For instance, in the case of *L C Services Limited v Brown*,[2] Andrew Brown, the sales director of LC Services, was found to have broken the fiduciary duty he owed to LC Services. He also breached the terms of his services agreement and misused confidential information belonging to LC Services. It appeared that Mr Brown altered or re-installed the operating system on his computer on 1 October 2003, at the time the claimants were pursuing disclosure documents from the defendants. A digital evidence professional was subsequently able to retrieve the residue of the text of the relevant database in dispute, and the remains of a number of emails sent by Mr Brown. The content of these emails showed that he was in breach of his fiduciary duties to LC Services.[3]

1 Ewa Huebner, Derek Bren and Cheong Kai Wee, 'Data hiding in the NTFS file system' (2006) 3(4) Digital Investigation 211; Dan H. Willoughby Jr, Rose Hunter Jones and Gregory R. Antine, 'Sanctions for e-discovery violations: by the numbers' (2010) 60(3) Duke Law Journal 789.
2 [2003] EWHC 3024 (QB), [2003] 12 WLUK 391.
3 Bruce J. Nikkel, 'Forensic acquisition and analysis of magnetic tapes' (2005) 2(1) Digital Investigation 8; Mayank R. Gupta, Michael D. Hoeschele and Marcus K. Rogers, 'Hidden disk areas: HPA and DCO' (2006) 5(1) International Journal of Digital Evidence.

9.79 There are several techniques that can be used to recover data that has been deleted. This can be done manually or through the use of tools, depending on the complexity of the problem faced by the specialist. For instance, some tools use a bit-for-bit copy of a disk to reconstruct the file system, including any files marked as deleted in the file allocation table, master file table or their equivalents. However, where files are fragmented and have been partially overwritten, it may be necessary to recover them by hand. A typical technique to recover deleted files (often called 'carving') involves searching unallocated space and swap files for such information as headers and footers. Although there are many types of file that can be recovered (carved) in this way with an appropriate tool, such as graphic files, word processing and executable files, recovery is limited to those files whose headers have not been deleted.[1]

1 Paul Alvarez, 'Using Extended File Information (EXIF) file headers in digital evidence examination' (2004) 2(3) International Journal of Digital Evidence.

Passwords and encryption

9.80 A number of tools are available that are capable of removing passwords and bypassing or recovering them. Some tools are available for guessing passwords if the encryption keys are small enough, and where it is not possible to obtain a password, it is sometimes possible to search for unencrypted versions of the data in other areas of the hard disk.[1] Passwords can be used simply to provide access control to unencrypted data, can be the 'key' that decrypts encrypted data, and can even be the 'key' that decrypts the actual key that is used to decrypt encrypted data. The methods used to bypass passwords or 'crack' the code needed to decrypt encrypted data are many and varied, but in general stronger encryption algorithms and larger 'keys' mean that very long processing times are required to gain access to the data, if indeed they can be accessed. Depending on the processing power available, it may be impossible to reveal the passphrase or gain access to encrypted materials in a realistic time frame. The techniques used to attempt to obtain access to encrypted or password-protected data are discussed in Chapter 8 on encrypted data. The increased use of encryption on (mobile telephone) file systems poses problems and has led to significant debate and developments in the field of police powers.

1 Eoghan Casey, 'Practical approaches to recovering encrypted digital evidence' (2002) 1(3) International Journal of Digital Evidence; Christopher Hargreaves and Howard Chivers, 'Recovery of encryption keys from memory using a linear scan', *Proceedings of the 2008 Third International Conference on Availability, Reliability and Security*, 2008, 1369–1376; Eoghan Casey, Geoff Fellows, Matthew Geiger and Gerasimos Stellatos, 'The growing impact of full disk encryption on digital forensics' (2011) 8(2) Digital Investigation, 129.

Traces of evidence

Network connections

9.81 One of the most significant difficulties faced by digital evidence professionals with computers and devices that are connected to a network such as the Internet, or a series of computers or devices that are connected in an organization, is the possibility that a hacker or malicious employee might enter the system without authority and undertake a series of actions that causes an innocent person to be accused of doing something he did not do.[1] This is where data logs can help. Two types of log, the application log and system event log, contain information about how users have used the computer. Scrutinizing these logs, either manually or with a tool, can help to obtain a clearer picture about the activities that took place on the system, although consideration must be given to the integrity of the logs themselves. Note that logs may also be present at other levels in the network, such as on a fileserver, an Internet proxy or a firewall. The availability of such logs may, however, vary a great deal. A typical problem in this area is the shared use of a single public IP address for Internet traffic by many different local users. These users will typically have their own, locally distributed (private) IP address. A setup like this is known as NAT (Network Address Translation) since it requires translation of the local user's (private) IP addresses to the public IP address and vice versa. Network-based logs only rarely contain enough data to identify the individual user, however.[2]

1 Srinivas Mukkamala and Andrew H. Sung, 'Identifying significant features for network forensic analysis using artificial intelligence techniques' (2003) 1(4) International Journal of Digital Evidence;

Bruce J. Nikkel, 'Domain name forensics: a systematic approach to investigating an internet presence' (2004) 1(4) Digital Investigation 247; Bruce J. Nikkel, 'Improving evidence acquisition from live network sources' (2006) 3(2) Digital Investigation 89; Eoghan Casey and Aaron Stanley, 'Tool review – remote forensic preservation and examination tools' (2004) 1(4) Digital Investigation 284; Omer Demir, Ping Ji and Jinwoo Kim, 'Packet marking and auditing for network forensics' (2007) 6(1) International Journal of Digital Evidence.

2 Hein Dries-Ziekenheiner and Iljitsch van Beijnum, 'Allocation and use of IP addresses', Study for the European Commission (December 2010, SMART 2010/14), http://bookshop.europa.eu/en/allocation-and-use-of-ip-addresses-pbKK0113063/.

Logs, files and printing

9.82 In addition, when a user uses his computer, a digital trace is left of the actions across a range of data logs and files.[1] A data log is capable of containing any type of data, depending on what the system is programmed to capture.[2] For instance, if a file is downloaded from the Internet, a date and time stamp will be added to the file to demonstrate when the file was downloaded onto the computer. When the file is moved, opened or modified, the time and date stamps will be altered to reflect these changes. In addition, the metadata can also help provide more information about the file, such as the location where it was stored on the disk, the printer on which the file was printed and the time and date the file was created. When a file is printed, the computer tends to store the print job in a temporary file before it is sent to the printer when the printer has the capacity to print the file. Once the command to print has been passed to the temporary store, the user can continue to work with the application – for instance, she can continue to type a new document while the previous document is waiting to be printed. The temporary print store retains valuable information, such as the name of the file to be printed, the type of application used, the name of the printer, the purported name of the person whose file is to be printed and the data itself. In addition, there is a date and time stamp added to the file to show when the file was printed. It should be noted, however, that the date and time stamp can be altered, which means it is important to ensure that the date and time stamp is corroborated by other methods.[3]

1 In relation to intrusion detection systems, see Peter Sommer, 'Intrusion detection systems as evidence' [2002] 3 CTLR 67; Vlasti Broucek and Paul Turner, 'Intrusion detection: issues and challenges in evidence acquisition' (2004) 18(2) International Review of Law, Computers & Technology 149; Jean-Marc Dinant, 'The long way from electronic traces to electronic evidence' (2004) 18(2) International Review of Law, Computers & Technology 173.

2 Erin E. Kenneally, 'Digital logs – proof matters' (2004) 1(2) Digital Investigation 94.

3 Karen Kent and Murugiah Souppaya, Guide to Computer Security Log Management (2006), Special Publication 800-92 at 2.1.3 fourth bullet point, http://nvlpubs.nist.gov/nistpubs/Legacy/SP/nistspecialpublication800-92.pdf.

Use of the Internet

9.83 When a person obtains access to the Internet, a range of data is created and retained on a computer or device, including the websites that have been visited, the contents a user has viewed and the data sources accessed.[1] Some systems, both in the network and on customer premises, also include a log of the times and dates of the Internet session and details of the device or connection that was used (such as the modem, network card or physical network port in the access network). With more services available online, it is important to be able to rely on information provided by network operators for investigation purposes. Typical information requests involve IP addresses, subscriber details and possibly payment information. Internet access logs may, furthermore, provide information as to where and how users were connected to a service, and may identify others involved in the same investigation. Finally, it is interesting to observe that CCTV systems are gradually being replaced by systems that use Internet Protocol technologies (IP) and wireless IP, which will in turn cause additional expense and increase the legal complexity (where the camera is capturing images in one country, and these images are being recorded or stored in another country) in obtaining access to such systems for the purposes of litigation or criminal proceedings.[2] The types of information available include those noted below.

1 Yeong Zee Kin, 'Computer misuse, forensics and evidence on the Internet' (2000) 5(5) Communications Law 153; Vivienne Mee, Theodore Tryfonas and Iain Sutherland, 'The Windows Registry as a forensic artefact: illustrating evidence collection for Internet usage' (2006) 3(3) Digital Investigation 166.

2 Fanny Coudert, 'Towards a new generation of CCTV networks: erosion of data protection safeguards?' (2009) 25(2) Computer Law & Security Review 145.

9.84 Browser cache When viewing a page on the Internet, the browser retains and takes copies of all the elements that make up the page, such as graphics and HTML text. This copy is called a cache. The computer or device gives the page a date and time stamp at the time the page was downloaded. The reason for doing this is that when the page is visited again, the cached file is used by the computer or device in place of obtaining access to the same page online and the date and time stamp is subsequently updated. Another item of information created and logged in some browser history databases is the number of times a web page was visited. It must not be assumed, however, that just because the computer or device has recorded certain types of web page that the user actually viewed such pages. This is because some websites, in particular those promoting pornography, will redirect a browser to different websites, and may even make unauthorized changes to the computer or device.[1] It is possible to recover these cached files, even if they are deleted. Recovered files can provide such information as when the computer or device was used to obtain access to web-based email, when sites were visited and if purchases were made or financial transactions undertaken.

1 Daniel Bilar, 'Known knowns, known unknowns and unknown unknowns: anti-virus issues, malicious software and internet attacks for non-technical audiences' (2009) 6 Digital Evidence and Electronic Signature Law Review 123.

9.85 Cookies Many websites keep a track of visits by users to their sites by placing this information in files on the users' computers or devices called cookies. If cookies have not been disabled, the information in the cookie directory can help with an investigation. As for websites included in the temporary cache file, it does not follow that just because there is a cookie on the computer or device that a user necessarily went to all of the websites included in the cookie directory. Some advertisements on a website may place a cookie on the user's computer or device, even though the user did not click on and view the particular website. Further, where the user's browser has been redirected without his permission, cookies can be added to the directory without the knowledge of the user.

9.86 Private browsing, VPN proxies and Tor In order to provide Internet users with more privacy, several browser manufacturers have introduced 'incognito modes' or 'private browsing' modes in their browser software. In this mode, no Internet history, cache entries or cookies (or any other artefacts) remain after the Internet session. This means it will be harder (if not impossible) to retrieve a reliable indication of a user's Internet usage and surfing behaviour from the information present in the local computer system. In practice, other systems such as access logs at service providers' services or browsed websites may still be able to identify the user by her IP address.[1]

1 For which see *United States v Bandy*, Slip Copy, 2021 WL 414830.

9.87 In order to further enhance user privacy and anonymity, services such as Tor (The Onion Router) and VPNs (Virtual Private Networks) are available that allow users to hide the origins of their connection to the services they use. In the case of Tor, this is achieved through a network of nodes operated by volunteers who anonymize connections to the Internet by providing a route across three or more anonymous nodes (including an entry and exit node, as they are called) on behalf of a Tor user. Since no logging is kept at any of the intermediary Tor nodes, this assures a relatively high level of anonymity. Similarly, VPNs and proxies can be used to connect to the Internet via a predetermined 'hop' in the network. Provided the VPN origin is not logged, this may effectively make tracing users by their network addresses impossible. Note that the use of other information and identifiers is still possible, so that various other measures may still reveal the users' actual names, addresses and Internet activities.

9.88 Email and instant messaging Email has become a dominant method of communication for the vast majority of organizations, although text-based 'chat' is used increasingly by individuals, and especially on smartphones. Nevertheless, a great deal of evidence can be discovered from email communications. Some software programs store email in plaintext files, while others use proprietary formats that will require the digital evidence professional to use a number of tools in order to read the messages. Other email systems utilize online storage only and leave very little communications data on the filesystem of computers or devices. It is sometimes possible to recover email messages that have been deleted but have not been removed from the email files.[1] Where it is impossible or difficult to restore emails from a single computer or device, it might be possible to track email traffic through the network it has travelled.[2] Organizations are beginning to recognize the importance of their email communications, and many larger organizations have archives of email communications that can be investigated in the event of electronic disclosure or electronic discovery requests.

1 See the criminal case of *R. v Khan (Adeel)* [2015] EWCA Crim 1816, [2015] 11 WLUK 550, [2016] 1 Cr App R (S) 47 where the only evidence was of screen shots of email messages, and screen shots of email messages were also adduced in *Cole v Carpenter* [2020] EWHC 3155 (Ch), [2020] 11 WLUK 318 regarding a dispute over the sale of a work of art by Pablo Picasso, known as 'Le Sauvetage' or 'The Rescue' (this was an application by the defendants for permission to make a contempt application against the claimant); see also *Vorotyntseva v Money-4 Ltd (t/a Nebeus.com)* [2018] EWHC 2596 (Ch), [2018] 9 WLUK 501.
2 Eoghan Casey, Troy Larson and H. Morrow Long, 'Network analysis' in Eoghan Casey (ed) *Handbook of Computer Crime Investigation Forensic Tools and Technology*, 234–239.

9.89 Instant messaging, in the meantime, has become the default method of communication for many people. This presents problems for the investigator. It is not only used on local desktop systems (where this technology is increasingly also used in business environments), but it has also seen a major surge in use on mobile devices in recent years. Due to the Snowden revelations in 2013 of the mass international surveillance by the NSA,[1] many instant messaging programs currently in widespread use have introduced end-to-end encryption, meaning that intermediaries do not have access to plaintext messages, but merely to an encrypted version of those messages. Each connected device has a unique public key and a private key that is unknown to the intermediary. In practice, this means that the only place where such communications can be viewed and decrypted to a readable format is at the end user's device.

1 David Cole, 'After Snowden: Regulating technology-aided surveillance in the digital age' (2016) 44 Capital University Law Review 677.

9.90 Mobile applications that are used for instant messaging typically include the ability to send photographs and videos. Social networks and mobile Internet messaging have become the default communication method used by children.[1] This creates an increased workload for investigators of child abuse-related cases, especially where they may need to view a home computer, as well as a multitude of other devices, to help determine why a child might have left home, or how he or she got into contact with a certain adult, for instance.[2] Another challenge is that these programs increasingly offer features that allow the user to determine a set time and date to destroy any images sent. Therefore, images are no longer stored on the filesystem of the device or telephone by default, but temporary copies only are displayed for a short period of time, after which they are deleted. This leaves fewer artefacts and creates further challenges in criminal investigations involving abusive images and children, particularly in relation to practices such as sexting, the sending of sexual images and messages, and grooming, where adults lure children typically for sexual abuse by acting as persons of the same age.

1 Sonia Livingstone, Leslie Haddon, Anke Görzig and Kjartan Ólafsson, 'Risks and safety on the internet: the perspective of European children: full findings and policy implications from the EU Kids Online survey of 9–16 year olds and their parents in 25 countries', EU Kids Online 2011 (LSE 2012), http://eprints.lse.ac.uk/33731/1/Risks%20and%20safety%20on%20the%20internet%28lsero%29.pdf.
2 Harlan Carvey, 'Instant messaging investigations on a live Windows XP system', (2004) 1(4) Digital Investigation 256; Mike Dickson, 'An examination into MSN Messenger 7.5 contact identification' (2006) 3(2) Digital Investigation 79; Mike Dickson, 'An examination into Yahoo Messenger 7.0 contact identification' (2006) 3(3) Digital Investigation 159; Paul Sanderson, 'Identifying an existing file KaZaA artefacts' (2006) 3(3) Digital Investigation 174; Mike Dickson, 'An examination into AOL Instant Messenger 5.5 contact identification' (2006) 3(4) Digital Investigation 227; Jessica Reust, 'Case study: AOL instant messenger trace evidence' (2006) 3(4) Digital Investigation 238.

9.91 Voice over Internet Protocol (known as VoIP) is another computer-to-computer technology that has expanded rapidly, and will need to be considered when conducting an investigation.[1] Contrary to the old telephony system (often referred to as POTS or Plain Old Telephone System), Internet-based calls can be made fairly anonymously and it is easy to deceive a person into thinking that a telephone number is genuine (called 'spoofing'), especially the number of the party initiating the call.[2] This makes telephone numbers increasingly unreliable as identifiers. The risk of wrongfully attributing the source of a telephone call on the basis of its originating telephone number has increased greatly, especially since many VoIP providers allow spoofing of outbound calls as a service feature, and special services have emerged that specialize in spoofing calls for various purposes. In most cases the connection will be encrypted, which means that the data packets flowing between the caller and the recipient of a VoIP call is not in decipherable voice form, and if intercepted midway, cannot be reconstructed to meaningful evidence.

1 Xinyuan Wang, Shiping Chen and Sushil Jajodia, 'Tracking anonymous peer-to-peer VoIP calls on the Internet', *Proceedings of the 12th ACM Conference on Computer and Communications Security* (2005), 81–91.
2 Richard Clayton, 'Can CLI be trusted?' (2007) 12(2) Information Security Technical Report 74, https://www.cl.cam.ac.uk/~rnc1/cli.pdf.

9.92 Digital and online wealth A special category of data is related to financial investigations and digital evidence. Once a small field with limited overlap to digital forensics, the advent of cryptocurrencies such as Bitcoin, electronic money such as PayPal, as well as many other types of digital assets and wealth stored online, have increased the need for specialized investigations into electronic evidence pertaining to wealth that is accessible through computer systems. It should be noted that, in contrast to electronic money, where a database containing a ledger (denominated in fiat currency such as pound and euro) is typically stored with a service provider, cryptocurrencies make it possible to store values in local wallets that are hosted on software present on a computer system or device. A special property of these currencies is that the cryptographic values in the wallet can be copied in order to make it possible to spend the currency from either one of the copies made. This complicates search and seizure for this type of evidence. Digital evidence professionals will need to have a good knowledge of the way in which such wallets are stored, as well as the most common online services related to the various types of financial activities that can be employed online, in order to proficiently and, indeed, forensically conduct financial investigations into data. From a legal perspective, it should be noted that the existing international standards make frequent use of the reversal of the burden of proof in cases of 'unexplained wealth'. These are cases where a predicate offence can be proven, yet significantly more 'unexplained' wealth is found to be present following a financial investigation. In such cases the burden of proof regarding the title to such wealth can be shifted to the suspect.[1]

1 This is sometimes called 'extended confiscation' (if such wealth is seized) and in the UK is implemented in the regime for UWO (Unexplained Wealth Orders) in s 6 (which only applies to England and Wales) of the Proceeds of Crime Act 2002.

Reporting

9.93 The findings, and any conclusions made by the digital evidence professional, will be set out in a report. Whether prepared for criminal or civil proceedings, the report should include a range of information that is pertinent to the case, including, but not limited to:

(1) Notes prepared during the examination phase of the investigation.

(2) Details about the way in which the investigation was conducted.

(3) Details about the continuity of custody.

(4) The validity of the procedures used.

(5) Details of what was discovered, including, but not limited to:

(a) Any specific files or data that were directly related to the investigation.

(b) Any further files or data that may support the conclusions reached by the specialist. This will include the recovery of any deleted files and the analysis of any graphic files.

(c) The types of search conducted, such as key word searches, and the programs searched.

(d) Any relevant evidence from the Internet, such as emails and the analysis of websites visited and log files.

(e) Indications of names that might demonstrate evidence of ownership of software, such as with whom the software was registered.

(f) Whether there was any attempt to hide data in any way, and if so, what methods were used.

9.94 Professor Casey refers to the following principles to guide the preparation of forensic reports: observation, hypothesis, prediction, experimentation/testing and conclusion.[1] Following from these principles, the report needs to reflect how the examination was conducted and what data were recovered. It may be that the digital evidence professional will have to give evidence about the conduct of the examination and the validity of the procedures and tools used. Essential to any report will be the conclusions reached by the professional. Where an opinion is offered, the opinion should set out the basis of the evidence. Consideration should also be given to rates of error, including the origin and timing of events that had been recorded, whether the digital evidence professional took care when reaching conclusions where data were lost, whether the professional was aware that digital evidence can be fabricated, and whether the professional evaluated the evidence based 'on the reliability of the system and processes that generate the records'.[2]

1 Casey, *Digital Evidence*, 204.

2 Eoghan Casey, 'Error, uncertainty, and loss in digital evidence' (2002) 1(2) International Journal of Digital Evidence.

9.95 As pointed out by Professor Sommer, it is important to be aware that digital evidence professionals have to use a variety of techniques to cope with the wide diversity of hardware and software encountered. Reliability is one factor to take into account. Another factor is the degree of reliance on the conclusions reached by a digital evidence professional. The digital evidence must be interpreted, and care should be taken to ensure the underlying rationale is sustainable.[1]

1 Peter Sommer, 'Digital footprints: assessing computer evidence' [1998] Crim LR Special Edition 65 and 69.

9.96 Assumptions should not form part of any report (except in Australia[1]) by a digital evidence professional, as occurred in some cases relating to the investigations by the UK police under the name Operation Ore. In this case, police forces in the UK investigated and prosecuted over 7,000 people for offences relating to the possession of abusive images of children and secured over 2,000 convictions.[2] This operation was instigated after the conviction of Thomas and Janice Reedy (the Landslide trial, named after their company) in the United States for operating a website selling access to abusive images of children.[3] After the trial, a copy of the database recording details of the payments received by Landslide was shared with a number of police forces across the world. This information formed the initial evidence for the purposes of the investigations that subsequently took place. There was evidence to suggest that stolen credit card numbers were used to steal money by 'buying' access to the illegal websites hosted by Reedy, who tried to prevent this without success.[4] Some of those prosecuted claimed that they did not use their credit cards to obtain access to abusive images of children, as in the case of Dr Paul Grout. No abusive images of children were found on his computers. He produced alibi evidence to demonstrate that at the time of the alleged links to the Landslide website, he was not at a computer terminal. The case was withdrawn from the jury.[5] On occasions, it was also assumed that if a credit card number was in the Landslide database, the person whose number it was had therefore paid for abusive images of children. Brian Cooper used his credit card to buy bicycle parts from a US website. His card details were obtained by Akip Anshori, an Indonesian, who successfully subscribed to the Landslide website until Mr Cooper alerted his credit card provider to the unauthorized payments. The police failed to find any abusive images of children on his computers.[6]

1 Nigel Wilson, 'Expert evidence in the Digital Age in Australia' (2012) 31(2) Civil Justice Quarterly 216.
2 For an outline (notwithstanding that the content may not be entirely accurate), see https://en.wikipedia.org/wiki/Operation_Ore.
3 *United States of America v Reedy*, 304 F.3d 358 (5th Cir. 2002), 2002 WL 1966498.
4 Duncan Campbell, 'Sex, lies and the missing videotape', *PC Pro* (June 2007), 18–21; Supplementary memorandum by Mr Jim Gamble dated 1 June 2007 submitted to the Science and Technology Committee – Fifth Report (Session 2006–07, 24 July 2007) (the evidence is published in Vol II (HL Paper 165-II)), where Mr Gamble challenges some of the assertions made by Mr Campbell.
5 'Invisible predator', BBC, Inside Out – Yorkshire & Lincolnshire, 4 October 2004.
6 Campbell, 'Sex, lies and the missing videotape', 19.

9.97 A similar case involved Jeremy Clifford, who was charged with making and being in possession of indecent images of children. The images were found in the temporary cache folder with random names such as 'FX7RA'. Such images generally appear as advertisements, and the user will not necessarily have clicked on them, nor will she be aware that they are on her machine. At his trial, Clifford was acquitted when the prosecution offered no evidence. Although he failed in his first legal action for malicious prosecution and misfeasance in public office,[1] his appeal succeeded,[2] and the police were subsequently found liable.[3] It transpired that the police and the digital evidence professional had made a number of erroneous assumptions about the Landslide databases, the evidence of Internet browsing and site visit history on Clifford's machine.[4]

1 *Clifford v The Chief Constable of the Hertfordshire Constabulary* [2008] EWHC 3154 (QB), [2008] 12 WLUK 568.
2 *Clifford v The Chief Constable of the Hertfordshire Constabulary* [2009] EWCA Civ 1259, [2009] 12 WLUK 16.
3 *Clifford v The Chief Constable of the Hertfordshire Constabulary* [2011] EWHC 815 (QB), [2011] 4 WLUK 7.
4 [2009] EWCA Civ 1259 at [67]–[76].

9.98 Great care must be given to the nature of the technical evidence, as demonstrated by the case of *R. v O'Shea (Anthony David)*,[1] a case that also centred on the Landslide database. The case had been publicized by the media as a public enquiry into the entire operation conducted by the police. It was not. It was an appeal against conviction by one man on the main ground that new evidence from one Bates, described as a computer expert, based on a forensic examination of the Landslide records, suggested that a third party had misappropriated the appellant's identity. The members of the Court of Appeal held that there was no evidence to support Bates' suggestion that the Landslide webmaster had access to the appellant's personal data that were used in the transactions, that there was no evidence to prove that the hypothetical fraudulent webmaster had obtained access to the Freeserve proxy servers to assume the appellant's identity, and noted the appellant had checked his credit card statements regularly and not challenged these transactions (he had challenged the debiting of his credit card account in relation to other amounts that were similar to those in question in this case).[2] Describing this additional evidence as 'mere assertion, unsupported by any published or other material or any reasoning,'[3] the members of the Court of Appeal concluded that the appellant's conviction was safe and dismissed the appeal.

1 [2010] EWCA Crim 2879, [2010] 12 WLUK 150; Stephen Mason, 'Digital evidence: beware of assuming too much' (2011) 22(2) Comps & Law 36.
2 [2010] EWCA Crim 2879 at [50]–[59].
3 [2010] EWCA Crim 2879 at [43].

Analysis of a failure

9.99 A prosecution in Wales in 2015 offers an illustrative case study to demonstrate what can go wrong when the police do not conduct a careful investigation, and the prosecution's failure to understand the weakness of the evidence upon which the charges are preferred. A number of nurses working at the Princess of Wales Hospital in Bridgend were indicted on charges relating to alleged falsification of patient notes regarding blood glucose levels. Professor Thimbleby, an expert witness for the defence, discussed the evidence in detail[1] where he outlined the correct, systematic procedure to be observed by the nurses.

1 Harold Thimbleby, 'Misunderstanding IT: hospital cybersecurity and IT problems reach the courts' (2018) 15 Digital Evidence and Electronic Signatures Law Review 11; Professor Angela Hopkins, 'Review of the blood glucometry investigations in Abertawe Bro Morgannwg University Health Board: establishing lessons learned' (ABM University Health Board, June – September 2016), http://www.wales.nhs.uk/sitesplus/documents/863/4.5%20Blood%20Glucometry.pdf.

9.100 The central record system had no records of many of the tests and their results the nurses had written on the paper notes for each patient. Because of this discrepancy, the police concluded that the nurses had written down fictitious readings and had not bothered to do their job. As an aside, nurses could not necessarily undertake the actions as set out above, because of problems with the software, and also because sometimes it was difficult for the software to read the patient's identity number. It turned out that a practical solution was to type 000 on the glucometer keyboard, or for the nurse to scan her own barcode in order for the glucometer to accept the data to be input as a valid patient, or to manually type in the name of the patient – but this action would not prevent the nurse from misspelling the patient's name. The glucometer accepted both of these methods of getting around the failure of the software code and would give a correct blood glucose reading. However, the hospital system rejected this data, the consequence of which required manual intervention for the data to be added to the central database – which might not happen or might introduce further errors.

9.101 On analysing the prosecution evidence – which was in the form of a CD of Excel spreadsheets and, on a later date, XML files of data logged on blood glucometers – it was discovered that the relevant data were not present. The prosecution asserted that because data was not present, it followed that the nurses had fabricated doing actual tests, because if they had actually done the tests, the data would be present in the spreadsheets.

9.102 The prosecution needed to prove that it was the failure of the nurses to input data that caused the data to be missing from the central database – that is, the absence of data proved fabrication, rather than any other possibility. The police and the prosecution lawyers assumed that the glucometers and hospital IT systems were reliable, even though they knew the systems required human intervention. The police did not question the management of the data, and there was no evidence about the day-to-day management of the data. The prosecution also claimed that the devices were accurate as blood glucose meters. This was not relevant. The relevant issue was whether the glucometers reliably transmitted test data to the hospital's patient record system. It did not appear that the police or the prosecution bothered to research this topic – if they had, they would have discovered a number of relevant articles that included reference to issues which were noted by Professor Thimbleby regarding the practical problems of the device and getting the data to the central computer.[1] The judge concluded that the prosecution evidence was unreliable and was therefore excluded.[2] The prosecution response was to offer no evidence.[3] In consequence, the nurses were acquitted.

1 Ksenia Tonyushkina and James H. Nichols, 'Glucose meters: a review of technical challenges to obtaining accurate results' (2009) 3(4) Journal of Diabetes Science and Technology 971; Suzanne Austin Boren and William L. Clarke, 'Analytical and clinical performance of blood glucose monitors' (2010) 4(1) Journal of Diabetes Science and Technology 84; James H. Nichols, 'Blood glucose testing in the hospital: error sources and risk management' (2011) 5(1) Journal of Diabetes Science and Technology 173; David C. Klonoff, 'Point-of-care blood glucose meter accuracy in the hospital setting' (2014) 27(3) Diabetes Spectrum 174.
2 Ruling in *R v Cahill; R v Pugh* 14 October 2014, Crown Court at Cardiff, T20141094 and T20141061 before HHJ Crowther QC (2017) 14 Digital Evidence and Electronic Signature Law Review 67.
3 'Nurses cleared of wilful neglect at Princess of Wales Hospital in Bridgend' *South Wales Evening Post*, 14 October 2015, http://www.southwales-eveningpost.co.uk/nurses-cleared-wilful-neglect-princess-wales/story-27983645-detail/story.html; 'Princess of Wales Hospital nurse neglect trial collapses' BBC News, 14 October 2015, http://www.bbc.co.uk/news/uk-wales-south-east-wales-34527845.

Anti-forensics and interpretation of evidence

9.103 As with all fields of forensic analysis, computer forensics is part of a continuous race of catch-up between investigators and criminals. Just as criminals quickly started to wear gloves once fingerprint evidence had reached the awareness of the wider public, computer criminals too began to use tools to hide or alter the traces of their activities. Anti-computer forensics has become the term for the possible countermeasures that criminals may take to prevent, delay or invalidate computer forensic efforts, a problem increasingly recognized by the research community.[1] Deletion of data as a classic anti-forensic technique may serve as an initial example to illustrate some of the issues computer crime investigations are increasingly confronted with. In the early days of the Internet, software that securely wiped data from all parts of the computer was the preserve of the experts, or governmental organizations with special security needs.

Today, tools that irretrievably delete files are now easily obtainable for free from various sources, and can be used quickly and reliably even by comparatively computer-illiterate users.[2] This example not only illustrates the proliferation of anti-forensic tools, it also highlights some of the complexities that are involved. Most anti-forensic tools are 'dual nature' tools, just as many hacking tools are. They have legitimate uses and are often even officially recommended, if not legally mandated, for instance, to protect the security and privacy of sensitive data. Computer software is regularly 'purpose neutral'. In other words, what works as a protection against criminals trying to obtain access to credit card details also works as a protection from the police trying to obtain access to private emails; what works for system administrators seeking to detect misuse of a computer by an employee also works for criminals obtaining access to commercially sensitive secrets. This has implications for the legal responses to anti-computer forensics, and also for the probative weight of evidence affected by any counter measures that were used by a suspect, and is further discussed below.

1 Chris B. Simmons, Danielle L. Jones and Lakisha L. Simmons, 'A framework and demo for preventing anti-computer forensics' (2011) 11(1) Issues in Information Systems 366; R. Harris, 'Arriving at an anti-forensics consensus: examining how to define and control the anti-forensics problem' (2006) 3(S) Digital Investigation S44.

2 Andy Jones and Christopher Meyler, 'What evidence is left after disk cleaners?', (2004) 1(3) Digital Investigation 183; Laurent Simon and Ross Anderson, 'Security analysis of android factory resets', http://www.cl.cam.ac.uk/~rja14/Papers/fr_most15.pdf.

9.104 As noted above, the social context is a crucial determinant for the interpretation of electronic evidence. In the early days of the Internet, finding that a suspect had acquired the specialist knowledge necessary to operate (or maybe even write) the software for a cleaning tool could be prima facie evidence that he had tried to hide traces of illegal activity. This inference is no longer sound, because secure cleaning of deleted data has become a standard operating procedure in many organizations to prevent data security breaches, and default settings on popular free tools such as CCleaner allow the effortless routine destruction of deleted files every time a computer is shut down.

9.105 The legal system and police investigators have reacted in several ways to this new reality. One approach is through technology – developing new investigative tools that either look for other types of data not yet protected by counter measures or are in some other way capable of undoing the damage of anti-forensic tools. However, this need to react rapidly to developments in the anti-computer forensic field can cause problems for the legal system, where rules on the admissibility of scientific evidence often require extensive testing and acceptance in the scientific community, supported by publication in peer-reviewed journals, together with robust methods of calibration, standardized procedures, accepted minimum criteria for training and proficiency with the new tools.[1] What is important to note for criminal prosecutions is that electronic evidence can serve a dual purpose: it can either directly support the prosecution's case, or it can be indirect evidence that the suspect took actions to hide some form of criminal activity – which in turn may also be direct evidence that he committed one of the various statutory offences that have been created to prevent the destruction or spoliation of data.

1 For the US, see Christopher V. Marsico, 'Computer evidence v. Daubert: the coming conflict' (2004) CERIAS Tech Report 2005-17; the issue was also discussed in the context of anti-forensics and the use of the 'Evidence Eliminator' programme in *State of Ohio v Starner*, Slip Copy, 2009 WL 3532306 (Ohio

App. 3 Dist.); Barbara Guttman, James R. Lyle and Richard Ayers, 'Ten years of computer forensic tool testing' (2011) 8 Digital Evidence and Electronic Signature Law Review 139; Computer Forensics Tool Testing (CFTT) Project, https://www.nist.gov/content/computer-forensics-tool-testing-cftt-project; DigitalCorpora.org, http://digitalcorpora.org.

9.106 With all this in mind, the following is an overview of the various approaches to anti-computer forensics, and the effects they have on the availability, reliability and interpretation of electronic evidence. Anti-computer forensics are understood here as any technique, hardware tool or software that prevents or delays the forensic analysis of a data carrier, and negatively affects the existence, amount, authenticity or quality of evidence from a computer or device. There are at least five different subcategories of anti-forensics: data destruction, data tampering, data hiding, trail obfuscation and attacks against the computer forensic tools themselves.

Data destruction

9.107 Data destruction is the most obvious and most widely discussed anti-forensics measure and has created a considerable legal and technological debate.[1] Unlike a physical object or piece of paper that can be destroyed effectively, it is much more difficult to completely obliterate a document in electronic form. A user simply clicks the 'delete' icon on a computer, in general terms, to remove the pointer to the data. The document or data remains, and it is possible to retrieve this data in certain circumstances, even if it is partly overwritten.[2] However, disk cleaning utilities that overwrite or 'shred' data have become increasingly available and easy to use for even unsophisticated users. These software-based tools write patterns of pseudo-random combinations of 1s and 0s (in other words, meaningless data) on to all of the sectors on a hard drive. This also includes a setting to wipe free space or unallocated or 'slack' space, which is where older 'deleted' data often reside. Slack space occurs when data is split between clusters on the hard disk. As files only rarely and by chance fill up every cluster, some space remains. Cleaning software also deletes much of the metadata that accumulates from using the computer – it wipes and cleans old file entries, recently used file lists and many other things including custom locations.

1 For an early article on this topic, see Matthew J. Bester, 'A wreck on the info-bhan: electronic mail and the destruction of evidence' (1998) 6 CommLaw Conspectus 75.

2 *Nucleus Information Systems v Palmer* [2003] EWHC 2013 (Ch), [2003] 7 WLUK 636, where employees used software in an attempt to overwrite the data on computers owned by the company before they were returned; *R v Smith (Graham Westgarth), R v Jayson (Mike)* [2002] EWCA Crim 683, [2002] 3 WLUK 178, [2003] 1 Cr App R 13, [2002] Crim LR 659, Times, 23 April 2002, [2002] CLY 819, in which Jayson deleted a number of abusive images of children that were subsequently recovered; *Prest v Marc Rich & Company Investment AG* [2006] EWHC 927 (Comm), [2006] 3 WLUK 109, where it was alleged the claimant deliberately deleted documents on his laptop computer; *R. v Porter (Ross Warwick)* [2006] EWCA Crim 560, [2006] 1 WLR 2633, [2007] 2 All ER 625, [2006] 3 WLUK 471, [2006] 2 Cr App R 25, [2006] Crim LR 748, (2006) 103(4) LSG 28, Times, 21 June 2006, [2006] CLY 858, where it was held that it is a matter for the members of a jury to determine whether files were in the 'possession' of the accused, where the accused placed the files in the recycle bin, and the recycle bin was then deleted – the files were incapable of being recovered (and thus viewed) without the use of specialist forensic techniques and equipment provided by the US Federal Government which was not available to the public; *R. v Grout (Philip)* [2011] EWCA Crim 299, [2011] 3 WLUK 5, [2011] 1 Cr App R 38, (2011) 175 JP 209, [2011] Crim LR 584, [2011] CLY 780, where the day before the appellant's arrest, he reformatted his computer, so that his computer contained no MSN history of any kind before that date.

9.108 In practice, a person might delete emails and files as a matter of routine, and the organization might fail to realize that it has backup copies of all the relevant data,[1] or the organization might have backup data to deal with situations where data is deleted, whether inadvertently or deliberately. For instance, in *Noble Resources SA v Gross*,[2] Mr Gross attempted to delete SMS messages that might have incriminated him. Several thousand of these messages were recovered from various places: from backups of his personal mobile telephone and the BlackBerry of the person to whom the messages were sent. Copies were also found in a backup file on his laptop computer shortly before trial; they were also on the forensic image of his laptop taken by his forensic experts, and on a CD of his personal files that he only disclosed during the course of the trial. Mrs Justice Gloster DBE said: 'with the assistance of one Jimmy Weston, an IT expert, Mr. Gross had deliberately changed the time settings on the laptop to conceal the fact that he himself had made the deletions; and that the last recorded logon time with his user ID reflected this'.[3]

1 As in *Fiona Trust & Holding Corporation v Privalov* [2010] EWHC 3199 (Comm), [2010] 12 WLUK 346, (2011) 108(3) LSG 17.
2 [2009] EWHC 1435 (Comm), [2009] 6 WLUK 558.
3 [2009] EWHC 1435 (Comm) at [54].

9.109 Data destruction adds a great deal of complexity to both civil litigation and the investigation of alleged crimes. On occasions, a party may have a reasonable suspicion that the other party might intend to delete files, or has already deleted files, although the technical issues relating to such allegations can serve to confuse.[1] In *United States of America v Triumph Capital Group, Inc.*,[2] McCarthy, the CEO and controlling shareholder of Triumph, Spadoni, Triumph's Vice President and General Counsel, together with a number of others, were accused of a variety of offences relating to racketeering, including bribery, obstruction of justice and witness tampering. It came to the notice of the US government that Spadoni was alleged to have purchased a software program to purge his computer of incriminating evidence. Triumph was ordered to deliver up the relevant computer for forensic tests. The tests revealed that relevant data had been deleted, and the deleted files were recovered. A search of the recovered Internet cache files revealed evidence of other offences. This caused the investigator to obtain a further warrant to search and seize evidence of the further crimes. In *L C Services v Brown*[3] the operating system on Brown's computer had been changed or re-installed at the time the claimants were pursuing disclosure of documents by the defendants, but a digital evidence professional was able to recover the remains of email communications. The recovered evidence was sufficient to incriminate him, and he was held liable for breach of fiduciary duties to the plaintiffs, his ex-employer.

1 The decision by the Supreme Court of Delaware in the case of *Genger v TR Investors, LLC*, 26 A.3d 180 (2011), 2011 WL 2802832, upholding a finding of spoliation by the trial judge, was examined in detail in Daniel B. Garrie and Bill Spernow, 'Legally correct but technologically off the mark' (2010 9(1) Northwestern Journal of Technology & Intellectual Property 1, in which the authors took the view that the judges failed to understand what had occurred in technical terms.
2 211 F.R.D. 31 (D.Conn. 2002).
3 [2003] EWHC 3024 (QB) at [53] and [54].

9.110 Where there is a reasonable suspicion that a party might delete files, as in the proceedings leading up to divorce in the case of *Ranta v Ranta*,[1] it may be possible to obtain an order to prevent a party from deleting, removing or uninstalling any programs, files or folders.[2] Sanctions may follow for deleting files, depending on the seriousness of the action, where a party deliberately wipes hard drives after a court has ordered their production, as in *Electronic Funds Solutions v Murphy*.[3] Furthermore, it is not inconceivable for a court to order a party to search for relevant documents in backup tapes and archives and to provide information about data that have been deleted.[4]

1 2004 WL 504588 (Conn.Super.).

2 See *Takenaka (UK) Ltd and Corfe v Frankl* [2001] EWCA Civ 348, [2001] 3 WLUK 163, [2001] EBLR 40, [2001] CLY 1819, where patterns of online behaviour were analysed to establish whether it was more likely that defamatory emails were sent to the defendant's wife, and used to show that certain pieces of software were used in close proximity to each other and therefore made it more likely that the suspect had sent the emails; *L C Services v Brown* [2003] EWHC 3024 (QB) at [60] and [68]; *Douglas v Hello! Ltd (No 3)* [2003] EWHC 55 (Ch), [2003] 1 All ER 1087 (Note), [2003] 1 WLUK 554, [2003] EMLR 29, (2003) 100(11) LSG 34, (2003) 153 NLJ 175, Times, 30 January 2003, [2003] CLY 390; *Crown Dilmun v Sutton* [2004] EWHC 52 (Ch), [2004] 1 WLUK 467, [2004] 1 BCLC 468, [2004] WTLR 497, (2004) 101(7) LSG 34, Times, 5 February 2004, [2004] CLY 456; *LTE Scientific Ltd v Thomas* [2005] EWHC 7 (QB), [2005] 1 WLUK 38; *Prest v Marc Rich & Company Investment AG* [2006] EWHC 927 (Comm), [2006] 3 WLUK 109; *Sectrack NV v Satamatics Ltd* [2007] EWHC 3003 (Comm), [2007] 12 WLUK 558; *Noble Resources SA v Gross* [2009] EWHC 1435 (Comm) at [53] and [57]–[58]; *First Conferences Services Ltd v Bracchi* [2009] EWHC 2176 (Ch), [2009] 8 WLUK 249; note also *Crowson Fabrics Limited v Rider* [2007] EWHC 2942 (Ch), [2007] 12 WLUK 602, [2008] IRLR 288, [2008] FSR 17, [2008] CLY 1280; *Rybak v Langbar International Ltd* [2010] EWHC 2015 (Ch), [2010] 7 WLUK 288. For the USA, see Shira A. Scheindlin and Kanchana Wangkeo, 'Electronic discovery sanctions in the twenty-first century' (2004) 11(1) Mich Telecomm Tech L Rev 71; *Arista Records, L.L.C. v Tschirhart*, 241 F.R.D. 462 (2006), 2006 WL 2728927; Willoughby and others, 'Sanctions for e-discovery violations; Charles W. Adams, 'Spoliation of electronic evidence: sanctions versus advocacy' (2011) 8(1) Mich Telecomm Tech L Rev 1.

3 134 Cal.App.4th 1161 (2005), 36 Cal.Rptr.3d 663 (Cal. Ct. App. 2005).

4 *Zhou v Pittsburg State University*, 2003 WL 1905988 (D.Kan.); in relation to digital audio files (including case law), see Alan F. Blakley, 'Digital audio files in litigation' (2007) 2(1) Journal of Legal Technology Risk Management 1.

9.111 As indicated above, the use of these tools has been the result of legal requirements to ensure data security and privacy protection, which means that increasingly they come with official guarantees that promise that the wiped data cannot be reconstructed by criminals[1] – and as a side effect, the police cannot reconstruct the data either. For instance, to provide legal entities with the assurance that they comply with the law, such programs typically allow default settings that erase data automatically every time a computer is shut down, or every time someone tries to obtain access to a file without the password. This makes it increasingly problematic to infer criminal intent to hide data when evidence of disk cleaning is found.

1 For instance, Richard Kissel, Andrew Regenscheid, Matthew Scholl and Kevin Stine, *Guidelines for Media Sanitization* (NIST Special Publication 800-88, Revision 1, December 2014), http://nvlpubs.nist.gov/nistpubs/SpecialPublications/NIST.SP.800-88r1.pdf.

9.112 The physical destruction of a computer, including the hard drive, will ensure the data (without investing in costly reconstruction and recovery services) is lost, as in *Strasser v Yalamanchi*.[1] In this case, it was claimed that a hard drive containing relevant data had been severely damaged by lightning, and an employee saw fit to dispose of the computer as a result. In response to the extensive pre-trial actions and the failure to provide an adequate reason for the destruction of the computer while litigation was under way, the trial judge subsequently instructed the members of the jury that the negligent destruction of evidence might be inferred from the failure of the appellant to preserve and maintain evidence. The appeal court subsequently upheld the decision.

1 783 So.2d 1087 (Fla.App. 4 Dist. 2001), 2001 WL 195056.

9.113 Generally speaking, the most secure way to prevent computer forensics is the physical destruction of the hard drive, or short of that, degaussing in a strong magnetic field. Degaussing with an approved degausser is, for some highly sensitive military or national security applications, the required method of data destruction.[1] As discussed above, in comparison to the deliberate attempt at destruction to prevent others from obtaining evidence, paper copy files of underlying source documents may be destroyed for perfectly legitimate reasons, and reliance might subsequently be made on the version held in electronic form. This tends to occur when organizations attempt to reduce the cost of storage of paper documents but fail to consider the cost of electronic storage and the need to deal with old data when a system is upgraded. In the case of *Heveafil Sdn. Bdh. v United States*,[2] the US Department of Commerce refused to accept a copy of a database containing a bill of materials stored on a computer diskette as a means of verifying the cost information in an investigation into anti-dumping extruded rubber. Heveafil claimed that the database held on the diskette had been taken from the mainframe, that it used the previous version in the course of normal business and that the database on the diskette contained an exact duplicate of the database developed on the mainframe computer. In an appeal from the US Court of International Trade, the Court of Appeals for the Federal Circuit accepted the argument by the Department of Commerce that it could reject the data on the diskette as not having been properly authenticated, and a finding of adverse inference was admissible in the circumstances. The assertions by Heveafil were not sufficient, because it failed to provide evidence of the veracity of the contents of the diskette, such as explanations of how the copy was made. The company merely copied data from the mainframe and then deleted the first in time data as well as the underlying paper versions. In doing so, it failed to provide a trail of evidence to demonstrate the procedures undertaken to provide for the veracity of the diskette copy.

1 https://www.nsa.gov/Portals/70/documents/resources/everyone/media-destruction/NSAEPLMagneticDegaussers%20June2019.pdf?ver=2019-07-03-090458-077.
2 58 Fed.Appx. 843, 2003 WL 1466193 (Fed.Cir.); 25 ITRD 1128.

9.114 As mentioned above, the social context can be crucial in interpreting electronic evidence. While clicking on the delete icon is not a way actually to destroy evidence, and can furthermore be seen as an intentional attempt to destroy evidence and pervert the course of justice, the opposite question also arises: under what circumstances can the law interpret a user's failed attempt to destroy a file as a sign that he wanted to rid himself of possession of an illegal item? An innocent user who accidentally downloads an illegal picture, or finds one on a second-hand computer, may think that by deleting the item he has successfully rid himself of it. The law on possession of illegal material may or may not take the same view, if, for an average user, it is very easy to recover the item in question, and it is thus possible to use the 'paper bin' as a convenient hidden storage space.

9.115 All the methods of data deletion described above have been developed for data stored on traditional magnetic media. But increasingly, new storage media look set to challenge anti-forensic measures and also thwart the efforts of investigators. With traditional magnetic storage media, 'bad sectors' can create inaccessible parts of the hard drive that are 'accidentally' protected from many cleaning utilities. Solid-state drives (SSDs), unlike traditional magnetic discs such as hard disk drives, do not have any moving mechanical components but use integrated circuits to store data persistently. Solid-state drives pose new problems for the recovery of data, because they store data in ways that are much more non-linear and complex than that of traditional hard disk drives.[1] However, programs such as Parted Magic claim to provide safe data cleaning for SSDs.

1 Bell and Boddington, 'Solid state drives'.

9.116 Several new filing systems increase data permanence either by design – to prevent accidental data loss – or by accident. For instance, journaling file systems record write operations in a number of different locations, which means data 'leftovers' may exist in places 'outside' the nominal file storage location. RAID and anti-fragmentation techniques may also result in file data being written to multiple locations. In SSDs, for instance, if the same part of the drive is written over and over again, this will have the effect of 'wearing it out' prematurely. To counteract that, technologies are built into SSDs called 'wear levelling', which relocates blocks of data between the time when they are originally written and the time when they are overwritten. This has the effect of preventing the 'true' erasure of data.

9.117 From a legal and evidential perspective, it is necessary to have some knowledge of the differences these storage media entail for data deletion and data retrieval to interpret correctly the findings of the digital evidence professional. The easier it is to securely delete data with off-the-shelf, easily customizable tools, the less convincing is the inference of an intentional attempt to hide evidence. Finding evidence for the deletion of data from traditional hard drives is therefore different from evidence of deletion from new and more advanced storage systems, where data erasure requires specialist knowledge and considerable efforts.

9.118 The question that remains is what inferences, if any, can be drawn from the *absence* of evidence if data have been successfully deleted. A defence lawyer may want to argue that according to the prosecution case, some traces of illegal activity *ought* to have been found on his client's computer, using the *absence* of such evidence as an argument to undermine the prosecution case. How convincing the argument is may well depend on the type of storage medium used and the nature of file systems employed. As noted with wear levelling, there are also increasingly automated 'housekeeping operations' being carried out by computers on files. In the past, finding that an illegal file, say of images of child sexual abuse, had been moved and copied to several places of a hard drive would have been evidence that the suspect knew of, and knowingly handled, the file in question. Increasingly, this inference depends on the storage medium, and if a number of copies at different parts of the drive existed, it is possible that these could have been the result of automated actions by the computer. Finally, for several legal purposes, a party may have to prove that it either took all reasonable steps to delete certain files, for instance in an action for damages after a data security breach, or that it took every reasonable effort to produce data, for instance, in response to a court order as part of the disclosure or discovery process. The type of evidence required to document that all reasonable steps were taken to either securely delete the data, or to recover lost data, will depend on the precise nature of the storage medium.

9.119 A separate way of destroying data at the filesystem level is by the deletion of filesystem-wide encryption keys. Mobile telephones and several desktop operating systems increasingly feature encrypted filesystems that use a private key for unlocking the data in the filesystem. This key has to be unlocked and made available for encryption and decryption each time the computer or telephone is booted, turned on after a longer delay, or after the key memory-retention period has expired. Data that is written to the persistent filesystem is encrypted using a unique (system specific, locally generated) private key, which is then secured (and unlocked upon demand) using a PIN, swipe pattern or fingerprint. Upon unlocking the telephone, this key is decrypted to enable full access. Destroying the private key, however, makes it virtually impossible to retrieve the data on the telephone, provided the cryptography and the implementation of this feature is done to exacting security standards. A modern smartphone may then destroy all data if a certain number of attempts are made to unlock the private key with a wrong or false fingerprint or access code.[1]

1 A good example is the implementation of this system in iOS for Apple smartphones. It is described extensively in the iOS 9.3 or later security guide (May 2016), https://www.apple.com/business/docs/iOS_Security_Guide.pdf.

Falsifying data

9.120 Tampering with electronic evidence is not new. An early example of erasing part of a tape recording and re-recording part of a conversation occurred in the UK in 1955.[1] In *R v Sinha (Arun Kumar)*,[2] medical data recorded on a computer was altered after the death of a patient, giving rise to a charge of perverting the course of justice. In the case of *Freemont (Denbigh) Ltd v Knight Frank LLP*,[3] one witness concocted evidence by creating documents in the form of a series of notes of discussions, which included statements that had not been made during the course of the discussions,[4] and to avoid detection, had the hard drives of older computers destroyed when the firm upgraded its computer systems.[5] Attempts to adduce fraudulent evidence before a court are rare, but increasing.[6] For instance, Bruce Hyman, who had been a prominent British television and radio producer before qualifying as a barrister later in life, created a false judgment for a friend. His deception was uncovered and he was subsequently convicted for perverting the course of justice and sentenced to a term of imprisonment of twelve months and ordered to pay £3,000 to his victim in compensation and Crown expenses of £3,745 – the first barrister to be so convicted, and he was subsequently disbarred by the Bar Standards Board.[7] In another case in Japan, a prosecutor altered electronic evidence in a case he was investigating, and was subsequently convicted and imprisoned for 18 months.[8]

1 'Recording as testimony to truth' [1955] Crim LR 2, [1954] SJ 98, 794.
2 [1994] 7 WLUK 34, [1998] Masons CLR 35, [1995] Crim LR 68 (CA), Times, 13 July 1994, Independent, 1 August 1994, [1994] CLY 1137.
3 [2014] EWHC 3347 (Ch), [2014] 10 WLUK 398, [2015] PNLR 4, [2015] CLY 1796.
4 Although the judge did not have to determine precisely how the evidence was concocted, and he considered the possibility of amended computer files at [56], he concluded on other evidence that the evidence was concocted, for which see [116], [123] and [140].
5 At [56]–[60].
6 *Premier Homes and Land Corporation v Cheswell, Inc.*, 240 F.Supp.2d 97 (D.Mass. 2002), 2002 WL 31907329 for fabrication of an email; *People v Superior Court of Sacramento County*, 2004 WL 1468698 (Cal.App. 3 Dist.) for fabrication of letters on a computer after the event; *ISTIL Group Inc v Zahoor* [2003] EWHC 165 (Ch), [2003] 2 All ER 252, [2003] 2 WLUK 476, [2003] CP Rep 39, Independent, April 7, 2003, [2003] CLY 451 for a forged document; *Fiona Trust & Holding Corporation v Privalov*

[2010] EWHC 3199 (Comm), [2010] 12 WLUK 346, (2011) 108(3) LSG 17 for a forged and backdated agreement and employment contract; for forged emails, *Apex Global Management Ltd v FI Call Ltd* [2015] EWHC 3269 (Ch), [2015] 11 WLUK 248; in a criminal context, see *R v Brooker* [2014] EWCA Crim 1998, also cited as *AG's Ref: 071 of 2014, R v B (R C A) (2014)* (available in the LexisNexis electronic database), where Brooker sent text messages from a second mobile telephone in her possession, claiming that her boyfriend sent them.

7 Angella Johnson, 'How my barrister forged evidence against my husband – and now faces jail' *The Mail*, 8 September 2007; Steven Morris, 'Barrister becomes first to be jailed for perverting justice' *The Guardian*, 20 September 2007; Simon de Bruxelles, 'Barrister jailed for trying to frame man with fake e-mail' Timesonline, 20 September 2007.

8 Hironao Kaneko, case translation and commentary in 'Heisei 22 Nen (Wa) 5356 Gou' (2012) 9 Digital Evidence and Electronic Signature Law Review 109.

9.121 However, it is conceivable, given the ease with which electronic data is so easily manipulated and altered, that attempts will be made in the future to falsify and alter documents even before a trial ever takes place, or to create vast swathes of 'evidence' of a complete set of legal proceedings. This happened in *Islamic Investment Company of the Gulf (Bahamas) Ltd v Symphony Gems NV.*[1] As explained the in judgment of Hamblen J:[2]

> From the end of October 2010 until December 2013 [the lawyer] conducted fictitious litigation for RM. That litigation involved fictitious hearings before the Commercial Court and the Court of Appeal; purported judgments of those courts; purported sealed court orders; a purported hearing transcript; purported skeleton arguments; purported correspondence with court officials and the Claimant's solicitors, Norton Rose; the fictitious instruction and engagement of various counsel, and telephone conferences involving the impersonation of his senior partner and of leading counsel. None of this reflected reality. Throughout that period there was in fact no contact with Norton Rose or the court.

1 [2014] EWHC 3777 (Comm), [2014] 11 WLUK 521.
2 [2014] EWHC 3777 (Comm) at [4].

9.122 Even such mundane matters such as proof of parking violations have been subject to the alteration of electronic evidence. In the case of Kevin Maguire, he had parked his car in Market Place in Bury town centre, Greater Manchester at 7.15 am on 31 August 2003. He returned at 5 pm to find he had been given a parking ticket at 9.15 am. Normally there were no restrictions on a Sunday, and when he parked his car, there were no signs to indicate there were any temporary restrictions in place. There were no signs because the NCP staff did not put them up on the previous night as there was a high likelihood that the signs could be pulled down or damaged by revellers overnight. In fact, the signs were put up after Mr Maguire had parked his car. When Mr Maguire complained to the NCP, it was asserted that he had parked illegally and he was sent a photograph of his parked car, which was dated 30 August 2003. Mr Maguire appealed against the parking fine. It transpired that one Gavin Moses, a member of the NCP staff, had altered the date on the digital photograph from 31 August to 30 August, so that it appeared that Mr Maguire had parked illegally. Mr Maguire was cleared of illegal parking and was awarded costs. Gavin Moses subsequently entered a plea of guilty when he was prosecuted for perverting the course of justice, and was sentenced to 150 hours of community service.[1]

1 BBC News online news item, '"Fit up" parking warden sentenced', 28 January 2005, http://news.bbc.co.uk/1/hi/england/manchester/4216539.stm. A further article was published by a Manchester website dated 27 January 2005, but the web page is no longer active.

9.123 In Singapore, for use in salary negotiations with his prospective employer, a solicitor Ruddy Lim altered the monthly salary on his payslip from DLA Piper Singapore Pte Ltd to read $65,000, rather than $25,000. The description of his method is set out in the judgment:[1]

> 'The Accused testified that he first created Exhibit P2 in his laptop computer some time between 12 and 14 November 2006. He was travelling in Jakarta at the time, and carried a soft copy of the DLA Piper logo in his laptop for preparing marketing materials. He created a document in the word-processing programme, Word, by typing out the text and numbers of the false payslip. He cut and pasted the DLA Piper logo onto the Word document. He then copied the image of the company stamp (with the office manager's signature) from his original payslip ... using software from Adobe, and electronically affixed the image onto the Word document. During this time, the Word document existed only in soft copy. When he returned to Singapore, he printed out the Word document on 14 November 2006, then scanned it into the Xerox machine so that a "pdf" version of the false payslip would be created. He wanted to convert it from Word document format into "pdf" because the former was "editable", while the latter was a "fixed format". He then emailed the resulting document ... to [his prospective employer].'

1 *PP v Rudy Lim* [2010] SGDC 174 at [17].

9.124 Considerably more attention will have to be paid to demonstrate the integrity of electronic data in the future, which in turn will help substantiate the claim for authenticity to reflect the reliability of the data.[1] In all of these cases, the changes to the data were carried out manually. Anti-computer forensics increasingly provides tools to alter data automatically, and in particular the crucial metadata, thus diminishing the evidential value of the data that can be recovered. 'Backtrack' or 'Transmogrify', for instance, can change the extension of files by turning .exe (application) files into .docx (Word document) files, thereby hiding their malicious character. 'Timestomp' can change the timestamps of files, the metadata that records the creation and alteration of a file.[2] Randomizers can automatically generate random file names, and criminals can use tools that replace Roman letters with identical-looking Cyrillic ones. Both approaches defeat data-mining techniques that look for 'known bad files' or signatures of known illegal images. Software developers who wanted to test the reliability of common forensic tools such as Encase developed many of these tools. Vincent Lui, one of the most prolific developers of tools with anti-forensic implications, concludes that the 'unfortunate truth' is that the presumption of reliability is 'unjustified' and the justice system is 'not sufficiently sceptical of that which is offered up as proof.'[3]

1 According to the conclusions on page 56 of *Report of Digital Forensic Analysis* (26 March 2012) by Stroz Friedberg and submitted as evidence in the case of *Paul D. Ceglia v Mark Zuckerberg, Individually, and Facebook, Inc.*, 600 Fed.Appx. 34 (2015), Stroz Friedberg determined that it had 'found direct and compelling digital forensic evidence that the documents relied upon by Mr. Ceglia to support his claim were forged', http://cdn.arstechnica.net/wp-content/uploads/2014/08/strozreport.pdf.
2 Hamid Jahankhani and Elidon Beqiri, 'Digital evidence manipulation using anti-forensic tools and techniques' in Hamid Jahankhani, David Lilburn Watson and Gianluigi Me (eds) *Handbook of Electronic Security and Digital Forensics* (World Scientific Publishing Co Pte Ltd 2010), 411–427.
3 Van Buskirk and Liu, 'Digital evidence', 25.

9.125 Other tools have legitimate objectives such as privacy protection. For instance, to prevent companies from obtaining data about individual behaviour when using a search engine, software can be used to create a large number of chance queries to create random noise.[1] A record of keyword searches can also have evidential value in a criminal trial. Thus to establish the interest of the suspect in certain poisons or drugs, these tools can be used to cast doubt on the reliability of the log data that documents the searches carried out on a suspect's computer. Since the search terms had been automatically generated, any inference that the user of the machine intentionally searched for a specific term becomes problematic.

1 Ye Shaozhi, Felix Wu, Raju Pandey and Hao Chen, 'Noise injection for search privacy protection' (2009) UC Davis Postprints, http://escholarship.org/uc/item/08k1004m.

9.126 Lastly, a specific type of falsification should be given consideration. In many countries around the world state security and intelligence services operate malware (see also the paragraph on the use of legal intrusion, which is increasingly used as a police power) which is capable, not only of surveillance of their targets, but, with a simple addition, could be used to plant falsified data. The presence, use, or even the evidence of existence of the use of such tools creates significant technical challenges.[1] In cases where unscrupulous people acting on behalf of a government have the political motive to use such tools, consideration should be given to the possibility that such falsifications may have been used.

1 See, for example, the case of Hacking Team, an Italian supplier of such capabilities that was found to have made a long list of rather 'unethical' and often illegal sales to governments: Andy Greenberg, 'Hacking Team breach shows a global spying firm run amok', Wired, 7 June 2015, https://www.wired.com/2015/07/hacking-team-breach-shows-global-spying-firm-run-amok/; Patrick Howell O'Neill, 'The fall and rise of a spyware empire', MIT Technology Review, 29 November 2019, https://www.technologyreview.com/2019/11/29/131803/the-fall-and-rise-of-a-spyware-empire/; for another example of such software, see the Israeli-made Pegasus malware, traced by the Toronto-based citizen lab (at the Munk School of the University of Toronto): Bill Marczak, John Scott-Railton, Sarah McKune, Bahr Abdul Razzak and Ron Deibert, 'HIDE AND SEEK tracking NSO group's Pegasus spyware to operations in 45 countries', 18 September 2018, https://citizenlab.ca/2018/09/hide-and-seek-tracking-nso-groups-pegasus-spyware-to-operations-in-45-countries/.

Hiding data

9.127 Tampering with and destroying data works best when the criminal no longer needs the data. For possession crimes such as the possession of illegal images, this is not possible. Hiding the data rather than destroying or altering it therefore becomes an important objective. Cryptography is the best known anti-forensic method to hide data from third parties. Due to its importance as a dual use technology with important roles for privacy and data security, and also because of the complex legal issues involved with cryptography, this is considered in the chapter on encrypted data.

9.128 Another well-known method of hiding data is steganography. Steganography is the method of hiding a message inside a digital object, which may be a graphic, a picture, a film or a sound clip. The sender is able to hide a message in a seemingly innocuous file, and the recipient can retrieve the message upon receipt. Other methods used to hide data include writing data to slack space or space that has not been allocated for use, hiding data on a hard drive in a secret partition, and the transmission of data under the cover of transmission protocols. Various types of commercial and free software are available to perform steganography on data. It can be relatively difficult to detect hidden data within a file, and the communication can be even more difficult to uncover if the message has been compressed and encrypted before being hidden in the carrier.

At present, it is unlikely that many investigators will undertake a routine examination for hidden data.[1]

1 Brent T. McBride, Gilbert L. Peterson and Steven C. Gustafson, 'A new blind method for detecting novel steganography' (2005) 2(1) Digital Investigation 50; a wide range of references on this topic is provided in Gary C. Kessler, 'An overview of steganography for the computer forensics examiner' (2004) 6(3) Forensic Science Communications– for an update of this article to February 2015, see http://www.garykessler.net/library/fsc_stego.html; Rachel Zax and Frank Adelstein, 'FAUST: forensic artifacts of uninstalled steganography tools' (2009) 6(1–2) Digital Investigation 25.

9.129 There are now various tools available that facilitate the hiding of data in places on the hard drive that are less likely to be inspected. In this sense, they are the mirror images of the deletion tools discussed above. Deletion tools aim to securely delete any trace of an incriminating file, regardless of where on the computer a copy may be hiding. Conversely, 'Slacker' breaks up a file and stores individual pieces of it in the slack space left at the end of files, making it look like random noise to forensic tools – imagine just two digits each of a stolen credit card number stored in the unused part of a legitimate file. Slacker then enables the data to be reassembled as required.[1] One of the problems with these tools is that they develop faster than it is possible to train digital evidence professionals, and even more importantly, faster than the development of sound, tested and agreed standards. This not only makes the detection of evidence more difficult; it also raises issues about the admissibility of the opinion evidence of forensic experts.

1 Hal Berghel, 'Hiding data, forensics, and anti-forensics' (2007) 50(4) Communications of the ACM 15.

Attacks against computer forensics

9.130 Arguably, the latest addition to the inventory of anti-computer forensics is attacks against the investigator's tools. As noted above, digital forensics is highly dependent on software tools. To create evidence that is admissible, these tools have to be evaluated and tested, and the results ideally published in openly available, peer-reviewed scientific publications. Indeed, some of the most popular tools are open source: that is, their source code is freely available. One of the benefits of this approach is not only a high degree of transparency when it comes to assessing the reliability of data generated by these tools, but also the ability for security professionals to improve them and to adapt them to local situations.[1] However, it also enables criminals to develop tools that interfere directly with the evidence collection process and infiltrate the software that tries to analyse a suspect's computer. This can either be done by undermining the integrity of the data that is collected, for instance by changing the hash value of the bit copy that the software creates (thus violating the continuity of evidence by casting reasonable doubt on the authenticity of the copy) or by forcing the analysis tool to either overlook incriminating data, or to report misleading information about it.[2] In doing so, it cannot be right to equate such a tool with, say, a photocopier.[3]

1 Kenneally, 'Gatekeeping out of the box'.
2 Chris K. Ridder, 'Evidentiary implications of potential security weaknesses in forensic software' (2009) 1(3) International Journal of Digital Crime and Forensics 80.
3 *Williford v State of Texas*, 127 S.W.3d 309 (Tex.App.-Eastland 2004), 2004 WL 67560.

Trail obfuscation

9.131 Trail obfuscation combines the deliberate attempt at tampering, deleting and hiding data with the taking of measures to frustrate investigations, conceal identities and evade enforcement actions.[1] In many investigations, the data held on the suspect's computer or device is only one part of the prosecution's case. The other, equally important, set of data will come from the Internet and relate to the suspect's browsing behaviour, or the victim's computer or device in the case of a hacking offence: the origin of the data, the websites visited, and the activities undertaken. Obfuscating the trail that such activities leave behind on the Internet is therefore an important aspect of anti-computer forensics. It includes various anonymity-protection tools such as VPNs or anonymous remailers to hide browsing activity, or the use of spoofed or zombified accounts when sending malicious emails or spam, or the launch of a denial of service attack. 'Zombified accounts', as discussed in more detail below, demonstrate a specific side effect of anti-computer forensics. One way for a criminal to hide illegal activities is to take over the computer of a third party, for instance, after inserting a Trojan horse program, discussed in more detail below, and using this third party machine to carry out illegal activities. This not only hides the true perpetrator from the investigators, it also creates data that can falsely incriminate an innocent party.[2]

1 In the civil context, see *EMI Records Ltd v British Sky Broadcasting Ltd* [2013] EWHC 379 (Ch), [2013] Bus LR 884, [2013] 2 WLUK 812, [2013] ECDR 8, [2013] Info TLR 133, [2013] FSR 31, Times, 23 April 2013, [2013] CLY 1752.
2 Mukkamala and Sung, 'Identifying significant features for network forensic analysis'; Nikkel, 'Domain name forensics'; Nikkel, 'Improving evidence acquisition from live network sources'; Casey and Stanley, 'Tool review – remote forensic preservation and examination tools'; Demir and others, 'Packet marking and auditing for network forensics'.

9.132 The range of tasks performed by such malicious software is probably only restricted by the imagination of the person who creates the program. A number of cases in the criminal courts where people have been accused of being in possession of abusive images of children on their computers have used the defence that some form of malicious software caused data to be downloaded to their computers or enabled a third party to obtain access to their computers without the permission of the computers' owners.[1] In the case of *R v Caffrey*,[2] the defendant was charged with causing unauthorized modification of computer material under s 3(1) of the Computer Misuse Act 1990. The prosecution alleged that the defendant sent a deluge of electronic data from his computer to a computer server operated in the Port of Houston, Texas, USA, the effect of which was to cause the computer at the Port of Houston to shut down. The defendant claimed, in his defence, that unknown hackers obtained control of his computer and then launched a number of programs to attack the computer at the Port of Houston. The forensic examiner for the prosecution could not find any evidence of a Trojan horse on the computer. The defence claimed that it was impossible for every file to have been tested, and that the Trojan horse file might have had a facility to destroy itself, leaving no traces of having resided on his computer. The forensic examiner for the prosecution disputed that, stating that a Trojan horse would leave a trace on the computer. The jury acquitted Mr Caffrey.[3]

1 *R v Schofield* (April 2003, unreported), Reading Crown Court, and *R v Green* (October 2003, unreported), Exeter Crown Court.
2 (October 2003, unreported), Southwark Crown Court.

3 Esther George, 'Casenote' (2004) 1(2) Digital Investigation 89; Susan Brenner, Brian Carrier and Jef Henninger, 'The Trojan horse defense in cybercrime cases' (2004) 21 Santa Clara High Tech LJ 1; the first Trojan horse case in the People' Republic of China was prosecuted in 2009: Jihong Chen, 'The first "Trojan horse" case prosecuted in China' (2010) 7 Digital Evidence and Electronic Signature Law Review 107; Alex Xia and Julia Peng, 'First "Trojan horse" case prosecuted for illegal invasion of computer systems in China' (2009) 25 Computer Law & Security Review 298.

9.133 It should be noted that just because an individual may have such materials on his computer, it does not follow that he was responsible for downloading them. It is important for any digital evidence professional to report on findings within the context of what the technology is capable of doing. For instance, it is possible to introduce malicious software through web pages without the permission of the website owner. When a person visits a website, software could redirect the computer to undesirable websites, and the computer will automatically download unwanted material onto the temporary cache file of the computer without the user's permission or knowledge.[1]

1 For which, see Bilar, 'Known knowns' (in which the author illustrates the ease by which third parties can obtain control of computers without the authority of the owner or user); Megan Carney and Marc Rogers, 'The Trojan made me do it: a first step in statistical based computer forensics event reconstruction' (2004) 2(4) International Journal of Digital Evidence.

9.134 A *Trojan horse* is a malicious software program containing hidden code that is designed to conceal itself in a computer as if it were legitimate software. When activated, the software will perform an operation that is not authorized by the user, such as the destruction of data (including the entire hard drive), the collection of data on a computer and transmission to a third party without the user being aware of what is happening, the counteraction of security measures installed on a computer, and the instruction of the computer to perform tasks such as to take part in a denial of service attack, or permit the creator of the program to obtain access to the computer. Just like the other large group of malware, viruses, Trojan horses pose a Janus-face conundrum for computer forensics. Finding a virus or a Trojan infection can be direct evidence amounting to an unauthorized modification of computer systems. At the same time, this can also be indirect evidence that the computer at the centre of an investigation has been tampered with and that the crime scene is 'contaminated'.

9.135 The dual use nature of many of the tools used for anti-computer forensics has been noted above. On the one hand, these tools protect our privacy against criminals, but they also protect the privacy of criminals from police investigations. A similar analysis applies to spyware such as Trojan horses. On the one hand, they allow criminals to obtain access to credit card details or passwords. On the other, they have the potential to allow the police to obtain access to the activities of criminals – that is, if the police succeed in planting such a program on the suspect's computer. Attempts to use malware for investigative purposes have caused legal controversy in some countries. In Germany, the Constitutional Court ruled against such clandestine surveillance after prosecutors applied for warrants to permit their use. In the discussion before the court, evidence was also given from computer specialists about the security and evidential implications of these 'Federal Trojans'. To work efficiently, they must not be detected by commercial anti-virus software. This can only be achieved either by the tacit collaboration of the anti-virus software vendors, or by using the ingenuity of programmers employed by the police. In either case, the result will be malware that cannot be easily detected. One obvious danger is that criminals can get hold of and in turn hijack the code for this 'official' malware once it was planted on their machines, which would give them in effect a 'master key' for all computer systems. In such an event, it would become much easier for the defence to mount 'Caffrey style' arguments, and all computers could become crime scenes with compromised integrity.[1]

1 Wiebke Abel and Burkhard Schafer, 'The German Constitutional Court on the right in confidentiality and integrity of information technology systems – a case report on BVerfG, NJW 2008, 822' (2009) 6(1) SCRIPT-ed 106.

9.136 A final complication is created by the desire to protect users against malware. The use of Trojans lies at the heart of distributed denial of service attacks, a significant threat to the functioning of the Internet. Preventing malware has therefore become a high priority for police and commerce. Ordinary users, who often fail to take appropriate steps to protect their computers and devices against interference by criminals, are the weakest link. The Trusted Computing Initiative is one possible answer to this problem. It would allow a coalition of software and hardware developers much more direct access to computers, ensuring that all their defence mechanisms work as specified, and that no unauthorized program is run on them. While this approach is promising in its potential to reduce computer criminality, for the interpretation of electronic evidence, it carries several challenges. Since computer forensic tools too are essentially a form of 'spyware', common forensic applications may not work any longer in a trusted computing environment. Even worse, the philosophy of trusted computing is premised on belief that to protect the user against criminal activities, the security and control of the computer or device is improved if it is determined by not just the user but also by organizations. This means that the number of people and organizations that at any given time would have access to users' computers and the data held therein would increase considerably, especially if the keys to users' computers and their devices are compromised. This could in turn cast doubt on the reliability and authenticity of the data found on a computer or device during a criminal investigation. At the moment, lawyers assume, often naively, that data found on a suspect's computer or device must have been put there by the person in physical control of the machine (typically, the owner); this inference would look increasingly doubtful in a trusted computer environment.[1]

1 Yianna Danidou and Burkhard Schafer, 'Trusted computing and the digital crime scene' (2011) 8 Digital Evidence and Electronic Signature Law Review 111.

An intellectual framework for analysing electronic evidence

9.137 However, as we have seen, despite these differences, evidence in digital form shares important features with other types of evidence. Eyewitness evidence, forensic trace evidence such as DNA and proof by document can all provide the basis for analogical reasoning to determine the evidentiary value of an item of digital evidence, if we are aware of the limitations of this analogy. The digital evidence professional, however, has a different job from that of a DNA analyst or a forensic entomologist and, in particular, deals with mathematical abstractions rather than empirical objects. Therefore, findings will not normally be in the form of matching probabilities or other quantifiable, generalized statements.[1] 'Universal' theories of evidence are regrettably either rare, or too abstract to be of much practical value. However, the 'hierarchy of propositions' promoted by the Forensic Science Service in the UK has the potential to provide such a framework, which can also help to illuminate further the distinguishing features of electronic evidence and what they mean for practice. To interpret evidence, the digital evidence professional (or the judge) has to consider propositions that represent respectively the prosecution or defence, or the pursuer or defendant. Evidential weight can only be ascertained if the propositions from both sides are considered, and the increase or decrease in likelihood for both is considered. Several studies have shown, with examples, how a hierarchical analysis can help in the evaluation of heterogeneous evidence, from eyewitnesses to DNA.[2] The nature of electronic evidence is such that on a like-by-like comparison and allowing for the machine-mediated nature of electronic evidence, the evidence will be several steps further removed from the reasoning associated with traditional evidence. All these steps have to be explored and the counterfactuals examined before electronic evidence can be said to be proved.

1 A potential problem for jurisdictions that follow the US decision in *Daubert v Merrell Dow Pharmaceuticals, Inc.*, 509 U.S. 579 (1993), 113 S.Ct. 2786 that requires that experts report confidence values and error rates, something that rarely applies in computer forensics.
2 I. W. Evett, G. Jackson and J. Lambert, 'More on the hierarchy of propositions: exploring the distinction between explanations and propositions' (2000) 40(1) Science & Justice 3.

Conclusions and future considerations

9.138 The widespread use of computers, the Internet, mobile telephones and smartphones means that most lawyers now have to deal with electronic evidence.[1] Increased use of specialized law enforcement capacities, the more traditional criminal justice system and advanced security and intelligence capabilities has created a field that is in constant flux. The weighing of the probative value of the evidence, can be straightforward only in simple cases, for which ample precedent and standards exist, but not otherwise where the parties challenge the data or new and innovative methods are in play. In these cases, the court often has to rely upon digital evidence professionals. This implies the need for a thorough analysis of the merits of each piece of data given in evidence. For this reason, lawyers must familiarize themselves with electronic evidence and understand not only the need to scrutinize the qualifications and conclusions of digital evidence professionals, but also the need to scrutinize the very evidence that they present and the manner in which it was obtained.

1 Graeme Horsman and Lynne R. Conniss, 'Investigating evidence of mobile phone usage by drivers in road traffic accidents' (2015) 12 Digital Investigation S30.

9.139 Cloud computing and trusted computing affect the way digital evidence professionals obtain evidence, which means that great care must be taken over how such evidence is obtained, which will doubtless be the subject of careful cross-examination.[1] In addition, the methods used by attackers in the digital environment will mean it is increasingly necessary to take into consideration the use of rarer techniques to obtain evidence in the future.[2]

1 Stephen Mason, 'Trusted computing and forensic investigations' (2005) 2(3) Digital Investigation 189: this article is merely an introduction to the topic that includes relevant references, and see also Stephen Mason, 'Trusting your computer to be trusted' (2005) Computer Fraud & Security 7,

with a number of additional references; see also a thesis in partial fulfilment of the requirements for the degree of Masters in Forensic Information Technology submitted to the graduate faculty of Computing and Mathematical Sciences at Auckland University of Technology by Michael E. Spence, 'Factors influencing digital evidence transfer across international borders: a case study' (2010), http://aut.researchgateway.ac.nz/handle/10292/1187; Ian Walden, 'Law enforcement access in a cloud environment' (Legal Studies Research Paper No 74/2011), http://papers.ssrn.com/sol3/papers.cfm?abstract_id=1781067; Josiah Dykstra and Alan T. Sherman, 'Acquiring forensic evidence from infrastructure-as-a-service cloud computing: exploring and evaluating tools, trust, and techniques' (2012) 9 Digital Investigation S90.

2 Kris Harms, 'Forensic analysis of System Restore points in Microsoft Windows XP' (2006) 3(3) Digital Investigation 151.

9.140 In response to these developments, anti-computer forensics has emerged over the last decade as a significant challenge to the investigation of crimes involving the use of computers and computer-like devices. The arms race between criminals and investigators on the one hand, and the dual use nature of the tools that permit and prevent digital investigations on the other, have created a highly complex interaction that requires careful reflection on the nature of electronic evidence in any individual case, a reflection that has to be constantly updated as new tools emerge. While this chapter posits various principles and standards for handling and analysing electronic evidence, technological advancements will undoubtedly create new challenges and conflicts for the process of collecting, evaluating and examining electronic evidence in a legal setting in the near future.

10

Competence of witnesses

Stephen Mason and Lynne Townley

The need for witnesses

10.1 Concern is sometimes expressed over the competence, knowledge and qualifications of the witness giving evidence as to the trustworthiness of digital data as evidence. In *Wood (Stanley William)*, the Lord Chief Justice explained this as follows:

> This computer was rightly described as a calculating tool. It did not contribute its own knowledge. It merely did a sophisticated calculation which could have been done manually by the chemist and was in fact done by the chemists using the computer programmed by Mr. Kellie whom the Crown called as a witness. The fact that the efficiency of a device is dependent on more than one person does not make any difference in kind. Virtually every device will involve the persons who made it, the persons who calibrated, programmed or set it up (for example with a clock the person who set it to the right time in the first place) and the person who uses or observes the device. In each particular case how many of these people it is appropriate to call must depend on the facts of, and the issues raised and concessions made in that case.[1]

1 (1983) 76 Cr App R 23 at 27.

10.2 The complexity of a computer, whatever the nature of the device (whether a hand-held device or a mainframe computer), will give rise to issues of authentication, but a wider range of challenges may also be raised:

> 1. There may be a question about the accuracy or otherwise of the human input. Where the accuracy of the information is challenged, two factors will be pertinent: whether the human beings responsible for inputting the information entered the correct information; and, regardless of the conclusions reached in answering the first point, whether the software harboured an error or a malicious code that acted to change the information that was entered by humans. In the first instance, evidence from those that were responsible for entering the data, if they can be found, will need to be called. In the second instance, the evidence of a suitably knowledgeable digital evidence professional or a suitable technician who is highly familiar with the system will be necessary.
>
> 2. The 'reliability' of the underlying operating system and application software may be at issue. This is a separate question to the first type of challenge, and will require a witness with different skills to the witnesses required in the first example. Here, it may be necessary to call the manufacturer of the hardware, or the developer of the operating system or application, or failing that, an expert in the specific operating or application software.
>
> 3. The mechanisms developed to ensure a system operates properly and efficiently may be at issue. A good example is that of bank ATMs. It is a notorious fact that attacks on ATMs are successful without the use of the card issued to

Stephen Mason and Lynne Townley, 'Competence of witnesses', in Stephen Mason and Daniel Seng (eds.), *Electronic Evidence and Electronic Signatures* (5th edn, University of London 2021) 488–499.

the customer. Because these systems are subject to outward-facing threats, the range of experts will be wider when challenges of this nature are made, and will include experts who work in a bank as well as experts who are familiar with the weaknesses of bank ATM systems.

10.3 The precise nature of the evidence to be given will be governed by the nature of the challenge by the defence in any one case. The observations made by the Lord Chief Justice in *Wood (Stanley William)* were later elaborated by Steyn J, as he then was, in *R v Minors*, specifically including an observation underlying the rationale for admitting such evidence without adding to the burden of the prosecution:

> The law of evidence must be adapted to the realities of contemporary business practice. Mainframe computers, minicomputers and microcomputers play a pervasive role in our society. Often the only record of a transaction, which nobody can be expected to remember, will be in the memory of a computer. The versatility, power and frequency of use of computers will increase. If computer output cannot relatively readily be used as evidence in criminal cases, much crime (and notably offences involving dishonesty) will in practice be immune from prosecution. On the other hand, computers are not infallible. They do occasionally malfunction. Software systems often have 'bugs'. Unauthorised alteration of information stored on a computer is possible. The phenomenon of a 'virus' attacking computer systems is also well established. Realistically, therefore, computers must be regarded as imperfect devices.[1]

1 *R v Minors (Craig), R v Harper (Giselle Gaile)* [1989] 1 WLR 441 at 443.

Separating data reliability from computer reliability

10.4 In the case of *R v Minors*, the appellant tendered a passbook with false entries purporting to show there was more money held in the account than the £1 that was actually recorded. An auditor, a member of the audit investigation department of the Alliance and Leicester Building Society who had 14 years' relevant experience and regularly worked with the particular computer, produced the computer record of the complete history of the appellant's account. The last four (forged) entries in the account book were not recorded in the computer printout. The evidence of the computer printout was relevant to the question whether there was, in fact, a balance of only £1 in the account. For technical reasons that no longer apply, it was held that the evidence of the building society auditor was wrongly admitted under the provisions of the Police and Criminal Evidence Act (PACE) 1984 that prevailed at the time.

10.5 In this case, it is pertinent to note that the auditor was properly qualified to testify as to the 'reliability' of the computer. However, it is suggested that the 'reliability' of the computer was not in issue in this case. The issue was whether the information entered into the computer was accurate, and if so, how the accuracy or otherwise of the information could be proved. The 'reliability' of the computer was a separate issue. All the auditor would be doing in such circumstances was to provide evidence as to how the information was transcribed from the passbook to the computer, and whether the methods used by the building society were capable of providing the assurance that the information was accurate.

10.6 In the case of *R v Harper*,[1] it was alleged that the appellant presented a stolen Capital Card when travelling on a London Transport bus. The relevant sequence of events were as follows. In February 1985 a batch of cards were stolen at Alexandra Palace railway station; appropriate entries were made by an employee in the 'Lost Book' at the station; the relevant entries were transferred to a computer belonging to British Rail at King's Cross railway station, and the entries were further transferred from this computer to a computer at Waterloo railway station owned by London Regional Transport. At trial, the prosecution relied on a computer printout from the Waterloo computer to show that the card was stolen. The printout was produced by a revenue protection official who worked at Baker Street station. The judge admitted the evidence, but it was held on appeal that it was incorrect to do so because the witness could not, from her own knowledge, testify to the 'reliability' of the computer, and also that the requirements of s 68 of PACE 1984 had not been satisfied.[2]

1 *R v Minors (Craig), R v Harper (Giselle Gaile)* [1989] 1 WLR 441, [1989] 1 All ER 208, [1988] 12 WLUK 161, (1989) 89 Cr App R 102, [1989] Crim LR 360, (1989) 133 SJ 420, [1989] CLY 546.

2 Section 68 of the Police and Criminal Evidence Act 1984 was repealed by the Criminal Justice Act 1988, Schedule 16.

10.7 This decision must be right. However, it is suggested that the 'reliability' of the computer was not relevant given this set of facts. The fatal problem in this instance was a break in the continuity of evidence, because the 'Lost Book' held at Alexandra Palace railway station was missing at the time of the trial. The witness may have been competent to give evidence of the procedures used to register and disseminate the knowledge of the loss of Capital Cards. However, on these facts, because there were so many separate connections in the chain, the prosecution ought to have obtained evidence from each person responsible for the process by which lost or stolen cards were brought to the attention of the relevant authority, and how the information was disseminated.[1]

1 See 'Evidence obtained from a computer' (1992) 56 Journal of Criminal Law 44 for a comparison between *Minors* and *Shephard* and 'touching wood'; Colin Tapper, 'Reform on the law of evidence in relation to the output from computers' (1995) 3(1) Intl J L & Info Tech 85. In *Odex Pte. Ltd. v Pacific Internet Ltd* [2007] SGDC, rev'd on other grounds, [2008] SGHC 35, [2008] 3 SLR 18, the lawyers could not even identify the correct person to prepare a witness statement; George Wei, 'Pre-commencement discovery and the Odex litigation: copyright versus confidentiality or is it privacy?' (2008) 20 SAcLJ 591; and Daniel Seng, 'Evidential issues from pre-action discoveries: *Odex Pte Ltd v Pacific Internet Ltd*' (2009) 6 Digital Evidence and Electronic Signature Law Review 25.

Lay experts as witnesses

10.8 In the case of *R v Spiby (John Eric)*,[1] the defence argued, unsuccessfully, that the sub-manager of a hotel could not discharge the burden under s 69 of PACE 1984 to show that the computer was working 'properly'. It was submitted that only a service engineer or an expert on the use of the particular computer system would have been able to say whether the machine was working 'correctly'.[2] Taylor LJ agreed with the decision of the trial judge, and considered that the positive evidence of the sub-manager that the device was working was sufficient in this instance. This cannot be correct. Only a service engineer or a suitably qualified professional with knowledge of the particular computer system would be in a position to determine whether the device was working 'properly'. The sub-manager was only competent to give evidence of his reliance on the output of the device for the purpose of submitting a record of the telephone calls made from particular extensions in the hotel and recorded by the machine – that is, for the purpose of billing customers for the calls made. An assertion that the output is considered reliable because the hotel relies on the output of the device does not prove the device is 'reliable'. These are separate questions.

1 [1990] 3 WLUK 150, (1990) 91 Cr App R 186, Times, 16 March 1990, Independent, 2 April 1990, Daily Telegraph, 30 March 1990, [1990] CLY 785. See Solomon E. Salako 'R v Spiby Revisited' (1991) 1(1) LTJ 29.
2 Colin Tapper, 'Evidence from computers' (1974) 8 Georgia Law Review 562, 595. Professor Tapper noted, at fn 193, 596, that 'An interesting trial dilemma regarding foundation testimony is that too much of a showing of error control may cause a jury to find the system so fraught with error that the system would be presumed to be unreliable, while too little testimony on that matter would cause a similar result'. Unfortunately, it does not follow that the latter result occurs.

10.9 Compare this case with the decision in *United States of America v Linn.*[1] A computer printout of telephone calls was admitted into evidence. The appellant argued that the printout was not admissible because it was an untrustworthy record generated by a computer. The appellant suggested that the Director of Communications of the Sheraton hotel 'did not understand the distinctions between "menus", "data bases", and computer "code", she was "confused and inadequately trained", and thus without personal knowledge of the way in which the computer printout was generated'.[2]

1 880 F.2d 209 (9th Cir. 1989).
2 880 F.2d 209 (9th Cir. 1989) at 216.

10.10 No evidence was offered to indicate why the content of the printout was considered to be unreliable or why it was relevant that the witness failed to understand how the printout was generated. Beezer CJ rejected the submission as frivolous. He pointed out that the telephone record was generated automatically and it was retained in the ordinary course of business; thus such records were considered business records under the relevant Federal Rules of Evidence.

10.11 In this case, two separate issues were conflated: first, the witness was not an expert witness and therefore not qualified to give the evidence, and second, the witness failed to understand the underlying working of the computer that produced the printout. If the 'reliability' of the computer was in issue, the appellant ought to have alleged the content of the printout could not be trusted, and have given sufficient reasons for the burden to fall to the prosecution to demonstrate the computer was working correctly.

10.12 It was not considered necessary for a computer expert to provide evidence that a till roll connected to a computer was 'working properly' in *R v Shephard (Hilda)*[1] under the provisions of s 69 of PACE 1984. The oral evidence of a store detective, who demonstrated how the prices of goods were added to the till roll, was considered sufficient by the members of the Court of Appeal and the House of Lords. It should be noted that the store detective was only capable of demonstrating the method by which the prices of goods were added to the till, not whether the software accurately replicated the list of goods purchased. In giving judgment in the Court of Appeal, Lloyd J said of the evidence given by the store detective:

> On the evidence in the court below in the present case, there was no doubt about the functioning of the computer. Mrs. McNicholas who gave detailed evidence as to how the cash tills worked, and explained the link with the central computer, was asked in chief

> 'Q. And what about the master computer? Did that malfunction?
>
> A. Touch wood, no. I have never known it break down since we have had it.'
>
> She was not cross-examined on the point. In addition, she has spent, as we have said, many hours examining the particular till rolls. She would have been the first to notice if there had been any internal evidence of malfunction. In those circumstances it was legitimate for the court to infer that the computer was operating properly.[2]

1 [1993] AC 380, [1993] 2 WLR 102, [1993] 1 All ER 225, [1992] 12 WLUK 273, (1993) 96 Cr App R 345, (1993) 157 JP 145, [1993] Crim LR 295, (1993) 143 NLJ 127, (1993) 137 SJLB 12, Times, 17 December 1992, Independent, 21 January 1993, [1993] CLY 636 (spelt 'Shepherd' in All ER and Crim LR); but see the highly relevant comments in 'Evidence obtained from a computer' (1992) 56 Journal of Criminal Law 44 in comparing the decision in this case against the decision in *R v Minors (Craig), R v Harper (Giselle Gaile)* [1989] 1 WLR 441; 'Admissibility of computer print-outs' (1993) 57(3) Journal of Criminal Law 277.
2 *R v Shephard* (1991) 93 Cr App R 139 at 143.

10.13 In rejecting the need for a computer expert to sign a certificate where oral evidence has been given that was open to cross-examination, Lord Griffiths offered the following comments in the House of Lords:

> Documents produced by computers are an increasingly common feature of all business and more and more people are becoming familiar with their uses and operation. Computers vary immensely in their complexity and in the operations they perform. The nature of the evidence to discharge the burden of showing that there has been no improper use of the computer and that it was operating properly will inevitably vary from case to case. The evidence must be tailored to suit the needs of the case. I suspect that it will very rarely be necessary to call an expert and that in the vast majority of cases it will be possible to discharge the burden by calling a witness who is familiar with the operation of the computer in the sense of knowing what the computer is required to do and who can say that it is doing it properly.[1]

1 [1993] AC 380 at 387 B–D; followed in *Public Prosecution Service v McGowan* [2008] NICA 13, [2009] NI 1.

10.14 Lord Griffiths went on to say:

> The computer in this case was of the simplest kind printing limited basic information on each till roll. The store detective was able to describe how the tills were operated, what the computer did, that there had been no trouble with the computer and how she had also examined all the till rolls which showed no evidence of malfunction either by the tills or by the central computer.[1]

1 [1993] AC 380 at 387E; the Crown Prosecution Service cites this decision by the House of Lords as if a lay person has any knowledge of the complexities of a computer system: 'The House of Lords has held that a store detective is competent to produce till rolls produced by a store's computer where the store detective was familiar with the operation of the tills and can say that the store had no difficulties caused by the operation of the computer', https://www.cps.gov.uk/legal-guidance/computer-records-evidence.

10.15 Dr Stephen Castell was engaged as an expert witness in litigation regarding a major electronic point of sale computer system for a national retailer in 1994, and he remarked that a centralized computer connected to remote tills in store branches is far from being a computer of the simplest kind.[1]

1 'Letter to the Editor', *Computer Law and Security Report* (May–June 1994), 158.

10.16 At the same time as this case was being heard in England, the Court of Appeals of Nebraska heard an appeal in the case of *State of Nebraska v Ford*.[1] The appellant was convicted of theft from hotel rooms. The hotel used a system controlled by a computer, by which both those staying at the hotel and members of staff gained entry to a room by way of a card with machine-readable code. A number of thefts from rooms were linked to the recorded use of a card issued to Ford. When challenged, Ford admitted to being in the rooms at the time, but not to theft. The prosecution adduced the business records under the hearsay exception, which provides that the evidence can be admitted if the activity recorded is of a type that regularly occurs in the course of the day-to-day activity of the business; and the record was made at or near the time of the events recorded, and the record is authenticated by a qualified witness. The defence challenged the qualifications of the witness, Glenda Willmon, the general manager of the hotel, who explained how the system worked. Connolly J, who gave the judgment for the court, rejected the submission by the defence that the witness was not suitably qualified. The judge said that it did not matter whether the witness could discuss the components or engineering principles of the computer.[2] This must be right. Unless there is a challenge to the accuracy of the evidence tendered that results from a computer or computer-like device, it does not necessarily follow that a person familiar with a computer system cannot give evidence of the output of the system.

1 501 N.W.2d 318 (Neb.App. 1993).
2 501 N.W.2d 318 at 321.

10.17 The view that an expert is not always required to attest to the proper working of a computer was repeated in *Darby (Yvonne Beatrice) v DPP*.[1] In this case, a police constable operating a speed-measuring device testified to the proper operation of the device, even though the device acted to corroborate his own testimony. In undertaking this task, the police constable merely outlined how the device was used, not whether it was accurate. Similarly, in *R. v Dean (Jeanette), R. v Bolden (Robert Allen)*,[2] Lt Cdr Quigley, a Maritime Law Enforcement and Liaison Officer at the Department of State, contacted the Coast Guard Command Center at US Coast Guard headquarters in Washington, DC to request a search of the vessel *Battlestar*. A search was made of the Marine Safety Information System, which was a database containing information on all US vessels. The Command Center also searched the databases of four coast states, and no record of this vessel was found. One ground of appeal centred on the submission that there was no evidence from the people who carried out the searches and the computers were operating properly, and as a result, the evidence was not admissible under s 69 of PACE 1984. The members of the Court of Appeal disagreed. It was considered that Lt Cdr Quigley could give evidence of the 'reliability' of the computers, because there were no reported problems with the databases, and searches on three separate occasions for the same name failed to bring up the name of the vessel. Dyson J gave judgment, and commented that: 'the fact that searches on three separate occasions produced the same result provided strong support for the conclusion that the computers were operating properly on each occasion.'[3]

1 [1994] 10 WLUK 343, [1995] RTR 294, (1995) 159 JP 533 (DC), Times, 4 November 1994, [1994] CLY 674.
2 [1998] 2 WLUK 562, (1998) 2 Cr App R 171, [1998] CLY 984.
3 (1998) 2 Cr App R 171 at 178E.

10.18 This conclusion ought to be reconsidered: the proposition should be that the database was searched on three occasions, and the failure to find an entry for the vessel enables the conclusion to be reached that the name of the vessel was not on the database.[1] This is a different issue to whether the computer was 'working properly', or in preference, returning verifiably correct results: the computer may not have been working completely to the expectation of the user, because it might have had any number of problems that did not necessarily affect the effectiveness of the search facility. The effectiveness of the search of the database can be independent of the ability of the computer to return generally verifiably correct results. If the 'reliability' of the computer is challenged, it must be necessary to provide a reasonable basis upon which the claim is made, and there ought to be some evidence proffered to demonstrate that the results produced by the computer might be so unreliable as to affect the output used in evidence.

1 *R. (on the application of Sedgefield BC) v Dickinson* [2009] EWHC 2758 (Admin), [2009] 10 WLUK 317, where a search of a database failed to reveal evidence of an entry, but this was insufficient to prove that the notification of a change of circumstances had not been received.

Qualification of witnesses

10.19 Where there is a reason that the content of the computer printout cannot be trusted, then the qualifications of the witness will be relevant, because of the nature of the evidence they will be required to give and be cross-examined upon. The degree of expertise required from a witness will vary according to the problem encountered. In *DPP v Barber*,[1] the first two characters of each line on the printout were missing, although the accuracy of the information recorded on the printout was not affected. However, the magistrate declined to hear the evidence of a service engineer who was able to explain the nature of the problem because he was not a computer expert, and the evidence of what he had seen at a later date was not relevant to the state of the device at the time the printout was produced. The appeal was allowed because the evidence of the service engineer should have been received. This must be right, given that an ancillary part of the device was apparently not working properly, and the defect did not affect the accuracy of the data.

1 [1998] 5 WLUK 294, (1999) 163 JP 457, [1999] CLY 886; 'Effect of intoximeter's defects' (1999) 63(6) Journal of Criminal Law 527.

10.20 The two issues are further illustrated in *R v Neville*,[1] where the Crown sought to adduce evidence of a computer printout showing telephone calls made on Neville's mobile telephone in connection with the hiring of a tractor unit and the employment of a driver to transport a large quantity of stolen hi-fi equipment. The mobile telephone was hired from Talkland, a subsidiary of ICL. A different company, Racal, undertook the telephone operations. The software in the Racal computer issued instructions to record the date, time and duration of each call automatically, and these details were passed on to Talkland. The computer belonging to Talkland included software code that enabled it to produce an itemized bill for their customers. When the bill was paid, the printout was stored on microfiche. The Crown sought to adduce the microfiche into evidence (or, presumably, a printout of the contents recorded on the microfiche), and the judge admitted it after a trial within a trial. The Crown then called a witness, an employee of Talkland with no apparent qualifications, to give evidence that she had checked all relevant records and had no reason to believe that the telephone bill was inaccurate because of any improper use of either of the computers involved, including the Racal computer. She also stated that the computer at her place of work was working properly so far as her enquiries led. This cannot be correct. The witness might have had the competence to give evidence of the procedures within her knowledge to provide for the accuracy of billing information at Talkland,[2] but was in no position (not being competent) to offer evidence of any material substance that the computers at Talkland were working properly, and certainly not in a position to offer the same evidence relating to the procedures at Racal, nor as to whether the computer belonging to Racal, of which she had no knowledge, never mind expert knowledge, was working properly.

1 [1990] 11 WLUK 143, [1991] Crim LR 288, [1991] CLY 623.
2 The evidence can be admitted under the provisions of s 117 of the Criminal Justice Act 2003.

10.21 Knowledge that is obtained from experience at work in the absence of formal qualifications is acceptable.[1] However, it is not helpful when a police officer is entrusted to conduct a forensic examination of a mobile telephone without the relevant knowledge or expertise, as in *R v Coultas (Kiera)*,[2] or where a mobile telephone analyst provides evidence that is tantamount to expert evidence where the members of a jury are presented with the appearance of cell site analysis, and then invited to infer facts without any of the technical knowledge required to substantiate any conclusions.[3] The degree of expertise required of a witness was the subject of the appeal in *R. v Stubbs (Paul Matthew)*.[4] The appellant was convicted of conspiracy to defraud, in that he was involved in fraudulent money transfers from HSBC Bank of around £11.8 million. The fraudulent activities were carried out using an online banking system called Hexagon. The appellant was a member of the password reset team, responsible for resetting customer passwords. The prosecution called Mr Richard Roddy, an employee of HSBC, to give evidence of the Hexagon system. Mr Roddy was not the only witness called to provide evidence of an expert nature. The defence objected at trial to the admissibility of parts of Mr Roddy's evidence on the basis that he lacked the expertise and independence to give expert opinion on the matters in question. It was accepted that he could give evidence about the processes within HSBC and the manner in which the system was designed to operate. However, it was contended that his detailed account of the actual activity within the system at the material times amounted to inadmissible opinion evidence. Following a trial within a trial, the judge ruled Mr Roddy's evidence to be admissible and declined to exclude it under s 78 of PACE 1984 or article 6 of the European Convention on Human Rights. The grounds of objection are set out in the judgment of Richards LJ:

> 48. Of particular importance was Mr Roddy's evidence that the activity reports all related to the same session, which had the reference number 'CC000051' and had been registered to the staff delegate identification PWRD on the morning of 24 July 2002. A session number would be allocated upon a user's log-on at a particular terminal. If all the transactions took place within one continuous session and there were legitimate transactions admittedly carried out by the appellant during that session just before and just after the illegitimate transactions, the prosecution could argue with force that the illegitimate transactions must have been carried out from the same terminal; and this also provided strong support for the argument that they must have been carried out by the appellant.

49. Mr Winter submitted that Mr Roddy did not have the expertise to give such evidence that the activity reports all related to a single session. The fact that they had the same number did not mean that it was a single session. There was evidence from the admitted expert, Mr Danbury, that *concurrent* log-ons (so as to target and hijack a live session) were not possible; but that left open the possibility of *non-concurrent* log-ons to the system under the same session number. This was something that Mr Roddy had not investigated and did not have the technical qualifications to investigate or to answer questions about.

50. Among the various points made by Mr Winter were these:

i) The activity reports themselves do not show when log-ons and log-offs occurred. For example, they do not show the undoubted log-off by the appellant at about 17.20. This leaves open the possibility that he had previously logged off at about 17.00, just before the illegitimate activity.

ii) There was no evidence about the appellant's log-on in the morning. Further, although Mr Roddy said that the computer timed out if the session was idle for a period, the evidence was not clear as to how long it needed before a timed log-off occurred. One would have expected a timed log-off when the appellant left the computer at lunchtime, but there was nothing to show whether there had been a log-off followed by a fresh log-on by the appellant after lunch. In short, there was simply no evidence about when or how the appellant's CC000051 session was created.

iii) Mr Roddy gave evidence that, once a session ended, the next session would not be given the same number again: the number reverted to a pool of numbers available to be allocated by the computer to new sessions. He said in cross-examination that there was a 1 in 100,000 chance of it being reallocated to a different session on the same day. Yet there was evidence of three instances the previous day in which session numbers had been reallocated to other sessions after discontinuance of the session to which they were originally allocated. Mr Roddy was unable to say how this could have happened.

iv) There were other pointers to the illegitimate activity having been carried out by someone other than the appellant. The illegitimate activity involved a random attack on five companies beginning with the letter 'A', whereas the appellant would have known or could have discovered the primary delegate identification for all the companies and would not have needed to do things in this way. Moreover, on two occasions in the course of the illegitimate activity the user deployed a shortcut that was never used by the appellant in the course of his legitimate transactions. The vulnerability of the system to attack by members of staff was illustrated by the fraud perpetrated by Mr Kareer earlier the same year, involving as it did the use of other people's terminals in their absence.[5]

1 *R. v Oakley (Trevor Alan)* [1979] 6 WLUK 43, (1980) 70 Cr App R 7, [1979] RTR 417, [1979] Crim LR 657, [1979] CLY 458, where a police officer, with 15 years' experience in the traffic division, attended and passed a course as an accident investigator, having attended over 400 fatal road traffic accidents; *R. v Murphy (William Francis)* [1980] 3 WLUK 64, (1980) 71 Cr App R 33, [1980] RTR 145, [1980] Crim LR 309, (1980) 124 SJ 189, [1980] CLY 2295, where a police officer offered an opinion as to the nature of a collision.

2 [2008] EWCA Crim 3261, [2008] 9 WLUK 352.

3 *R. v Turner (Andrew Neil)* [2020] EWCA Crim 1241, [2020] 9 WLUK 308. On similar facts, a differently composed Court of Appeal determined the position correctly in *R. v Calland (Sean Thomas)* [2017] EWCA Crim 2308, [2017] 12 WLUK 706. (For some inexplicable reason, *Calland* was not cited in *Turner*.) On cell site analysis, see Matthew Tart, Iain Brodie, Nicholas Gleed and James Matthews,

'Historic cell site analysis – overview of principles and survey methodologies' (2012) 8(3–4) Digital Investigation185; R. P. Coutts and H. Selby, 'Problems with cell phone evidence tendered to "prove" the location of a person at a point in time' (2016) 13 Digital Evidence and Electronic Signature Law Review 76; Reg Coutts and Hugh Selby, '"Mobile ping data" – metadata for tracking' (2017) 14 Digital Evidence and Electronic Signature Law Review 22; Matthew Tart, Sue Pope, David Baldwin and Robert Bird, 'Cell site analysis: roles and interpretation' (2019) 59(5) Science & Justice 558; Matthew Tart, 'Opinion evidence in cell site analysis' (2020) 60(4) Science & Justice 363.

4 [2006] EWCA Crim 2312, [2006] 10 WLUK 328.

5 [2006] EWCA Crim 2312 at [48]–[50], original emphasis.

10.22 In reaching the decision to admit the evidence, the trial judge applied the tests in *R v Bonython*.[1] Richards LJ agreed that it was not in dispute that the first test was satisfied, because the Hexagon system was a subject for expert testimony, and he went on to say, of the second question:

> In our judgment he was also right to give an affirmative answer to the second question, holding that Mr Roddy had acquired sufficient knowledge of the subject to render his opinion of value in resolving the issues before the court concerning the operation of the Hexagon system. This was an assessment properly made after hearing Mr Roddy's evidence on the *voir dire*. The extent of Mr Roddy's experience of the Hexagon system, as summarised above, enabled him to give valuable assistance on the interpretation of the data taken from the central computer and set out in the activity reports. It was accepted that he was not an IT specialist in any wider sense and that his technical knowledge of the system was limited. But this did not preclude his being regarded as an expert to the extent indicated by the judge.[2]

1 [1984] SASR 45.

2 *R. v Stubbs (Paul Matthew)* [2006] EWCA Crim 2312 at [55]. For how courts consider the qualifications of experts, see Sean E. Goodison, Robert C. Davis and Brian A. Jackson, *Digital Evidence and the U.S. Criminal Justice System: Identifying Technology and Other Needs to More Effectively Acquire and Utilize Digital Evidence* (RAND Corporation 2013), 13, and Peter Sommer, 'Certification, registration, assessment of digital forensic experts: the UK experience' (2011) 2(1) Digital Investigation 98.

10.23 The members of the jury were informed of the limitations in the evidence that Mr Roddy was able to give, and it was a matter for them to determine whether they should accept and place weight on his evidence. It was submitted that Mr Roddy's evidence went to admissibility because he was an employee of HSBC and represented the victim of the fraud, and therefore he was not an independent witness. The court rejected this submission. Expertise and independence are separate issues, and it was pointed out that although he made a concession to his lack of objectivity, no attention was given to any feature of his evidence that would support a case of conscious bias or lack of objectivity. Richard LJ indicated:

> In any event it was a matter for the jury to determine whether there was any conscious or unconscious bias or lack of objectivity that might render his evidence unreliable. This was, as the judge said, a matter going to weight rather than admissibility. The circumstances did not warrant a refusal by the judge to admit the relevant parts of Mr Roddy's evidence at all.[1]

1 [2006] EWCA Crim 2312 at [59]. In England and Wales, both the Civil Procedure Rules 2020, part 35 and the Criminal Procedure Rules 2020, part 19 make provision for a single joint expert in certain circumstances. Therefore, there is an onus on the parties to agree expert evidence where they can. For an analysis of the potential problems with this, see Peter Sommer, 'Meetings between experts: a route to simpler, fairer trials?' (2009) 5(3–4), Digital Investigation 146.

10.24 The technical evidence offered by Mr Roddy was not the only evidence of relevance that was led by the prosecution. There was supporting evidence for the prosecution case, for instance: the appellant left the building sometime after 17.00 and returned at 17.27. He claimed he returned to collect his umbrella and that it had been raining, yet the evidence from a CCTV located outside an office a few minutes away from the entrance revealed it was bright and sunny at the material time. The appellant also failed to produce relevant paperwork authorizing the change in passwords, lied during his internal interviews and the evidence he gave to the police when questioned was also inconsistent.

10.25 In addition to the evidence of Mr Roddy, the prosecution also called a Mr Alan Danbury, a computer expert who had been responsible for introducing the system into the UK in the early 1990s, and the manager of the support team until he retired in 2004. During the trial within a trial, the judge also heard evidence from a witness for the defence, a Mr Michael Turner. Mr Turner was not able to provide a report because of a lack of information for a variety of reasons, as set out by Richards LJ:

> the appellant's workstation had not been retained or imaged; there was no computer running the 2002 version of the Hexagon system which could be analysed; he had been provided with no information as to how the HSBC computers operated or produced the audit logs relied on by Mr Roddy; and he did not have the underlying data from which he could safely reach any conclusion.[1]

1 [2006] EWCA Crim 2312 at [44].

10.26 These comments highlight the problems faced by the defence in attempting to elicit cooperation with the victim when legitimate questions need to be investigated to enable the cross-examination of prosecution witnesses to undermine the evidence they give. This is a particular problem when challenging a bank, because the defence has a legitimate interest in challenging the ability of a particular system to withstand an attack or an attempt at subversion. Conversely, the bank cannot, when confronted with evidence that fraud may have taken place, suspend the operation of the system or disrupt it in such a way as to cause it to stop working, no matter how short a time it would take. If a bank were required to pay more attention to the gathering of forensic evidence at a sufficient standard to satisfy criminal proceedings, then they, together with other organizations that may suffer similar attempts, will either be obliged to train employees, or call in suitably qualified experts to conduct an investigation at the time the suspicion is raised. Apart from the added cost and the marginal utility of taking such steps, the victim must decide at the time suspicion is raised whether the integrity of the system will be at issue, which in turn requires the victim to have hindsight of the future challenges.

10.27 In this case, a balance had to be struck between adducing evidence of the system and how it operated within the knowledge of the person responsible for it at the bank, and whether it was necessary to require a more in-depth analysis from a person expert in the relevant system. The dividing line between the need for an expert in the operation of the computer system to give evidence, and the evidence of someone who is familiar with the day-to-day operation of the system is a fine one, and it will depend on the nature of the case as to whether one expert is to be preferred over another.[1] In many cases, as this particular prosecution illustrates, the expert evidence, both internal and external, will not be conclusive. The members of the jury can be appraised of the conflicting technical evidence, and will then be required to consider the technical evidence against the other evidence in reaching their decision. In this instance, it can be argued that the technical evidence, which was not conclusive, was supported by the inconsistencies in the appellant's behaviour.

1 In *RTA v McNaughton* [2006] NSWSC 115, a witness was not permitted or sufficiently expert to give evidence of the position a vehicle was in at the material time.

10.28 Arguably, there is a distinction between the competence, knowledge and qualifications of a witness tendered to give evidence of the trustworthiness of evidence in digital data. If the defence challenges the accuracy of the evidence, it will be necessary to call a witness with relevant competence, knowledge and suitable qualifications to give evidence. The decision in the case of *R v Shephard* must be right, but not because of the rationale offered by the members of the House of Lords. The defence did not challenge the truth of claims made by the witness, only the qualifications of the witness to testify. From the law reports, it appeared that the witness had sufficient knowledge to offer the evidence he did. Had the defence challenged the system that the till roll was connected to, and questioned whether the entire system was trustworthy, including what, if any, errors had been found in operating it across a number of shops connected to a central server, then the witness would not have been competent or qualified to give evidence.

Appendix 1

Draft Convention on Electronic Evidence

The Draft Convention was published in the *Digital Evidence and Electronic Signature Law Review* (2016) 13 S1–S11 (the online version includes further information relating to the process by which it was written).

Summary

The Draft Convention is the first treaty dealing with the status of electronic evidence, covering civil and criminal proceedings, the investigation and examination of electronic evidence, and general provisions regarding the recognition and admissibility of electronic evidence from foreign jurisdictions.

Convention on Electronic Evidence

London,

Preamble

[The States signatory hereto],

Considering that the aim of the Drafting Committee is to encourage judges and lawyers to appreciate the concept of evidence in electronic form;

Recognising the value of promoting international co-operation with [the other States that are Parties] to this Convention;

Convinced of the need to pursue, as a matter of priority, a common policy on electronic evidence;

Conscious that the profound changes brought about by the machine and software code (collectively 'digital systems') have altered the means by which evidence is authenticated, in that the medium and the content are no longer bound together as with paper, and that the rules established for paper do not always apply to evidence in electronic form;

Concerned by the risk that electronic evidence can be misunderstood and misinterpreted;

Recognising that evidence in electronic form has unique characteristics that are significantly different to paper and other objects, which raise complex questions about the integrity and reliability of data in electronic form;

Recognising the need to facilitate the co-operation between States for the proper receipt, handling and authentication of electronic evidence;

Believing that it is in the interests of justice to provide for fairness in legal proceedings;

Have agreed as follows:

Part I – Use of terms

Article 1 – Definitions

For the purposes of this Convention:

'adjudicator' means any person that is lawfully appointed as a judge, arbitrator or to any other role that requires the holder of the office to act in a judicious and unbiased manner;

'attribution' means the assigning of responsibility for or tracing the origin of an act purported to have been performed or committed using or through a computer device, system or network;

'authentication' means the process by which any electronic record, document, statement or other thing is proven to be what it claims to be;

'computer' means any device capable of performing mathematical or logical instructions;

'court' means any international court, national court, statutory arbitral or other tribunal, board or commission according to national law of the contracting state;

'electronic evidence' means evidence derived from data contained in or produced by any device the functioning of which depends on a software program or from data stored on or communicated over a computer system or network;

'electronic record' means data that is recorded or stored on any medium in or by a device programmed by software code and that can be read or perceived by a person or any such device, and includes a display, printout or other output that represents the data;

'device' means any apparatus or tool operating alone or connected to other apparatus or tools, that processes information or data in electronic form;

'digital' means anything that relies on technology based on a binary system or any future development or replacement technology of the same;

'digital evidence practitioner' means a person who is appropriately qualified, and where the law requires, authorized, to investigate and examine evidence in electronic form;

'legal proceeding' means any formal procedure that takes place before any court, national or international, a statutory arbitral or other tribunal, board or commission according to national law and charged with legally defined duties and obligations, or any other formal legal process;

'metadata' means data that describe other data;

'program' means any set of instructions stored in a machine-readable format that can be used to perform a function in a repeatable and reproducible manner;

'relevant legal proceedings' means the legal proceedings for which data in electronic form is requested under a Mutual Legal Assistance Treaty or any other bilateral or multilateral instrument;

'tool' means any device or software program that can be used to identify, secure, examine and analyse electronic evidence.

Part II – Status of electronic evidence

Article 2 – Admissibility of electronic evidence

1. Evidence in electronic form shall be admitted into legal proceedings.

2. Article 2(1) does not modify any existing national rule that applies to the admissibility of evidence, except in relation to the rules relating to authenticity and best evidence.

Article 3 – Agreement on the admissibility of electronic evidence

1. Unless otherwise provided in any law operating in the relevant jurisdiction, an electronic record or document may be tendered, subject to the discretion and rules of the court, if the Parties to the proceedings have expressly agreed to its introduction.

2. Notwithstanding the provisions of Article 3(1), an agreement between the Parties on the admissibility of an electronic record or document does not render the record admissible in a criminal proceeding if at the time the agreement was made

(a) the accused person or any of the persons accused in the proceeding was not represented by a lawyer;

(b) except where the adjudicator finds that admitting the record or document into evidence does not prejudice the case for the accused.

Article 4 – Authentication of electronic evidence

1. The party seeking to introduce electronic evidence in any legal proceeding has the burden of proving it is what it claims to be.

2. The matters set out below are to be considered when assessing that evidence in electronic form is what it claims to be:

(a) The data (both the content and associated metadata) relied upon in any legal proceedings can be shown to be an accurate representation of the prevailing and existing state of those data at the time relevant to the legal proceedings.

(b) If the data have changed from the moment they were identified (and possibly seized) as potential evidence in legal proceedings, there is an accurate and reliable method of documenting any such changes, including the reasons for any such modifications.

(c) The continuity of the data between the moment in time the data were obtained for legal purposes and their submission as an exhibit in legal proceedings can be demonstrated.

(d) Any techniques that were used to obtain, secure and process the data can be tested and shown to have been appropriate for the purpose for which they were applied.

(e) The technical and organizational evidence demonstrates that the integrity of the data is trustworthy, and can therefore be considered reliable and complete (insofar as the data can be complete), which in turn will depend on the circumstances surrounding the data at the time they were identified as being potentially relevant in legal proceedings.

Article 5 – Best evidence

1. In any legal proceeding, where any printout, document or other physical manifestation of the result or output or appearance of any electronic process, record or any other representation of that process or record has been manifestly or consistently acted on, relied upon, or used as the record of the information represented by or stored on the printout, the printout or other physical manifestation shall be considered the best evidence and admitted as evidence subject to satisfactory proof of its integrity.

2. Where the output of a process is relied upon, and it remains in electronic form, the best evidence rule remains, subject to the provisions of Article 4(2).

3. Article 5(1) and (2) do not modify any domestic rule that applies to the admission of evidence.

Part III – Investigation and examination of digital evidence

Article 6 – Digital evidence practitioner

1. Since digital evidence practitioners are required to make informed judgements about the appropriateness of the tools and techniques they use to secure and preserve electronic evidence, the Parties shall establish minimum standards for their formal education and training.

2. A digital evidence practitioner must be able to provide, in compliance with the necessary court and legal requirements:

(a) an analysis of their findings, setting out the scientifically agreed basis upon which their judgement is based; and

(b) shall identify and explain any data that appear to be inconsistent with their findings.

3. The primary duty of the digital evidence practitioner is to the court.

Article 7 – The use of good practice guidelines for electronic evidence

1. The Parties to the Convention shall establish a Forum for the development of good practice and guidelines in the acquisition, handling and otherwise processing of electronic evidence in the form of a set of agreed common requirements.

2. The forum shall:

(a) Include participation from at least two thirds of all Parties to the Convention.

(b) Establish its own rules of procedure and may establish subcommittees to consider specific issues.

(c) Be funded on a basis to be agreed.

(d) Submit the first edition of its agreed common requirements to the Parties within two (2) years of this Convention coming into force for subsequent adoption by the Parties.

(e) Produce updates and amendments to the agreed common requirements as deemed desirable and necessary by the Forum and in any case every two years, or a statement that an update is not currently necessary.

3. Except where incompatible or inconsistent with national legislation, codes or procedure, the Parties to this Convention shall implement agreed common requirements on the acquisition, obtaining, packaging, processing and examination of electronic evidence.

4. The agreed common requirements shall be:

(a) Drafted by reference to the guidelines established by the Forum.

(b) Adopted within [time period to be agreed] of accession to this Convention or within [time period to be agreed] of the publication of the first version of the agreed common requirements by the Forum, wherever is the sooner.

(c) Implemented by all national and government departments charged with legal duties and obligations involving the use, handling or processing of electronic evidence.

5. Any authority responsible for investigating a matter involving the criminal law shall apply and follow the agreed common requirements unless there are exceptional or extenuating circumstances where they cannot be followed.

6. Where, under Article 7(5) above, the agreed common requirements have not been complied with for exceptional circumstances, those circumstances and the reasons shall be recorded in writing at the time of the departure from the agreed common requirements and the written record shall be admissible in legal proceedings.

Part IV – Treatment of electronic evidence upon receipt

Article 8 – The requesting party

1. The provisions of this Article apply where the requesting party makes a request for evidence in electronic form to the sending party.

2. When the requesting party makes a request for evidence in electronic form, regardless of the mechanism by which the evidence is requested, the requesting party

shall provide a legally binding undertaking in writing to the sending party to include the following:

(a) An assurance that the data shall be dealt with in accordance with how evidence in legal proceedings is normally dealt with in the requesting parties' jurisdiction under the relevant legislation, procedural rules and rules of professional conduct.

(b) Copies of the data shall only be given to parties authorized to receive the data that are part of the relevant legal proceedings.

(c) Data provided under the provisions of Article 8 shall only be used for purposes related to the relevant legal proceedings.

(d) The sending party may waive the provisions of Article 8(2)(b). The terms of any such waiver shall be decided by the parties in a form and to the extent that they determine.

3. Notwithstanding the provisions contained in Article 8(2) above, all data in electronic form that is provided to the requesting party shall be the subject of all the relevant laws of the requesting party, including, but not limited to, confidentiality, the protection of data and the security of data.

4. The assurances provided by the receiving party under the provisions of Article 8(2) above may be provided in physical or electronic form as is agreed between the parties.

5. The provisions of Article 8(3) shall also apply to any other receiving party authorised to receive the data that are part of the relevant legal proceedings.

Part V – General provisions

Article 9 – Admissibility of electronic evidence from other jurisdictions

1. Where electronic evidence originates in another jurisdiction, its admissibility is not impaired if the electronic evidence is proven in accordance with Article 3 or the authenticity of the evidence is otherwise demonstrated.

2. The provisions of Article 9 do not modify any domestic rule that applies to evidence in electronic form obtained contrary to relevant human rights legislation or data protection legislation.

Article 10 – Recognition of foreign electronic evidence and signatures

1. In determining whether or not, or to what extent, data in electronic form are legally effective, no regard shall be had to the geographical location where the data were created or used or to the place of business of their creation, provided those data are located in the domestic jurisdiction.

2. Where the electronic record or document is located in a foreign jurisdiction, Article 10(1) above does not apply unless –

(a) the party who adduces evidence of the contents of an electronic record or document has, not less than 14 days before the day on which the evidence is adduced, served on each other party a copy of the electronic record or document proposed to be tendered, except where exceptional, urgent and exigent circumstances apply;

(b) the court directs that it is to apply; or

(c) there is an international treaty in effect establishing recognition of electronic records or documents or of electronic signatures located in the foreign jurisdiction.

3. Notwithstanding the provisions of Article 10(2)(a) above, what constitutes exceptional, urgent or exigent circumstances for the purposes of this Article is a matter for the court seized with the matter.

4. Notwithstanding the provisions of Article 10(2) above, an adjudicator may admit data in electronic form that are located in a foreign jurisdiction if domestic law so provides.

Article 11 – Interpretation

1. Where the meaning of a word or phrase in this Convention differs from the meaning of a word or phrase defined in any information technology literature, the adjudicator shall interpret the meaning in accordance with the domestic law on the interpretation of words and phrases.

Article 12 – Entering into force

1. The Convention shall enter into force on the thirtieth day following the date of deposit with the [*name of sponsoring organization*].

2. For each State ratifying or acceding to the Convention after the deposit of the [*third*] instrument of ratification or accession, the Convention shall enter into force on the thirtieth day after the deposit by such State of its instrument of ratification or accession.

Explanatory notes to the Draft Convention on Electronic Evidence

1. The main objective is to pursue a common policy towards electronic evidence, taking into account the differences in the treatment of evidence in individual jurisdictions. This Convention does not seek to harmonize judicial systems. The aim is to encourage judges and lawyers to more fully understand the concept of electronic evidence in the interests of providing for fairness in legal proceedings; to promote adequate procedures in legal proceedings; to implement appropriate legislation where necessary, and to promote international co-operation.

2. Part I Article 1 provides a number of definitions. The aim is to provide definitions that transcend legal cultures. Although the definition of 'authentication' does not include reference to relevant international or domestic guidelines and standards, it does not preclude the use of such guidelines and standards in demonstrating authenticity. The definition of 'electronic evidence' is taken to be synonymous with the term 'digital evidence'.

3. Part II considers the status of electronic evidence, covering the admissibility of electronic evidence (Article 2 and Article 3), authentication (Article 4) and best evidence (Article 5).

4. Article 2 aims to provide minimum rules to the admissibility of electronic evidence. The purpose of Article 2(1) is to prevent a party from seeking to exclude evidence in electronic form because it is in electronic form. Article 2(2) does not modify any domestic rule relating to the admissibility of electronic evidence other than in relation to authenticity and best evidence.

5. Article 3, regarding the agreement on admissibility of electronic evidence, is taken and adapted from the *Commonwealth Draft Model Law on Electronic Evidence* and *Electronic Evidence: Model Policy Guidelines & Legislative Texts* (Harmonization of ICT Policies, Legislation and Regulatory Procedures in the Caribbean, International Telecommunication Union Telecommunication Development Bureau, Geneva, 2013).

6. The provisions of Article 3(1) aim to permit the parties to a legal proceeding to agree on the authenticity of the evidence. The purpose of this Article is to simplify the legal process by reducing the time that might be spent in authenticating documents and records in electronic form that both parties rely on. There is no point in increasing the time (and costs) spent on unnecessary actions.

7. Article 4(1) deals with the process of proving that data in electronic form is what it claims to be. The word authenticity is used, even though this may be considered to be irrelevant and out-of-date. To establish whether an electronic record, document or other thing is proven to be what it claims to be, the tests regarding the integrity, reliability and completeness of the data and therefore trustworthiness is more important. It is for the adjudicator to assess the evidence before them to determine whether the data is what it claims to be. The term 'authentic' is used by many jurisdictions in other contexts, such as the provision of an 'authentic' record. The word 'authentication' remains, but it should not be taken to override the domestic methods of determining whether an electronic record, document or other thing is proven to be what it claims to be – nor does it refer to the 'authentic' record.

8. Article 4(2) was initially taken from Stephen Mason, *Electronic Evidence* (3rd edn, LexisNexis Butterworths, 2012), 4.21. Both the *Commonwealth Draft Model Law on Electronic Evidence* and *Electronic Evidence: Model Policy Guidelines & Legislative Texts* (Harmonization of ICT Policies, Legislation and Regulatory Procedures in the Caribbean, International Telecommunication Union Telecommunication Development Bureau, Geneva, 2013) provide for a presumption (the term 'judicial notice' is also used in some jurisdictions – this term has a similar effect to the presumption) that electronic evidence is 'reliable' or that a computer system or other similar device was 'operating properly'. No lawyer or judicial authority has put any evidence forward to establish what 'reliability' means in relation to computers and computer like devices, or what 'operating properly' means. Because a minority of jurisdictions adopt this presumption in the absence of any evidence that such a presumption is justified, it is considered more appropriate to refrain from including such a presumption in the Draft Convention.

9. The provisions of Article 4(2) operate to require a party to demonstrate whether the data in electronic form is what it claims to be, and conversely, for the challenging party to cross examine to establish that the data is not an accurate presentation of what it claims to be.

10. Article 5 specifically refers to the common law concept of best evidence. The term 'original' has deliberately not been included in this Draft Convention. This is because the word 'original' has different meanings for lawyers and notaries, and also in different jurisdictions. The term 'original' is not helpful when analysing evidence in electronic form. This is because every item of data in electronic form is a copy. There can be no original.

11. Part III deals with the investigation and examination of electronic evidence in Articles 6 and 7.

12. Article 6 provides for the formal education and training of digital evidence practitioners. People that investigate, seize and analyse evidence in electronic form ought to be educated and trained through a formal process. This is in the interests of justice and fairness between the parties, and because evidence in electronic form is now ubiquitous and an every-day part of legal proceedings.

13. Article 7 provides for the creation of a Forum to develop appropriate guidelines or standards for the process of investigating evidence in electronic form. A number of guidelines exist at present. It is in the interests of justice that such guidelines are not only publicly available, but are developed by representatives from internationally respected bodies. By developing a set of internationally recognized guidelines,

adjudicators will be better informed when assessing evidence in electronic form. The development of common guidelines or standards will also promote confidence in and acceptance of the quality of evidence especially where obtained in another jurisdiction.

14. Part IV provides for the transmission of data in electronic form between jurisdictions. The terms of Article 8 do not affect the provision of any Mutual Legal Assistance Treaty, bilateral or multilateral instrument, or of any other method of requesting evidence from a foreign jurisdiction. The purpose of this provision is to reassure the sending party that the evidence sent will be dealt with appropriately and in accordance with the norms of the receiving jurisdiction relating to evidence in legal proceedings. Some jurisdictions are wary of sending evidence without suitable provision for the security and the protection of the people mentioned in the data.

15. Part V deals with general provisions. In particular, Article 9 on the admissibility of electronic evidence from other jurisdictions attempts to deal with the difficult question of which set of legal requirements apply to evidence in electronic form – whether it is of the State in which the evidence is geographically located, or the State in which the evidence is to be submitted in a legal proceeding. Article 9(1) seeks to indicate that if the evidence is proven in accordance with the provisions of Article 4, the matter of the geographical location is irrelevant. Alternatively, an adjudicator can admit the evidence as being authentic where the authenticity of the evidence is demonstrated in some other manner that is accepted by the adjudicator.

16. Article 10 provides that evidence in electronic form that ostensibly originates in a foreign jurisdiction can be admitted, notwithstanding that it was not actually located in the domestic jurisdiction. The aim is to enable the admission into a legal proceeding of electronic evidence and electronic signatures that might otherwise not be admitted because of lack of formalities.

17. Although the provisions of Article 11(1) may appear to be open to interpretation, the clause mirrors many such clauses in legislation relating to electronic commerce and communications across the world. Article 11(2) deals with the inevitable disagreement between the meaning of words in a technical sense and a legal sense. When this occurs, it is for the adjudicator to determine the meaning in accordance with the relevant provisions in domestic law on interpretation. There has been no attempt to incorporate technical definitions into the Convention, because doing so might cause greater uncertainty than is intended.

Appendix 2

Cumulative vignettes

Each of the vignettes appearing in the first three editions are set out below.

First edition, 2007

The abacus

'Your honour, I seek to exhibit the abacus.'

The judge looked over his spectacles 'Which form of abacus is it?'

The barrister looked perplexed and turned to his solicitor and whispered 'Which form of abacus? How do I know? Are there different types of abacus?'

'Oh yes', whispered the solicitor, 'it's a Chinese abacus.' 'Oh, right. Thanks.' 'It's a Chinese abacus, your honour.'

'Thank you, Mr Puffington. And what is the purpose of exhibiting the abacus?'

'Well, your honour, it's the item upon which the calculations were made to perpetrate the alleged fraud.'

'Indeed, but that does not mean the abacus ought to be exhibited. Have you a submission on this matter Miss Jawleyford?'

Miss Jawleyford stood as Mr Puffington sat down.

'Well, your honour, the defence does not seek to argue about an inanimate object.'

'Quite.'

'But what we must look to, in my submission, is the reason for admitting the abacus as an exhibit, your honour.'

'Indeed.'

'We have already had the opportunity of viewing the abacus, and take no point on the object itself. It is admitted that the defendant used the device. As a material object, it can be admitted into evidence. But the question is, what purpose is served in admitting the device. It is my submission that the presence of the abacus serves no purpose, because the device is merely a device. There is no record of what, if any, calculations might have been made on the device.'

Miss Jawleyford sat down. Mr Puffington stood.

'Your honour, in our submission, it's important to exhibit the abacus, because it will serve to make the members of the jury ask themselves why the defendant, a finance director earning over a million-pound salary a year, deliberately used such a device. It is our case that he used the abacus to avoid the creation of records that would implicate him in the alleged fraud. To that end, it's an important exhibit that ought to be admitted into evidence.'

Second edition, 2010

The 'forged' document

'The problem with the email submitted by the witness, madam, is that the signature cannot be trusted. For this reason, the evidence cannot be admitted.'

Mr Tulkinghorn sat down. Mr Tangle stood up.

'With the deepest possible respect, madam, my learned friend has let his usual penetrating insight into the analysis of evidence fail him. If this was a letter, for instance, the first question will be "Is the letter genuine?" If the letter is a forgery, then the signature matters not – unless it is genuine and intended to deceive the recipient. If the letter is genuine, *then* the question arises as to whether the signature is a forgery. Thus it must be with the email. If my learned friend claims that the email is a forgery, the status of the signature is irrelevant. Is my learned friend suggesting that the email is a forgery?'

Mr Tangle sat down.

Her Honour Judge Flite QC looked at Mr Tulkinghorn. 'Well? It strikes me that this must be correct. Are you suggesting the email is a forgery?'

Mr Tulkinghorn stood up.

'In this instance, my learned friend has indicated an error of logic on my part, which I concede. The point is, anybody can forge an email and write any name as an electronic signature. If we cannot trust the signature, then we cannot trust the email.'

Her Honour Judge Flite QC continued the questioning, 'But the authenticity of the email must come before the verification of the signature? Mr Tangle?'

Mr Tulkinghorn sat down. Mr Tangle stood up.

'Where the authenticity of a document is challenged, a wide range of tests can be made to determine whether it is a forgery. I acknowledge that the contents can help determine whether it is a forgery. But if it was a letter, the paper, ink, and the type face might all be the subject of tests. In the case of an email, the technical information relating to the status of the document is of the utmost relevance. In my submission, determining whether to trust the signature can only follow *after* it has been established whether the email is genuine or a forgery.'

Third edition, 2012

The 'competent' witness

'My learned friend for the prosecution has established that you are the sub-manager of the hotel, that you are familiar with the functions of the machine that controls the telephone system, and that you know how it works and what it is supposed to do?'

'Yes.'

'And the printouts you have brought to court purport to indicate when the telephone was used in room 2820?'

'Yes.'

'For this reason, my learned friend considers your evidence is all that is needed to establish the reliability of the telephone system. Let me ask you this, how does the direct inward system access work?'

'Er, I don't know.'

'You don't know what happens, or you don't know what the direct inward system access is?'

'I don't know what it is.'

'So, by implication, you don't know what the password is?'

'No.'

'By implication, you won't know if thieves have used the password to route telephone calls through the hotel telephone system?'

'No.'

'Can you tell me the purpose of the latest software update, whether it included a security fix, and when it was downloaded?'

'Er, no, I don't know any of that.'

'Why do you not know?'

'Well, because the IT people do all of that stuff.'

'So you are asserting, by bringing along the printouts of the telephone calls, that these telephone calls were actually made, and they were made from room 2820.'

'Well, yes, if you say so.'

'I do not say so, you do. You also claim that because none of your customers have ever complained about their bills, it follows that the telephone system is reliable and therefore trustworthy?'

'Well, I wouldn't put it quite like that.'

'Thank you, Mr Prunsquallor.'

Judge Sepulchrave turned to prosecuting counsel, 'Unless you have any questions in re-examination Mrs Groan?'

Mrs Groan stood up. 'Your honour, no,' and sat down.

'Very well, you may leave the witness stand, Mr Prunsquallor. Yes, Mr Rottcodd?'

'Thank you, your honour. My learned friend for the prosecution would have us believe that because the information printed on the piece of paper apparently looks sensible, it therefore follows that the contents must not only be reliable, but represent the truth. My learned friend also suggests that because Mr Prunsquallor uses the hotel's telephone system in the performance of his duties, this is a sufficient foundation as a qualification as a competent witness. With your honour's leave, I will address the latter point first ...'

Fourth edition, 2017

Business records

Judge Nuri Efendi looked over his spectacles. 'Now we have covered the main matters to be dealt with in this case management conference, you may address the business records point, Mr Ayarcı.'

Mr Halit Ayarcı stood up. 'Your honour, thank you. My learned friend intends to submit a number of spreadsheets into evidence. There are problems with this. The first of which is that he only intends to submit printouts of the spreadsheet application or program, whatever our technical friends consider a spreadsheet to be. My learned friend has declined to provide copies to the defence in electronic form. My application is for the prosecution to provide copies of the relevant spreadsheets in electronic form.'

Mr Hayri İrdal stood up. Mr Halit Ayarcı sat down.

'Your honour, I must protest. A printout is real evidence, and is to be received as prima facie evidence of the entries. The defence is attempting to add to the costs in this case by making an unreasonable request.'

Judge Nuri Efendi interjected. 'Mr Ayarcı, please elaborate your point.'

Mr Hayri İrdal sat down. Mr Halit Ayarcı stood up.

'My submission is that the technical literature clearly demonstrates that all spreadsheets have significant error rates, and it is our contention that it is obvious that there must be some errors in the documents that affect the figures that my learned friend wishes to have admitted. Indeed, as I have made it clear to my learned friend, the collapse of the banking system in Jamaica in the late 1990s was partly due to the use of spreadsheets and the failure to manage and control them. On this issue alone, I submit that it cannot be right to admit these documents under the bankers' books exception without the electronic versions of the files being subject to analysis by appropriately qualified digital evidence professionals.'

Mr Halit Ayarcı sat down. Mr Hayri İrdal stood up.

'Your honour, as my learned friend is only too well aware, the evidence also benefits from the presumption that mechanical instruments were in order at the material time – a presumption which, I do not need to remind your honour, intentionally included computers. I most strongly resist this potentially expensive and unnecessary challenge regarding the authenticity of the spreadsheets on the basis that this presumption applies.'

Mr Hayri İrdal sat down.

Judge Nuri Efendi considered the submission. 'Mr Ayarcı, notwithstanding the legislative provisions governing business records, the presumption of equipment being properly constructed and operating correctly must be strong, and it is a particularly strong presumption in the case of equipment within the control of the party. Please address this particular issue.'

Mr Halit Ayarcı stood up.

'I appreciate the nature of the presumption, your honour. The exception permits records to be adduced because, in the past, employees entered information into physical books by hand, and this meant they could be relied upon as a record made at that point in time, and one could ascertain at a glance whether somebody tried to change the entries. The justification was that such records were more reliable than the memory of a witness. This might have been so, but records in electronic form are notorious for being inaccurate for a variety of reasons, and it must be common sense that this rule cannot be relied upon in the twenty-first century.

Let me ask my learned friend what he means that computers are reliable. For instance:

Does my learned friend mean that the spreadsheets are authentic, in that they are the right ones, and they have not been tampered with?

Does he mean that the spreadsheets are valid, in that they contain the information that is claimed of them?

Perhaps he means that the spreadsheets are internally valid, in that the spreadsheets work? If this is the case, what evidence is there that the users of the spreadsheet application checked that the algorithms were correct? My learned friend might also like to confirm if the presumption that computers are reliable includes the maintenance of the spreadsheets and who wrote them, and what qualifications they had to be able to program 'reliably'.

But perhaps he means that the software code of the operating system is reliable? How does he know? How many updates have there been since the spreadsheets began to operate? Were all updates applied? When updates occurred, how did they affect the application software? What is his measure of reliability?

Does he mean that there are no errors of logic that can lead to an incorrect result? What evidence does he have of this, taking into account the number of software code updates to the spreadsheets? Perhaps my learned friend can kindly indicate the number and purpose of each software update since its inception.

Perhaps he means that the employees who input the figures are always accurate? And I presume the system is so reliable that inaccurate inputs are recognized and corrected, and that these corrections are recorded?

No doubt my learned friend can also confirm, because the spreadsheet programs are deemed to be reliable, that there are no errors of omission where the formula is wrong because one or more of its input cells is blank or otherwise incorrect such as referring to the wrong cells?

I ask my learned friend, which part of this process is reliable? All of it? Parts of it? If part of it, which part and for what reason?

But let me finish with another question on the basis that your honour is against my request for electronic versions of the spreadsheets – perhaps my learned friend can assure the court, if only paper versions of the record are to be admitted, that the full information will be provided. That is, he will provide the respective algorithms that undertake the calculations – after all, one does not admit the body of a motor vehicle on its own into evidence to demonstrate the cause of a collision where it is claimed that the brakes failed – one needs to know how the brakes worked and to view the evidence of the braking system. But that is exactly what my learned friend is asking the court to admit: the unsupported assertions of the truth of the contents of spreadsheet programs in the absence of the mechanism by which the data was created.

Finally, before my learned friend responds, we have to consider the requirement that the book is in the custody or control of the bank. This is a significant issue, because, as we now understand it, the spreadsheets in question are maintained in the cloud ...'

Index

www.ingramcontent.com/pod-product-compliance
Ingram Content Group UK Ltd.
Pitfield, Milton Keynes, MK11 3LW, UK
UKHW021854100926
8556IPUK00020B/1215

9 781911 507222